Flexible Organization

Macroeconomics, sixth edition is organized around two central parts: A core and a set of two major extensions. The text's **flexible organization** emphasizes an integrated view of macroeconomics, while enabling professors to focus on the theories, models, and applications that they deem central to their particular course.

The flowchart below quickly illustrates how the chapters are organized and fit within the book's overall structure. For a more detailed explanation of the **Organization**, and for an extensive list of **Alternative Course Outlines**, see pages **xiii–xv** in the preface.

INTRODUCTION

A Tour of the World **Chapter 1**
A Tour of the Book **Chapter 2**

THE CORE

The Short Run
The Goods Market **Chapter 3**
Financial Markets **Chapter 4**
Goods and Financial Markets: The *IS-LM* Model **Chapter 5**

The Medium Run
The Labor Market **Chapter 6**
Putting All Markets Together: The *AS-AD* Model **Chapter 7**
The Natural Rate of Unemployment and The Phillips Curve **Chapter 8**
The Crisis **Chapter 9**

The Long Run
The Facts of Growth **Chapter 10**
Saving, Capital Accumulation, and Output **Chapter 11**
Technological Progress and Growth **Chapter 12**
Technological Progress: The Short, the Medium, and the
Long Run **Chapter 13**

EXTENSIONS

EXPECTATIONS
Expectations: The Basic Tools **Chapter 14**
Financial Markets and Expectations **Chapter 15**
Expectations, Consumption, and Investment **Chapter 16**
Expectations, Output, and Policy **Chapter 17**

THE OPEN ECONOMY
Openness in Goods and Financial Markets **Chapter 18**
The Goods Market in an Open Economy **Chapter 19**
Output, the Interest Rate, and the Exchange Rate **Chapter 20**
Exchange Rate Regimes **Chapter 21**

BACK TO POLICY

Should Policy Makers Be Restrained? **Chapter 22**
Fiscal Policy: A Summing Up **Chapter 23**
Monetary Policy: A Summing Up **Chapter 24**

EPILOGUE

The Story of Macroeconomics **Chapter 25**

Sixth Edition

MACROECONOMICS

Olivier Blanchard
International Monetary Fund
Massachusetts Institute of Technology

David R. Johnson
Wilfrid Laurier University

PEARSON

Boston   Columbus   Indianapolis   New York   San Francisco   Upper Saddle River
Amsterdam   Cape Town   Dubai   London   Madrid   Milan   Munich   Paris   Montréal   Toronto
Delhi   Mexico City   São Paulo   Sydney   Hong Kong   Seoul   Singapore   Taipei   Tokyo

Editor in Chief: Donna Battista
AVP/Executive Editor: David Alexander
Senior Editorial Project Manager: Lindsey Sloan
Executive Marketing Manager: Lori DeShazo
Senior Managing Editor: Nancy Fenton
Senior Production Project Manager: Nancy
  Freihofer
Senior Manufacturing Buyer: Carol Melville
Cover Designer: Jonathan Boylan
Cover Photo: © Alan Z. Uster/Fotolia

Permissions Specialist: Jill Dougan
Image Manager: Rachel Youdelman
Executive Media Producer: Melissa Honig
MyEconLab Content Lead: Noel Lotz
Project Management, Page Makeup, and Design:
  PreMediaGlobal
Printer/Binder: R.R. Donnelley / Willard
Cover Printer: Lehigh Phoenix
Text Font: Utopia 10/12

Credits and acknowledgments borrowed from other sources and reproduced, with permission, in this text-book appear on the appropriate page within text and on pages C-1–C-3.

Cataloging-in-Publication Data is on file at the Library of Congress

10 9 8 7 6 5 4 3 2 1

ISBN-13: 978-0-13-306165-9
ISBN-10: 0-13-306165-5

To Noelle and Susan

About the Authors

Olivier Blanchard is the Robert M. Solow Professor of Economics at the Massachusetts Institute of Technology. He did his undergraduate work in France and received a Ph.D. in economics from MIT in 1977. He taught at Harvard from 1977 to 1982 and has taught at MIT since 1983. He has frequently received the award for best teacher in the department of economics. He is currently on leave from MIT and serves as the Chief Economist at the International Monetary Fund.

He has done research on many macroeconomic issues, including the effects of fiscal policy, the role of expectations, price rigidities, speculative bubbles, unemployment in Western Europe, transition in Eastern Europe, the role of labor market institutions, and the various aspects of the current crisis. He has done work for many governments and many international organizations, including the *World Bank*, the *IMF*, the *OECD*, the *EU Commission*, and the *EBRD*. He has published over 150 articles and edited or written over 20 books, including *Lectures on Macroeconomics* with Stanley Fischer.

He is a research associate of the National Bureau of Economic Research, a fellow of the Econometric Society, a member of the American Academy of Arts and Sciences, and a past Vice President of the American Economic Association.

He currently lives in Washington, D.C. with his wife, Noelle. He has three daughters: Marie, Serena, and Giulia.

David Johnson is Professor of Economics at Wilfrid Laurier University and Education Policy Scholar at the C. D. Howe Institute.

Professor Johnson's areas of specialty are macroeconomics, international finance, and, more recently, the economics of education. His published work in macroeconomics includes studies of Canada's international debt, the influence of American interest rates on Canadian interest rates, and the determination of the exchange rate between Canada and the United States. His 2005 book *Signposts of Success*, a comprehensive analysis of elementary school test scores in Ontario, was selected as a finalist in 2006 for both the Donner Prize and the Purvis Prize. He has also written extensively on inflation targets as part of monetary policy in Canada and around the world. His primary teaching area is macroeconomics. He is coauthor with Olivier Blanchard of *Macroeconomics* (fourth Canadian edition).

Professor Johnson received his undergraduate degree from the University of Toronto, his Master's degree from the University of Western Ontario, and his Ph.D. in 1983 from Harvard University, where Olivier Blanchard served as one of his supervisors. He has worked at the Bank of Canada and visited at the National Bureau of Economic Research, Cambridge University, and most recently at the University of California, Santa Barbara as Canada-U.S. Fulbright Scholar and Visiting Chair.

Professor Johnson lives in Waterloo, Ontario, with his wife Susan, who is also an economics professor. They have shared the raising of two children, Sarah and Daniel. When not studying or teaching economics, David plays Oldtimers' Hockey and enjoys cross-country skiing in the winter and sculling in the summer. For a complete change of pace, Professor Johnson has been heavily involved in the Logos program, an after-school program for children and youth at First Mennonite Church in Kitchener, Ontario.

Brief Contents

Contents

The Medium Run 109

Focus Boxes

Preface

We had two main goals in writing this book:

- To make close contact with current macroeconomic events. What makes macroeconomics exciting is the light it sheds on what is happening around the world, from the major economic crisis which has engulfed the world since 2008, to the budget deficits of the United States, to the problems of the Euro area, to high growth in China. These events—and many more—are described in the book, not in footnotes, but in the text or in detailed boxes. Each box shows how you can use what you have learned to get an understanding of these events. Our belief is that these boxes not only convey the "life" of macroeconomics, but also reinforce the lessons from the models, making them more concrete and easier to grasp.

- To provide an integrated view of macroeconomics. The book is built on one underlying model, a model that draws the implications of equilibrium conditions in three sets of markets: the goods market, the financial markets, and the labor market. Depending on the issue at hand, the parts of the model relevant to the issue are developed in more detail while the other parts are simplified or lurk in the background. But the underlying model is always the same. This way, you will see macroeconomics as a coherent whole, not a collection of models. And you will be able to make sense not only of past macroeconomic events, but also of those that unfold in the future.

New to this Edition

- Chapter 1 starts with a history of the crisis, giving a sense of the landscape, and setting up the issues to be dealt with throughout the book.

- A new Chapter 9, which comes after the short- and medium-run architecture have been put in place, focuses specifically on the crisis. It shows how one can use and extend the short-run and medium run analysis to understand the various aspects of the crisis, from the role of the financial system to the constraints on macroeconomic policy.

- Material on depressions and slumps has been relocated from later chapters to Chapter 9, and the material on very high inflation has been reduced and included in Chapter 23.

- A rewritten Chapter 23, on fiscal policy, focuses on the current debt problems of the United States.

- Chapters 23, 24, and 25 draw the implications of the crisis for the conduct of fiscal and monetary policy in particular, and for macroeconomics in general.

- Many new Focus boxes have been introduced and look at various aspects of the crisis, among them the following: "The Lehman Bankruptcy, Fears of Another Great Depression, and Shifts in the Consumption Function" in Chapter 3; "Bank Runs, Deposit Insurance, and Wholesale Funding" in Chapter 4; "The Liquidity Trap, Quantitative Easing, and the Role of Expectations" in Chapter 17; "The G20 and the 2009 Fiscal Stimulus" in Chapter 19; "How Countries Decreased Their Debt Ratios after World War II" in Chapter 23; and "LTV Ratios and Housing Price Increases from 2000 to 2007 in Chapter 24.

- Figures and tables have been updated using the latest data available.

Organization

The book is organized around two central parts: A core, and a set of two major extensions. An introduction precedes the core. The two extensions are followed by a review of the role of policy. The book ends with an epilogue. A flowchart on the front endpaper makes it easy to see how the chapters are organized, and fit within the book's overall structure.

- Chapters 1 and 2 introduce the basic facts and issues of macroeconomics. Chapter 1 focuses on the crisis, and then takes a tour of the world, from the United States, to Europe, to China. Some instructors will prefer to cover Chapter 1 later, perhaps after Chapter 2, which introduces basic concepts, articulates the notions of short run, medium run, and long run, and gives the reader a quick tour of the book.

While Chapter 2 gives the basics of national income accounting, we have put a detailed treatment of national income accounts to Appendix 1 at the end of the book. This decreases the burden on the beginning reader, and allows for a more thorough treatment in the appendix.

■ Chapters 3 through 13 constitute the **core**. Chapters 3 through 5 focus on the **short run**. These three chapters characterize equilibrium in the goods market and in the financial markets, and they derive the basic model used to study short–run movements in output, the *IS–LM* model.

Chapters 6 through 8 focus on the **medium run**. Chapter 6 focuses on equilibrium in the labor market and introduces the notion of the natural rate of unemployment. Chapters 7 and 8 develop a model based on aggregate demand and aggregate supply and show how that model can be used to understand movements in activity and movements in inflation, both in the short and in the medium run.

The current crisis is a sufficiently important and complex event that it deserves its own chapter. Building on and extending Chapters 6 to 8, Chapter 9 focuses on the origins of the crisis, the role of the financial system, and the constraints facing fiscal and monetary policy, such as the liquidity trap and the high level of public debt.

Chapters 10 through 13 focus on the **long run**. Chapter 10 describes the facts, showing the evolution of output across countries and over long periods of time. Chapters 11 and 12 develop a model of growth and describe how capital accumulation and technological progress determine growth. Chapter 13 focuses on the effects of technological progress not only in the long run, but also in the short run and in the medium run. This topic is typically not covered in textbooks but is important. And the chapter shows how one can integrate the short run, the medium run, and the long run—a clear example of the payoff to an integrated approach to macroeconomics.

■ Chapters 14 through 21 cover the two major **extensions**.

Chapters 14 through 17 focus on the role of **expectations** in the short run and in the medium run.

Expectations play a major role in most economic decisions, and, by implication, play a major role in the determination of output.

Chapters 18 through 21 focus on the implications of **openness** of modern economies. Chapter 21 focuses on the implications of different exchange rate regimes, from flexible exchange rates, to fixed exchange rates, currency boards, and dollarization.

■ Chapters 22 through 24 return to macroeconomic **policy**. Although most of the first 21 chapters constantly discuss macroeconomic policy in one form or another, the purpose of Chapters 22 through 24 is to tie the threads together. Chapter 22 looks at the role and the limits of macroeconomic policy in general. Chapters 23 and 24 review monetary policy and fiscal policy. Some instructors may want to use parts of these chapters earlier. For example, it is easy to move forward the discussion of the government budget constraint in Chapter 23 or the discussion of inflation targeting in Chapter 24.

■ Chapter 25 serves as an **epilogue**; it puts macroeconomics in historical perspective by showing the evolution of macroeconomics in the last 70 years, discussing current directions of research, and the lessons of the crisis for macroeconomics.

Changes from the Fifth to the Sixth Edition

The structure of the sixth edition, namely the organization around a core and two extensions, is fundamentally the same as that of the fifth edition. This edition is, however, dominated in many ways by the crisis, and the many issues it raises. Thus, in addition to a first discussion of the crisis in Chapter 1, and numerous boxes and discussions throughout the book, we have added a new chapter, Chapter 9, specifically devoted to the crisis.

At the same time, we have removed the two chapters on pathologies in the fifth edition. The reason is simple, and in some ways, ironic. While we thought that it was important for macroeconomic students to know about such events as the Great Depression, or the long slump in Japan, we did not expect the world to be confronted with many of the same issues any time soon. While far from being as bad as the Great Depression, the crisis raises many of the same issues as the Great Depression did. Thus, much of the material covered in the chapters on pathologies in the fifth edition has been moved to the core and to the two extensions.

We have also removed Chapter 9 of the fifth edition, which developed a framework to think about the relation between growth, unemployment, and inflation. This was in response to teachers who found the framework too difficult for students to follow. Again, some of the material in that chapter has been kept and integrated elsewhere, in particular in Chapter 8.

Alternative Course Outlines

Within the book's broad organization, there is plenty of opportunity for alternative course organizations. We have made the chapters shorter than is standard in textbooks, and, in our experience, most chapters can be covered in an hour and a half. A few (Chapters 5 and 7 for example) might require two lectures to sink in.

- Short courses. (15 lectures or less)

  A short course can be organized around the two introductory chapters and the core (Chapter 13 can be excluded at no cost in continuity). Informal presentations of one or two of the extensions, based, for example, on Chapter 17 for expectations (which can be taught as a stand alone), and on Chapter 18 for the open economy, can then follow, for a total of 14 lectures.

  A short course might leave out the study of growth (the long run). In this case, the course can be organized around the introductory chapters and Chapters 3 through 9 in the core; this gives a total of 9 lectures, leaving enough time to cover, for example, Chapter 17 on expectations, Chapters 18 through 20 on the open economy, for a total of 13 lectures.

- Longer courses (20 to 25 lectures)

  A full semester course gives more than enough time to cover the core, plus one or both of the two extensions, and the review of policy.

  The extensions assume knowledge of the core, but are otherwise mostly self contained. Given the choice, the order in which they are best taught is probably the order in which they are presented in the book. Having studied the the role of expectations first helps students to understand the interest parity condition, and the nature of exchange rate crises.

Features

We have made sure never to present a theoretical result without relating it to the real world. In addition to discussions of facts in the text itself, we have written a large number of **Focus** boxes, which discuss particular macroeconomic events or facts, from the United States or from around the world.

We have tried to re-create some of the student–teacher interactions that take place in the classroom by the use of **margin notes**, which run parallel to the text. The margin notes create a dialogue with the reader and, in so doing, smooth the more difficult passages and give a deeper understanding of the concepts and the results derived along the way.

For students who want to explore macroeconomics further, we have introduced the following two features:

- **Short appendixes** to some chapters, which expand on points made within the chapter.

- A **Further Readings** section at the end of most chapters, indicating where to find more information, including a number of key Internet addresses.

Each chapter ends with three ways of making sure that the material in the chapter has been digested:

- A **summary** of the chapter's main points.

- A list of **key terms**.

- A series of **end-of-chapter exercises**. "Quick Check" exercises are easy. "Dig Deeper" exercises are a bit harder, and "Explore Further" typically require either access to the Internet or the use of a spreadsheet program.

A list of symbols on the back endpapers makes it easy to recall the meaning of the symbols used in the text.

The Teaching and Learning Package

The book comes with a number of supplements to help both students and instructors.

For Instructors:

- **Instructor's Manual**. The Instructor's manual discusses pedagogical choices, alternative ways of presenting the material, and ways of reinforcing students' understanding. Chapters in the manual include six main sections: objectives, in the form of a motivating question; why the answer matters; key tools, concepts, and assumptions; summary; and pedagogy. Many chapters also include sections focusing on extensions and observations. The Instructor's Manual also includes the answers to all end-of-chapter questions and exercises.

- **Test Item File**. The test bank is completely revised with additional new multiple-choice questions for each chapter.

- **TestGen**—The printed Test Item File is designed for use with the computerized TestGen package, which allows instructors to customize, save, and generate classroom tests. The test program permits instructors to edit, add, or delete questions from the test bank; edit existing graphics and create new graphics; analyze test results; and organize a database of tests and student results. This software allows for extensive flexibility and ease of use. It provides many options for organizing and displaying tests, along with search and sort features. The software and the Test Item File can be downloaded from the Instructor's Resource Center. (**www.pearsonhighered.com/blanchard**)

- **Digital Image Library**—We have digitized the complete set of figures, graphs, and charts from the book. These files can be downloaded from the Instructor's Resource Center. (**www.pearsonhighered.com/ blanchard**)

- **PowerPoint Lecture Slides**—These electronic slides provide section titles, tables, equations, and graphs for each chapter and can be downloaded from the Instructor's Resource Center. (**www.pearsonhighered. com/blanchard**)

MyEconLab®

MyEconLab delivers rich online content and innovative learning tools in your classroom. Instructors who use MyEconLab gain access to powerful communication and assessment tools, and their students receive access to the additional learning resources described below.

- **Students and MyEconLab**—This online homework and tutorial system puts students in control of their own learning through a suite of study and practice tools correlated with the online, interactive version of the textbook and other media tools. Within MyEconLab's structured environment, students practice what they learn, test their understanding, and then pursue a study plan that MyEconLab generates for them based on their performance on practice tests.

- **Instructors and MyEconLab**—MyEconLab provides flexible tools that allow instructors to easily and effectively customize online course materials to suit their needs. Instructors can create and assign tests, quizzes,

or homework assignments. MyEconLab saves time by automatically grading all questions and tracking results in an online gradebook. MyEconLab can even grade assignments that require students to draw a graph.

- **Real-Time Data**—The real-time data problems are new. These problems load the latest available data from FRED, a comprehensive up-to-date data set maintained by the Federal Reserve Bank of St. Louis. The questions are graded with feedback in exactly the same way as those based on static data.

After registering for MyEconLab, instructors have access to downloadable supplements such as an Instructor's Manual, PowerPoint lecture notes, and a Test Item File. The Test Item File can also be used with MyEconLab, giving instructors ample material from which they can create assignments.

MyEconLab is delivered in Pearson's MyLab Mastering system, which offers advanced communication and customization features. Instructors can upload course documents and assignments and use advanced course management features. For more information about MyEconLab or to request an instructor access code, visit www.myeconlab.com.

Acknowledgments and Thanks

This book owes much to many. We thank Adam Ashcraft, Peter Berger, Peter Benczur, Efe Cakarel, Harry Gakidis, David Hwang, Kevin Nazemi, David Reichsfeld, Jianlong Tan, Stacy Tevlin, Gaurav Tewari, Corissa Thompson, John Simon, and Jeromin Zettelmeyer for their research assistance over the years. We thank the generations of students in 14.02 at MIT who have freely shared their reactions to the book over the years.

We have benefited from comments from many colleagues and friends. Among them are John Abell, Daron Acemoglu, Tobias Adrian, Chuangxin An, Roland Benabou, Samuel Bentolila, and Juan Jimeno (who have adapted the book for a Spanish edition); Francois Blanchard, Roger Brinner, Ricardo Caballero, Wendy Carlin, Martina Copelman, Henry Chappell, Ludwig Chincarini, and Daniel Cohen (who has adapted the book for a French edition); Larry Christiano, Bud Collier, Andres Conesa, Peter Diamond, Martin Eichenbaum, Gary Fethke, David Findlay, Francesco Giavazzi, and Alessia Amighini (who have adapted the book for an Italian edition); Andrew Healy, Steinar Holden, and Gerhard Illing (who has adapted the book for a German edition); Yannis Ioannides, Angelo Melino (who has adapted the book for a Canadian edition); P. N. Junankar, Sam Keeley, Bernd Kuemmel, Paul

Krugman, Antoine Magnier, Peter Montiel, Bill Nordhaus, Tom Michl, Dick Oppermann, Athanasios Orphanides, and Daniel Pirez Enri (who has adapted the book for a Latin American edition); Michael Plouffe, Zoran Popovic, Jim Poterba, and Jeff Sheen (who has adapted the book for an Australasian edition); Ronald Schettkat, and Watanabe Shinichi (who has adapted the book for a Japanese edition); Francesco Sisci, Brian Simboli, Changyong Rhee, Julio Rotemberg, Robert Solow, Andre Watteyne, and Michael Woodford.

We have benefited from comments from many readers, reviewers, and class testers. Among them:

- John Abell, Randolph, Macon Woman's College
- Carol Adams, Cabrillo College
- Gilad Aharonovitz, School of Economic Sciences
- Terence Alexander, Iowa State University
- Roger Aliaga-Diaz, Drexel University
- Robert Archibald, College of William & Mary
- John Baffoe-Bonnie, La Salle University
- Fatolla Bagheri, University of North Dakota
- Stephen Baker, Capital University
- Erol Balkan, Hamilton College
- Jennifer Ball, Washburn University
- Richard Ballman, Augustana College
- King Banaian, St. Cloud State University
- Charles Bean, London School of Economics and Political Science
- Scott Benson, Idaho State University
- Gerald Bialka, University of North Florida
- Robert Blecker, American University
- Scott Bloom, North Dakota State University
- Pim Borren, University of Canterbury, New Zealand
- LaTanya Brown-Robertson, Bowie State University
- James Butkiewicz, University of Delaware
- Colleen Callahan, American University
- Bruce Carpenter, Mansfield University
- Kyongwook Choi, Ohio University College
- Michael Cook, William Jewell College

- Nicole Crain, Lafayette College
- Rosemary Cunningham, Agnes Scott College
- Evren Damar, Pacific Lutheran University
- Dale DeBoer, University of Colorado at Colorado Springs
- Adrian de Leon-Arias, Universidad de Guadalajara
- Brad DeLong, UC Berkeley
- Firat Demir, University of Oklahoma
- Wouter Denhaan, UC San Diego
- John Dodge, King College
- F. Trenery Dolbear, Brandeis University
- Patrick Dolenc, Keene State College
- Brian Donhauser, University of Washington
- Michael Donihue, Colby College
- Vincent Dropsy, California State University
- Justin Dubas, St. Norbert College
- Amitava Dutt, University of Notre Dame
- John Edgren, Eastern Michigan University
- Eric Elder, Northwestern College
- Sharon J. Erenburg, Eastern Michigan University
- Antonina Espiritu, Hawaii Pacific University
- J. Peter Federer, Clark University
- Rendigs Fels, Vanderbilt University
- John Flanders, Central Methodist University
- Marc Fox, Brooklyn College
- Yee-Tien (Ted) Fu, Stanford University
- Yee-Tien Fu, National Cheng-Chi University, Taiwan
- Scott Fullwiler, Wartburg College
- Julie Gallaway, University of Missouri–Rolla
- Bodhi Ganguli, Rutgers, The State University of NJ
- Fabio Ghironi, Boston College
- Alberto Gomez-Rivas, University of Houston–Downtown
- Fidel Gonzalez, Sam Houston State University
- Harvey Gram, Queen College, City University of New York

- Randy Grant, Linfield College
- Alan Gummerson, Florida International University
- Reza Hamzaee, Missouri Western State College
- Michael Hannan, Edinboro University
- Kenneth Harrison, Richard Stockton College
- Mark Hayford, Loyola University
- Thomas Havrilesky, Duke University
- George Heitmann, Muhlenberg College
- Ana Maria Herrera, Michigan State University
- Peter Hess, Davidson College
- Eric Hilt, Wellesley College
- John Holland, Monmouth College
- Mark Hopkins, Gettysburg College
- Takeo Hoshi, University of California, San Diego
- Ralph Husby, University of Illinois, Urbana–Champaign
- Yannis Ioannides, Tufts University
- Aaron Jackson, Bentley College
- Bonnie Johnson, California Lutheran University
- Louis Johnston, College of St. Benedict
- Barry Jones, SUNY Binghamton
- Fred Joutz, George Washington University
- Cem Karayalcin, Florida International University
- Okan Kavuncu, University of California
- Miles Kimball, University of Michigan
- Paul King, Denison University
- Michael Klein, Tufts University
- Mark Klinedinst, University of Southern Mississippi
- Shawn Knabb, Western Washington University
- Todd Knoop, Cornell College
- Paul Koch, Olivet Nazarene University
- Ng Beoy Kui, Nanyang Technical University, Singapore
- Leonard Lardaro, University of Rhode Island
- James Leady, University of Notre Dame
- Charles Leathers, University of Alabama
- Hsien-Feng Lee, National Taiwan University
- Jim Lee, Texas A&M University–Corpus Christi
- John Levendis, Loyola University New Orleans
- Frank Lichtenberg, Columbia University
- Mark Lieberman, Princeton University
- Shu Lin, Florida Atlantic University
- Maria Luengo-Prado, Northeastern University
- Mathias Lutz, University of Sussex
- Bernard Malamud, University of Nevada, Las Vegas
- Ken McCormick, University of Northern Iowa
- William McLean, Oklahoma State University
- B. Starr McMullen, Oregon State University
- Mikhail Melnik, Niagara University
- O. Mikhail, University of Central Florida
- Fabio Milani, University of California, Irvine
- Rose Milbourne, University of New South Wales
- Roger Morefield, University of Saint Thomas
- Shahriar Mostashari, Campbell University
- Eshragh Motahar, Union College
- Nick Noble, Miami University
- Ilan Noy, University of Hawaii
- John Olson, College of St. Benedict
- Brian O'Roark, Robert Morris University
- Jack Osman, San Francisco State University
- Emiliano Pagnotta, Northwestern University
- Biru Paksha Paul, SUNY Cortland
- Andrew Parkes, Mesa State College
- Allen Parkman, University of Mexico
- Jim Peach, New Mexico State University
- Gavin Peebles, National University of Singapore
- Michael Quinn, Bentley College
- Charles Revier, Colorado State University
- Jack Richards, Portland State University
- Raymond Ring, University of South Dakota

- Monica Robayo, University of North Florida
- Malcolm Robinson, Thomas Moore College
- Brian Rosario, University of California, Davis
- Kehar Sangha, Old Dominion University
- Ahmad Saranjam, Bridgewater State College
- Carol Scotese, Virginia Commonwealth University
- John Seater, North Carolina State University
- Peter Sephton, University of New Brunswick
- Ruth Shen, San Francisco State University
- Kwanho Shin, University of Kansas
- Tara Sinclair, The George Washington University
- Aaron Smallwood, University of Texas, Arlington
- David Sollars, Auburn University
- Liliana Stern, Auburn University
- Edward Stuart, Northeastern Illinois University
- Abdulhanid Sukaar, Cameron University
- Peter Summers, Texas Tech University
- Mark Thomas, University of Maryland Baltimore County
- Brian Trinque, The University of Texas at Austin
- Marie Truesdell, Marian College
- David Tufte, Southern Utah University
- Abdul Turay, Radford University
- Frederick Tyler, Fordham University
- Pinar Uysal, Boston College
- Evert Van Der Heide, Calvin College
- Kristin Van Gaasbeck, California State University, Sacramento
- Lee Van Scyoc, University of Wisconsin, Oshkosh
- Paul Wachtel, New York University Stern Business School
- Susheng Wang, Hong Kong University
- Donald Westerfield, Webster University
- Christopher Westley, Jacksonville State University
- David Wharton, Washington College
- Jonathan Willner, Oklahoma City University

- Mark Wohar, University of Nebraska, Omaha
- Steven Wood, University of California, Berkeley
- Michael Woodford, Princeton University
- Ip Wing Yu, University of Hong Kong
- Chi-Wa Yuen, Hong Kong University of Science and Technology
- Christian Zimmermann, University of Connecticut
- Liping Zheng, Drake University

They have helped us beyond the call of duty, and each has made a difference to the book.

We have many people to thank at Pearson/Prentice Hall: David Alexander, executive editor for Economics; Lindsey Sloan, editorial project manager; Emily Brodeur, editorial assistant; Nancy Freihofer, production editor; and Lori DeShazo, the marketing manager for Economics, and Lauren Foster at PreMediaGlobal.

Thanks from Olivier

I want to single out Steve Rigolosi, the editor for the first edition; Michael Elia, the editor to the second and third editions; Amy Ray, the editor of the fourth edition; and Chris Rogers, the editor of the fifth edition. Steve forced me to clarify. Michael forced me to simplify. Amy forced me to simplify further. Together, they have made all the difference to the process and to the book. I thank all of them deeply.

At MIT, I continue to thank John Arditi for his absolute reliability.

I have also benefited from often-stimulating suggestions from my daughters, Serena, Giulia and Marie: I did not, however, follow all of them. At home, I continue to thank Noelle for preserving my sanity.

Olivier Blanchard
Cambridge, MIT
June 2012

Thanks from David

I have to thank Olivier for encouraging me to write the Canadian editions of this book over the past decade. I enjoyed that work and I enjoyed teaching out of the Canadian edition. I appreciated the opportunity to participate in the sixth American edition.

I would like to thank the many students in intermediate macroeconomics at Wilfrid Laurier University whom I have taught over the years. I was blessed with four excellent instructors in macroeconomics at the graduate level:

David Laidler, Michael Parkin, Benjamin Friedman and Olivier Blanchard. These professors taught macroeconomics in a way that made it engaging and exciting.

Alastair Robertson, who was a superb colleague for many years in teaching intermediate macroeconomics at WLU, taught me a lot about teaching.

Finally I would like to thank my wife Susan. I benefit so much from her love and support.

David Johnson,
Wilfred Laurier University
Waterloo, Ontario,
June 2012

Introduction

The first two chapters of this book introduce you to the issues and the approach of macroeconomics.

Chapter 1

Chapter 1 takes you on a macroeconomic tour of the world. It starts with a look at the economic crisis that has dominated the world economy since the late 2000s. The tour stops at each of the world's major economic powers: the United States, the Euro area, and China.

Chapter 2

Chapter 2 takes you on a tour of the book. It defines the three central variables of macroeconomics: output, unemployment, and inflation. It then introduces the three time periods around which the book is organized: the short run, the medium run, and the long run.

A Tour of the World

What is macroeconomics? The best way to answer is not to give you a formal definition, but rather to take you on an economic tour of the world, to describe both the main economic evolutions and the issues that keep macroeconomists and macroeconomic policy makers awake at night.

The truth is, at the time of this writing (the fall of 2011), policy makers are not sleeping well and have not slept well in a long time. In 2008, the world economy entered a major macroeconomic crisis, the largest one since the Great Depression. World output growth, which typically runs at 4 to 5% a year, was actually negative in 2009. Since then, growth has turned positive, and the world economy is slowly recovering. But the crisis has left a number of scars, and many worries remain.

Our goal is in this chapter is to give you a sense of these events and of some of the macroeconomic issues confronting different countries today. There is no way we can take you on a full tour, so, after an overview of the crisis, we focus on the three main economic powers of the world: the United States, the Euro area, and China.

Section 1-1 looks at the crisis.

Section 1-2 looks at the United States.

Section 1-3 looks at the Euro area.

Section 1-4 looks at China.

Section 1-5 concludes and looks ahead.

Read this chapter as you would read an article in a newspaper. Do not worry about the exact meaning of the words or about understanding all the arguments in detail: The words will be defined, and the arguments will be developed in later chapters. Regard this chapter as background, intended to introduce you to the issues of macroeconomics. If you enjoy reading this chapter, you will probably enjoy reading this book. Indeed, once you have read the book, come back to this chapter; see where you stand on the issues, and judge how much progress you have made in your study of macroeconomics. ●

1-1 The Crisis

Table 1-1 gives you output growth rates for the world economy, for advanced economies and for other countries separately, since 2000. As you can see, from 2000 to 2007 the world economy had a sustained expansion. Annual average world output growth was 3.2%, with advanced economies (the group of 30 or so richest countries in the world) growing at 2.6% per year, and emerging and developing economies (the other 150 or so other countries in the world) growing at an even faster 6.5% per year.

In 2007 however, signs that the expansion might be coming to an end started to appear. U.S. housing prices, which had doubled since 2000, started declining. In mid-2007, as we wrote the previous edition of this book, we described how economists were divided as to whether this might lead to a recession—a decrease in output. Optimists believed that, while lower housing prices might lead to lower housing construction and to lower spending by consumers, the Fed (the short name for the U.S. central bank, formally known as the *Federal Reserve Board*) could lower interest rates to stimulate demand and avoid a recession. Pessimists believed that the decrease in interest rates might not be enough to sustain demand, and that the United States may go through a short recession.

Even the pessimists turned out not to be pessimistic enough. As housing prices continued to decline, it became clear that many of the mortgage loans that had been given out during the earlier expansion were of poor quality. Many of the borrowers had taken too large a loan and were increasingly unable to make mortgage payments. And, with declining housing prices, the value of their mortgage often exceeded the price of the house, giving them an incentive to default. This was not the worst of it: The banks that had issued the mortgages had often bundled and packaged them together into new securities and then sold these securities to other banks and investors. These securities had often been repackaged into yet new securities, and so on. The result is that many banks, instead of holding the mortgages themselves, held these securities, which were so complex that their value was nearly impossible to assess.

This complexity and opaqueness turned a housing price decline into a major financial crisis, a development that very few economists had anticipated. Not knowing the quality of the assets that other banks had on their balance sheets, banks became very reluctant to lend to each other for fear that the bank to which they lent might not be able to repay. Unable to borrow, and with assets of uncertain value, many banks found themselves in trouble. On September 15, 2008, a major bank, Lehman Brothers, went bankrupt. The effects were dramatic. Because the links between Lehman and other banks were so opaque, many other banks looked appeared

> "Banks" here actually means "banks and other financial institutions." But this is too long to write and we do not want to go into these complications in Chapter 1.

Table 1-1 World Output Growth since 2000						
Percent	2000–2007 (average)	2008	2009	2010	2011*	2012*
World	3.2	1.5	−2.3	4.0	3.0	3.2
Advanced economies	2.6	0.1	−3.7	3.0	1.6	1.9
Emerging and developing economies	6.5	6.0	2.8	7.3	6.4	6.0

Output growth: Annual rate of growth of gross domestic product (GDP). *The numbers for 2011 and 2012 are forecasts, as of the fall of 2011.

Source: World Economic Outlook database, September 2011

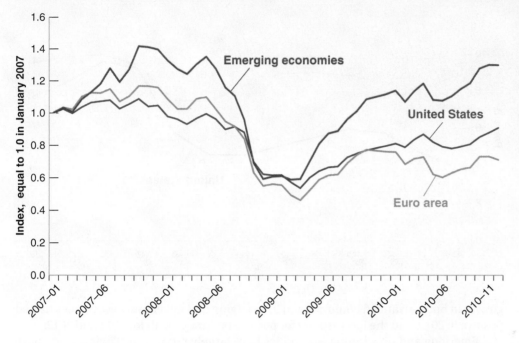

Figure 1-1

Stock prices in the United States, the Euro area, and emerging economies, 2007–2010

Source: Haver Analytics USA (S111ACD), Eurogroup (S023ACD), all emerging markets (S200ACD), all monthly averages)

at risk of going bankrupt as well. For a few weeks, it looked as if the whole financial system might collapse.

This financial crisis quickly turned into a major economic crisis. Stock prices collapsed. Figure 1-1 plots the evolution of three stock price indexes, for the United States, for the Euro area, and for emerging economies, from the beginning of 2007 on. The indexes are set equal to 1 in January 2007. Note how, by the end of 2008, stock prices had lost half or more of their value from their previous peak. Note also that, despite the fact that the crisis originated in the United States, European and emerging market stock prices decreased by as much as their U.S. counterparts; we shall return to this later.

Hit by the decrease in housing prices and the collapse in stock prices, and worried that this might be the beginning of another Great Depression, people sharply cut their consumption. Worried about sales and uncertain about the future, firms ◄ sharply cut back investment. With housing prices dropping and many vacant homes on the market, very few new homes were built. Despite strong actions by the Fed, which cut interest rates all the way down to zero, and by the U.S. government, which cut taxes and increased spending, demand decreased, and so did output. In the third quarter of 2008, U.S. output growth turned negative and remained so in 2009.

The Great Depression saw four years of negative output growth from 1929 to 1932. The unemployment rate peaked at 24.9%.

One might have hoped that the crisis would remain largely contained in the United States. As Table 1-1 and Figure 1-1 both show, this was not the case. The U.S. crisis quickly became a world crisis. Other countries were affected through two channels. The first channel was trade. As U.S. consumers and firms cut spending, part of the decrease fell on imports of foreign goods. Looking at it from the viewpoint of countries exporting to the United States, their exports went down, and so, in turn, did their output. The second channel was financial. U.S. banks, badly needing funds in the United States, repatriated funds from other countries, creating problems for banks in those countries as well. The result was not just a U.S. but a world recession. By 2009, average growth in advanced economies was −3.7%, by far the lowest annual growth rate since the Great Depression. Growth in emerging and developing economies remained positive but was nearly 4 percentage points lower than the 2000–2007 average.

Since then, thanks to strong monetary and fiscal policies and to the slow repair of the financial system, most economies have turned around. As you can see from Table 1-1,

Figure 1-2

Unemployment rates in the United States and the Euro area, 2000–2012

Source: World Economic Outlook database, September 2011

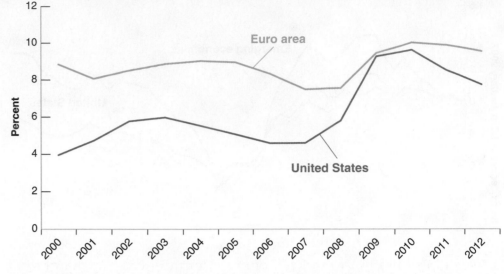

growth in both advanced countries and in emerging and developing economies turned positive in 2010, and the forecasts are for positive but low growth for 2011 and 2012.

Emerging and developing economies have largely recovered. Their exports have increased and foreign funds have returned. Indeed, some of these countries are starting to see increasing inflation, which is an indication that they may be overheating.

In advanced countries, however, many problems remain. As shown in Figure 1-2, both in the United States and the Euro area, unemployment increased a lot in the crisis and remains very high. The increase in the unemployment rate in the United States is particularly striking, increasing from 4.6% in 2007 to 9.6% in 2010, with forecasts implying only a slow decrease in 2011 and 2012. What is behind this persistently high unemployment is low output growth, and behind this low growth are many factors: Housing prices are still declining, and housing investment remains very low. Banks are still not in great shape, and bank lending is still tight. Consumers who have seen the value of their housing and their financial wealth fall are cutting consumption. And the crisis has led to serious fiscal problems. As output declined during the crisis, so did government revenues, leading to a large increase in budget deficits. Deficits have led in turn to a large increase in public debt over time. Countries must now reduce their deficits, and this is proving difficult. There are serious worries that, in some European countries, governments may not be able to adjust and may default on their debt. This, in turn, makes economists and policy makers worry that we may see yet another financial and economic crisis in the near future.

In short, while the worst of the crisis is probably over, it has left many problems in its wake, which will keep macroeconomists and policy makers busy for many years to come. We shall return to these issues in more detail at many points in the book. In the rest of the chapter, we take a closer look at the three main economic powers of the world: the United States, the Euro area, and China.

1-2 The United States

When economists first look at a country, the first two questions they ask are: How big is the country, from an economic point of view? And what is its standard of living? To answer the first, they look at output—the level of production of the country as a whole. To answer the second, they look at output per person. The

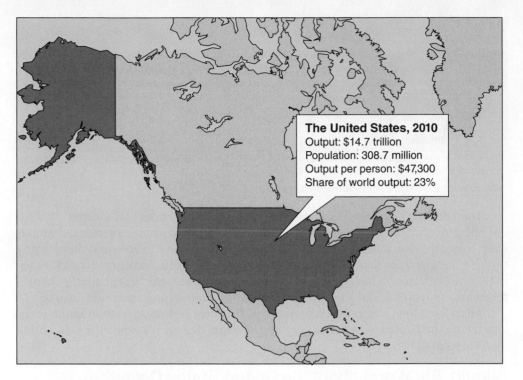

Figure 1-3

The United States

The United States, 2010
Output: $14.7 trillion
Population: 308.7 million
Output per person: $47,300
Share of world output: 23%

answers, for the United States, are given in Figure 1-3: The United States is very large, with an output of $14.7 trillion in 2010, accounting for 23% of world output. This makes it the largest country in the world, in economic terms. And the standard of living in the United States is very high: Output per person is $47,300. It is not the country with the highest output per person in the world, but it is close to the top.

When economists want to dig deeper and look at the state of health of the country, they look at three basic variables:

■ *Output growth*—the rate of change of output
■ The *unemployment rate*—the proportion of workers in the economy who are not employed and are looking for a job
■ The *inflation rate*—the rate at which the average price of the goods in the economy is increasing over time

Can you guess some of the countries with a higher standard of living than the United States? *Hint*: Think of oil producers and financial centers. For the answers, go to www.imf.org/external/pubs/ft/weo/2011/01/weodata/weo-selgr.aspx and look for "Gross Domestic Product per capita, in current prices."

Numbers for the three variables for the U.S. economy are given in Table 1-2. To put current numbers in perspective, the first column gives the average value of the rate of growth of output, the unemployment rate, and the inflation rate in the United States for the period 1980 to 1999. The next columns look at the more recent years, giving you first average numbers for the period 2000 to 2007, and then numbers for each year from 2008 to 2012. The numbers for 2011 and 2012 are forecasts as of the fall of 2011.

By looking at the first two columns, you can see why, in 2007, just before the crisis, economists felt good about the U.S. economy. The rate of growth of the economy since 2000 was 2.6%, admittedly a bit lower than the previous 20-year average, but still fairly high for an advanced country. Importantly, the average unemployment rate since 2000 was 5.0%, substantially lower than in the previous 20 years. And inflation was low, 2.8% on average since 2000, again substantially lower than it had been in the past.

Table 1-2 Growth, Unemployment, and Inflation in the United States, 1980–2012

Percent	1980–1999 (average)	2000–2007 (average)	2008	2009	2010	2011	2012
Output growth rate	3.0	2.6	0.0	–3.5	3.0	1.5	1.8
Unemployment rate	6.5	5.0	5.8	9.3	9.6	9.1	9.0
Inflation rate	4.2	2.8	3.8	–0.3	1.7	2.9	1.2

Output growth rate: annual rate of growth of output (GDP). Unemployment rate: average over the year. Inflation rate: annual rate of change of the price level (GDP deflator).

Source: World Economic Outlook database, September 2011

Then the crisis came, and you can see it in the numbers from 2008 onward. Output did not grow in 2008 and declined by 3.5% in 2009. Unemployment increased dramatically, to nearly 10%. Inflation declined, being slightly negative in 2009 and then staying positive but low since then. The economy rebounded in 2010, with growth of 3%. Since then, however, growth has decreased again, becoming so weak that unemployment is forecast to remain high for a long time to come. Inflation is forecast to remain low.

Apart from high unemployment, perhaps the most serious macroeconomic problem facing the United States is its very large budget deficit. We now turn to it, and to some of its implications.

Should You Worry about the United States Deficit?

Figure 1-4 shows the evolution of the U.S. federal budget surplus (a negative value represents a deficit) since 1990. You can see that after an increase in deficits due to the 1990–1991 recession, the rest of the decade was associated with a steady improvement and by 1998, the budget had actually gone from deficit to surplus. The main reasons for the steady improvement were twofold. First, strong output growth

Figure 1-4

U.S. Federal Budget surpluses as a percent of GDP since 1990

Source: Table B-79 Economic Report of the President 2010. Values for 2011 and 2012 are estimates.

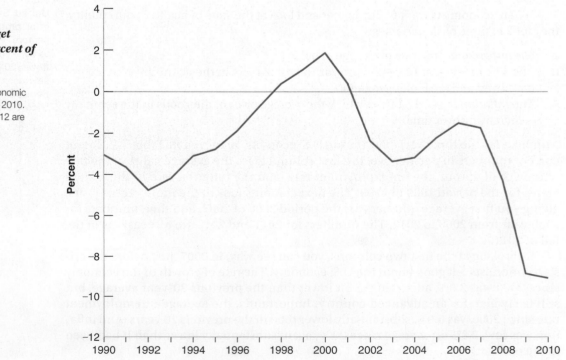

for most of the decade led to strong growth of government revenues. Second, rules were devised and implemented to contain government spending, from the use of spending caps on some categories of spending to the requirement that any new spending program be associated with an equal increase in revenues. Once budget surpluses appeared, however, Congress became increasingly willing to break its own rules and allow for more spending. At the same time, the Bush administration convinced Congress to cut taxes, with the stated intent of spurring growth. The result was a return to budget deficits. On the eve of the crisis, in 2007, the deficit was equal to 1.7% of GDP, not very large but still a deficit. The crisis had a dramatic effect on the deficit, which increased to 9% of GDP in 2010 and appears likely to be even higher in 2011. The factors behind the increase are straightforward. Lower output has led to lower government revenues. Federal revenues, which were equal to 18.9% of GDP in 2007, had declined to 16.2% of GDP in 2010. Federal spending, which was equal to 20.6% in 2007, had increased to 25.3% in 2010. This reflects not only an increase in transfers, such as higher unemployment benefits, but a more general increase in spending across the board as the government tried to counteract the decrease in private demand through an increase in public spending.

You may conclude that, as output recovers further and unemployment decreases, revenues will increase and some of the spending will be phased out. This is indeed likely to be the case, and forecasts are for a reduction in the deficit to around 5% by the middle of the decade. A 5% deficit, however, is still too a large number and creates a steadily increasing debt. Budget forecasts for the more distant future are even gloomier. The U.S. population is getting older, and Social Security benefits will increase substantially in the future. And, even more importantly, health expenditures are growing very fast and, with them, spending in government programs such as Medicare and Medicaid. So there is wide agreement that the budget deficit must be reduced further. But there is disagreement as to both when and how.

- Some economists argue that deficit reduction should start now and proceed rapidly. They argue that the credibility of the U.S. government is at stake, and that only a strong reduction will convince people that the government will do what is needed to stabilize the debt. Other economists argue, however, that too fast a reduction in the deficit would be dangerous. A reduction in the deficit can be achieved by a combination of an increase in taxes and a decrease in spending. Either one, they argue, will decrease demand and slow down growth at a time when unemployment is still very high. Their recommendation is thus to reduce the deficit, but to do it slowly and steadily.
- Even if there is agreement on the need for deficit reduction, there is much less agreement on how it should be achieved. The disagreement is along political lines. Republicans believe that it should be done primarily through decreases in spending. They suggest the elimination of a number of government programs and caps on such programs as Medicare. Democrats believe that most existing programs are justified, and they are more inclined to want to do the adjustment through an increase in taxes. The worry, at this juncture, is that these positions are hard to reconcile, and that, as a result, large deficits may continue for a long time to come.

1-3 The Euro Area

In 1957, six European countries decided to form a common European market—an economic zone where people and goods could move freely. Since then, 21 more countries have joined, bringing the total to 27. This group is now known as the **European Union**, or EU for short.

Until a few years ago, the official name was the *European Community*, or EC. You may still encounter that name. ◄

In 1999, the European Union decided to go one step further and started the process of replacing national currencies with one common currency, called the *Euro*. Only eleven countries participated at the start; since then, six more have joined. Some countries, in particular the United Kingdom, have decided not to join, at least for the time being. The official name for the group of member countries is the **Euro area**. The transition took place in steps. On January 1, 1999, each of the 11 countries fixed the value of its currency to the Euro. For example, 1 Euro was set equal to 6.56 French francs, to 166 Spanish pesetas, and so on. From 1999 to 2002, prices were quoted both in national currency units and in Euros, but the Euro was not yet used as currency. This happened in 2002, when Euro notes and coins replaced national currencies. Seventeen countries now belong to this *common currency* area.

▶ The area also goes by the names of "Euro zone" or "Euroland." The first sounds too technocratic, and the second reminds one of Disneyland. We shall avoid them.

As you can see from Figure 1-5, the Euro area is a strong economic power. Its output is nearly equal to that of the United States, and its standard of living is not far behind. (The European Union as a whole has an output that exceeds that of the United States.) As the numbers in Table 1-3 show, however, it is not doing very well.

▶ The Euro area has existed only since 1999 and membership has increased; numbers for 1980 to 1999 are constructed by adding national numbers for each of the 17 current member countries.

Look at the first two columns of Table 1-3. Even during the pre-crisis period, from 2000 to 2007, the Euro area was not doing very well compared to the United States. Output growth was lower than in the United States over the same period. Unemployment was substantially higher than in the United States. Admittedly, inflation was lower than in the United States and fell over the decade after 2000. The overall picture was of a slowly growing economy with high unemployment. Not surprisingly, the crisis made things worse. Growth was negative in 2009, and while it has turned positive, the forecasts for 2011 and 2012 are of very low growth. Unemployment has increased to 10% and, because of low growth, is forecast to decrease only slowly. The Euro area faces two main issues today. First (and this is a problem it shares with the rest of Europe) is how to reduce unemployment. Second is how to function efficiently as a **common currency area**. We consider these two issues in turn.

How Can European Unemployment Be Reduced?

The increase in European unemployment since 2007 is primarily due to the crisis, and it is reasonable to expect that the unemployment rate will eventually return to its pre-crisis level. But this pre-crisis level was already high, 8.5% for the Euro area over the period 2000–2007. Why is this? Despite a large amount of research, there is still no full agreement on the answers.

Some politicians blame macroeconomic policy. They argue that the monetary policy followed by the European Central Bank has kept interest rates too high, leading to low demand and high unemployment. According to them, the central bank should decrease interest rates and allow for an increase in demand, and unemployment would decrease.

Table 1-3 Growth, Unemployment, and Inflation in the Euro Area, 1980–2012							
Percent	1980–1999 (average)	2000–2007 (average)	2008	2009	2010	2011	2012
Output growth rate	2.2	2.2	0.4	−4.2	1.8	1.6	1.1
Unemployment rate	9.6	8.5	7.6	9.5	10.1	9.9	9.9
Inflation rate	5.2	2.3	3.2	0.3	1.6	2.5	1.5

Source: World Economic Outlook database, September 2011

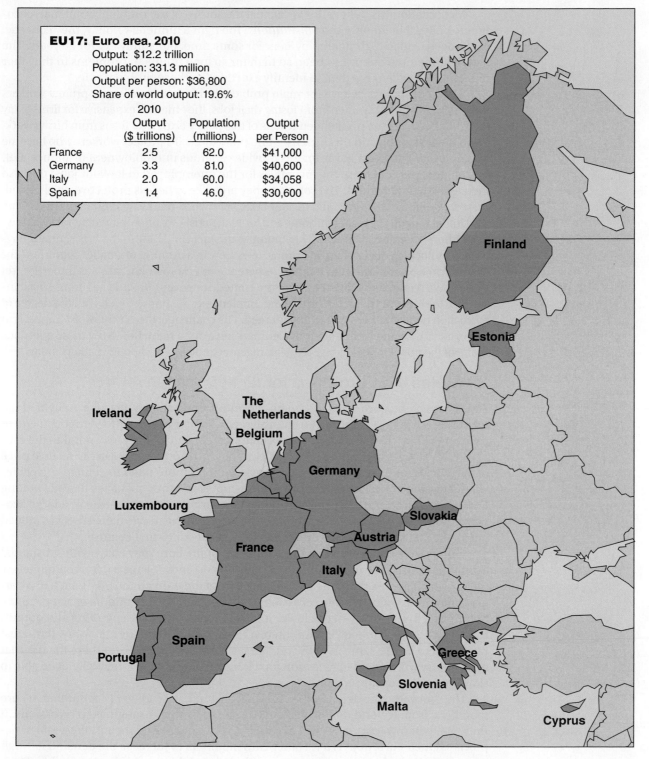

EU17: Euro area, 2010
Output: $12.2 trillion
Population: 331.3 million
Output per person: $36,800
Share of world output: 19.6%

	2010 Output ($ trillions)	Population (millions)	Output per Person
France	2.5	62.0	$41,000
Germany	3.3	81.0	$40,600
Italy	2.0	60.0	$34,058
Spain	1.4	46.0	$30,600

Figure 1-5

The Euro area

Most economists believe, however, that the source of the problem is not macroeconomic policy, but *labor market institutions*. Too tight a monetary policy, they concede, can indeed lead to high unemployment for some time, but surely not for 20 years. The fact that unemployment has been so high for so long points to problems in the labor market. The challenge is then to identify exactly what these problems are.

Some economists believe the main problem is that European states protect workers too much. To prevent workers from losing their jobs, they make it expensive for firms to lay off workers. One of the unintended results of this policy is to deter firms from hiring workers in the first place, and this increases unemployment. To protect workers who become unemployed, European governments provide generous unemployment insurance. But, by doing so, they decrease the incentives for the unemployed to look for jobs; this also increases unemployment. The solution, they argue, is to be less protective, to eliminate these *labor market rigidities*, and to adopt U.S.-style labor-market institutions. This is what the United Kingdom has largely done, and, until the crisis, its unemployment rate was low.

Others are more skeptical. They point to the fact that, before the crisis, unemployment was not high everywhere in Europe. It was low in a number of smaller countries—for example, the Netherlands or Denmark, where the unemployment rate was under 4%. Yet these countries are very different from the United States and provide generous social insurance to workers. This suggests that the problem may lie not so much with the degree of protection but with the way it is implemented. The challenge, these economists argue, is to understand what the Netherlands or Denmark have done right. Resolving these questions is one of the major tasks facing European macroeconomists and policy makers today.

What Has the Euro Done for Its Members?

Supporters of the euro point first to its enormous symbolic importance. In light of the many past wars among European countries, what better proof of the permanent end to military conflict than the adoption of a common currency? They also point to the economic advantages of having a common currency: no more changes in the relative price of currencies for European firms to worry about, no more need to change currencies when crossing borders. Together with the removal of other obstacles to trade among European countries, the euro contributes, they argue, to the creation of a large economic power in the world. There is little question that the move to the euro was indeed one of the main economic events of the start of the twenty-first century.

Others worry, however, that the symbolism of the euro may come with substantial economic costs. They point out that a common currency means a common monetary policy, which means the same interest rate across the euro countries. What if, they argue, one country plunges into recession while another is in the middle of an economic boom? The first country needs lower interest rates to increase spending and output; the second country needs higher interest rates to slow down its economy. If interest rates have to be the same in both countries, what will happen? Isn't there the risk that one country will remain in recession for a long time or that the other will not be able to slow down its booming economy?

Until recently, the debate was somewhat abstract. It no longer is. A number of euro members, from Ireland, to Portugal, to Greece, are going through deep recessions. If they had their own currency, they likely would have decreased their interest rate or depreciated their currency vis à vis other euro members to increase the demand for their exports. Because they share a currency with their neighbors, this is not possible. Thus, some economists argue that they should drop out of the euro. Others argue that such an exit would be both unwise, as it would give up on the other advantages of being in the euro, and extremely disruptive, leading to even deeper problems for the country that has exited. This issue is likely to remain a hot one for some time to come.

1-4 China

China is in the news every day. It is increasingly seen as one of the major economic powers in the world. Is the attention justified? A first look at the numbers in Figure 1-6 suggests it may not be. True, the population of China is enormous, more than four times that of the United States. But its output, expressed in dollars by multiplying the number in yuans (the Chinese currency) by the dollar–yuan exchange rate, is only 5.8 trillion dollars, less than half that of the United States. Output per person is only $4,300, roughly one-tenth of output per person in the United States.

So why is so much attention paid to China? There are two reasons. To understand the first, we need to go back to the number for output per person. When comparing output per person in a rich country like the United States and a relatively poor country like China, one must be careful. The reason is that many goods are cheaper in poor countries. For example, the price of an average restaurant meal in New York City is about 20 dollars; the price of an average restaurant meal in Beijing is about 25 yuans, or, at the current exchange rate, about 4 dollars. Put another way, the same income (expressed in dollars) buys you much more in Beijing than in New York City. If we want to compare standards of living, we have to correct for these differences; measures which do so are called PPP (for *purchasing power parity*) measures. Using such a measure, output per person in China is estimated to be about $7,500, roughly one-sixth of the output per person in the United States. This gives a more accurate picture of the standard of living in China. It is obviously still much lower than that of the United States or other rich countries. But it is higher than suggested by the numbers in Figure 1-6.

Second, and more importantly, China has been growing rapidly for more than three decades. This is shown in Table 1-4, which gives output growth, unemployment, and inflation for the periods 1980–1999, 2000–2007, and each of the years 2008 to 2012. The numbers for 2011 and 2012 are forecasts as of the fall of 2011.

Look at the first two columns of Table 1-4. The most impressive numbers are those for output growth. Since 1980, China's output has grown at roughly 10% a year. This

◄ The issue is less important when comparing two rich countries. Thus, this was not a major issue when comparing standards of living in the United States and the euro area earlier.

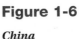

Figure 1-6

China

China, 2010
Output: $5.8 trillion
Population: 1,340 million
Output per person: $4,300
Share of world output: 9.3%

Table 1-4 Growth and Inflation in China, 1980–2012							
Percent	1980–1999 (average)	2000–2007 (average)	2008	2009	2010	2011	2012
Output growth rate	9.8	10.5	9.6	9.2	10.3	9.5	9.0
Unemployment rate	2.7	3.9	4.2	4.3	4.1	4.0	4.0
Inflation rate	8.1	1.6	5.9	–0.6	3.3	5.5	3.3

Output growth rate: annual rate of growth of output (GDP). Inflation rate: annual rate of change of the price level (GDP deflator).

Source: *World Economic Outlook* database, September 2011

represents a doubling of output every seven years. Compare this number to the numbers for the United States and for Europe we saw earlier, and you understand why the importance of the emerging economies in the world economy, China being the main one, is increasing so rapidly. Turn to unemployment. Numbers for unemployment are typically less reliable in poorer countries, so you should take those numbers with a grain of salt: Many workers stay in the countryside rather than being unemployed in the cities. Nevertheless, the numbers suggest consistently low unemployment. And inflation, which was high before 2000, is now relatively low.

Another striking aspect of Table 1-4 is how difficult it is to see the effects of the crisis in the data. Growth has barely decreased, and unemployment has barely increased since 2007. The reason is not that China is closed to the rest of the world. Chinese exports slowed during the crisis. But the adverse effect on demand was nearly fully offset by a major fiscal expansion by the Chinese government, with, in particular, a major increase in public investment. The result was sustained growth of demand and, in turn, of output.

This sustained growth performance raises obvious questions. The first is whether the numbers are for real. Could it be that growth has been overstated? After all, China is still officially a communist country, and government officials may have incentives to overstate the economic performance of their sector or their province. Economists who have looked at this carefully conclude that this is probably not the case. The statistics are not as reliable as they are in richer countries, but there is no obvious bias. Output growth is indeed very high in China.

So where does the growth come from? It clearly comes from two sources:

■ The first is high accumulation of capital. The investment rate (the ratio of investment to output) in China exceeds 40% of output, a high number. For comparison, the investment rate in the United States is only 17%. More capital means higher productivity and higher output.

■ The second is rapid technological progress. One of the strategies followed by the Chinese government has been to encourage foreign firms to relocate and produce in China. As foreign firms are typically much more productive than Chinese firms, this has increased productivity and output. Another aspect of the strategy has been to encourage joint ventures between foreign and Chinese firms. By making Chinese firms work with and learn from foreign firms, the productivity of the Chinese firms has increased dramatically.

When described in this way, achieving high productivity and high output growth appears easy, a recipe that every poor country could and should follow. In fact, things are less obvious. China is one of a number of countries that made the transition from central planning to a market economy. Most of the other countries, from Central Europe to Russia and the other former Soviet republics, experienced a large decrease in output at the time of transition. Most still have growth rates far below that of China. In many countries, widespread corruption and poor property rights make firms unwilling to invest. So why has China fared so much better? Some economists believe that this is the result of a slower transition: The first Chinese reforms took place in agriculture as early as 1980, and even today, many firms remain owned by the state. Others argue that the fact that the communist party has remained in control has actually helped the economic transition; tight political control has allowed for a better protection of property rights, at least for new firms, giving them incentives to invest. Getting the answers to these questions, and thus learning what other poor countries can take from the Chinese experience, can clearly make a huge difference, not only for China but for the rest of the world.

1-5 Looking Ahead

This concludes our world tour. There are many other regions of the world we could have looked at:

- India, another poor and large country, with a population of 1,200 million people, which, like China, is now growing very fast. In 2010, India's output growth rate was 10%.
- Japan, whose growth performance for the 40 years following World War II was so impressive that it was referred to as an economic miracle, but has done very poorly in the last two decades. Since a stock market crash in the early 1990s, Japan has been in a prolonged slump, with average output growth under 1% per year.
- Latin America, which went from very high inflation to low inflation in the 1990s. Many countries, such as Chile and Brazil, appear to be in good economic shape and have done relatively well in the crisis. Argentina, which went through a collapse of its exchange rate and a major banking crisis in the early 2000s, has now largely recovered and is also growing rapidly.
- Central and Eastern Europe, which shifted from central planning to a market system in the early 1990s. In most countries, the shift was characterized by a sharp decline in output at the start of transition. Some countries, such as Poland, now have high growth rates; others, such as Bulgaria or Romania, are still struggling.
- Africa, which has suffered decades of economic stagnation, but where, contrary to common perceptions, growth has been high since 2000, averaging 5.5% per year during the decade and reflecting growth in most of the countries of the continent.

There is a limit to how much you can absorb in this first chapter. Think about the questions to which you have been exposed:

- The big issues triggered by the crisis: What caused the crisis? Why did it transmit so fast from the United States to the rest of the world? In retrospect, what could and should have been done to prevent it? Were the monetary and fiscal responses appropriate? Why is the recovery so slow in advanced countries? How was China able to maintain high growth?
- Can monetary and fiscal policies be used to avoid recessions? At what rate should the United States reduce its budget deficit? What are the pros and cons of joining a common currency area such as the euro area? What measures could be taken in Europe to reduce persistently high unemployment?
- Why do growth rates differ so much across countries, even over long periods of time? Can other countries emulate China and grow at the same rate?

The purpose of this book is to give you a way of thinking about these questions. As we develop the tools you need, we shall show you how to use them by returning to these questions and showing you the answers the tools suggest.

Key Terms

European Union (EU), 9
euro area, 10

common currency area, 10

Questions and Problems

QUICK CHECK

All Quick Check questions and problems are available on MyEconLab.

1. Using the information in this chapter, label each of the following statements true, false, or uncertain. Explain briefly.

a. Output growth was negative in both advanced as well as emerging and developing countries in 2009.

b. Stock prices fell between 2007 and 2010 around the world.

c. In the 1960s and early 1970s, the United States had a higher rate of unemployment than Europe, but today it has a much lower rate of unemployment.

d. China's seemingly high growth rate is a myth, a product solely of misleading official statistics.

e. The high rate of unemployment in Europe started when a group of major European countries adopted a common currency.

f. The Federal Reserve lowers interest rates when it wants to avoid recession and raises interest rates when it wants to slow the rate of growth in the economy.

g. Output per person is very different in the euro area, the United States, and China.

h. The United States federal government has never run a budget surplus in the last two decades.

2. Macroeconomic policy in Europe

Beware of simplistic answers to complicated macroeconomic questions. Consider each of the following statements and comment on whether there is another side to the story.

a. There is a simple solution to the problem of high European unemployment: Reduce labor market rigidities.

b. What can be wrong about joining forces and adopting a common currency? The euro is obviously good for Europe.

DIG DEEPER

All Dig Deeper questions and problems are available on MyEconLab.

3. Chinese economic growth is the outstanding feature of the world economic scene over the past two decades.

a. In 2010, U.S. output was $14.7 trillion, and Chinese output was $5.8 trillion. Suppose that from now on, the output of China grows at an annual rate of 10.5% per year, while the output of the United States grows at an annual rate of 2.6% per year. These are the values in each country for the period 2000–2007 as stated in the text. Using these assumptions and a spreadsheet, calculate and plot U.S. and Chinese output from 2010 over the next 100 years. How many years will it take for China to have a total level of output equal to that of the United States?

b. When China catches up with the United States in total output, will residents of China have the same standard of living as U.S. residents? Explain.

c. Another word for standard of living is output per person. How has China raised its output per person in the last two decades? Are these methods applicable to the United States?

d. Do you think China's experience in raising its standard of living (output per person) provides a model for developing countries to follow?

4. Deficit reduction was identified as the major issue facing the United States as of the writing of this chapter.

a. Go to the most recent Economic Report of the President to ascertain whether deficits as a percent of GDP have increased or decreased compared to what was expected for 2011 and 2012 as of the writing of the chapter.

b. Calculate the total change in the deficit as a percent of GDP between 2011 and most recent data. Now split the change in the deficit since 2011 into (1) the changes in tax revenue as a percent of GDP, (2) the change in expenditures as a percent of GDP.

c. Use the data entitled Economic and Financial Indicators found in *The Economist* to find the country with largest budget deficit and largest budget surplus. In this list the budget deficit is called the "Budget Balance." Then find the OECD member in this list with the largest budget deficit and largest budget surplus.

EXPLORE FURTHER

5. U.S. postwar recessions

*This question looks at the recessions over the past 40 years. To work this problem, first obtain quarterly data on U.S. output growth for the period 1960 to the most recent date from the Web site **www.bea.gov**. Table 1.1.1 presents the percent change in real gross domestic product. This data can be downloaded to a spreadsheet. Plot the quarterly GDP growth rates from 1960:1 to the latest observations. Did any quarters have negative growth? Using the definition of a recession as two or more consecutive quarters of negative growth, answer the following questions.*

a. How many recessions has the U.S. economy undergone since 1960, quarter 2?

b. How many quarters has each recession lasted?

c. In terms of length and magnitude, which two recessions have been the most severe?

6. From Problem 5, write down the quarters in which the six traditional recessions started. Find the monthly series in the Federal Reserve Bank of St. Louis (FRED) database for the seasonally adjusted unemployment rate. Retrieve the monthly data series on the unemployment rate for the period 1969 to the end of the data. Make sure all data series are seasonally adjusted.

   a. Look at each recession since 1969. What was the unemployment rate in the first month of the first quarter of negative growth? What was the unemployment rate in the last month of the last quarter of negative growth? By how much did the unemployment rate increase?

   b. Which recession had the largest increase in the rate of unemployment? Begin with the month before the quarter in which output first falls and measure to the highest level of the unemployment rate before the next recession.

Further Reading

- The best way to follow current economic events and issues is to read *The Economist*, a weekly magazine published in England. The articles in *The Economist* are well informed, well written, witty, and opinionated. Make sure to read it regularly.

APPENDIX: Where to Find the Numbers

Suppose you want to find the numbers for inflation in Germany over the past five years. Fifty years ago, the answer would have been to learn German, find a library with German publications, find the page where inflation numbers were given, write them down, and plot them by hand on a clean sheet of paper. Today, improvements in the collection of data, the development of computers and electronic databases, and access to the Internet make the task much easier. This appendix will help you find the numbers you are looking for, be it inflation in Malaysia last year, or consumption in the United States in 1959, or unemployment in Ireland in the 1980s. In most cases, the data can be downloaded to spreadsheets for further treatment.

For a Quick Look at Current Numbers

- The best source for the most recent numbers on output, unemployment, inflation, exchange rates, interest rates, and stock prices for a large number of countries is the last four pages of *The Economist*, published each week (www.economist.com). The Web site, like many of the Web sites listed below, contains both information available free to anyone and information available only to subscribers.

- A good source for recent numbers about the U.S. economy is *National Economic Trends*, published monthly by the Federal Reserve Bank of Saint Louis (www.research.stlouisfed.org/publications/net/).

For More Detail about the U.S. Economy

- A convenient database, with numbers often going back to the 1960s, for both the United States and other countries, is the *Federal Reserve Economic Database* (called *FRED*), maintained by the Federal Reserve Bank of Saint Louis. Access is free, and much of the data used in this book comes from that database. (www.research.stlouisfed.org/fred2/)

- Once a year, the *Economic Report of the President*, written by the Council of Economic Advisers and published by the U.S. Government Printing Office in Washington, D.C., gives a description of current evolutions, as well as numbers for most major macroeconomic variables, often going back to the 1950s. (It contains two parts, a report on the economy, and a set of statistical tables. Both can be found at www.origin.www.gpoaccess.gov/eop/.)

- A detailed presentation of the most recent numbers for national income accounts is given in the *Survey of Current Business*, published monthly by the U.S. Department of Commerce, Bureau of Economic Analysis (www.bea.gov). A user's guide to the statistics published by the Bureau of Economic Analysis is given in the *Survey of Current Business*, April 1996.

- The standard reference for national income accounts is the *National Income and Product Accounts of the United States*. Volume 1, 1929–1958, and Volume 2, 1959–1994, are published by the U.S. Department of Commerce, Bureau of Economic Analysis (www.bea.gov).

- For data on just about everything, including economic data, a precious source is the *Statistical Abstract of the United States*, published annually by the U.S. Department of Commerce, Bureau of the Census (www.census.gov/prod/www/statistical-abstract.html).

Numbers for Other Countries

The **Organization for Economic Cooperation and Development**, OECD for short, located in Paris, France (www.oecd.org), is an organization that includes most of the rich countries in the world (Australia, Austria, Belgium, Canada, Chile, the Czech Republic, Denmark, Estonia, Finland, France, Germany, Greece, Hungary, Iceland, Israel, Italy, Japan, Korea,

Luxembourg, Mexico, the Netherlands, New Zealand, Norway, Poland, Portugal, the Slovak Republic, Slovenia, Spain, Sweden, Switzerland, Turkey, the United Kingdom, and the United States). Together, these countries account for about 70% of the world's output. One strength of the OECD data is that, for many variables, the OECD tries to make the variables comparable across member countries (or tells you when they are not comparable). The OECD puts out three useful publications, all available on the OECD site:

■ The first is the *OECD Economic Outlook*, published twice a year. In addition to describing current macroeconomic issues and evolutions, it includes a data appendix, with data for many macroeconomic variables. The data typically go back to the 1980s and are reported consistently, both across time and across countries.

■ The second is the *OECD Employment Outlook*, published annually. It focuses more specifically on labor-market issues and numbers.

■ Occasionally, the OECD puts together current and past data, and publishes a set of OECD Historical Statistics in which various years are grouped together.

The main strength of the publications of the **International Monetary Fund** (IMF for short, located in Washington, D.C.) is that they cover nearly all of the countries of the world. The IMF has 187 member countries and provides data on each of them (www.imf.org).

■ A particularly useful IMF publication is the *World Economic Outlook* (WEO for short), which is published twice a year and which describes major economic events in the world and in specific member countries. Selected series associated with the Outlook are available in the WEO database, available on the IMF site (www.imf.org/external/data.htm). Most of the data shown in this chapter come from this database.

■ Two other useful publications are the *Global Financial Stability Report* (GFSR for short), which focuses on financial developments, and the *Fiscal Monitor*, which focuses on

fiscal developments. All three publications are available on the IMF Web site (www.imf.org/external/index.htm).

Historical Statistics

■ For long-term historical statistics for the United States, the basic reference is *Historical Statistics of the United States, Colonial Times to 1970*, Parts 1 and 2, published by the U.S. Department of Commerce, Bureau of the Census (www.census.gov/prod/www/abs/statab.html).

■ For long-term historical statistics for several countries, a precious data source is Angus Maddison's *Monitoring the World Economy*, 1820–1992, Development Centre Studies, OECD, Paris, 1995. This study gives data going back to 1820 for 56 countries. Two even longer and broader sources are *The World Economy: A Millenial Perspective*, Development Studies, OECD, 2001, and *The World Economy: Historical Statistics*, Development Studies, OECD 2004, both also by Angus Maddison.

Current Macroeconomic Issues

A number of Web sites offer information and commentaries about the macroeconomic issues of the day. In addition to *The Economist* Web site mentioned earlier, the site maintained by Nouriel Roubini (www.rgemonitor.com) offers an extensive set of links to articles and discussions on macroeconomic issues (by subscription).

Finally, if you still have not found what you were looking for, a site maintained by Bill Goffe at the State University of New York (SUNY) (www.rfe.org), lists not only many more data sources, but also sources for economic information in general, from working papers, to data, to jokes, to jobs in economics, and to blogs.

Key Terms

Organization for Economic Cooperation and Development (OECD), 17
International Monetary Fund (IMF), 18

A Tour of the Book

T he words *output, unemployment,* and *inflation* appear daily in newspapers and on the evening news. So when we used these words in Chapter 1, you knew roughly what we were talking about. It is now time to define these words more precisely, and this is what we do in the first three sections of this chapter.

Section 2-1 looks at output.

Section 2-2 looks at the unemployment rate.

Section 2-3 looks at the inflation rate.

Section 2-4 introduces two important relations between these three variables: Okun's law and the Phillips curve.

Section 2-5 then introduces the three central concepts around which the book is organized:

■ The *short run*: What happens to the economy from year to year

■ The *medium run*: What happens to the economy over a decade or so

■ The *long run*: What happens to the economy over a half century or longer

Building on these three concepts, Section 2-6 gives you the road map to the rest of the book. ●

2-1 Aggregate Output

Economists studying economic activity in the nineteenth century or during the Great Depression had no measure of aggregate activity (*aggregate* is the word macroeconomists use for *total*) on which to rely. They had to put together bits and pieces of information, such as the shipments of iron ore or sales at some department stores, to try to infer what was happening to the economy as a whole.

Two economists, Simon Kuznets, from Harvard University, and Richard Stone, ▶ from Cambridge University, were given the Nobel Prize for their contributions to the development of the national income and product accounts—a gigantic intellectual and empirical achievement.

It was not until the end of World War II that **national income and product accounts** (or national income accounts, for short) were put together. Measures of aggregate output have been published on a regular basis in the United States since October 1947. (You will find measures of aggregate output for earlier times, but these have been constructed retrospectively.)

Like any accounting system, the national income accounts first define concepts and then construct measures corresponding to these concepts. You need only to look at statistics from countries that have not yet developed such accounts to realize that precision and consistency in such accounts are crucial. Without precision and consistency, numbers that should add up do not; trying to understand what is going on feels like trying to balance someone else's checkbook. We shall not burden you with the details of national income accounting here. But because you will occasionally need to know the definition of a variable and how variables relate to each other, Appendix 1 at the end of the book gives you the basic accounting framework used in the United States (and, with minor variations, in most other countries) today. You will find it useful whenever you want to look at economic data on your own.

You may come across another term, **gross national product**, or **GNP**. There is a subtle difference between "domestic" and "national," and thus between GDP and GNP. We examine the distinction in Chapter 18 and ▶ in Appendix 1 at the end of the book. For now, ignore it.

GDP: Production and Income

The measure of **aggregate output** in the national income accounts is called the **gross domestic product**, or **GDP**, for short. To understand how GDP is constructed, it is best to work with a simple example. Consider an economy composed of just two firms:

In reality, not only workers ▶ and machines are required for steel production, but so are iron ore, electricity, and so on. We shall ignore these to keep the example simple.

- Firm 1 produces steel, employing workers and using machines to produce the steel. It sells the steel for $100 to Firm 2, which produces cars. Firm 1 pays its workers $80, leaving $20 in profit to the firm.
- Firm 2 buys the steel and uses it, together with workers and machines, to produce cars. Revenues from car sales are $200. Of the $200, $100 goes to pay for steel and $70 goes to workers in the firm, leaving $30 in profit to the firm.

We can summarize this information in a table:

Steel Company (Firm 1)			Car Company (Firm 2)		
Revenues from sales		$100	Revenues from sales		$200
Expenses		$80	Expenses		$170
Wages	$80		Wages	$70	
			Steel purchases	$100	
Profit		$20	Profit		$30

An intermediate good is a good used in the production of another good. Some goods can be both final goods and intermediate goods. Potatoes sold directly to consumers are final goods. Potatoes used to produce potato chips are intermediate goods. Can you ▶ think of other examples?

How would you define aggregate output in this economy? As the sum of the values of all goods produced in the economy—the sum of $100 from the production of steel and $200 from the production of cars, so $300? Or as just the value of cars, which is equal to $200?

Some thought suggests that the right answer must be $200. Why? Because steel is an **intermediate good**: It is used in the production of cars. Once we count the production of cars, we do not want to count the production of the goods that went into the production of these cars.

This motivates the first definition of GDP:

1. GDP Is the Value of the Final Goods and Services Produced in the Economy during a Given Period.

The important word here is **final**. We want to count only the production of final goods, not intermediate goods. Using our example, we can make this point in another way. Suppose the two firms merged, so that the sale of steel took place inside the new firm and was no longer recorded. The accounts of the new firm would be given by the following table:

Steel and Car Company	
Revenues from sales	$200
Expenses (wages)	$150
Profit	$50

All we would see would be one firm selling cars for $200, paying workers $80 + $70 = $150, and making $20 + $30 = $50 in profits. The $200 measure would remain unchanged—as it should. We do not want our measure of aggregate output to depend on whether firms decide to merge or not.

This first definition gives us one way to construct GDP: by recording and adding up the production of all final goods—and this is indeed roughly the way actual GDP numbers are put together. But it also suggests a second way of thinking about and constructing GDP:

2. GDP Is the Sum of Value Added in the Economy during a Given Period.

The term **value added** means exactly what it suggests. The value added by a firm is defined as the value of its production minus the value of the intermediate goods used in production.

In our two-firms example, the steel company does not use intermediate goods. Its value added is simply equal to the value of the steel it produces, $100. The car company, however, uses steel as an intermediate good. Thus, the value added by the car company is equal to the value of the cars it produces minus the value of the steel it uses in production, $200 − $100 = $100. Total value added in the economy, or GDP, equals $100 + $100 = $200. (Note that aggregate value added would remain the same if the steel and car firms merged and became a single firm. In this case, we would not observe intermediate goods at all—as steel would be produced and then used to produce cars within the single firm—and the value added in the single firm would simply be equal to the value of cars, $200.)

This definition gives us a second way of thinking about GDP. Put together, the two definitions imply that the value of final goods and services—the first definition of GDP—can also be thought of as the sum of the value added by all the firms in the economy—the second definition of GDP.

So far, we have looked at GDP from the *production side*. The other way of looking at GDP is from the *income side*. Go back to our example and think about the revenues left to a firm after it has paid for its intermediate goods: Some of the revenues go to pay workers—this component is called *labor income*. The rest goes to the firm—that component is called *capital income* or *profit income*.

Of the $100 of value added by the steel manufacturer, $80 goes to workers (labor income) and the remaining $20 goes to the firm (capital income). Of the $100 of value added by the car manufacturer, $70 goes to labor income and $30 to capital income. For the economy as a whole, labor income is equal to $150 ($80 + $70), capital income is equal to $50 ($20 + $30). Value added is equal to the sum of labor income and capital income is equal to $200 ($150 + $50).

The labor share in the example is thus 75%. In advanced countries, the share of labor is indeed typically between 65 ◀ and 75%.

This motivates the third definition of GDP:

3. GDP Is the Sum of Incomes in the Economy during a Given Period.

To summarize: You can think about aggregate output— *GDP*—in three different but equivalent ways.

Two lessons to remember:

i. GDP is the measure of ▶ aggregate output, which we can look at from the production side (aggregate production), or the income side (aggregate income); and

ii. Aggregate production and aggregate income are always equal.

- From the *production side*: GDP equals the value of the final goods and services produced in the economy during a given period.
- Also from the *production side*: GDP is the sum of value added in the economy during a given period.
- From the *income side*: GDP is the sum of incomes in the economy during a given period.

Nominal and Real GDP

U.S. GDP was $14,660 billion in 2010, compared to $526 billion in 1960. Was U.S. output really 28 times higher in 2010 than in 1960? Obviously not: Much of the increase reflected an increase in prices rather than an increase in quantities produced. This leads to the distinction between nominal GDP and real GDP.

Nominal GDP is the sum of the quantities of final goods produced times their current price. This definition makes clear that nominal GDP increases over time for two reasons:

- First, the production of most goods increases over time.
- Second, the prices of most goods also increase over time.

If our goal is to measure production and its change over time, we need to eliminate the effect of increasing prices on our measure of GDP. That's why **real GDP** is constructed as the sum of the quantities of final goods times *constant* (rather than *current*) prices.

If the economy produced only one final good, say, a particular car model, constructing real GDP would be easy: We would use the price of the car in a given year and then use it to multiply the quantity of cars produced in each year. An example will help here. Consider an economy that only produces cars—and to avoid issues we shall tackle later, assume the same model is produced every year. Suppose the number and the price of cars in three successive years are given by:

Nominal GDP, which is equal to the quantity of cars times their price, goes up from $200,000 in 2004 to $288,000 in 2005—a 44% increase—and from $288,000 in 2005 to $338,000 in 2006—a 16% increase.

Year	Quantity of Cars	Price of Cars	Nominal GDP	Real GDP (in 2005 dollars)
2004	10	$20,000	$200,000	$240,000
2005	12	$24,000	$288,000	$288,000
2006	13	$26,000	$338,000	$312,000

- To construct real GDP, we need to multiply the number of cars in each year by a *common* price. Suppose we use the price of a car in 2005 as the common price. This approach gives us in effect *real GDP in 2005 dollars.*
- Using this approach, real GDP in 2004 (in 2005 dollars) equals 10 cars × $24,000 per car = $240,000. Real GDP in 2005 (in 2005 dollars) equals 12 cars × $24,000 per car = $288,000, the same as nominal GDP in 2005. Real GDP in 2006 (in 2005 dollars) is equal to 13 × $24,000 = $312,000.

Warning! People often use *nominal* to denote small amounts. Economists use ▶ *nominal* for variables expressed in current prices. And they surely do not refer to small amounts: The numbers typically run in the billions or trillions of dollars.

So real GDP goes up from $240,000 in 2004 to $288,000 in 2005—a 20% increase—and from $288,000 in 2005 to $312,000 in 2006—an 8% increase.

■ How different would our results have been if we had decided to construct real GDP using the price of a car in, say, 2006 rather than 2005? Obviously, the level of real GDP in each year would be different (because the prices are not the same in 2006 as in 2005); but its rate of change from year to year would be the same as above.

To be sure, compute real GDP in 2006 dollars, and compute ◀ the rate of growth from 2004 to 2005, and from 2005 to 2006.

The problem in constructing real GDP in practice is that there is obviously more than one final good. Real GDP must be defined as a weighted average of the output of all final goods, and this brings us to what the weights should be.

The *relative prices* of the goods would appear to be the natural weights. If one good costs twice as much per unit as another, then that good should count for twice as much as the other in the construction of real output. But this raises the question: What if, as is typically the case, relative prices change over time? Should we choose the relative prices of a particular year as weights, or should we change the weights over time? More discussion of these issues, and of the way real GDP is constructed in the United States, is left to the appendix to this chapter. Here, what you should know is that the measure of real GDP in the U.S. national income accounts uses weights that reflect relative prices and which change over time. The measure is called **real GDP in chained (2005) dollars**. We use 2005 because, as in our example above, 2005 is the year when, by construction, real GDP is equal to nominal GDP. It is our best measure of the output of the U.S. economy, and its evolution shows how U.S. output has increased over time.

Figure 2-1 plots the evolution of both nominal GDP and real GDP since 1960. By construction, the two are equal in 2005. The figure shows that real GDP in 2010 was about 4.7 times its level of 1960—a considerable increase, but clearly much less than the 28-fold increase in nominal GDP over the same period. The difference between the two results comes from the increase in prices over the period.

Suppose real GDP was measured in 2000 dollars rather ◀ than 2005 dollars. Where would the nominal GDP and real GDP lines on the graph intersect?

The terms *nominal GDP* and *real GDP* each have many synonyms, and you are likely to encounter them in your readings:

■ Nominal GDP is also called **dollar GDP** or **GDP in current dollars**.

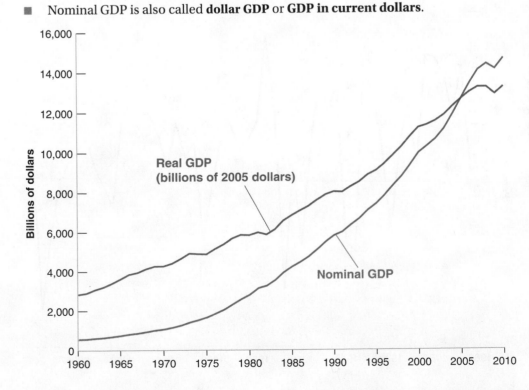

Figure 2-1

Nominal and real U.S. GDP, 1960–2010

From 1960 to 2010, nominal GDP increased by a factor of 28. Real GDP increased by a factor of about 5.

Source: Series GDPCA,GDPA: Federal Reserve Economic Data (FRED) http://research.stlouisfed.org/fred2/

- Real GDP is also called **GDP in terms of goods**, **GDP in constant dollars**, **GDP adjusted for inflation**, or **GDP in (chained) 2005 dollars** or **GDP in 2005 dollars**—if the year in which real GDP is set equal to nominal GDP is 2005, as is the case in the United States at this time.

In the chapters that follow, unless we indicate otherwise,

- GDP will refer to *real GDP* and Y_t will denote *real GDP in year t*.
- Nominal GDP, and variables measured in current dollars, will be denoted by a dollar sign in front of them—for example, $\$Y_t$ for nominal GDP in year *t*.

GDP: Level versus Growth Rate

We have focused so far on the level of real GDP. This is an important number that gives the economic size of a country. A country with twice the GDP of another country is economically twice as big as the other country. Equally important is the level of **real GDP per person**, the ratio of real GDP to the population of the country. It gives us the average standard of living of the country.

Warning: One must be careful about how one does the comparison: Recall the discussion in Chapter 1 about the standard of living in China. This is discussed further in Chapter 10.

In assessing the performance of the economy from year to year, economists focus, however, on the rate of growth of real GDP, often called just **GDP growth**. Periods of positive GDP growth are called **expansions**. Periods of negative GDP growth are called **recessions**.

The evolution of GDP growth in the United States since 1960 is given in Figure 2-2. GDP growth in year *t* is constructed as $(Y_t - Y_{t-1})/Y_{t-1}$ and expressed as a percent. The figure shows how the U.S. economy has gone through a series of expansions, interrupted by short recessions. Again, you can see the effects of the crisis: zero growth in 2008, and a large negative growth rate in 2009.

It is actually the subject of one of the boxes in Chapter 5.

The figure raises a small puzzle. According to the graph, growth was positive in 2001. But you may have heard people refer to the "recession of 2001." Why do they do so? Because they look at GDP growth quarter by quarter, rather than year by year. There

Figure 2-2

Growth rate of U.S. GDP, 1960–2010

Since 1960, the U.S. economy has gone through a series of expansions, interrupted by short recessions. The most recent recession was the most severe recession in the period from 1960 to 2010.

Source: Calculated using series GDPCA in Figure 2-1

Real GDP, Technological Progress, and the Price of Computers

A tough problem in computing real GDP is how to deal with changes in quality of existing goods. One of the most difficult cases is computers. It would clearly be absurd to assume that a personal computer in 2010 is the same good as a personal computer produced in 1981 (the year in which the IBM PC was introduced): The same amount of money can clearly buy much more computing in 2010 than it could in 1981. But how much more? Does a 2010 computer provide 10 times, 100 times, or 1,000 times the computing services of a 1981 computer? How should we take into account the improvements in internal speed, the size of the random access memory (RAM) or of the hard disk, the fact that computers can access the Internet, and so on?

The approach used by economists to adjust for these improvements is to look at the market for computers and how it values computers with different characteristics in a given year. Example: Suppose the evidence from prices of different models on the market shows that people are willing to pay 10% more for a computer with a speed of 3 GHz (3,000 megahertz) rather than 2 GHz. (The first edition of this book, published in 1996, compared two computers, with speeds of 50 and 16 megaherz, respectively. This change is a good indication of technological progress. A further indication of technological progress is that, for the past few years, progress has not been made by increasing the speed of processors, but rather by using multicore processors. We shall leave this aspect aside here, but people in charge of national income accounts cannot; they have to take this change into account as well.) Suppose

new computers this year have a speed of 3 GHz compared to a speed of 2 GHz for new computers last year. And suppose the dollar price of new computers this year is the same as the dollar price of new computers last year. Then economists in charge of computing the adjusted price of computers will conclude that new computers are in fact 10% cheaper than last year.

This approach, which treats goods as providing a collection of characteristics—for computers, speed, memory, and so on—each with an implicit price, is called hedonic pricing ("hedone" means "pleasure" in Greek). It is used by the Department of Commerce—which constructs real GDP—to estimate changes in the price of complex and fast changing goods, such as automobiles and computers. Using this approach, the Department of Commerce estimates that, for a given price, the quality of new computers has increased on average by 18% a year since 1981. Put another way, a typical personal computer in 2010 delivers $1.18^{29} = 121$ times the computing services a typical personal computer delivered in 1981.

Not only do computers deliver more services, they have become cheaper as well: Their dollar price has declined by about 10% a year since 1981. Putting this together with the information in the previous paragraph, this implies that their quality-adjusted price has fallen at an average rate of 18% + 10% = 28% per year. Put another way, a dollar spent on a computer today buys $1.28^{29} = 1,285$ times more computing services than a dollar spent on a computer in 1981.

is no official definition of what constitutes a recession, but the convention is to refer to a "recession" if the economy goes through at least two consecutive quarters of negative growth. Although GDP growth was positive for 2001 as a whole, it was negative during each of the first three quarters of 2001; thus 2001 qualifies as a (mild) recession.

2-2 The Unemployment Rate

Because it is a measure of aggregate activity, GDP is obviously the most important macroeconomic variable. But two other variables, unemployment and inflation, tell us about other important aspects of how an economy is performing. This section focuses on the unemployment rate.

We start with two definitions: **Employment** is the number of people who have a job. **Unemployment** is the number of people who do not have a job but are looking for one. The **labor force** is the sum of employment and unemployment:

$$L = N + U$$
$$\text{labor force} = \text{employment} + \text{unemployment}$$

The **unemployment rate** is the ratio of the number of people who are unemployed to the number of people in the labor force:

$$u = \frac{U}{L}$$

unemployment rate $=$ unemployment/labor force

Constructing the unemployment rate is less obvious than you might have thought. The cartoon above not withstanding, determining whether somebody is employed is straightforward. Determining whether somebody is unemployed is harder. Recall from the definition that, to be classified as unemployed, a person must meet two conditions: that he or she does not have a job, and he or she is looking for one; this second condition is harder to assess.

Until the 1940s in the United States, and until more recently in most other countries, the only available source of data on unemployment was the number of people registered at unemployment offices, and so only those workers who were registered in unemployment offices were counted as unemployed. This system led to a poor measure of unemployment. How many of those looking for jobs actually registered at the unemployment office varied both across countries and across time. Those who had no incentive to register—for example, those who had exhausted their unemployment benefits—were unlikely to take the time to come to the unemployment office, so they were not counted. Countries with less generous benefit systems were likely to have fewer unemployed registering, and therefore smaller measured unemployment rates.

Today, most rich countries rely on large surveys of households to compute the unemployment rate. In the United States, this survey is called the **Current Population Survey (CPS)**. It relies on interviews of 50,000 households every month. The survey classifies a person as employed if he or she has a job at the time of the interview; it classifies a person as unemployed if he or she does not have a job *and has been looking for a job in the last four weeks*. Most other countries use a similar definition of unemployment. In the United States, estimates based on the CPS show that, during 2010, an average of 139.0 million people were employed, and 14.8 million people were unemployed, so the unemployment rate was $14.8/(139.0 + 14.8) = 9.6\%$.

Note that only those *looking for a job* are counted as unemployed; those who do not have a job and are not looking for one are counted as **not in the labor force**. When unemployment is high, some of the unemployed give up looking for a job and therefore are no longer counted as unemployed. These people are known as **discouraged workers.** Take an extreme example: If all workers without a job gave up looking for one, the

Figure 2-3

U.S. unemployment rate, 1960–2010

Since 1960, the U.S. unemployment rate has fluctuated between 3 and 10%, going down during expansions, and going up during recessions. The effect of the crisis is highly visible, with the unemployment rate reaching close to 10%, the highest such rate since the 1980s.

Source: Series UNRATE: Federal Reserve Economic Data (FRED) http://research.stlouisfed.org/fred2/

unemployment rate would equal zero. This would make the unemployment rate a very poor indicator of what is happening in the labor market. This example is too extreme; in practice, when the economy slows down, we typically observe both an increase in unemployment and an increase in the number of people who drop out of the labor force. Equivalently, a higher unemployment rate is typically associated with a lower **participation rate**, defined as the ratio of the labor force to the total population of working age. ◄

At the start of economic reform in Eastern Europe in the early 1990s, unemployment increased dramatically. But equally dramatic was the fall in the participation rate. In Poland in 1990, 70% of the decrease in employment was reflected in early retirements—by people dropping out of the labor force rather than becoming unemployed.

Figure 2-3 shows the evolution of unemployment in the United States since 1970. Since 1960, the U.S. unemployment rate has fluctuated between 3 and 10%, going up during recessions and down during expansions. Again, you can see the effect of the crisis, with the unemployment rate reaching a peak at nearly 10% in 2010, the highest such rate since the 1980s.

Why Do Economists Care about Unemployment?

Economists care about unemployment for two reasons. First, they care about unemployment because of its direct effect on the welfare of the unemployed. Although unemployment benefits are more generous today than they were during the Great Depression, unemployment is still often associated with financial and psychological suffering. How much suffering depends on the nature of the unemployment. One image of unemployment is that of a stagnant pool, of people remaining unemployed for long periods of time. In normal times, in the United States, this image is not right: Every month, many people become unemployed, and many of the unemployed find jobs. When unemployment increases, however, as is the case now, the image becomes more accurate. Not only are more people unemployed, but also many of them are unemployed for a long time. For example, the mean duration of unemployment, which was 9 weeks on average during 2000–2007, increased to 33 weeks in 2010. In short, when the unemployment increases, not only does unemployment become both more widespread, but it also becomes more painful.

Did Spain Have a 24% Unemployment Rate in 1994?

· ·

In 1994, the official unemployment rate in Spain reached 24%. (It then decreased steadily, reaching a low of 8% in 2007, only to increase dramatically again since the beginning of the crisis. It now exceeds 20% and is still increasing. Thus, many of the issues in this Focus box are becoming relevant again.) This was roughly the same unemployment rate as in the United States in 1933, the worst year of the Great Depression. Yet Spain in 1994 looked nothing like the United States in 1933: There were few homeless, and most cities looked prosperous. Can we really believe that nearly one-fifth of the Spanish labor force was looking for work?

To answer this question, we must first examine how the Spanish unemployment number is put together. Like the CPS in the United States, unemployment is measured using a large survey of 60,000 households. People are classified as unemployed if they indicate that they are not working but are seeking work.

Can we be sure that people tell the truth? No. Although there is no obvious incentive to lie—answers to the survey are confidential and are not used to determine whether people are eligible for unemployment benefits—those who are working in the underground economy may prefer to play it safe and report that they are unemployed instead.

The size of the underground economy—the part of economic activity that is not measured in official statistics, either because the activity is illegal or because firms and workers would rather not report it and thus not pay taxes—is an old issue in Spain. And because of that, we actually know more about the underground economy in Spain than in many other countries: In 1985, the Spanish government tried to find out more and organized a detailed survey of 60,000 individuals. To try to elicit the truth from those interviewed, the questionnaire asked interviewees for an extremely precise account of the use of their time, making it more difficult to misreport. The answers were interesting. The underground economy in Spain—defined as the number of people working without declaring it to the social security administration—accounted for between 10 and 15% of employment. But it was composed mostly of people who already had a job and were taking a second or even a third job. The best estimate from the survey was that only about 15% of the unemployed were in fact working. This implied that the unemployment rate, which was officially 21% at the time, was in fact closer to 18%, still a very high number. In short, the Spanish underground economy was significant, but it just was not the case that most of the Spanish unemployed work in the underground economy.

How did the unemployed survive? Did they survive because unemployment benefits were unusually generous in Spain? No. Except for very generous unemployment benefits in two regions, Andalusia and Extremadura—which, not surprisingly, had even higher unemployment than the rest of the country—unemployment benefits were roughly in line with unemployment benefits in other OECD countries. Benefits were typically 70% of the wage for the first six months, and 60% thereafter. They were given for a period of 4 to 24 months, depending on how long people had worked before becoming unemployed. The 30% of the unemployed who had been unemployed for more than two years did not receive unemployment benefits.

So how did they survive? A key to the answer lies with the Spanish family structure. The unemployment rate was highest among the young: In 1994, it was close to 50% for those between 16 and 19, and around 40% for those between 20 and 24. The young typically stay at home until their late 20s, and have increasingly done so as unemployment increased. Looking at households rather than at individuals, the proportion of households where nobody was employed was less than 10% in 1994; the proportion of households that received neither wage income nor unemployment benefits was around 3%. In short, the family structure, and transfers from the rest of the family, were the factors that allowed many of the unemployed to survive.

Second, economists also care about the unemployment rate because it provides a signal that the economy may not be using some of its resources efficiently. Many workers who want to work do not find jobs; the economy is not utilizing its human resources efficiently. From this viewpoint, can very low unemployment also be a problem? The answer is yes. Like an engine running at too high a speed, an economy in which unemployment is very low may be overutilizing its resources and run into labor shortages. How low is "too low"? This is a difficult question, a question we will take up at more length later in the book. The question came up in 2000 in the United States. At the end of 2000, some economists worried that the unemployment rate, 4% at the time, was indeed too low. So, while they did not advocate triggering a recession, they favored lower (but positive) output growth for some time, so as to allow the unemployment rate to increase to a somewhat higher level. It turned out that they got more than they had asked for: a recession rather than a slowdown.

It is probably because of statements like this that economics is known as the "dismal science."

2-3 The Inflation Rate

Inflation is a sustained rise in the general level of prices—the **price level**. The **inflation rate** is the rate at which the price level increases. (Symmetrically, **deflation** is a sustained decline in the price level. It corresponds to a negative inflation rate).

The practical issue is how to define the price level so the inflation rate can be measured. Macroeconomists typically look at two measures of the price level, at two *price indexes*: the GDP deflator and the Consumer Price Index.

> Deflation is rare, but it happens. Japan has had deflation, off and on, since the late 1990s. The United States experienced deflation in the 1930s during the Great Depression.

The GDP Deflator

We saw earlier how increases in nominal GDP can come either from an increase in real GDP, or from an increase in prices. Put another way, if we see nominal GDP increase faster than real GDP, the difference must come from an increase in prices.

This remark motivates the definition of the GDP deflator. The **GDP deflator** in year t, P_t, is defined as the ratio of nominal GDP to real GDP in year t:

$$P_t = \frac{\text{Nominal GDP}_t}{\text{Real GDP}_t} = \frac{\$Y_t}{Y_t}$$

Note that, in the year in which, by construction, real GDP is equal to nominal GDP (2005 at this point in the United States), this definition implies that the price level is equal to 1. This is worth emphasizing: The GDP deflator is called an **index number**. Its level is chosen arbitrarily—here it is equal to 1 in 2005—and has no economic interpretation. But its rate of change, $(P_t - P_{t-1})/P_{t-1}$ (which we shall denote by π_t in the rest of the book), has a clear economic interpretation: It gives the rate at which the general level of prices increases over time—the rate of inflation.

One advantage to defining the price level as the GDP deflator is that it implies a simple relation among *nominal GDP*, *real GDP*, and the *GDP deflator*. To see this, reorganize the previous equation to get:

$$\$Y_t = P_t Y_t$$

Nominal GDP is equal to the GDP deflator times real GDP. Or, putting it in terms of rates of change: The rate of growth of nominal GDP is equal to the rate of inflation plus the rate of growth of real GDP.

> Index numbers are often set equal to 100 (in the base year) rather than to 1. If you look at the Economic Report of the President (see Chapter 1) you will see that the GDP deflator, reported in Table B-3, is equal to 100 for 2005 (the base year), 103.2 in 2006, and so on.

> Compute the GDP deflator and the associated rate of inflation from 2004 to 2005 and from 2005 to 2006 in our car example in Section 2-1, when real GDP is constructed using the 2005 price of cars as the common price.

> For a refresher, see Appendix 2, Proposition 7.

The Consumer Price Index

The GDP deflator gives the average price of output—the final goods *produced* in the economy. But consumers care about the average price of consumption—the goods they *consume*. The two prices need not be the same: The set of goods produced in the economy is not the same as the set of goods purchased by consumers, for two reasons:

- Some of the goods in GDP are sold not to consumers but to firms (machine tools, for example), to the government, or to foreigners.
- Some of the goods bought by consumers are not produced domestically but are imported from abroad.

To measure the average price of consumption, or, equivalently, the **cost of living**, macroeconomists look at another index, the **Consumer Price Index, or CPI.** The CPI has been in existence in the United States since 1917 and is published monthly (in contrast, numbers for GDP and the GDP deflator are only constructed and published quarterly).

The CPI gives the cost in dollars of a specific list of goods and services over time. The list, which is based on a detailed study of consumer spending, attempts to

> Do not confuse the CPI with the PPI, or *producer price index*, which is an index of prices of domestically produced goods in manufacturing, mining, agriculture, fishing, forestry, and electric utility industries.

Figure 2-4

Inflation rate, using the CPI and the GDP deflator, 1960–2010

The inflation rates, computed using either the CPI or the GDP deflator, are largely similar.

Source: Calculated using series GDPDEF, CPI-AUSCL Federal Reserve Economic Data (FRED) http://research.stlouisfed.org/fred2/

> Do not ask why such a strange base period was chosen. Nobody seems to remember.

> You may wonder why the effect of the increases in the price of oil since 1999 is much less visible in the figure. The answer: The increases have taken place more slowly over time, and other factors have worked in the opposite direction.

represent the consumption basket of a typical urban consumer and is updated roughly only once every 10 years.

Each month, Bureau of Labor Statistics (BLS) employees visit stores to find out what has happened to the price of the goods on the list; prices are collected in 87 cities, from about 23,000 retail stores, car dealerships, gas stations, hospitals, and so on. These prices are then used to construct the Consumer Price Index.

Like the GDP deflator (the price level associated with aggregate output, GDP), the CPI is an index. It is set equal to 100 in the period chosen as the base period and so its level has no particular significance. The current base period is 1982 to 1984, so the average for the period 1982 to 1984 is equal to 100. In 2010, the CPI was 222.8; thus, it cost more than twice as much in dollars to purchase the same consumption basket than in 1982–1984.

You may wonder how the rate of inflation differs depending on whether the GDP deflator or the CPI is used to measure it. The answer is given in Figure 2-4, which plots the two inflation rates since 1960 for the United States. The figure yields two conclusions:

- The CPI and the GDP deflator move together most of the time. In most years, the two inflation rates differ by less than 1%.
- But there are clear exceptions. In 1979 and 1980, the increase in the CPI was significantly larger than the increase in the GDP deflator. The reason is not hard to find. Recall that the GDP deflator is the price of goods *produced* in the United States, whereas the CPI is the price of goods *consumed* in the United States. That means when the price of imported goods increases relative to the price of goods produced in the United States, the CPI increases faster than the GDP deflator. This is precisely what happened in 1979 and 1980. The price of oil doubled. And although the United States is a producer of oil, it produces much less than it consumes: It was and still is a major oil importer. The result was a large increase in the CPI compared to the GDP deflator.

In what follows, we shall typically assume that the two indexes move together so we do not need to distinguish between them. we shall simply talk about *the price level* and denote it by P_t, without indicating whether we have the CPI or the GDP deflator in mind.

Why Do Economists Care about Inflation?

If a higher inflation rate meant just a faster but proportional increase in all prices and wages—a case called *pure inflation*—inflation would be only a minor inconvenience, as relative prices would be unaffected.

Take, for example, the workers' *real wage*—the wage measured in terms of goods rather than in dollars. In an economy with 10% more inflation, prices would increase by 10% more a year. But wages would also increase by 10% more a year, so real wages would be unaffected by inflation. Inflation would not be entirely irrelevant; people would have to keep track of the increase in prices and wages when making decisions. But this would be a small burden, hardly justifying making control of the inflation rate one of the major goals of macroeconomic policy.

So why do economists care about inflation? Precisely because there is no such thing as pure inflation:

- During periods of inflation, not all prices and wages rise proportionately. Because they don't, inflation affects income distribution. For example, retirees in many countries receive payments that do not keep up with the price level, so they lose in relation to other groups when inflation is high. This is not the case in the United States, where Social Security benefits automatically rise with the CPI, protecting retirees from inflation. But during the very high inflation that took place in Russia in the 1990s, retirement pensions did not keep up with inflation, and many retirees were pushed to near starvation.

- Inflation leads to other distortions. Variations in relative prices also lead to more uncertainty, making it harder for firms to make decisions about the future, such as investment decisions. Some prices, which are fixed by law or by regulation, lag behind the others, leading to changes in relative prices. Taxation interacts with inflation to create more distortions. If tax brackets are not adjusted for inflation, for example, people move into higher and higher tax brackets as their nominal income increases, even if their real income remains the same. ◄ This is known as *bracket creep*. In the United States, the tax brackets are adjusted automatically for inflation: If inflation is 5%, all tax brackets also go up by 5%—in other words, there is no bracket creep.

If inflation is so bad, does this imply that deflation (negative inflation) is good?

The answer is no. First, high deflation (a large negative rate of inflation) would create many of the same problems as high inflation, from distortions to increased uncertainty. Second, as we shall see later in the book, even a low rate of deflation limits the ability of monetary policy to affect output. So what is the "best" rate of inflation? Most macroeconomists believe that the best rate of inflation is a low and stable rate of inflation, somewhere between 1 and 4%. We shall look at the pros and cons of different rates of inflation later in the book. ◄ Newspapers sometimes confuse deflation and recession. They may happen together but they are not the same. Deflation is a decrease in the price level. A recession is a decrease in real output.

2-4 Output, Unemployment, and the Inflation Rate: Okun's Law and the Phillips Curve

We have looked separately at the three main dimensions of aggregate economic activity: output growth, the unemployment rate, and the inflation rate. Clearly they are not independent, and much of this book will be spent looking at the relations among them in detail. But it is useful to have a first look now.

Okun's Law

Intuition suggests that if output growth is high, unemployment will decrease, and this is indeed true. This relation was first examined by American economist Arthur Okun and for this reason has become known as **Okun's law**. Figure 2-5 plots the change in the unemployment rate on the vertical axis against the rate of growth of output on the horizontal axis for the United States since 1960. It also draws the line that best fits the cloud of points in the figure. Looking at the figure and the line suggests two conclusions: ◄ Arthur Okun was an adviser to President Kennedy in the 1960s. Okun's law is, of course, not a law, but an empirical regularity.

- The line is downward sloping and fits the cloud of points quite well. Put in economic terms: There is a tight relation between the two variables: Higher output

Figure 2-5

Changes in the unemployment rate versus output growth in the United States, 1960–2010

Output growth that is higher than usual is associated with a reduction in the unemployment rate; output growth that is lower than usual is associated with an increase in the unemployment rate.

Source: See Figures 2-2 and 2-3.

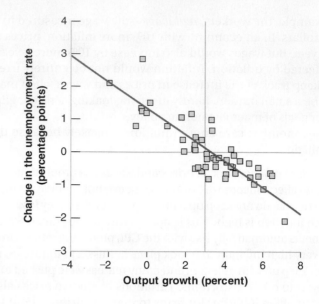

Such a graph, plotting one ▶ variable against another, is called a scatterplot. The line is called a regression line. For more on regressions, see Appendix 3.

growth leads to a decrease in unemployment. The slope of the line is −0.4. This implies that, on average, an increase in the growth rate of 1% decreases the unemployment rate by roughly −0.4%. This is why unemployment goes up in recessions and down in expansions. This relation has a simple but important implication: The key to decreasing unemployment is a high enough rate of growth.

■ This vertical line crosses the horizontal axis at the point where output growth is roughly equal to 3%. In economic terms: It takes a growth rate of about 3% to keep unemployment constant. This is for two reasons. The first is that population, and thus the labor force, increases over time, so employment must grow over time just to keep the unemployment rate constant. The second is that output per worker is also increasing with time, which implies that output growth is higher than employment growth. Suppose, for example, that the labor force grows at 1% and that output per worker grows at 2%. Then output growth must be equal to 3% (1% + 2%) just to keep the unemployment rate constant.

The Phillips Curve

Okun's law implies that, with strong enough growth, one can decrease the unemployment rate to very low levels. But intuition suggests that, when unemployment becomes very low, the economy is likely to overheat, and that this will lead to upward pressure on inflation. And, to a large extent, this is true. This relation was first explored in 1958 by a New Zealand economist, A. W. Phillips, and has become known as the **Phillips curve**. Phillips plotted the rate of inflation against the unemployment rate. Since then, the Phillips curve has been redefined as a relation between the *change in the rate of inflation* and the unemployment rate. Figure 2-6 plots the change in the inflation rate (measured using the CPI) on the vertical axis against the unemployment rate on the horizontal axis, together with the line that fits the cloud of points best, for the United States since 1960. Looking at the figure again suggests two conclusions:

It should probably be known ▶ as the Phillips relation, but it is too late to change that.

■ The line is downward sloping, although the fit is not as tight as it was for Okun's law: Higher unemployment leads, on average, to a decrease in inflation; lower unemployment leads to an increase in inflation. But this is only true on average. Sometimes, high unemployment is associated with an increase in inflation.

Figure 2-6

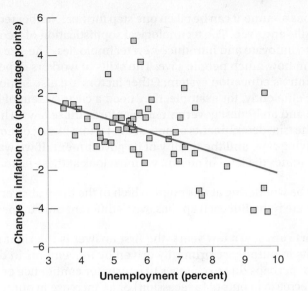

Changes in the inflation rate versus the unemployment rate in the United States, 1960–2010

A low unemployment rate leads to an increase in the inflation rate, a high unemployment rate to a decrease in the inflation rate.

Source: See Figures 2-3 and 2-4.

- The line crosses the horizontal axis at the point where the unemployment rate is roughly equal to 6%. In economic terms: When unemployment has been below 6%, inflation has typically increased, suggesting that the economy was overheating, operating above its potential. When unemployment has been above 6%, inflation has typically decreased, suggesting that the economy was operating below potential. But, again here, the relation is not tight enough that the unemployment rate at which the economy overheats can be pinned down very precisely. This explains why some economists believe that we should try to maintain a lower unemployment rate, say 4 or 5%, and others believe that it may be dangerous, leading to overheating and increasing inflation.

Clearly, a successful economy is an economy that combines high output growth, low unemployment, and low inflation. Can all these objectives be achieved simultaneously? Is low unemployment compatible with low and stable inflation? Do policy makers have the tools to sustain growth, to achieve low unemployment while maintaining low inflation? These are the questions we shall take up as we go through the book. The next two sections give you the road map.

2-5 The Short Run, the Medium Run, the Long Run

What determines the level of aggregate output in an economy?

- Reading newspapers suggests a first answer: Movements in output come from movements in the demand for goods. You probably have read news stories that begin like this: "Production and sales of automobiles were higher last month due to a surge in consumer confidence, which drove consumers to showrooms in record numbers." Stories like these highlight the role demand plays in determining aggregate output; they point to factors that affect demand, ranging from consumer confidence to interest rates.
- But, surely, no amount of Indian consumers rushing to Indian showrooms can increase India's output to the level of output in the United States. This suggests a second answer: What matters when it comes to aggregate output is the supply side—how much the economy can produce. How much can be produced depends on how advanced the technology of the country is, how much capital it is using, and the size and the skills of its labor force. These factors—not consumer confidence—are the fundamental determinants of a country's level of output.

- The previous argument can be taken one step further: Neither technology, nor capital, nor skills are given. The technological sophistication of a country depends on its ability to innovate and introduce new technologies. The size of its capital stock depends on how much people save. The skills of workers depend on the quality of the country's education system. Other factors are also important: If firms are to operate efficiently, for example, they need a clear system of laws under which to operate and an honest government to enforce those laws. This suggests a third answer: The true determinants of output are factors like a country's education system, its saving rate, and the quality of its government. If we want to understand what determines the level of output, we must look at these factors.

You might be wondering at this point, which of the three answers is right? The fact is that all three are right. But each applies over a different time frame:

- In the **short run**, say, a few years, the first answer is the right one. Year-to-year movements in output are primarily driven by movements in demand. Changes in demand, perhaps due to changes in consumer confidence or other factors, can lead to a decrease in output (a recession) or an increase in output (an expansion).
- In the **medium run**, say, a decade, the second answer is the right one. Over the medium run, the economy tends to return to the level of output determined by supply factors: the capital stock, the level of technology, and the size of the labor force. And, over a decade or so, these factors move sufficiently slowly that we can take them as given.
- In the **long run**, say, a few decades or more, the third answer is the right one. To understand why China has been able to achieve such a high growth rate since 1980, we must understand why both the capital stock and the level of technology in China are increasing so fast. To do so, we must look at factors like the education system, the saving rate, and the role of the government.

This way of thinking about the determinants of output underlies macroeconomics, and it underlies the organization of this book.

2-6 A Tour of the Book

The book is organized in three parts: A core; two extensions; and, finally, a comprehensive look at the role of macroeconomic policy. This organization is shown in Figure 2-7. We now describe it in more detail.

The Core

The core is composed of three parts—the short run, the medium run, and the long run.

- Chapters 3 to 5 look at how output is determined in the short run. To focus on the role of demand, we assume that firms are willing to supply any quantity at a given price. In other words, we ignore supply constraints. Chapter 3 looks at the goods market. Chapter 4 focuses on financial markets. Chapter 5 puts the goods and financial markets together. The resulting framework is known as the *IS–LM* model. Developed in the late 1930s, the *IS–LM* model still provides a simple way of thinking about the determination of output in the short run, and it remains a basic building block of macroeconomics. It also allows for a first pass at studying the effects of fiscal policy and monetary policy on output.

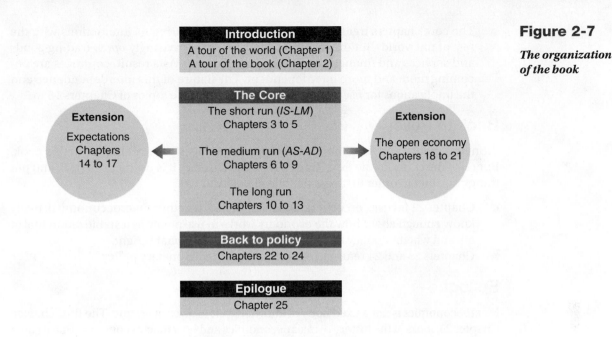

Figure 2-7

The organization of the book

- Chapters 6 to 9 develop the supply side and look at how output is determined in the medium run. Chapter 6 introduces the labor market. Chapter 7 puts together goods, financial, and labor markets and shows you how to think about the determination of output both in the short run and in the medium run. The resulting framework is called the aggregate supply–aggregate demand *AS–AD* model and, together with the *IS–LM*, is another workhorse of macroeconomics. Chapter 8 focuses on the relation between unemployment, inflation, and money growth. By then, you will have all the elements we need to take a first detailed look at the crisis. The crisis is unusual in a number of ways. The initial shock is a major shock to the financial system. Both monetary and fiscal policies are facing sharp constraints. As a result, the crisis is much deeper than a standard recession, and the recovery is proving to be very slow. This is the subject of Chapter 9.
- Chapters 10 to 13 focus on the long run. Chapter 10 introduces the relevant facts by looking at the growth of output both across countries and over long periods of time. Chapters 11 and 12 discuss how both capital accumulation and technological progress determine growth. Chapter 13 looks at the interaction among technological progress, wages, and unemployment.

Extensions

The core chapters give you a way of thinking about how output (and unemployment, and inflation) is determined over the short, medium, and long run. However, they leave out several elements, which are explored in two extensions:

- Expectations play an essential role in macroeconomics. Nearly all the economic decisions people and firms make—whether or not to buy a car, whether to buy bonds or to buy stocks, whether or not to build a new plant—depend on their expectations about future income, future profits, future interest rates, and so on. Fiscal and monetary policy affect economic activity not only through their direct effects, but also through their effects on people's and firms' expectations. While we touch on these issues in the core, Chapters 14 to 17 offer a more detailed treatment and draw the implications for fiscal and monetary policy.

- The core chapters treat the economy as *closed*, ignoring its interactions with the rest of the world. But the fact is, economies are increasingly *open*, trading goods and services and financial assets with one another. As a result, countries are becoming more and more interdependent. The nature of this interdependence and the implications for fiscal and monetary policy are the topics of Chapters 18 to 21.

Back to Policy

Monetary policy and fiscal policy are discussed in nearly every chapter of this book. But once the core and the extensions have been covered, it is useful to go back and put things together in order to assess the role of policy.

- Chapter 22 focuses on general issues of policy, whether macroeconomists really know enough about how the economy works to use policy as a stabilization tool at all, and whether policy makers can be trusted to do what is right.
- Chapters 23 and 24 return to the role of fiscal and monetary policy.

Epilogue

Macroeconomics is not a fixed body of knowledge. It evolves over time. The final chapter, Chapter 25, looks at the history of macroeconomics and how macroeconomists have come to believe what they believe today. From the outside, macroeconomics sometimes looks like a field divided among schools—"Keynesians," "monetarists," "new classicals," "supply-siders," and so on—hurling arguments at each other. The actual process of research is more orderly and more productive than this image suggests. We identify what we see as the main differences among macroeconomists, the set of propositions that define the core of macroeconomics today, and the challenges posed to macroeconomists by the crisis.

Summary

- We can think of GDP, the measure of aggregate output, in three equivalent ways: (1) GDP is the value of the final goods and services produced in the economy during a given period; (2) GDP is the sum of value added in the economy during a given period; and (3) GDP is the sum of incomes in the economy during a given period.

- Nominal GDP is the sum of the quantities of final goods produced times their current prices. This implies that changes in nominal GDP reflect both changes in quantities and changes in prices. Real GDP is a measure of output. Changes in real GDP reflect changes in quantities only.

- A person is classified as unemployed if he or she does not have a job and is looking for one. The unemployment rate is the ratio of the number of people unemployed to the number of people in the labor force. The labor force is the sum of those employed and those unemployed.

- Economists care about unemployment because of the human cost it represents. They also look at unemployment because it sends a signal about how efficiently the economy is using its resources. High unemployment indicates that the country is not utilizing its resources efficiently.

- Inflation is a rise in the general level of prices—the price level. The inflation rate is the rate at which the price level increases. Macroeconomists look at two measures of the price level. The first is the GDP deflator, which is the average price of the goods produced in the economy. The second is the Consumer Price Index (CPI), which is the average price of goods consumed in the economy.

- Inflation leads to changes in income distribution, to distortions, and to increased uncertainty.

- There are two important relations among output, unemployment, and inflation. The first, called Okun's law, is a relation between output growth and the change in unemployment: High output growth typically leads to a decrease in the unemployment rate. The second, called the Phillips curve, is a relation between unemployment and inflation: A low unemployment rate typically leads to an increase in the inflation rate.

- Macroeconomists distinguish between the short run (a few years), the medium run (a decade), and the long run (a few decades or more). They think of output as being determined by demand in the short run. They think of output as being determined by the level of technology, the capital stock, and the labor force in the medium run. Finally, they think of output as being determined by factors like education, research, saving, and the quality of government in the long run.

Key Terms

Questions and Problems

QUICK CHECK
All Quick Check questions and problems are available on MyEconLab.

1. Using the information in this chapter, label each of the following statements true, false, or uncertain. Explain briefly.

a. U.S. GDP was 28 times higher in 2010 than it was in 1960.

b. When the unemployment rate is high, the participation rate is also likely to be high.

c. The rate of unemployment tends to fall during expansions and rise during recessions.

d. If the Japanese CPI is currently at 108 and the U.S. CPI is at 104, then the Japanese rate of inflation is higher than the U.S. rate of inflation.

e. The rate of inflation computed using the CPI is a better index of inflation than the rate of inflation computed using the GDP deflator.

f. Okun's law shows that when output growth is lower than normal, the unemployment rate tends to rise.

g. Periods of negative GDP growth are called recessions.

h. When the economy is functioning normally, the unemployment rate is zero.

i. The Phillips curve is a relation between the level of inflation and the level of unemployment.

2. Suppose you are measuring annual U.S. GDP by adding up the final value of all goods and services produced in the economy. Determine the effect on GDP of each of the following transactions.

a. A seafood restaurant buys $100 worth of fish from a fisherman.

b. A family spends $100 on a fish dinner at a seafood restaurant.

c. Delta Air Lines buys a new jet from Boeing for $200 million.

d. The Greek national airline buys a new jet from Boeing for $200 million.

e. Delta Air Lines sells one of its jets to Denzel Washington for $100 million.

3. During a given year, the following activities occur:

i. A silver mining company pays its workers $200,000 to mine 75 pounds of silver. The silver is then sold to a jewelry manufacturer for $300,000.

ii. The jewelry manufacturer pays its workers $250,000 to make silver necklaces, which the manufacturer sells directly to consumers for $1,000,000.

a. Using the production-of-final-goods approach, what is GDP in this economy?

b. What is the value added at each stage of production? Using the value-added approach, what is GDP?

c. What are the total wages and profits earned? Using the income approach, what is GDP?

4. An economy produces three goods: cars, computers, and oranges. Quantities and prices per unit for years 2005 and 2006 are as follows:

	2005		2006	
	Quantity	Price	Quantity	Price
Cars	10	$2000	12	$3000
Computers	4	$1000	6	$500
Oranges	1000	$1	1000	$1

a. What is nominal GDP in 2005 and in 2006? By what percentage does nominal GDP change from 2005 to 2006?

b. Using the prices for 2005 as the set of common prices, what is real GDP in 2005 and in 2006? By what percentage does real GDP change from 2005 to 2006?

c. Using the prices for 2006 as the set of common prices, what is real GDP in 2005 and in 2006? By what percentage does real GDP change from 2005 to 2006?

d. Why are the two output growth rates constructed in (b) and (c) different? Which one is correct? Explain your answer.

5. Consider the economy described in Problem 4.

a. Use the prices for 2005 as the set of common prices to compute real GDP in 2005 and in 2006. Compute the GDP deflator for 2005 and for 2006 and compute the rate of inflation from 2005 to 2006.

b. Use the prices for 2006 as the set of common prices to compute real GDP in 2005 and in 2006. Compute the GDP deflator for 2005 and for 2006 and compute the rate of inflation from 2005 to 2006.

c. Why are the two rates of inflation different? Which one is correct? Explain your answer.

6. Consider the economy described in Problem 4.

a. Construct real GDP for years 2005 and 2006 by using the average price of each good over the two years.

b. By what percentage does real GDP change from 2005 to 2006?

c. What is the GDP deflator in 2005 and 2006? Using the GDP deflator, what is the rate of inflation from 2005 to 2006?

d. Is this an attractive solution to the problems pointed out in Problems 4 and 5 (i.e., two different growth rates and two different inflation rates, depending on which set of prices is used)? (The answer is yes and is the basis for the construction of chained-type deflators. See the appendix to this chapter for more discussion.)

7. Using macroeconomic relations:

a. Okun's law stated that when output growth is higher than usual, the unemployment rate tends to fall. Explain why usual output growth is positive.

b. In which year, a year where output growth is 2% or a year where output growth is –2%, will the unemployment rate rise more?

c. The Phillips curve is a relation between the change in the inflation rate and the level of the unemployment rate. Using the Phillips curve, is the unemployment rate zero when the rate of inflation is neither rising nor falling.

d. The Phillips curve is often portrayed a line with a negative slope. In the text, the slope is –0.4. In your opinion, is this a "better" economy if the line has a large slope, say –0.8, or a smaller slope, say –0.2?

DIG DEEPER
All Dig Deeper questions and problems are available on MyEconLab.

8. Hedonic pricing

As the first Focus box in this chapter explains, it is difficult to measure the true increase in prices of goods whose characteristics change over time. For such goods, part of any price increase can be attributed to an increase in quality. Hedonic pricing offers a method to compute the quality-adjusted increase in prices.

a. Consider the case of a routine medical checkup. Name some reasons you might want to use hedonic pricing to measure the change in the price of this service.

Now consider the case of a medical checkup for a pregnant woman. Suppose that a new ultrasound method is introduced. In the first year that this method is available, half of doctors offer the new method, and half offer the old method. A checkup using the new method costs 10% more than a checkup using the old method.

b. In percentage terms, how much of a quality increase does the new method represent over the old method? (Hint: Consider the fact that some women choose to see a doctor offering the new method when they could have chosen to see a doctor offering the old method.)

Now, in addition, suppose that in the first year the new ultrasound method is available, the price of checkups using the new method is 15% higher than the price of checkups in the previous year (when everyone used the old method).

c. How much of the higher price for checkups using the new method (as compared to checkups in the previous year) reflects a true price increase of checkups and how much represents a quality increase? In other words, how much higher is the quality-adjusted price of checkups using the new method as compared to the price of checkups in the previous year?

In many cases, the kind of information we used in parts (b) and (c) is not available. For example, suppose that in the year the new ultrasound method is introduced, all doctors adopt the new method, so the old method is no longer used. In addition, continue to assume that the price of checkups in the year the new method is introduced is 15% higher than the price of checkups in the previous year (when everyone used the old method). Thus, we observe a 15% price increase in checkups, but we realize that the quality of checkups has increased.

d. Under these assumptions, what information required to compute the quality-adjusted price increase of checkups is lacking? Even without this information, can we say anything about the quality-adjusted price increase of checkups? Is it more than 15%? less than 15%? Explain.

9. Measured and true GDP

Suppose that instead of cooking dinner for an hour, you decide to work an extra hour, earning an additional $12. You then purchase some (takeout) Chinese food, which costs you $10.

a. By how much does measured GDP increase?

b. Do you think the increase in measured GDP accurately reflects the effect on output of your decision to work? Explain.

EXPLORE FURTHER

10. Comparing the recessions of 2009 and 2001:

One very easy source for data is the Federal Reserve Bank of St. Louis FRED database. The series that measures real GDP is GDPC1, real GDP in each quarter of the year expressed at a seasonally adjusted annual rate (denoted SAAR). The monthly series for the unemployment rate is UNRATE. You can download these series in a variety of ways from this database.

a. Look at the data on quarterly real GDP growth from 1999 through 2001 and then from 2007 through 2009. Which recession has larger negative values for GDP growth, the recession centered on 2000 or the recession centered on 2008?

b. The unemployment rate is series UNRATE. Is the unemployment rate higher in the 2001 recession or the 2009 recession?

c. The National Bureau of Economic Research (NBER), which dates recessions, identified a recession beginning in March 2001 and ending in November 2001. The equivalent dates for the next, longer recession were December 2007 ending June 2009. In other words, according to the NBER, the economy began a recovery in November 2001 and in June 2009. Given your answers to parts (a) and (b), do you think the labor market recovered as quickly as GDP? Explain.

For more on NBER recession dating, visit www.nber.org. This site provides a history of recession dates and some discussion of their methodology.

Further Readings

- If you want to learn more about the definition and the construction of the many economic indicators that are regularly reported on the news—from the help-wanted index to the retail sales index—two easy-to-read references are:
  The *Guide to Economic Indicators*, by Norman Frumkin, 3rd edition, M.E. Sharpe, 4th edition, New York, 2005.
  The Economist Guide to Economic Indicators, by the staff of *The Economist*, 6th edition, Bloomberg, New York, 2007.

- In 1995, the U.S. Senate set up a commission to study the construction of the CPI and make recommendations about potential changes. The commission concluded that the rate of inflation computed using the CPI was on average about 1% too high. If this conclusion is correct, this implies in particular that real wages (nominal wages divided by the CPI) have grown 1% more per year than is currently being reported. For more on the conclusions of the commission and some of the exchanges that followed, read *Consumer Prices, the Consumer Price Index, and the Cost of Living*, by Michael Boskin et al., *Journal of Economic Perspectives*, 1998, 12(1): pp. 3–26.

- For a short history of the construction of the National Income Accounts, read *GDP: One of the Great Inventions of the 20th Century*, Survey of Current Business, January 2000, 1–9. (www.bea.gov/bea/articles/beawide/2000/0100od.pdf)

- For a discussion of some of the problems involved in measuring activity, read "What We Don't Know Could Hurt Us; Some Reflections on the Measurement of Economic Activity," by Katherine Abraham, *Journal of Economic Perspectives*, 2005, 19(3): pp. 3–18.

- To see why it is hard to measure the price level and output correctly, read "Viagra and the Wealth of Nations" by Paul Krugman, 1998 (www.pkarchive.org/theory/viagra.html). (Paul Krugman is an economist at Princeton University and a columnist at the New York Times. His columns are opinionated, insightful, and fun to read.)

APPENDIX: The Construction of Real GDP, and Chain-Type Indexes

The example we used in the chapter had only one final good—cars—so constructing real GDP was easy. But how do we construct real GDP when there is more than one final good? This appendix gives the answer.

To understand how real GDP in an economy with many final goods is constructed, all you need to do is look at an economy where there are just two final goods. What works for two goods works just as well for millions of goods.

Suppose that an economy produces two final goods, say wine and potatoes:

- In year 0, it produces 10 pounds of potatoes at a price of $1 a pound, and 5 bottles of wine at a price of $2 a bottle.
- In year 1, it produces 15 pounds of potatoes at a price of $1 a pound, and 5 bottles of wine at a price of $3 a bottle.
- Nominal GDP in year 0 is therefore equal to $20. Nominal GDP in year 1 is equal to $30.

This information is summarized in the following table.

Nominal GDP in Year 0 and in Year 1.

	Year 0		
	Quantity	$ Price	$ Value
Potatoes (pounds)	10	1	10
Wine (bottles),	5	5	10
Nominal GDP			20

	Year 1		
	Quantity	$ Price	$ Value
Potatoes (pounds)	15	1	15
Wine (bottles)	5	3	15
Nominal GDP			30

The rate of growth of nominal GDP from year 0 to year 1 is equal to $(\$30 - \$20)/\$20 = 50\%$. But what is the rate of growth of real GDP?

Answering this question requires constructing real GDP for each of the two years. The basic idea behind constructing real GDP is to evaluate the quantities in each year using the *same set of prices.*

Suppose we choose, for example, the prices in year 0. Year 0 is then called the **base year**. In this case, the computation is as follows:

- Real GDP in year 0 is the sum of the quantity in year 0 times the price in year 0 for both goods: $(10 \times \$1) + (5 \times \$2) = \$20$.
- Real GDP in year 1 is the sum of the quantity in year 1 times the price in year 0 for both goods: $(15 \times \$1) + (5 \times \$2) = \$25$.
- The rate of growth of real GDP from year 0 to year 1 is then $(\$25 - \$20)/\$20$, or 25%.

This answer raises however an obvious issue: Instead of using year 0 as the base year, we could have used year 1, or any other year. If, for example, we had used year 1 as the base year, then:

- Real GDP in year 0 would be equal to $(10 \times \$1 + 5 \times \$3) = \$25$.
- Real GDP in year 1 would be equal to $(15 \times \$1 + 5 \times \$3) = \$30$.
- The rate of growth of real GDP from year 0 to year 1 would be equal to $\$5/\$25$, or 20%.

The answer using year 1 as the base year would therefore be different from the answer using year 0 as the base year. So if the choice of the base year affects the constructed percentage rate of change in output, which base year should one choose?

Until the mid-1990s in the United States—and still in most countries today—the practice was to choose a base year and change it infrequently, say, every five years or so. For example, in the United States, 1987 was the base year used from December 1991 to December 1995. That is, measures of real GDP published, for example, in 1994 for both 1994 and for all earlier years were constructed using 1987 prices. In December 1995, national income accounts shifted to 1992 as a base year; measures of real GDP for all earlier years were recalculated using 1992 prices.

This practice was logically unappealing. Every time the base year was changed and a new set of prices was used, all past real GDP numbers—and all past real GDP growth rates—were recomputed: Economic history was, in effect, rewritten every five years! Starting in December 1995, the U.S. Bureau of Economic Analysis (BEA)—the government office that produces the GDP numbers—shifted to a new method that does not suffer from this problem.

The method requires four steps:

- Constructing the rate of change of real GDP from year t to year $t + 1$ in two different ways. First using the prices from year t as the set of common prices; second, using the prices from year $t + 1$ as the set of common prices. For example, the rate of change of GDP from 2006 to 2007 is computed by:

  (1) Constructing real GDP for 2006 and real GDP for 2007 using 2006 prices as the set of common prices, and computing a first measure of the rate of growth of GDP from 2006 to 2007.

  (2) Constructing real GDP for 2006 and real GDP for 2007 using 2007 prices as the set of common prices, and computing a second measure of the rate of growth of GDP from 2006 to 2007.

- Constructing the rate of change of real GDP as the average of these two rates of change.

- Constructing an index for the level of real GDP by *linking*— or *chaining*—the constructed rates of change for each year. The index is set equal to 1 in some arbitrary year. At the time this book is written, the arbitrary year is 2005. Given that the constructed rate of change from 2005 to 2006 by the BEA is 2.6%, the index for 2006 equals $(1 + 2.6\%) = 1.026$. The index for 2006 is then obtained by multiplying the index for 2005 by the rate of change from 2005 to 2006, and so on. (You will find the value of this index—multiplied by 100—in the second column of Table B3 in the Economic Report of the President. Check that it is 100 in 2005 and 102.6 in 2006, and so on.)

- Multiplying this index by nominal GDP in 2005 to derive *real GDP in chained (2005) dollars.* As the index is 1 in 2005, this implies that real GDP in 2005 equals nominal GDP in 2005.

  Chained refers to the chaining of rates of change described above. *(2005)* refers to the year where, by construction, real GDP is equal to nominal GDP. (You will find the value of real GDP in chained (2005) dollars in the first column of Table B2 of the Economic Report of the President.)

  This index is more complicated to construct than the indexes used before 1995. (To make sure you understand the steps, construct real GDP in chained (year 0) dollars for year 1 in our example.) But it is clearly better conceptually: The prices used to evaluate real GDP in two adjacent years are the right prices, namely the average prices for those two years. And, because the rate of change from one year to the next is constructed using the prices in those two years rather than the set of prices in an arbitrary base year, history will not be rewritten every five years—as it used to be when, under the previous method for constructing real GDP, the base year was changed every five years.

(For more details, go to www.bea.doc.gov/bea/ARTICLES/NATIONAL/NIPA/1995/0795od.pdf)

Key Term

base year, 40

The Short Run

In the short run, demand determines output. Many factors affect demand, from consumer confidence to fiscal and monetary policy.

Chapter 3

Chapter 3 looks at equilibrium in the goods market and the determination of output. It focuses on the interaction among demand, production, and income. It shows how fiscal policy affects output.

Chapter 4

Chapter 4 looks at equilibrium in financial markets and the determination of the interest rate. It shows how monetary policy affects the interest rate.

Chapter 5

Chapter 5 looks at the goods market and financial markets together. It shows what determines output and the interest rate in the short run. It looks at the role of fiscal and monetary policy. The model developed in Chapter 5 is called the *IS–LM* model and is one of the workhorses of macroeconomics.

The Goods Market

When economists think about year-to-year movements in economic activity, they focus on the interactions among *production, income, and demand*:

■ **Changes in the demand for goods lead to changes in production.**

■ **Changes in production lead to changes in income.**

■ **Changes in income lead to changes in the demand for goods.**

Nothing makes the point better than the cartoon below:

This chapter looks at these interactions and their implications.

Section 3-1 looks at the composition of GDP and the different sources of the demand for goods.

Section 3-2 looks at the determinants of the demand for goods.

Section 3-3 shows how equilibrium output is determined by the condition that the production of goods must be equal to the demand for goods.

Section 3-4 gives an alternative way of thinking about the equilibrium, based on the equality of investment and saving.

Section 3-5 takes a first pass at the effects of fiscal policy on equilibrium output. ●

3-1 The Composition of GDP

The purchase of a machine by a firm, the decision to go to a restaurant by a consumer, and the purchase of combat airplanes by the federal government are clearly very different decisions and depend on very different factors. So, if we want to understand what determines the demand for goods, it makes sense to decompose aggregate output (GDP) from the point of view of the different goods being produced, and from the point of view of the different buyers for these goods.

The decomposition of GDP typically used by macroeconomists is shown in Table 3-1 (a more detailed version, with more precise definitions, appears in Appendix 1 at the end of the book).

"Output" and "production" are synonymous. There is no rule for using one or the other. Use ▶ the one that sounds better.

- First comes **consumption** (which we will denote by the letter C when we use algebra below and throughout this book). These are the goods and services purchased by consumers, ranging from food to airline tickets, to new cars, and so on. Consumption is by far the largest component of GDP. In 2010, it accounted for 70.5% of GDP.

Warning! To most people, "investment" refers to the purchase of assets like gold or shares of General Motors. Economists use "investment" to refer to the purchase of new capital goods, such as (new) machines, (new) buildings, or (new) houses. When economists refer to the purchase of ▶ gold, or shares of General Motors, or other financial assets, they use the term "financial investment."

- Second comes **investment** (I), sometimes called **fixed investment** to distinguish it from inventory investment (which we will discuss below). Investment is the sum of **nonresidential investment**, the purchase by firms of new plants or new machines (from turbines to computers), and **residential investment**, the purchase by people of new houses or apartments.

  Nonresidential investment and residential investment, and the decisions behind them, have more in common than might first appear. Firms buy machines or plants to produce output in the future. People buy houses or apartments to get *housing services* in the future. In both cases, the decision to buy depends on the services these goods will yield in the future, so it makes sense to treat them together. Together, nonresidential and residential investment accounted for only 12.0% of GDP in 2010.

This ratio is historically low and reflects the very low level of residential investment, ▶ which itself is the result of the sharp decrease in housing prices since 2007.

- Third comes **government spending** (G). This represents the purchases of goods and services by the federal, state, and local governments. The goods range from airplanes to office equipment. The services include services provided by government employees: In effect, the national income accounts treat the government as buying the services provided by government employees—and then providing these services to the public, free of charge.

  Note that G does not include **government transfers**, like Medicare or Social Security payments, nor interest payments on the government debt. Although these are clearly government expenditures, they are not purchases of goods and services. That is why the number for government spending on goods and services in Table 3-1, 20.4% of GDP, is smaller than the number for total government spending including transfers

Table 3-1	The Composition of U.S. GDP, 2010	Billions of Dollars	Percent of GDP
	GDP (Y)	14,660	100
1	Consumption (C)	10,348	70.5
2	Investment (I)	1,756	12.0
	Nonresidential	1,415	9.7
	Residential	341	2.3
3	Government spending (G)	3,001	20.4
4	Net exports	−516	−3.5
	Exports (X)	1,838	12.5
	Imports (IM)	−2,354	−16.0
5	Inventory investment	71	0.5

Source: Survey of Current Business, May 2010, Table 1-1-5

and interest payments. That number, in 2010, was approximately 39% of GDP when transfers and interest payments of federal, state, and local governments are combined.

■ The sum of lines 1, 2, and 3 gives the *purchases of goods and services by U.S. consumers, U.S. firms, and the U.S. government.* To determine the *purchases of U.S. goods and services*, two more steps are needed:

First, we must subtract **imports** (IM), the purchases of foreign goods and services by U.S. consumers, U.S. firms, and the U.S. government.

Second, we must add **exports** (X), the purchases of U.S. goods and services by foreigners.

The difference between exports and imports, $(X - IM)$, is called **net exports**, or the **trade balance**. If exports exceed imports, the country is said to run a **trade surplus**. If exports are less than imports, the country is said to run a **trade deficit**. In 2010, U.S. exports accounted for 12.5% of GDP. U.S. imports were equal to 16.0% of GDP, so the United States was running a trade deficit equal to 3.5% of GDP.

◀ Exports > imports
      ⇔ trade surplus

Exports < imports
      ⇔ trade deficit

■ So far we have looked at various sources of purchases (sales) of U.S. goods and services in 2010. To determine U.S. production in 2010, we need to take one last step:

In any given year, production and sales need not be equal. Some of the goods produced in a given year are not sold in that year, but in later years. And some of the goods sold in a given year may have been produced in an earlier year. The difference between goods produced and goods sold in a given year—the difference between production and sales, in other words—is called **inventory investment**. If production exceeds sales and firms accumulate inventories as a result, then inventory investment is said to be positive. If production is less than sales and firms' inventories fall, then inventory investment is said to be negative. Inventory investment is typically small—positive in some years and negative in others. In 2010, inventory investment was positive, equal to just $71 billion. Put another way, production was higher than sales by an amount equal to $71 billion.

Make sure you understand each of these three equivalent ways of stating the relations among production, sales, and
◀ inventory investment:

Inventory investment =
   production − sales
Production   =
   sales + inventory investment
Sales   =
   production − inventory
   investment

We now have what we need to develop our first model of output determination.

3-2 The Demand for Goods

Denote the total demand for goods by Z. Using the decomposition of GDP we saw in Section 3-1, we can write Z as

$$Z \equiv C + I + G + X - IM$$

Recall that inventory invest-ment is not part of demand. ▶

A model nearly always starts with "Assume" (or "Suppose"). This is an indication that real-ity is about to be simplified to focus on the issue at hand. ▶

This equation is an **identity** (which is why it is written using the symbol "≡" rather than an equals sign). It *defines* Z as the sum of consumption, plus investment, plus govern-ment spending, plus exports, minus imports.

We now need to think about the determinants of Z. To make the task easier, let's first make a number of simplifications:

■ Assume that all firms produce the same good, which can then be used by consum-ers for consumption, by firms for investment, or by the government. With this (big) simplification, we need to look at only one market—the market for "the" good—and think about what determines supply and demand in that market.

■ Assume that firms are willing to supply any amount of the good at a given price level P. This assumption allows us to focus on the role demand plays in the determination of output. As we shall see later in the book, this assumption is valid only in the short run. When we move to the study of the medium run (starting in Chapter 6), we shall abandon it. But for the moment, it will simplify our discussion.

■ Assume that the economy is *closed*—that it does not trade with the rest of the world: Both exports and imports are zero. This assumption clearly goes against the facts: Modern economies trade with the rest of the world. Later on (starting in Chapter 18), we will abandon this assumption as well and look at what hap-pens when the economy is open. But, for the moment, this assumption will also simplify our discussion because we won't have to think about what determines exports and imports.

Under the assumption that the economy is closed, $X = IM = 0$, so the demand for goods Z is simply the sum of consumption, investment, and government spending:

$$Z \equiv C + I + G$$

Let's discuss each of these three components in turn.

Consumption (C)

Consumption decisions depend on many factors. But the main one is surely income, or, more precisely, **disposable income**, the income that remains once con-sumers have received transfers from the government and paid their taxes. When their disposable income goes up, people buy more goods; when it goes down, they buy fewer goods.

Let C denote consumption, and Y_D denote disposable income. We can then write:

$$C = C(Y_D) \qquad (3.1)$$
$$(+)$$

This is a formal way of stating that consumption C is a function of disposable in-come Y_D. The function $C(Y_D)$ is called the **consumption function**. The positive sign below Y_D reflects the fact that when disposable income increases, so does consumption. Economists call such an equation a **behavioral equation** to indicate that the equation captures some aspect of behavior—in this case, the behavior of consumers.

We will use functions in this book as a way of representing relations between vari-ables. What you need to know about functions—which is very little—is described in Appendix 2 at the end of the book. This appendix develops the mathematics you need to go through this book. Not to worry: we shall always describe a function in words when we introduce it for the first time.

It is often useful to be more specific about the form of the function. Here is such a case. It is reasonable to assume that the relation between consumption and disposable income is given by the simpler relation:

$$C = c_0 + c_1 Y_D \tag{3.2}$$

In other words, it is reasonable to assume that the function is a **linear relation.** The relation between consumption and disposable income is then characterized by two **parameters**, c_0 and c_1:

- The parameter c_1 is called the **propensity to consume.** (It is also called the *marginal propensity to consume.* I will drop the word "marginal" for simplicity.) It gives the effect an additional dollar of disposable income has on consumption. If c_1 is equal to 0.6, then an additional dollar of disposable income increases consumption by $1 \times 0.6 = 60$ cents.

   A natural restriction on c_1 is that it be positive: An increase in disposable income is likely to lead to an increase in consumption. Another natural restriction is that c_1 be less than 1: People are likely to consume only part of any increase in disposable income and save the rest.

- The parameter c_0 has a literal interpretation. It is what people would consume if their disposable income in the current year were equal to zero: If Y_D equals zero in equation (3.2), $C = c_0$. If we use this interpretation, a natural restriction is that, if current income were equal to zero, consumption would still be positive: With or without income, people still need to eat! This implies that c_0 is positive. How can people have positive consumption if their income is equal to zero? Answer: They dissave. They consume either by selling some of their assets or by borrowing.

◀ Think about your own consumption behavior. What are your values of c_0 and c_1?

- The parameter c_0 has a less literal and more frequently used interpretation. Changes in c_0 reflect changes in consumption for a given level of disposable income. Increases in c_0 reflect an increase in consumption given income, decreases in c_0 a decrease. There are many reasons why people may decide to consume more or less, given their disposable income. They may, for example, find it easier or more difficult to borrow, or may become more or less optimistic about the future. An example of a decrease in c_0 is given in the Focus Box, "The Lehman Bankruptcy, Fears of Another Great Depression, and Shifts in the Consumption Function."

The relation between consumption and disposable income shown in equation (3.2) is drawn in Figure 3-1. Because it is a linear relation, it is represented by a

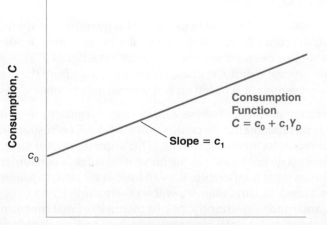

Figure 3-1

Consumption and disposable income

Consumption increases with disposable income, but less than one for one. A lower value of c_0 will shift the entire line down.

straight line. Its intercept with the vertical axis is c_0; its slope is c_1. Because c_1 is less than 1, the slope of the line is less than 1: Equivalently, the line is flatter than a 45–degree line. If the value of c_0 increases, then the line shifts up by the same amount. (A refresher on graphs, slopes, and intercepts is given in Appendix 2.)

Next we need to define disposable income Y_D. Disposable income is given by

$$Y_D \equiv Y - T$$

where Y is income and T is taxes paid minus government transfers received by consumers. For short, we will refer to T simply as taxes—but remember that it is equal to taxes minus transfers. Note that the equation is an identity, indicated by "$\equiv$".

Replacing Y_D in equation (3.2) gives

$$C = c_0 + c_1(Y - T) \tag{3.3}$$

Equation (3.3) tells us that consumption C is a function of income Y and taxes T. Higher income increases consumption, but less than one for one. Higher taxes decrease consumption, also less than one for one.

Investment (I)

Models have two types of variables. Some variables depend on other variables in the model and are therefore explained within the model. Variables like these are called **endogenous**. This was the case for consumption above. Other variables are not explained within the model but are instead taken as given. Variables like these are called **exogenous**. This is how we will treat investment here. We will take investment as given and write:

$$I = \bar{I} \tag{3.4}$$

Endogenous variables—explained within the model
Exogenous variables—taken as given

Putting a bar on investment is a simple typographical way to remind us that we take investment as given.

We take investment as given to keep our model simple. But the assumption is not innocuous. It implies that, when we later look at the effects of changes in production, we will assume that investment does not respond to changes in production. It is not hard to see that this implication may be a bad description of reality: Firms that experience an increase in production might well decide they need more machines and increase their investment as a result. For now, though, we will leave this mechanism out of the model. In Chapter 5 we will introduce a more realistic treatment of investment.

Government Spending (G)

The third component of demand in our model is government spending, G. Together with taxes T, G describes **fiscal policy**—the choice of taxes and spending by the government. Just as we just did for investment, we will take G and T as exogenous. But the reason why we assume G and T are exogenous is different from the reason we assumed investment is exogenous. It is based on two distinct arguments:

Recall: "Taxes" stand for taxes minus government transfers.

■ First, governments do not behave with the same regularity as consumers or firms, so there is no reliable rule we could write for G or T corresponding to the rule we wrote, for example, for consumption. (This argument is not airtight, though. Even if governments do not follow simple behavioral rules as consumers do, a good part of their behavior is predictable. We will look at these issues later, in particular in Chapters 22 and 23. Until then, we will set them aside.)

■ Second, and more importantly, one of the tasks of macroeconomists is to think about the implications of alternative spending and tax decisions. We want to be able to say, "If the government were to choose these values for G and T, this is what would happen." The approach in this book will typically treat G and T as variables chosen by the government and will not try to explain them within the model. ◄

Because we will (nearly always) take G and T as exogenous, we won't use a bar to denote their values. This will keep the notation lighter.

3-3 The Determination of Equilibrium Output

Let's put together the pieces we have introduced so far.

Assuming that exports and imports are both zero, the demand for goods is the sum of consumption, investment, and government spending:

$$Z \equiv C + I + G$$

Replacing C and I from equations (3.3) and (3.4), we get

$$Z = c_0 + c_1(Y - T) + \bar{I} + G \qquad (3.5)$$

The demand for goods Z depends on income Y, taxes T, investment $\bar{I}$, and government spending G.

Let's now turn to **equilibrium** in the goods market, and the relation between production and demand. If firms hold inventories, then production need not be equal to demand: For example, firms can satisfy an increase in demand by drawing upon their inventories—by having negative inventory investment. They can respond to a decrease in demand by continuing to produce and accumulating inventories—by having positive inventory investment. Let's first ignore this complication, though, and begin by assuming that firms do not hold inventories. In this case, inventory investment is always equal to zero, and **equilibrium in the goods market** requires that production Y be equal to the demand for goods Z: ◄

Think of an economy that produces only haircuts. There cannot be inventories of haircuts—haircuts produced but not sold?—so production must always be equal to demand.

$$Y = Z \qquad (3.6)$$

This equation is called an **equilibrium condition**. Models include three types of equations: identities, behavioral equations, and equilibrium conditions. You now have seen examples of each: The equation defining disposable income is an identity, the consumption function is a behavioral equation, and the condition that production equals demand is an equilibrium condition. ◄

There are three types of equations:
  Identities
  Behavioral equations
  Equilibrium conditions

Replacing demand Z in (3.6) by its expression from equation (3.5) gives

$$Y = c_0 + c_1(Y - T) + \bar{I} + G \qquad (3.7)$$

Equation (3.7) represents algebraically what we stated informally at the beginning of this chapter:

In equilibrium, production, Y (the left side of the equation), is equal to demand (the right side). Demand in turn depends on income, Y, which is itself equal to production. ◄

Relate this statement to the cartoon at the start of the chapter.

Note that we are using the same symbol Y for production and income. This is no accident! As you saw in Chapter 2, we can look at GDP either from the production side or from the income side. Production and income are identically equal.

Having constructed a model, we can solve it to look at what determines the level of output—how output changes in response to, say, a change in government spending. Solving a model means not only solving it algebraically, but also understanding why the results are what they are. In this book, solving a model will also mean characterizing the results using graphs—sometimes skipping the algebra altogether—and describing the results and the mechanisms in words. Macroeconomists always use these three tools:

1. Algebra to make sure that the logic is correct

2. Graphs to build the intuition

3. Words to explain the results

Make it a habit to do the same.

Using Algebra

Rewrite the equilibrium equation (3.7):

$$Y = c_0 + c_1 Y - c_1 T + \bar{I} + G$$

Move $c_1 Y$ to the left side and reorganize the right side:

$$(1 - c_1) Y = c_0 + \bar{I} + G - c_1 T$$

Divide both sides by $(1 - c_1)$:

$$Y = \frac{1}{1 - c_1} [c_0 + \bar{I} + G - c_1 T] \tag{3.8}$$

Equation (3.8) characterizes equilibrium output, the level of output such that production equals demand. Let's look at both terms on the right, beginning with the second term.

"Autonomous" means independent—in this case, independent of output.

■ The term $[c_0 + \bar{I} + G - c_1 T]$ is that part of the demand for goods that does not depend on output. For this reason, it is called **autonomous spending**.

Can we be sure that autonomous spending is positive? We cannot, but it is very likely to be. The first two terms in brackets, c_0 and $\bar{I}$, are positive. What about the last two, $G - c_1 T$? Suppose the government is running a **balanced budget**—taxes equal government spending. If $T = G$, and the propensity to consume (c_1) is less than 1 (as we have assumed), then $(G - c_1 T)$ is positive and so is autonomous spending. Only if the government were running a very large budget surplus—if taxes were much larger than government spending—could autonomous spending be negative. We can safely ignore that case here.

If $T = G$, then $(G - c_1 T) = (T - c_1 T) = (1 - c_1) T > 0$.

■ Turn to the first term, $1/(1 - c_1)$. Because the propensity to consume (c_1) is between zero and 1, $1/(1 - c_1)$ is a number greater than one. For this reason, this number, which *multiplies* autonomous spending, is called the **multiplier**. The closer c_1 is to 1, the larger the multiplier.

What does the multiplier imply? Suppose that, for a given level of income, consumers decide to consume more. More precisely, assume that c_0 in equation (3.3) increases by \$1 billion. Equation (3.8) tells us that output will increase by more than \$1 billion. For example, if c_1 equals 0.6, the multiplier equals $1/(1 - 0.6) = 1/0.4 = 2.5$, so that output increases by $2.5 \times \$1$ billion $= \$2.5$ billion.

We have looked at an increase in consumption, but equation (3.8) makes it clear that any change in autonomous spending—from a change in investment, to a change in government spending, to a change in taxes—will have the same qualitative effect: It will change output by more than its direct effect on autonomous spending.

Where does the multiplier effect come from? Looking back at equation (3.7) gives us the clue: An increase in c_0 increases demand. The increase in demand then leads to an increase in production. The increase in production leads to an equivalent increase in income (remember the two are identically equal). The increase in income further increases consumption, which further increases demand, and so on. The best way to describe this mechanism is to represent the equilibrium using a graph. Let's do that.

Using a Graph

Let's characterize the equilibrium graphically.

- First, plot production as a function of income.

    In Figure 3-2, measure production on the vertical axis. Measure income on the horizontal axis. Plotting production as a function of income is straightforward: Recall that production and income are identically equal. Thus, the relation between them is the 45-degree line, the line with a slope equal to 1.

- Second, plot demand as a function of income.

    The relation between demand and income is given by equation (3.5). Let's rewrite it here for convenience, regrouping the terms for autonomous spending together in the term in parentheses:

$$Z = (c_0 + \bar{I} + G - c_1 T) + c_1 Y \qquad (3.9)$$

    Demand depends on autonomous spending and on income—via its effect on consumption. The relation between demand and income is drawn as ZZ in the graph. The intercept with the vertical axis—the value of demand when income is equal to zero—equals autonomous spending. The slope of the line is the propensity to consume, c_1: When income increases by 1, demand increases by c_1. Under the restriction that c_1 is positive but less than 1, the line is upward sloping but has a slope of less than 1.

- In equilibrium, production equals demand.

    Equilibrium output, Y, therefore occurs at the intersection of the 45-degree line and the demand function. This is at point A. To the left of A, demand exceeds production; to the right of A, production exceeds demand. Only at A are demand and production equal.

Figure 3-2

Equilibrium in the goods market

Equilibrium output is determined by the condition that production be equal to demand.

Suppose that the economy is at the initial equilibrium, represented by point A in the graph, with production equal to Y.

Now suppose c_0 increases by \$1 billion. At the initial level of income (the level of disposable income associated with point A since T is unchanged in this example), consumers increase their consumption by \$1 billion. This makes use of the second interpretation of the value of c_0. What happens is shown in Figure 3-3, which builds on Figure 3-2.

Equation (3.9) tells us that, for any value of income, demand is higher by \$1 billion. Before the increase in c_0, the relation between demand and income was given by the line ZZ. After the increase in c_0 by \$1 billion, the relation between demand and income is given by the line ZZ', which is parallel to ZZ but higher by \$1 billion. In other words, the demand curve shifts up by \$1 billion. The new equilibrium is at the intersection of the 45-degree line and the new demand relation, at point A'.

Look at the vertical axis. The distance between Y and Y' on the vertical axis is larger than ► the distance between A and B—which is equal to \$1 billion.

Equilibrium output increases from Y to Y'. The increase in output, $(Y' - Y)$, which we can measure either on the horizontal or the vertical axis, is larger than the initial increase in consumption of \$1 billion. This is the multiplier effect.

With the help of the graph, it becomes easier to tell how and why the economy moves from A to A'. The initial increase in consumption leads to an increase in demand of \$1 billion. At the initial level of income, Y, the level of demand is shown by point B: Demand is \$1 billion higher. To satisfy this higher level of demand, firms increase production by \$1 billion. This increase in production of \$1 billion implies that income increases by \$1 billion (recall: income = production), so the economy moves to point C. (In other words, both production and income are higher by \$1 billion.) But this is not the end of the story. The increase in income leads to a further increase in demand. Demand is now shown by point D. Point D leads to a higher level of production, and so on, until the economy is at A', where production and demand are again equal. This is therefore the new equilibrium.

We can pursue this line of explanation a bit more, which will give us another way to think about the multiplier.

■ The first–round increase in demand, shown by the distance AB in Figure 3-3— equals \$1 billion.

Figure 3-3

The effects of an increase in autonomous spending on output

An increase in autonomous spending has a more than one-for-one effect on equilibrium output.

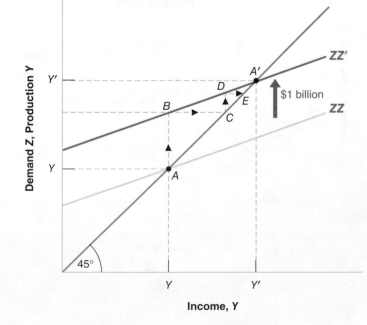

- This first–round increase in demand leads to an equal increase in production, or $1 billion, which is also shown by the distance AB.
- This first–round increase in production leads to an equal increase in income, shown by the distance BC, also equal to $1 billion.
- The second–round increase in demand, shown by the distance CD, equals $1 billion (the increase in income in the first round) times the propensity to consume, c_1—hence, $\$c_1$ billion.
- This second–round increase in demand leads to an equal increase in production, also shown by the distance CD, and thus an equal increase in income, shown by the distance DE.
- The third–round increase in demand equals $\$c_1$ billion (the increase in income in the second round), times c_1, the marginal propensity to consume; it is equal to $\$c_1 \times c_1 = \$c_1^2$ billion, and so on.

Following this logic, the total increase in production after, say, $n + 1$ rounds equals $1 billion times the sum:

$$1 + c_1 + c_1^2 + \cdots + c_1^n$$

Such a sum is called a **geometric series**. Geometric series will frequently appear in this book. A refresher is given in Appendix 2 at the end of the book. One property of geometric series is that, when c_1 is less than one (as it is here) and as n gets larger and larger, the sum keeps increasing but approaches a limit. That limit is $1/(1 - c_1)$, making the eventual increase in output $\$1/(1 - c_1)$ billion.

The expression $1/(1 - c_1)$ should be familiar: It is the multiplier, derived another way. This gives us an equivalent, but more intuitive way of thinking about the multiplier. We can think of the original increase in demand as triggering successive increases in production, with each increase in production leading to an increase in income, which leads to an increase in demand, which leads to a further increase in production, which leads ... and so on. The multiplier is the sum of all these successive increases in production.

Trick question: Think about the multiplier as the result of these successive rounds. What would happen in each successive round if c_1, the propensity to consume, were larger than one?

Using Words

How can we summarize our findings in words?

Production depends on demand, which depends on income, which is itself equal to production. An increase in demand, such as an increase in government spending, leads to an increase in production and a corresponding increase in income. This increase in income leads to a further increase in demand, which leads to a further increase in production, and so on. The end result is an increase in output that is larger than the initial shift in demand, by a factor equal to the multiplier.

The size of the multiplier is directly related to the value of the propensity to consume: The higher the propensity to consume, the higher the multiplier. What is the value of the propensity to consume in the United States today? To answer this question, and more generally to estimate behavioral equations and their parameters, economists use **econometrics**, the set of statistical methods used in economics. To give you a sense of what econometrics is and how it is used, read Appendix 3 at the end of this book. This appendix gives you a quick introduction, along with an application estimating the propensity to consume. A reasonable estimate of the propensity to consume in the United States today is around 0.6 (the regressions in Appendix 3 yield two estimates, 0.5 and 0.8). In other words, an additional dollar of disposable income leads on average to an increase in consumption of 60 cents. This implies that the multiplier is equal to $1/(1 - c_1) = 1/(1 - 0.6) = 2.5$.

How Long Does It Take for Output to Adjust?

Let's return to our example one last time. Suppose that c_0 increases by $1 billion. We know that output will increase by an amount equal to the multiplier $1/(1 - c_1)$ times $1 billion. But how long will it take for output to reach this higher value?

Under the assumptions we have made so far, the answer is: Right away! In writing the equilibrium condition (3.6), I have assumed that production is always equal to demand. In other words, I have assumed that production responds to demand instantaneously. In writing the consumption function (3.2), I have assumed that consumption responds to changes in disposable income instantaneously. Under these two assumptions, the economy goes instantaneously from point A to point A' in Figure 3-3: The increase in demand leads to an immediate increase in production, the increase in income associated with the increase in production leads to an immediate increase in demand, and so on. There is nothing wrong in thinking about the adjustment in terms of successive rounds as we did earlier, even though the equations indicate that all these rounds happen at once.

In the model we saw earlier, we ruled out this possibility by assuming firms did not hold ▶ inventories, and so could not rely on drawing down inventories to satisfy an increase demand.

This instantaneous adjustment isn't really plausible: A firm that faces an increase in demand might well decide to wait before adjusting its production, meanwhile drawing down its inventories to satisfy demand. A worker who gets a pay raise might not adjust her consumption right away. These delays imply that the adjustment of output will take time.

Formally describing this adjustment of output over time—that is, writing the equations for what economists call the **dynamics** of adjustment, and solving this more complicated model—would be too hard to do here. But it is easy to do it in words:

- Suppose, for example, that firms make decisions about their production levels at the beginning of each quarter. Once their decisions are made, production cannot be adjusted for the rest of the quarter. If purchases by consumers are higher than production, firms draw down their inventories to satisfy the purchases. On the other hand, if purchases are lower than production, firms accumulate inventories.

- Now suppose consumers decide to spend more, that they increase c_0. During the quarter in which this happens, demand increases, but production—because we assumed it was set at the beginning of the quarter—doesn't yet change. Therefore, income doesn't change either.

- Having observed an increase in demand, firms are likely to set a higher level of production in the following quarter. This increase in production leads to a corresponding increase in income and a further increase in demand. If purchases still exceed production, firms further increase production in the following quarter, and so on.

- In short, in response to an increase in consumer spending, output does not jump to the new equilibrium, but rather increases over time from Y to Y'.

   How long this adjustment takes depends on how and how often firms revise their production schedule. If firms adjust their production schedules more frequently in response to past increases in purchases, the adjustment will occur faster.

We will often do in this book what I just did here. After we have looked at changes in equilibrium output, we will then describe informally how the economy moves from one equilibrium to the other. This will not only make the description of what happens in the economy feel more realistic, but it will often reinforce your intuition about why the equilibrium changes.

We have focused in this section on increases in demand. But the mechanism, of course, works both ways: Decreases in demand lead to decreases in output. The recent

The Lehman Bankruptcy, Fears of Another Great Depression, and Shifts in the Consumption Function

Why would consumers decrease consumption if their disposable income has not changed? Or, in terms of equation (3.2), why might c_0 decrease—leading in turn to a decrease in demand, output, and so on?

One of the first reasons that comes to mind is that, even if their current income has not changed, they start worrying about the future and decide to save more. This is precisely what happened at the start of the crisis, in late 2008 and early 2009. The basic facts are shown in Figure 1 below. The figure plots, from the first quarter of 2008 to the last quarter of 2009, the behavior of three variables, disposable income, total consumption, and consumption of durables—the part of consumption that falls on goods such as cars, computers, and so on (Appendix 1 at the end of the book gives a more precise definition). To make things visually simple, all three variables are normalized to equal 1 in the first quarter of 2008.

You should note two things about the figure. First, despite the fact that the crisis led to a large fall in GDP, during that period, disposable income did not initially move much. It even increased in the first quarter of 2008. But consumption was unchanged from quarter 1 to quarter 2 and then fell before disposable income fell. Consumption fell by more than disposable income, by 3 percentage points in 2009 relative to 2008. The distance between the line for disposable income and the line for consumption

increased. Second, during the third and especially the fourth quarters of 2008, the consumption of durables dropped sharply. By the fourth quarter of 2008, it was down 10% relative to the first quarter, before recovering in early 2009 and decreasing again later.

Why did consumption, and especially, consumption of durables, decrease at the end of 2008 despite relatively small changes in disposable income? A number of factors were at play, but the main one was the psychological fallout of the financial crisis. Recall, from Chapter 1, that, on September 15, Lehman Brothers, a very large bank, went bankrupt, and that, in the ensuing weeks, it appeared that many more banks might follow suit and the financial system might collapse. For most people, the main sign of trouble was what they read in newspapers: Even though they still had their job and received their monthly income checks, the events reminded them of the stories of the Great Depression and the pain that came with it. One way to see this is to look at the Google Trends series that gives the number of searches for "Great Depression," from January 2008 to September 2009, and is plotted in Figure 2 below. The series is normalized so its average value is 1 over the two years. Note how sharply the series peaked in October 2008 and then slowly decreased over the course of 2009, as it became clear that, while the crisis was a serious one, policy makers were going to do whatever they could do to avoid a repeat of the Great Depression.

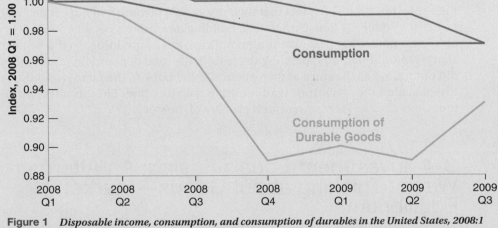

Figure 1 *Disposable income, consumption, and consumption of durables in the United States, 2008:1 to 2009:3*

Source: Calculated using series DPIC96, PCECC96, PCDGCC96: Federal Reserve Economic Data (FRED) http://research.stlouisfed.org/fred2/

If you felt that the economy might go into another Great Depression, what would you do? Worried that you might become unemployed or that your income might decline in the future, you would probably cut consumption, even if your disposable income had not changed yet. And, given the uncertainty about what was going on, you might also delay the purchases you could afford to delay; for example, the purchase of a new car or a new TV. As Figure 1 in this box shows, this is exactly what consumers did in late 2008: Total consumption decreased, and consumption of durables collapsed. In 2009, as the smoke slowly cleared and the worse scenarios became increasingly unlikely, consumption of durables picked up. But, by then, many other factors were contributing to the crisis.

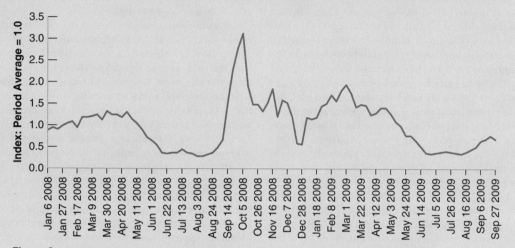

Figure 2 *Google search volume for "Great Depression," January 2008 to September 2009*

Source: Google Trends, "Great Depression."

recession was the result of two of the four components of autonomous spending dropping by a large amount at the same time. To remind you, the expression for autonomous spending is $[c_0 + I + G - c_1 T]$. The Focus box "The Lehman Bankruptcy, Fears of Another Great Depression, and Shifts in the Consumption Function" above shows how, when the crisis started, worries about the future led consumers to cut on their spending despite the fact that their disposable income had not yet declined; that is, c_0 fell in value. As house prices fell, building new homes became much less desirable. New homes are part of autonomous investment spending, so the value of I fell sharply. As autonomous spending decreased, the total demand for goods fell, and so did output. We shall return at many points in the book to the factors and the mechanisms behind the crisis and steadily enrich our story line. But this effect on autonomous spending will remain a central element of the story.

3-4 Investment Equals Saving: An Alternative Way of Thinking about Goods—Market Equilibrium

Thus far, we have been thinking of equilibrium in the goods market in terms of the equality of the production and the demand for goods. An alternative—but equivalent—way of thinking about equilibrium focuses instead on investment and saving. This is how John Maynard Keynes first articulated this model in 1936, in *The General Theory of Employment, Interest and Money*.

Let's start by looking at saving. Saving is the sum of private saving and public ◀ Saving = Private + Public saving? saving.

■ By definition, **private saving** (S), saving by consumers, is equal to their disposable income minus their consumption:

$$S \equiv Y_D - C$$

Using the definition of disposable income, we can rewrite private saving as income minus taxes minus consumption:

$$S \equiv Y - T - C$$

■ By definition, **public saving** is equal to taxes (net of transfers) minus government spending, $T - G$. If taxes exceed government spending, the government is running a **budget surplus**, so public saving is positive. If taxes are less than govern- ◀ Public saving ⇔ Budget surplus? ment spending, the government is running a **budget deficit**, so public saving is negative.

■ Now return to the equation for equilibrium in the goods market that we derived earlier. Production must be equal to demand, which, in turn, is the sum of consumption, investment, and government spending:

$$Y = C + I + G$$

Subtract taxes (T) from both sides and move consumption to the left side:

$$Y - T - C = I + G - T$$

The left side of this equation is simply private saving (S), so

$$S = I + G - T$$

Or, equivalently,

$$I = S + (T - G) \tag{3.10}$$

On the left is investment. On the right is saving, the sum of *private saving* and *public saving*.

Equation (3.10) gives us another way of thinking about equilibrium in the goods market: It says that equilibrium in the goods market requires that investment equal **saving**— the sum of private and public saving. This way of looking at equilibrium explains why the equilibrium condition for the goods market is called the *IS* **relation**, which stands for "**I**nvestment equals **S**aving": What firms want to invest must be equal to what people and the government want to save.

To understand equation (3.10), imagine an economy with only one person who has to decide how much to consume, invest, and save—a "Robinson Crusoe" economy, for example. For Robinson Crusoe, the saving and the investment decisions are one and the same: What he invests (say, by keeping rabbits for breeding rather than having them for dinner), he automatically saves. In a modern economy, however, investment decisions are made by firms, whereas saving decisions are made by consumers and the government. In equilibrium, equation (3.10) tells us, all these decisions have to be consistent: Investment must equal saving.

To summarize: There are two equivalent ways of stating the condition for equilibrium in the goods market:

$$Production = Demand$$

$$Investment = Saving$$

Earlier, we characterized the equilibrium using the first condition, equation (3.6). We now do the same using the second condition, equation (3.10). The results will be the same, but the derivation will give you another way of thinking about the equilibrium.

- Note first that *consumption and saving decisions are one and the same*: Given their disposable income, once consumers have chosen consumption, their saving is determined, and vice versa. The way we specified consumption behavior implies that private saving is given by:

$$S = Y - T - C$$
$$= Y - T - c_0 - c_1(Y - T)$$

Rearranging, we get

$$S = -c_0 + (1 - c_1)(Y - T) \qquad (3.11)$$

- In the same way that we called c_1 the propensity to consume, we can call $(1 - c_1)$ the **propensity to save**. The propensity to save tells us how much of an additional unit of income people save. The assumption we made earlier—that the propensity to consume (c_1) is between zero and one implies that the propensity to save ($1 - c_1$) is also between zero and one. Private saving increases with disposable income, but by less than one dollar for each additional dollar of disposable income.

  In equilibrium, investment must be equal to saving, the sum of private and public saving. Replacing private saving in equation (3.10) by its expression from above,

$$I = -c_0 + (1 - c_1)(Y - T) + (T - G)$$

Solving for output,

$$Y = \frac{1}{1 - c_1}[c_0 + \bar{I} + G - c_1 T] \qquad (3.12)$$

Equation (3.12) is exactly the same as equation (3.8). This should come as no surprise. We are looking at the same equilibrium condition, just in a different way. This alternative way will prove useful in various applications later in the book. The Focus box "The Paradox of Saving" looks at such an application, which was first emphasized by Keynes and is often called the "paradox of saving."

3-5 Is the Government Omnipotent? A Warning

Equation (3.8) implies that the government, by choosing the level of spending (G) or the level of taxes (T), can choose the level of output it wants. If it wants output to be higher by, say, $1 billion, all it needs to do is to increase G by $$(1 - c_1)$ billion; this increase in government spending, in theory, will lead to an output increase of $$(1 - c_1)$ billion times the multiplier $1/(1 - c_1)$, or $1 billion.

Can governments really choose the level of output they want? Obviously not: If they could, and it was as easy as it sounds in the previous paragraph, why would the American government have allowed growth to stall in 2008 and output to actually fall in 2009? Why wouldn't the government increase the growth rate now, so as to decrease unemployment more rapidly? There are many aspects of reality that we have not yet incorporated in our model, and all of them complicate the governments' task. We shall do so in due time. But it is useful to list them briefly here:

For a glimpse at the longer list, go to Section 23-1, "What You Have Learned," in Chapter 23.

- Changing government spending or taxes is not easy. Getting the U.S. Congress to pass bills always takes time, often becoming a president's nightmare (Chapters 22 and 23).

The Paradox of Saving

As we grow up, we are told about the virtues of thrift. Those who spend all their income are condemned to end up poor. Those who save are promised a happy life. Similarly, governments tell us, an economy that saves is an economy that will grow strong and prosper! The model we have seen in this chapter, however, tells a different and surprising story.

Suppose that, at a given level of disposable income, consumers decide to save more. In other words, suppose consumers decrease c_0, therefore decreasing consumption and increasing saving at a given level of disposable income. What happens to output and to saving?

Equation (3.12) makes it clear that equilibrium output decreases: As people save more at their initial level of income, they decrease their consumption. But this decreased consumption decreases demand, which decreases production.

Can we tell what happens to saving? Let's return to the equation for private saving, equation (3.11) (recall that we assume no change in public saving, so saving and private saving move together):

$$S = -c_0 + (1 - c_1)(Y - T)$$

On the one hand, $-c_0$ is higher (less negative): Consumers are saving more at any level of income; this tends to increase saving. But, on the other hand, their income Y is lower: This decreases saving. The net effect would seem to be ambiguous. In fact, we can tell which way it goes:

To see how, go back to equation (3.10), the equilibrium condition that investment and saving must be equal:

$$I = S + (T - G)$$

By assumption, investment does not change: $I = \bar{I}$. Nor do T or G. So the equilibrium condition tells us that in equilibrium, private saving S cannot change either. Although people want to save more at a given level of income, their income decreases by an amount such that their saving is unchanged.

This means that as people attempt to save more, the result is both a decline in output and unchanged saving. This surprising pair of results is known as the **paradox of saving** (or the paradox of thrift).

So should you forget the old wisdom? Should the government tell people to be less thrifty? No. The results of this simple model are of much relevance in the short run. The desire of consumers to save more is an important factor in many of the U.S. recessions, including, as we saw in the Focus box earlier, the current crisis. But—as we will see later in this book when we look at the medium run and the long run—other mechanisms come into play over time, and an increase in the saving rate is likely to lead over time to higher saving and higher income. A warning remains, however: Policies that encourage saving might be good in the medium run and in the long run, but they can lead to a reduction in demand and in output, and perhaps even a recession, in the short run.

■ We have assumed that investment remained constant. But investment is also likely to respond in a variety of ways. So are imports: Some of the increased demand by consumers and firms will not be for domestic goods but for foreign goods. The exchange rate may change. All these responses are likely to be associated with complex, dynamic effects, making it hard for governments to assess the effects of their policies with much certainty (Chapters 5 and 7, and 19 to 22).

■ Expectations are likely to matter. For example, the reaction of consumers to a tax cut is likely to depend on whether they think of the tax cut as transitory or permanent. The more they perceive the tax cut as permanent, the larger will be their consumption response (Chapters 15 to 17).

■ Achieving a given level of output can come with unpleasant side effects. Trying to achieve too high a level of output can, for example, lead to increasing inflation and, for that reason, be unsustainable in the medium run (Chapters 7 and 8).

■ Cutting taxes or increasing government spending, as attractive as it may seem in the short run, can lead to large budget deficits and an accumulation of public debt. A large debt has adverse effects in the long run. This is a hot issue in the United States today and in almost every advanced country in the world (Chapters 9, 11, 17, and 23).

In short, the proposition that, by using fiscal policy, the government can affect demand and output in the short run is an important and correct proposition. But as we refine our analysis, we will see that the role of the government in general, and the successful use of fiscal policy in particular, becomes increasingly difficult: Governments will never again have it so good as they have had in this chapter.

Summary

What you should remember about the components of GDP:

- GDP is the sum of consumption, investment, government spending, inventory investment, and exports minus imports.
- Consumption (C) is the purchase of goods and services by consumers. Consumption is the largest component of demand.
- Investment (I) is the sum of nonresidential investment—the purchase of new plants and new machines by firms—and of residential investment—the purchase of new houses or apartments by people.
- Government spending (G) is the purchase of goods and services by federal, state, and local governments.
- Exports (X) are purchases of U.S. goods by foreigners. Imports (IM) are purchases of foreign goods by U.S. consumers, U.S. firms, and the U.S. government.
- Inventory investment is the difference between production and purchases. It can be positive or negative.

What you should remember about our first model of output determination:

- In the short run, demand determines production. Production is equal to income. Income in turn affects demand.

- The consumption function shows how consumption depends on disposable income. The propensity to consume describes how much consumption increases for a given increase in disposable income.
- Equilibrium output is the level of output at which production equals demand. In equilibrium, output equals autonomous spending times the multiplier. Autonomous spending is that part of demand that does not depend on income. The multiplier is equal to $1/(1 - c_1)$, where c_1 is the propensity to consume.
- Increases in consumer confidence, investment demand, government spending, or decreases in taxes all increase equilibrium output in the short run.
- An alternative way of stating the goods–market equilibrium condition is that investment must be equal to saving—the sum of private and public saving. For this reason, the equilibrium condition is called the IS relation (I for investment, S for saving).

Key Terms

Questions and Problems

QUICK CHECK

All Quick Check questions and problems are available on MyEconLab.

1. Using the information in this chapter, label each of the following statements true, false, or uncertain. Explain briefly.
   a. The largest component of GDP is consumption.
   b. Government spending, including transfers, was equal to 20.4% of GDP in 2010.
   c. The propensity to consume has to be positive, but otherwise it can take on any positive value.
   d. *Fiscal policy* describes the choice of government spending and taxes and is treated as exogenous in our goods market model.
   e. The equilibrium condition for the goods market states that consumption equals output.
   f. An increase of one unit in government spending leads to an increase of one unit in equilibrium output.
   g. An increase in the propensity to consume leads to a decrease in output.

2. Suppose that the economy is characterized by the following behavioral equations:

$$C = 160 + 0.6Y_D$$
$$I = 150$$
$$G = 150$$
$$T = 100$$

Solve for the following variables.
   a. Equilibrium GDP (Y)
   b. Disposable income (Y_D)
   c. Consumption spending (C)

3. Use the economy described in Problem 2.
   a. Solve for equilibrium output. Compute total demand. Is it equal to production? Explain.
   b. Assume that G is now equal to 110. Solve for equilibrium output. Compute total demand. Is it equal to production? Explain.
   c. Assume that G is equal to 110, so output is given by your answer to (b). Compute private plus public saving. Is the sum of private and public saving equal to investment? Explain.

DIG DEEPER

All Dig Deeper questions and problems are available on MyEconLab.

4. *The balanced budget multiplier*
   For both political and macroeconomic reasons, governments are often reluctant to run budget deficits. Here, we examine whether policy changes in G and T that maintain a balanced budget are macroeconomically neutral. Put another way, we examine whether it is possible to affect output through changes in G and T so that the government budget remains balanced. Start from equation (3.8).
   a. By how much does *Y* increase when *G* increases by one unit?
   b. By how much does *Y* decrease when *T* increases by one unit?

   c. Why are your answers to (a) and (b) different?
   Suppose that the economy starts with a balanced budget: G = T. *If the increase in* G *is equal to the increase in* T, *then the budget remains in balance. Let us now compute the balanced budget multiplier.*
   d. Suppose that *G* and *T* increase by one unit each. Using your answers to (a) and (b), what is the change in equilibrium GDP? Are balanced budget changes in *G* and *T* macroeconomically neutral?
   e. How does the specific value of the propensity to consume affect your answer to (a)? Why?

5. *Automatic stabilizers*
   So far in this chapter, we have assumed that the fiscal policy variables G and T are independent of the level of income. In the real world, however, this is not the case. Taxes typically depend on the level of income and so tend to be higher when income is higher. In this problem, we examine how this automatic response of taxes can help reduce the impact of changes in autonomous spending on output.
   Consider the following behavioral equations:

$$C = c_0 + c_1 Y_D$$
$$T = t_0 + t_1 Y$$
$$Y_D = Y - T$$

   G *and* I *are both constant. Assume that* t_1 *is between 0 and 1.*
   a. Solve for equilibrium output.
   b. What is the multiplier? Does the economy respond more to changes in autonomous spending when t_1 is 0 or when t_1 is positive? Explain.
   c. Why is fiscal policy in this case called an automatic stabilizer?

6. *Balanced budget versus automatic stabilizers*
   It is often argued that a balanced budget amendment would actually be destabilizing. To understand this argument, consider the economy in Problem 5.
   a. Solve for equilibrium output.
   b. Solve for taxes in equilibrium.
   Suppose that the government starts with a balanced budget and that there is a drop in c_0.
   c. What happens to *Y*? What happens to taxes?
   d. Suppose that the government cuts spending in order to keep the budget balanced. What will be the effect on *Y*? Does the cut in spending required to balance the budget counteract or reinforce the effect of the drop in c_0 on output? (Don't do the algebra. Use your intuition and give the answer in words.)

7. *Taxes and transfers*
   Recall that we define taxes, T, as net of transfers. In other words,

$$T = Taxes - Transfer\ Payments$$

   a. Suppose that the government increases transfer payments to private households, but these transfer payments are not financed by tax increases. Instead, the government borrows to pay for the transfer payments. Show in a diagram (similar to Figure 3-2) how this policy affects equilibrium output. Explain.

b. Suppose instead that the government pays for the increase in transfer payments with an equivalent increase in taxes. How does the increase in transfer payments affect equilibrium output in this case?

c. Now suppose that the population includes two kinds of people: those with high propensity to consume and those with low propensity to consume. Suppose the transfer policy increases taxes on those with low propensity to consume to pay for transfers to people with high propensity to consume. How does this policy affect equilibrium output?

d. How do you think the propensity to consume might vary across individuals according to income? In other words, how do you think the propensity to consume compares for people with high income and people with low income? Explain. Given your answer, do you think tax cuts will be more effective at stimulating output when they are directed toward high-income or toward low-income taxpayers?

8. Investment and income

This problem examines the implications of allowing investment to depend on output. Chapter 5 carries this analysis much further and introduces an essential relation—the effect of the interest rate on investment—not examined in this problem.

a. Suppose the economy is characterized by the following behavioral equations:

$$C = c_0 + c_1 Y_D$$
$$Y_D = Y - T$$
$$I = b_0 + b_1 Y$$

Government spending and taxes are constant. Note that investment now increases with output. (Chapter 5 discusses the reasons for this relation.) Solve for equilibrium output.

b. What is the value of the multiplier? How does the relation between investment and output affect the value of the multiplier? For the multiplier to be positive, what condition must $(c_1 + b_1)$ satisfy? Explain your answers.

c. Suppose that the parameter b_0, sometimes called *business confidence*, increases. How will equilibrium output be affected? Will investment change by more or less than the change in b_0? Why? What will happen to national saving?

EXPLORE FURTHER

9. The paradox of saving revisited

You should be able to complete this question without doing any algebra, although you may find making a diagram helpful for part (a). For this problem, you do not need to calculate the magnitudes of changes in economic variables—only the direction of change.

a. Consider the economy described in Problem 8. Suppose that consumers decide to consume less (and therefore to save more) for any given amount of disposable income. Specifically, assume that consumer confidence (c_0) falls. What will happen to output?

b. As a result of the effect on output you determined in part (a), what will happen to investment? What will happen to public saving? What will happen to private saving? Explain. (*Hint*: Consider the saving-equals-investment characterization of equilibrium.) What is the effect on consumption?

c. Suppose that consumers had decided to increase consumption expenditure, so that c_0 had increased. What would have been the effect on output, investment, and private saving in this case? Explain. What would have been the effect on consumption?

d. Comment on the following logic: "When output is too low, what is needed is an increase in demand for goods and services. Investment is one component of demand, and saving equals investment. Therefore, if the government could just convince households to attempt to save more, then investment, and output, would increase."

Output is not the only variable that affects investment. As we develop our model of the economy, we will revisit the paradox of saving in future chapter problems.

10. Using fiscal policy in this first (and simplest model) to avoid the recession of 2010:

In this chapter, Table 3-1 shows GDP in 2010 was roughly $15,000 billion. You learned in Chapter 1 that GDP fell by approximately 3 percentage points in 2009.

a. How many billion dollars is 3 percentage points of $15,000 billion?

b. If the propensity to consume were 0.5, by how much would government spending have to have increased to prevent a decrease in output?

c. If the propensity to consume were 0.5, by how much would taxes have to have been cut to prevent any decrease in output?

d. Suppose Congress had chosen to both increase government spending and raise taxes by the same amount in 2009. What increase in government spending and taxes would have been required to prevent the decline in output in 2009?

11. The "exit strategy" problem

In fighting the recession associated with the crisis, taxes were cut and government spending was increased. The result was a very large government deficit. To reduce that deficit, taxes must be increased or government spending must be cut. This is the "exit strategy" from the large deficit.

a. How will reducing the deficit in either way affect the equilibrium level of output in the short run?

b. Which will change equilibrium output more: (i) cutting G by $100 billion (ii) raising T by $100 billion?

c. How does your answer to part (b) depend on the value of the marginal propensity to consume?

d. You hear the argument that a reduction in the deficit will increase consumer and business confidence and thus reduce the decline in output that would otherwise occur with deficit reduction. Is this argument valid?

Financial Markets

Barely a day goes by without the media speculating whether the **Fed** (short for **Federal Reserve Bank**, the U.S central bank) is going to change the interest rate, and what the change is likely to do to the economy. Ben Bernanke, the chairman of the Fed, is widely perceived as the most powerful policy maker in the United States, if not in the world.

The model of economic activity we developed in Chapter 3 did not include an interest rate, so there was no role for the Fed and its chair. This was a strong simplification, and it is time to relax it. In this chapter, we shall introduce the simplest model needed to think about the determination of the interest rate and the role of the central bank, a model in which people face a simple portfolio choice, whether to hold money or to hold bonds. In that model, we can think of the interest rate as determined by the demand of money and the supply for money. Then, in the next chapter, we shall look at how the interest rate in turn affects demand and output. This simple model does not, however, do justice to the complexity of the financial system. When we focus on the crisis in Chapter 9, we shall look at the financial sector in more detail.

The chapter has four sections:

Section 4-1 looks at the demand for money.

Section 4-2 assumes that the central bank directly controls the supply of money and shows how the interest rate is determined by the condition that the demand for money be equal to its supply.

Section 4-3 introduces banks as suppliers of money, revisits interest rates and how they are determined, and describes the role of the central bank in this process.

Section 4-4, an optional section, presents two alternative ways of looking at the equilibrium. One focuses on the federal funds market. The other focuses on the money multiplier. ●

◀ Before becoming Chairman of the Fed, Bernanke already had an impressive academic reputation. See Chapter 25.

4-1 The Demand for Money

This section looks at the determinants of *the demand for money*. A warning before we start: Words such as "money" or "wealth" have very specific meanings in economics, often not the same meanings as in everyday conversations. The purpose of the Focus box "Semantic Traps: Money, Income, and Wealth" is to help you avoid some of these traps. Read it carefully, and come back to it once in a while.

Suppose, as a result of having steadily saved part of your income in the past, your financial wealth today is $50,000. You may intend to keep saving in the future and increase your wealth further, but its value today is given. Suppose also that you only have the choice between two assets, money and bonds:

Make sure you see the difference between the decision about how much to save (a decision that determines how your wealth changes over time) and the decision about how to allocate a given stock of wealth between money and bonds.

- *Money*, which you can use for transactions, pays no interest. In the real world, there are two types of money: **currency**, coins and bills, and **checkable deposits**, the bank deposits on which you can write checks. The sum of currency and checkable deposits is called **M1**. The distinction between the two will be important when we look at the supply of money. For the moment, however, the distinction does not matter and we can ignore it.
- **Bonds** pay a positive interest rate, i, but they cannot be used for transactions. In the real world, there are many types of bonds and other financial assets, each associated with a specific interest rate. For the time being, we will also ignore this aspect of reality and assume that there is just one type of bond and that it pays, i, the rate of interest.

Assume that buying or selling bonds implies some cost; for example, a phone call to your broker and the payment of a transaction fee. How much of your $50,000 should you hold in money, and how much in bonds? On the one hand, holding all your wealth in the form of money is clearly very convenient. You won't ever need to call a broker or pay transaction fees. But it also means you will receive no interest income. On the other hand, if you hold all your wealth in the form of bonds, you will earn interest on the full amount, but you will have to call your broker frequently—whenever you need money to take the subway, pay for a cup of coffee, and so on. This is a rather inconvenient way of going through life.

Therefore, it is clear that you should hold both money and bonds. But in what proportions? This will depend mainly on two variables:

- Your *level of transactions*. You will want to have enough money on hand to avoid having to sell bonds whenever you need money. Say, for example, that you typically spend $3,000 a month. In this case, you might want to have, on average, say, two months worth of spending on hand, or $6,000 in money, and the rest, $50,000 − $6,000 = $44,000, in bonds. If, instead, you typically spend $4,000 a month, you might want to have, say, $8,000 in money and only $42,000 in bonds.
- *The interest rate on bonds*. The only reason to hold any of your wealth in bonds is that they pay interest. If bonds paid zero interest, you would want to hold all of your wealth in the form of money because it is more convenient.

  The higher the interest rate, the more you will be willing to deal with the hassle and costs associated with buying and selling bonds. If the interest rate is very high, you might even decide to squeeze your money holdings to an average of only two weeks' worth of spending, or $1,500 (assuming your monthly spending is $3,000). This way, you will be able to keep, on average, $48,500 in bonds and earn more interest as a result.

Let's make this last point more concrete. Many of you probably do not hold bonds; few of you have a broker. However, many of you likely do hold bonds indirectly if you

Semantic Traps: Money, Income, and Wealth

In everyday conversation, we use "money" to denote many different things. We use it as a synonym for income: "making money." We use it as a synonym for wealth: "She has a lot of money." In economics, you must be more careful. Here is a basic guide to some terms and their precise meanings in economics.

Money is what can be readily used to pay for transactions. Money is currency and checkable deposits at banks. **Income** is what you earn from working plus what you receive in interest and dividends. It is a flow—something expressed in units of time: weekly income, monthly income, or yearly income, for example. J. Paul Getty was once asked what his income was. Getty answered: "$1,000." He meant but did not say: $1,000 per minute!

Saving is that part of after-tax income that you do not spend. It is also a flow. If you save 10% of your income, and your income is $3,000 per month, then you save $300 per month. **Savings** (plural) is sometimes used as a synonym for wealth—the value of what you have accumulated over time. To avoid confusion, we will not use "savings" in this book.

Your **financial wealth**, or simply **wealth**, is the value of all your financial assets minus all your financial liabilities. In contrast to income or saving, which are flow variables, financial wealth is a stock variable. It is the value of wealth at a given moment in time.

At a given moment in time, you cannot change the total amount of your financial wealth. It can only change over time as you save or dissave, or as the value of your assets and liabilities change. But you can change the composition of your wealth; you can, for example, decide to pay back part of your mortgage by writing a check against your checking account. This leads to a decrease in your liabilities (a smaller mortgage) and a corresponding decrease in your assets (a smaller checking account balance); but, at that moment, it does not change your wealth.

Financial assets that can be used directly to buy goods are called money. Money includes currency and checkable deposits—deposits against which you can write checks. Money is also a stock. Someone who is wealthy might have only small money holdings—say, $1,000,000 in stocks but only $500 in a checking account. It is also possible for a person to have a large income but only small money holdings—say, an income of $10,000 monthly but only $1,000 in his checking account.

Investment is a term economists reserve for the purchase of new capital goods, from machines to plants to office buildings. When you want to talk about the purchase of shares or other financial assets, you should refer them as a **financial investment**.

Learn how to be economically correct:

> Do not say "Mary is making a lot of money"; say "Mary has a high income."

> Do not say "Joe has a lot of money"; say "Joe is very wealthy."

---

have a money market account with a financial institution. **Money market funds** (the full name is *money market mutual funds*) pool together the funds of many people. The funds are then used to buy bonds—typically government bonds. Money market funds pay an interest rate close to but slightly below the interest rate on the bonds they hold—the difference coming from the administrative costs of running the funds and from their profit margins.

When the interest rate on these funds reached 14% per year in the early 1980s (a very high interest rate by today's standards), many people who had previously kept all of their wealth in their checking accounts (which paid little or no interest) realized how much interest they could earn by moving some of it into money market accounts instead. As a result, accounts like these became very popular. Since then, however, interest rates have fallen. By the mid 2000s, just before the crisis, the average interest rate paid by money market funds was only around 5%. This was better than zero—the rate paid on many checking accounts—but is much less attractive than the rate in the early 1980s. Since the crisis, the interest rate has further decreased, and, in 2010, the average interest rate on money market funds was less than 1%. As a result, people are now less careful about putting as much as they can in their money market funds. Put another way, for a given level of transactions, people now keep more of their wealth in money than they did in the early 1980s.

◄ An economy where the interest rate is equal or very close to zero is said to be in a liquidity trap. More on this in Chapter 9.

Deriving the Demand for Money

Let's go from this discussion to an equation describing the demand for money.

Denote the amount of money people want to hold—their *demand for money*—by M^d (the superscript d stands for *demand*). The demand for money in the economy as a whole is just the sum of all the individual demands for money by the people in the economy. Therefore, it depends on the overall level of transactions in the economy and on the interest rate. The overall level of transactions in the economy is hard to measure, but it is likely to be roughly proportional to nominal income (income measured in dollars). If nominal income were to increase by 10%, it is reasonable to think that the dollar value of transactions in the economy would also increase by roughly 10%. So we can write the relation between the demand for money, nominal income, and the interest rate as:

$$M^d = \$Y\, L(i) \tag{4.1}$$
$$(-)$$

where $\$Y$ denotes nominal income. Read this equation in the following way: *The demand for money M^d is equal to nominal income $\$Y$ times a function of the interest rate i, with the function denoted by $L(i)$.* The minus sign under i in $L(i)$ captures the fact that the interest rate has a negative effect on money demand: An increase in the interest rate *decreases* the demand for money, as people put more of their wealth into bonds.

Equation (4.1) summarizes what we have discussed so far:

- First, the demand for money increases in proportion to nominal income. If nominal income doubles, increasing from $\$Y$ to $\$2Y$, then the demand for money also doubles, increasing from $\$Y\,L(i)$ to $\$2Y\,L(i)$.
- Second, the demand for money depends negatively on the interest rate. This is captured by the function $L(i)$ and the negative sign underneath: An increase in the interest rate decreases the demand for money.

Revisit Chapter 2's example of an economy composed of a steel company and a car company. Calculate the total value of transactions in that economy. If the steel and the car companies doubled in size, what would happen to transactions and to GDP? ▶

What matters here is nominal income—income in dollars, not real income. If real income does not change but prices double, leading to a doubling of nominal income, people will need to hold twice as much money to buy the same consumption basket. ▶

Figure 4-1

The Demand for Money

For a given level of nominal income, a lower interest rate increases the demand for money. At a given interest rate, an increase in nominal income shifts the demand for money to the right.

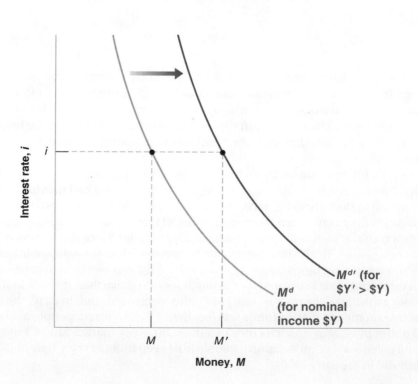

Who Holds U.S. Currency?

According to household surveys in 2006 the average U.S. household held $1,600 in currency (dollar bills and coins). Multiplying by the number of households in the U.S. economy (about 110 million), this implies that the total amount of currency held by U.S. households was around $170 billion.

According to the Federal Reserve Board, however—which issues the dollar bills and therefore knows how much is in circulation—the amount of currency in circulation was actually a much higher $750 billion. Here lies the puzzle: If it was not held by households, where was all this currency?

Clearly some currency was held by firms, rather than by households. And some was held by those involved in the underground economy or in illegal activities. When dealing with drugs, dollar bills, not checks, are the way to settle accounts. Surveys of firms and IRS estimates of the underground economy suggest, however, that this can only account for another $80 billion at the most. This leaves $500 billion, or 66% of the total, unaccounted for. So where was it? The answer: Abroad, held by foreigners:

A few countries, Ecuador and El Salvador among them, have actually adopted the dollar as their own currency. So people in these countries use dollar bills for transactions. But these countries are just too small to explain the puzzle.

In a number of countries that have suffered from high inflation in the past, people have learned that their domestic currency may quickly become worthless and they may see dollars as a safe and convenient asset. This is, for example, the case of Argentina and of Russia. Estimates by the U.S. Treasury suggest that Argentina holds more than $50 billion in dollar bills, Russia more than $80 billion—so together, more than the holdings of U.S. households.

In yet other countries, people who have emigrated to the United States bring home U.S. dollar bills; or tourists pay some transactions in dollars, and the bills stay in the country. This is, for example, the case for Mexico or Thailand.

The fact that foreigners hold such a high proportion of the dollar bills in circulation has two main macroeconomic implications. First, the rest of the world, by being willing to hold U.S. currency, is making in effect an interest-free loan to the United States of $500 billion. Second, while we shall think of money demand (which includes both currency and checkable deposits) as being determined by the interest rate and the level of transactions in the country, it is clear that U.S. money demand also depends on other factors. Can you guess, for example, what would happen to U.S. money demand if the degree of civil unrest increased in the rest of the world?

The relation between the demand for money, nominal income, and the interest rate implied by equation (4.1) is shown in Figure 4-1. The interest rate, i, is measured on the vertical axis. Money, M, is measured on the horizontal axis.

The relation between the demand for money and the interest rate *for a given level of nominal income* $\$Y$ is represented by the M^d curve. The curve is downward sloping: The lower the interest rate (the lower i), the higher the amount of money people want to hold (the higher M).

For a given interest rate, an increase in nominal income increases the demand for money. In other words, an increase in nominal income shifts the demand for money to the right, from M^d to $M^{d'}$. For example, at interest rate i, an increase in nominal income from $\$Y$ to $\$Y'$ increases the demand for money from M to M'.

4-2 Determining the Interest Rate: I

Having looked at the demand for money, we now look at the supply of money and then at the equilibrium.

In the real world, there are two types of money: checkable deposits, which are supplied by banks, and currency, which is supplied by the central bank. In this section, we will assume that checkable deposits do not exist—that the only money in the economy is currency. In the next section, we will reintroduce checkable deposits, and look at the role banks play. Introducing banks makes the discussion more realistic, but it also makes the mechanics of money supply more complicated. It is better to build up the discussion in two steps.

Money Demand, Money Supply, and the Equilibrium Interest Rate

Suppose the central bank decides to supply an amount of money equal to M, so

$$M^s = M$$

Throughout this section, "money" stands for "central bank money," or "currency." ▶ The superscript s stands for *supply*. (Let's disregard, for the moment, the issue of how exactly the central bank supplies this amount of money. We shall return to it in a few paragraphs.)

Equilibrium in financial markets requires that money supply be equal to money demand, that $M^s = M^d$. Then, using $M^s = M$, and equation (4.1) for money demand, the equilibrium condition is

$$\text{Money supply} = \text{Money demand}$$
$$M = \$Y\, L(i) \tag{4.2}$$

This equation tells us that the interest rate i must be such that, given their income $\$Y$, people are willing to hold an amount of money equal to the existing money supply M. This equilibrium relation is called the ***LM* relation**. As for the *IS* relation, the name of the *LM* relation is more than 50 years old. The letter L stands for **liquidity**: Economists use liquidity as a measure of how easily an asset can be exchanged for money. Money is *fully liquid*; other assets less so.

How liquid depends on the asset: Bonds are typically fairly liquid. Houses are much less liquid. It takes time to sell ▶ them, and the selling price is often hard to know prior to the final sale. Transaction costs to sell a house are much higher than those to sell a bond.

We can think of the demand for money as a demand for liquidity. The letter M stands for money. The demand for liquidity must equal the supply of money.

This equilibrium condition is represented graphically in Figure 4-2. As in Figure 4-1, money is measured on the horizontal axis, and the interest rate is measured

Figure 4-2

The Determination of the Interest Rate

The interest rate must be such that the supply of money (which is independent of the interest rate) is equal to the demand for money (which does depend on the interest rate).

Figure 4-3

The Effects of an Increase in Nominal Income on the Interest Rate

An increase in nominal income leads to an increase in the interest rate.

on the vertical axis. The demand for money, M^d, drawn for a given level of nominal income, $\$Y$, is downward sloping: A higher interest rate implies a lower demand for money. The supply of money is drawn as the vertical line denoted M^s: The money supply equals M and is independent of the interest rate. Equilibrium occurs at point A, and the equilibrium interest rate is given by i.

Now that we have characterized the equilibrium, we can look at how changes in nominal income or changes in the money supply by the central bank affect the equilibrium interest rate.

■ Figure 4-3 shows the effects of an increase in nominal income on the interest rate.

The figure replicates Figure 4-2, and the initial equilibrium is at point A. An increase in nominal income from $\$Y$ to $\$Y'$ increases the level of transactions, which increases the demand for money at any interest rate. The money demand curve *shifts* to the right, from M^d to $M^{d'}$. The equilibrium moves from A up to A', and the equilibrium interest rate increases from i to i'.

In words: *An increase in nominal income leads to an increase in the interest rate.* The reason: At the initial interest rate, the demand for money exceeds the supply. An increase in the interest rate is needed to decrease the amount of money people want to hold and to reestablish equilibrium.

■ Figure 4-4 shows the effects of an increase in the money supply on the interest rate.

The initial equilibrium is at point A, with interest rate i. An increase in the money supply, from $M^s = M$ to $M^{s'} = M'$, leads to a shift of the money supply curve to the right, from M^s to $M^{s'}$. The equilibrium moves from A down to A'; the interest rate decreases from i to i'.

In words: *an increase in the supply of money by the central bank leads to a decrease in the interest rate.* The decrease in the interest rate increases the demand for money so it equals the now larger money supply.

Figure 4-4

The Effects of an Increase in the Money Supply on the Interest Rate

An increase in the supply of money leads to a decrease in the interest rate.

Monetary Policy and Open Market Operations

We can get a better understanding of the results in Figures 4-3 and 4-4 by looking more closely at how the central bank actually changes the money supply, and what happens when it does so.

Open market operations. In modern economies, the way central banks change the supply of money is by buying or selling bonds in the bond market. If a central bank wants to increase the amount of money in the economy, it buys bonds and pays for them by creating money. If it wants to decrease the amount of money in the economy, it sells bonds and removes from circulation the money it receives in exchange for the bonds. These actions are called **open market operations** because they take place in the "open market" for bonds.

▶ The balance sheet of the central bank is given in Figure 4-5. The assets of the central bank are the bonds it holds in its portfolio. Its liabilities are the stock of money in the economy. Open market operations lead to equal changes in assets and liabilities.

If the central bank buys, say, $1 million worth of bonds, the amount of bonds it holds is higher by $1 million, and so is the amount of money in the economy. Such an operation is called an **expansionary open market operation**, because the central bank increases (*expands*) the supply of money.

If the central bank sells $1 million worth of bonds, both the amount of bonds held by the central bank and the amount of money in the economy are lower by $1 million. Such an operation is called a **contractionary open market operation**, because the central bank decreases (*contracts*) the supply of money.

The balance sheet of a bank (or firm, or individual) is a list of its assets and liabilities at a point in time. The assets are the sum of what the bank owns and what is owed to it by others. The liabilities are what the bank owes to others.

Bond Prices and Bond Yields

We have focused so far on the interest rate on bonds. In fact, what is determined in bond markets is not interest rates, but bond *prices*; in this section we show that the interest rate on a bond can then be inferred from the price of the bond. Understanding

Figure 4-5

The Balance Sheet of the Central Bank and the Effects of an Expansionary Open Market Operation

The assets of the central bank are the bonds it holds. The liabilities are the stock of money in the economy. An open market operation in which the central bank buys bonds and issues money increases both assets and liabilities by the same amount.

this relation between the interest rate and bond prices will prove useful both here and later in this book.

■ Suppose the bonds in our economy are one-year bonds—bonds that promise a payment of a given number of dollars, say $100, a year from now. In the United States, bonds issued by the government promising payment in a year or less are called **Treasury bills** or **T-bills**. Let the price of a bond today be $\$P_B$, where the subscript B stands for "bond." If you buy the bond today and hold it for a year, the rate of return on holding the bond for a year is $(\$100 - \$P_B)/\$P_B$. Therefore, the interest rate on the bond is given by

$$i = \frac{\$100 - \$P_B}{\$P_B}$$

The interest rate is what you get for the bond a year from now ($100) minus what you pay for the bond today ($\$P_B$), divided by the price of the bond today, ($\$P_B$).

If $\$P_B$ is $99, the interest rate equals $\$1/\$99 = 0.010$, or 1.0% per year. If $\$P_B$ is $90, the interest rate is $\$1/\$90 = 11.1\%$ per year. *The higher the price of the bond, the lower the interest rate.*

■ If we are given the interest rate, we can figure out the price of the bond using the same formula. Reorganizing the formula above, the price today of a one-year bond paying $100 a year from today is given by

$$\$P_B = \frac{\$100}{1 + i}$$

The price of the bond today is equal to the final payment divided by 1 plus the interest rate. If the interest rate is positive, the price of the bond is less than the final payment. The higher the interest rate, the lower the price today. You may read or hear that "bond markets went up today." This means that *the prices of bonds went up*, and therefore that *interest rates went down.*

We are now ready to return to the effects of an open market operation and its effect on equilibrium in the money market.

Consider first an expansionary open market operation, in which the central bank buys bonds in the bond market and pays for them by creating money. As the central bank buys bonds, the demand for bonds goes up, increasing their price. Conversely, the interest rate on bonds goes down. Note that by paying for the bonds with money, the central bank has increased the money supply.

Consider instead a contractionary open market operation, in which the central bank decreases the supply of money. It sells bonds in the bonds market. This leads to a decrease in their price, and an increase in the interest rate. Note that by selling the bonds in exchange for money previously held by households, the central bank has reduced the money supply.

Let's summarize what we have learned in the first two sections:

■ The interest rate is determined by the equality of the supply of money and the demand for money.

■ By changing the supply of money, the central bank can affect the interest rate.

■ The central bank changes the supply of money through open market operations, which are purchases or sales of bonds for money.

■ Open market operations in which the central bank increases the money supply by buying bonds lead to an increase in the price of bonds and a decrease in the interest rate. In Figure 4-2, the purchase of bonds by the central bank shifts the money supply to the right.

■ Open market operations in which the central bank decreases the money supply by selling bonds lead to a decrease in the price of bonds and an increase in the interest rate. In Figure 4-2, the purchase of bonds by the central bank shifts the money supply to the left.

Let us take up two more issues before moving on.

Choosing Money or Choosing the Interest Rate?

We have described the central bank as choosing the money supply and letting the interest rate be determined at the point where money supply equals money demand. Instead, we could have described the central bank as choosing the interest rate and then adjusting the money supply so as to achieve the interest rate it has chosen.

To see this, return to Figure 4-4. Figure 4-4 showed the effect of a decision by the central bank to increase the money supply from M^s to $M^{s'}$, causing the interest rate to fall from i to i'. However, we could have described the figure in terms of the central bank decision to lower the interest rate from i to i' by increasing the money supply from M^s to $M^{s'}$.

Suppose nominal income increases, as in Figure 4-3, and that the central bank wants ▶ to keep the interest rate unchanged. How does it need to adjust the money supply?

Why is it useful to think about the central bank as choosing the interest rate? Because this is what modern central banks, including the Fed, typically do. They typically think about the interest rate they want to achieve, and then move the money supply so as to achieve it. This is why, when you listen to the news, you do not hear: "The Fed decided to increase the money supply today." Instead you hear: "The Fed decided to decrease the interest rate today." The way the Fed did it was by increasing the money supply appropriately.

Money, Bonds, and Other Assets

We have been looking at an economy with only two assets, money and bonds. This is obviously a much simplified version of actual economies with their many financial assets and many financial markets. But, as you will see in later chapters, the basic lessons we have just learned apply very generally. The only change we will have to make is replacing "interest rate" in our conclusions with "short-term interest rate on government bonds." You will see that the short-term interest rate is determined by the condition we just discussed—the equilibrium between money supply and money demand. The central bank can, through open market operations, change the short-term interest rate; and open market operations are indeed the basic tool used by most modern central banks, including the Fed, to affect interest rates.

The complication: The short-term interest rate—the rate directly controlled by the Fed—is not the only interest rate that affects spending. We return to this issue first in Chapter 9, and then in Chapters 15 to 17.

There is one dimension, however, to which our model must be extended. We have assumed that all money in the economy consisted of currency, supplied by the central bank. In the real world, money includes not only currency but also checkable deposits. Checkable deposits are supplied not by the central bank but by (private) banks. How the presence of banks and checkable deposits changes our conclusions is the topic of the next section.

4-3 Determining the Interest Rate: II

To understand what determines the interest rate in an economy with both currency and checkable deposits, we must first look at what banks do.

What Banks Do

Modern economies are characterized by the existence of many types of **financial intermediaries**—institutions that receive funds from people and firms and use these funds to buy financial assets or to make loans to other people and firms. The assets of these institutions are the financial assets they own and the loans they have made. Their liabilities are what they owe to the people and firms from whom they have received funds.

Banks are one type of financial intermediary. What makes banks special—and the reason we focus on banks here rather than on financial intermediaries in general—is that their liabilities are money: People can pay for transactions by writing checks up to the amount of their account balance. Let's look more closely at what banks do.

The balance sheet of banks is shown in the bottom half of Figure 4-6, Figure 4-6b.

■ Banks receive funds from people and firms who either deposit funds directly or have funds sent to their checking accounts (via direct deposit of their paychecks, for example.) At any point in time, people and firms can write checks or withdraw up to the full amount of their account balances. The liabilities of the banks are therefore equal to the value of these *checkable deposits*.

■ Banks keep as **reserves** some of the funds they receive. They are held partly in cash and partly in an account the banks have at the central bank, which they can draw on when they need to. Banks hold reserves for three reasons:

On any given day, some depositors withdraw cash from their checking accounts while others deposit cash into their accounts. There is no reason for the inflows and outflows of cash to be equal, so the bank must keep some cash on hand.

Let us give you the bottom line in case you want to skip the section: Even in this more complicated case, the central bank can, by changing the amount of central bank money, control the short-term interest rate.

Banks have other types of liabilities in addition to checkable deposits, and they are engaged in more activities than just holding bonds or making loans. Ignore these complications for the moment. We consider these complications in Chapter 9.

(a)
Central Bank

Assets	Liabilities
Bonds	Central Bank Money = Reserves + Currency

(b)
Banks

Assets	Liabilities
Reserves Loans Bonds	Checkable deposits

Figure 4-6

The Balance Sheet of Banks, and the Balance Sheet of the Central Bank Revisited

In the same way, on any given day, people with accounts at the bank write checks to people with accounts at other banks, and people with accounts at other banks write checks to people with accounts at the bank. What the bank, as a result of these transactions, owes the other banks can be larger or smaller than what the other banks owe to it. For this reason also, the bank needs to keep reserves.

The first two reasons imply that the banks would want to keep some reserves even if they were not required to do so. But, in addition, banks are subject to reserve requirements, which require them to hold reserves in some proportion of their checkable deposits. In the United States, reserve requirements are set by the Fed. The actual **reserve ratio**—the ratio of bank reserves to bank checkable deposits—is about 10% in the United States today. Banks can use the other 90% to make loans or buy bonds.

■ Loans represent roughly 70% of banks' nonreserve assets. Bonds account for the rest, 30%. The distinction between bonds and loans is unimportant for our purposes in this chapter—which is to understand how the money supply is determined. For this reason, to keep the discussion simple, we will assume in this chapter that banks do not make loans, that they hold only reserves and bonds as assets. But the distinction between loans and bonds is important for other purposes, from the possibility of "bank runs" to the role of federal deposit insurance. These topics are first explored in the Focus box, "Bank Runs, Deposit Insurance, and Wholesale Funding," and then at more length in Chapter 9 on the crisis.

Figure 4-6a returns to the balance sheet of the central bank, in an economy in which there are banks. It is very similar to the balance sheet of the central bank we saw in Figure 4-5. The asset side is the same as before: The assets of the central bank are the bonds it holds. The liabilities of the central bank are the money it has issued, **central bank money**. The new feature is that not all of central bank money is held as currency by the public. Some of it is held as reserves by banks.

The Supply and the Demand for Central Bank Money

The easiest way to think about how the interest rate in this economy is determined is by thinking in terms of the supply and the demand for *central bank money*:

■ The demand for central bank money is equal to the demand for currency by people plus the demand for reserves by banks.
■ The supply of central bank money is under the direct control of the central bank.
■ The equilibrium interest rate is such that the demand and the supply for central bank money are equal.

Figure 4-7 shows the structure of the demand and the supply of central bank money in more detail. (Ignore the equations for the time being. Just look at the boxes.) Start on the left side. The demand for money by people is for both checkable deposits and currency. Because banks have to hold reserves against checkable deposits, the demand for checkable deposits leads to a demand for reserves by banks. Consequently, the demand for central bank money is equal to the demand for reserves by banks plus the demand for currency. Go to the right side: The supply of central bank money is determined by the central bank. Look at the equal sign: The interest rate must be such that the demand and the supply of central bank money are equal.

Bank Runs, Deposit Insurance, and Wholesale Funding

Is bank money (checkable deposits) just as good as central bank money (currency)? To answer this question, we must look at what banks do with their funds, and at the distinction between making loans or holding bonds.

Making a loan to a firm or buying a government bond are more similar than they may seem. In one case, the bank lends to a firm. In the other, the bank lends to the government. This is why, for simplicity, we assumed in the text that banks held only bonds.

But, in one respect, making a loan is very different from buying a bond. Bonds, especially government bonds, are very liquid: If need be, they can be sold easily in the bond market. Loans, on the other hand, are often not liquid at all. Calling them back may be impossible. Firms have probably already used their loans to buy inventories or new machines, so they no longer have the cash on hand. Likewise, individuals likely have used their loans to purchase cars, houses, or other things. The bank could in principle sell the loans to a third party to get cash. However, selling them might be very difficult because potential buyers would know little about how reliable the borrowers are.

This fact has one important implication: Take a healthy bank, a bank with a portfolio of good loans. Suppose rumors start that the bank is not doing well and some loans will not be repaid. Believing that the bank may fail, people with deposits at the bank will want to close their accounts and withdraw cash. If enough people do so, the bank will run out of reserves. Given that the loans cannot be called back, the bank will not be able to satisfy the demand for cash, and it will have to close.

Conclusion: Fear that a bank will close can actually cause it to close—even if all its loans are good. The financial history of the United States up to the 1930s is full of such **bank runs**. One bank fails for the right reason (because it has made bad loans). This causes depositors at other banks to panic and withdraw money from their banks, forcing them to close. You have probably seen *It's a Wonderful Life*, an old movie with James Stewart that runs on TV every year around Christmas. After another bank in Stewart's town fails, depositors at the savings and loan he manages get scared and want to withdraw their money too. Stewart successfully persuades them this is not a good idea. It's a Wonderful Life has a happy ending. But in real life, most bank runs didn't.

What can be done to avoid bank runs? One solution is called **narrow banking**. Narrow banking would restrict banks to holding liquid and safe government bonds, like T-bills. Loans would have to be made by financial intermediaries other than banks. This would eliminate bank runs, as well as the need for federal insurance. Some recent changes in U.S. regulation have gone in that direction, restricting banks that rely on deposits from engaging in some financial operations, but they stop far short of imposing narrow banking.

Another solution, and one that has been adopted by governments in most advanced countries, is deposit insurance. The United States, for example, introduced federal deposit insurance in 1934. The U.S. government now insures each account up to a ceiling, which, since 2008, is $250,000. (In response to the crisis, all accounts are currently fully insured, regardless of the amount, but this is scheduled to end in December 2012.) As a result, there is no reason for depositors to run and withdraw their money.

Federal deposit insurance leads, however, to problems of its own: Depositors, who do not have to worry about their deposits, no longer look at the activities of the banks in which they have their accounts. Banks may then misbehave, by making loans they wouldn't have made in the absence of deposit insurance. And, as the crisis has unfortunately shown, deposit insurance is no longer enough. The reason is that banks have increasingly relied on other sources of funds, often borrowing overnight from other financial institutions and investors, a method of financing known as **wholesale funding**. Wholesale funding, just before the crisis, accounted for close to 30% of total funding for U.S. banks. These funds were not insured, and when, in late 2008, doubts increased about the quality of the assets held by banks, there was in effect a run on many banks, this time not from the traditional depositors but from wholesale funders. To avoid more bank collapses, the Fed had no choice than to provide funds to banks on a very large scale.

Since then, banks have reduced their reliance on wholesale funding, which is down to roughly 25% in the United States. In parallel, regulation is being considered that would force banks to hold enough liquid assets to be able to withstand a large decrease in their wholesale funding. This is one of the challenges facing bank regulators today.

FOCUS

We now go through each of the boxes in Figure 4-7 and ask:

- What determines the demand for checkable deposits and the demand for currency?
- What determines the demand for reserves by banks?
- What determines the demand for central bank money?
- How does the condition that the demand for and the supply of central bank money be equal determine the interest rate?

Be careful to distinguish among:
Demand for money (demand for currency and checkable deposits)
Demand for bank money (demand for checkable deposits)
Demand for central bank money (demand for currency by people and demand for reserves by banks)

Figure 4-7

Determinants of the Demand and the Supply of Central Bank Money

The Demand for Money

When people can hold both currency and checkable deposits, the demand for money involves *two* decisions. First, people must decide how much money to hold. Second, they must decide how much of this money to hold in currency and how much to hold in checkable deposits.

It is reasonable to assume that the overall demand for money (currency plus checkable deposits) is given by the same factors as before. People will hold more money the higher the level of transactions and the lower the interest rate on bonds. So we can assume that overall money demand is given by the same equation as before (equation (4.1)):

$$M^d = \$Y\, L(i) \qquad (4.3)$$
$$(-)$$

That brings us to the second decision. How do people decide how much to hold in currency, and how much in checkable deposits? Currency is more convenient for small transactions (it is also more convenient for illegal transactions.) Checks are more convenient for large transactions. Holding money in your checking account is safer than holding cash.

Let's assume people hold a fixed proportion of their money in currency—call this proportion c—and, by implication, hold a fixed proportion $(1 - c)$ in checkable deposits. Call the demand for currency CU^d (CU for currency, and d for demand). Call the demand for checkable deposits D^d (D for deposits, and d for demand). The two demands are given by

$$CU^d = cM^d \qquad (4.4)$$

$$D^d = (1 - c)M^d \qquad (4.5)$$

Equation (4.4) shows the first component of the demand for central bank money—the demand for currency by the public. Equation (4.5) shows the demand for checkable deposits.

We now have a description of the first box, "Demand for Money," on the left side of Figure 4-7: Equation (4.3) shows the overall demand for money. Equations (4.4) and (4.5) show the demand for checkable deposits and the demand for currency, respectively.

The demand for checkable deposits leads to a demand by banks for reserves, the second component of the demand for central bank money. To see how, let's turn to the behavior of banks.

The Demand for Reserves

The larger the amount of checkable deposits, the larger the amount of reserves the banks must hold, both for precautionary and for regulatory reasons. Let θ (the Greek lowercase letter theta) be the reserve ratio, the amount of reserves banks hold per dollar of checkable deposits. Let R denote the reserves of banks. Let D denote the dollar amount of checkable deposits. Then, by the definition of θ, the following relation holds between R and D:

$$R = \theta D \qquad (4.6)$$

We saw earlier that, in the United States today, the reserve ratio is roughly equal to 10%. Thus, θ is roughly equal to 0.1.

If people want to hold D^d in deposits, then, from equation (4.6), banks must hold θD^d in reserves. Combining equations (4.5) and (4.6), the second component of the demand for central bank money—the demand for reserves by banks—is given by

$$R^d = \theta(1 - c)M^d \qquad (4.7)$$

We now have the equation corresponding to the second box, "Demand for Reserves by Banks," on the left side of Figure 4-7.

The Demand for Central Bank Money

Call H^d the demand for central bank money. This demand is equal to the sum of the demand for currency and the demand for reserves:

$$H^d = CU^d + R^d \qquad (4.8)$$

Replace CU^d and R^d by their expressions from equations (4.4) and (4.7) to get

$$H^d = cM^d + \theta(1 - c)M^d = [c + \theta(1 - c)]M^d$$

Finally, replace the overall demand for money, M^d, by its expression from equation (4.3) to get:

$$H^d = [c + \theta(1 - c)]\$Y\, L(i) \qquad (4.9)$$

This gives us the equation corresponding to the third box, "Demand for Central Bank Money," on the left side of Figure 4-7.

◀ Suppose banks doubled the number of locations of ATMs, making them more convenient to use for their customers. What would happen to the demand for central bank money?

The Determination of the Interest Rate

We are now ready to characterize the equilibrium. Let H be the supply of central bank money; H is directly controlled by the central bank; just like in the previous section, the central bank can change the amount of H through open market operations. The equilibrium condition is that the supply of central bank money be equal to the demand for central bank money:

$$H = H^d \qquad (4.10)$$

Or, using equation (4.9):

$$H = [c + \theta(1 - c)]\$Y\ L(i) \tag{4.11}$$

The supply of central bank money (the left side of equation (4.11)) is equal to the demand for central bank money (the right side of equation (4.11)), which is equal to the term in brackets times the overall demand for money.

Look at the term in brackets more closely:

Suppose that people held only currency, so $c = 1$. Then, the term in brackets would be equal to 1, and the equation would be exactly the same as equation (4.2) in Section 4-2 (with the letter H replacing the letter M on the left side, but H and M both stand for the supply of central bank money). In this case, people would hold only currency, and banks would play no role in the supply of money. We would be back to the case we looked at in Section 4-2.

Assume instead that people did not hold currency at all, but held only checkable deposits, so $c = 0$. Then, the term in brackets would be equal to θ. Suppose, for example, that $\theta = 0.1$, so that the term in brackets was equal to 0.1. Then the demand for central bank money would be equal to one-tenth of the overall demand for money. This is easy to understand: People would hold only checkable deposits. For every dollar they wanted to hold, banks would need to have 10 cents in reserves. In other words, the demand for reserves would be one-tenth of the overall demand for money.

Leaving aside these two extreme cases, note that, as long as people hold some checkable deposits (so that $c < 1$), the term in brackets is less than 1: This means the demand for central bank money is less than the overall demand for money. This is due to the fact that the demand for reserves by banks is only a fraction of the demand for checkable deposits.

We can represent the equilibrium condition, equation (4.11), graphically, and we do this in Figure 4-8. The figure looks the same as Figure 4-2, but with central bank money rather than money on the horizontal axis. The interest rate is measured on the vertical axis. The demand for central bank money, $CU^d + R^d$, is drawn for a given level of

Figure 4-8

Equilibrium in the Market for Central Bank Money and the Determination of the Interest Rate

The equilibrium interest rate is such that the supply of central bank money is equal to the demand for central bank money.

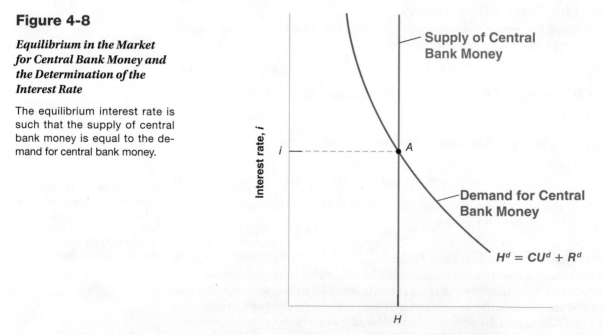

nominal income. A higher interest rate implies a lower demand for central bank money for two reasons: (1) The demand for currency by people goes down; (2) the demand for checkable deposits by people also goes down. This leads to lower demand for reserves by banks. The supply of money is fixed and is represented by a vertical line at H. Equilibrium is at point A, with interest rate i.

The effects of either changes in nominal income or changes in the supply of central bank money are qualitatively the same as in the previous section. In particular, an increase in the supply of central bank money leads to a shift in the vertical supply line to the right. This leads to a lower interest rate. As before, an increase in central bank money leads to a decrease in the interest rate. Conversely, a decrease in central bank money leads to an increase in the interest rate.

Suppose people get worried about the possibility of bank runs and decide to hold a higher proportion of money in the form of currency. If the central bank keeps the money supply constant, what will happen to the interest rate?

4-4 Two Alternative Ways of Looking at the Equilibrium*

In Section 4-3, we looked at the equilibrium through the condition that the supply and the demand of central bank money be equal. There are two other ways of looking at the equilibrium. While they are all equivalent, each provides a different way of thinking about the equilibrium, and going through each one will strengthen your understanding of how monetary policy affects the interest rate.

The Federal Funds Market and the Federal Funds Rate

Instead of thinking in terms of the supply and the demand for central bank money, we can think in terms of the supply and the demand for bank reserves:

The supply of reserves is equal to the supply of central bank money H, minus the demand for currency by the public, CU^d. The demand for reserves by banks is R^d. So the equilibrium condition that the supply and the demand for bank reserves be equal is given by:

$$H - CU^d = R^d$$

Notice that, if we move CU^d from the left side to the right side of the equation and use the fact that the demand for central bank money H^d is given by $H^d = CU^d + R^d$, then this equation becomes $H = H^d$. In other words, looking at the equilibrium in terms of the supply and the demand for reserves is equivalent to looking at the equilibrium in terms of the supply and the demand for central bank money—the approach we followed in Section 4-3.

Nevertheless, this alternative way of looking at the equilibrium is attractive because, in the United States, there is indeed an actual market for bank reserves, where the interest rate adjusts to balance the supply and demand for reserves. This market is called the **federal funds market**. Banks that have excess reserves at the end of the day lend them to banks that have insufficient reserves. In equilibrium, the total demand for reserves by all banks taken together, R^d, must be equal to the supply of reserves to the market, $H - CU^d$—the equilibrium condition stated above.

The interest rate determined in this market is called the **federal funds rate**. Because the Fed can in effect choose the federal funds rate it wants by changing the supply of central bank money, H, the federal funds rate is typically thought of as the main indicator of U.S. monetary policy. This is why so much attention is focused on it, and why changes in the federal funds rate typically make front page news.

In short, the Fed determines the federal funds rate.

*This section is optional

The Supply of Money, the Demand for Money, and the Money Multiplier

Remember: All three ways are equivalent in the sense that they yield the same answer. ▶ But each gives us a different way of thinking about the answer and strengthens our intuition.

We have seen how we can think of the equilibrium in terms of the equality of the supply and demand of central bank money, or in terms of the equality of the supply and demand of reserves. There is yet another way of thinking about the equilibrium which is sometimes very useful. We can think about the equilibrium in terms of the equality of the overall supply and the overall demand for money (currency and checkable deposits).

To derive an equilibrium condition in terms of the overall supply and the overall demand for money, start with the equilibrium condition (4.11) (which states that the supply of central bank money must equal the demand for central bank money) and divide both sides by $[c + \theta(1 - c)]$:

$$\frac{1}{[c + \theta(1 - c)]} H = \$Y \, L(i) \tag{4.12}$$

Supply of money = Demand for money

The right side of equation (4.12) is the overall demand for money (currency plus checkable deposits). The left side is the overall supply of money (currency plus checkable deposits). Basically the equation says that, in equilibrium, the overall supply and the overall demand of money must be equal.

- If you compare equation (4.12) with equation (4.2), the equation characterizing the equilibrium in an economy without banks, you will see that the only difference is that the overall supply of money is not equal just to central bank money but to central bank money times a constant term $1/(c + \theta(1 - c))$.

   Notice also that, because $(c + \theta(1 - c))$ is less than one, its inverse—the constant term on the left of the equation—is greater than one. For this reason, this constant term is called the **money multiplier**. The overall supply of money is therefore equal to central bank money times the money multiplier. If the money multiplier is 4, for example, then the overall supply of money is equal to 4 times the supply of central bank money.

- To reflect the fact that the overall supply of money depends in the end on the amount of central bank money, central bank money is sometimes called **high-powered money** (this is where the letter H we used to denote central bank money comes from), or the **monetary base**. The term *high-powered* reflects the fact that increases in H lead to more than one-for-one increases in the overall money supply, and are therefore "high-powered." In the same way, the term *monetary base* reflects the fact that the overall money supply depends ultimately on a "base"—the amount of central bank money in the economy.

The presence of a multiplier in equation (4.12) implies that a given change in central bank money has a larger effect on the money supply—and in turn a larger effect on the interest rate—in an economy with banks than in an economy without banks. To understand why, it is useful to return to the description of open market operations, this time in an economy with banks.

Understanding the Money Multiplier

To make the arithmetic easier, let's consider a special case where people hold only checkable deposits, so $c = 0$. In this case, the multiplier is $1/\theta$. In other words, an increase of a dollar of high powered money leads to an increase of $1/\theta$ dollars in the money supply. Assume further that $\theta = 0.1$, so that the multiplier equals $1/0.1 = 10$.

The purpose of what follows is to help you understand where this multiplier comes from, and, more generally, to help you understand how the initial increase in central bank money leads to a ten-fold increase in the overall money supply.

Suppose the Fed buys $100 worth of bonds in an open market operation. It pays the seller—call him seller 1—$100. To pay the seller, the Fed creates $100 in central bank money. The increase in central bank money is $100. When we looked earlier at the effects of an open market operation in an economy in which there were no banks, this was the end of the story. Here, it is just the beginning:

- Seller 1 (who, we have assumed, does not want to hold any currency) deposits the $100 in a checking account at his bank—call it bank A. This leads to an increase in checkable deposits of $100.
- Bank A keeps $100 times $0.1 = $10 in reserves and buys bonds with the rest, $100 times $0.9 = $90. It pays $90 to the seller of those bonds—call her seller 2.
- Seller 2 deposits $90 in a checking account in her bank—call it bank B. This leads to an increase in checkable deposits of $90.
- Bank B keeps $90 times $0.1 = $9 in reserves and buys bonds with the rest, $90 times $0.9 = $81. It pays $81 to the seller of those bonds, call him seller 3.
- Seller 3 deposits $81 in a checking account in his bank, call it bank C.
- And so on.

By now, the chain of events should be clear. What is the eventual increase in the money supply? The increase in checkable deposits is $100 when seller 1 deposits the proceeds of his sale of bonds in bank A, plus $90 when seller 2 deposits the proceeds of her sale of bonds in bank B, plus $81 when seller 3 does the same, and so on. Let's write the sum as:

$$\$100\,(1 + 0.9 + 0.9^2 + \ldots)$$

The series in parentheses is a geometric series, so its sum is equal to $1/(1 - 0.9) = 10$ (see Appendix 2 at the end of this book for a refresher on geometric series). The money supply increases by $1,000—10 times the initial increase in central bank money.

This derivation gives us another way of thinking about the money multiplier: We can think of the ultimate increase in the money supply as the result of *successive rounds of purchases of bonds*—the first started by the Fed in its open market operation, the following rounds by banks. Each successive round leads to an increase in the money supply, and eventually the increase in the money supply is equal to 10 times the initial increase in the central bank money. Note the parallel between our interpretation of the money multiplier as the result of successive purchases of bonds and the interpretation of the goods market multiplier (Chapter 3) as the result of successive rounds of spending. Multipliers can often be interpreted as the result of successive rounds of decisions and derived as the sum of a geometric series. This interpretation often gives a better understanding of how the process works.

Summary

- The demand for money depends positively on the level of transactions in the economy and negatively on the interest rate.
- The interest rate is determined by the equilibrium condition that the supply of money be equal to the demand for money.

- For a given supply of money, an increase in income leads to an increase in the demand for money and an increase in the interest rate. An increase in the supply of money for a given income leads to a decrease in the interest rate.

- The way the central bank changes the supply of money is through open market operations.
- Expansionary open market operations, in which the central bank increases the money supply by buying bonds, lead to an increase in the price of bonds and a decrease in the interest rate.
- Contractionary open market operations, in which the central bank decreases the money supply by selling bonds, lead to a decrease in the price of bonds and an increase in the interest rate.
- When money includes both currency and checkable deposits, we can think of the interest rate as being determined by the condition that the supply of central bank money be equal to the demand for central bank money.
- The supply of central bank money is under the control of the central bank. The demand for central bank money depends on the overall demand for money, the proportion of money people keep as currency, and the ratio of reserves to checkable deposits chosen by banks.
- Another, but equivalent, way to think about the determination of the interest rate is in terms of the equality of the supply and demand for bank reserves. The market for bank reserves is called the federal funds market. The interest rate determined in that market is called the federal funds rate.
- Yet another way to think about the determination of the interest rate is in terms of the equality of the overall supply of and the overall demand for money. The overall supply of money is equal to central bank money times the money multiplier.

Key Terms

Questions and Problems

QUICK CHECK

All Quick Check questions and problems are available on MyEconLab.

1. Using the information in this chapter, label each of the following statements true, false, or uncertain. Explain briefly.

a. Income and financial wealth are both examples of stock variables.

b. The term *investment*, as used by economists, refers to the purchase of bonds and shares of stock.

c. The demand for money does not depend on the interest rate because only bonds earn interest.

d. About two-thirds of U.S. currency is held outside the United States.

e. The central bank can increase the supply of money by selling bonds in the market for bonds.

f. The Federal Reserve can determine the money supply, but it cannot determine interest rates—not even the federal funds rate—because interest rates are determined in the private sector.

g. Bond prices and interest rates always move in opposite directions.

h. Since the Great Depression, the United States has relied on federal deposit insurance to help solve the problem of bank runs.

2. Suppose that a person's yearly income is $60,000. Also suppose that this person's money demand function is given by

$$M^d = \$Y(.35 - i)$$

a. What is this person's demand for money when the interest rate is 5%? 10%?

b. Explain how the interest rate affects money demand.

c. Suppose that the interest rate is 10%. In percentage terms, what happens to this person's demand for money if her yearly income is reduced by 50%?

d. Suppose that the interest rate is 5%. In percentage terms, what happens to this person's demand for money if her yearly income is reduced by 50%?

e. Summarize the effect of income on money demand. In percentage terms, how does this effect depend on the interest rate?

3. *Consider a bond that promises to pay $100 in one year.*

a. What is the interest rate on the bond if its price today is $75? $85? $95?

b. What is the relation between the price of the bond and the interest rate?

c. If the interest rate is 8%, what is the price of the bond today?

4. *Suppose that money demand is given by*

$$M^d = \$Y(.25 - i)$$

where $Y is $100. Also, suppose that the supply of money is $20.

a. What is the equilibrium interest rate?

b. If the Federal Reserve Bank wants to increase i by 10 percentage points (e.g., from 2% to 12%), at what level should it set the supply of money?

DIG DEEPER
All Dig Deeper questions and problems are available on MyEconLab.

5. *Suppose that a person's wealth is $50,000 and that her yearly income is $60,000. Also suppose that her money demand function is given by*

$$M^d = \$Y(.35 - i)$$

a. Derive the demand for bonds. Suppose the interest rate increases by 10 percentage points. What is the effect on the demand for bonds?

b. What are the effects of an increase in wealth on the demand for money and the demand for bonds? Explain in words.

c. What are the effects of an increase in income on the demand for money and the demand for bonds? Explain in words.

d. Consider the statement "When people earn more money, they obviously will hold more bonds." What is wrong with this statement?

6. *The demand for bonds*

In this chapter, you learned that an increase in the interest rate makes bonds more attractive, so it leads people to hold more of their wealth in bonds as opposed to money. However, you also learned that an increase in the interest rate reduces the price of bonds.

How can an increase in the interest rate make bonds more attractive and reduce their price?

7. *ATMs and credit cards*
This problem examines the effect of the introduction of ATMs and credit cards on money demand. For simplicity, let's examine a person's demand for money over a period of four days.

Suppose that before ATMs and credit cards, this person goes to the bank once at the beginning of each four-day period and withdraws from her savings account all the money she needs for four days. Assume that she needs $4 per day.

a. How much does this person withdraw each time she goes to the bank? Compute this person's money holdings for days 1 through 4 (in the morning, before she needs any of the money she withdraws).

b. What is the amount of money this person holds, on average?

Suppose now that with the advent of ATMs, this person withdraws money once every two days.

c. Recompute your answer to part (a).

d. Recompute your answer to part (b).

Finally, with the advent of credit cards, this person pays for all her purchases using her card. She withdraws no money until the fourth day, when she withdraws the whole amount necessary to pay for her credit card purchases over the previous four days.

e. Recompute your answer to part (a).

f. Recompute your answer to part (b).

g. Based on your previous answers, what do you think has been the effect of ATMs and credit cards on money demand?

8. *The money multiplier*
The money multiplier is described in Section 4-4. Assume the following:

i. The public holds no currency.

ii. The ratio of reserves to deposits is 0.1.

iii. The demand for money is given by

$$M^d = \$Y(.8 - 4i)$$

Initially, the monetary base is $100 billion, and nominal income is $5 trillion.

a. What is the demand for central bank money?

b. Find the equilibrium interest rate by setting the demand for central bank money equal to the supply of central bank money.

c. What is the overall supply of money? Is it equal to the overall demand for money at the interest rate you found in part (b)?

d. What is the impact on the interest rate if central bank money is increased to $300 billion?

e. If the overall money supply increases to $3,000 billion, what will be the impact on i? [*Hint*: Use what you discovered in part (c).]

9. *Bank runs and the money multiplier preferring to hold on to their cash.*

During the Great Depression, the U.S. economy experienced many bank runs, to the point where people became unwilling to keep their money in banks, preferring to hold on to their cash cash.

How would you expect such a shift away from checkable deposits toward currency to affect the size of the money multiplier?

EXPLORE FURTHER
10. *Current monetary policy*

Go to the Web site for the Federal Reserve Board of Governors (**www.federalreserve.gov**) and download the most recent monetary policy press release of the Federal Open Market Committee (FOMC). Make sure you get the most recent FOMC press release and not simply the most recent Fed press release.

a. What is the current stance of monetary policy? (Note that policy will be described in terms of increasing or decreasing the federal funds rate as opposed to increasing or decreasing the money supply.)

b. If the federal funds rate has changed recently, what does the change imply about the bond holdings of the Federal Reserve? Has the Fed been increasing or decreasing its bond holdings?

Finally you can visit the Fed's website and find various statements explaining the Fed's current policy on interest rates. These statements set the stage for the analysis in Chapter 5. Some parts of these statement should make more complete sense at the end Chapter 5.

Further Readings

- While we shall return to many aspects of the financial system throughout the book, you may want to dig deeper and read a textbook on money and banking. Here are four of them: *Money, Banking, and Financial Markets*, by Laurence Ball (Worth, 2010); *Money, Banking, and Financial Markets*, by Stephen Cecchetti and Kermit Schoenholtz (McGraw-Hill/Irwin, 2010); *Money, the Financial System and the Economy*, by R. Glenn Hubbard (Addison-Wesley, 2007); *The Economics of Money, Banking, and the Financial System*, by Frederic Mishkin, (Pearson, 9th edition, 2010).

- The Fed maintains a useful Web site, which contains not only data on financial markets but also information on what the Fed does, on recent testimonies by the Fed Chairman, and so on (http://www.federalreserve.gov).

Goods and Financial Markets: The *IS-LM* Model

In Chapter 3, we looked at the goods market. In Chapter 4, we looked at financial markets. We now look at goods and financial markets together. By the end of this chapter you will have a framework to think about how output and the interest rate are determined in the short run.

In developing this framework, we follow a path first traced by two economists, John Hicks and Alvin Hansen, in the late 1930s and the early 1940s. When the economist John Maynard Keynes published his *General Theory* in 1936, there was much agreement that his book was both fundamental and nearly impenetrable. (Try to read it, and you will agree.) There were (and still are) many debates about what Keynes "really meant." In 1937, John Hicks summarized what he saw as one of Keynes's main contributions: the joint description of goods and financial markets. His analysis was later extended by Alvin Hansen. Hicks and Hansen called their formalization the *IS–LM* model.

Macroeconomics has made substantial progress since the early 1940s. This is why the *IS–LM* model is treated in this and the next chapter rather than in Chapter 26 of this book. (If you had taken this course 40 years ago, you would be nearly done!) But to most economists, the *IS–LM* model still represents an essential building block—one that, despite its simplicity, captures much of what happens in the economy in the *short run*. This is why the *IS–LM* model is still taught and used today.

This chapter develops the basic version of the *IS–LM* model. It has five sections:

Section 5-1 looks at equilibrium in the goods market and derives the *IS* relation.

Section 5-2 looks at equilibrium in financial markets and derives the *LM* relation.

Sections 5-3 and 5-4 put the *IS* and the *LM* relations together and use the resulting *IS–LM* model to study the effects of fiscal and monetary policy—first separately, then together.

Section 5-5 introduces dynamics and explores how the *IS–LM* model captures what happens in the economy in the short run. ●

5-1 The Goods Market and the *IS* Relation

Let's first summarize what we learned in Chapter 3:

- We characterized equilibrium in the goods market as the condition that production, Y, be equal to the demand for goods, Z. We called this condition the *IS* relation.
- We defined demand as the sum of consumption, investment, and government spending. We assumed that consumption was a function of disposable income (income minus taxes), and took investment spending, government spending, and taxes as given:

$$Z = C(Y - T) + \bar{I} + G$$

(In Chapter 3, we assumed, to simplify the algebra, that the relation between consumption, C, and disposable income, $Y - T$, was linear. Here, we shall not make this assumption but use the more general form $C = C(Y - T)$ instead).

- The equilibrium condition was thus given by

$$Y = C(Y - T) + \bar{I} + G$$

- Using this equilibrium condition, we then looked at the factors that moved equilibrium output. We looked in particular at the effects of changes in government spending and of shifts in consumption demand.

The main simplification of this first model was that the interest rate did not affect the demand for goods. Our first task in this chapter is to abandon this simplification and introduce the interest rate in our model of equilibrium in the goods market. For the time being, we focus only on the effect of the interest rate on investment and leave a discussion of its effects on the other components of demand until later.

Much more on the effects of interest rates on both consumption and investment in Chapter 16. ▶

Investment, Sales, and the Interest Rate

In Chapter 3, investment was assumed to be constant. This was for simplicity. Investment is in fact far from constant and depends primarily on two factors:

- The level of sales. Consider a firm facing an increase in sales and needing to increase production. To do so, it may need to buy additional machines or build an additional plant. In other words, it needs to invest. A firm facing low sales will feel no such need and will spend little, if anything, on investment.
- The interest rate. Consider a firm deciding whether or not to buy a new machine. Suppose that to buy the new machine, the firm must borrow. The higher the interest rate, the less attractive it is to borrow and buy the machine. (For the moment, and to keep things simple, we make two simplifications. First, we assume that all firms can borrow at the same interest rate—namely, the interest rate on bonds as determined in Chapter 4. In fact, many firms borrow from banks, possibly at a different rate. We return to this in Chapter 9. We also leave aside the distinction between the nominal interest rate—the interest rate in terms of dollars—and the real interest rate—the interest rate in terms of goods. The distinction is important, however, and we return to it in Chapter 14).

At a high enough interest rate, the additional profits from using the new machine will not cover interest payments, and the new machine will not be worth buying.

The argument still holds if the firm uses its own funds: The higher the interest rate, the more attractive it is to lend the funds ▶ rather than to use them to buy the new machine.

To capture these two effects, we write the investment relation as follows:

$$I = I(Y, i) \qquad (5.1)$$
$$(+, -)$$

Equation (5.1) states that investment I depends on production Y and the interest rate i. (We continue to assume that inventory investment is equal to zero, so sales and production are always equal. As a result, Y denotes sales, and it also denotes production.) The positive sign under Y indicates that an increase in production (equivalently, an increase in sales) leads to an increase in investment. The negative sign under the interest rate i indicates that an increase in the interest rate leads to a decrease in investment.

An increase in output leads to an increase in investment. ◄ An increase in the interest rate leads to a decrease in investment.

Determining Output

Taking into account the investment relation (5.1), the condition for equilibrium in the goods market becomes

$$Y = C(Y - T) + I(Y, i) + G \qquad (5.2)$$

Production (the left side of the equation) must be equal to the demand for goods (the right side). Equation (5.2) is our expanded *IS relation*. We can now look at what happens to output when the interest rate changes.

Start with Figure 5-1. Measure the demand for goods on the vertical axis. Measure output on the horizontal axis. For a given value of the interest rate i, demand is an increasing function of output, for two reasons:

- An increase in output leads to an increase in income and thus to an increase in disposable income. The increase in disposable income leads to an increase in consumption. We studied this relation in Chapter 3.
- An increase in output also leads to an increase in investment. This is the relation between investment and production that we have introduced in this chapter.

In short, an increase in output leads, through its effects on both consumption and investment, to an increase in the demand for goods. This relation between demand and output, for a given interest rate, is represented by the upward-sloping curve ZZ. Note two characteristics of ZZ in Figure 5-1:

- Since we have not assumed that the consumption and investment relations in equation (5.2) are linear, ZZ is in general a curve rather than a line. Thus, we have drawn it as a curve in Figure 5-1. All the arguments that follow would apply if we

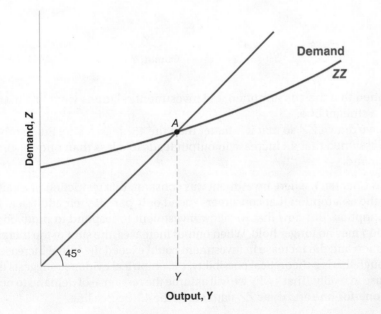

Figure 5-1

Equilibrium in the Goods Market

The demand for goods is an increasing function of output. Equilibrium requires that the demand for goods be equal to output.

Figure 5-2

The Derivation of the IS Curve

(a) An increase in the interest rate decreases the demand for goods at any level of output, leading to a decrease in the equilibrium level of output.
(b) Equilibrium in the goods market implies that an increase in the interest rate leads to a decrease in output. The *IS* curve is therefore downward sloping.

assumed that the consumption and investment relations were linear and that ZZ were a straight line.

■ We have drawn ZZ so that it is flatter than the 45-degree line. Put another way, we have assumed that an increase in output leads to a less than one-for-one increase in demand.

Make sure you understand why the two statements mean ▶ the same thing.

In Chapter 3, where investment was constant, this restriction naturally followed from the assumption that consumers spend only part of their additional income on consumption. But now that we allow investment to respond to production, this restriction may no longer hold. When output increases, the sum of the increase in consumption and the increase in investment could exceed the initial increase in output. Although this is a theoretical possibility, the empirical evidence suggests that it is not the case in reality. That's why we will assume the response of demand to output is less than one-for-one and draw ZZ flatter than the 45-degree line.

88   The Short Run   **The Core**

Equilibrium in the goods market is reached at the point where the demand for goods equals output; that is, at point A, the intersection of ZZ and the 45-degree line. The equilibrium level of output is given by Y.

So far, what we have done is extend, in straightforward fashion, the analysis of Chapter 3. But we are now ready to derive the IS curve.

Deriving the *IS* Curve

We have drawn the demand relation, ZZ, in Figure 5-1 for a given value of the interest rate. Let's now derive in Figure 5-2 what happens if the interest rate changes.

Suppose that, in Figure 5-2(a), the demand curve is given by ZZ, and the initial equilibrium is at point A. Suppose now that the interest rate increases from its initial value i to a new higher value i'. At any level of output, the higher interest rate leads to lower investment and lower demand. The demand curve ZZ shifts down to ZZ': At a given level of output, demand is lower. The new equilibrium is at the intersection of the lower demand curve ZZ' and the 45-degree line, at point A'. The equilibrium level of output is now equal to Y'.

In words: The increase in the interest rate decreases investment. The decrease in investment leads to a decrease in output, which further decreases consumption and investment, through the multiplier effect.

Can you show graphically what the size of the multiplier is? (*Hint*: Look at the ratio of the decrease in equilibrium output to the initial decrease in investment.)

Using Figure 5-2(a), we can find the equilibrium value of output associated with *any* value of the interest rate. The resulting relation between equilibrium output and the interest rate is drawn in Figure 5-2(b).

Figure 5-2(b) plots equilibrium output Y on the horizontal axis against the interest rate on the vertical axis. Point A in Figure 5-2(b) corresponds to point A in Figure 5-2(a), and point A' in Figure 5-3(b) corresponds to A' in Figure 5-2(a). The higher interest rate is associated with a lower level of output.

This relation between the interest rate and output is represented by the downward–sloping curve in Figure 5-2(b). This curve is called the ***IS* curve**.

Equilibrium in the goods market implies that an increase in the interest rate leads to a decrease in output. This relation is represented by the downward–sloping *IS* curve.

Shifts of the *IS* Curve

We have drawn the IS curve in Figure 5-2 taking as given the values of taxes, T, and government spending, G. Changes in either T or G will shift the IS curve.

To see how, consider Figure 5-3. The IS curve gives the equilibrium level of output as a function of the interest rate. It is drawn for given values of taxes and spending. Now

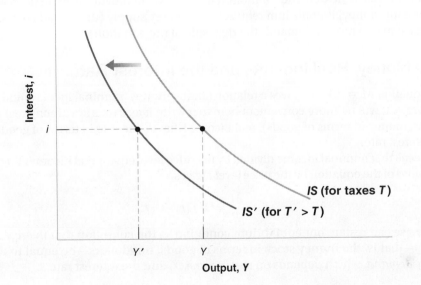

Figure 5-3

Shifts of the IS Curve

An increase in taxes shifts the *IS* curve to the left.

IS (for taxes T)

IS′ (for $T' > T$)

Interest, i

Output, Y

i

Y' Y

consider an increase in taxes, from T to T'. At a given interest rate, say i, disposable income decreases, leading to a decrease in consumption, leading in turn to a decrease in the demand for goods and a decrease in equilibrium output. The equilibrium level of output decreases from Y to Y'. Put another way, the *IS* curve shifts to the left: At a given interest rate, the equilibrium level of output is lower than it was before the increase in taxes.

For a given interest rate, an increase in taxes leads to a decrease in output. In graphic ▶ terms: An increase in taxes shifts the *IS* curve to the left.

More generally, any factor that, for a given interest rate, decreases the equilibrium level of output causes the *IS* curve to shift to the left. We have looked at an increase in taxes. But the same would hold for a decrease in government spending, or a decrease in consumer confidence (which decreases consumption given disposable income). Symmetrically, any factor that, for a given interest rate, increases the equilibrium level of output—a decrease in taxes, an increase in government spending, an increase in consumer confidence—causes the *IS* curve to shift to the right.

Suppose that the government announces that the Social Security system is in trouble, and it may have to cut retirement ▶ benefits in the future. How are consumers likely to react? What is then likely to happen to demand and output today?

Let's summarize:

- Equilibrium in the goods market implies that an increase in the interest rate leads to a decrease in output. This relation is represented by the downward-sloping *IS* curve.
- Changes in factors that decrease the demand for goods given the interest rate shift the *IS* curve to the left. Changes in factors that increase the demand for goods given the interest rate shift the *IS* curve to the right.

5-2 Financial Markets and the *LM* Relation

Let's now turn to financial markets. We saw in Chapter 4 that the interest rate is determined by the equality of the supply of and the demand for money:

$$M = \$Y\,L(i)$$

The variable M on the left side is the nominal money stock. We will ignore here the details of the money-supply process that we saw in Sections 4-3 and 4-4, and simply think of the central bank as controlling M directly.

The right side gives the demand for money, which is a function of nominal income, $\$Y$, and of the nominal interest rate, i. As we saw in Section 4-1, an increase in nominal income increases the demand for money; an increase in the interest rate decreases the demand for money. Equilibrium requires that money supply (the left side of the equation) be equal to money demand (the right side of the equation).

Real Money, Real Income, and the Interest Rate

The equation $M = \$Y\,L(i)$ gives a relation among money, nominal income, and the interest rate. It will be more convenient here to rewrite it as a relation among real money (that is, money in terms of goods), real income (that is, income in terms of goods), and the interest rate.

From Chapter 2:
Nominal GDP = Real GDP multiplied by the GDP deflator: $\$Y = YP$.
Equivalently:
Real GDP = Nominal GDP divided by the GDP deflator: $\$Y/P = Y$.

Recall that nominal income divided by the price level equals real income, Y. Dividing both sides of the equation by the price level P gives

$$\frac{M}{P} = Y\,L(i) \tag{5.3}$$

Hence, we can restate our equilibrium condition as the condition that the *real money supply*—that is, the money stock in terms of goods, not dollars—be equal to the *real money demand*, which depends on real income, Y, and the interest rate, i.

The notion of a "real" demand for money may feel a bit abstract, so an example will help. Think not of your demand for money in general but just of your demand for coins. Suppose you like to have coins in your pocket to buy two cups of coffee during the day. If a cup costs $1.20, you will want to keep about $2.40 in coins: This is your nominal demand for coins. Equivalently, you want to keep enough coins in your pocket to buy two cups of coffee. This is your demand for coins in terms of goods—here in terms of cups of coffee.

From now on, we shall refer to equation (5.3) as the *LM relation*. The advantage of writing things this way is that *real income*, Y, appears on the right side of the equation instead of *nominal income*, $\$Y$. And real income (equivalently real output) is the variable we focus on when looking at equilibrium in the goods market. To make the reading lighter, we will refer to the left and right sides of equation (5.3) simply as "money supply" and "money demand" rather than the more accurate but heavier "real money supply" and "real money demand." Similarly, we will refer to income rather than "real income."

Deriving the LM Curve

To see the relation between output and the interest rate implied by equation (5.3), let's use Figure 5-4. Look first at Figure 5-4(a). Let the interest rate be measured on the vertical axis and (real) money be measured on the horizontal axis. (Real) money supply is given by the vertical line at M/P and is denoted M^s. For a given level of (real) income, Y, (real) money demand is a decreasing function of the interest rate. It is drawn as the downward-sloping curve denoted M^d. Except for the fact that we measure real rather than nominal money on the horizontal axis, the figure is similar to Figure 4-3 in Chapter 4. The equilibrium is at point A, where money supply is equal to money demand, and the interest rate is equal to i.

Now consider an increase in income from Y to Y', which leads people to increase their demand for money at any given interest rate. Money demand shifts to the right, to $M^{d'}$. The new equilibrium is at A', with a higher interest rate, i'. Why does an increase in income lead to an increase in the interest rate? When income increases, money demand increases; but the money supply is given. Thus, the interest rate must go up until the two opposite effects on the demand for money—the increase in income that leads people to want to hold more money and the increase in the interest rate that leads

(a) (Real) Money, *M/P*

(b) Income, *Y*

Figure 5-4

The Derivation of the LM Curve

(a) An increase in income leads, at a given interest rate, to an increase in the demand for money. Given the money supply, this increase in the demand for money leads to an increase in the equilibrium interest rate.
(b) Equilibrium in the financial markets implies that an increase in income leads to an increase in the interest rate. The LM curve is therefore upward sloping.

people to want to hold less money—cancel each other. At that point, the demand for money is equal to the unchanged money supply, and financial markets are again in equilibrium.

Using Figure 5-4(a), we can find the value of the interest rate associated with *any* value of income for a given money stock. The relation is derived in Figure 5-4(b).

Figure 5-4(b) plots the equilibrium interest rate i on the vertical axis against income on the horizontal axis. Point A in Figure 5-4(b) corresponds to point A in Figure 5-4(a), and point A' in Figure 5-4(b) corresponds to point A' in Figure 5-4(a). More generally, equilibrium in financial markets implies that the higher the level of output, the higher the demand for money, and therefore the higher the equilibrium interest rate.

Equilibrium in financial markets implies that, for a given money stock, the interest rate is an increasing function of the level of income. This relation is represented by the upward-sloping *LM* curve.

This relation between output and the interest rate is represented by the upward-sloping curve in Figure 5-4(b). This curve is called the **LM curve**. Economists sometimes characterize this relation by saying, "higher economic activity puts pressure on interest rates." Make sure you understand the steps behind this statement.

Shifts of the *LM* Curve

We have derived the *LM* curve in Figure 5-4, taking both the nominal money stock, M, and the price level, P—and, by implication, their ratio, the real money stock, M/P—as given. Changes in M/P, whether they come from changes in the nominal money stock, M, or from changes in the price level, P, will shift the *LM* curve.

For a given level of output, an increase in the money supply leads to a decrease in the interest rate. In graphic terms: An increase in the money supply shifts the *LM* curve down.

To see how, let us look at Figure 5-5 and consider an increase in the nominal money supply, from M to M'. Given the fixed price level, the real money supply increases from M/P to M'/P. Then, at any level of income, say Y, the interest rate consistent with equilibrium in financial markets is lower, going down from i to, say, i'. The *LM* curve shifts down, from *LM* to *LM'*. By the same reasoning, at any level of income, a decrease in the money supply leads to an increase in the interest rate. It causes the *LM* curve to shift up.

Why do we think about shifts of the *IS* curve to the left or to the right but about shifts of the *LM* curve up or down? The reason:

We think of the goods market as determining Y given i; so we want to know what happens to Y when an exogenous variable changes. Y is on the horizontal axis, and moves right or left.

We think of financial markets as determining i given Y; so we want to know what happens to i when an exogenous variable changes. i is on the vertical axis, and moves up or down.

Let's summarize:

- Equilibrium in financial markets implies that, for a given real money supply, an increase in the level of income, which increases the demand for money, leads to an increase in the interest rate. This relation is represented by the upward-sloping *LM* curve.

- An increase in the money supply shifts the *LM* curve down; a decrease in the money supply shifts the *LM* curve up.

Figure 5-5

Shifts of the LM Curve

An increase in money causes the *LM* curve to shift down.

5-3 Putting the *IS* and the *LM* Relations Together

The *IS* relation follows from the condition that the supply of goods must be equal to the demand for goods. It tells us how the interest rate affects output. The *LM* relation follows from the condition that the supply of money must be equal to the demand for money. It tells us how output in turn affects the interest rate. We now put the *IS* and *LM* relations together. At any point in time, the supply of goods must be equal to the demand for goods, and the supply of money must be equal to the demand for money. Both the *IS* and *LM* relations must hold. Together, they determine both output and the interest rate.

IS relation: $$Y = C(Y - T) + I(Y, i) + G$$

LM relation: $$\frac{M}{P} = Y L(i)$$

Figure 5-6 plots both the *IS* curve and the *LM* curve on one graph. Output—equivalently, production or income—is measured on the horizontal axis. The interest rate is measured on the vertical axis.

Any point on the downward-sloping *IS* curve corresponds to equilibrium in the goods market. *Any point* on the upward-sloping *LM* curve corresponds to equilibrium in financial markets. *Only at point A* are both equilibrium conditions satisfied. That means point *A*, with the associated level of output *Y* and interest rate *i*, is the overall equilibrium—the point at which there is equilibrium in both the goods market and the financial markets.

The *IS* and *LM* relations that underlie Figure 5-6 contain a lot of information about consumption, investment, money demand, and equilibrium conditions. But you may ask: So what if the equilibrium is at point *A*? How does this fact translate into anything directly useful about the world? Don't despair: Figure 5-6 holds the answer to many questions in macroeconomics. Used properly, it allows us to study what happens to output and the interest rate when the central bank decides to increase the money stock, or when the government decides to increase taxes, or when consumers become more pessimistic about the future, and so on.

Let's now see what the *IS–LM* model can do.

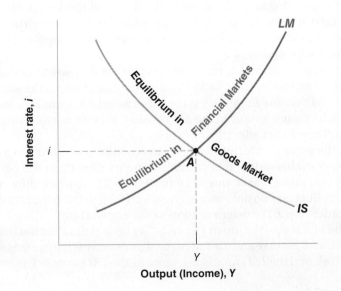

Interest rate, *i*

i

Equilibrium in Financial Markets

Equilibrium in Goods Market

LM

IS

A

Y

Output (Income), Y

Figure 5-6

The IS–LM Model

Equilibrium in the goods market implies that an increase in the interest rate leads to a decrease in output. This is represented by the *IS* curve. Equilibrium in financial markets implies that an increase in output leads to an increase in the interest rate. This is represented by the *LM* curve. Only at point *A*, which is on both curves, are both goods and financial markets in equilibrium.

Fiscal Policy, Activity, and the Interest Rate

Suppose the government decides to reduce the budget deficit and does so by increasing taxes while keeping government spending unchanged. Such a change in fiscal policy is often called a **fiscal contraction** or a **fiscal consolidation**. (An *increase* in the deficit, either due to an increase in government spending or to a decrease in taxes, is called a **fiscal expansion**.) What are the effects of this fiscal contraction on output, on its composition, and on the interest rate?

Decrease in $G - T$ ⇔ fiscal contraction ⇔ fiscal consolidation
Increase in $G - T$ ⇔ fiscal expansion

When you answer this or any question about the effects of changes in policy, always go through the following three steps:

1. Ask how the change affects equilibrium in the goods market and how it affects equilibrium in the financial markets. Put another way: How does it shift the *IS* and/or the *LM* curves?

2. Characterize the effects of these shifts on the intersection of the *IS* and the *LM* curves. What does this do to equilibrium output and the equilibrium interest rate?

3. Describe the effects in words.

And when you feel really confident, put on a bow tie and go explain events on TV. (Why so many TV economists actually wear bow ties is a mystery.) ▶

With time and experience, you will often be able to go directly to step 3. By then you will be ready to give an instant commentary on the economic events of the day. But until you get to that level of expertise, go step by step.

■ Start with step 1. The first question is how the increase in taxes affects equilibrium in the goods market—that is, how it affects the *IS* curve.

Let's draw, in Figure 5-7(a), the *IS* curve corresponding to equilibrium in the goods market before the increase in taxes. Now take an arbitrary point, *B*, on this *IS* curve. By construction of the *IS* curve, output Y_B and the corresponding interest rate i_B are such that the supply of goods is equal to the demand for goods.

At the interest rate i_B, ask what happens to output if taxes increase from T to T'. We saw the answer in Section 5-1. Because people have less disposable income, the increase in taxes decreases consumption, and through the multiplier, decreases output. At interest rate i_B output decreases from Y_B to Y_C. More generally, at *any* interest rate, higher taxes lead to lower output. Consequently, the *IS* curve shifts to the left, from *IS* to *IS'*.

Taxes appear in the *IS* relation ⇔ Taxes shift the *IS* curve. ▶

Next, let's see if anything happens to the *LM* curve. Figure 5-7(b) draws the *LM* curve corresponding to equilibrium in the financial markets before the increase in taxes. Take an arbitrary point, *F*, on this *LM* curve. By construction of the *LM* curve, the interest rate i_F and income Y_F are such that the supply of money is equal to the demand for money.

What happens to the *LM* curve when taxes are increased? The answer: Nothing. At the given level of income Y_F the interest rate at which the supply of money is equal to the demand for money is the same as before, namely i_F. In other words, because taxes do not appear in the *LM* relation, they do not affect the equilibrium condition. They do not affect the *LM* curve.

Taxes do not appear in the *LM* relation ⇔ Taxes do not shift ▶ the *LM* curve.

A reminder: An exogenous variable is a variable we take ▶ as given, unexplained within the model. Here, taxes.

Note the general principle here: A curve shifts in response to a change in an exogenous variable only if this variable appears directly in the equation represented by that curve. Taxes enter in equation (5.2), so, when they change, the *IS* curve shifts. But taxes do not enter in equation (5.3), so the *LM* curve does not shift.

■ Now consider step 2, the determination of the equilibrium.

Let the initial equilibrium in Figure 5-7(c) be at point *A*, at the intersection between the initial *IS* curve and the *LM* curve. The *IS* curve is the same as the *IS* curve in Figure 5-7(a), and the *LM* curve is the same as the *LM* curve in Figure 5-7(b).

Figure 5-7

The Effects of an Increase in Taxes

An increase in taxes shifts the *IS* curve to the left and leads to a decrease in the equilibrium level of output and the equilibrium interest rate.

After the increase in taxes, the *IS* curve shifts to the left—from *IS* to *IS'*. The new equilibrium is at the intersection of the new *IS* curve and the unchanged *LM* curve, or point *A'*. Output decreases from *Y* to *Y'*. The interest rate decreases from *i* to *i'*. Thus, as the *IS* curve *shifts*, the economy *moves along* the *LM* curve, from *A* to *A'*. The reason these words are italicized is that it is important always to distinguish between the *shift of* a curve (here the shift of the *IS* curve) and the *movement along* a curve (here the movement along the *LM* curve). Many mistakes come from not distinguishing between the two.

The increase in taxes shifts the *IS* curve. The *LM* curve does not shift. The economy moves along the *LM* curve. ▶

■ Step 3 is to tell the story in words:

The increase in taxes leads to lower disposable income, which causes people to decrease their consumption. This decrease in demand leads, in turn, to a decrease in output and income. At the same time, the decrease in income reduces the demand for money, leading to a decrease in the interest rate. The decline in the interest rate reduces but does not completely offset the effect of higher taxes on the demand for goods.

If the interest rate did not decline, the economy would go from point *A* to point *D* in Figure 5-7(c), and output would be directly below point *D*. Because of the decline in the interest rate—which stimulates investment—the decline in activity is only to point *A'*. ▶

What happens to the components of demand? By assumption, government spending remains unchanged (we have assumed that the reduction in the budget deficit takes place through an increase in taxes). Consumption surely goes down: Taxes go up and income goes down, so disposable income goes down on both counts. The last question is, what happens to investment? On the one hand, lower output means lower sales and lower investment. On the other, a lower interest rate leads to higher investment. Without knowing more about the exact form of the investment relation, equation (5.1), we cannot tell which effect dominates: If investment depended only on the interest rate, then investment would surely increase; if investment depended only on sales, then investment would surely decrease. In general, investment depends on both the interest rate and on sales, so we cannot tell. (The case where investment falls as the deficit rises is sometimes called the **crowding out** of investment by the deficit. If investment instead rises when the deficit rises, there is **crowding in** of investment by the deficit.) Contrary to what is often stated by politicians, a reduction in the budget deficit does not necessarily lead to an increase in investment. The Focus box, "Deficit Reduction: Good or Bad for Investment?" discusses this in more detail.

We shall return to the relation between fiscal policy and investment many times in this book and we shall qualify this first answer in many ways. But the result that, *in the short run, a reduction of the budget deficit may or may not decrease investment*, will remain.

Monetary Policy, Activity, and the Interest Rate

An increase in the money supply is called a **monetary expansion**. A decrease in the money supply is called a **monetary contraction** or **monetary tightening**.

Increase in *M* ⇔ monetary expansion. Decrease in *M* ⇔ monetary contraction ⇔ monetary tightening. ▶

Let's take the case of a monetary expansion. Suppose that the central bank increases nominal money, *M*, through an open market operation. Given our assumption that the price level is fixed in the short run, this increase in nominal money leads to a one-for-one increase in real money, *M/P*. Let us denote the initial real money supply by *M/P*, the new higher one by *M'/P*, and trace in Figure 5-8 the effects of the money supply increase on output and the interest rate.

For a given price level *P*: *M* increases by 10% ⇒ *M/P* increases by 10%. ▶

■ Again, step 1 is to see whether and how the *IS* and the *LM* curves shift.

Let's look at the *IS* curve first. The money supply does not *directly* affect either the supply of or the demand for goods. In other words, *M* does not appear in the *IS* relation. Thus, a change in *M* does not shift the *IS* curve.

Deficit Reduction: Good or Bad for Investment?

You may have heard this argument in some form before: "Private saving goes either toward financing the budget deficit or financing investment. It does not take a genius to conclude that reducing the budget deficit leaves more saving available for investment, so investment increases."

This argument sounds simple and convincing. How do we reconcile it with what we just saw, namely that a deficit reduction may decrease rather than increase investment?

To make progress, first go back to Chapter 3, equation (3.10). There we learned that we can also think of the goods-market equilibrium condition as

$$\text{Investment} = \text{Private saving} + \text{Public saving}$$
$$I = S + (T - G)$$

In equilibrium, investment is indeed equal to private saving plus public saving. If public saving is positive, the government is said to be running a budget surplus; if public saving is negative, the government is said to be running a budget deficit. So

it is true that given private saving, if the government reduces its deficit—either by increasing taxes or reducing government spending so that $T - G$ goes up—investment must go up: Given S, $T - G$ going up implies that I goes up.

The crucial part of this statement, however, is "given private saving." The point is that a fiscal contraction affects private saving as well: The contraction leads to lower output and therefore to lower income. As consumption goes down by less than income, private saving also goes down. And it may go down by more than the reduction in the budget deficit, leading to a decrease rather than an increase in investment. In terms of the equation above: If S decreases by more than $T - G$ increases, then I will decrease, not increase.

To sum up, a fiscal contraction may decrease investment. Or, looking at the reverse policy, a *fiscal expansion*— a decrease in taxes or an increase in spending—may actually increase investment.

Money enters the *LM* relation, however, so the *LM* curve shifts when the money supply changes. As we saw in Section 5-2, an increase in the money supply shifts the *LM* curve down, from *LM* to *LM'*: At a given level of income, an increase in money leads to a decrease in the interest rate.

- Step 2 is to see how these shifts affect the equilibrium. The monetary expansion shifts the *LM* curve. It does not shift the *IS* curve. The economy moves along the *IS*

◀ Money does not appear in the *IS* relation ⇔ Money does not shift the *IS* curve.

◀ Money appears in the *LM* relation ⇔ Money shifts the *LM* curve.

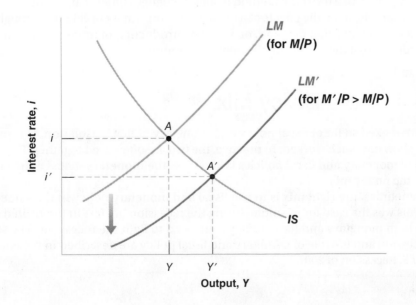

Figure 5-8

The Effects of a Monetary Expansion

A monetary expansion leads to higher output and a lower interest rate.

Table 5-1 The Effects of Fiscal and Monetary Policy

	Shift of *IS*	Shift of *LM*	Movement in Output	Movement in Interest Rate
Increase in taxes	left	none	down	down
Decrease in taxes	right	none	up	up
Increase in spending	right	none	up	up
Decrease in spending	left	none	down	down
Increase in money	none	down	up	down
Decrease in money	none	up	down	up

The increase in *M* shifts the *LM* curve down. It does not shift the *IS* curve. The economy moves along the *IS* curve.

curve, and the equilibrium moves from point *A* to point *A'*. Output increases from *Y* to *Y'*, and the interest rate decreases from *i* to *i'*.

■ Step 3 is to say it in words: The increase in money leads to a lower interest rate. The lower interest rate leads to an increase in investment and, in turn, to an increase in demand and output.

In contrast to the case of fiscal contraction, we can tell exactly what happens to the different components of demand after a monetary expansion: Because income is higher and taxes are unchanged, disposable income goes up, and so does consumption. Because sales are higher and the interest rate is lower, investment also unambiguously goes up. So a monetary expansion is more investment friendly than a fiscal expansion.

Let's summarize:

■ You should remember the three-step approach (characterize the shifts, show the effect on the equilibrium, tell the story in words) we have developed in this section to look at the effects of changes in policy on activity and the interest rate. We shall use it throughout the book.

■ Table 5-1 summarizes what we have learned about the effects of fiscal and monetary policy. Use the same method to look at changes other than changes in policy. For example, trace the effects of a decrease in consumer confidence through its effect on consumption demand, or, say, the introduction of more convenient credit cards through their effect on the demand for money.

5-4 Using a Policy Mix

How U.S. monetary and fiscal policy have been used during this crisis is the main topic of the next chapter.

We have looked so far at fiscal policy and monetary policy in isolation. Our purpose was to show how each worked. In practice, the two are often used together. The combination of monetary and fiscal policies is known as the **monetary–fiscal policy mix**, or simply the **policy mix**.

Sometimes, the right mix is to use fiscal and monetary policy in the same direction. This was the case for example during the recession of 2001 in the United States, where both monetary and fiscal policy were used to fight the recession. The story of the recession and the role of monetary and fiscal policy are described in the Focus box "The U.S. Recession of 2001."

Focus: The U.S. Recession of 2001

In 1992, the U.S. economy embarked on a long expansion. For the rest of the decade, GDP growth was positive and high. In 2000, however, the expansion came to an end. From the third quarter of 2000 to the fourth quarter of 2001, GDP growth was either positive and close to zero or negative. Based on data available at the time, it was thought that growth was negative through the first three quarters of 2001. Based on revised data, shown in Figure 1, which gives the growth rate for each quarter from 1999–1 to 2002–4, measured at annual rate, it appears that growth was actually small but positive in the second quarter. (These data revisions happen often, so that what we see when we look back is not always what national income statisticians perceived at the time.) The National Bureau of Economic Research (known as the NBER for short), a nonprofit organization that has traditionally dated U.S. recessions and expansions, concluded that the U.S. economy had indeed had a recession in 2001, starting in March 2001 and ending in December 2001; this period is represented by the shaded area in the figure.

What triggered the recession was a sharp decline in investment demand. Nonresidential investment—the demand for plant and equipment by firms—decreased by 4.5% in 2001. The cause was the end of what Alan Greenspan, the chairman of the Fed at the time, had dubbed a period of "irrational exuberance": During the second part of the 1990s, firms had been extremely optim istic about the future, and the rate of investment had been very high—the average yearly growth rate of investment from 1995 to 2000 exceeded 10%. In 2001, however, it became clear to firms that they had been overly optimistic and had invested too much. This led them to cut back on investment, leading to a decrease in demand and, through the multiplier, a decrease in GDP.

The recession could have been much worse. But it was met by a strong macroeconomic policy response, which certainly limited the depth and the length of the recession.

Take monetary policy first. Starting in early 2001, the Fed, feeling that the economy was slowing down, started increasing the money supply and decreasing the federal funds rate aggressively. (Figure 2 shows the behavior of the federal funds rate, from 1991–1 to 2002–4.) It continued to do so throughout the year. The funds rate, which stood at 6.5% in January, stood at less than 2% at the end of the year.

Turn to fiscal policy. During the 2000 Presidential campaign, then candidate George Bush had run on a of lower taxes. The argument was that the federal budget was in surplus, and so there was room to reduce tax rates while keeping the budget in balance. When President Bush took office in 2001 and it became clear that the economy was slowing down, he had an additional rationale to cut tax rates, namely the use of lower taxes to increase demand and fight the recession. Both the 2001 and the 2002 budgets included substantial reductions in tax rates. On the spending side, the events of September 11, 2001 led to an increase in spending, mostly on defense and homeland security.

Figure 3 shows the evolution of federal government revenues and spending during 1999–1 to 2002–4, both

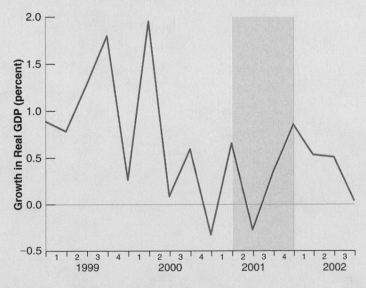

Figure 1   *The U.S. Growth Rate, 1999–1 to 2002–4*

Source: Calculated using Series GDPC1, Federal Reserve Economic Data (FRED)
http://research.stlouisfed.org/fred2/

Figure 2 *The Federal Funds Rate, 1999–1 to 2002–4*

Source: Series FEDFUNDS, Federal Reserve Economic Data (FRED) http://research. stlouisfed.org/fred2/

expressed as ratios to GDP. Note the dramatic decrease in revenues starting in the third quarter of 2001. Even without decreases in tax rates, revenues would have gone down during the recession: Lower output and lower income mechanically imply lower tax revenues. But, because of the tax cuts, the decrease in revenues in 2001 and 2002 was much larger than can be explained by the recession. Note also the smaller but steady increase in spending starting

around the same time. As a result, the budget surplus—the difference between revenues and spending—went from positive up until 2000, to negative in 2001 and, much more so, in 2002.

The effects of the initial decrease in investment demand and the monetary and fiscal responses can be represented using the *IS-LM* model. In Figure 4, assume that the equilibrium at the end of 2000 is represented by

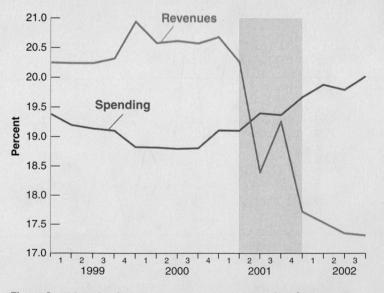

Figure 3 *U.S. Federal Government Revenues and Spending (as Ratios to GDP), 1999–1 to 2002–4*

Source: Calculated using Series GDP, FGRECPY, FGEXPND, Federal Reserve Economic Data (FRED) http://research.stlouisfed.org/fred2/

point A, at the intersection of the initial *IS* and the initial *LM* curves. What happened in 2001 was the following:

- The decrease in investment demand led to a sharp shift of the *IS curve* to the left, from *IS* to *IS"*. Absent policy reactions, the economy would have been at point *A"*, with output *Y"*.
- The increase in the money supply led to a downward shift of the *LM* curve, from *LM* to *LM'* .
- The decrease in tax rates and the increase in spending both led to a shift of the *IS* curve to the right, from *IS"* to *IS'*.

As a result of the decrease in investment demand and of the two policy responses, the economy in 2001 ended up at point *A'*, with a decrease in output, and a much lower interest rate. The output level associated with *A'* was lower than the output level associated with *A*—there was a recession— but it was much higher than the output level associated with *A"*, the level that would have prevailed in the absence of policy responses.

Let us end by taking up four questions you might be asking yourself at this point:

- Why weren't monetary and fiscal policy used to avoid rather than just to limit the size of the recession?

The reason is that changes in policy affect demand and output only over time (more on this in Section 5-5). Thus, by the time it became clear that the U.S. economy was entering a recession, it was already too late to use policy to avoid it. What the policy did was to reduce both the depth and the length of the recession.

- Weren't the events of September 11, 2001 also a cause of the recession?

The answer, in short, is no. As we have seen, the recession started long before September 11, and ended soon after. Indeed, GDP growth was positive in the last quarter of 2001. One might have expected—and, indeed, most economists expected—the events of September 11 to have large adverse effects on output, leading, in particular, consumers and firms to delay spending decisions until the outlook was clearer. In fact, the drop in spending was short and limited. Decreases in the federal funds rate after September 11—and large discounts by automobile producers in the last quarter of 2001— are believed to have been crucial in maintaining consumer confidence and consumer spending during that period.

- Was the monetary–fiscal mix used to fight the recession a textbook example of how policy should be conducted?

On this, economists differ. Most economists give high marks to the Fed for strongly decreasing interest rates as soon as the economy slowed down. But most economists are worried that the tax cuts introduced in 2001 and 2002 led to large and persistent budget deficits. They argue that the tax cuts should have been temporary, helping the U.S. economy get out of the recession but stopping thereafter. While the current crisis is mostly responsible for the large deficits we have today, the tax cuts have made the situation worse. As we saw in Chapter 1, reducing the budget deficit is perhaps the main item on the U.S. policy agenda.

- Why were monetary and fiscal policy unable to avoid the current crisis and the large decrease in U.S. output in 2009?

The answer, in short, is twofold. The shocks were much larger, and much harder to react to. And the room for policy responses was more limited. We shall return to these two aspects in Chapter 9.

Figure 4 *The U.S. Recession of 2001*

Sometimes, the right mix is to use the two policies in opposite directions, for example, combining a fiscal contraction with a monetary expansion. This was the case in the early 1990s in the United States. When Bill Clinton was elected President in 1992, one of his priorities was to reduce the budget deficit using a combination of cuts in spending and increases in taxes. Clinton was worried, however, that, by itself, such a fiscal contraction would lead to a decrease in demand and trigger another recession. The right strategy was to combine a fiscal contraction (so as to get rid of the deficit) with a monetary expansion (to make sure that demand and output remained high). This was the strategy adopted and carried out by Bill Clinton (who was in charge of fiscal policy) and Alan Greenspan (who was in charge of monetary policy). The result of this strategy—and a bit of economic luck—was a steady reduction of the budget deficit (which turned into a budget surplus at the end of the 1990s) and a steady increase in output throughout the rest of the decade.

Make sure you can tell the story using the *IS-LM* diagram. Which curves shifted? ▶ What was the effect on the equilibrium?

5-5 How Does the *IS-LM* Model Fit the Facts?

We have so far ignored dynamics. For example, when looking at the effects of an increase in taxes in Figure 5-7—or the effects of a monetary expansion in Figure 5-8—we made it look as if the economy moved instantaneously from A to A', as if output went instantaneously from Y to Y'. This is clearly not realistic: The adjustment of output clearly takes time. To capture this time dimension, we need to reintroduce dynamics.

Introducing dynamics formally would be difficult. But, as we did in Chapter 3, we can describe the basic mechanisms in words. Some of the mechanisms will be familiar from Chapter 3, some are new:

■ Consumers are likely to take some time to adjust their consumption following a change in disposable income.
■ Firms are likely to take some time to adjust investment spending following a change in their sales.
■ Firms are likely to take some time to adjust investment spending following a change in the interest rate.
■ Firms are likely to take some time to adjust production following a change in their sales.

So, in response to an increase in taxes, it takes some time for consumption spending to respond to the decrease in disposable income, some more time for production to decrease in response to the decrease in consumption spending, yet more time for investment to decrease in response to lower sales, for consumption to decrease in response to the decrease in income, and so on.

In response to a monetary expansion, it takes some time for investment spending to respond to the decrease in the interest rate, some more time for production to increase in response to the increase in demand, yet more time for consumption and investment to increase in response to the induced change in output, and so on.

Describing precisely the adjustment process implied by all these sources of dynamics is obviously complicated. But the basic implication is straightforward: Time is needed for output to adjust to changes in fiscal and monetary policy. How much time? This question can only be answered by looking at the data and using econometrics. Figure 5-9 shows the results of such an econometric study, which uses data from the United States from 1960 to 1990.

We discussed the federal funds market and the federal ▶ funds rate in Section 4-4.
The study looks at the effects of a decision by the Fed to increase the *federal funds rate* by 1%. It traces the typical effects of such an increase on a number of macroeconomic variables.

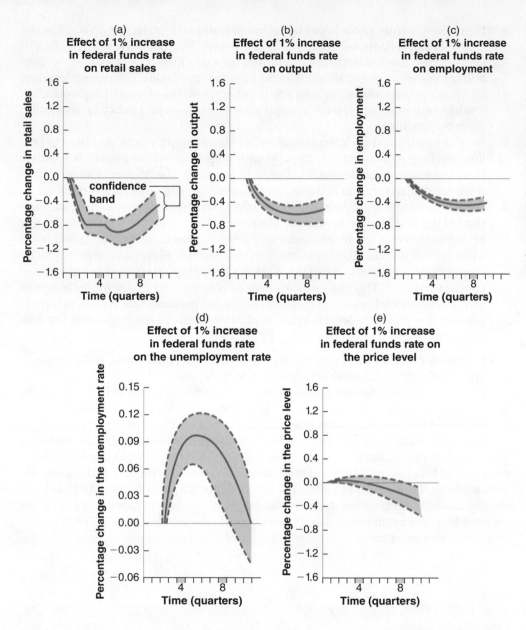

Figure 5-9

The Empirical Effects of an Increase in the Federal Funds Rate

In the short run, an increase in the federal funds rate leads to a decrease in output and to an increase in unemployment, but it has little effect on the price level.

Source: Lawrence Christiano, Martin Eichenbaum, and Charles Evans, "The Effects of Monetary Policy Shocks: Evidence From the Flow of Funds," *Review of Economics and Statistics*. 1996, 78 (February): pp. 16–34.

Each panel in Figure 5-9 represents the effects of the change in the interest rate on a given variable. Each panel plots three lines. The solid line in the center of a band gives the best estimate of the effect of the change in the interest rate on the variable we look at in the panel. The two dashed lines and the tinted space between the dashed lines represents a **confidence band**, a band within which the true value of the effect lies with 60% probability.

■ Panel 5-9(a) shows the effects of an increase in the federal funds rate of 1% on retail sales over time. The percentage change in retail sales is plotted on the vertical axis; time, measured in quarters, is on the horizontal axis.

Focusing on the best estimate—the solid line—we see that the increase in the federal funds rate of 1% leads to a decline in retail sales. The largest decrease in retail sales, −0.9%, is achieved after five quarters.

There is no such thing in econometrics as learning the exact value of a coefficient or the exact effect of one variable on another. Rather, what econometrics does is to provide us a best estimate—here, the thick line—and a measure of confidence we can have in the estimate—here, the confidence band.

This explains why monetary policy could not prevent the 2001 recession (See the ▶ Focus box: The U.S. Recession of 2001.) When at the start of 2001, the Fed starting decreasing the federal funds rate, it was already too late for these cuts to have much effect in 2001.

■ Figure 5-9(b) shows how lower sales lead to lower output. In response to the decrease in sales, firms cut production, but by less than the decrease in sales. Put another way, firms accumulate inventories for some time. The adjustment of production is smoother and slower than the adjustment of sales. The largest decrease, −0.7%, is reached after eight quarters. In other words, monetary policy works, but it works with long lags. It takes nearly two years for monetary policy to have its full effect on production.

■ Panel 5-9(c) shows how lower output leads to lower employment: As firms cut production, they also cut employment. As with output, the decline in employment is slow and steady, reaching –0.5% after eight quarters. The decline in employment is reflected in an increase in the unemployment rate, shown in Panel 5-9(d).

■ Panel 5-9(e) looks at the behavior of the price level. Remember, one of the *assumptions* of the *IS–LM* model is that the price level is given, and so it does not change in response to changes in demand. Panel 5-9(b) shows that this assumption is not a bad approximation of reality in the short run. The price level is nearly unchanged for the first six quarters or so. Only after the first six quarters does the price level appear to decline. This gives us a strong hint as to why the *IS–LM* model becomes less reliable as we look at the medium run: In the medium run, we can no longer assume that the price level is given, and movements in the price level become important.

Figure 5-9 provides two important lessons. First, it gives us a sense of the dynamic adjustment of output and other variables to monetary policy.

Second, and more fundamentally, it shows that what we observe in the economy is consistent with the implications of the *IS–LM* model. This does not *prove* that the *IS–LM* model is the right model. It may be that what we observe in the economy is the result of a completely different mechanism, and the fact that the *IS–LM* model fits well is a coincidence. But this seems unlikely. The *IS–LM* model looks like a solid basis on which to build when looking at movements in activity in the short-run. Later on, we shall extend the model to look at the role of expectations (Chapters 14 to 17) and the implications of openness in goods and financial markets (Chapters 18 to 21). But we must first understand what determines output in the medium run. This is the topic of the next four chapters.

Summary

. . . .

■ The *IS–LM model* characterizes the implications of equilibrium in both the goods and the financial markets.

■ The *IS* relation and the *IS* curve show the combinations of the interest rate and the level of output that are consistent with equilibrium in the goods market. An increase in the interest rate leads to a decline in output. Consequently, the *IS* curve is downward sloping.

■ The *LM* relation and the *LM* curve show the combinations of the interest rate and the level of output consistent with equilibrium in financial markets. Given the real money supply, an increase in output leads to an increase in the interest rate. Consequently, the *LM* curve is upward sloping.

■ A fiscal expansion shifts the *IS* curve to the right, leading to an increase in output and an increase in the interest rate. A fiscal contraction shifts the *IS* curve to the left, leading to a decrease in output and a decrease in the interest rate.

■ A monetary expansion shifts the *LM* curve down, leading to an increase in output and a decrease in the interest rate. A monetary contraction shifts the *LM* curve up, leading to a decrease in output and an increase in the interest rate.

■ The combination of monetary and fiscal policies is known as the monetary–fiscal policy mix, or simply the policy mix. Sometimes monetary and fiscal policy are used in the same direction. This was the case during the 2001 U.S. recession. Sometimes, they are used in opposite directions. Fiscal contraction and monetary expansion can, for example, achieve a decrease in the budget deficit while avoiding a decrease in output.

■ The *IS–LM* model appears to describe well the behavior of the economy in the short run. In particular, the effects of monetary policy appear to be similar to those implied by the *IS–LM* model once dynamics are introduced in the model. An increase in the interest rate due to a monetary contraction leads to a steady decrease in output, with the maximum effect taking place after about eight quarters.

Key Terms

IS curve, 89
LM curve, 92
fiscal contraction, fiscal consolidation, 94
fiscal expansion, 94
crowding out, crowding in, 96

monetary expansion, 96
monetary contraction, monetary tightening, 96
monetary–fiscal policy mix, (policy mix), 98
confidence band, 103

Questions and Problems

QUICK CHECK
All Quick Check questions and problems are available on MyEconLab.

1. *Using the information in this chapter, label each of the following statements true, false, or uncertain. Explain briefly.*

  a. The main determinants of investment are the level of sales and the interest rate.

  b. If all the exogenous variables in the *IS* relation are constant, then a higher level of output can be achieved only by lowering the interest rate.

  c. The *IS* curve is downward sloping because goods market equilibrium implies that an increase in taxes leads to a lower level of output.

  d. If government spending and taxes increase by the same amount, the *IS* curve does not shift.

  e. The *LM* curve is upward sloping because a higher level of the money supply is needed to increase output.

  f. An increase in government spending leads to a decrease in investment.

  g. Government policy can increase output without changing the interest rate only if both monetary and fiscal policy variables change.

2. *Consider first the goods market model with constant investment that we saw in Chapter 3. Consumption is given by*

$$C = c_0 + c_1(Y - T)$$

and I, G, and T are given.

  a. Solve for equilibrium output. What is the value of the multiplier?
  Now let investment depend on both sales and the interest rate:

$$I = b_0 + b_1 Y - b_2 i$$

  b. Solve for equilibrium output. At a given interest rate, is the effect of a change in autonomous spending bigger than what it was in part (a)? Why? (Assume $c_1 + b_1 < 1$.)
  Next, write the LM *relation as*

$$M/P = d_1 Y - d_2 i$$

  c. Solve for equilibrium output. (Hint: Eliminate the interest rate from the *IS* and *LM* relations.) Derive the multiplier (the effect of a change of one unit in autonomous spending on output).

  d. Is the multiplier you obtained in part (c) smaller or larger than the multiplier you derived in part (a)? Explain how your answer depends on the parameters in the behavioral equations for consumption, investment, and money demand.

3. *The response of investment to fiscal policy*

  a. Using the *IS–LM* diagram, show the effects on output and the interest rate of a decrease in government spending. Can you tell what happens to investment? Why?
  Now consider the following IS–LM *model:*

$$C = c_0 + c_1(Y - T)$$
$$I = b_0 + b_1 Y - b_2 i$$
$$M/P = d_1 Y - d_2 i$$

  b. Solve for equilibrium output. Assume $c_1 + b_1 < 1$. (*Hint*: You may want to re-work through Problem 2 if you are having trouble with this step.)

  c. Solve for the equilibrium interest rate. (*Hint*: Use the *LM* relation.)

  d. Solve for investment.

  e. Under what conditions on the parameters of the model (i.e., c_0, c_1, and so on) will investment increase when *G* decreases? (Hint: If *G* decreases by one unit, by how much does *I* increase? Be careful; you want the change in *I* to be positive when the change in *G* is negative.)

  f. Explain the condition you derived in part (e).

4. *Consider the following IS–LM model:*

$$C = 200 + .25Y_D$$
$$I = 150 + .25Y - 1000i$$
$$G = 250$$
$$T = 200$$
$$(M/P)^d = 2Y - 8000i$$
$$M/P = 1600$$

a. Derive the *IS* relation. (*Hint:* You want an equation with Y on the left side and everything else on the right.)

b. Derive the *LM* relation. (*Hint:* It will be convenient for later use to rewrite this equation with *i* on the left side and everything else on the right.)

c. Solve for equilibrium real output. (*Hint:* Substitute the expression for the interest rate given by the *LM* equation into the *IS* equation and solve for output.)

d. Solve for the equilibrium interest rate. (*Hint:* Substitute the value you obtained for *Y* in part (c) into either the *IS* or *LM* equations and solve for *i*. If your algebra is correct, you should get the same answer from both equations.)

e. Solve for the equilibrium values of *C* and *I*, and verify the value you obtained for *Y* by adding *C, I,* and *G.*

f. Now suppose that the money supply increases to $M/P =$ 1,840. Solve for *Y, i, c,* and *T,* and describe in words the effects of an expansionary monetary policy.

g. Set *M/P* equal to its initial value of 1,600. Now suppose that government spending increases to $G = 400$. Summarize the effects of an expansionary fiscal policy on *Y, i,* and *C.*

DIG DEEPER

All Dig Deeper questions and problems are available on MyEconLab.

5. Investment and the interest rate

The chapter argues that investment depends negatively on the interest rate because an increase in the cost of borrowing discourages investment. However, firms often finance their investment projects using their own funds.

If a firm is considering using its own funds (rather than borrowing) to finance investment projects, will higher interest rates discourage the firm from undertaking these projects? Explain. (Hint: Think of yourself as the owner of a firm that has earned profits and imagine that you are going to use the profits either to finance new investment projects or to buy bonds. Will your decision to invest in new projects in your firm be affected by the interest rate?)

6. The Bush–Greenspan policy mix
In 2001, the Fed pursued a very expansionary monetary policy. At the same time, President George W. Bush pushed through legislation that lowered income taxes.

a. Illustrate the effect of such a policy mix on output.

b. How does this policy mix differ from the Clinton–Greenspan mix?

c. What happened to output in 2001? How do you reconcile the fact that both fiscal and monetary policies were expansionary with the fact that growth was so low in 2002? (Hint: What else happened?)

7. Policy mixes
Suggest a policy mix to achieve each of the following objectives.

a. Increase *Y* while keeping *i* constant.

b. Decrease the fiscal deficit while keeping *Y* constant. What happens to *i*? To investment?

8. The (less paradoxical) paradox of saving
A chapter problem at the end of Chapter 3 considered the effect of a drop in consumer confidence on private saving and

investment, when investment depended on output but not on the interest rate. Here, we consider the same experiment in the context of the IS–LM *framework, in which investment depends on the interest rate and output.*

a. Suppose households attempt to save more, so that consumer confidence falls. In an *IS–LM* diagram, show the effect of the fall in consumer confidence on output and the interest rate.

b. How will the fall in consumer confidence affect consumption, investment, and private saving? Will the attempt to save more necessarily lead to more saving? Will this attempt necessarily lead to less saving?

EXPLORE FURTHER

9. The Clinton–Greenspan policy mix

As described in this chapter, during the Clinton administration the policy mix changed toward more contractionary fiscal policy and more expansionary monetary policy. This question explores the implications of this change in the policy mix, both in theory and fact.

a. Suppose *G* falls, *T* rises, and *M* increases and that this combination of policies has no effect on output. Show the effects of these policies in an *IS–LM* diagram. What happens to the interest rate? What happens to investment?

b. Go to the Web site of the *Economic Report of the President* (**www.gpoaccess.gov/eop/**). Look at Table B-79 in the statistical appendix. What happened to federal receipts (tax revenues), federal outlays, and the budget deficit as a percentage of GDP over the period 1992 to 2000? (Note that federal outlays include transfer payments, which would be excluded from the variable *G*, as we define it in our *IS–LM* model. Ignore the difference.)

c. The Federal Reserve Board of Governors posts the recent history of the federal funds rate at http://**www.federalreserve. gov/releases/h15/data.htm.** You will have to choose to look at the rate on a daily, weekly, monthly, or annual interval. Look at the years between 1992 and 2000. When did monetary policy become more expansionary?

d. Go to Table B-2 of the *Economic Report of the President* and collect data on real GDP and real gross domestic investment for the period 1992 to 2000. Calculate investment as a percentage of GDP for each year. What happened to investment over the period?

e. Finally, go to Table B-31 and retrieve data on real GDP per capita (in chained 2005 dollars) for the period. Calculate the growth rate for each year. What was the average annual growth rate over the period 1992 to 2000? In Chapter 10 you will learn that the average annual growth rate of U.S. real GDP per capita was 2.6% between 1950 and 2004. How did growth between 1992 and 2000 compare to the Post World War II average?

10. Consumption, investment, and the recession of 2001

This question asks you to examine the movements of investment and consumption before, during, and after the recession of 2001. It also asks you to consider the response of investment and consumption to the events of September 11, 2001.

*Go to the Web site of the Bureau of Economic Analysis (**www.bea.gov**). Find the NIPA tables, in particular the* quarterly versions of Table 1.1.1, which shows the percentage change in real GDP and its components, and Table 1.1.2, which shows the contribution of the components of GDP to the overall percentage change in GDP. Table 1.1.2 weighs the percentage change of the components by their size. Investment is more variable than consumption, but consumption is much bigger than investment, so smaller percentage changes in consumption can have the same impact on GDP as much larger percentage changes in investment. Note that the quarterly percentage changes are annualized (i.e., expressed as annual rates). Retrieve the quarterly data on real GDP, consumption, gross private domestic investment, and non-residential fixed investment for the years 1999 to 2002 from Tables 1.1.1 and 1.1.2.

  a. Identify the quarters of negative growth in 2000 and 2001.
  b. Track consumption and investment around 2000 and 2001. From Table 1.1.1, which variable had the bigger percentage change around this time? Compare non-residential fixed investment with overall investment. Which variable had the bigger percentage change?
  c. From Table 1.1.2, get the contribution to GDP growth of consumption and investment for 1999 to 2001. Calculate

the average of the quarterly contributions for each variable for each year. Now calculate the change in the contribution of each variable for 2000 and 2001 (i.e., subtract the average contribution of consumption in 1999 from the average contribution of consumption in 2000, subtract the average contribution of consumption in 2000 from the average contribution of consumption in 2001, and do the same for investment for both years). Which variable had the largest decrease in its contribution to growth? What do you think was the proximate cause of the recession of 2001? (Was it a fall in investment demand or a fall in consumption demand?)

  d. Now look at what happened to consumption and investment after the events of September 11th in the third and fourth quarters of 2001 and in the first two quarters of 2002. Does the drop in investment at the end of 2001 make sense to you? How long did this drop in investment last? What happened to consumption about this time? How do you explain, in particular, the change in consumption in the fourth quarter of 2001? Did the events of September 11, 2001 cause the recession of 2001? Use the discussion in the chapter and your own intuition as guides in answering these questions.

Further Reading

■ A description of the U.S. economy, from the period of "irrational exuberance" to the 2001 recession and the role of fiscal and monetary policy, is given by Paul Krugman, in *The*

Great Unraveling, W.W. Norton, 2003. New York, (Warning: Krugman did not like the Bush administration or its policies!)

APPENDIX: An Alternative Derivation of the *LM* Relation as an Interest Rate Rule

In the text, we derived the *LM* relation under the assumption that *the money stock remained constant*. This gave us the positive relation between the interest rate and income shown, for example, in Figure 5-4(b).

As we discussed in Chapter 4, however, the assumption that the central bank keeps the money stock constant and lets the interest rate adjust when income changes is not a good description of what modern central banks do. Most central banks think instead in terms of setting the interest rate, adjusting the money supply so as to achieve the interest rate they want. Thus, we may want to derive the *LM* relation under the alternative assumption that the central bank sets the interest rate and adjusts the money supply as needed to achieve that goal.

To see what this implies, turn to Figure 1(a). Like Figure 5-4(a), the panel plots money supply and money demand,

with the interest rate on the vertical axis and money on the horizontal axis. The money supply is given by the vertical line M^s, money demand by the downward-sloping curve M^d. The initial equilibrium is at point A, with interest rate i_A.

Now consider an increase in income that shifts money demand from M^d to $M^{d'}$. If the central bank does not change the money supply, then the equilibrium will move from A to B, and the interest rate will increase from i_A to i_B. The implied *LM* curve, *LM*, the relation between the interest rate and income, is drawn in Figure 1(b). It is exactly the same as in Figure 5-4(a).

Suppose, however, that the central bank wants to keep the interest rate constant in the face of the increase in income. Can it do it? Yes. How can it do it? By increasing the money supply in response to the increase in income, from M^s to $M^{s'}$. If it

Figure 1

The LM Relation as an Interest Rate Rule

(a) Depending on whether and by how much the central bank increases the money supply in response to shift in money demand coming from changes in income, the interest rate may remain constant, or increase a little, or increase a lot.

(b) We can think of the *LM* curve as showing whether and by how much the central bank allows the interest rate to increase in response to increases in income.

does so, the interest rate will remain constant. The equilibrium will move from *A* to *D*, and the interest rate will remain constant at i_A. The resulting *LM* curve, denoted by *LM'* in Figure 1(b), will be horizontal: In response to the increase in income, the central bank will adjust the money supply so as to keep the interest rate constant.

This may be too extreme a policy. Perhaps the central bank wants to allow the interest rate to increase, but by less than it would if the central bank kept the money supply constant. For example, in response to the increase in income, the central bank may choose to increase the money supply by $M^{s''} < M^{s'}$. In this case, the equilibrium will move from *A* to *C*, and the interest rate will increase from i_A to i_C. The resulting *LM* curve, denoted by *LM''* in Figure 1(b), will be upward sloping but flatter than *LM*.

To summarize: The *LM* relation we derived in the text gave us the relation between the interest rate and income for a *given money supply*. The *LM* relation derived in the appendix gives us the relation between the interest rate and income when the central bank follows a given **interest rate rule**, and

lets the money supply adjust as needed. Its slope then depends on how much the central bank increases the interest rate in response to increases in income.

Which *LM* relation should you use? It depends on the question at hand. Take, for example, the case of an increase in the deficit, shifting the *IS* curve to the right. You may want to know what would happen to output and the interest rate if the central bank money supply remained constant, in which case you will use the *LM* relation derived in the text. But you may know that, for example, the central bank is likely to keep the interest rate constant, in which case you will use the the *LM* relation we derived in this appendix—in this particular case, an horizontal *LM* curve. ▲

Under which of the two assumptions will fiscal policy have the strongest effect on output?

Key Term

interest rate rule, 108

The Medium Run

In the medium run, the economy returns to a level of output associated with the natural rate of unemployment.

Chapter 6

Chapter 6 looks at equilibrium in the labor market. It characterizes the natural rate of unemployment—the unemployment rate to which the economy tends to return in the medium run. Associated with the natural rate of unemployment is a natural level of output.

Chapter 7

Chapter 7 looks at equilibrium in all three markets—goods, financial, labor—together. It shows that, while output typically deviates from the natural level of output in the short run, it returns to this natural level in the medium run. The model developed in Chapter 7 is called the *AS–AD* model, and, together with the *IS–LM* model, is one of the workhorses of macroeconomics.

Chapter 8

Chapter 8 looks more closely at the relation between inflation and unemployment, a relation known as the Phillips curve. In the short run, the behavior of inflation depends on the deviation of unemployment from its natural rate. In the medium run, unemployment returns to the natural rate independent of inflation. Inflation is determined by money growth in the medium run.

Chapter 9

Chapter 9 looks at why the current crisis has been so deep and prolonged. It shows how an initial shock in the housing market was amplified through its effects in the financial system. It shows how the room for policy to help output return to its natural level is limited in two ways: Monetary policy is limited by the presence of a liquidity trap. Fiscal policy is limited by the presence of a high level of public debt.

6

The Labor Market

Think about what happens when firms respond to an increase in demand by increasing production: Higher production leads to higher employment. Higher employment leads to lower unemployment. Lower unemployment leads to higher wages. Higher wages increase production costs, leading firms to increase prices. Higher prices lead workers to ask for higher wages. Higher wages lead to further increases in prices, and so on.

So far, we have simply ignored this sequence of events: By assuming a constant price level in the *IS–LM* model, we in effect assumed that firms were able and willing to supply any amount of output at a given price level. So long as our focus was on the *short run*, this assumption was acceptable. But, as our attention turns to the *medium run*, we must now abandon this assumption, explore how prices and wages adjust over time, and how this, in turn, affects output. This will be our task in this and the next three chapters.

At the center of the sequence of events described in the first paragraph is *the labor market*, the market in which wages are determined. This chapter focuses on the labor market. It has six sections:

Section 6-1 provides an overview of the labor market.

Section 6-2 focuses on unemployment, how it moves over time, and how its movements affect individual workers.

Sections 6-3 and **6-4** look at wage and price determination.

Section 6-5 then looks at equilibrium in the labor market. It characterizes the *natural rate of unemployment*, the rate of unemployment to which the economy tends to return in the medium run.

Section 6-6 gives a map of where we will be going next. ●

6-1 A Tour of the Labor Market

The total U.S. population in 2010 was 308.7 million (Figure 6-1). Excluding those who were either under working age (under 16), in the armed forces, or behind bars, the number of people potentially available for civilian employment, the **noninstitutional civilian population**, was 237.8 million.

The civilian **labor force**—the sum of those either working or looking for work— was only 153.8 million. The other 84 million people were **out of the labor force**, neither working in the market place nor looking for work. The **participation rate**, defined as the ratio of the labor force to the noninstitutional civilian population, was therefore 153.8/237.8, or 64.7%. The participation rate has steadily increased over time, reflecting mostly the increasing participation rate of women: In 1950, one woman out of three was in the labor force; now the number is close to two out of three.

Of those in the labor force, 139 million were employed, and 14.8 million were unemployed—looking for work. The **unemployment rate**, defined as the ratio of the unemployed to the labor force, was therefore 14.8/153.8 = 9.6. As we shall see later, 9.6% is a very high unemployment rate by historical standards.

Work in the home, such as cooking or raising children, is not classified as work in the official statistics. This is a reflection of the difficulty of measuring these activities— not a value judgment about what constitutes work and what doesn't.

The Large Flows of Workers

To get a sense of what a given unemployment rate implies for individual workers, consider the following analogy:

Take an airport full of passengers. It may be crowded because many planes are coming and going, and many passengers are quickly moving in and out of the airport. Or it may be because bad weather is delaying flights and passengers are stranded, waiting for the weather to improve. The number of passengers in the airport will be high in both cases, but their plights are quite different. Passengers in the second scenario are likely to be much less happy.

Figure 6-1

Population, Labor Force, Employment, and Unemployment in the United States (in millions), 2010

Source: Current Population Survey http://www.bls.gov/cps/

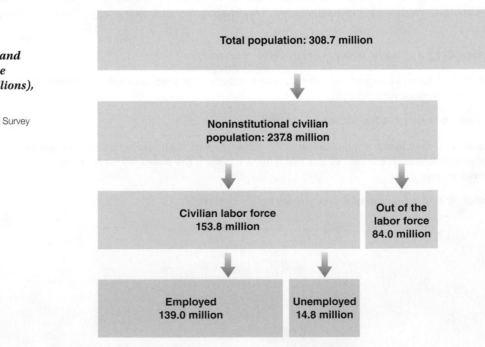

In the same way, a given unemployment rate may reflect two very different realities. It may reflect an active labor market, with many **separations** and many **hires**, and so with many workers entering and exiting unemployment; or it may reflect a sclerotic labor market, with few separations, few hires, and a stagnant unemployment pool.

Finding out which reality hides behind the aggregate unemployment rate requires data on the movements of workers. The data are available in the United States from a monthly survey called the **Current Population Survey (CPS)**. Average monthly flows, computed from the CPS for the United States from 1994 to 2011, are reported in Figure 6-2. (For more on the ins and outs of the CPS, see the Focus box "The Current Population Survey.")

Figure 6-2 has three striking features:

■ The flows of workers in and out of employment are very large.

On average, there are 8.5 million separations each month in the United States (out of an employment pool of 132.4 million), 3.1 million change jobs (shown by the circular arrow at the top), 3.6 million move from employment to out of the labor force (shown by the arrow from employment to out of the labor force), and 1.8 million move from employment to unemployment (shown by the arrow from employment to unemployment).

Why are there so many separations each month? About three-fourths of all separations are usually **quits**—workers leaving their jobs for what they perceive as a better alternative. The remaining one-fourth are **layoffs**. Layoffs come mostly from changes in employment levels across firms: The slowly changing aggregate employment numbers hide a reality of continual job destruction and job creation across firms. At any given time, some firms are suffering decreases in demand and decreasing their employment; other firms are enjoying increases in demand and increasing employment.

■ The flows in and out of unemployment are large relative to the number of unemployed: The average monthly flow out of unemployment each month is 4.0 million: 2.1 million people get a job, and 1.9 million stop searching for a job and drop out of the labor force. Put another way, the proportion of unemployed leaving unemployment equals 4.0/8.4 or about 47% each month. Put yet another way, the

Sclerosis, a medical term, means hardening of the arteries. By analogy, it is used in economics to describe markets that function poorly and have few transactions.

The numbers for employment, unemployment, and those out of the labor force in Figure 6-1 referred to 2010. The numbers for the same variables in Figure 6-2 refer to averages from 1994 to 2011. This is why they are different.

Put another, and perhaps more dramatic way: On average, every day in the United States, about 60,000 workers become unemployed.

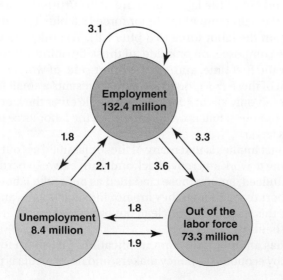

Figure 6-2

Average Monthly Flows between Employment, Unemployment, and Nonparticipation in the United States, 1994 to 2011 (millions)

(1) The flows of workers in and out of employment are large; (2) The flows in and out of unemployment are large relative to the number of unemployed; (3) There are also large flows in and out of the labor force, much of it directly to and from employment.

Source: Calculated from the series constructed by Fleischman and Fallick, http://www.federalreserve.gov/econresdata/researchdata.htm

The Current Population Survey

The Current Population Survey (CPS) is the main source of statistics on the labor force, employment, participation, and earnings in the United States.

When the CPS began in 1940, it was based on interviews of 8,000 households. The sample has grown considerably, and now about 60,000 households are interviewed every month. (The CPS was redesigned in 1994, which is why, for consistency, Figures 6-2, 6-4, and 6-5 start only in 1994.) The households are chosen so that the sample is representative of the U.S. population. Each household stays in the sample for four months, leaves the sample for the following eight months, then comes back for another four months before leaving the sample permanently.

The survey is now based on computer-assisted interviews. Interviews are either done in person, in which case interviewers use laptop computers, or by phone. Some questions are asked in every survey. Other questions are specific to a particular survey and are used to find out about particular aspects of the labor market.

The Labor Department uses the data to compute and publish numbers on employment, unemployment, and participation by age, sex, education, and industry. Economists use these data, which are available in large computer files, in two ways:

The first is to get snapshots of how things are at various points in time, to answer such questions as: What is the distribution of wages for Hispanic–American workers with only primary education, and how does it compare with the same distribution 10 or 20 years ago?

The second way, of which Figure 6-2 is an example, is answered by the fact that the survey follows people through time. By looking at the same people in two consecutive months, economists can find out, for example, how many of those who were unemployed last month are employed this month. This number gives them an estimate of the probability of somebody who was unemployed last month found a job this month.

For more on the CPS, you can go to the CPS homepage. (www.bls.gov/cps/home.htm)

The average duration of unemployment equals the inverse of the proportion of unemployed leaving unemployment each month. To see why, consider an example. Suppose the number of unemployed is constant and equal to 100, and each unemployed person remains unemployed for two months. So, at any given time, there are 50 people who have been unemployed for one month and 50 who have been unemployed for two months. Each month, the 50 unemployed who have been unemployed for two months leave unemployment. In this example, the proportion of unemployed leaving unemployment each month is 50/100, or 50%. The duration of unemployment is two months—the inverse of 1/50%.

average **duration of unemployment**—the average length of time people spend unemployed—is between two and three months.

This fact has an important implication. You should not think of unemployment in the United States as a stagnant pool of workers waiting indefinitely for jobs. For most (but obviously not all) of the unemployed, being unemployed is more a quick transition than a long wait between jobs. One needs, however, to make two remarks at this point. First, the United States is unusual in this respect: In many European countries, the average duration is much longer than in the United States. Second, as we shall see below, even in the United States, when unemployment is high, such as is the case today, the average duration of unemployment becomes much longer. Being unemployed becomes much more painful.

■ The flows in and out of the labor force are also surprisingly large: Each month, 5.5 million workers drop out of the labor force (3.6 plus 1.9), and a slightly larger number, 5.1, join the labor force (3.3 plus 1.8). You might have expected these two flows to be composed, on one side, of those finishing school and entering the labor force for the first time, and, on the other side, of workers going into retirement. But each of these two groups actually represents a small fraction of the total flows. Each month only about 400,000 new people enter the labor force, and about 300,000 retire. But the actual flows in and out of the labor force are 10.6 million, so about 15 times larger.

What this fact implies is that many of those classified as "out of the labor force" are in fact willing to work and move back and forth between participation and nonparticipation. Indeed, among those classified as out of the labor force, a very large proportion report that although they are not looking, they "want a job." What they really mean by this statement is unclear, but the evidence is that many do take jobs when offered them.

This fact has another important implication. The sharp focus on the unemployment rate by economists, policy makers, and news media is partly misdirected.

Some of the people classified as "out of the labor force" are very much like the unemployed. They are in effect **discouraged workers**. And while they are not actively looking for a job, they will take it if they find one.

This is why economists sometimes focus on the **employment rate**, the ratio of employment to the population available for work, rather than on the unemployment rate. The higher unemployment, or the higher the number of people out of the labor force, the lower the employment rate.

We shall follow tradition in this book and focus on the unemployment rate as an indicator of the state of the labor market, but you should keep in mind that the unemployment rate is not the best estimate of the number of people available for work.

Working in the opposite direction: Some of the unemployed may be unwilling to accept any job offered to them and should probably not be counted as unemployed since they are not really looking for a job.

In 2010, employment was 139 million and the population available for work was 237.8 million. The employment rate was 58.5%. The employment rate is sometimes called the employment to population ratio.

6-2 Movements in Unemployment

Let's now look at movements in unemployment. Figure 6-3 shows the average value of the U.S. unemployment rate over the year, for each year, all the way back to 1948. The shaded areas represent years during which there was a recession.

Figure 6-3 has two important features:

■ Until the mid-1980s, it looked as if the U.S. unemployment rate was on an upward trend, from an average of 4.5% in the 1950s to 4.7% in the 1960s, 6.2% in the 1970s, and 7.3% in the 1980s. From the 1980s on however, the unemployment rate steadily declined for more than two decades. By 2006, the unemployment rate was 4.6%. These decreases led a number of economists to conclude that the trend from 1950 to the 1980s had been reversed, and that the normal rate of unemployment in the United States had fallen. How much of the large increase in the unemployment rate since 2007 is temporary, and whether we can return to the low rates of the mid-2000s, remains to be seen.

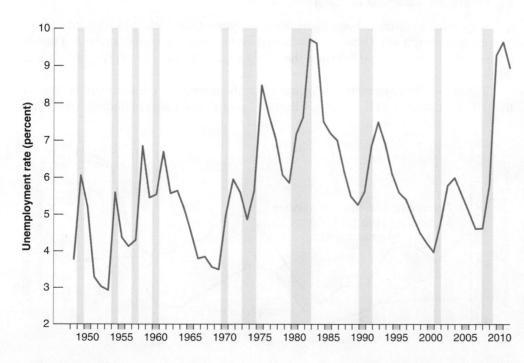

Figure 6-3

Movements in the U.S. Unemployment Rate, 1948–2010

Since 1948, the average yearly U.S. unemployment rate has fluctuated between 3% and 10%.

Source: Series UNRATE: Federal Reserve Economic Data (FRED) http://research.stlouisfed.org/fred2/

- Leaving aside these trend changes, year-to-year movements in the unemployment rate are closely associated with recessions and expansions. Look, for example, at the last four peaks in unemployment in Figure 6-3. The most recent peak, at 9.6% is in 2010, is the result of the crisis. The previous two peaks, associated with the recessions of 2001 and 1990–1991 recessions, had much lower unemployment rate peaks, around 7%. Only the recession of 1982, where the unemployment rate reached 9.7%, is comparable to the current crisis. (Annual averages can mask larger values within the year. In the 1982 recession, while the average unemployment rate over the year was 9.7%, the unemployment rate actually reached 10.8% in November 1982. Similarly, the monthly unemployment rate in the crisis peaked at 10.0% in October 2009.)

How do these fluctuations in the *aggregate unemployment rate* affect *individual workers*? This is an important question because the answer determines both:

- The effect of movements in the aggregate unemployment rate on the welfare of individual workers, and
- The effect of the aggregate unemployment rate on wages.

Let's start by asking how firms can decrease their employment in response to a decrease in demand. They can hire fewer new workers, or they can lay off the workers they currently employ. Typically, firms prefer to slow or stop the hiring of new workers first, relying on quits and retirements to achieve a decrease in employment. But doing only this may not be enough if the decrease in demand is large, so firms may then have to lay off workers.

Now think about the implications for both employed and unemployed workers.

- If the adjustment takes place through fewer hires, the chance that an unemployed worker will find a job diminishes. Fewer hires means fewer job openings; higher unemployment means more job applicants. Fewer openings and more applicants combine to make it harder for the unemployed to find jobs.
- If the adjustment takes place instead through higher layoffs, then employed workers are at a higher risk of losing their job.

In general, as firms do both, higher unemployment is associated with both a lower chance of finding a job if one is unemployed and a higher chance of losing it if one is employed. Figures 6-4 and 6-5 show these two effects at work over the period 1994 to 2010.

Figure 6-4 plots two variables against time: the unemployment rate (measured on the left vertical axis); and the proportion of unemployed workers finding a job each

Note also that the unemployment rate sometimes peaks in the year after the recession, ▶ not in the actual recession year. This occurred, for example, in the 2001 recession. The reason is that, while output is higher and growth is positive, so the economy is technically no longer in recession, the additional output does not require enough new hires to reduce the unemployment rate.

Figure 6-4

The Unemployment Rate and the Proportion of Unemployed Finding Jobs, 1994–2010

When unemployment is high, the proportion of unemployed finding jobs within one month is low. Note that the scale on the right is an inverse scale.

Source: See Figure 6-2.

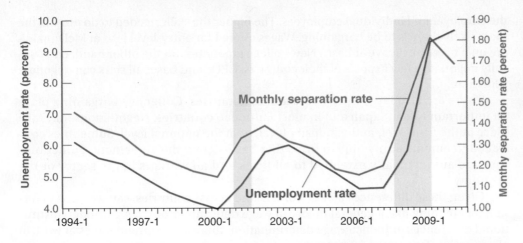

Figure 6-5

The Unemployment Rate and the Monthly Separation Rate from Employment, 1994–2010

When unemployment is high, a higher proportion of workers lose their jobs.

Source: See Figure 6-2.

month (measured on the right vertical axis). This proportion is constructed by dividing the flow from unemployment to employment during each month by the number of unemployed. To show the relation between the two variables more clearly, the proportion of unemployed finding jobs is plotted on an inverted scale: Be sure you see that on the right vertical scale, the proportion is lowest at the top and highest at the bottom.

The relation between movements in the proportion of unemployed workers finding jobs and the unemployment rate is striking: Periods of higher unemployment are associated with much lower proportions of unemployed workers finding jobs. In 2010, for example, with unemployment close to 10%, only about 18% of the unemployed found a job within a month, as opposed to 28% in 2007, when unemployment was much lower.

Similarly, Figure 6-5 plots two variables against time: the unemployment rate (measured on the left vertical axis); and the monthly separation rate from employment (measured on the right vertical axis). The monthly separation rate is constructed by dividing the flow from employment (to unemployment and to "out of the labor force") during each month by the number of employed in the month. The relation between the separation rate and the unemployment rate plotted is quite strong: Higher unemployment implies a higher separation rate—that is, a higher chance of employed workers losing their jobs. The probability nearly doubles between times of low unemployment and times of high unemployment.

Let's summarize:

When unemployment is high, workers are worse off in two ways:

■ Employed workers face a higher probability of losing their job.
■ Unemployed workers face a lower probability of finding a job; equivalently, they can expect to remain unemployed for a longer time.

To be slightly more precise, we only learn from Figure 6-5 that, when unemployment is higher, separations into unemployment and out of the labor force are higher. Separations equal quits plus layoffs. ◄ We know from other sources that quits are lower when unemployment is high: It is more attractive to quit when there are plenty of jobs. So, if separations go up and quits go down, this implies that layoffs (which equal separations minus quits) go up even more than separations.

6-3 Wage Determination

Having looked at unemployment, let's turn to wage determination, and to the relation between wages and unemployment.

Wages are set in many ways. Sometimes they are set by **collective bargaining**; that is, bargaining between firms and unions. In the United States, however, collective bargaining plays a limited role, especially outside the manufacturing sector. Today, barely more than 10% of U.S. workers have their wages set by collective bargaining agreements. For the rest, wages are either set by employers or by bargaining between

◄ Collective bargaining: bargaining between a union (or a group of unions) and a firm (or a group of firms).

the employer and individual employees. The higher the skills needed to do the job, the more likely there is to be bargaining. Wages offered for entry-level jobs at McDonald's are on a take-it-or-leave-it basis. New college graduates, on the other hand, can typically negotiate a few aspects of their contracts. CEOs and baseball stars can negotiate a lot more.

There are also large differences across countries. Collective bargaining plays an important role in Japan and in most European countries. Negotiations may take place at the firm level, at the industry level, or at the national level. Sometimes contract agreements apply only to firms that have signed the agreement. Sometimes they are automatically extended to all firms and all workers in the sector or the economy.

Given these differences across workers and across countries, can we hope to formulate anything like a general theory of wage determination? Yes. Although institutional differences influence wage determination, there are common forces at work in all countries. Two sets of facts stand out:

■ Workers are typically paid a wage that exceeds their **reservation wage**, the wage that would make them indifferent between working or being unemployed. In other words, most workers are paid a high enough wage that they prefer being employed to being unemployed.
■ Wages typically depend on labor-market conditions. The lower the unemployment rate, the higher the wages. (We shall state this more precisely in the next section.)

To think about these facts, economists have focused on two broad lines of explanation. The first is that even in the absence of collective bargaining, workers have some bargaining power, which they can and do use to obtain wages above their reservation wages. The second is that firms themselves may, for a number of reasons, want to pay wages higher than the reservation wage. Let's look at each explanation in turn.

Bargaining

How much **bargaining power** a worker has depends on two factors. The first is how costly it would be for the firm to replace him, were he to leave the firm. The second is how hard it would be for him to find another job, were he to leave the firm. The more costly it is for the firm to replace him, and the easier it is for him to find another job, the more bargaining power he will have. This has two implications:

■ How much bargaining power a worker has depends first on the nature of his job. Replacing a worker at McDonald's is not very costly: The required skills can be taught quickly, and typically a large number of willing applicants have already filled out job application forms. In this situation, the worker is unlikely to have much bargaining power. If he asks for a higher wage, the firm can lay him off and find a replacement at minimum cost. In contrast, a highly skilled worker who knows in detail how the firm operates may be very difficult and costly to replace. This gives him more bargaining power. If he asks for a higher wage, the firm may decide that it is best to give it to him.
■ How much bargaining power a worker has also depends on labor market conditions. When the unemployment rate is low, it is more difficult for firms to find acceptable replacement workers. At the same time, it is easier for workers to find other jobs. Under these conditions, workers are in a stronger bargaining position and may be able to obtain a higher wage. Conversely, when the unemployment rate is high, finding good replacement workers is easier for firms, while finding another job is harder for workers. Being in a weak bargaining position, workers may have no choice but to accept a lower wage.

Peter Diamond, Dale Mortensen, and Christopher Pissarides received the 2010 Nobel Prize in economics precisely for working out the characteristics of a labor market with large flows and wage bargaining.

Henry Ford and Efficiency Wages

In 1914, Henry Ford—the builder of the most popular car in the world at the time, the Model-T—made a stunning announcement. His company would pay all qualified employees a minimum of $5 a day for an eight-hour day. This was a very large salary increase for most employees, who had been earning an average $2.30 for a nine-hour day. From the point of view of the Ford company, this increase in pay was far from negligible—it represented about half of the company's profits at the time.

What Ford's motivations were is not entirely clear. Ford himself gave too many reasons for us to know which ones he actually believed. The reason was not that the company had a hard time finding workers at the previous wage. But the company clearly had a hard time retaining workers. There was a very high turnover rate, as well as high dissatisfaction among workers.

Whatever the reasons behind Ford's decision, the results of the wage increase were astounding, as Table 1 shows:

Table 1	Annual Turnover and Layoff Rates (%) at Ford, 1913–1915		
	1913	1914	1915
Turnover rate	370	54	16
Layoff rate	62	7	0.1

The annual turnover rate (the ratio of separations to employment) plunged from a high of 370% in 1913 to a low of 16% in 1915. (An annual turnover rate of 370% means that on average 31% of the company's workers left each month, so that over the course of a year the ratio of separations to employment was $31\% \times 12 = 370\%$.) The layoff rate collapsed from 62% to nearly 0%. The average rate of absenteeism (not shown in the table), which ran at close to 10% in 1913, was down to 2.5% one year later. There is little question that higher wages were the main source of these changes.

Did productivity at the Ford plant increase enough to offset the cost of increased wages? The answer to this question is less clear. Productivity was much higher in 1914 than in 1913. Estimates of the productivity increases range from 30% to 50%. Despite higher wages, profits were also higher in 1914 than in 1913. But how much of this increase in profits was due to changes in workers' behavior and how much was due to the increasing success of Model-T cars is harder to establish.

While the effects support efficiency wage theories, it may be that the increase in wages to $5 a day was excessive, at least from the point of view of profit maximization. But Henry Ford probably had other objectives as well, from keeping the unions out—which he did—to generating publicity for himself and the company—which he surely did.

Source: Dan Raff and Lawrence Summers, "Did Henry Ford Pay Efficiency Wages?" *Journal of Labor Economics* 1987 5 (No. 4 Part 2): pp. S57–S87.

Efficiency Wages

Regardless of workers' bargaining power, firms may want to pay more than the reservation wage. They may want their workers to be productive, and a higher wage can help them achieve that goal. If, for example, it takes a while for workers to learn how to do a job correctly, firms will want their workers to stay for some time. But if workers are paid only their reservation wage, they will be indifferent between their staying or leaving. In this case, many of them will quit, and the turnover rate will be high. Paying a wage above the reservation wage makes it more attractive for workers to stay. It decreases turnover and increases productivity.

Behind this example lies a more general proposition: Most firms want their workers to feel good about their jobs. Feeling good promotes good work, which leads to higher productivity. Paying a high wage is one instrument the firm can use to achieve these goals. (See the Focus box "Henry Ford and Efficiency Wages.") Economists call the theories that link the *productivity* or the *efficiency* of workers to the wage they are paid **efficiency wage theories.**

◀ Before September 11, 2001, the approach to airport security was to hire workers at low wages and accept the resulting high turnover. Now that airport security has become a much higher priority, the approach is to make the jobs more attractive and higher paid, so as to get more motivated and more competent workers and reduce turnover.

Like theories based on bargaining, efficiency wage theories suggest that wages depend on both the nature of the job and on labor-market conditions:

■ Firms—such as high-tech firms—that see employee morale and commitment as essential to the quality of their work will pay more than firms in sectors where workers' activities are more routine.

■ Labor-market conditions will affect the wage. A low unemployment rate makes it more attractive for employed workers to quit: When unemployment is low, it is easy to find another job. That means, when unemployment decreases, a firm that wants to avoid an increase in quits will have to increase wages to induce workers to stay with the firm. When this happens, lower unemployment will again lead to higher wages. Conversely, higher unemployment will lead to lower wages.

Wages, Prices, and Unemployment

We capture our discussion of wage determination by using the following equation:

$$W = P^e F(u, z) \tag{6.1}$$
$$(-, +)$$

The aggregate nominal wage W depends on three factors:

■ The expected price level P^e
■ The unemployment rate u
■ A catchall variable z that stands for all other variables that may affect the outcome of wage setting.

Let's look at each factor.

The Expected Price Level

First, ignore the difference between the expected and the actual price level and ask: Why does the price level affect nominal wages? The answer: Because both workers and firms care about *real wages*, not nominal wages.

■ Workers do not care about how many dollars they receive but about how many goods they can buy with those dollars. In other words, they do not care about the nominal wages they receive, but about the nominal wages (W) they receive relative to the price of the goods they buy (P). They care about W/P.

■ In the same way, firms do not care about the nominal wages they pay but about the nominal wages (W) they pay relative to the price of the goods they sell (P). So they also care about W/P.

Think of it another way: If workers expect the price level—the price of the goods they buy—to double, they will ask for a doubling of their nominal wage. If firms expect the price level—the price of the goods they sell—to double, they will be willing to double the nominal wage. So, if both workers and firms expect the price level to double, they will agree to double the nominal wage, keeping the real wage constant. This is captured in equation (6.1): A doubling in the expected price level leads to a doubling of the nominal wage chosen when wages are set.

An increase in the expected price level leads to an increase in the nominal wage, in ▶ the same proportion.

Return now to the distinction we set aside at the start of the paragraph: Why do wages depend on the *expected price level*, P^e, rather than the *actual price level*, P?

Because wages are set in nominal (dollar) terms, and when they are set, the relevant price level is not yet known.

For example, in some union contracts in the United States, nominal wages are set in advance for three years. Unions and firms have to decide what nominal wages will be over the following three years based on what they expect the price level to be over those three years. Even when wages are set by firms, or by bargaining between the firm and each worker, nominal wages are typically set for a year. If the price level goes up unexpectedly during the year, nominal wages are typically not readjusted. (How workers and firms form expectations of the price level will occupy us for much of the next three chapters; we will leave this issue aside for the moment.)

The Unemployment Rate

Also affecting the aggregate wage in equation (6.1) is the unemployment rate u. The minus sign under u indicates that an increase in the unemployment rate *decreases* wages.

The fact that wages depend on the unemployment rate was one of the main conclusions of our earlier discussion. If we think of wages as being determined by bargaining, then higher unemployment weakens workers' bargaining power, forcing them to accept lower wages. If we think of wages as being determined by efficiency wage considerations, then higher unemployment allows firms to pay lower wages and still keep workers willing to work.

An increase in unemployment leads to a decrease in the ◀ nominal wage.

The Other Factors

The third variable in equation (6.1), z, is a catchall variable that stands for all the factors that affect wages given the expected price level and the unemployment rate. By convention, we will define z so that an increase in z implies an increase in the wage (thus, the positive sign under z in the equation). Our earlier discussion suggests a long ◀ list of potential factors here.

By the definition of z, an increase in z leads to an increase in the nominal wage.

Take, for example, **unemployment insurance**—the payment of unemployment benefits to workers who lose their jobs. There are very good reasons why society should provide some insurance to workers who lose their job and have a hard time finding another. But there is little question that, by making the prospects of unemployment less distressing, more generous unemployment benefits do increase wages at a given unemployment rate. To take an extreme example, suppose unemployment insurance did not exist. Some workers would have little to live on and would be willing to accept very low wages to avoid remaining unemployed. But unemployment insurance does exist, and it allows unemployed workers to hold out for higher wages. In this case, we can think of z as representing the level of unemployment benefits: At a given unemployment rate, higher unemployment benefits increase the wage.

It is easy to think of other factors. An increase in the minimum wage may increase not only the minimum wage itself, but also wages just above the minimum wage, leading to an increase in the average wage, W, at a given unemployment rate. Or take an increase in **employment protection**, which makes it more expensive for firms to lay off workers. Such a change is likely to increase the bargaining power of workers covered by this protection (laying them off and hiring other workers is now more costly for firms), increasing the wage for a given unemployment rate.

We will explore some of these factors as we go along.

6-4 Price Determination

Having looked at wage determination, let's now turn to price determination.

The prices set by firms depend on the costs they face. These costs depend, in turn, on the nature of the **production function**—the relation between the inputs used in production and the quantity of output produced—and on the prices of these inputs.

For the moment, we will assume firms produce goods using labor as the only factor of production. We will write the production function as follows:

$$Y = AN$$

where Y is output, N is employment, and A is labor productivity. This way of writing the production function implies that **labor productivity**—output per worker—is constant and equal to A.

It should be clear that this is a strong simplification. In reality, firms use other factors of production in addition to labor. They use capital—machines and factories. They use raw materials—oil, for example. Moreover, there is technological progress, so that labor productivity (A) is not constant but steadily increases over time. We shall introduce these complications later. We will introduce raw materials in Chapter 7 when we discuss changes in the price of oil. We will focus on the role of capital and technological progress when we turn to the determination of output in the *long run* in Chapters 10 through 13. For the moment, though, this simple relation between output and employment will make our lives easier and still serve our purposes.

Given the assumption that labor productivity, A, is constant, we can make one further simplification. We can choose the units of output so that one worker produces one unit of output—in other words, so that $A = 1$. (This way we do not have to carry the letter A around, and this will simplify notation.) With this assumption, the production function becomes

$$Y = N \tag{6.2}$$

The production function $Y = N$ implies that the cost of producing one more unit of output is the cost of employing one more worker, at wage W. Using the terminology introduced in your microeconomics course: The marginal cost of production—the cost of producing one more unit of output—is equal to W.

If there were perfect competition in the goods market, the price of a unit of output would be equal to marginal cost: P would be equal to W. But many goods markets are not competitive, and firms charge a price higher than their marginal cost. A simple way of capturing this fact is to assume that firms set their price according to

$$P = (1 + m)W \tag{6.3}$$

where m is the **markup** of the price over the cost. If goods markets were perfectly competitive, m would be equal to zero, and the price P would simply equal the cost W. To the extent they are not competitive and firms have market power, m is positive, and the price P will exceed the cost W by a factor equal to $(1 + m)$.

6-5 The Natural Rate of Unemployment

Let's now look at the implications of wage and price determination for unemployment.

For the rest of this chapter, we shall do so under the assumption that nominal wages depend on the actual price level, P, rather than on the expected price level, P^e (why we make this assumption will become clear soon). Under this additional

Using a term from microeconomics: This assumption implies constant returns to labor in production. If firms double the number of workers they employ, they double the amount of output they produce.

The rest of the chapter is based on the assumption that $P^e = P$.

assumption, wage setting and price setting determine the equilibrium (also called "natural") rate of unemployment. Let's see how.

The Wage-Setting Relation

Given the assumption that nominal wages depend on the actual price level (P) rather than on the expected price level (P^e), equation (6.1), which characterizes wage determination, becomes:

$$W = PF(u, z)$$

Dividing both sides by the price level,

$$\frac{W}{P} = F(u, z) \qquad (6.4)$$

$$(-, +)$$

Wage determination implies a negative relation between the real wage, W/P, and the unemployment rate, u: *The higher the unemployment rate, the lower the real wage chosen by wage setters*. The intuition is straightforward: The higher the unemployment rate, the weaker the workers' bargaining position, and the lower the real wage will be.

This relation between the real wage and the rate of unemployment—let's call it the **wage-setting relation**—is drawn in Figure 6-6. The real wage is measured on the vertical axis. The unemployment rate is measured on the horizontal axis. The wage-setting relation is drawn as the downward–sloping curve *WS* (for wage setting): The higher the unemployment rate, the lower the real wage.

"Wage setters": Unions and firms if wages are set by collective bargaining; individual workers and firms if wages are set on a case-by-case basis; firms if wages are set on a take-it-or-leave-it basis.

The Price–Setting Relation

Let's now look at the implications of price determination. If we divide both sides of the price–determination equation, (6.3), by the nominal wage, we get

$$\frac{P}{W} = 1 + m \qquad (6.5)$$

The ratio of the price level to the wage implied by the price-setting behavior of firms equals 1 plus the markup. Now invert both sides of this equation to get the implied real wage:

$$\frac{W}{P} = \frac{1}{1 + m} \qquad (6.6)$$

Note what this equation says: *Price-setting decisions determine the real wage paid by firms*. An increase in the markup leads firms to increase their prices given the wage they have to pay; equivalently, it leads to a decrease in the real wage.

The step from equation (6.5) to equation (6.6) is algebraically straightforward. But how price setting actually determines the real wage paid by firms may not be intuitively obvious. Think of it this way: Suppose the firm you work for increases its markup and therefore increases the price of its product. Your real wage does not change very much: You are still paid the same nominal wage, and the product produced by the firm is at most a small part of your consumption basket.

Now suppose that not only the firm you work for, but all the firms in the economy increase their markup. All the prices go up. Even if you are paid the same nominal

Figure 6-6

Wages, Prices, and the Natural Rate of Unemployment

The natural rate of unemployment is the unemployment rate such that the real wage chosen in wage setting is equal to the real wage implied by price setting.

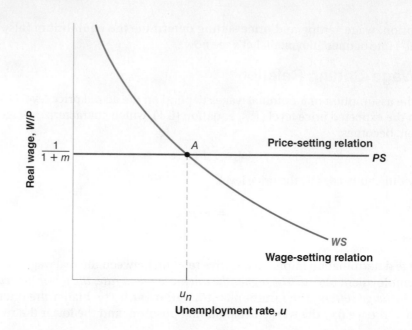

wage, your real wage goes down. So, the higher the markup set by firms, the lower your (and everyone else's) real wage will be. This is what equation (6.6) says.

The **price-setting relation** in equation (6.6) is drawn as the horizontal line *PS* (for price setting) in Figure 6-6. The real wage implied by price setting is $1/(1 + m)$; it does not depend on the unemployment rate.

Equilibrium Real Wages and Unemployment

Equilibrium in the labor market requires that the real wage chosen in wage setting be equal to the real wage implied by price setting. (This way of stating equilibrium may sound strange if you learned to think in terms of labor supply and labor demand in your microeconomics course. The relation between wage setting and price setting, on the one hand, and labor supply and labor demand, on the other, is closer than it looks at first and is explored further in the appendix at the end of this chapter.) In Figure 6-6, equilibrium is therefore given by point *A*, and the equilibrium unemployment rate is given by u_n.

We can also characterize the equilibrium unemployment rate algebraically; eliminating W/P between equations (6.4) and (6.6) gives

$$F(u_n, z) = \frac{1}{1 + m} \tag{6.7}$$

The equilibrium unemployment rate, u_n, is such that the real wage chosen in wage setting—the left side of equation (6.7)—is equal to the real wage implied by price setting—the right side of equation (6.7).

The equilibrium unemployment rate, u_n is called the **natural rate of unemployment** (which is why we have used the subscript *n* to denote it). The terminology has become standard, so we shall adopt it, but this is actually a bad choice of words. The word "natural" suggests a constant of nature, one that is unaffected by institutions and policy. As its derivation makes clear, however, the "natural" rate of unemployment is anything but natural. The positions of the wage-setting and price-setting curves, and thus the equilibrium unemployment rate, depend on both *z* and *m*. Consider two examples:

"Natural," in *Webster's Dictionary*, means "in a state provided by nature, without ► man-made changes."

■ An increase in unemployment benefits. An increase in unemployment benefits can be represented by an increase in *z*: Since an increase in benefits makes the

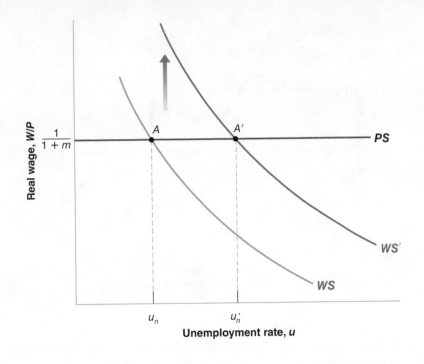

Figure 6-7

Unemployment Benefits and the Natural Rate of Unemployment

An increase in unemployment benefits leads to an increase in the natural rate of unemployment.

prospect of unemployment less painful, it increases the wage set by wage setters at a given unemployment rate. So it shifts the wage-setting relation up, from WS to WS' in Figure 6-7. The economy moves along the PS line, from A to A'. The natural rate of unemployment increases from u_n to u_n'.

In words: At a given unemployment rate, higher unemployment benefits lead to a higher real wage. A higher unemployment rate is needed to bring the real wage back to what firms are willing to pay.

- A less stringent enforcement of existing antitrust legislation. To the extent that this allows firms to collude more easily and increase their market power, it will lead to an increase in their markup—an increase in m. The increase in m implies a decrease in the real wage paid by firms, and so it shifts the price-setting relation down, from PS to PS' in Figure 6-8. The economy moves along WS. The equilibrium moves from A to A', and the natural rate of unemployment increases from u_n to u_n'.

In words: By letting firms increase their prices given the wage, less stringent enforcement of antitrust legislation leads to a decrease in the real wage. Higher unemployment is required to make workers accept this lower real wage, leading to an increase in the natural rate of unemployment.

Factors like the generosity of unemployment benefits or antitrust legislation can hardly be thought of as the result of nature. Rather, they reflect various characteristics of the structure of the economy. For that reason, a better name for the equilibrium rate of unemployment would be the **structural rate of unemployment**, but so far the name has not caught on.

From Unemployment to Employment

Associated with the natural rate of unemployment is a **natural level of employment**, the level of employment that prevails when unemployment is equal to its natural rate.

An increase in unemployment benefits shifts the wage setting curve up. The economy ◀ moves along the price-setting curve. Equilibrium unemployment increases.

◀ This has led some economists to call unemployment a "discipline device": Higher unemployment is the device that forces wages to correspond to what firms are willing to pay.

◀ An increase in the markup shifts the price setting curve (line in this case). The economy moves along the wage-setting curve. Equilibrium unemployment increases.

◀ This name has been suggested by Edmund Phelps, from Columbia University. Phelps was awarded the Nobel Prize in 2006. For more on some of his contributions, see Chapters 8 and 25.

Figure 6-8

Markups and the Natural Rate of Unemployment

An increase in markups decreases the real wage and leads to an increase in the natural rate of unemployment.

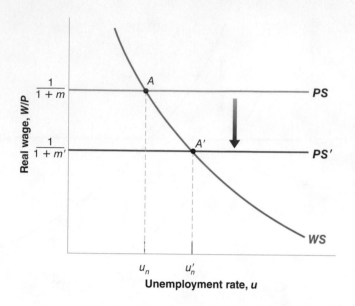

Let's review the relation among unemployment, employment, and the labor force. Let U denote unemployment, N denote employment, and L the labor force. Then:

$$u \equiv \frac{U}{L} = \frac{L - N}{L} = 1 - \frac{N}{L}$$

The first step follows from the definition of the unemployment rate (u). The second follows from the fact that, from the definition of the labor force, the level of unemployment (U) equals the labor force (L) minus employment (N). The third step follows from simplifying the fraction. Putting all three steps together: The unemployment rate u equals 1 minus the ratio of employment N to the labor force L.

$L = N + U \Rightarrow U = L - N$ ▶

Rearranging to get employment in terms of the labor force and the unemployment rate gives:

$$N = L(1 - u)$$

Employment N is equal to the labor force L, times 1 minus the unemployment rate u. So, if the natural rate of unemployment is u_n and the labor force is equal to L, the natural level of employment N_n is given by

$$N_n = L(1 - u_n)$$

For example, if the labor force is 150 million and the natural rate of unemployment is, say, 5%, then the natural level of employment is $150 \times (1 - 0.05) = 142.5$ million.

From Employment to Output

Finally, associated with the natural level of employment is the **natural level of output**, the level of production when employment is equal to the natural level of employment. Given the production function we have used in this chapter ($Y = N$), the natural level of output Y_n is easy to derive. It is given by

$$Y_n = N_n = L(1 - u_n)$$

Using equation (6.7) and the relations among the unemployment rate, employment, and the output we just derived, the natural level of output satisfies the following equation:

$$F\left(1 - \frac{Y_n}{L}, z\right) = \frac{1}{1 + m} \tag{6.8}$$

The natural level of output (Y_n) is such that, at the associated rate of unemployment $(u_n = 1 - Y_n/L)$, the real wage chosen in wage setting—the left side of equation (6.8)—is equal to the real wage implied by price setting—the right side of equation (6.8). As you will see, equation (6.8) will turn out to be very useful in the next chapter. Make sure you understand it.

We have gone through many steps in this section. Let's summarize:

Assume that the expected price level is equal to the actual price level. Then:

- The real wage chosen in wage setting is a decreasing function of the unemployment rate.
- The real wage implied by price setting is constant.
- Equilibrium in the labor market requires that the real wage chosen in wage setting be equal to the real wage implied by price setting. This determines the equilibrium unemployment rate.
- This equilibrium unemployment rate is known as the natural rate of unemployment.
- Associated with the natural rate of unemployment is a natural level of employment and a natural level of output.

6-6 Where We Go from Here

We have just seen how equilibrium in the labor market determines the equilibrium unemployment rate (we have called it the natural rate of unemployment), which in turn determines the level of output (we have called it the natural level of output).

So, you may ask, what did we do in the previous four chapters? If equilibrium in the labor market determines the unemployment rate and, by implication, the level of output, why did we spend so much time looking at the goods and financial markets? What about our earlier conclusions that the level of output was determined by factors such as monetary policy, fiscal policy, consumer confidence, and so on—all factors that do not enter equation (6.8) and therefore do not affect the natural level of output?

The key to the answer lies in the difference between the short run and the medium run:

- We have derived the natural rate of unemployment and the associated levels of employment and output under two assumptions. First, we have assumed equilibrium in the labor market. Second, we have assumed that the price level was equal to the expected price level.
- However, there is no reason for the second assumption to be true in the *short run*. The price level may well turn out to be different from what was expected when nominal wages were set. Hence, in the short run, there is no reason for unemployment to be equal to the natural rate or for output to be equal to its natural level.

As we will see in the next chapter, the factors that determine movements in output *in the short run* are indeed the factors we focused on in the preceding three chapters: monetary policy, fiscal policy, and so on. Your time (and mine) was not wasted.

In the short run, the factors that determine movements in output are the factors we focused on in the preceding three chapters: monetary policy, fiscal policy, and so on.

In the medium run, output tends to return to the natural level, and the factors that determine output are the factors we have focused on this chapter. ▷

■ But expectations are unlikely to be systematically wrong (say, too high or too low) forever. That is why, in the medium run, unemployment tends to return to the natural rate, and output tends to return to the natural level. *In the medium run*, the factors that determine unemployment and output are the factors that appear in equations (6.7) and (6.8).

These, in short, are the answers to the questions asked in the first paragraph of this chapter. Developing these answers in detail will be our task in the next three chapters.

Summary

■ The labor force consists of those who are working (employed) or looking for work (unemployed). The unemployment rate is equal to the ratio of the number of unemployed to the number in the labor force. The participation rate is equal to the ratio of the labor force to the working-age population.

■ The U.S. labor market is characterized by large flows between employment, unemployment, and "out of the labor force." On average, each month, about 47% of the unemployed move out of unemployment, either to take a job or to drop out of the labor force.

■ Unemployment is high in recessions and low in expansions. During periods of high unemployment, the probability of losing a job increases and the probability of finding a job decreases.

■ Wages are set unilaterally by firms or by bargaining between workers and firms. They depend negatively on the unemployment rate and positively on the expected price level. The reason why wages depend on the expected price level is that they are typically set in nominal terms for some period of time. During that time, even if the price level turns out to be different from what was expected, wages are typically not readjusted.

■ The price set by firms depends on the wage and on the markup of prices over wages. The higher the markup chosen by firms, the higher the price given the wage, and thus the lower the real wage implied by price-setting decisions.

■ Equilibrium in the labor market requires that the real wage chosen in wage setting be equal to the real wage implied by price setting. Under the additional assumption that the expected price level is equal to the actual price level, equilibrium in the labor market determines the unemployment rate. This unemployment rate is known as the *natural rate of unemployment*.

■ In general, the actual price level may turn out to be different from the price level expected by wage setters. Therefore, the unemployment rate need not be equal to the natural rate.

■ The coming chapters will show that:
In the short run, unemployment and output are determined by the factors we focused on in the previous three chapters, but, in the medium run, unemployment tends to return to the natural rate, and output tends to return to its natural level.

Key Terms

Questions and Problems

1. Using the information in this chapter, label each of the following statements true, false, or uncertain. Explain briefly.

a. Since 1950, the participation rate in the United States has remained roughly constant at 60%.

b. Each month, the flows into and out of employment are very small compared to the size of the labor force.

c. Fewer than 10% of all unemployed workers exit the unemployment pool each year.

d. The unemployment rate tends to be high in recessions and low in expansions.

e. Most workers are typically paid their reservation wage.

f. Workers who do not belong to unions have no bargaining power.

g. It may be in the best interest of employers to pay wages higher than their workers' reservation wage.

h. The natural rate of unemployment is unaffected by policy changes.

2. Answer the following questions using the information provided in this chapter.

a. As a percentage of the employed workers, what is the size of the flows into and out of employment (i.e., hires and separations) each month?

b. As a percentage of the unemployed workers, what is the size of the flows from unemployment into employment each month?

c. As a percentage of the unemployed, what is the size of the total flows out of unemployment each month? What is the average duration of unemployment?

d. As a percentage of the labor force, what is the size of the total flows into and out of the labor force each month?

e. In the text we say that there is an average of 400,000 new workers entering the labor force each month. What percentage of total flows into the labor force do new workers entering the labor force constitute?

3. The natural rate of unemployment

Suppose that the markup of goods prices over marginal cost is 5%, and that the wage-setting equation is

$$W = P(1 - u),$$

where u is the unemployment rate.

a. What is the real wage, as determined by the price-setting equation?

b. What is the natural rate of unemployment?

c. Suppose that the markup of prices over costs increases to 10%. What happens to the natural rate of unemployment? Explain the logic behind your answer.

4. Reservation wages

In the mid-1980s, a famous supermodel once said that she would not get out of bed for less than $10,000 (presumably per day).

a. What is your own reservation wage?

b. Did your first job pay more than your reservation wage at the time?

c. Relative to your reservation wage at the time you accept each job, which job pays more: your first one or the one you expect to have in 10 years?

d. Explain your answers to parts (a) through (c) in terms of the efficiency wage theory.

e. Part of the policy response to the crisis was to extend the length of time workers could receive unemployment benefits. How would this affect reservation wages if this change was made permanent?

5. Bargaining power and wage determination

Even in the absence of collective bargaining, workers do have some bargaining power that allows them to receive wages higher than their reservation wage. Each worker's bargaining power depends both on the nature of the job and on the economy-wide labor market conditions. Let's consider each factor in turn.

a. Compare the job of a delivery person and a computer network administrator. In which of these jobs does a worker have more bargaining power? Why?

b. For any given job, how do labor market conditions affect a worker's bargaining power? Which labor-market variable would you look at to assess labor-market conditions?

c. Suppose that for given labor-market conditions [the variable you identified in part (b)], worker bargaining power throughout the economy increases. What effect would this have on the real wage in the medium run? in the short run? What determines the real wage in the model described in this chapter?

6. The existence of unemployment

a. Suppose the unemployment rate is very low. How easy is it for firms to find workers to hire? How easy is it for workers to find jobs? What do your answers imply about the relative bargaining power of workers and firms when the unemployment rate is very low? What do your answers imply about what happens to the wage as the unemployment rate gets very low?

b. Given your answer to part (a), why is there unemployment in the economy? (What would happen to real wages if the unemployment rate were equal to zero?)

7. The informal labor market

You learned in Chapter 2 that informal work at home (e.g., preparing meals, taking care of children) is not counted as part of GDP. Such work also does not constitute employment in labor-market statistics. With these observations in mind, consider two economies, each with 100 people, divided into 25 households, each composed of four people. In each household, one person stays at home and prepares the food, two people work in the nonfood sector, and one person is unemployed. Assume that the workers outside food preparation produce the same actual and measured output in both economies.

In the first economy, EatIn, the 25 food-preparation work-ers (one per household) cook for their families and do not work outside the home. All meals are prepared and eaten at home. The 25 food-preparation workers in this economy do not seek work in the formal labor market (and when asked, they say they are not looking for work). In the second economy, EatOut, the 25 food-preparation workers are employed by restaurants. All meals are purchased in restaurants.

a. Calculate measured employment and unemployment and the measured labor force for each economy. Calculate the measured unemployment rate and participation rate for each economy. In which economy is measured GDP higher?

b. Suppose now that EatIn's economy changes. A few restau-rants open, and the food preparation workers in 10 house-holds take jobs restaurants. The members of these 10 households now eat all of their meals in restaurants. The food-preparation workers in the remaining 15 households continue to work at home and do not seek jobs in the for-mal sector. The members of these 15 households continue to eat all of their meals at home. Without calculating the numbers, what will happen to measured employment and unemployment and to the measured labor force, unem-ployment rate, and participation rate in EatIn? What will happen to measured GDP in EatIn?

c. Suppose that you want to include work at home in GDP and the employment statistics. How would you measure the value of work at home in GDP? How would you alter the definitions of *employment*, *unemployment*, and *out of the labor force*?

d. Given your new definitions in part (c), would the labor-market statistics differ for EatIn and EatOut? Assuming that the food produced by these economies has the same value, would measured GDP in these economies differ? Under your new definitions, would the experiment in part (b) have any effect on the labor market or GDP statistics for EatIn?

EXPLORE FURTHER

8. Unemployment spells and long-term unemployment

According to the data presented in this chapter, about 47% of unemployed workers leave unemployment each month.

a. What is the probability that an unemployed worker will still be unemployed after one month? two months? six months?

Now consider the composition of the unemployment pool. We will use a simple experiment to determine the proportion of the unemployed who have been unem-ployed six months or more. Suppose the number of unem-ployed workers is constant and equal to x (where x is some constant). Each month, 47% of the unemployed find jobs, and an equivalent number of previously employed work-ers become unemployed.

b. Consider the group of x workers who are unemployed this month. After a month, what percentage of this group will still be unemployed? (*Hint*: If 47% of unemployed workers find jobs every month, what percentage of the original x unemployed workers did not find jobs in the first month?)

c. After a second month, what percentage of the original x unemployed workers has been unemployed for at least two months? [*Hint*: Given your answer to part (b), what percentage of those unemployed for at least one month do not find jobs in the second month?] After the sixth month, what percentage of the original x unemployed workers has been unemployed for at least six months?

d. Using Table B-44 of the *Economic Report of the President* (**www.gpoaccess.gov/eop/**), compute the proportion of un-employed who have been unemployed six months or more (27 weeks or more) for each year between 1996 and 2010. How do these numbers compare with the answer you obtained in part (c)? Can you guess what may account for the difference between the actual numbers and the answer you obtained in this problem? (*Hint*: Suppose that the probability of exiting unemployment goes down the longer you are unemployed.)

e. Part of the policy response to the crisis was an extension of the length of time that an unemployed worker could re-ceive unemployment benefits. How would you predict this change would affect the proportion of those unemployed more than six months?

9. Go to the Web site maintained by the U.S. Bureau of Labor Statistics (**www.bls.gov**). Find the latest Employment Situation Summary. Look under the link "National Employment."

a. What are the latest monthly data on the size of the U.S. ci-vilian labor force, on the number of unemployed, and on the unemployment rate?

b. How many people are employed?

c. Compute the change in the number of unemployed from the first number in the table to the most recent month in the table. Do the same for the number of employed work-ers. Is the decline in unemployment equal to the increase in employment? Explain in words.

10. *The typical dynamics of unemployment over a recession.*

The table below shows the behavior of annual real GDP growth during three recessions. These data are from Table B-4 of the Economic Report of the President:

Year	Real GDP Growth	Unemployment Rate
1981	2.5	
1982	−1.9	
1983	4.5	
1990	1.9	
1991	−0.2	
1992	3.4	
2008	0.0	
2009	−2.6	
2010	2.9	

Use Table B-35 from the Economic Report of the President to fill in the annual values of the unemployment rate in the table above and consider these questions.

a. When is the unemployment rate in a recession higher, the year of declining output or the following year?

b. Explain the pattern of the unemployment rate after a recession if the production function is not linear in the workforce.

c. Explain the pattern of the unemployment rate after a recession if discouraged workers return to the labor force as the economy recovers.

d. The rate of unemployment remains substantially higher after the crisis-induced recession in 2009. In that recession, unemployment benefits were extended in length from 6 months to 12 months. What does the model predict the effect of this policy will be on the natural rate of unemployment? Do the data support this prediction in any way?

Further Reading

- A further discussion of unemployment along the lines of this chapter is given by Richard Layard, Stephen Nickell, and Richard Jackman in *The Unemployment Crisis* (Oxford: Oxford University Press, 1994).

APPENDIX: Wage- and Price-Setting Relations versus Labor Supply and Labor Demand

If you have taken a microeconomics course, you probably saw a representation of labor-market equilibrium in terms of labor supply and labor demand. You may therefore be asking yourself: How does the representation in terms of wage setting and price setting relate to the representation of the labor market I saw in that course?

In an important sense, the two representations are similar:

To see why, let's redraw Figure 6-6 in terms of the real wage on the vertical axis, and the level of *employment* (rather than the unemployment rate) on the horizontal axis. We do this in Figure 1.

Employment, N, is measured on the horizontal axis. The level of employment must be somewhere between zero and L, the labor force: Employment cannot exceed the number of people available for work, (i.e., the labor force). For any employment level N, unemployment is given by $U = L - N$. Knowing this, we can measure unemployment by starting from L and *moving to the left* on the horizontal axis: Unemployment is given by the distance between L and N. The lower is employment, N, the higher is unemployment, and by implication the higher is the unemployment rate, u.

Let's now draw the wage-setting and price-setting relations and characterize the equilibrium:

- An increase in employment (a movement to the right along the horizontal axis) implies a decrease in unemployment and therefore an increase in the real wage chosen in wage setting. Thus, the wage-setting relation is now *upward sloping*: Higher employment implies a higher real wage.
- The price-setting relation is still a horizontal line at $W/P = 1/(1 + m)$.

- The equilibrium is given by point A, with "natural" employment level N_n (and an implied natural unemployment rate equal to $u_n = (L - N_n)/L$).

In this figure the wage-setting relation looks like a labor-supply relation. As the level of employment increases, the real wage paid to workers increases as well. For that reason, the wage-setting relation is sometimes called the "labor-supply" relation (in quotes).

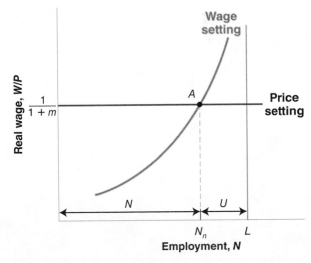

Figure 1

Wage and Price Setting and the Natural Level of Employment

What we have called the price-setting relation looks like a flat labor-demand relation. The reason it is flat rather than downward sloping has to do with our simplifying assumption of constant returns to labor in production. Had we assumed, more conventionally, that there were decreasing returns to labor in production, our price-setting curve would, like the standard labor-demand curve, be downward sloping: As employment increased, the marginal cost of production would increase, forcing firms to increase their prices given the wages they pay. In other words, the real wage implied by price setting would decrease as employment increased.

But, in a number of ways, the two approaches are different:

■ The standard labor-supply relation gives the wage at which a given number of workers are willing to work: The higher the wage, the larger the number of workers who are willing to work.

In contrast, the wage corresponding to a given level of employment in the wage-setting relation is the result of a process of bargaining between workers and firms, or unilateral wage setting by firms. Factors like the structure of collective bargaining or the use of wages to deter quits affect the wage-setting relation. In the real world, they seem to play an important role. Yet they play no role in the standard labor-supply relation.

■ The standard labor-demand relation gives the level of employment chosen by firms at a given real wage. It is derived under the assumption that firms operate in competitive goods and labor markets and therefore take wages and prices—and by implication the real wage—as given.

In contrast, the price-setting relation takes into account the fact that in most markets firms actually set prices. Factors such as the degree of competition in the goods market affect the price-setting relation by affecting the markup. But these factors aren't considered in the standard labor-demand relation.

■ In the labor supply–labor demand framework, those unemployed are *willingly unemployed*: At the equilibrium real wage, they prefer to be unemployed rather than work.

In contrast, in the wage setting–price setting framework, unemployment is likely to be involuntary. For example, if firms pay an efficiency wage—a wage above the reservation wage—workers would rather be employed than unemployed. Yet, in equilibrium, there is still involuntary unemployment. This also seems to capture reality better than does the labor supply–labor demand framework.

These are the three reasons why we have relied on the wage-setting and the price-setting relations rather than on the labor supply–labor demand approach to characterize equilibrium in this chapter.

Putting All Markets Together: The *AS–AD* Model

I n Chapter 5, we looked at the determination of output in the short run. In Chapter 6, we looked at the determination of output in the medium run. We are now ready to put the two together and look at the determination of output in both the short run and the medium run.

To do so, we use the equilibrium conditions for *all* the markets we have looked at so far—the goods and financial markets in Chapter 5, the labor market in Chapter 6.

Then, using these equilibrium conditions, we derive two relations:

The first relation, which we call the *aggregate supply relation*, captures the implications of equilibrium in the labor market; it builds on what you saw in Chapter 6.

The second relation, which we call the *aggregate demand relation*, captures the implications of equilibrium in both the goods market and financial markets; it builds on what you saw in Chapter 5.

Combining these two relations gives us the *AS–AD* model (for aggregate supply–aggregate demand). This chapter presents the basic version of the model. When confronted with a macroeconomic question, this is the version we typically use to organize our thoughts. For some questions—if we want to focus on the behavior of inflation, for example, or understand the role of the financial system in the current crisis—the basic *AS–AD* model must be extended. But it provides a base on which one can build, and this is what we shall do in the next two chapters.

This chapter is organized as follows:

Section 7-1 derives the aggregate supply relation, and Section 7-2 derives the aggregate demand relation.

Section 7-3 combines the two to characterize equilibrium output in the short run and in the medium run.

Section 7-4 looks at the dynamic effects of monetary policy.

Section 7-5 looks at the dynamic effects of fiscal policy.

Section 7-6 looks at the effects of an increase in the price of oil.

Section 7-7 summarizes.

7-1 Aggregate Supply

The **aggregate supply relation** captures the effects of output on the price level. It is derived from the behavior of wages and prices we described in Chapter 6.

In Chapter 6, we derived the following equation for wage determination (equation (6.1)):

$$W = P^e F(u, z)$$

The nominal wage W, set by wage setters, depends on the expected price level P^e, on the unemployment rate u, and on the catchall variable z for all the other factors that affect wage determination, from unemployment benefits to the form of collective bargaining.

Also in Chapter 6, we derived the following equation for price determination (equation (6.3)):

$$P = (1 + m)W$$

The price P set by firms (equivalently, the price level) is equal to the nominal wage W, times 1 plus the markup m.

We then used these two relations together with the additional assumption that the actual price level was equal to the expected price level. Under this additional assumption, we derived the natural rate of unemployment and, by implication, the natural level of output.

The difference in this chapter is that we will not impose this additional assumption. (It will turn out that the price level is equal to the expected price level in the medium run but will typically not be equal to the expected price level in the short run.) Without this additional assumption, the price-setting relation and the wage-setting relation give us a relation, which we now derive, among the price level, the output level, and the expected price level.

The first step is to eliminate the nominal wage W between the two equations. Replacing the nominal wage in the second equation above by its expression from the first gives

$$P = P^e (1 + m) F(u, z) \tag{7.1}$$

The price level P depends on the expected price level P^e, on the unemployment rate u (as well as on the markup m and on the catchall variable z; but we will assume both m and z are constant here).

The second step is to replace the unemployment rate u with its expression in terms of output. To replace u, recall the relation between the unemployment rate, employment, and output we derived in Chapter 6:

$$u = \frac{U}{L} = \frac{L - N}{L} = 1 - \frac{N}{L} = 1 - \frac{Y}{L}$$

The first equality follows from the definition of the unemployment rate. The second equality follows from the definition of unemployment ($U \equiv L - N$). The third equality just simplifies the fraction. The fourth equality follows from the specification of the production function, which says that to produce one unit of output requires one worker, so that $Y = N$. What we get then is

$$u = 1 - \frac{Y}{L}$$

A better name would be "the labor market relation." But because the relation looks graphically like a supply curve (there is a positive relation between output and the price), it is called "the aggregate supply relation." we follow this tradition.

In words: For a given labor force, the higher the output, the lower the unemployment rate.

Replacing u by $1 - (Y/L)$ in equation (7.1) gives us the *aggregate supply relation, or AS relation for short*:

$$P = P^e (1 + m) F\left(1 - \frac{Y}{L}, z\right) \tag{7.2}$$

The price level P depends on the expected price level P^e and the level of output Y (and also on the markup m, the catchall variable z, and the labor force L, which we all take as constant here). The AS relation has two important properties:

The first property is that, given the expected price level, an increase in output leads to an increase in the price level. This is the result of four underlying steps:

An increase in Y leads to an increase in P.

1. An increase in output leads to an increase in employment.

2. The increase in employment leads to a decrease in unemployment and therefore to a decrease in the unemployment rate.

3. The lower unemployment rate leads to an increase in the nominal wage.

4. The increase in the nominal wage leads to an increase in the prices set by firms and therefore to an increase in the price level.

The second property is that, given unemployment, an increase in the expected price level leads, one for one, to an increase in the actual price level. For example, if the expected price level doubles, then the price level will also double. This effect works through wages:

An increase in P^e leads to an increase in P.

1. If wage setters expect the price level to be higher, they set a higher nominal wage.

2. The increase in the nominal wage leads to an increase in costs, which leads to an increase in the prices set by firms and a higher price level.

If output is equal to the natural level of output, the price level is equal to the expected price level.

The relation between the price level P and output Y, for a given value of the expected price level P^e, is represented by the curve AS in Figure 7-1. The AS curve has three properties that will prove useful in what follows:

■ The aggregate supply curve is upward sloping. Put another way, an increase in output Y leads to an increase in the price level P. You saw why earlier.

Put informally: High economic activity puts pressure on prices.

■ The aggregate supply curve goes through point A, where $Y = Y_n$ and $P = P^e$. Put another way: When output Y is equal to the natural level of output Y_n, the price level P turns out to be exactly equal to the expected price level P^e.

　　How do we know this? From the definition of the natural level of output in Chapter 6. Recall that we defined the natural rate of unemployment (and by implication the natural level of output) as the rate of unemployment (and by implication the level of output) that prevails if the price level and the expected price level are equal.

Figure 7-1

The Aggregate Supply Curve

Given the expected price level, an increase in output leads to an increase in the price level.

Figure 7-2

The Effect of an Increase in the Expected Price Level on the Aggregate Supply Curve

An increase in the expected price level shifts the aggregate supply curve up.

This property—that the price level equals the expected price level when output is equal to the natural level of output—has two straightforward implications:

When output is above the natural level of output, the price level turns out to be higher than expected. In Figure 7-1: If Y is to the right of Y_n, P is higher than P^e. Conversely: When output is below the natural level of output, the price level turns to be lower than expected. In Figure 7-1: If Y is to the left of Y_n, P is lower than P^e.

■ An increase in the expected price level P^e shifts the aggregate supply curve up. Conversely: A decrease in the expected price level shifts the aggregate supply curve down.

This third property is shown in Figure 7-2. Suppose the expected price level increases from P^e to $P^{e'}$. At a given level of output, and, correspondingly, at a given unemployment rate, the increase in the expected price level leads to an increase in wages, which leads in turn to an increase in prices. So, at any level of output, the price level is higher: The aggregate supply curve shifts up. In particular, instead of going through point A (where $Y = Y_n$ and $P = P^e$), the aggregate supply curve now goes through point A' (where $Y = Y_n$, $P = P^{e'}$).

 Recall: When output equals the natural level of output, the price level turns out to be equal to the expected price level.

Let's summarize:

■ Starting from wage determination and price determination in the labor market, we have derived the *aggregate supply relation*.

■ This relation implies that for a given expected price level, the price level is an increasing function of the level of output. It is represented by an upward-sloping curve, called the *aggregate supply curve*.

■ Increases in the expected price level shift the aggregate supply curve up; decreases in the expected price level shift the aggregate supply curve down.

7-2 Aggregate Demand

The **aggregate demand relation** captures the effect of the price level on output. It is derived from the equilibrium conditions in the goods and financial markets we described in Chapter 5.

In Chapter 5, we derived the following equation for goods-market equilibrium (equation (5.2)):

$$Y = C(Y - T) + I(Y, i) + G$$

Equilibrium in the goods market requires that output equal the demand for goods—the sum of consumption, investment, and government spending. This is the *IS* relation.

Also in Chapter 5, we derived the following equation for equilibrium in financial markets (equation (5.3)):

$$\frac{M}{P} = Y L(i)$$

Equilibrium in financial markets requires that the supply of money equal the demand for money. This is the *LM* relation.

Recall that what appears on the left side of the *LM* equation is the real money stock, M/P. We focused in Chapters 5 and 6 on changes in the real money stock that came from changes in nominal money M by the Fed. But changes in the real money stock M/P can also come from changes in the price level P. A 10% increase in the price level P has the same effect on the real money stock as a 10% decrease in the stock of nominal money M : Either leads to a 10% decrease in the real money stock.

Using the *IS* and *LM* relations, we can derive the relation between the price level and the level of output implied by equilibrium in the goods and financial markets. We do this in Figure 7-3.

■ Figure 7-3(a) draws the *IS* curve and the *LM* curve. The *IS* curve is drawn for given values of G and T. It is downward sloping: An increase in the interest rate leads to a decrease in output. The *LM* curve is drawn for a given value of M/P. It is upward sloping: An increase in output increases the demand for money, and the interest rate

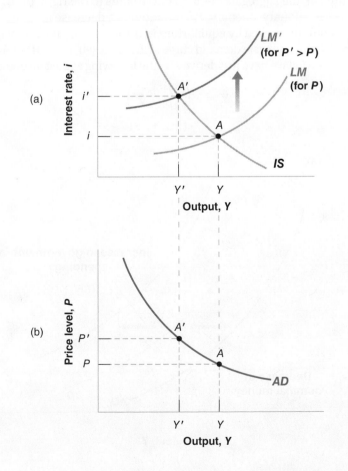

Figure 7-3

The Derivation of the Aggregate Demand Curve

An increase in the price level leads to a decrease in output.

increases so as to maintain equality of money demand and the (unchanged) money supply. The point at which the goods market and the financial markets are both in equilibrium is at the intersection of the *IS* curve and the *LM* curve, at point *A*.

Now consider the effects of an increase in the price level from *P* to *P'*. Given the stock of nominal money, *M*, the increase in the price level *P* decreases the real money stock, *M/P*. This implies that the *LM* curve shifts up: At a given level of output, the lower real money stock leads to an increase in the interest rate. The economy moves along the *IS* curve, and the equilibrium moves from *A* to *A'*. The interest rate increases from *i* to *i'*, and output decreases from *Y* to *Y'*. In short: The increase in the price level leads to a decrease in output.

In words: The increase in the price level leads to a decrease in the real money stock. This monetary contraction leads to an increase in the interest rate, which leads in turn to a lower demand for goods and lower output.

■ The negative relation between output and the price level is drawn as the down-sloping *AD* curve in Figure 7-3(b). Points *A* and *A'* in Figure 7-3(b) correspond to points *A* and *A'* in Figure 7-3(a). An increase in the price level from *P* to *P'* leads to a decrease in output from *Y* to *Y'*. This curve is called the *aggregate demand curve*. The underlying negative relation between output and the price level is called the *aggregate demand relation*.

Any variable other than the price level that shifts either the IS curve or the LM curve also shifts the aggregate demand relation.

Take, for example, an increase in government spending *G*. At a given price level, the level of output implied by equilibrium in the goods and the financial markets is higher: In Figure 7-4, the aggregate demand curve shifts to the right, from *AD* to *AD'*.

Or take a contractionary, open market operation—a decrease in *M*. At a given price level, the level of output implied by equilibrium in the goods and the financial markets is lower. In Figure 7-4, the aggregate demand curve shifts to the left, from *AD* to *AD"*.

Let's represent what we have just derived by the following aggregate demand relation:

$$Y = Y\left(\frac{M}{P}, G, T\right) \tag{7.3}$$
$$(+, \ +, -)$$

A better name would be "the goods market and financial markets relation." But, because it is a long name, and because the relation looks graphically like a demand ▶ curve (that is, a negative relation between output and the price), it is called the "aggregate demand relation." We shall, again, follow tradition.

Recall that open market operations are the means through ▶ which the Fed changes the nominal money stock.

Figure 7-4

Shifts of the Aggregate Demand Curve

At a given price level, an increase in government spending increases output, shifting the aggregate demand curve to the right. At a given price level, a decrease in nominal money decreases output, shifting the aggregate demand curve to the left.

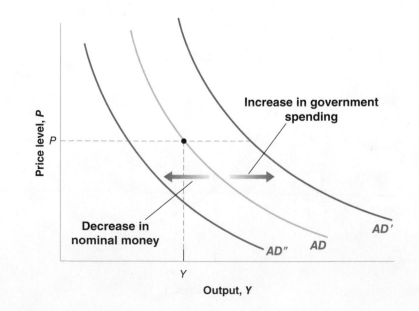

Output Y is an increasing function of the real money stock M/P, an increasing function of government spending G, and a decreasing function of taxes, T.

Given monetary and fiscal policy—that is, given M, G, and T—an increase in the price level P leads to a decrease in the real money stock, M/P, which leads to a decrease in output. This is the relation captured by the AD curve in Figure 7-3(b).

Let's summarize:

■ Starting from the equilibrium conditions for the goods and financial markets, we have derived the *aggregate demand relation*.

■ This relation implies that the level of output is a decreasing function of the price level. It is represented by a downward-sloping curve, called the *aggregate demand curve*.

■ Changes in monetary or fiscal policy—or, more generally, in any variable, other than the price level, that shifts the IS or the LM curves—shift the aggregate demand curve.

7-3 Equilibrium in the Short Run and in the Medium Run

The next step is to put the AS and the AD relations together. From Sections 7-1 and 7-2, the two relations are given by

$$AS \text{ relation} \qquad P = P^e (1 + m) F\left(1 - \frac{Y}{L}, z\right)$$

$$AD \text{ relation} \qquad Y = Y\left(\frac{M}{P}, G, T\right)$$

For a given value of the expected price level, P^e (which enters the aggregate supply relation), and for given values of the monetary and fiscal policy variables M, G, and T (which enter the aggregate demand relation), these two relations determine the equilibrium values of output, Y, and the price level, P.

Note the equilibrium depends on the value of P^e. The value of P^e determines the position of the aggregate supply curve (go back to Figure 7-2), and the position of the aggregate supply curve affects the equilibrium. In the short run, we can take P^e, the price level expected by wage setters when they last set wages, as given. But, over time, P^e is likely to change, shifting the aggregate supply curve and changing the equilibrium. With this in mind, we first characterize equilibrium in the short run—that is, taking P^e as given. We then look at how P^e changes over time, and how that change affects the equilibrium.

Equilibrium in the Short Run

The short–run equilibrium is characterized in Figure 7-5:

■ The aggregate supply curve AS is drawn for a given value of P^e. It is upward sloping: The higher the level of output, the higher the price level. The position of the curve depends on P^e. Recall from Section 7-1 that, when output is equal to the natural level of output, the price level is equal to the expected price level. This means that, in Figure 7-5, the aggregate supply curve goes through point B : If $Y = Y_n$, then $P = P^e$.

■ The aggregate demand curve AD is drawn for given values of M, G, and T. It is downward sloping: The higher the price level, the lower the level of output.

The equilibrium is given by the intersection of the AS and AD curves at point A. By construction, at point A, the goods market, the financial markets, and the labor market are *all* in equilibrium. The fact that the labor market is in equilibrium is because point

Figure 7-5

The Short-Run Equilibrium

The equilibrium is given by the intersection of the aggregate supply curve and the aggregate demand curve. At point A, the labor market, the goods market, and financial markets are all in equilibrium.

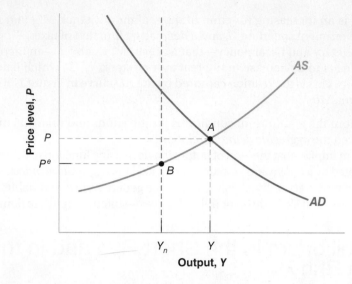

A is on the aggregate supply curve. That fact that the goods and financial markets are in equilibrium is because point A is on the aggregate demand curve. The equilibrium level of output and price level are given by Y and P.

There is no reason why, in general, equilibrium output Y should be equal to the natural level of output Y_n. Equilibrium output depends both on the position of the aggregate supply curve (and therefore on the value of P^e) and on the position of the aggregate demand curve (and therefore on the values of M, G, and T). As we have drawn the two curves, Y is greater than Y_n: In other words, the equilibrium level of output exceeds the natural level of output. But clearly we could have drawn the AS and the AD curves so equilibrium output Y was smaller than the natural level of output Y_n.

Figure 7-5 gives us our first important conclusion: In the *short run*, there is no reason why output should equal the natural level of output. Whether it does depends on the specific values of the expected price level and the values of the variables affecting the position of aggregate demand.

We must now ask, What happens over time? More precisely: Suppose, in the short run, output is above the natural level of output—as is the case in Figure 7-5. What will happen over time? Will output eventually return to the natural level of output? If so, how? These are the questions we take up in the rest of this section.

From the Short Run to the Medium Run

If you live in an economy where the inflation rate is typically positive, then, even if the price level this year turns out equal to what you expected, you may still take into account the presence of inflation and expect the price level to be higher next year. In this chapter, we look ▶ at an economy in which there is no steady inflation. We will focus on the dynamics of output and inflation in the next chapter.

To think about what happens over time, consider Figure 7-6. The curves denoted AS and AD are the same as in Figure 7-5, and so the short–run equilibrium is at point A—which corresponds to point A in Figure 7-5. Output is equal to Y, and is higher than the natural level of output Y_n.

At point A, output exceeds the natural level of output. So we know from Section 7-1 that the price level is higher than the expected price level—higher than the price level wage setters expected when they set nominal wages.

The fact that the price level is higher than wage setters expected is likely to lead them to revise upward their expectations of what the price level will be in the future. So, next time they set nominal wages, they are likely to make that decision based on a higher expected price level, say based on $P^{e'}$, where $P^{e'} > P^e$.

This increase in the expected price level implies that in the next period, the aggregate supply curve shifts up, from AS to AS': At a given level of output, wage setters expect a higher price level. They set a higher nominal wage, which in turn leads firms to set a higher price. The price level therefore increases.

Figure 7-6

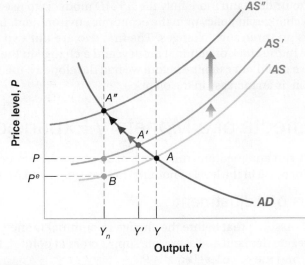

The Adjustment of Output over Time

If output is above the natural level of output, the *AS* curve shifts up over time until output has fallen back to the natural level of output.

This upward shift in the *AS* curve implies that the economy moves up along the *AD* curve. The equilibrium moves from *A* to *A′*. Equilibrium output decreases from *Y* to *Y′*.

The adjustment does not end at point *A′*. At *A′*, output *Y′* still exceeds the natural level of output Y_n, so the price level is still higher than the expected price level. Because of this, wage setters are likely to continue to revise upwards their expectation of the price level.

This means that as long as equilibrium output exceeds the natural level of output Y_n, the expected price level increases, shifting the *AS* curve upward. As the *AS* curve shifts upward and the economy moves up along the *AD* curve, equilibrium output continues to decrease.

Does this adjustment eventually come to an end? Yes. It ends when the *AS* curve has shifted all the way to *AS″*, when the equilibrium has moved all the way to *A″*, and the equilibrium level of output is equal to Y_n. At *A″*, equilibrium output is equal to the natural level of output, so the price level is equal to the expected price level. At this point, wage setters have no reason to change their expectations; the *AS* curve no longer shifts, and the economy stays at *A″*.

In words: So long as output exceeds the natural level of output, the price level turns out to be higher than expected. This leads wage setters to revise their expectations of the price level upward, leading to an increase in the price level. The increase in the price level leads to a decrease in the real money stock, which leads to an increase in the interest rate, which leads to a decrease in output. The adjustment stops when output is equal to the natural level of output. At that point, the price level is equal to the expected price level, expectations no longer change, and, output remains at the natural level of output. Put another way, in the *medium run*, output returns to the natural level of output.

We have looked at the dynamics of adjustment starting from a case in which initial output was higher than the natural level of output. Clearly, a symmetric argument holds when initial output is below the natural level of output. In this case, the price level is lower than the expected price level, leading wage setters to lower their expectations of the price level. Lower expectations of the price level cause the *AS* curve to shift down and the economy to move down the *AD* curve until output has increased back to the natural level of output.

Let's summarize:

■ In the *short run*, output can be above or below the natural level of output. Changes in any of the variables that enter either the aggregate supply relation or the aggregate demand relation lead to changes in output and to changes in the price level. ◀ In the short run, $Y \neq Y_n$.

■ In the *medium run*, output eventually returns to the natural level of output. The adjustment works through changes in the price level. When output is above the natural level of output, the price level increases. The higher price level decreases demand and output. When output is below the natural level of output, ◀ In the medium run, $Y = Y_n$. the price level decreases, increasing demand and output.

The best way to understand more fully the *AS–AD* model is to use it to look at the dynamic effects of changes in policy or in the economic environment. In the next three sections, we focus on three such changes. The first two are our two favorite policy changes: a change in the stock of nominal money; and a change in the budget deficit. The third, which we could not examine before we had developed a theory of wage and price determination, is an increase in the oil price.

7-4 The Effects of a Monetary Expansion

What are the short-run and medium-run effects of an expansionary monetary policy, say of a one-time increase in the level of nominal money from M to M'?

The Dynamics of Adjustment

Look at Figure 7-7. Assume that before the change in nominal money, output is at its natural level. Aggregate demand and aggregate supply cross at point A, the level of output at A equals Y_n, and the price level equals P.

Now consider an increase in nominal money. Recall the specification of aggregate demand from equation (7.3):

$$Y = Y\left(\frac{M}{P}, G, T\right)$$

For a given price level P, the increase in nominal money M leads to an increase in the real money stock M/P, leading to an increase in output. The aggregate demand curve shifts to the right, from AD to AD'. In the short run, the economy goes from point A to A'. Output increases from Y_n to Y', and the price level increases from P to P'.

Over time, the adjustment of price level expectations comes into play. As output is higher than the natural level of output, the price level is higher than wage setters expected. They then revise their expectations, which causes the aggregate supply curve to shift up over time. The economy moves up along the aggregate demand curve AD'. The adjustment process stops when output has returned to the natural level of output. At that point, the price level is equal to the expected price level. In the medium run, the aggregate supply curve is given by AS'', and the economy is at point A'': Output is back to Y_n, and the price level is equal to P''.

We think of shifts in the *AD* curve as shifts to the right or to the left because we think of the *AD* relation as telling us what output is for a given price level. We then ask: At a given price level, does output increase (a shift to the right) or decrease (a shift to the left)?

We think of shifts in the *AS* curve as shifts up or down because we think of the *AS* relation as telling us what the price level is for a given level of output. We then ask: At a given output level, does the price level increase (a shift up) or decrease (a shift down)?

Figure 7-7

The Dynamic Effects of a Monetary Expansion

A monetary expansion leads to an increase in output in the short run but has no effect on output in the medium run.

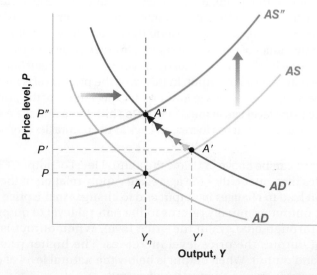

We can actually pin down the exact size of the eventual increase in the price level. If output is back to the natural level of output, the real money stock must also be back to its initial value. In other words, the proportional increase in prices must be equal to ◀ the proportional increase in the nominal money stock: If the initial increase in nominal money is equal to 10%, then the price level ends up 10% higher.

Go back to equation (7.3): If Y is unchanged (and G and T are also unchanged), then M/P must also be unchanged.

If M/P is unchanged, it must be that M and P each increase in the same proportion.

Going Behind the Scenes

To get a better sense of what is going on, it is useful to go behind the scenes to see what happens not only to output and to the price level, but also what happens to the interest rate. We can do this by looking at what happens in terms of the IS–LM model.

Figure 7-8(a) reproduces Figure 7-7 (leaving out the AS'' curve to keep things simple) and shows the adjustment of output and the price level in response to the increase in nominal money. Figure 7-8(b) shows the adjustment of output and the interest rate by looking at the same adjustment process, but in terms of the IS–LM model.

Look first at Figure 7-8(b). Before the change in nominal money, the equilibrium is given by the intersection of the IS and LM curves; that is, at point A—which corresponds to point A in Figure 7-8(a). Output is equal to the natural level of output, Y_n, and the interest rate is given by i.

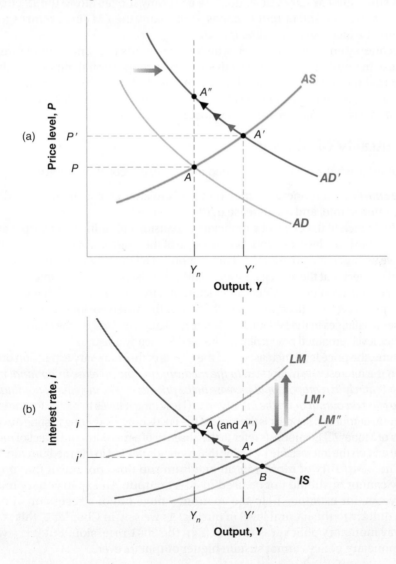

Figure 7-8

The Dynamic Effects of a Monetary Expansion on Output and the Interest Rate

The increase in nominal money initially shifts the LM curve down, decreasing the interest rate and increasing output. Over time, the price level increases, shifting the LM curve back up until output is back at the natural level of output.

The short–run effect of the monetary expansion is to shift the *LM* curve down from *LM* to *LM'*, moving the equilibrium from point *A* to point *A'*—which corresponds to point *A'* in Figure 7-8(a). The interest rate is lower, and output is higher.

Note that there are two effects at work behind the shift from *LM* to *LM'*: One is due to the increase in nominal money. The other, which partly offsets the first, is due to the increase in the price level. Let's look at these two effects more closely:

■ If the price level did not change, the increase in nominal money would shift the *LM* curve down to *LM''*. So, if the price level did not change—as was our assumption in Chapter 5—the equilibrium would be at the intersection of *IS* and *LM''*, or point *B*.

■ But even in the short run, the price level increases—from *P* to *P'* in Figure 7-8(a). This increase in the price level shifts the *LM* curve upward from *LM''* to *LM'*, partially offsetting the effect of the increase in nominal money.

■ The net effect of these two shifts—down from *LM* to *LM''* in response to the increase in nominal money, and up from *LM''* to *LM'* in response to the increase in the price level—is a shift of the *LM* curve from *LM* to *LM'*, and the equilibrium is given by *A'*.

Over time, the fact that output is above its natural level implies that the price level continues to increase. As the price level increases, it further reduces the real money stock and shifts the *LM* curve back up. The economy moves along the *IS* curve: The interest rate increases and output declines. Eventually, the *LM* curve returns to where it was before the increase in nominal money.

The economy ends up at point *A*, which corresponds to point *A''* in Figure 7-8(a): The increase in nominal money is exactly offset by a proportional increase in the price level. The real money stock is therefore unchanged. With the real money stock unchanged, output is back to its initial value, Y_n, which is the natural level of output, and the interest rate is also back to its initial value, *i*.

The Neutrality of Money

Let's summarize what we have just learned about the effects of monetary policy:

■ In the *short run*, a monetary expansion leads to an increase in output, a decrease in the interest rate, and an increase in the price level.

How much of the effect of a monetary expansion falls initially on output and how much on the price level depends on the slope of the aggregate supply curve. In Chapter 5, we assumed the price level did not respond at all to an increase in output—we assumed in effect that the aggregate supply curve was flat. Although we intended this as a simplification, empirical evidence does show that the initial effect of changes in output on the price level is indeed quite small. We saw this when we looked at estimated responses to changes in the Federal Funds rate in Figure 5-9: Despite the change in output, the price level remained practically unchanged for nearly a year.

■ Over time, the price level increases, and the effects of the monetary expansion on output and on the interest rate disappear. *In the medium run, the increase in nominal money is reflected entirely in a proportional increase in the price level. The increase in nominal money has no effect on output or on the interest rate.* (How long it takes in reality for the effects of money on output to disappear is the topic of the Focus box "How Long Lasting Are the Real Effects of Money?") Economists refer to the absence of a medium–run effect of money on output and on the interest rate by saying that money is neutral in the medium run.

The **neutrality of money** in the medium run does not mean that monetary policy cannot or should not be used to affect output. An expansionary monetary policy can, for example, help the economy move out of a recession and return more quickly to the natural level of output. As we saw in Chapter 5, this is exactly the way monetary policy was used to fight the 2001 recession. But it is a warning that monetary policy cannot sustain higher output forever.

Why only partially? Suppose the price level increased in the same proportion as the increase in nominal money, leaving the real money stock unchanged. If the real money stock were unchanged, output would remain unchanged as well. But if output were unchanged, the price level would not increase, contradicting our premise.

Actually, the way the proposition is typically stated is that money is neutral in the long run. This is because many economists use "long run" to refer to what we call in this book the "medium run."

How Long Lasting Are the Real Effects of Money?

To determine how long lasting the real effects of money are, economists use **macroeconometric models.** These models are larger-scale versions of the aggregate supply and aggregate demand model in this chapter.

The model we examine in this box was built in the early 1990s by John Taylor, at Stanford University.

The Taylor model is substantially larger than the model we studied in this chapter. On the aggregate supply side, it has separate equations for price and for wage setting. On the demand side, it has separate equations for consumption, for investment, for exports, and for imports. (Recall that, so far, we have assumed the economy is closed, so we have ignored exports and imports altogether.) In addition, instead of looking at just one country as we have done here, it looks at eight countries (the United States, and seven major OECD countries) and solves for equilibrium in all eight countries simultaneously. Each equation, for each country, is estimated using econometrics, and allows for a richer dynamic structure than the equations we have relied on in this chapter.

The implications of the model for the effects of money on output are shown in Figure 1. The simulation looks at the effects of an increase in nominal money of 3% over the initial year, taking place over four quarters—0.1% in the first quarter, 0.6% in the second, 1.2% in the third, and 1.1% in the fourth. After these four step increases, nominal money remains at its new higher level forever.

The effects of money on output reach a maximum after three quarters. By then, output is 1.8% higher than it would have been without the increase in nominal money. Over time, however, the price level increases and output returns to the natural level of output. In year 4, the price level is up by 2.5%, while output is up by only 0.3%. Therefore, the Taylor model suggests, it takes roughly four years for output to return to its natural level, or, put another way, four years for changes in nominal money to become neutral.

Do all macroeconometric models give the same answer? No. Because they differ in the way they are constructed, in the way variables are chosen, and in the way equations are estimated, their answers are different. But most of them have the following implications in common: The effects of an increase in money on output build up for one to two years and then decline over time. (To get a sense of how the answers might differ across models, see the Focus box "Twelve Macroeconometric Models" in Chapter 22.)

Source: Figure 1 is reproduced from John Taylor, Macroeconomic Policy in a World Economy (W.W. Norton, 1993) Figure 5-1A, p. 138.

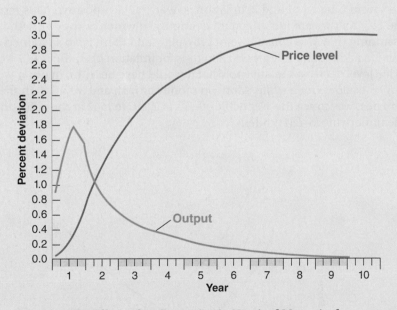

Figure 1 *The Effects of an Expansion in Nominal Money in the Taylor Model*

7-5 A Decrease in the Budget Deficit

The policy we just looked at—a monetary expansion—led to a shift in aggregate demand coming from a shift in the *LM* curve. Let's now look at the effects of a shift in aggregate demand coming from a shift in the *IS* curve.

Recall, from Chapter 5, that a reduction in the budget deficit is also called a fiscal contraction, or a fiscal consolidation.

Suppose the government is running a budget deficit and decides to reduce it by decreasing its spending from G to G' while leaving taxes T unchanged. How will this affect the economy in the short run and in the medium run?

Assume that output is initially at the natural level of output, so that the economy is at point A in Figure 7-9: Output equals Y_n. The decrease in government spending from G to G' shifts the aggregate demand curve to the left, from AD to AD': For a given price level, output is lower. In the short run, the equilibrium moves from A to A' ; output decreases from Y_n to Y' and the price level decreases from P to P'.

The initial effect of the deficit reduction triggers lower output. We first derived this result in Chapter 3, then in Chapter 5, and it holds here as well.

What happens over time? As long as output is below the natural level of output, we know that the aggregate supply curve keeps shifting down. The economy moves down along the aggregate demand curve AD' until the aggregate supply curve is given by AS'' and the economy reaches point A''. By then, the recession is over, and output is back at Y_n.

Like an increase in nominal money, a reduction in the budget deficit does not affect output forever. Eventually, output returns to its natural level. But there is an important difference between the effects of a change in money and the effects of a change in the deficit. At point A'', not everything is the same as before: Output is back to the natural level of output, but the price level and the interest rate are lower than before the shift. (The fact that the price level decreases may feel strange given that, as we saw in Chapters 1 and 2, inflation is nearly always positive. This result comes from the fact that we are looking at an economy in which money growth is zero—we are assuming that M is constant, not growing—and there is no sustained inflation. If we were to allow for money growth and thus for inflation, then the result would be that the price level decreases relative to what it would have been, or, in other words, that inflation goes down for a while. More on money growth and inflation in the next chapter.) The best way to see these specific effects is again to look at the adjustment in terms of the underlying *IS–LM* model.

Figure 7-9

The Dynamic Effects of a Decrease in the Budget Deficit

A decrease in the budget deficit leads initially to a decrease in output. Over time, however, output returns to the natural level of output.

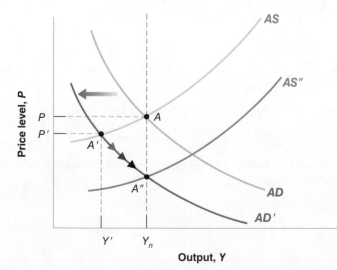

Deficit Reduction, Output, and the Interest Rate

Figure 7-10(a) reproduces Figure 7-9, showing the adjustment of output and the price level in response to the increase in the budget deficit (but leaving out AS'' to keep things visually simple). Figure 7-10(b) shows the adjustment of output and the interest rate by looking at the same adjustment process, but in terms of the IS–LM model.

Look first at Figure 7-10(b). Before the change in fiscal policy, the equilibrium is given by the intersection of the IS curve and the LM curve, at point A—which corresponds to point A in Figure 7-10(a). Output is equal to the natural level of output, Y_n, and the interest rate is given by i.

As the government reduces the budget deficit, the IS curve shifts to the left, to IS'. If the price level did not change (the assumption we made in Chapter 5), the economy would move from point A to point B. But, because the price level declines in response to the decrease in output, the real money stock increases, leading to a partially offsetting shift of the LM curve, down to LM'. So, the initial effect of deficit reduction is to move the economy from point A to point A'. (Point A' in Figure 7-10(b) corresponds to point A' in Figure 7-10(a).) Both output and the interest rate are lower than before the

Figure 7-10

The Dynamic Effects of a Decrease in the Budget Deficit on Output and the Interest Rate

A deficit reduction leads in the short run to a decrease in output and to a decrease in the interest rate. In the medium run, output returns to its natural level, while the interest rate declines further.

fiscal contraction. Note that, just as was the case in Chapter 5, we cannot tell whether investment increases or decreases in the short run: Lower output decreases investment, but the lower interest rate increases investment.

So long as output remains below the natural level of output, the price level continues to decline, leading to a further increase in the real money stock. The *LM* curve continues to shift down. In Figure 7-10(b), the economy moves down from point A' along *IS'*, and eventually reaches A'' (which corresponds to A'' in Figure 7-10(a)). At A'', the *LM* curve is given by *LM''*.

At A'', output is back at the natural level of output. But the interest rate is lower than it was before deficit reduction, down from i to i''. The composition of output is also different: To see how and why, let's rewrite the *IS* relation, taking into account that at A'', output is back at the natural level of output, so that $Y = Y_n$

$$Y_n = C(Y_n - T) + I(Y_n, i) + G$$

Because income Y_n and taxes T are unchanged, consumption C is the same as before the deficit reduction. By assumption, government spending G is lower than before. Therefore investment I must be higher than before the deficit reduction—higher by an amount exactly equal to the decrease in G. Put another way, in the medium run, a reduction in the budget deficit unambiguously leads to a decrease in the interest rate and an increase in investment.

Budget Deficits, Output, and Investment

Let's summarize what you have just learned about the effects of fiscal policy:

Recall the discussion of the ▶ policy mix in Chapter 5.

■ In the *short run*, a budget deficit reduction, if implemented alone—that is, without an accompanying change in monetary policy—leads to a decrease in output and may lead to a *decrease* in investment.

Go back to Figure 7-10. What ▶ would the Fed need to do in order to avoid a short run decrease in output in response to the fiscal contraction?

   Note the qualification "without an accompanying change in monetary policy": In principle, these adverse short-run effects on output can be avoided by using the right monetary–fiscal policy mix. What is needed is for the central bank to increase the money supply enough to offset the adverse effects of the decrease in government spending on aggregate demand. This is what happened in the United States in the 1990s. As the Clinton administration reduced budget deficits, the Fed made sure that, even in the short run, the deficit reduction did not lead to a recession and lower output.

■ In the *medium run*, output returns to the natural level of output, and the interest rate is lower. In the medium run, a deficit reduction leads unambiguously to an *increase* in investment.

Effects of a deficit reduction:

Short run: Y decreases, I increases or decreases.

Medium run: Y unchanged, ▶ I increases.

Long run: Y increases, I increases.

   We have not taken into account so far the effects of investment on capital accumulation and the effects of capital on production (we will do so in Chapters 10 to 13 when we look at the long run). But it is easy to see how our conclusions would be modified if we did take into account the effects on capital accumulation. In the long run, the level of output depends on the capital stock in the economy. So if a lower government budget deficit leads to more investment, it will lead to a higher capital stock, and the higher capital stock will lead to higher output.

Everything we have just said about the effects of deficit reduction through a fiscal consolidation would apply equally to policy measures aimed at increasing private saving. An increase in the private saving rate—that is, lower consumption at the same level of disposable income—decreases demand and output in the short run, leaves output unchanged in the medium run, and, through increases in the capital stock from increased investment, increases output in the long run.

Disagreements among economists about the effects of measures aimed at increasing either public saving or private saving often come from differences in time frames. Those who are concerned with short-run effects worry that measures to increase saving, public or private, might create a recession and decrease saving and investment for some time. Those who look beyond the short run see the eventual increase in saving and investment and emphasize the favorable medium-run and long-run effects on output.

7-6 An Increase in the Price of Oil

So far we have looked so far at shocks that shift the aggregate demand curve: an increase in the money supply, or a reduction in the budget deficit. There are other shocks, however, that affect both aggregate demand and aggregate supply and play an important role in fluctuations. An obvious candidate is movements in the price of oil. To see why, turn to Figure 7-11.

Figure 7-11 plots two series. The first, represented by the red line, is the dollar price of oil—that is, the price of a barrel of oil in dollars— since 1970. It is measured on the vertical axis on the left. This is the series that is quoted in the newspapers, more or less every day. What matters, however, for economic decisions is not the dollar price, but the real price of oil; that is, the dollar price of oil divided by the price level. Thus, the second series in the figure, represented by the blue line, shows the real price of oil, constructed as the dollar price of oil divided by the U.S. consumer price index. Note that the real price is an index; it is normalized to equal 100 in 1970. It is measured on the vertical axis on the right.

What is perhaps most striking in the figure is the large increase in the real price of oil in the 2000s: In 10 years, from 1998 to 2008, the index for the real price went from about 100 to more than 500, a more than five-fold increase. As the figure shows, however, there were two similar increases in the price of oil in the 1970s, the first in 1973–1975 and the second in 1977–1981. Just as in the more recent episode, the real price of oil increased from 100 in 1970 (this is the normalization we have chosen) to more than 500 in 1981.

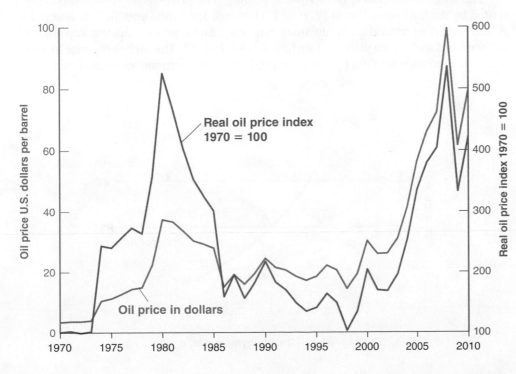

Figure 7-11

The Nominal and the Real Price of Oil, 1970–2010

Over the last 40 years, there have been three sharp increases in the real price of oil. The first two increases took place in the 1970s. The more recent one took place in the 2000s, until the crisis hit.

Source: Series OILPRICE, CPIAUSCL Federal Reserve Economic Data (FRED) http://research.stlouisfed.org/fred2/. The value of the index is set equal to 100 in 1970.)

What was behind these large increases? In the 1970s, the main factors were the formation of **OPEC** (the Organization of Petroleum Exporting Countries), a cartel of oil producers that was able to act as a monopoly and increase prices, and disruptions due to wars and revolutions in the Middle East. In the 2000s, the main factor was quite different, namely the fast growth of emerging economies, in particular China, which led to a rapid increase in the world demand for oil and, by implication, a steady increase in real oil prices. Whether coming from changes in supply in the 1970s or from changes in the demand from emerging countries in the 2000s, the implication for U.S. firms and consumers was the same: more expensive oil, more expensive energy.

In thinking about the macroeconomic effects of such increases, it is clear that we face a serious problem in using the model we have developed so far: The price of oil appears neither in our aggregate supply relation nor in our aggregate demand relation! The reason is that, until now, we have assumed that output was produced using only labor. One way to extend our model would be to recognize explicitly that output is produced using labor *and* other inputs (including energy), and then figure out what effect an increase in the price of oil has on the price set by firms and on the relation between output and employment. An easier way, and the way we shall go here, is simply to capture the increase in the price of oil by an increase in m—the markup of the price over the nominal wage. The justification is straightforward: Given wages, an increase in the price of oil increases the cost of production, forcing firms to increase prices.

Having made this assumption, we can then track the dynamic effects of an *increase in the markup* on output and the price level. It will be easiest here to work backward in time, first asking what happens in the medium run, and then working out the dynamics of adjustment from the short run to the medium run.

Effects on the Natural Rate of Unemployment

Let's start by asking what happens to the natural rate of unemployment when the real price of oil increases (for simplicity, we shall drop "real" in what follows). Figure 7-12 reproduces the characterization of labor-market equilibrium from Figure 6-8 in Chapter 6:

The wage-setting curve is downward sloping. The price-setting relation is represented by the horizontal line at $W/P = 1/(1 + m)$. The initial equilibrium is at point A, and the initial natural unemployment rate is u_n. An increase in the markup leads to a downward shift of the price-setting line, from PS to PS': The higher the markup, the lower the real wage implied by price setting. The equilibrium moves from A to A'. The

Figure 7-12

The Effects of an Increase in the Price of Oil on the Natural Rate of Unemployment

An increase in the price of oil leads to a lower real wage and a higher natural rate of unemployment.

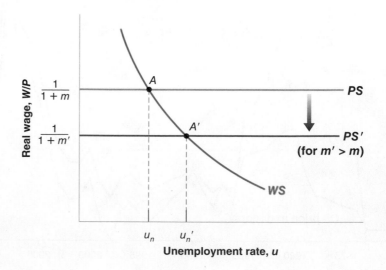

real wage is lower. The natural unemployment rate is higher: Getting workers to accept the lower real wage requires an increase in unemployment.

The increase in the natural rate of unemployment leads in turn to a decrease in the natural level of employment. If we assume that the relation between employment and output is unchanged—that is, that each unit of output still requires one worker in addition to the energy input—then the decrease in the natural level of employment leads to an identical decrease in the natural level of output. Putting things together: An increase in the price of oil leads to a decrease in the natural level of output.

This assumes that the increase in the price of oil is permanent. If, in the medium run, the price of oil goes back to its initial value, then the natural rate is clearly unaffected.

The Dynamics of Adjustment

Let's now turn to dynamics. Suppose that before the increase in the price of oil, the aggregate demand curve and the aggregate supply curve are given by AD and AS, respectively, so the economy is at point A in Figure 7-13, with output at the natural level of output, Y_n, and by implication $P = P^e$.

We have just established that the increase in the price of oil decreases the natural level of output. Call this lower level Y'_n. We now want to know what happens in the short run and how the economy moves from Y_n to Y'_n.

To think about the short run, recall that the aggregate supply relation is given by

$$P = P^e (1 + m) F\left(1 - \frac{Y}{L}, z\right)$$

Recall that we capture the effect of an increase in the price of oil by an increase in the markup m. So, in the short run (given P^e), the increase in the price of oil shows up as an increase in the markup m. This increase in the markup leads firms to increase their prices, leading to an increase in the price level P at any level of output Y. The aggregate supply curve shifts up.

We can be more specific about the size of the shift, and knowing the size of this shift will be useful in what follows. We know from Section 7-1 that the aggregate supply curve always goes through the point such that output equals the natural level of output and the price level equals the expected price level. Before the increase in the price of oil, the aggregate supply curve in Figure 7-13 goes through point A, where output equals Y_n and the price level is equal to P^e. After the increase in the price of oil, the new aggregate supply curve goes through point B, where output equals the new lower

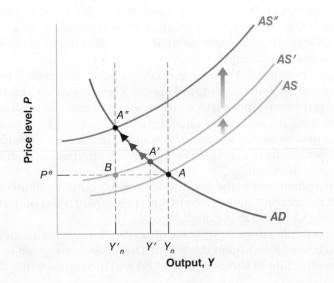

Figure 7-13

The Dynamic Effects of an Increase in the Price of Oil

An increase in the price of oil leads, in the short run, to a decrease in output and an increase in the price level. Over time, output decreases further and the price level increases further.

Figure 7-14

Oil Price Increases and Inflation in the United States since 1970

The oil price increases of the 1970s were associated with large increases in inflation. This was however not the case in the 2000s.

Source: Real Oil Price Index—see Figure 7-10. *Inflation calculated as annual rate of change of series,* CPIAUSCL Federal Reserve Economic Data (FRED) http://research.stlouisfed.org/fred2/

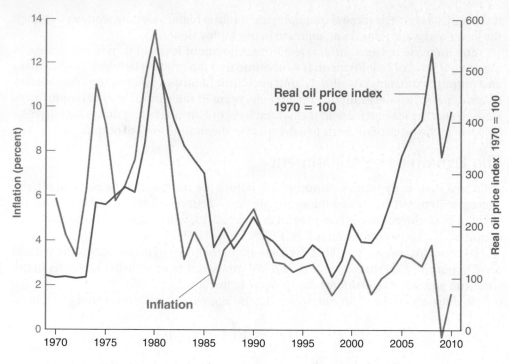

natural level of output Y'_n and the price level equals the expected price level, P^e. The aggregate supply curve shifts left from *AS* to *AS'*.

Does the aggregate demand curve shift as a result of the increase in the price of oil? The answer is: maybe. There are many channels through which demand might be affected at a given price level: The higher price of oil may lead firms to change their investment plans, canceling some investment projects and/or shifting to less energy-intensive equipment. The increase in the price of oil also redistributes income from oil buyers to oil producers. Oil producers may spend less than than oil buyers, leading to a decrease in consumption demand. Let's take the easy way out: Because some of the effects shift the aggregate demand curve to the right and others shift the aggregate demand curve to the left, let's simply assume that the effects cancel each other out and that aggregate demand does not shift.

▶ Higher gas prices may lead you to get rid of your gas guzzler.

▶ This is indeed typically the case. Oil producers realize that high oil revenues might not last forever. This leads them to save a large proportion of the income from oil revenues.

Under this assumption, in the short run, only the *AS* shifts. The economy therefore moves along the *AD* curve, from *A* to *A'*. Output decreases from Y_n to Y'. The increase in the price of oil leads firms to increase their prices. This increase in the price level then decreases demand and output.

What happens over time? Although output has fallen, the natural level of output has fallen even more: At point *A'*, output Y' is still above the new natural level of output Y'_n, so the aggregate supply curve continues to shift up. The economy therefore moves over time along the aggregate demand curve, from *A'* to *A''*. At point *A''*, output Y' is equal to the new lower natural level of output Y'_n, and the price level is higher than before the oil shock: Shifts in aggregate supply affect output not only in the short run but in the medium run as well.

To summarize: Increases in the price of oil decrease output and increase prices in the short run. If the increase in the price of oil is permanent, then output is lower not only in the short run, but also in the medium run.

How do these implications fit what we observed in response to increases in the price of oil both in the 1970s and in the 2000s? The answers are given by Figure 7-14, which plots the evolution of the real price of oil and inflation—using the CPI—and

Oil Price Increases: Why Were the 2000s so Different from the 1970s?

FOCUS

The question raised by Figures 7-14 and 7-15 is an obvious one: Why is it that oil price increases were associated with stagflation in the 1970s, but have had so little apparent effect on the economy in the 2000s?

A first line of explanation is that shocks other than the increase in the price of oil were at work in the 1970s and in the 2000s.

In the 1970s, not only did the price of oil increase, but so did the price of many other raw materials. This implies that the aggregate supply relation shifted up by more than implied by just the increase in the price of oil, and so the adverse effect on output was stronger than in the 2000s.

In the 2000s, many economists believe that, partly because of globalization and foreign competition, workers bargaining power weakened. If true, this implies that, while the increase in oil prices shifted the aggregate supply curve up, the decrease in bargaining power of workers shifted it down, dampening or even eliminating the adverse effects of the oil price increase on output and the price level.

Econometric studies suggest, however, that more was at work, and that, even after controlling for the presence of these other factors, the effects of the price of oil have changed since the 1970s. Figure 1 shows the effects of a 100% increase in the price of oil on output and on the price level, estimated using data from two different periods. The black and blue lines show the effects of an increase in the price of oil on the CPI deflator and on GDP, based on data from 1970:1 to 1986:4; the green and red lines do the same, but based on data from 1987:1 to 2006:4 (the time scale on the horizontal axis is in quarters). The figure suggests two main conclusions. First, in both periods, as predicted by our model, the increase in the price of oil leads to an increase in the CPI and a decrease in GDP. Second, the effects of the increase in the price of oil on both the CPI and on GDP have become smaller, roughly half of what they were earlier.

Why have the adverse effects of the increase in the price of oil become smaller? This is still very much a topic of research. But, at this stage, two hypotheses appear plausible:

The first hypothesis is that, today, U.S. workers have less bargaining power than they did in the 1970s. Thus, as the price of oil has increased, workers have been more willing to accept a reduction in wages, limiting the upward shift in the aggregate supply curve, and thus limiting the adverse effect on the price level and on output. (Make sure you understand this statement; use Figure 7-13 to increase your understanding.)

The second hypothesis concerns monetary policy. When the price of oil increased in the 1970s, people started expecting much higher prices in general, and P^e increased dramatically. The result was further shifts of the aggregate supply curve, leading to a larger increase in the price level and a larger decrease in output. In the 2000s, monetary policy was conducted in a very different way than in the 1970s, and expectations were that the Fed would not let the increase in the price of oil lead to a much higher price level. Thus, P^e barely increased over time, leading to a smaller shift of the aggregate supply curve, and thus a smaller effect on output and the price level than in the 1970s. (Again, use Figure 7-13 to make sure you understand this statement.)

Figure 1   *The Effects of a 100% Permanent Increase in the Price of Oil on the CPI and on GDP. The effects of an increase in the price of oil on output and the price level are smaller than they used to be*

Figure 7-15

Oil Price Increases and Unemployment in the United States since 1970

The oil price increases of the 1970s were associated with large increases in unemployment. This was however not the case in the 2000s.

Source: Real Oil Price Index—see Figure 7-11. Unemployment rate Series UNRATE: Federal Reserve Economic Data (FRED) http://research.stlouisfed.org/fred2/

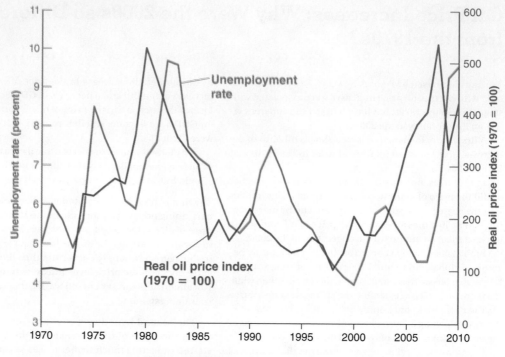

True, output decreased dramatically, starting in 2008. But it is clear that this was not due ▶ to the earlier increase in oil prices, but due instead to the financial crisis.

Figure 7-15, which plots the evolution of the real price of oil and the unemployment rate, in the United States since 1970.

First, the good news (for our model, although surely not for the U.S. economy at the time): Note how both of the increases in the price of oil of the 1970s were followed by major increases in inflation and in unemployment. This fits our conclusions very well. Now, the bad news (for our model, but not for the U.S. economy): Note how the increase in the price of oil in the 2000s was associated with neither an increase in inflation nor an increase in unemployment. In light of what happened in the 1970s, this lack of an effect has come as a surprise to macroeconomists. The state of research, and various hypotheses being explored, are discussed in the Focus box "Oil Price Increases: Why Were the 2000s so Different from the 1970s?". A summary of the conclusions goes like this: Oil price increases still decrease output and increase inflation. Because of decreases in the use of oil in production, because of changes in the labor market, and because of improvements in the conduct of monetary policy, the effect of oil price increases on both output and inflation was smaller in the 2000s than it was in the 1970s. And the reason it is hard to see an adverse effect on output and on inflation in the 2000s in Figures 7-14 and 7-15 is that these oil price shocks were largely offset by other, favorable shocks.

7-7 Conclusions

This chapter has covered a lot of ground. Let us repeat some key ideas and develop some of the earlier conclusions.

The Short Run versus the Medium Run

One key message of this chapter is that changes in policy typically have different effects in the short run and in the medium run. The main results of this chapter are summarized in Table 7-1. A monetary expansion, for example, affects output in the short run but not in the medium run. In the short run, a reduction in the budget deficit decreases output and decreases the interest rate and may decrease investment. But in

Table 7-1	Short-Run Effects and Medium-Run Effects of a Monetary Expansion and a Budget Deficit Reduction on Output, the Interest Rate, and the Price Level					

	Short Run			Medium Run		
	Output Level	Interest Rate	Price Level	Output Level	Interest Rate	Price Level
Monetary expansion	increase	decrease	increase (small)	no change	no change	increase
Deficit reduction	decrease	decrease	decrease (small)	no change	decrease	decrease

the medium run, the interest rate decreases and output returns to the natural level of output, and investment unambiguously increases.

Disagreements among economists about the effects of various policies often come from differences in the time frame they have in mind. If you are worried about output and investment in the short run, you might be reluctant to proceed with fiscal consolidation. But if your focus is on the medium or the long run, you will see the consolidation as helping investment and eventually, through higher capital accumulation, increasing output. One implication is that where you stand depends in particular on how fast you think the economy adjusts to shocks. If you believe that it takes a long time for output to return to its natural level, you will naturally focus more on the short run and be willing to use policies that increase output in the short run, even if medium-run effects are nil or negative. If you believe instead that output returns to its natural level quickly, you will put more emphasis on the medium-run implications and will, by implication, be more reluctant to use those policies.

Shocks and Propagation Mechanisms

This chapter also gives you a general way of thinking about **output fluctuations** (sometimes called **business cycles**)—movements in output around its trend (a trend that we have ignored so far but on which we will focus in Chapters 10 to 13):

You can think of the economy as being constantly hit by **shocks**. These shocks may be shifts in consumption coming from changes in consumer confidence, shifts in investment, shifts in the demand for money, and so on. Or they may come from changes in policy—from the introduction of a new tax law, to a new program of infrastructure investment, to a decision by the central bank to fight inflation by tightening the money supply.

Each shock has dynamic effects on output and its components. These dynamic effects are called the **propagation mechanism** of the shock. Propagation mechanisms are different for different shocks. The effects of a shock on activity may build up over time, affecting output in the medium run. Or the effects may build up for a while and then decrease and disappear. We saw, for example, that the effects of an increase in money on output reach a peak after six to nine months and then slowly decline afterward as the price level eventually increases in proportion to the increase in nominal money. At times, some shocks are sufficiently large or come in sufficiently bad combinations that they create a recession. The two recessions of the 1970s were due largely to increases in the price of oil; the recession of the early 1980s was due to a sharp contraction in money; the recession of the early 1990s was due primarily to a sudden decline in consumer confidence; the recession of 2001 was due to a sharp drop in investment spending. The current crisis and the sharp decrease in output in 2010 had its origins in

How to define *shocks* is harder than it looks. Suppose a failed economic program in an Eastern European country leads to political chaos in that country, which leads to increased risk of nuclear war in the region, which leads to a fall in consumer confidence in the United States, which leads to a recession in the United States. What is the "shock"? The failed program? The fall of democracy? The increased risk of nuclear war? Or the decrease in consumer confidence? In practice, we have to cut the chain of causation somewhere. Thus, we may refer to the drop in consumer confidence as "the shock" and ignore its underlying causes.

the problems of the housing market, which then led to a major financial shock, and in turn to a sharp reduction in output. What we call economic fluctuations are the result of these shocks and their dynamic effects on output.

Where We Go from Here

■ We assumed in this chapter that the nominal money stock was constant, that there was no nominal money growth. This led to a constant price level in the medium run. What we observe most of the time, however, is positive inflation, namely a steady increase in the price level. This in turn requires us to extend our analysis to the case where money growth is positive and to revisit the relation among output, unemployment, inflation, and money growth. We take this up in Chapter 8.

■ The *AS–AD* model we constructed in this chapter has a reassuring property. While shocks move output away from its natural level in the short run, there are forces that tend to take it back to its natural level over time. Output below its natural level leads to a decrease in the price level, which leads in turn to an increase in the real money stock, a decrease in the interest rate, and an increase in demand and in output. This process takes place until output has returned to its natural level and there is no longer pressure on the price level to adjust further. And, if this process is too slow, fiscal and monetary policies can help accelerate the return to the natural rate. The crisis and the very slow recovery (recall the facts presented in Chapter 1) we are experiencing force us to reconsider these conclusions. This is what we do in Chapter 9.

Summary

· ·

■ The model of aggregate supply and aggregate demand describes the movements in output and the price level when account is taken of equilibrium in the goods market, the financial markets, and the labor market.

■ The aggregate supply relation captures the effects of output on the price level. It is derived from equilibrium in the labor market. It is a relation among the price level, the expected price level, and the level of output. An increase in output decreases unemployment; the decrease in unemployment increases wages and, in turn, increases the price level. An increase in the expected price level leads, one for one, to an increase in the actual price level.

■ The aggregate demand relation captures the effects of the price level on output. It is derived from equilibrium in goods and financial markets. An increase in the price level decreases the real money stock, increasing the interest rate and decreasing output.

■ In the short run, movements in output come from shifts in either aggregate demand or aggregate supply. In the medium run, output returns to the natural level of output, which is determined by equilibrium in the labor market.

■ An expansionary monetary policy leads in the short run to an increase in the real money stock, a decrease in the interest rate, and an increase in output. Over time, the price level increases, and the real money stock decreases until output has returned to its natural level. In the medium run, money does not affect output, and changes in money are reflected in proportional increases in the price level. Economists refer to this fact by saying that, in the medium run, money is neutral.

■ A reduction in the budget deficit leads in the short run to a decrease in the demand for goods and therefore to a decrease in output. Over time, the price level decreases, leading to an increase in the real money stock and a decrease in the interest rate. In the medium run, output increases back to the natural level of output, but the interest rate is lower and investment is higher.

■ An increase in the price of oil leads, in both the short run and in the medium run, to a decrease in output. In the short run, it leads to an increase in the price level, which decreases the real money stock and leads to a contraction of demand and output. In the medium run, an increase in the price of oil decreases the real wage paid by firms, increases the natural rate of unemployment, and therefore decreases the natural level of output.

■ The difference between short-run effects and medium-run effects of policies is one of the reasons economists disagree in their policy recommendations. Some economists believe the economy adjusts quickly to its medium-run equilibrium, so they emphasize medium-run implications of policy. Others believe the adjustment mechanism through which output returns to the natural level of output is a slow process at best, and so they put more emphasis on the short-run effects of policy.

■ Economic fluctuations are the result of a continual stream of shocks to aggregate supply or to aggregate demand and of the dynamic effects of each of these shocks on output. Sometimes the shocks are sufficiently adverse, alone or in combination, that they lead to a recession.

Key Terms

aggregate supply relation, 134
aggregate demand relation, 136
neutrality of money, 144
macroeconometric models, 145
Organization of Petroleum Exporting Countries (OPEC), 150

output fluctuations, 155
business cycles, 155
shocks, 155
propagation mechanism, 155

Questions and Problems

QUICK CHECK
All Quick Check questions and problems are available on MyEconLab.

1. Using the information in this chapter, label each of the following statements true, false, or uncertain. Explain briefly.

a. The aggregate supply relation implies that an increase in output leads to an increase in the price level.

b. The natural level of output can be determined by looking solely at the aggregate supply relation.

c. The aggregate demand relation is downward sloping because at a higher price level, consumers wish to purchase fewer goods.

d. In the absence of changes in fiscal or monetary policy, the economy will always remain at the natural level of output.

e. Expansionary monetary policy has no effect on the level of output in the medium run.

f. Fiscal policy cannot affect investment in the medium run because output always returns to its natural level.

g. In the medium run, output and the price level always return to the same value.

2. Aggregate demand shocks and the medium run

Suppose the economy begins with output equal to its natural level. Then, there is a reduction in income taxes.

a. Using the *AS–AD* model developed in this chapter, show the effects of a reduction in income taxes on the position of the *AD*, *AS*, *IS*, and *LM* curves in the medium run.

b. What happens to output, the interest rate, and the price level in the medium run? What happens to consumption and investment in the medium run?

3. Aggregate supply shocks and the medium run

Consider an economy with output equal to the natural level of output. Now suppose there is an increase in unemployment benefits.

a. Using the model developed in this chapter, show the effects of an increase in unemployment benefits on the

position of the *AD* and *AS* curves in the short run and in the medium run.

b. How will the increase in unemployment benefits affect output and the price level in the short run and in the medium run?

4. The neutrality of money

a. In what sense is money neutral? How is monetary policy useful if money is neutral?

b. Fiscal policy, like monetary policy, cannot change the natural level of output. Why then is monetary policy considered neutral but fiscal policy is not?

c. Discuss the statement "Because neither fiscal nor monetary policy can affect the natural level of output, it follows that, in the medium run, the natural level of output is independent of all government policies."

DIG DEEPER
All DIG Deeper questions and problems are available on MyEconLab.

5. The paradox of saving, one more time

In chapter problems at the end of Chapters 3 and 5, we examined the paradox of saving in the short run, under different assumptions about the response of investment to output and the interest rate. Here we consider the issue one last time in the context of the AS–AD *model.*

Suppose the economy begins with output equal to its natural level. Then there is a decrease in consumer confidence as households attempt to increase their saving for a given level of disposable income.

a. In *AS–AD* and *IS–LM* diagrams, show the effects of the decline in consumer confidence in the short run and the medium run. Explain why the curves shift in your diagrams.

b. What happens to output, the interest rate, and the price level in the short run? What happens to consumption, investment, and private saving in the short run? Is it possible that the decline in consumer confidence will actually lead to a fall in private saving in the short run?

c. Repeat part (b) for the medium run. Is there any paradox of saving in the medium run?

6. *Suppose that the interest rate has no effect on investment.*

a. Can you think of a situation in which this may happen?

b. What does this imply for the slope of the *IS* curve?

c. What does this imply for the slope of the *LM* curve?

d. What does this imply for the slope of the *AD* curve?

   Continue to assume that the interest rate has no effect on investment. Assume that the economy starts at the natural level of output. Suppose there is a shock to the variable z, so that the AS curve shifts up.

e. What is the short-run effect on output and the price level? Explain in words.

f. What happens to output and the price level over time? Explain in words.

7. *Demand shocks and demand management*

   Assume that the economy starts at the natural level of output. Now suppose there is a decline in business confidence, so that investment demand falls for any interest rate.

a. In an *AS–AD* diagram, show what happens to output and the price level in the short run and the medium run.

b. What happens to the unemployment rate in the short run? in the medium run?

   Suppose that the Federal Reserve decides to respond immediately to the decline in business confidence in the short run. In particular, suppose that the Fed wants to prevent the unemployment rate from changing in the short run after the decline in business confidence.

a. What should the Fed do? Show how the Fed's action, combined with the decline in business confidence, affects the *AS–AD* diagram in the short run and the medium run.

b. How do short-run output and the short-run price level compare to your answers from part (a)?

c. How do the short-run and medium-run unemployment rates compare to your answers from part (b)?

8. *Supply shocks and demand management*

   Assume that the economy starts at the natural level of output. Now suppose there is an increase in the price of oil.

a. In an *AS–AD* diagram, show what happens to output and the price level in the short run and the medium run.

b. What happens to the unemployment rate in the short run? in the medium run?

   Suppose that the Federal Reserve decides to respond immediately to the increase in the price of oil. In particular, suppose that the Fed wants to prevent the unemployment rate from changing in the short run after the increase in the price of oil. Assume that the Fed changes the money supply once—immediately after the increase in the price of oil—and then does not change the money supply again.

c. What should the Fed do to prevent the unemployment rate from changing in the short run? Show how the Fed's action, combined with the decline in business confidence, affects the *AS–AD* diagram in the short run and the medium run.

d. How do output and the price level in the short run and the medium run compare to your answers from part (a)?

e. How do the short-run and medium-run unemployment rates compare to your answers from part (b)?

9. *Based on your answers to Problems 7 and 8 and the material from the chapter, comment on the following statement:*

   "The Federal Reserve has the easiest job in the world. All it has to do is conduct expansionary monetary policy when the unemployment rate increases and contractionary monetary policy when the unemployment rate falls."

10. *Taxes, oil prices, and workers*

   Everyone in the labor force is concerned with two things: whether they have a job and, if so, their after-tax income from that job (i.e., their after-tax real wage). An unemployed worker may also be concerned with the availability and amount of unemployment benefits, but we will leave that issue aside for this problem.

a. Suppose there is an increase in oil prices. How will this affect the unemployment rate in the short run and the medium run? How will it affect the real wage (W/P)?

b. Suppose there is a reduction in income taxes. How will this affect the unemployment rate in the short run and the medium run? How about the real wage? For a given worker, how will after-tax income be affected?

c. According to our model, what policy tools does the government have available to increase the real wage?

d. During 2003 and 2004, oil prices increased more or less at the same time that income taxes were reduced. A popular joke at the time was that people could use their tax refunds to pay for the higher gas prices. How do your answers to this problem make sense of this joke?

EXPLORE FURTHER

11. *Adding energy prices to the AS curve*

   In this problem, we incorporate the price of energy inputs (e.g., oil) explicitly into the AS curve.

   Suppose the price-setting equation is given by

$$P = (1 + m)W^a P_E^{1-a}$$

where P_E is the price of energy resources and $0 < a < 1$. Ignoring a multiplicative constant, $W^a P_E^{1-a}$ is the marginal cost function that would result from the production technology, $Y = N^a E^{1-a}$, where N is employed labor and E represents units of energy resources used in production.

   As in the text, the wage-setting relation is given by

$$W = P^e F(u, z)$$

   Make sure to distinguish between P_E, the price of energy resources, and P^e, the expected price level for the economy as a whole.

a. Substitute the wage-setting relation into the price-setting relation to obtain the aggregate supply relation.

b. Let $x = P_E/P$, the real price of energy. Observe that $P \times x = P_E$ and substitute for P_E in the *AS* relation you derived in part (a). Solve for *P* to obtain

$$P = P^e (1 + m)^{1/a} F(u, z) x^{(1-a)/a}$$

c. Graph the *AS* relation from part (b) for a given P^e and a given x.

d. Suppose that $P = P^e$. How will the natural rate of unemployment change if x, the real price of energy, increases? [*Hint*: You can solve the *AS* equation for x to obtain the answer, or you can use your intuition. If $P = P^e$, how must $F(u, z)$ change when x increases to maintain the equality in part (b)? How must u change to have the required effect on $F(u, z)$?]

e. Suppose that the economy begins with output equal to the natural level of output. Then the real price of energy increases. Show the short-run and medium-run effects of the increase in the real price of energy in an *AS–AD* diagram.

   The text suggests that a change in expectations about monetary policy may help explain why increases in oil prices over the past few years have had less of an adverse effect on the economy than the oil price shocks of the 1970s. Let us examine how such a change in expectations would alter the effect of an oil price shock.

f. Suppose there is an increase in the real price of energy. In addition, despite the increase in the real price of energy, suppose that the expected price level (i.e., P^e) does not change. After the short-run effect of the increase in the real price of energy, will there be any further adjustment of the economy over the medium run? In order for the expected price level not to change, what monetary action must wage-setters be expecting after an increase in the real price of energy?

12. *Growth and fluctuations: some economic history*

   When economists think about history, fluctuations often stand out—oil shocks and stagflation in the 1970s, a recession followed by a long expansion in the 1980s, a recession followed by an extraordinary low-unemployment, low-inflation boom in the 1990s. This question puts these fluctuations into some perspective.

   *Go to the Web site of the Bureau of Economic Analysis (**www.bea.gov**) and retrieve the quarterly version of NIPA Table 1.1.6, real GDP in chained (2005) dollars. Get real GDP for the fourth quarter of 1959, 1969, 1979, 1989, 1999, 2000, and 2010 as well as for the fourth quarter of the most recent year available.*

a. Using the real GDP numbers for 1959 and 1969, calculate the decadal growth rate of real GDP for the 1960s. Do the same for the 1970s, 1980s, 1990s, and the 2000s and for the available years of the most recent decade.

b. How does growth in the 1970s compare to growth in the later decades? How does growth in the 1960s compare to the later decades? Which decade looks most unusual?

The Phillips Curve, the Natural Rate of Unemployment, and Inflation

I n 1958, A. W. Phillips drew a diagram plotting the rate of inflation against the rate of unemployment in the United Kingdom for each year from 1861 to 1957. He found clear evidence of a negative relation between inflation and unemployment: When unemployment was low, inflation was high, and when unemployment was high, inflation was low, often even negative.

Two years later, Paul Samuelson and Robert Solow replicated Phillips's exercise for the United States, using data from 1900 to 1960. Figure 8-1 reproduces their findings using CPI inflation as a measure of the inflation rate. Apart from the period of very high unemployment during the 1930s (the years from 1931 to 1939 are denoted by triangles and are clearly to the right of the other points in the figure), there also appeared to be a negative relation between inflation and unemployment in the United States. This relation, which Samuelson and Solow labeled the **Phillips curve**, rapidly became central to macroeconomic thinking and policy. It appeared to imply that countries could choose between different combinations of unemployment and inflation. A country could achieve low unemployment if it were willing to tolerate higher inflation, or it could achieve price level stability—zero inflation—if it were willing to tolerate higher unemployment. Much of the discussion about macroeconomic policy became a discussion about which point to choose on the Phillips curve.

In the 1970s, however, this relation broke down. In the United States and most OECD countries, there was both high inflation *and* high unemployment, clearly contradicting the original Phillips curve. A relation reappeared, but it reappeared as a relation between the unemployment rate and the *change* in the inflation rate. Today in the United States, high unemployment typically

Figure 8-1

During the period 1900–1960 in the United States, a low unemployment rate was typically associated with a high inflation rate, and a high unemployment rate was typically associated with a low or negative inflation rate.

Source: Historical Statistics of the United States. http://hsus.cambridge.org/HSUSWeb/index.do

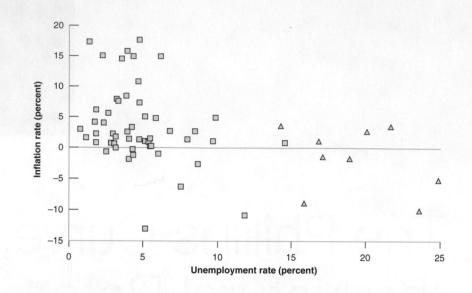

leads not to low inflation, but to a decrease in inflation over time. Conversely, low unemployment doesn't lead to high inflation, but to an increase in inflation over time.

The purpose of this chapter is to explore the mutations of the Phillips curve and, more generally, to understand the relation between inflation and unemployment. You will see that what Phillips discovered was the aggregate supply relation, and that the mutations of the Phillips curve came from changes in the way people and firms formed expectations.

The chapter has three sections:

Section 8-1 shows how we can think of the aggregate supply relation as a relation between inflation, expected inflation, and unemployment.

Section 8-2 uses this relation to interpret the mutations in the Phillips curve over time. It shows the relation between the actual unemployment rate, the natural unemployment rate, and inflation. It then draws two central implications of the Phillips curve for the medium run: In the medium run, unemployment returns to the natural rate, independent of inflation. The inflation rate is determined by the rate of money growth.

Section 8-3 further discusses the relation between unemployment and inflation across countries and over time. ●

8-1 Inflation, Expected Inflation, and Unemployment

We then replaced the unemployment rate by its expression in terms of output to obtain a relation between the price level, the expected price level, and output. As our focus is on the relation between unemployment (rather than output) and inflation, we do not need to take this step here.

Our first step will be to show that the aggregate supply relation we derived in Chapter 7 can be rewritten as a relation between *inflation, expected inflation,* and the *unemployment rate*.

To rewrite, go back to the aggregate supply relation between the price level, the expected price level, and the unemployment rate we derived in Chapter 7 (equation (7.1)).

$$P = P^e (1 + m) F(u, z)$$

Recall that the function F captures the effects on the wage of the unemployment rate, u, and of the other factors that affect wage setting represented by the catchall variable z. m is the markup of prices over wages. It will be convenient here to assume a specific form for this function:

$$F(u, z) = 1 - \alpha u + z$$

The function F comes from the wage-setting relation, equation (6.1):

$$W = P^e F(u, z).$$

This captures the notion that the higher the unemployment rate, the lower the wage; and the higher z (for example, the more generous unemployment benefits are), the higher the wage. The parameter α (the Greek lowercase letter alpha) captures the strength of the effect of unemployment on the wage.

Replace the function F by this specific form in the aggregate supply relation above:

$$P = P^e(1 + m)(1 - \alpha u + z) \qquad (8.1)$$

Finally, let π denote the *inflation rate*, and π^e denote the expected inflation rate. Then equation (8.1) can be rewritten as

$$\pi = \pi^e + (m + z) - \alpha u \qquad (8.2)$$

Deriving equation (8.2) from equation (8.1) is not difficult, but it is tedious, so it is left to an appendix at the end of this chapter. What is important is that you understand each of the effects at work in equation (8.2):

From now on, to lighten your reading, we shall often refer ◀ to "the inflation rate" simply as "inflation," and to "the unemployment rate" simply as "unemployment."

■ *An increase in expected inflation, π^e, leads to an increase in actual inflation, π.*

To see why, start from equation (8.1). An increase in the expected price level P^e leads, one for one, to an increase in the actual price level P: If wage setters expect a higher price level, they set a higher nominal wage, which leads to an increase in the price level.

Now note that, given last period's price level, a higher price level this period implies a higher rate of increase in the price level from last period to this period— that is, higher inflation. Similarly, given last period's price level, a higher expected price level this period implies a higher expected rate of increase in the price level from last period to this period—that is, higher expected inflation. So the fact that an increase in the expected price level leads to an increase in the actual price level can be restated as: An increase in expected inflation leads to an increase in inflation.

◀ Increase in $\pi^e \Rightarrow$ Increase in π.

■ *Given expected inflation, π^e, an increase in the markup m, or an increase in the factors that affect wage determination—an increase in z—leads to an increase in inflation, π.*

From equation (8.1): Given the expected price level P^e, an increase in either m or z increases the price level P. Using the same argument as in the previous bullet to restate this proposition in terms of inflation and expected inflation: Given expected inflation π^e, an increase in either m or z leads to an increase in inflation π.

◀ Increase in m or $z \Rightarrow$ Increase in π.

■ *Given expected inflation, π^e, an increase in the unemployment rate u leads to a decrease in inflation π.*

From equation (8.1): Given the expected price level P^e, an increase in the unemployment rate u leads to a lower nominal wage, which leads to a lower price level P. Restating this in terms of inflation and expected inflation: Given expected inflation π^e, an increase in the unemployment rate u leads to a decrease in inflation π.

◀ Increase in $u \Rightarrow$ Decrease in π.

We need one more step before we return to a discussion of the Phillips curve: When we look at movements in inflation and unemployment in the rest of the chapter, it will often be convenient to use time indexes so that we can refer to variables like inflation, or expected inflation, or unemployment, in a specific year. So we rewrite equation (8.2) as:

$$\pi_t = \pi_t^e + (m + z) - \alpha u_t \qquad (8.3)$$

The variables π_t, π_t^e, and u_t refer to inflation, expected inflation, and unemployment in year t. Be sure you see that there are no time indexes on m and z. This is because we shall typically think of both m and z as constant while we look at movements in inflation, expected inflation, and unemployment over time.

8-2 The Phillips Curve

Let's start with the relation between unemployment and inflation as it was first discovered by Phillips, Samuelson, and Solow, around 1960.

The Early Incarnation

Imagine an economy where inflation is positive in some years, negative in others, and is on average equal to zero. This is not the way things have been for some time: Since 1960, inflation has been positive in all years but one, 2009, when it was negative, but small. But as we shall see later in this chapter, average inflation *was* close to zero during much of the period Phillips, Samuelson, and Solow were studying.

In such an environment, how will wage setters choose nominal wages for the coming year? With the average inflation rate equal to zero in the past, it is reasonable for wage setters to expect that inflation will be equal to zero over the next year as well. So, let's assume that expected inflation is equal to zero—that $\pi_t^e = 0$. Equation (8.3) then becomes

$$\pi_t = (m + z) - \alpha u_t \tag{8.4}$$

This is precisely the negative relation between unemployment and inflation that Phillips found for the United Kingdom and Solow and Samuelson found for the United States. The story behind it is simple: Given the expected price level, which workers simply take to be last year's price level, lower unemployment leads to a higher nominal wage. A higher nominal wage leads to a higher price level. Putting the steps together, lower unemployment leads to a higher price level this year relative to last year's price level—that is, to higher inflation. This mechanism has sometimes been called the **wage–price spiral**, an expression that captures well the basic mechanism at work:

- Low unemployment leads to a higher nominal wage.
- In response to the higher nominal wage, firms increase their prices. The price level increases.
- In response to the higher price level, workers ask for a higher nominal wage the next time the wage is set.
- The higher nominal wage leads firms to further increase their prices. As a result, the price level increases further.
- In response to this further increase in the price level, workers, when they set the wage again, ask for a further increase in the nominal wage.
- And so the race between prices and wages results in steady wage and price inflation.

Mutations

The combination of an apparently reliable empirical relation, together with a plausible story to explain it, led to the adoption of the Phillips curve by macroeconomists and policy makers. During the 1960s, U.S. macroeconomic policy was aimed at maintaining unemployment in the range that appeared consistent with moderate inflation. And, throughout the 1960s, the negative relation between unemployment and inflation provided a reliable guide to the joint movements in unemployment and inflation.

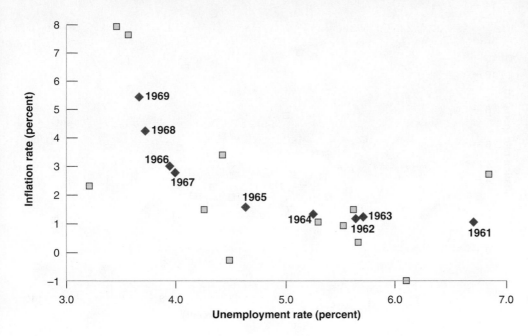

Figure 8-2

Inflation versus Unemployment in the United States, 1948–1969

The steady decline in the U.S. unemployment rate throughout the 1960s was associated with a steady increase in the inflation rate.

Source: Series UNRATE, CPIAUSCL Federal Reserve Economic Data (FRED) http://research. stlouisfed.org/fred2/

Figure 8-2 plots the combinations of the inflation rate and the unemployment rate in the United States for each year from 1948 to 1969. Note how well the Phillips relation held during the long economic expansion that lasted throughout most of the 1960s. During the years 1961 to 1969, denoted by black diamonds in the figure, the unemployment rate declined steadily from 6.8% to 3.4%, and the inflation rate steadily increased, from 1.0% to 5.5%. Put informally, from 1961 to 1969, the U.S. economy moved up along the Phillips curve.

Around 1970, however, the relation between the inflation rate and the unemployment rate, so visible in Figure 8-2, broke down. Figure 8-3 shows the combination of the inflation rate and the unemployment rate in the United States for each year since 1970. The points are scattered in a roughly symmetric cloud: There is no visible relation between the unemployment rate and the inflation rate.

Why did the original Phillips curve vanish? There are two main reasons:

■ The United States was hit twice in the 1970s by a large increase in the price of oil (see Chapter 7). The effect of this increase in nonlabor costs was to force firms to increase their prices relative to the wages they were paying—in other words, to increase the markup m. As shown in equation (8.3), an increase in m leads to an increase in inflation, even at a given rate of unemployment, and this happened twice in the 1970s. The main reason for the breakdown of the Phillips curve relation, however, lay elsewhere:

■ Wage setters changed the way they formed their expectations. This change came, in turn, from a change in the behavior of inflation. Look at Figure 8-4, which shows the U.S. inflation rate since 1914. Starting in the 1960s (the decade shaded in the figure), you can see a clear change in the behavior of the rate of inflation. First, rather than being sometimes positive and sometimes negative, as it had for the first part of the century, the rate of inflation became consistently positive. Second, inflation became more persistent: High inflation in one year became more likely to be followed by high inflation the next year.

■ The persistence of inflation led workers and firms to revise the way they formed their expectations. When inflation is consistently positive year after year, expecting

Figure 8-3

Inflation versus Unemployment in the United States, 1970–2010

Beginning in 1970, the relation between the unemployment rate and the inflation rate disappeared in the United States.

Source: See Figure 8-2.

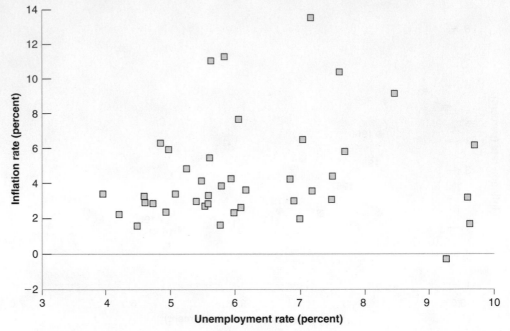

that the price level this year will be the same as the price level last year—which is the same as expecting zero inflation—becomes systematically incorrect; worse, it becomes foolish. People do not like to make the same mistake repeatedly. So, as inflation became consistently positive and more persistent, people, when forming expectations, started to take into account the presence and the persistence of inflation. This change in expectation formation changed the nature of the relation between unemployment and inflation.

Figure 8-4

U.S. Inflation, since 1914

Since the 1960s, the U.S. inflation rate has been consistently positive. Inflation has also become more persistent: A high inflation rate this year is more likely to be followed by a high inflation rate next year.

Source: Years 1900–1914, Historical Statistics of the United States. After 1914: Series CPIAUNS, Federal Reserve Economic Data (FRED) http://research.stlouisfed.org/fred2/

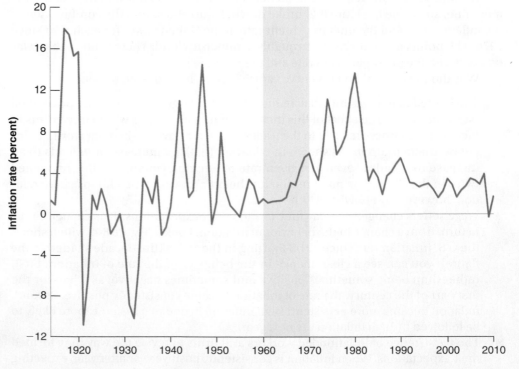

Let's look at the argument in the previous paragraph more closely. First, suppose expectations of inflation are formed according to

$$\pi_t^e = \theta\,\pi_{t-1} \tag{8.5}$$

The value of the parameter θ (the Greek lowercase theta) captures the effect of last year's inflation rate, π_{t-1}, on this year's expected inflation rate, π_t^e. The higher the value of θ, the more last year's inflation leads workers and firms to revise their expectations of what inflation will be this year, and so the higher the expected inflation rate is. We can think of what happened in the 1970s as an increase in the value of θ over time:

- As long as inflation was low and not very persistent, it was reasonable for workers and firms to ignore past inflation and to assume that the price level this year would be roughly the same as price level last year. For the period that Samuelson and Solow had looked at, θ was close to zero, and expectations were roughly given by $\pi_t^e = 0$.
- But, as inflation became more persistent, workers and firms started changing the way they formed expectations. They started assuming that if inflation had been high last year, inflation was likely to be high this year as well. The parameter θ, the effect of last year's inflation rate on this year's expected inflation rate, increased. The evidence suggests that, by the mid-1970s, people expected this year's inflation rate to be the same as last year's inflation rate—in other words, that θ was now equal to 1.

▸ Think about how you form expectations. What do you expect inflation to be next year? How did you come to this conclusion?

Now turn to the implications of different values of θ for the relation between inflation and unemployment. To do so, substitute equation (8.5) for the value of π_t^e into equation (8.3):

$$\pi_t = \overbrace{\theta\pi_{t-1}}^{\pi_t^e} + (m + z) - \alpha u_t$$

- When θ equals zero, we get the original Phillips curve, a relation between the inflation rate and the unemployment rate:

$$\pi_t = (m + z) - \alpha u_t$$

- When θ is positive, the inflation rate depends not only on the unemployment rate but also on last year's inflation rate:

$$\pi_t = \theta\pi_{t-1} + (m + z) - \alpha u_t$$

- When θ equals 1, the relation becomes (moving last year's inflation rate to the left side of the equation)

$$\pi_t - \pi_{t-1} = (m + z) - \alpha u_t \tag{8.6}$$

So, when $\theta = 1$, the unemployment rate affects not *the inflation rate*, but rather the *change in the inflation rate*: High unemployment leads to decreasing inflation; low unemployment leads to increasing inflation.

This discussion is the key to what happened from 1970 onward. As θ increased from 0 to 1, the simple relation between the unemployment rate and the inflation rate disappeared. This disappearance is what we saw in Figure 8-3. But a new relation emerged, this time between the unemployment rate and the change in the inflation

This line, called a regression line, is obtained using econometrics. (See Appendix 3 at the end of the book.) Note the line does not fit the cloud ▶ of points very tightly. There are years when the change in inflation is much larger than implied by the line and years when the change in inflation is much smaller than implied by the line. We return to this point later.

Original Phillips curve:
Increase in $u_t \Rightarrow$ Lower inflation.
(Modified) Phillips curve:
Increase in $u_t \Rightarrow$ Decreasing ▶ inflation.

rate—as predicted by equation (8.6). This relation is shown in Figure 8-5, which plots the change in the inflation rate versus the unemployment rate observed for each year since 1970. The figure shows a negative relation between the unemployment rate and the change in the inflation rate. The line that best fits the scatter of points for the period 1970–2010 is given by

$$\pi_t - \pi_{t-1} = 3.3\% - 0.55\, u_t \tag{8.7}$$

The line is drawn in Figure 8-5. For low unemployment, the change in inflation is positive. For high unemployment, the change in inflation is negative. This is the form the Phillips curve relation between unemployment and inflation takes today.

To distinguish it from the original Phillips curve (equation (8.4)), equation (8.6) or its empirical counterpart, equation (8.7) is often called the **modified Phillips curve**, or the **expectations-augmented Phillips curve** (to indicate that π_{t-1} stands for expected inflation), or the **accelerationist Phillips curve** (to indicate that a low unemployment rate leads to an increase in the inflation rate and thus *an acceleration* of the price level). We shall simply call equation (8.6) the Phillips curve and refer to the earlier incarnation, equation (8.4), as the *original* Phillips curve.

Figure 8-5

Change in Inflation versus Unemployment in the United States, 1970–2010

Since 1970, there has been a negative relation between the unemployment rate and the change in the inflation rate in the United States.

Source: Series CPIUNSCL, UNRATE: Federal Reserve Economic Data (FRED) http://research.stlouisfed.org/fred2/

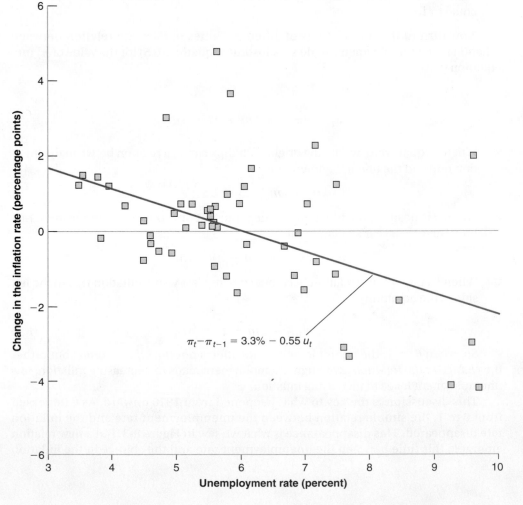

The Phillips Curve and the Natural Rate of Unemployment

The history of the Phillips curve is closely related to the discovery of the concept of the natural unemployment rate that we introduced in Chapter 6.

The original Phillips curve implied that there was no such thing as a natural unemployment rate: If policy makers were willing to tolerate a higher inflation rate, they could maintain a lower unemployment rate forever.

In the late 1960s, while the original Phillips curve still gave a good description of the data, two economists, Milton Friedman and Edmund Phelps, questioned the existence of such a trade-off between unemployment and inflation. They questioned it on logical grounds, arguing that such a trade-off could exist only if wage setters systematically underpredicted inflation, and that they were unlikely to make the same mistake forever. Friedman and Phelps also argued that if the government attempted to sustain lower unemployment by accepting higher inflation, the trade-off would ultimately disappear; the unemployment rate could not be sustained below a certain level, a level they called the "natural rate of unemployment." Events proved them right, and the trade-off between the unemployment rate and the inflation rate indeed disappeared. (See the Focus box "Theory ahead of the Facts: Milton Friedman and Edmund Phelps.") Today, most economists accept the notion of a *natural rate of unemployment*—subject to the many caveats we will see in the next ◀ section.

> Friedman was awarded the Nobel Prize in 1976. Phelps was awarded the Nobel Prize in 2006.

Let's make explicit the connection between the Phillips curve and the natural rate of unemployment.

By definition (see Chapter 6), the natural rate of unemployment is the unemployment rate such that the actual price level is equal to the expected price level. Equivalently, and more conveniently here, the natural rate of unemployment is the unemployment rate such that the actual inflation rate is equal to the expected inflation rate. Denote the natural unemployment rate by u_n (the index n stands for "natural"). Then, imposing the condition that actual inflation and expected inflation be the same ($\pi_t = \pi_t^e$) in equation (8.3) gives

$$0 = (m + z) - \alpha u_n$$

Solving for the natural rate u_n,

$$u_n = \frac{m + z}{\alpha} \tag{8.8}$$

The higher the markup, m, or the higher the factors that affect wage setting, z, the higher the natural rate of unemployment.

Now rewrite equation (8.3) as

$$\pi_t - \pi_t^e = -\alpha \left(u_t - \frac{m + z}{\alpha} \right)$$

Note from equation (8.8) that the fraction on the right side is equal to u_n, so we can rewrite the equation as

$$\pi_t - \pi_t^e = -\alpha(u_t - u_n) \tag{8.9}$$

If—as is the case in the United States today—the expected rate of inflation, π_t^e, is well approximated by last year's inflation rate, π_{t-1}, the equation finally becomes

$$\pi_t - \pi_{t-1} = -\alpha(u_t - u_n) \tag{8.10}$$

Theory Ahead of Facts: Milton Friedman and Edmund Phelps

Economists are usually not very good at predicting major changes before they happen, and most of their insights are derived after the fact. Here is an exception.

In the late 1960s—precisely as the original Phillips curve relation was working like a charm—two economists, Milton Friedman and Edmund Phelps, argued that the appearance of a trade-off between inflation and unemployment was an illusion.

Here are a few quotes from Milton Friedman. About the Phillips curve, he said:

"Implicitly, Phillips wrote his article for a world in which everyone anticipated that nominal prices would be stable and in which this anticipation remained unshaken and immutable whatever happened to actual prices and wages. Suppose, by contrast, that everyone anticipates that prices will rise at a rate of more than 75% a year—as, for example, Brazilians did a few years ago. Then, wages must rise at that rate simply to keep real wages unchanged. An excess supply of labor [by this, Friedman means high unemployment] will be reflected in a less rapid rise in nominal wages than in anticipated prices, not in an absolute decline in wages."

He went on:

"To state [my] conclusion differently, there is always a temporary trade-off between inflation and unemployment; there is no permanent trade-off. The temporary trade-off comes not from inflation per se, but from a rising rate of inflation."

He then tried to guess how much longer the apparent trade-off between inflation and unemployment would last in the United States:

"But how long, you will say, is "temporary"? . . . I can at most venture a personal judgment, based on some examination of the historical evidence, that the initial effect of a higher and unanticipated rate of inflation lasts for something like two to five years; that this initial effect then begins to be reversed; and that a full adjustment to the new rate of inflation takes as long for employment as for interest rates, say, a couple of decades."

Friedman could not have been more right. A few years later, the original Phillips curve started to disappear, in exactly the way Friedman had predicted.

Source: Milton Friedman, "The Role of Monetary Policy," American Economic Review 1968 58(1): pp. 1-17. (The article by Phelps, "Money-Wage Dynamics and Labor-Market Equilibrium," *Journal of Political Economy* 1968 76(4–part 2): pp. 678–711, made many of the same points more formally.)

Equation (8.10) is an important relation, for two reasons:

■ It gives us another way of thinking about *the Phillips curve*, as a relation between the actual unemployment rate u_t, the natural unemployment rate u_n, and the change in the inflation rate $\pi_t - \pi_{t-1}$:

The change in the inflation rate depends on the difference between the actual and the natural unemployment rates. When the actual unemployment rate is higher than the natural unemployment rate, the inflation rate decreases; when the actual unemployment rate is lower than the natural unemployment rate, the inflation rate increases.

$$u_t < u_n \Rightarrow \pi_t > \pi_{t-1}$$
$$u_t > u_n \Rightarrow \pi_t < \pi_{t-1}$$

■ It also gives us another way of thinking about the *natural rate of unemployment*:

The natural rate of unemployment is the rate of unemployment required to keep the inflation rate constant. This is why the natural rate is also called the **non-accelerating inflation rate of unemployment**, or **NAIRU**.

Calling the natural rate "the non-accelerating inflation rate of unemployment" is actually wrong: It should be called "the non-increasing inflation rate of unemployment," or NIIRU. But NAIRU has now become so standard that it is too late to change it.

What has been the natural rate of unemployment in the United States since 1970? Put another way: What has been the unemployment rate that, on average, has led to constant inflation?

To answer this question, all we need to do is to return to equation (8.7), the estimated relation between the change in inflation and the unemployment rate since 1970. Setting the change in inflation equal to zero in that equation implies a value for the natural unemployment rate of 3.3%/0.55 = 6%. In words: The evidence suggests that, since 1970 in the United States, the average rate of unemployment required to keep inflation constant has been equal to 6%.

The Neutrality of Money, Revisited

In Chapter 7, we looked at the effects of a change in the *level of nominal money* on output and on the price level in the medium run. We derived two propositions. First, output returned to its natural level, unaffected by the level of nominal money. Second, the price level moved in proportion to the nominal money stock, leaving the real money stock unchanged. We are now ready to extend these results and look at the effects of changes in the *rate of growth of nominal money* on unemployment and on inflation in the medium run.

Let us first look at unemployment and go back to equation (8.9). In the medium run, expected inflation must be equal to actual inflation. Thus the unemployment rate must be equal to the natural rate, which is clearly independent of the rate of growth of money.

Recall the derivation of the natural rate in Chapter 6. The natural rate depends on such factors as the markup of firms and the nature of bargaining in the labor market. Nowhere does the growth rate of money appear in the determination of the natural rate.

Now turn to inflation, and go back to the aggregate demand relation we derived in Chapter 7, equation (7.3):

$$Y = Y\left(\frac{M}{P}, G, T\right)$$

As we have done in previous chapters, we continue to ignore output growth, and thus assume that output is constant in the medium run.

If unemployment returns to the natural rate, u_n, it follows that output must return to its natural level, Y_n. So the relation becomes:

$$Y_n = Y\left(\frac{M}{P}, G, T\right)$$

If Y_n is constant, for this equality to hold (that is, for aggregate demand to be equal to the natural level of output), the right-hand side of the equation must be constant. If we assume unchanged fiscal policy (that is, constant G and constant T), this implies that the real money stock must also be constant. This implies in turn that the rate of inflation must be equal to the rate of money growth.

$$\pi = g_M$$

See Proposition 8 in Appendix 2. g_M is the notation for the rate of growth of the nominal money stock.

This is an important result: In the medium run, the rate of inflation is determined by the rate of money growth. Milton Friedman put it this way: *Inflation is always and everywhere a monetary phenomenon.* As we have seen, factors such as the monopoly power of firms, strong unions, strikes, fiscal deficits, and increases in the price of oil do affect the price level and, by implication, do affect inflation in the short run. But, unless they affect the rate of money growth, they have no effect on inflation in the medium run.

8-3 A Summary and Many Warnings

Let's take stock of what we have learned about the relation between inflation and unemployment:

- The aggregate supply relation is well captured in the United States today by a relation between the change in the inflation rate and the deviation of the unemployment rate from the natural rate of unemployment (equation (8.8)).
- When the unemployment rate exceeds the natural rate of unemployment, the inflation rate typically decreases. When the unemployment rate is below the natural rate of unemployment, the inflation rate typically increases.

The "unless" is important here. It could be, for example, that some of these shocks lead to a change in the rate of money growth. For example, a wage explosion or a large budget deficit may lead to higher money creation (more on deficits and inflation in Chapter 24). If this is the case, these shocks will, indirectly, affect inflation even in the medium run.

This relation has held quite well since 1970. But evidence from its earlier history, as well as the evidence from other countries, points to the need for a number of warnings.

All of them are on the same theme: The relation between inflation and unemployment can and does vary across countries and time.

Variations in the Natural Rate across Countries

Recall from equation (8.8) that the natural rate of unemployment depends on: all the factors that affect wage setting, represented by the catchall variable z; the markup set by firms m; and the response of inflation to unemployment, represented by α. If these factors differ across countries, there is no reason to expect all countries to have the same natural rate of unemployment. And natural rates indeed differ across countries, sometimes considerably.

Go back and look at Table 1-3 ▶ in Chapter 1.

Take, for example, the unemployment rate in the Euro area, which has averaged close to 9% since 1980. A high unemployment rate for a few years may well reflect a deviation of the unemployment rate from the natural rate. A high average unemployment rate for 30 years surely reflects a high natural rate. This tells us where we should look for explanations: in the factors determining the wage-setting and the price-setting relations.

Is it easy to identify the relevant factors? One often hears the statement that one of the main problems of Europe is its **labor-market rigidities**. These rigidities, the argument goes, are responsible for its high unemployment. While there is some truth to this statement, the reality is more complex. The Focus box, "What Explains European Unemployment?" discusses these issues further.

Variations in the Natural Rate over Time

In writing equation (8.6) and estimating equation (8.7), we treated $m + z$ as a constant. But there are good reasons to believe that m and z vary over time. The degree of monopoly power of firms, the structure of wage bargaining, the system of unemployment benefits, and so on are likely to change over time, leading to changes in either m or z and, by implication, changes in the natural rate of unemployment.

Changes in the natural unemployment rate over time are hard to measure. Again, the reason is that we do not observe the natural rate, only the actual rate. But broad evolutions can be established by comparing average unemployment rates, say across decades. Using this approach, the Focus box "What Explains European Unemployment?" discusses how and why the natural rate of unemployment had increased in Europe since the 1960s. The U.S. natural rate has moved much less than that in Europe. Nevertheless, it is also far from constant. Go back and look at Figure 6-3. You can see that, from the 1950s to the 1980s, the unemployment rate fluctuated around a slowly increasing trend: Average unemployment was 4.5% in the 1950s, and 7.3% in the 1980s. Then, from 1990 on, and until the crisis, the trend was reversed, with an average unemployment rate of 5.7% in the 1990s, and an average unemployment rate of 5.0% from 2000 to 2007. In 2007, the unemployment rate was 4.6%, and inflation was roughly constant, suggesting that unemployment was close to the natural rate. Why the U.S. natural rate of unemployment fell from the early 1990s on and what the effects of the crisis may be for the future are discussed in the Focus box "Changes in the U.S. Natural Rate of Unemployment since 1990". We draw two conclusions from the behavior of the U.S. unemployment rate since 1990 and these conclusions parallel the conclusion from our look at European unemployment in the earlier box: The determinants of the natural rate are many. We can identify a number of them, but knowing their respective role and drawing policy lessons is not easy.

Disinflation, Credibility, and Unemployment

In 1979, U.S. unemployment was 5.8%, roughly equal to the natural rate at the time. But the inflation rate, measured using the CPI, was running above 13%. Some of this

What Explains European Unemployment?

What do critics have in mind when they talk about the "labor-market rigidities" afflicting Europe? They have in mind in particular:

■ A generous system of **unemployment insurance**. The replacement rate—that is, the ratio of unemployment benefits to the after-tax wage—is often high in Europe, and the duration of benefits—the period of time for which the unemployed are entitled to receive benefits—often runs in years.

  Some unemployment insurance is clearly desirable. But generous benefits are likely to increase unemployment in at least two ways: They decrease the incentives the unemployed have to search for jobs. They may also increase the wage that firms have to pay. Recall our discussion of efficiency wages in Chapter 6. The higher unemployment benefits are, the higher the wages firms have to pay in order to motivate and keep workers.

■ A high degree of employment protection. By **employment protection**, economists have in mind the set of rules that increase the cost of layoffs for firms. These range from high severance payments, to the need for firms to justify layoffs, to the possibility for workers to appeal the decision and have it reversed.

  The purpose of employment protection is to decrease layoffs, and thus to protect workers from the risk of unemployment. What it also does, however, is to increase the cost of labor for firms and thus to reduce hires and make it harder for the unemployed to get jobs. The evidence suggests that, while employment protection does not necessarily increase unemployment, it changes its nature: The flows in and out of unemployment decrease, but the average duration of unemployment increases. Such long duration increases the risk that the unemployed lose skills and morale, decreasing their employability.

■ Minimum wages. Most European countries have national minimum wages. And in some countries, the ratio of the minimum wage to the median wage can be quite high. High minimum wages clearly run the risk of decreasing employment for the least-skilled workers, thus increasing their unemployment rate.

■ Bargaining rules. In most European countries, labor contracts are subject to **extension agreements**. A contract agreed to by a subset of firms and unions can be automatically extended to all firms in the sector. This considerably reinforces the bargaining power of unions, as it reduces the scope for competition by nonunionized firms. As we saw in Chapter 6, stronger bargaining power on the part of the unions may result in higher unemployment: Higher unemployment is needed to reconcile the demands of workers with the wages paid by firms.

Do these labor-market institutions really explain high unemployment in Europe? Is the case open and shut? Not quite. Here it is important to recall two important facts:

Fact 1: Unemployment was not always high in Europe. In the 1960s, the unemployment rate in the four major continental European countries was lower than that in the United States, around 2–3%. U.S. economists would cross the ocean to study the "European unemployment miracle"! The natural rate in these countries today is around 8–9%. How do we explain this increase?

One hypothesis is that institutions were different then, and that labor-market rigidities have only appeared in the last 40 years. This turns out not to be the case, however. It is true that, in response to the adverse shocks of the 1970s (in particular the two recessions following the increases in the price of oil), many European governments increased the generosity of unemployment insurance and the degree of employment protection. But, even in the 1960s, European labor-market institutions looked nothing like U.S. labor-market institutions. Social protection was much higher in Europe; yet unemployment was lower.

A more convincing line of explanation focuses on the interaction between institutions and shocks. Some labor-market institutions may be benign in some environments, yet very costly in others. Take employment protection. If competition between firms is limited, the need to adjust employment in each firm may be limited as well, and so the cost of employment protection may be low. But if competition, either from other domestic firms or from foreign firms, increases, the cost of employment protection may become very high. Firms that cannot adjust their labor force quickly may simply be unable to compete and go out of business.

Fact 2: Until the current crisis started, a number of European countries actually had low unemployment. This is shown in Figure 1, which gives the unemployment rate for 15 European countries (the 15 members of the European Union before the increase in membership to 27) in 2006. We chose 2006 because, in all these countries, inflation was stable, suggesting that the unemployment rate was roughly equal to the natural rate.

As you can see, the unemployment rate was indeed high in the large four continental countries: France, Spain, Germany, and Italy. But note how low the unemployment rate was in some of the other countries, in particular Denmark, Ireland, and the Netherlands.

Is it the case that these low unemployment countries had low benefits, low employment protection, weak unions? Things are unfortunately not so simple: Countries such as Ireland or the United Kingdom indeed have labor-market institutions that resemble those of the United States: limited benefits, low employment

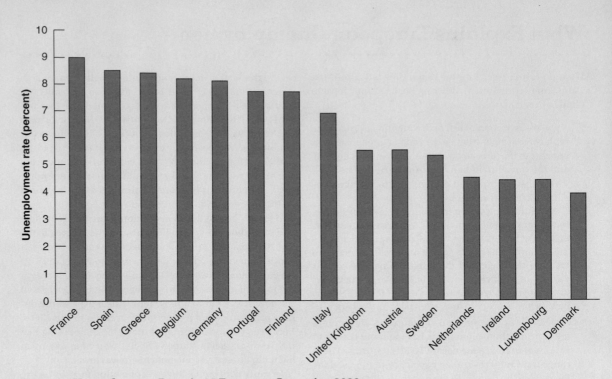

Figure 1 *Unemployment Rates in 15 European Countries, 2006*

protection, and weak unions. But countries like Denmark or the Netherlands have a high degree of social protection (in particular high unemployment benefits) and strong unions.

So what is one to conclude? An emerging consensus among economists is that the devil is in the details: Generous social protection is consistent with low unemployment. But it has to be provided efficiently. For example, unemployment benefits can be generous, so long as the unemployed are, at the same time, forced to take jobs if such jobs are available. Some employment protection (for example, in the form of generous severance payments) may be consistent with low

unemployment, so long as firms do not face the prospect of long administrative or judicial uncertainty when they lay off workers. Countries such as Denmark appear to have been more successful in achieving these goals. Creating incentives for the unemployed to take jobs and simplifying the rules of employment protection are on the reform agenda of many European governments. One may hope they will lead to a decrease in the natural rate in the future.

For more information on European unemployment, read Olivier Blanchard, "European Unemployment. The Evolution of Facts and Ideas," Economic Policy, 2006 (1): pp. 1–54.

was due to the large increase in oil prices, but, leaving this effect aside, underlying inflation was running at close to 10%. The question the Federal Reserve faced was no longer whether or not it should reduce inflation, but how fast it should reduce it. In August 1979, President Carter appointed Paul Volcker as Chairman of the Federal Reserve Board. Volcker, who had served in the Nixon administration, was considered an extremely qualified chairman who would and could lead the fight against inflation.

Fighting inflation implied tightening monetary policy, decreasing output growth, and thus accepting higher unemployment for some time. The question arose of how much unemployment, and for how long, would likely be needed to achieve a lower level of inflation, say 4%—which is the rate Volcker wanted to achieve.

Make sure to distinguish between deflation: a decrease in the price level (equivalently, negative inflation), and disinflation: a decrease in the inflation rate.

▶ ■ Some economists argued that such a **disinflation** would likely be very costly. Their starting point was equation (8.10):

$$\pi_t - \pi_{t-1} = -\alpha(u_t - u_n)$$

Changes in the U.S. Natural Rate of Unemployment since 1990

From 2000 to 2007, the average unemployment rate was under 5%, and inflation was stable. It thus appeared that the natural rate was around 5%, so roughly 2% lower than it had been in the 1980s. Since the beginning of the crisis, the unemployment rate has increased to reach more than 9% and is forecast to remain high for many years. While most of this increase clearly reflects an increase in the actual unemployment rate over the natural rate, the long period of high actual unemployment raises the issue of whether we can hope to go back to the pre-crisis rate.

Start with the first issue, namely why the natural rate decreased from the 1980s on. Researchers have offered a number of explanations:

■ Increased globalization and stronger competition between U.S. and foreign firms may have led to a decrease in monopoly power and a decrease in the markup. Also, the fact that firms can more easily move some of their operations abroad surely makes them stronger when bargaining with their workers. The evidence that unions in the U.S. economy are becoming weaker: The unionization rate in the United States, which stood at 25% in the mid 1970s, is below 15% today. As we saw, weaker bargaining power on the part of workers is likely to lead to lower unemployment.

■ The nature of the labor market has changed. In 1980, employment by temporary help agencies accounted for less than 0.5% of total U.S. employment. Today, it accounts for more than 2%. This is also likely to have reduced the natural rate of unemployment. In effect, it allows many workers to look for jobs while being employed rather than unemployed. The increasing role of Internet-based job sites, such as Monster.com, has also made matching of jobs and workers easier, leading to lower unemployment.

Some of the other explanations may surprise you. For example, researchers have also pointed to:

■ The aging of the U.S. population. The proportion of young workers (workers between the ages of 16 and 24) fell from 24% in 1980 to 14% in 2006. This reflects the end of the baby boom, which ended in the mid-1960s. Young workers tend to start their working life by going from job to job and typically have a higher unemployment rate. So, a decrease in the proportion of young workers leads to a decrease in the overall unemployment rate.

■ An increase in the incarceration rate. The proportion of the population in prison or in jail has tripled in the last 20 years in the United States. In 1980, 0.3% of the U.S. population of working age was in prison. In 2006, the proportion had increased to 1.0%. Because many of those in prison would likely have been unemployed were they not incarcerated, this is likely to have had an effect on the unemployment rate.

■ The increase in the number of workers on disability. A relaxation of eligibility criteria since 1984 has led to a steady increase in the number of workers receiving disability insurance, from 2.2% of the working age population in 1984 to 3.8% in 2006. It is again likely that, absent changes in the rules, some of the workers on disability insurance would have been unemployed instead.

Will the natural rate of unemployment remain low in the future? Globalization, aging, prisons, temporary help agencies, and the increasing role of the Internet are probably here to stay, suggesting that the natural rate should indeed remain low. Since the beginning of the crisis, however, there is an increasing worry, that the increase in the actual unemployment rate may eventually translate into an increase in the natural unemployment rate. The mechanism through which this may happen is known as **hysteresis** (in economics, hysteresis is used to mean that, after a shock, a variable does not return to its initial value, even when the shock has gone away):

Workers who have been unemployed for a long time may lose their skills, or their morale, and become, in effect, unemployable, leading to a higher natural rate. This is a very relevant concern. As we saw in Chapter 6, in 2010, the average duration of unemployment was 33 weeks, an exceptionally high number by historical standards. Forty-three percent of the unemployed had been unemployed for more than six months, 28% for more than a year. This raises two important questions. First, when the economy picks up, how many of them will be scarred by their unemployment experience and hard to reemploy? Second, are there policies which should be put in place now to help the long-term unemployed get back to work?

For more on the decrease in the natural rate, read "The High-Pressure U.S. Labor Market of the 1990s," by Lawrence Katz and Alan Krueger, *Brookings Papers on Economic Activity*, 1999 (1): pp. 1–87.

According to this equation, the only way to bring down inflation is to accept unemployment above the natural rate for some time. We saw earlier that α is estimated to be equal to 0.55. The equation therefore implies that, to decrease inflation by one percentage point, the unemployment rate has to be higher than the natural unemployment rate by 1/0.55, or about 1.8 percentage points for a year. Or to decrease inflation from 10% to 4%, the unemployment rate has to be higher than the natural rate by about 10 ((10 − 4)/0.55) percentage points for a year, or, more realistically, if inflation was decreased from 10% to 6% in five years, by about 2 (10/5) percentage points for five years. The natural conclusion was that it would make sense to go slowly, so as not to increase unemployment by too much in a given year.

Robert Lucas was awarded the Nobel Prize in 1995 and teaches at the University of Chicago.

■ Some economists argued that disinflation might in fact be much less costly. In what has become known as the **Lucas critique**, Lucas pointed out that when trying to predict the effects of a major policy change—like the change considered by too much the Fed at the time—it could be very misleading to take as given the relations estimated from past data. In the case of the Phillips curve, taking equation (8.10) as given was equivalent to assuming that wage setters would keep expecting inflation in the future to be the same as it was in the past, that the way wage setters formed their expectations would not change in response to the change in policy. This was an unwarranted assumption, Lucas argued: Why shouldn't wage setters take policy changes directly into account? If wage setters believed that the Fed was committed to lower inflation, they might well expect inflation to be lower in the future than in the past. They argued that the relevant equation was not equation (8.10) but equation (8.9). And equation (8.9) implied that, if the Fed was fully credible, the decrease in inflation might not require *any* increase in the unemployment rate. If wage setters expected inflation to now be 4%, then actual inflation would decrease to 4%, with unemployment remaining at the natural rate:

$$\pi_t = \pi_t^e - \alpha(u_t - u_n)$$
$$4\% = 4\% - \quad 0\%$$

Thomas Sargent was awarded the Nobel Prize in 2011 and now teaches at New York University.

Lucas did not believe that disinflation could really take place without some increase in unemployment. But Thomas Sargent, looking at the historical evidence on the end of several very high inflations, concluded that the increase in unemployment could be small. The essential ingredient of successful disinflation, he argued, was **credibility** of monetary policy—the belief by wage setters that the central bank was truly committed to reducing inflation. Only credibility would cause wage setters to change the way they formed their expectations. Furthermore, he argued, a clear and quick disinflation program was more likely to be credible than a protracted one that offered plenty of opportunities for reversal and political infighting along the way.

Who turned out to be right? In September 1979, Paul Volcker started increasing the interest rate so as to slow down the economy and reduce inflation. From 9% in 1979, the three-month Treasury bill rate was increased to 15% in August 1981. The effects on inflation, output growth, and unemployment are shown in Table 8-1. The table makes clear that there was no credibility miracle: Disinflation was associated with a sharp recession, with negative growth in both 1980 and 1982, and with a large and long-lasting increase in unemployment. The average unemployment rate was above 9% in both 1982 and 1983,

Table 8-1	Inflation and Unemployment, 1979–1985						
	1979	1980	1981	1982	1983	1984	1985
CPI inflation (%)	13.3	12.5	8.9	3.8	3.8	3.9	3.8
GDP growth (%)	2.5	−0.5	1.8	−2.2	3.9	6.2	3.2
Unemployment rate (%)	5.8	7.1	7.6	9.7	9.6	7.5	7.2

peaking at 10.8% in the month of December 1982. If we assume a natural rate of 6% and add the excess of unemployment above the natural rate (so 7.1% − 6.0% = 1.1% for 1980, 7.6% − 6.0% = 1.6% for 1981, etc.), total excess unemployment from 1979 to 1985 was 12.7%, a number no better than what equation (8.10) predicted.

Does this settle the issue of how much credibility matters? Not really. Those who argued before the fact that credibility would help argued after the fact that Volcker had not been fully credible. After increasing the interest rate from September 1979 to April 1980 and inducing a sharp decrease in growth, he appeared to have second thoughts, reversing course and sharply decreasing the interest rate from April to September, only to increase it again in 1981. This lack of consistency, some argued, reduced his credibility and increased the unemployment cost of the disinflation. A larger lesson still stands: The behavior of inflation depends very much on how people and firms form expectations. The Lucas critique still stands: The past relation between unemployment and inflation may be a poor guide to what happens when policy changes.

High Inflation and the Phillips Curve Relation

Recall how, in the 1970s, the U.S. Phillips curve changed as inflation became more persistent and wage setters changed the way they formed inflation expectations. The lesson is a general one: The relation between unemployment and inflation is likely to change with the level and the persistence of inflation. Evidence from countries with high inflation confirms this lesson. Not only does the way workers and firms form their expectations change, but so do institutional arrangements:

When the inflation rate becomes high, inflation also tends to become more variable. As a result, workers and firms become more reluctant to enter into labor ◄ contracts that set nominal wages for a long period of time: If inflation turns out higher than expected, real wages may plunge and workers will suffer a large cut in their living standard. If inflation turns out lower than expected, real wages may go up sharply. Firms may not be able to pay their workers. Some may go bankrupt.

For this reason, the terms of wage agreements change with the level of inflation. Nominal wages are set for shorter periods of time, down from a year to a month or even less. **Wage indexation**, a provision that automatically increases wages in line with inflation, becomes more prevalent.

These changes lead in turn to a stronger response of inflation to unemployment. To see this, an example based on wage indexation will help. Imagine an economy that has two types of labor contracts. A proportion λ (the Greek lowercase letter lambda) of labor contracts is indexed: Nominal wages in those contracts move one for one with variations in the actual price level. A proportion $1 - \lambda$ of labor contracts is not indexed: Nominal wages are set on the basis of expected inflation.

Under this assumption, equation (8.9) becomes

$$\pi_t = [\lambda \pi_t + (1 - \lambda)\pi_t^e] - \alpha(u_t - u_n)$$

The term in brackets on the right reflects the fact that a proportion λ of contracts is indexed and thus responds to actual inflation, π_t, and a proportion, $1 - \lambda$, responds to expected inflation, π_t^e. If we assume that this year's expected inflation is equal to last year's actual inflation, $\pi_t^e = \pi_{t-1}$, we get

$$\pi_t = [\lambda \pi_t + (1 - \lambda)\pi_{t-1}] - \alpha(u_t - u_n) \tag{8.11}$$

When $\lambda = 0$, all wages are set on the basis of expected inflation—which is equal to last year's inflation, π_{t-1}—and the equation reduces to equation (8.10):

$$\pi_t - \pi_{t-1} = -\alpha(u_t - u_n)$$

More concretely: When inflation runs on average at 3% a year, wage setters can be reasonably confident inflation will be between 1% and 5%. When inflation runs on average at 30% a year, wage setters can be confident inflation will be between 20% and 40%. In the first case, the real wage may end up 2% higher or lower than they expected when they set the nominal wage. In the second case, it may end up 10% higher or lower than they expected. There is much more uncertainty in the second case.

When λ is positive, however, a proportion λ of wages is set on the basis of actual inflation rather than expected inflation. To see what this implies, reorganize equation (8.11): Move the term in brackets to the left, factor $(1 - \lambda)$ on the left of the equation, and divide both sides by $1 - \lambda$ to get

$$\pi_t - \pi_{t-1} = -\frac{\alpha}{(1 - \lambda)}(u_t - u_n)$$

Wage indexation increases the effect of unemployment on inflation. The higher the proportion of wage contracts that are indexed—the higher λ—the larger the effect the unemployment rate has on the change in inflation—the higher the coefficient $\alpha/(1 - \lambda)$.

The intuition is as follows: Without wage indexation, lower unemployment increases wages, which in turn increases prices. But because wages do not respond to prices right away, there is no further increase in prices within the year. With wage indexation, however, an increase in prices leads to a further increase in wages within the year, which leads to a further increase in prices, and so on, so that the effect of unemployment on inflation within the year is higher.

If, and when, λ gets close to 1—which is when most labor contracts allow for wage indexation—small changes in unemployment can lead to very large changes in inflation. Put another way, there can be large changes in inflation with nearly no change in unemployment. This is what happens in countries where inflation is very high: The relation between inflation and unemployment becomes more and more tenuous and eventually disappears altogether.

Deflation and the Phillips Curve Relation

We have just looked at what happens to the Phillips curve when inflation is very high. Another issue is what happens when inflation is low, and possibly negative—when there is deflation.

The motivation for asking this question is given by an aspect of Figure 8-1 we mentioned at the start of the chapter but then left aside. In that figure, note how the points corresponding to the 1930s (they are denoted by triangles) lie to the right of the others. Not only is unemployment unusually high—this is no surprise because we are looking at the years corresponding to the Great Depression—but, *given the high unemployment rate*, the inflation rate is surprisingly high. In other words, given the very high unemployment rate, we would have expected not merely deflation, but a large rate of deflation. In fact, deflation was limited, and from 1934 to 1937, despite still very high unemployment, inflation actually turned positive.

How do we interpret this fact? There are two potential explanations.

One is that the Great Depression was associated with an increase not only in the actual unemployment rate, but also in the natural unemployment rate. This seems unlikely. Most economic historians see the Great Depression primarily as the result of a large adverse shift in aggregate demand leading to an increase in the actual unemployment rate over the natural rate of unemployment, rather than an increase in the natural rate of unemployment itself.

The other is that, when the economy starts experiencing deflation, the Phillips curve relation breaks down. One possible reason: The reluctance of workers to accept decreases in their nominal wages. Workers will unwittingly accept a cut in their real wages that occurs when their nominal wages increase more slowly than inflation. However, they are likely to fight the same cut in their real wages if it results from an overt cut in their nominal wages. If this argument is correct, this implies that the Phillips curve

Consider two scenarios. In one, inflation is 4%, and your nominal wage goes up by 2%. In the other, inflation is 0%, and your nominal wage is cut by 2%. Which do you dislike most? You should be indifferent between the two: In both cases, your real wage goes down by 2%. There is some evidence, however, that most people find the first scenario less painful, and thus suffer from money illusion, a term made more explicit in Chapter 24.

relation between the change in inflation and unemployment may disappear, or at least become weaker, when the economy is close to zero inflation.

This issue is not just of historical interest: In many countries today, unemployment is very high, and inflation is low. Whether inflation will turn into deflation is one of the developments closely watched by macroeconomists today.

Why deflation is potentially dangerous, and why policy makers want to avoid it, will have to wait until we introduce the distinction between nominal and real interest rates. We shall do this and return to this issue in Chapter 14.

Summary

■ The aggregate supply relation can be expressed as a relation between inflation, expected inflation, and unemployment. Given unemployment, higher expected inflation leads to higher inflation. Given expected inflation, higher unemployment leads to lower inflation.

■ When inflation is not very persistent, expected inflation does not depend very much on past inflation. Thus, the aggregate supply relation becomes a relation between inflation and unemployment. This is what Phillips in the United Kingdom and Solow and Samuelson in the United States discovered when they looked, in the late 1950s, at the joint behavior of unemployment and inflation.

■ As inflation became more persistent in the 1970s and 1980s, expectations of inflation became based more and more on past inflation. In the United States today, the aggregate supply relation takes the form of a relation between unemployment and the change in inflation. High unemployment leads to decreasing inflation; low unemployment leads to increasing inflation.

■ The natural unemployment rate is the unemployment rate at which the inflation rate remains constant. When the actual unemployment rate exceeds the natural rate of unemployment, the inflation rate typically decreases; when the actual unemployment rate is less than the natural unemployment rate, the inflation rate typically increases.

■ The natural rate of unemployment depends on many factors that differ across countries and can change over time. This is why the natural rate of unemployment varies across countries: It is higher in Europe than in the United States. Also, the natural unemployment rate varies over time: In Europe, the natural unemployment rate has greatly increased since the 1960s. In the United States, the natural unemployment rate increased from the 1960s to the 1980s and appears to have decreased since.

■ Changes in the way the inflation rate varies over time affect the way wage setters form expectations and also affects how much they use wage indexation. When wage indexation is widespread, small changes in unemployment can lead to very large changes in inflation. At high rates of inflation, the relation between inflation and unemployment disappears altogether.

■ At very low or negative rates of inflation, the Phillips curve relation appears to become weaker. During the Great Depression even very high unemployment led only to limited deflation. The issue is important because many countries have both high unemployment and low inflation today.

Key Terms

Questions and Problems

QUICK CHECK

All Quick Check questions and problems are available on MyEconLab.

1. Using the information in this chapter, label each of the following statements true, false, or uncertain. Explain briefly.

a. The original Phillips curve is the negative relation between unemployment and inflation that was first observed in the United Kingdom.

b. The original Phillips curve relation has proven to be very stable across countries and over time.

c. The aggregate supply relation is consistent with the Phillips curve as observed before the 1970s, but not since.

d. Policy makers can exploit the inflation–unemployment trade-off only temporarily.

e. In the late 1960s, the economists Milton Friedman and Edmund Phelps said that policy makers could achieve as low a rate of unemployment as they wanted.

f. The expectations-augmented Phillips curve is consistent with workers and firms adapting their expectations after the macroeconomic experience of the 1960s.

g. The natural rate of unemployment is constant over time within a country.

h. The natural rate of unemployment is the same in all countries.

i. Disinflation means that the rate of inflation is negative.

j. If Lucas was right, and if monetary policy was fully credible, there would be no relation between inflation and unemployment (i.e., no Phillips curve relation).

2. Discuss the following statements.

a. The Phillips curve implies that when unemployment is high, inflation is low, and vice versa. Therefore, we may experience either high inflation or high unemployment, but we will never experience both together.

b. As long as we do not mind having high inflation, we can achieve as low a level of unemployment as we want. All we have to do is increase the demand for goods and services by using, for example, expansionary fiscal policy.

3. Mutations of the Phillips curve

Suppose that the Phillips curve is given by

$$\pi_t = \pi_t^e + 0.1 - 2u_t$$

a. What is the natural rate of unemployment?

Assume

$$\pi_t^e = \theta\pi_{t-1}$$

and suppose that θ is initially equal to 0. Suppose that the rate of unemployment is initially equal to the natural rate. In year t, the authorities decide to bring the unemployment rate down to 3% and hold it there forever.

b. Determine the rate of inflation in years t, $t + 1$, $t + 2$, and $t + 5$.

c. Do you believe the answer given in (b)? Why or why not?

(Hint: Think about how people are likely to form expectations of inflation.)

Now suppose that in year t *+ 5, θ increases from 0 to 1. Suppose that the government is still determined to keep* u *at 3% forever.*

d. Why might θ increase in this way?

e. What will the inflation rate be in years $t + 5$, $t + 6$, and $t + 7$?

f. Do you believe the answer given in (e)? Why or why not?

4. The neutrality of money revisited

a. Fill in the empty spaces after Year 1 in the chart below:

Year	M Nominal Money Supply (billions)	g_M Growth Rate of Nominal Money Supply (percent)	P Price Level (index) Year 2 = 100	Inflation (percent)
1	380.95		95.2	
2	400			
3	420		105.0	
4	441		110.25	

b. What is the growth rate of the nominal money supply between years 1 and 2, 2 and 3, and 3 and 4?

c. What is the rate of inflation between years 1 and 2, 2 and 3, and 3 and 4?

d. What is the change in the real money supply between years 1 and 2, 2 and 3, and 3 and 4?

e. What assumption has been made about real output growth if this data describe the medium run?

5. The effects of a permanent decrease in the rate of nominal money growth

Suppose that the economy can be described by the following three equations:

$$u_t - u_{t-1} = -0.4(g_{yt} - 3\%) \quad \text{Okun's law}$$
$$\pi_t - \pi_{t-1} = -(u_t - 5\%) \quad \text{Phillips curve}$$
$$g_{yt} = g_{mt} - \pi_t \quad \text{Aggregate demand}$$

a. Reduce the three equations to two by substituting g_{yt} from the aggregate demand equation into Okun's law. (Okun's law was presented in Chapter 2.)

Assume initially that $u_t = u_{t-1} = 5\%$, $g_{mt} = 13\%$, *and* $\pi_t = 10\%$.

b. Explain why these values are consistent with the statement *"Inflation is always and everywhere a monetary phenomenon."*

Now suppose that money growth is permanently reduced from 13% to 3%, starting in year *t.*

c. Compute (using a calculator or a spreadsheet program) unemployment and inflation in years $t, t + 1, \ldots, t + 10$.

d. Does inflation decline smoothly from 10% to 3%? Why or why not?

e. Compute the values of the unemployment rate and the inflation rate in the medium run.

f. Is the statement that *"Inflation is always and everywhere a monetary phenomenon"* a statement that refers to the medium run or the short run?

DIG DEEPER

All Dig Deeper questions and problems are available on MyEconLab.

6. *The macroeconomic effects of the indexation of wages*

Suppose that the Phillips curve is given by

$$\pi_t - \pi_t^e = 0.1 - 2u_t$$

where

$$\pi_t^e = \pi_{t-1}$$

Suppose that inflation in year $t - 1$ is zero. In year t, the authorities decide to keep the unemployment rate at 4% forever.

a. Compute the rate of inflation for years $t, t + 1, t + 2$, and $t + 3$. *Now suppose that half the workers have indexed labor contracts.*

b. What is the new equation for the Phillips curve?

c. Based on your answer to part (b), recompute your answer to part (a).

d. What is the effect of wage indexation on the relation between π and u?

7. *Supply shocks and wage flexibility*

Suppose that the Phillips curve is given by

$$\pi_t - \pi_{t-1} = -\alpha(u_t - u_n)$$

where

$$u_n = (m + z)/\alpha.$$

Recall that this Phillips curve was derived in this chapter under the assumption that the wage-bargaining equation took the form

$$W = P^e(1 - \alpha u_t + z)$$

We can think of α as a measure of wage flexibility—the higher α the greater the response of the wage to a change in the unemployment rate, u_t.

a. Suppose $m = 0.03$ and $z = 0.03$. What is the natural rate of unemployment if $\alpha = 1$? if $\alpha = 2$? What is the relation between α and the natural rate of unemployment? Interpret your answer.

In Chapter 7, the text suggested that a reduction in the bargaining power of workers may have something to do with the economy's relatively mild response to the increases in oil prices in the past few years as compared to the economy's response to increases in oil prices in the 1970s. One manifestation of a reduction in worker bargaining power could be an overall increase in wage flexibility (i.e., an increase in α).

b. Suppose that as a result of an oil price increase, m increases to 0.06. What is the new natural rate of unemployment if $\alpha = 1$? if $\alpha = 2$? Would an increase in wage flexibility tend to weaken the adverse effect of an oil price increase?

EXPLORE FURTHER

8. *Estimating the natural rate of unemployment*

To answer this question, you will need data on the annual U.S. unemployment and inflation rates since 1970, which can be obtained very easily from the Economic Report of the President Web site http://**www.gpoaccess.gov**/eop/index.html Excel tables of the values can be downloaded.

Retrieve the annual data for the civilian unemployment rate from Table B-35. In addition, retrieve the annual percentage increase for the consumer price index (CPI), all urban consumers from Table B-63. You can access the same data at the Federal Reserve Bank of St. Louis FRED Web site.

a. Plot the data for all the years since 1970 on a diagram, with the change in inflation on the vertical axis and the rate of unemployment on the horizontal axis. Is your graph similar to Figure 8-5?

b. Using a ruler, draw the line that appears to fit best the points in the figure. Approximately what is the slope of the line? What is the intercept? Write down your equation.

c. According to your analysis in (b), what has been the natural rate of unemployment since 1970?

9. *Changes in the natural rate of unemployment*

a. Repeat Problem 8 but now draw separate graphs for the period 1970 to 1990 and the period since 1990.

b. Do you find that the relation between inflation and unemployment is different in the two periods? If so, how has the natural rate of unemployment changed?

10. *Money growth and the growth in real output over time*

a. Fill in the empty spaces after Year 1 in the chart. This economy is in medium-run equilibrium in every year:

Year	M Nominal Money Supply (billions)	g_M Growth Rate of Nominal Money Supply (percent)	P Price level (index) Year 2 = 100	Inflation	Real GDP (billions of Year 2 dollars)
1	367		95.2		1500
2	400				1560
3	436		105.0		1622.4
4	475.3		110.25		1687.3

b. What is the growth rate of the nominal money supply between years 1 and 2, years 2 and 3, and years 3 and 4?
c. What is the rate of inflation between years 1 and 2, 2 and 3, and 3 and 4?
d. What is the change in the real money supply between years 1 and 2, 2 and 3, and 3 and 4?
e. Why does the equation that says that the rate of inflation and the rate of growth of money must be equal NOT hold

in this case? (*Hint*: Think about what must happen to real money growth if real output, and thus the demand for real money is increasing over time? If real money growth must be positive, what does this imply about the relation between nominal money growth and inflation?)

APPENDIX: From the Aggregate Supply Relation to a Relation between Inflation, Expected Inflation, and Unemployment

This appendix shows how to go from the relation between the price level, the expected price level, and the unemployment rate given by equation (8.1),

$$P = P^e(1 + m)(1 - \alpha u + z)$$

to the relation between inflation, expected inflation, and the unemployment rate given by equation (8.2),

$$\pi = \pi^e + (m + z) - \alpha u$$

First, introduce time subscripts for the price level, the expected price level, and the unemployment rate, so P_t, P_t^e, and u_t refer to the price level, the expected price level, and the unemployment rate in year t. Equation (8.1) becomes

$$P_t = P_t^e(1 + m)(1 - \alpha u_t + z)$$

Next, go from an expression in terms of price levels to an expression in terms of inflation rates. Divide both sides by last year's price level, P_{t-1}:

$$\frac{P_t}{P_{t-1}} = \frac{P_t^e}{P_{t-1}}(1 + m)(1 - \alpha u_t + z) \qquad (8A.1)$$

Take the fraction P_t/P_{t-1} on the left side and rewrite it as

$$\frac{P_t}{P_{t-1}} = \frac{P_t - P_{t-1} + P_{t-1}}{P_{t-1}} = 1 + \frac{P_t - P_{t-1}}{P_{t-1}} = 1 + \pi_t$$

where the first equality follows from actually subtracting and adding P_{t-1} in the numerator of the fraction, the second equality follows from the fact that $P_{t-1}/P_{t-1} = 1$, and the third follows from the definition of the inflation rate ($\pi_t \equiv (P_t - P_{t-1})/P_{t-1}$).

Do the same for the fraction P_t^e/P_{t-1} on the right side, using the definition of the expected inflation rate ($\pi_t^e \equiv (P_t^e - P_{t-1})/P_{t-1}$):

$$\frac{P_t^e}{P_{t-1}} = \frac{P_t^e - P_{t-1} + P_{t-1}}{P_{t-1}} = 1 + \frac{P_t^e - P_{t-1}}{P_{t-1}} = 1 + \pi_t^e$$

Replacing P_t/P_{t-1} and P_t^e/P_{t-1} in equation (8A.1) by the expressions we have just derived,

$$(1 + \pi_t) = (1 + \pi_t^e)(1 + m)(1 - \alpha u_t + z)$$

This gives us a relation between inflation, π_t, expected inflation, π_t^e, and the unemployment rate, u_t. The remaining steps make the relation look more friendly: Divide both sides by $(1 + \pi_t^e)(1 + m)$:

$$\frac{(1 + \pi_t)}{(1 + \pi_t^e)(1 + m)} = 1 - \alpha u_t + z$$

So long as inflation, expected inflation, and the markup are not too large, a good approximation to the left side of this equation is given by $1 + \pi_t - \pi_t^e - m$ (see Propositions 3 and 6 in Appendix 2 at the end of the book). Replacing in the equation above and rearranging gives

$$\pi_t = \pi_t^e + (m + z) - \alpha u_t$$

Dropping the time indexes, this is equation (8.2) in the text. With the time indexes kept, this is equation (8.3) in the text.

The inflation rate π_t depends on the expected inflation rate π_t^e and the unemployment rate u_t. The relation also depends on the markup, m, on the factors that affect wage setting, z, and on the effect of the unemployment rate on wages, α.

The Crisis

When, in late 2006, U.S. housing prices started to decline, most economists forecast that this would affect housing investment and consumption adversely, and thus slow down growth. A few forecast that it might lead to a mild recession. Very few anticipated that it might lead to the largest economic crisis since the Great Depression. But it did.

What happened, and what few had anticipated, is that the decline in housing prices triggered a major financial crisis. The financial system was much more fragile than had been perceived, and within a few months, many banks and other financial institutions found themselves either bankrupt or near bankruptcy. As a result, banks became unable or unwilling to lend. The interest rates at which consumers and firms could borrow increased dramatically, leading to a fall in spending, and a fall in output.

As the extent of the economic crisis became clear, policy makers responded with financial, monetary, and fiscal measures: Central banks decreased the interest rates under their control. Governments embarked on major fiscal expansions. It is likely that these policies avoided what would have been an even larger decline in output.

Over time, however, both monetary and fiscal policies have run into sharp limits. The interest rates directly controlled by central banks are close to zero and cannot decline further: Many economies are in a "liquidity trap." The fiscal expansions, and the drop in government revenues from lower output, have led to large and worrisome increases in public debt. These limits make it harder to use policy to help the economy recover. While growth has turned positive since 2010, the recovery is slow, and unemployment is forecast to remain high for a long time.

We had a first look at the sequence of events in Chapter 1. Now that we have developed some of the basic tools, we can look at the events in more detail in this chapter. We focus on the United States in this chapter. Later on, when we have developed tools to look at the open economy, we shall look at the crisis in the rest of the world.

This chapter has three sections.

Section 9-1 looks at the start of the crisis, the decline in housing prices, and its effects on the financial system.

Section 9-2 examines the macroeconomic effects of the housing and financial crises, the evolution of output, and the policy responses.

Section 9-3 turns to the recovery.

In the process of analyzing the crisis, you will see how we use the *IS–LM* and the *AS–AD* models we developed in the previous chapters. We shall need to extend both, but you will see how we can build on them, and how they help organize both facts and thoughts. ●

9-1 From a Housing Problem to a Financial Crisis

When, in 2006, housing prices started declining in the United States, most economists forecast that this would lead to a decrease in aggregate demand and a slowdown in growth. Only a few economists anticipated that it would lead to a major macroeconomic crisis. What most had not anticipated was the effect of the decline of housing prices on the financial system. This is the focus of this section.

Housing Prices and Subprime Mortgages

Type "Case-Shiller" on the Internet if you want to find the index and see its recent evolution. You can also see what has happened to prices in the city in which you live. ▶

Figure 9-1 shows the evolution of an index of U.S. housing prices from 2000 on. The index is known as the Case-Shiller index, named for the two economists who have constructed it. The index is normalized to equal 100 in January 2000. You can see the large increase in prices the early 2000s, followed by a large decrease since then. From a value of 100 in 2000, the index increased to 226 in mid 2006. Starting in 2006, however, the index first stabilized and declined slightly in 2006, then, from 2007, starting declining rapidly. By the end of 2008, at the start of the financial crisis, the index was down to 162. It continued to decline and, at the time of this writing, it is roughly stable, at around 150.

Was the sharp price increase from 2000 to 2006 justified? In retrospect, and given the ensuing collapse, surely not. But, at the time, when prices were increasing, economists were not so sure. *Some* increase in prices was clearly justified:

Even if people did not finance the purchase of a house by taking a mortgage, low interest rates would lead to an increase in the price of houses. More on this when we discuss present discounted values in Chapter 14. ▶

■ The 2000s were a period of unusually low interest rates. As a result, mortgage rates were also low, increasing the demand for housing and thus pushing up the price.

■ Other factors were also at work. **Mortgage lenders** became increasingly willing to make loans to more risky borrowers. These mortgages, known as **subprime mortgages**, or **subprimes** for short, had existed since the mid-1990s but became more prevalent in the 2000s. By 2006, about 20% of all U.S. mortgages were subprimes. Was it necessarily bad? Again, at the time, this was seen by most economists as a positive development: It allowed more people to buy homes, and, under the assumption that housing prices would continue to increase, so the value of the mortgage would decrease over time relative to the price of the house, it looked safe both for lenders and

Figure 9-1

U.S. Housing Prices since 2000

Housing prices increased sharply from 2000 to 2006, only to decline since then.

Source: Case-Shiller Home Price Indices, http://www.standardandpoors.com/indices/main/en/us

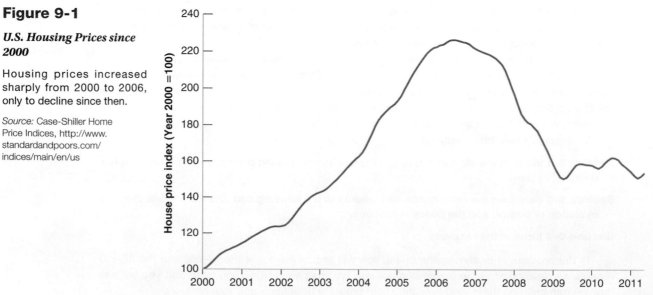

for borrowers. Judging from the past, the assumption that housing prices would not decrease also seemed reasonable: As you can see from Figure 9-1, housing prices had not decreased during the 2000–2001 recession.

In retrospect, again, these developments were much less benign than most economists thought. First, housing prices could go down, as became evident from 2006 on. When this happened, many borrowers found themselves in a situation where the mortgage they owed now exceeded the value of their house (when the value of the mortgage exceeds the value of the house, the mortgage is said to be **underwater**). Second, it became clear that, in many cases, the mortgages were in fact much riskier than either the lender pretended or the borrower understood. In many cases, borrowers had taken mortgages with low initial interest rates and thus low initial interest payments, probably not fully realizing that payments would increase sharply over time. Even if house prices had not declined, many of these borrowers would have been unable to meet their mortgage payments.

Some economists were worried even as prices were going up. Robert Shiller, one of the two economists behind the Case-Shiller index, was among them, warning that the price increase was a bubble that would most likely crash.

Some of these loans became known as NINJA loans (for no income, no job, no assets).

Some mortgages offered very low interest rates at the beginning. The low rates were known as "teaser rates." The rates then increased sharply after a few months or a few years.

Thus, as house prices turned around and many borrowers defaulted, many banks found themselves faced with large losses. In mid-2008, losses on mortgages were estimated to be around 300 billion dollars. This is obviously a large number, but, relative to the size of the U.S. economy, it is not a very large one: 300 billion dollars is only about 2% of U.S. GDP. One might have thought that the U.S. financial system could absorb the shock and that the adverse effect on output would be limited.

This was not to be. While the trigger of the crisis was indeed the decline in housing prices, its effects were enormously amplified. Even those economists who had anticipated the housing price decline did not realize how strong the amplification mechanisms would be. To understand them, we must return to the role of banks.

The Role of Banks

In Chapter 4, we looked at the role of banks in the determination of the money supply. Their important characteristic in that context was that they issued money, or, more precisely, that they had checkable deposits as liabilities. Here, we shall focus on their more general role as **financial intermediaries**, institutions that receive funds from those who wish to save and use those funds to make loans to those who wish to borrow.

See Section 4-3.

Figure 9-2 shows a (much simplified) bank balance sheet. The bank has assets of 100, liabilities of 80, and capital of 20. You can think of the owners of the bank has having directly invested 20 of their own funds, borrowed 80, and bought various assets for 100. As we saw in Chapter 4, the liabilities may be checkable deposits, or borrowing from investors and other banks. The assets may be reserves (central bank money), loans to consumers, loans to firms, loans to other banks, mortgages, government bonds, or other forms of securities. In Chapter 4, we ignored capital. But, for our purposes, introducing capital is important here. Suppose that a bank did not hold any capital. Then, if, for any reason, the assets it held went down in value and the liabilities remained the same, liabilities would exceed assets, and the bank would be bankrupt. It is thus essential for the bank to hold enough capital to limit the risk of bankruptcy.

One wishes that the balance sheets of banks were this simple and transparent. Had it been the case, the crisis would have been much more limited.

How can things go wrong even if the bank holds some capital, as in our example? First, the assets may decline in value by so much that the capital the bank holds is not

Assets 100	Liabilities 80
	Capital 20

Figure 9-2

Bank Assets, Capital, and Liabilities

enough to cover its losses. In our example, this will happen if the value of the assets decreases below 80. The bank will become insolvent. This is not, however, the only way the bank can get in trouble. Suppose that some of the investors that have loaned to the bank (made a deposit in the bank) want their funds back right away. If the bank can sell some of its assets, it can get the funds and pay the depositors. But it may be difficult for the bank to sell the assets quickly: Calling back loans is difficult; some securities may be hard to sell. The problem of the bank in this case is not **solvency**, but **illiquidity**. The bank is still solvent, but it is illiquid. The more liquid its liabilities, or the less liquid its assets, the more likely the bank is to find itself in trouble.

See the Focus box "Bank Runs, Deposit Insurance, and Wholesale Funding" in ▶ Chapter 4.

What happened in this crisis is a combination of all these factors: Banks had too little capital. Liabilities, both deposits and other securities issued by banks, were very liquid. Assets were often very illiquid. The outcome was a combination of both solvency and liquidity problems, which quickly paralyzed the financial system. We now look at three specific aspects of the crisis that affected banks (and other financial intermediaries) in more detail.

Leverage

Consider two banks. As in Figure 9-2, bank A has assets of 100, liabilities of 80, and capital of 20. Its **capital ratio** is defined as the ratio of capital to assets and is thus equal to 20%. Its **leverage ratio** is defined as the ratio of assets to capital (the inverse of the capital ratio) and is thus equal to 5. Bank B has assets of 100, liabilities of 95, and capital of 5. Thus, its capital ratio is equal to 5%, and its leverage ratio to 20.

Now suppose that some of the assets in each of the two banks go bad. For example, some borrowers cannot repay their loans. Suppose, as a result, that for both banks, the value of the assets decreases from 100 to 90. Bank A now has assets of 90, liabilities of 80, and capital of $90 - 80 = 10$. Bank B has assets of 90, liabilities of 95, and thus *negative* capital of $90 - 95 = -5$. Its liabilities exceed its assets: In other words, it is bankrupt. This is indeed what happened during the crisis: Many banks had such a high leverage ratio that even limited losses on assets greatly increased the risk of bankruptcy.

Some liabilities may actually pay a zero rate of return. Recall from Chapter 4 that a ▶ large part of these liabilities is checking deposits, which typically pay at most a low interest rate.

Why was leverage so high? The example suggests a simple answer: Higher leverage means higher expected profit. Suppose, for example, that assets pay an expected rate of return of 5%, and liabilities pay an expected rate of return of 4%. Then the owners of bank A have an expected rate of return on their capital of $(100 \times 5\% - 80 \times 4\%)/20 = 9\%$, and the owners of bank B have an expected rate of return of $(100 \times 5\% - 95 \times 4\%)/5 = 24\%$, so more than twice as high. But, as the example we just saw also makes clear, leverage also increases risk: The higher the leverage, the more likely the bank is to go bankrupt. What happened throughout the 2000s is that banks decided to get a higher return and thus to take on more risk as well.

Why did banks opt to take on more risk? This is the subject of much discussion. There appears to be a number of reasons: First, banks probably underestimated the risk they were taking: Times were good, and, in good times, banks, just like people, tend to underestimate the risk of bad times. Second, the compensation and bonus system also gave incentives to managers to go for high expected returns without fully taking the risk of bankruptcy into account. Third, while financial regulation required banks to keep their capital ratio above some minimum, banks found new ways of avoiding the regulation, by creating new financial structures such as *SIVs*. What these are and how banks used them is explained in the Focus box "Increasing Leverage and Alphabet Soup".

Complexity

Another important development of the 1990s and the 2000s was the growth of **securitization**. Traditionally, the financial intermediaries that made loans or issued mortgages kept them on their own balance sheet. This had obvious drawbacks. A local bank, with local loans and mortgages on its books, was very much exposed to the local economic situation. When, for example, oil prices had come down sharply in the mid-1980s and Texas was in recession, many local banks went bankrupt. Had they had a more diversified portfolio of mortgages, say mortgages from many parts of the country, these banks might have avoided bankruptcy.

This is the idea behind securitization. Securitization is the creation of securities based on a bundle of assets (for example, a bundle of loans, or a bundle of mortgages). For instance, a **mortgage-based security**, or **MBS** for short, is a title to the returns from a bundle of mortgages, with the number of underlying mortgages often in the tens of thousands. The advantage is that many investors, who would not want to hold individual mortgages, will be willing to buy and hold these securities. This increase in the supply of funds from investors is, in turn, likely to decrease the cost of borrowing.

One can think of further forms of securitization. For example, instead of issuing identical claims to the returns on the underlying bundle of assets, one can issue different types of securities. For example, one can issue two types of securities: **senior securities**, which have first claims on the returns from the bundle, and **junior securities**, which come after and pay only if something is left after the senior securities have been paid. Senior securities will appeal to investors who want little risk; junior securities will appeal to investors who are willing to take more risk. Such securities, known as **collateralized debt obligations**, or **CDOs**, were first issued in the late 1980s but, again, grew in importance in the 1990s and 2000s. Securitization went even further, with the creation of CDOs using previously created CDOs, or CDO^2. This could go on and on!

Securitization would seem like a good idea, a way of diversifying risk and getting a larger group of investors involved in lending to households or firms. And, indeed, it is. But it also came with a large cost, which became clear only during the crisis. It was a risk that **rating agencies**, those firms that assess the risk of various securities, had largely missed: When underlying mortgages went bad, assessing the value of the underlying bundles in the MBSs, or, even more so, of the underlying MBSs in the CDOs, was extremely hard to do. These assets came to be known as **toxic assets**. It led investors to assume the worst and be very reluctant either to hold them or to continue lending to those institutions that did hold them.

Liquidity

Yet another development of the 1990s and 2000s was the development of other sources of finance than checkable deposits by banks (the 80 dollars they borrowed in our example above). Increasingly, they relied on borrowing from other banks or other investors, in the form of short-term debt, to finance the purchase of their assets, a process known as **wholesale funding**. SIVs, the financial entities set up by banks, which we saw earlier, were entirely funded through such wholesale funding.

Wholesale funding again would seem like a good idea, giving banks more flexibility in the amount of funds they can use to make loans or buy assets. But it has a cost, which again became clear during the crisis. If investors or other banks, worried about the value of the assets held by the bank, decide to stop lending to the bank, the bank may find itself short of funds and be forced to sell some of its assets. If these assets are complex and hard to sell, it may have to sell them at very low prices, often referred to as **fire sale prices**.

We now have all the elements we need to explain what happened when housing prices declined, and why this led to a major financial crisis.

This is the modern equivalent of bank runs, when people ran to the bank to take their money out. Deposit insurance has largely eliminated that risk. But, now, it is the investors who lend to the bank in the form of short-term securities, not depositors, who can decide to take their money out. See the Focus box "Bank Runs, Deposit Insurance, and Wholesale Funding" in Chapter 4.

Increasing Leverage and Alphabet Soup: SIVs, AIG, and CDSs

SIV stands for **structured investment vehicle**. Think of it as a virtual bank, created by an actual bank. On the liability side, it borrows from investors, typically in the form of short-term debt. On the asset side, it holds various forms of securities. To reassure the investors that they will get repaid, the SIV typically had a guarantee from the actual bank that, if needed, the bank will provide funds to the SIV.

While the first SIV was set up by Citigroup in 1988, SIVs rapidly grew in size in the 2000s. You may ask why banks did not simply do all these things on their own balance sheet rather than create a separate vehicle. The main reason was to be able to increase leverage. If the banks had done these operations themselves, the operations would have appeared on their balance sheet and been subject to regulatory capital requirements, forcing them to hold enough capital to limit the risk of bankruptcy. But, it turns out, doing these operations through an SIV did not require banks to put capital down. For that reason, through setting up an SIV, banks could increase leverage and increase expected profits, and they did.

When housing prices started declining, and many mortgages turned bad, the securities held by the SIVs decreased in value. Investors became reluctant to lend to the SIVs, out of fear that they may be insolvent. The banks that had created the SIVs had to honor their obligations by paying investors, but had limited capital to do so. It became clear that banks had in effect created a **shadow banking system**, and that leverage of the banking system as a whole (i.e, including the shadow banking part) was much higher than had been perceived. Small losses could lead to bankruptcies. As of October 2008, no SIVs were left; they had either closed, or all their assets and liabilities had been transferred to the banks that had created them.

AIG stands for American International Group. It is an insurance company that, in the 2000s, had what looked like a good idea at the time. It would sell not only regular insurance, but also insurance against default risk, through the sale of **credit default swaps**, or CDSs for short. If a bank was worried about default on a security it held in its portfolio, it could buy a CDS from AIG that promised to pay the bank in case of default on the security. For this, AIG charged the bank a price supposed to reflect the probability of such a default. For banks, it was an attractive deal, because by buying insurance, the securities they held became riskless and thus decreased the capital that banks had to hold (the less risky the asset, the smaller the amount of capital required by regulation). AIG, being an insurance company rather than a bank, did not have to hold capital against the promises it was making.

When housing prices started declining and mortgages began to default, AIG had to make good on many of its promises. AIG, however, did not have the funds to make the payments on the CDSs they had issued. Thus, suddenly, banks realized that, without the insurance payout, their assets were much riskier than they had assumed, and that they did not have the capital needed to sustain losses. Again, leverage of the financial system (including now the banks, the SIVs, and CDS issuers such as AIG) was much higher than had been perceived. As we shall see below, the U.S. government decided it had to provide funds to AIG to make payments on the CDSs. The alternative would have led to default of AIG, but also the potential default of many banks holding CDSs. As of the end of 2009, the government had advanced more than $180 billion to AIG, which AIG used to pay the banks as promised. Since then, AIG has been steadily reimbursing the U.S. government and is expected to fully repay the loan.

Amplification Mechanisms

As the crisis worsened, solvency and liquidity concerns increased sharply, each reinforcing the other.

- When housing prices declined, and some mortgages went bad, high leverage implied a sharp decline in the capital of banks. This in turn forced them to sell some of their assets. Because these assets were often hard to value, they had to sell them at fire sale prices. This, in turn, decreased the value of similar assets remaining on their balance sheet, or on the balance sheet of other banks, leading to a further decline in capital ratio and forcing further sales of assets and further declines in prices.

- The complexity of the securities (MBSs, CDOs) and of the true balance sheets of banks (banks and their SIVs) made it very difficult to assess the solvency of banks and their risk of bankruptcy. Thus, investors became very reluctant to continue to lend to them, and wholesale funding came to a stop, forcing further asset sales

Figure 9-3

The Ted Spread since 2007

The rate spread, which reflects the risk banks perceive
in lending to each other, went
sharply up in September
2008.

Source: Bloomberg L.P.

and price declines. Even banks became very reluctant to lend to each other. This is shown in Figure 9-3, which shows the difference between the riskless rate (measured by the rate of three-month government bonds), which you can think of as the rate determined by monetary policy, and the rate at which banks are willing to lend to each other (known as the **Libor rate**). This difference is known as the **Ted spread**.

If banks perceived no risk in lending to each other, the Ted spread would be equal to zero. And, indeed, until mid-2007, it was very close to zero. Note, however, how it became larger in the second half of 2007 and then increased sharply in September 2008. Why then? Because, on September 15, 2008, Lehman Brothers, a major bank with more than $600 billion in assets, declared bankruptcy, leading financial participants to conclude that many, if not most, other banks and financial institutions were indeed at risk.

By mid-September 2008, both mechanisms were in full force. The financial system had become paralyzed: Banks had basically stopped lending to each other or to anyone else. Quickly, what had been largely a financial crisis turned into a macroeconomic crisis.

9-2 The Use and Limits of Policy

The immediate effects of the financial crisis on the macro economy were two-fold: first, a large increase in the interest rates at which people and firms could borrow; second, a dramatic decrease in confidence.

- Figure 9-4 shows the effect of the financial crisis on different interest rates. The first interest rate is the rate on 10-year U.S. government bonds. The second and third are the rates charged by the bond markets to two different types of firms, corresponding to different risk ratings. Firms with a **AAA (triple A)** rating are considered the safest, firms with a **BBB (triple B)** are considered less safe. In normal times, AAA firms can borrow at a rate close to the rate on government bonds; BBB firms borrow at a higher rate, but the difference is typically small, on the order of 1%. You can see that this was indeed the case at the start of 2007. But, as you can also see, the difference increased from mid-2007 on, and, while the rate on government bonds remained very low, the rates on both AAA and BBB bonds jumped

Figure 9-4

Yields on 10-Year U.S. Government Treasury, AAA, and BBB Corporate Bonds, since 2007

In September 2008, the financial crisis led to a sharp increase in the rates at which firms could borrow.

Source: Bloomberg L.P.

in September 2008 to very high levels. Suddenly, borrowing became extremely expensive for most firms. And for the many firms too small to issue bonds and thus depending on bank credit, it became nearly impossible to borrow at all.

In short, the interest rate charged to borrowers became very high (in some cases borrowers were completely shut out from borrowing) relative to the interest rate controlled by monetary policy.

■ Figure 9-5 shows the effects of the financial crisis on expectations. The events of September 2008 triggered wide anxiety among consumers and firms. Thoughts of another Great Depression and, more generally, confusion and fear about what was happening in the financial system, led to a large drop in confidence. The evolution of consumer confidence and business confidence indexes for the United States are shown in Figure 9-5. Both indexes are normalized to equal 100 in January 2007. Note how consumer confidence, which had started declining in mid-2007, took a sharp drop in the fall of 2008 and reached a low of 22 in early 2009, a level far below previous historical lows. The result of lower confidence and lower housing and stock prices was a sharp decrease in consumption.

See the Focus box "The Lehman Bankruptcy, Fears of Another Great Depression, and Shifts in the Consumption Function" in Chapter 3. ▶

Figure 9-5

U.S. Consumer and Business Confidence, since 2007

The financial crisis led to a sharp drop in confidence, which bottomed in early 2009.

Source: Bloomberg L.P.

Initial Policy Responses

The high cost of borrowing, lower stock prices, and lower confidence all combined to decrease the demand for goods. In terms of the *IS–LM* model, there was a sharp adverse shift of the *IS* curve. In the face of this large decrease in demand, policy makers did not remain passive.

The most urgent measures were aimed at strengthening the financial system:

- In order to prevent a run by depositors, federal deposit insurance was increased from $100,000 to $250,000 per account. Recall, however, that much of banks' funding came not from deposits but from the issuance of short-term debt to investors. In order to allow the banks to continue to fund themselves through wholesale funding, the Federal government offered a program guaranteeing new debt issues by banks.

- The Federal Reserve provided widespread liquidity to the financial system. We have seen that, if investors wanted to take their funds back, the banks had no alternative than to sell some of their assets, often at fire sale prices. In many cases, this would have meant bankruptcy. To avoid this, the Fed put in place a number of **liquidity facilities** to make it easier to borrow from the Fed. It allowed not only banks, but also other financial institutions to borrow from the Fed. Finally, it increased the set of assets that financial institutions could use as **collateral** when borrowing from the Fed (*collateral* refers to the asset a borrower pledges when borrowing from a lender. If the borrower defaults, the asset then goes to the lender). Together, these facilities allowed banks and financial institutions to pay back investors without having to sell their assets. It also decreased the incentives of investors to ask for their funds, as these facilities decreased the risk that banks would go bankrupt.

- The government introduced a program, called the **Troubled Asset Relief Program**, or **TARP**, aimed at cleaning up banks. The initial goal of the $700 billion program, introduced in October 2008, was to remove the complex assets from the balance sheet of banks, thus decreasing uncertainty, reassuring investors, and making it easier to assess the health of each bank. The Treasury, however, faced the same problems as private investors. If these complex assets were going to be exchanged for, say, Treasury bills, at what price should the exchange be done? Within a few weeks, it became clear that the task of assessing the value of each of these assets was extremely hard and would take a long time, and the initial goal was abandoned. The new goal became to increase the capital of banks. This was done by the government acquiring shares and thus providing funds to most of the largest U.S. banks. By increasing their capital ratio, and thus decreasing leverage, the goal of the program was to allow the banks to avoid bankruptcy and, over time, return to normal. As of the end of September 2009, total spending under the TARP was $360 billion, of which $200 billion was spent through the purchase of shares in banks. At the time of writing, most banks have bought back their shares and have reimbursed the government. The final cost of TARP is expected to be small, perhaps even zero.

- All these measures were aimed at providing liquidity to financial institutions, avoiding unnecessary bankruptcies, and allowing the financial system to function again. Worried, however, that some markets were slow to recover, the Fed directly intervened by purchasing private securities in these markets. In particular, given the importance of the housing sector in the crisis, it bought mortgage-backed securities. At the time of writing, the Fed is still the main buyer of these securities.

Fiscal and monetary policies were used aggressively as well.

- Figure 9-6 shows the evolution of the T-bill rate from January 2006 on. Starting ◄ in the summer of 2007, the Fed began to worry about a slowdown in growth and

> The specific interest rate used in the figure is the rate on T-bills with a maturity of three months, called the three-month T-bill rate. The interest rate is expressed as an annual rate.

Figure 9-6

The T-Bill Rate, since 2007

From mid-2007 to December 2008, the Fed decreased the T-bill rate from 5% to zero.

Source: Series TB3MS Federal Reserve Economic Data (FRED) http://research.stlouisfed.org/fred2/

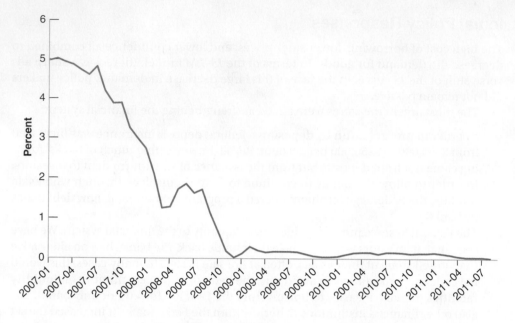

For technical reasons, the T-bill rate has not been quite equal to zero, but has typically been slightly positive. For all practical purposes, this has the same effect as a zero rate. ▶ ■

Figure 1-4 in Chapter 1 showed the path of the U.S. budget deficits since 1990. ▶ You can see how unusually large these deficits are.

started decreasing the T-bill rate. By September 2008, the rate stood at 1.7%, down from about 5% in July 2007. And, when it became clear in the fall of 2008 that demand was falling quickly, the Fed decreased the rate further. By December 2008, the rate was down to zero, and still is equal to zero at the time of this writing.

When the size of the adverse shock became clear, the U.S. government turned to fiscal policy, using a combination of reductions in taxes and increases in spending. When the Obama administration assumed office in 2009, its first priority was to design a fiscal program that would increase demand and reduce the size of the recession. Such a fiscal program, called the **American Recovery and Reinvestment Act**, was passed in February 2009. It called for $780 billion in new measures, in the form of both tax reductions and spending increases, over 2009 and 2010. The U.S. budget deficit increased from 1.7% of GDP in 2007 to a very high 9.0% in 2010. The increase was largely the mechanical effect of the crisis, as the decrease in output led automatically to a decrease in tax revenues and to an increase in transfer programs such as unemployment benefits. But it was also the result of the specific measures in the fiscal program aimed at increasing either private or public spending.

Still, this combination of financial, fiscal, and monetary measures was not enough to avoid a large decrease in output, with U.S. GDP falling by 3.5% in 2009 and recovering only slowly thereafter. One would hope that fiscal and monetary policies could help strengthen the recovery. But, as we shall see now, both face sharp limits.

The Limits of Monetary Policy: The Liquidity Trap

Since December 2008, the Fed has kept the T-bill rate at zero. Could it do more? More generally, what happens if the interest rate is equal to zero and the central bank further increases the supply of money?

To answer this question, we must first go back first to our characterization of the demand and the supply of money in Chapter 4. There we drew the demand for money, for a given level of income, as a decreasing function of the interest rate. The lower the interest rate, the larger the demand for money—equivalently, the smaller the demand for bonds. What we did not ask in Chapter 4 is what happens to the demand for money

Figure 9-7

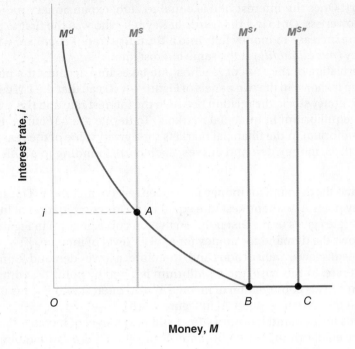

Money Demand, Money Supply, and the Liquidity Trap

When the interest rate is equal to zero, and once people have enough money for transaction purposes, they become indifferent between holding money and holding bonds. The demand for money becomes horizontal. This implies that, when the interest rate is equal to zero, further increases in the money supply have no effect on the interest rate.

when the interest rate becomes equal to zero. The answer: Once people hold enough money for transaction purposes, they are then indifferent between holding the rest of their financial wealth in the form of money or in the form of bonds. The reason they are indifferent is that both money and bonds pay the same interest rate, namely zero. Thus, the demand for money is as shown in Figure 9-7:

If you look at Figure 4-1, you will see that we avoided the issue by not drawing the demand for money for interest rates close to zero.

- As the interest rate decreases, people want to hold more money (and thus less bonds): The demand for money increases.
- As the interest rate becomes equal to zero, people want to hold an amount of money at least equal to the distance OB: this is what they need for transaction purposes. But they are willing to hold even more money (and therefore hold less bonds) because they are indifferent between money and bonds. Therefore, the demand for money becomes horizontal beyond point B.

Now consider the effects of an increase in the money supply.

- Consider the case where the money supply is M^s, so the interest rate consistent with financial market equilibrium is positive and equal to i. (This is the case we considered in Chapter 4.) Starting from that equilibrium, an increase in the money supply—a shift of the M^s line to the right—leads to a decrease in the interest rate.
- Now consider the case where the money supply is $M^{s'}$, so the equilibrium is at point B; or the case where the money supply is $M^{s''}$, so the equilibrium is given at point C. In either case, the initial interest rate is zero. And, in either case, an increase in the money supply has no effect on the interest rate. Think of it this way:

Suppose the central bank increases the money supply. It does so through an open market operation in which it buys bonds and pays for them by creating money. As the interest rate is zero, people are indifferent to how much money or bonds they hold, so they are willing to hold less bonds and more money at the same interest rate, namely zero. The money supply increases, but with no effect on the interest rate—which remains equal to zero.

From Chapter 4: The central bank changes the money stock through open market operations, in which it buys or sells bonds in exchange for money.

In short: Once the interest rate is equal to zero, expansionary monetary policy becomes powerless. Or to use the words of Keynes, who was the first to point out the problem, the increase in money falls into a **liquidity trap**: People are willing to hold more money (*more liquidity*) at the same interest rate.

The derivation of the *LM* curve when one takes into account the possibility of a liquidity trap is shown in the two panels of Figure 9-8. Recall that the *LM* curve gives, for a given real money stock, the relation between the interest rate and the level of income implied by equilibrium in financial markets. To derive the *LM* curve, Figure 9-8(a) looks at equilibrium in the financial markets for a given value of the real money stock and draws three money demand curves, each corresponding to a different level of income:

■ M^d shows the demand for money for a given level of income Y. The equilibrium is given by point A, with interest rate equal to i. This combination of income Y and interest rate i gives us the first point on the *LM* curve, point A in Figure 9-8(b).
■ $M^{d'}$ shows the demand for money for a lower level of income, $Y' < Y$. Lower income means fewer transactions and, therefore, a lower demand for money at any interest rate. In this case, the equilibrium is given by point A', with interest rate equal to i'. This combination of income Y' and interest rate i' gives us the second point on the *LM* curve, point A' in Figure 9-8(b).

So far, the derivation of the
LM curve is exactly the same
as in Chapter 5. It is only when ▶
income is lower than Y'', that
things become different.

■ $M^{d''}$ gives the demand for money for a still lower level of income $Y'' < Y'$. In this case, the equilibrium is given by point A'' in Figure 9-8(a), with interest rate equal to zero. Point A'' in Figure 9-8(b) corresponds to A'' in Figure 9-9(a).
■ What happens if income decreases below Y'', shifting the demand for money further to the left in Figure 9-8(a)? The intersection between the money supply curve and the money demand curve takes place on the horizontal portion of the money demand curve. The interest rate remains equal to zero.

Let's summarize: In the presence of a liquidity trap, the *LM* curve is given by Figure 9-8(b). For values of income greater than Y'', it is upward sloping—just as it was in Chapter 5 when we first characterized the *LM* curve. For values of income less than Y'', it is flat at $i = 0$. Intuitively: The interest rate cannot go below zero.

Figure 9-8

The Derivation of the LM Curve in the Presence of a Liquidity Trap

For low levels of output, the *LM* curve is a flat segment, with an interest rate equal to zero. For higher levels of output, it is upward sloping: An increase in income leads to an increase in the interest rate.

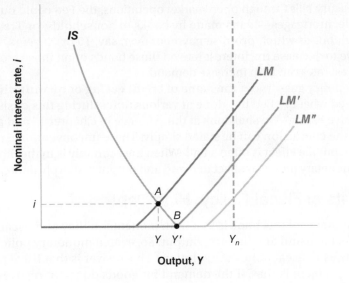

Figure 9-9

The IS–LM Model and the Liquidity Trap

In the presence of a liquidity trap, there is a limit to how much monetary policy can increase output.

Having derived the *LM* curve in the presence of a liquidity trap, we can look at the properties of the *IS–LM* model modified in this way. Suppose the economy is initially at point *A* in Figure 9-9. Equilibrium is at point *A*, at the intersection of the *IS* curve and the *LM* curve, with output *Y* and interest rate *i*. And suppose that this level of output is very low. The question is: Can monetary policy help the economy return to a higher level of output, say to Y_n?

Suppose the central bank increases the money supply, shifting the *LM* curve from *LM* to *LM'*. The equilibrium moves from point *A* down to point *B*. The interest rate decreases from *i* to zero, and output increases from *Y* to *Y'*. Thus, to this extent, expansionary monetary policy can indeed increase output.

What happens, however, if starting from point *B*, the central bank increases the money supply further, shifting the *LM* curve from *LM'* to, say, *LM"*? The intersection of *IS* and *LM"* remains at point *B*, and output remains equal to *Y'*. Expansionary monetary policy no longer has an effect on output; it cannot therefore help output increase to Y_n.

In words: When the interest rate is equal to zero, the economy falls into a *liquidity trap*: The central bank can increase *liquidity*—that is, increase the money supply. But this *liquidity* falls into a *trap*: The additional money is willingly held by people at an unchanged interest rate, namely zero. If, at this zero interest rate, the demand for goods is still too low, then there is nothing further conventional monetary policy can do to increase output.

You will note that, in the previous paragraph, we referred to the limits of *conventional* monetary policy; that is, monetary policy using open market operations aimed at decreasing the interest rate typically controlled by the Fed—in the United States, policy aimed at decreasing the interest rate on T-bills. The question is whether some *unconventional* measures may still be used. This is what the Fed (and other central banks around the world) have explored since 2008.

In the simple *IS–LM* model presented in Chapter 5, there was only one type of bond and one interest rate, and thus, once this rate was down to zero, there was nothing more monetary policy could do. But, in reality, there are many types of bonds and many interest rates. Some of these interest rates are higher than the interest rate on T-bills. This suggests the following unconventional monetary policy: Rather than

See for example the different interest rates facing AAA and BBB firms in Figure 9.4.

buying Treasury bills through open market operations, the Fed could buy other bonds; for example, mortgages—loans made by banks to households, or Treasury bonds—government bonds which promise payment over, say, 10 or 20 years. By doing so, it may be able to decrease the interest rate on those bonds or on those mortgages. These lower interest rates can help increase demand.

Such a policy goes under the name of **credit easing** or **quantitative easing**, and this is indeed what the Fed has done at various times during this crisis. How helpful is quantitative easing? We shall look at the evidence in Chapter 17 and again in Chapter 24. But the conclusion can be stated simply. These unconventional measures have some effect, but the effect is often small. When the economy is in the liquidity trap, the scope for monetary policy to affect demand and output is sharply limited.

The Limits of Fiscal Policy: High Debt

A recurrent theme of this book is that both monetary policy and fiscal policy can be used to affect demand and, in turn, output. So, even if monetary policy has reached sharp limits, isn't fiscal policy the solution? The answer is that fiscal policy also has limits. The problem is that, if the demand for goods does not recover over time by itself, if people or firms do not eventually become more optimistic and increase spending, the government must continue to run deficits to sustain higher demand and output. Continuing large deficits lead, however, to steadily higher public debt.

We shall look at the precise relation between debt and deficits in Chapter 23. But ▶ the notion that deficits lead to higher debt is straightforward.

In advanced countries, the ratio of government debt to GDP has increased from 46% in 2006 to 70% in 2011; in the United States, the ratio has increased from 42% in 2006 to 72% in 2011. High debt implies that, sooner or later, either taxes will have to increase, or spending will have to decrease, or the government will be unable to repay the debt. And when investors become worried about repayment of the debt, they start asking for higher interest rates on government bonds, making it even harder for the government to repay the debt. These worries are already leading

More on this in Chapter 23. ▶

to higher interest rates on government bonds in a number of European countries. They have not yet led to higher interest rates on government bonds in the United States. But the risk that interest rates might rise in the future is forcing the U.S. government to look for ways to begin to reduce its budget deficit now. This limits the contribution of fiscal policy to demand and to the recovery.

9-3 The Slow Recovery

While output growth is now positive in the United States, the recovery is very slow. Under current forecasts, unemployment is predicted to remain high for many years. There are increasing worries of a "lost decade." Looking at what has happened in Japan since the 1990s, these worries are justified: For nearly two decades, Japan has been in an economic slump. As the Focus box "Japan, the Liquidity Trap, and Fiscal Policy" shows, zero interest rates and large budget deficits have not succeeded in getting the Japanese economy back to normal.

We saw in Chapter 7 how some shocks, such as a permanent increase in the price of oil, can lead to a lower ▶ natural level of output. The financial crisis provides another potential example.

Why has the recovery from the crisis so slow in the United States? Some economists point to the aggregate supply side. They argue that the banking crisis has decreased the natural level of output, so that it would be wrong to think that we can go back to the pre-crisis level of output. More accurately, taking into account that output typically grows over time, it would be wrong to think that output can return to its old pre-crisis trend line. The weak recovery that we observe may be the best the economy can deliver. Indeed, the evidence from a large number of past banking crises, summarized in the Focus box "Do Banking Crises Affect Output in the

Japan, the Liquidity Trap, and Fiscal Policy

In the early 1990s, the Japanese stock market, which had boomed earlier, suddenly crashed. The Nikkei index, a broad index of Japanese stock prices, had gone up from 7,000 in 1980 to 35,000 at the beginning of 1990. Then, within two years, it went down to 16,000 and continued to decline after that, reaching a trough of 7,000 in 2003 (as we write, the Nikkei index is around 9,000). This decline in stock prices was followed by a decline in spending, and, in response to the decline in spending, the Japanese central bank cut the interest rate. As you can see from Figure 1, by the mid-1990s, the interest rate was down to less than 1%, and it has remained below 1% since.

With little room left for using monetary policy, fiscal policy was used to sustain demand. Figure 2 shows the evolution of government spending and revenues as a percentage of GDP since 1990. You can see the dramatic increase in spending from the early 1990s on. Much of the increased spending has taken the form of public works projects, and a joke circulating in Japan is that, by the time the Japanese economy has recovered, the entire shoreline of the Japanese archipelago will be covered in concrete. The result of this strong fiscal expansion, however, has been a sharp increase in debt. The ratio of government debt to GDP, which stood at 13% of GDP in 1991, is now above 120%. Meanwhile, the Japanese economy is still in a slump: GDP growth, which averaged 4.4% in the 1980s, was down to 1.4% in the 1990s, and 0.9% in the 2000s. What has happened in Japan since 1990 is a tough warning to other advanced countries that it may take a long time to recover.

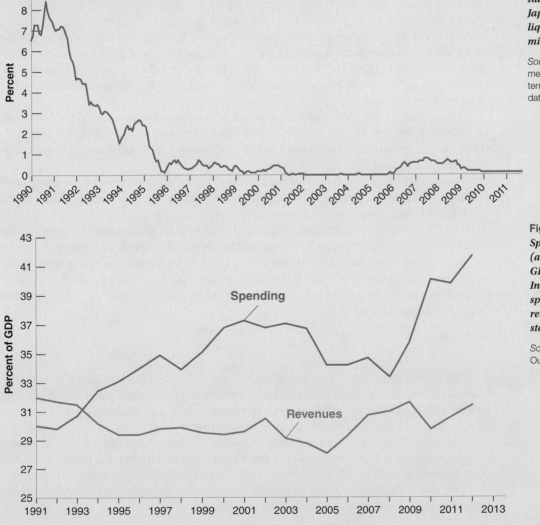

Figure 1 *The Interest Rate in Japan since 1990. Japan has been in a liquidity trap since the mid-1990s.*

Source: One-year government bond rate, DLX, International Monetary Fund database

Figure 2 *Government Spending and Revenues (as a percentage of GDP), Japan, since 1990. Increasing government spending and decreasing revenues have led to steadily larger deficits.*

Source: IMF World Economic Outlook database

Medium Run?" suggests that indeed output remains below its old pre-crisis trend line for many years. One can think of a number of reasons why this may be the case. The banking crisis may affect the efficiency of the banking system for a long time, leading to lower productivity (again relative to trend): Some of the new regulations introduced to decrease the risk of another financial crisis, such as increases in the capital ratio that banks must maintain, may indeed decrease risk; but they may also make intermediation between borrowers and lenders more costly, thus decreasing the natural level of output.

It may indeed be that the economy cannot return to its pre-crisis trend line. But in the context of the United States, this does not appear sufficient to explain the slow recovery from the crisis. In 2011, unemployment was around 9%. Pre-crisis, most estimates of the natural rate of unemployment were about 6%. It is unlikely that such a large increase in unemployment is entirely due to an increase in the natural rate of unemployment. In other words, what we are observing seems to be a rate of unemployment far above the underlying natural rate and, by implication, a level of output far below its natural level. So, most economists point also to the aggregate demand side. For the time being, insufficient aggregate demand, they argue, is the issue.

They point first to the limits of policy we have examined earlier. In a typical recovery, monetary and fiscal policy can be used to hasten the return of output to its natural level. In the current crisis, they can play a limited role at best. There is no room left for conventional monetary policy, and the effects of unconventional monetary policy are limited and uncertain. Worries about debt are putting strong pressure on the government to reduce the deficit, to pursue fiscal consolidation rather than fiscal expansion.

They also point out that, in the presence of the liquidity trap, not only does conventional monetary policy not work, but the process of adjustment that typically takes output back to its natural level in the medium run also fails. Recall from Chapter 7 how the mechanism typically works:

A decrease in output below its natural level leads to a decrease in the price level (at least relative to its trend). This leads to an increase in the real money stock, which in turn leads to a decrease in the interest rate. The decrease in the interest rate leads then to an increase in spending, which in turn leads to an increase in output. The process goes on until output has returned to its natural level. The process can be made faster by using either monetary policy (that is, by increasing the money stock, which leads to a larger decrease in the interest rate) or fiscal policy, which increases demand directly. At the core of the adjustment is the aggregate demand relation (equation (8.3) in Chapter 8):

$$Y = Y\left(\frac{M}{P}, G, T\right)$$

Now think about what happens when the economy is in the liquidity trap, with the interest rate equal to zero. In this case, an increase in the real money stock, M/P, whether it comes from an increase in M or from a decrease in P, has no effect on the interest rate, which remains equal to zero. So not only does monetary policy not affect spending, but the adjustment mechanism that returns output to its natural level in the AS–AD model also does not work: The decrease in the price level leads to a higher real money stock but does not lead to a lower interest rate and does not lead to higher spending.

Let's formally introduce this in our AS–AD model. If the economy is in the liquidity trap, the aggregate demand relation takes the following form:

$$Y = Y(G, T)$$

Figure 9-10

The Liquidity Trap and Adjustment Failure

If the economy is in the liquidity trap and output is below its natural level, the price level may decrease over time, but output does not increase.

As before, increases in government spending or decreases in taxes increase demand. But in the liquidity trap, aggregate demand no longer depends on the real money stock.

What may then happen to the economy is represented in Figure 9-10, using the *AS–AD* model. Aggregate supply is still represented by an upward sloping curve in the figure: The higher the level of output, the higher the price level, given the expected price level. Conversely, and more relevant for our case, the lower the output, the lower the price level. The aggregate demand relation is now vertical. For given values of *G*, *T*, aggregate demand does not depend on the real money stock and thus does not depend on the price level. Suppose that the initial aggregate supply and demand curves are given by *AS* and *AD*, respectively, so the initial equilibrium is at point *A*, with output *Y* below the natural level *Y_n*. In other words, output is low, and the economy is in the liquidity trap. As output is below its natural level, the aggregate supply curve shifts down over time. (Recall the mechanism: Low output implies high unemployment, which puts downward pressure on wages, and in turn on prices.) The equilibrium moves over time from A to B to C: The price level keeps decreasing, but this does not lead to an increase in output.

So is there hope that the U.S. economy will eventually return to normal? Yes. There are a number of reasons to think that aggregate demand will eventually recover. Eventually, the damage done to the banking system should be repaired. Very low housing investment and thus a decreasing housing stock, together with a growing population, should eventually lead to an increase in prices and higher housing investment in the future. Also, some types of consumption and investment cannot be deferred forever. Low purchases of consumer durables and of equipment now imply higher purchases later: Eventually, cars and machines break down and must be replaced. Economists sometimes refer to this mechanism as **pent-up demand**: Demand that does not take place today is *pent up* and increases demand in the future. Still, this may all take time, and, at the time of writing, a strong recovery appears to be far in the future.

Do Banking Crises Affect the Natural Level of Output?

Leaving aside the current crisis, there is a lot of evidence that banking crises lead to large decreases in output in the short run. But do they have an effect on output in the medium run? Or, put in terms of our model, do they affect the natural level of output?

To answer this question, researchers at the IMF looked at a number of banking crises across many countries from 1970 to 2002. They defined banking crises as episodes where there were either bank runs or a large number of bank failures. They identified 88 such crises. In each case, they looked at the behavior of GDP in the years following each crisis.

Using econometrics, they reached two conclusions: First, financial crises typically lead to a decrease in output relative to trend, even in the medium run. Second, while this conclusion holds on average, there is a lot of variation across countries. Some countries go back to trend, while others suffer large decreases.

The flavor of their results is given in Figure 1, which shows what happened in four countries following a banking crisis: Mexico after 1994, Korea after 1997, Sweden after 1991, and Thailand after 1997. In all four cases, there were major bank failures. For each country, the figure shows the evolution of GDP (the blue line) relative to the pre-crisis trend (dashed red line). You can see that, in three of the cases—Korea, Sweden, and Thailand—there was a large decrease in output relative to the pre-crisis trend, and this decrease was still largely present five years after the crisis. In other words, five years after the crisis, the rate of growth of GDP was roughly the same as before the crisis, but the level of GDP was lower than it would have been absent the crisis.

Can we tell why banking crises affect output, even in the medium run? The same researchers also looked at what happened to employment and what happened to productivity as a result of the crisis. They concluded that, on average, the decline in output could be broken down as follows: one-third related to a decrease in employment; two-thirds related to a decrease in productivity (both relative to trend). This suggests that the banking system plays an important role in the economy. Banking crises weaken the ability of the banking system to allocate funds to the right borrowers. This, in turn, makes the economy less productive.

Source: International Monetary Fund World Economic Outlook, October 2009, Chapter 4.

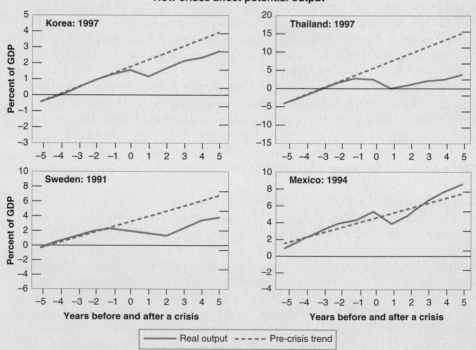

Figure 1   *The Evolution of Output after Four Banking Crises*

Summary

- The trigger of the crisis was a decrease in housing prices.
- The effect of lower housing prices was considerably amplified by the effects on the banking system. Because they had very low capital ratios, some banks became insolvent. Because the assets they held were highly complex, their value in the face of a decrease in housing prices and defaults on mortgages was highly uncertain, investors became reluctant to lend to banks, and many banks became illiquid. Banks became unwilling to lend to each other or to anyone else.
- Much higher interest rates for borrowers and, in some cases, the inability to borrow at all, led to a large decrease in spending. Worries about another Great Depression led to sharp declines in confidence and a further decrease in spending. The financial crisis led to a macroeconomic crisis and a large decline in output.
- Policies—fiscal, monetary, and financial—were used. They probably prevented an even larger decline in output but did not prevent the recession. Both fiscal and monetary policies now face sharp limits. Conventional monetary policy no longer works. The interest rate on T-bills has been decreased to zero, and the U.S. economy is in a liquidity trap. Large budget deficits have led to a large increase in debt, and there is strong pressure on the U.S. government to start reducing deficits now.
- The recovery is slow, and unemployment is expected to remain high for some time. It may be that the financial crisis has done lasting damage to the banking system, and the natural level of output may have decreased relative to trend. At this stage, however, the problem is on the demand side. The limits of policy, and the failure of the standard adjustment mechanism to return the economy to its natural level, imply that demand is likely to remain weak, and the recovery is likely to remain slow for some time to come.

Key Terms

mortgage lenders, 184

subprime mortgages (subprimes), 184

underwater mortgage, 185

financial intermediaries, 185

solvency, 186

illiquidity, 186

capital ratio, 186

leverage ratio, 186

securitization, 186

mortgage-based security (MBS), 187

senior securities, 187

junior securities, 187

collateralized debt obligation (CDO), 187

rating agencies, 187

toxic assets, 187

wholesale funding, 187

fire sale prices, 187

structured investment vehicle (SIV), 188

shadow banking system, 188

American International Group (AIG), 188

credit default swap (CDS), 188

Libor rate, 189

TED spread, 189

AAA (triple A), BBB (triple B), 189

liquidity facilities, 191

collateral, 191

Troubled Asset Relief Program (TARP), 191

American Recovery and Reinvestment Act, 192

liquidity trap, 194

credit easing, 196

quantitative easing, 196

Nikkei index, 197

pent-up demand, 199

Questions and Problems

QUICK CHECK
All Quick Check questions and problems are available on MyEconLab.

1. Using information in this chapter, label each of the following statements true, false, or uncertain. Explain briefly.

a. The loss in output that resulted from the financial crisis is many times larger than the losses on mortgages held by U.S. financial institutions.

b. An increase in a bank's leverage ratio tends to increase both the expected profit of the bank and the risk of the bank going bankrupt.

c. The high degree of securitization in the U.S. financial system helped to diversify risk and probably lessened the economic effect of the fall in housing prices.

d. Since the financial crisis ultimately led to a global recession, the policy measures (adopted in many countries) that provided substantial liquidity to financial institutions and that recapitalized banks (through the purchase of shares by governments) failed.

e. The fiscal stimulus programs adopted by many countries in response to the financial crisis helped offset the decline in aggregate demand and reduce the size of the recession.

f. The fiscal stimulus program adopted by many countries in response to the financial crisis did not lead to a large increase in the debt-to-GDP ratio.

g. Fiscal and monetary policy successfully saved Japan from a decade of slow growth following its financial crisis in the early 1990s.

2. *Traditional monetary and fiscal policy—the IS–LM view*
   Consider an economy described by Figure 9-9, with output lower than the natural level of output and the nominal interest rate at zero.

a. Draw Figure 9-9 using the *LM* curve passing through Point A.

b. If the Federal Reserve increases the money supply, what will happen to the *IS–LM* diagram you drew in part (a)? Will equilibrium output move closer to the natural level?

c. Given your answer to part (b), what policy options are available to the government to try to increase output? Consider traditional policy options only, and not financial policies. How does your answer relate to the policy decisions of the Obama administration and the U.S. Congress in February 2009?

3. *Traditional monetary and fiscal policy—the AS–AD view*
   Consider an economy described by Figure 9-10, with output lower than the natural level of output and the nominal interest rate at zero.

a. Draw Figure 9-10 and explain why the *AD* curve has a vertical portion.

b. If the Federal Reserve increases the money supply, what will happen to the *AS–AD* diagram you drew in part (a)? Will equilibrium output move closer to the natural level?

c. Given your answers to part (b), what policy options are available to the government to try to increase output? Consider traditional policy options only, and not financial policies. How does your answer relate to the policy decisions of the Obama administration and the U.S. Congress in February 2009?

DIG DEEPER

All Dig Deeper questions and problems are available on MyEconLab.

4. *Nontraditional macroeconomic policy: financial policy and quantitative easing*
   Consider again the economy described in Figure 9-9, and suppose that the IS and LM relations are

IS: $Y = C(Y - T, confidence) + I(Y, confidence,$
       $i + premium) + G$
LM: $M/P = YL(i)$

Interpret the interest rate as the federal funds rate, the policy interest rate of the Federal Reserve. Assume that the rate at which firms can borrow is much higher than the federal funds rate, equivalently that the premium in the IS equation is high.

a. Suppose that the government takes action to improve the solvency of the financial system. If the government's action is successful and banks become more willing to lend—both to one another and to nonfinancial firms—what is likely to happen to the premium? What will happen to the *IS–LM* diagram? Can we consider financial policy as a kind of macroeconomic policy?

b. Faced with a zero nominal interest rate, suppose the Fed decides to purchase securities directly to facilitate the flow of credit in the financial markets. This policy is called quantitative easing. If quantitative easing is successful, so that it becomes easier for financial and nonfinancial firms to obtain credit, what is likely to happen to the premium? What effect will this have on the *IS–LM* diagram? If quantitative easing has some effect, is it true that the Fed has no policy options to stimulate the economy when the federal funds rate is zero?

5. *Modern bank runs*
   Consider a simple bank that has assets of 100, capital of 20, and checking deposits of 80. Recall from Chapter 4 that checking deposits are liabilities of a bank.

a. Set up the bank's balance sheet.

b. Now suppose that the perceived value of the bank's assets falls by 10. What is the new value of the bank's capital?

c. Suppose the deposits are insured by the government. Despite the decline in the value of bank capital, is there any immediate reason for depositors to withdraw their funds from the bank? Would your answer change if the perceived value of the bank's assets fell by 15? 20? 25? Explain.

   Now consider a different sort of bank, still with assets of 100 and capital of 20, but now with short-term credit of 80 instead of checkable deposits. Short-term credit must be repaid or rolled over (borrowed again) when it comes due.

d. Set up this bank's balance sheet.

e. Again suppose the perceived value of the bank's assets falls. If lenders are nervous about the solvency of the bank, will they be willing to continue to provide short-term credit to the bank at low interest rates?

f. Assuming that the bank cannot raise additional capital, how can it raise the funds necessary to repay its debt coming due? If many banks are in this position at the same time (and if banks hold similar kinds of assets), what will likely happen to the value of the assets of these banks? How will this affect the willingness of lenders to provide short-term credit?

6. *The Troubled Asset Relief Program (TARP)*
   Consider a bank that has assets of 100, capital of 20, and short-term credit of 80. Among the bank's assets are securitized assets whose value depends on the price of houses. These assets have a value of 50.

a. Set up the bank's balance sheet.
   Suppose that as a result of a housing price decline, the value of the bank's securitized assets falls by an uncertain amount, so that these assets are now worth somewhere between 25

and 45. Call the securitized assets "troubled assets." The value of the other assets remains at 50. As a result of the uncertainty about the value of the bank's assets, lenders are reluctant to provide any short-term credit to the bank.

b. Given the uncertainty about the value of the bank's assets, what is the range in the value of the bank's capital?

As a response to this problem, the government considers purchasing the troubled assets, with the intention of reselling them again when the markets stabilize. (This is the original version of the TARP.)

c. If the government pays 25 for the troubled assets, what will be the value of the bank's capital? How much would the government have to pay for the troubled assets to ensure that the bank's capital does not have a negative value? If the government pays 45 for the troubled assets, but the true value turns out to be much lower, who bears the cost of this mistaken valuation? Explain.

Suppose instead of buying the troubled assets, the government provides capital to the bank by buying ownership shares, with the intention of reselling the shares again when the markets stabilize. (This is what the TARP ultimately became.) The government exchanges treasury bonds (which become assets for the bank) for ownership shares.

d. Suppose the government exchanges 25 of Treasury bonds for ownership shares. Assuming the worst-case scenario (so that the troubled assets are worth only 25), set up the new balance sheet of the bank. (Remember that the firm now has three assets: 50 of untroubled assets, 25 of troubled assets, and 25 of Treasury bonds.) What is the total value of the bank's capital? Will the bank be insolvent?

e. Given your answers and the material in the text, why might recapitalization be a better policy than buying the troubled assets?

EXPLORE FURTHER

7. *The TED spread*

The text described the fluctuations in the Ted spread that occurred during the financial crisis. Do an internet search and find the recent history of the Ted spread. You can find this information easily from various sources.

a. Consult Figure 9-3 to compare the current value of the Ted spread to its value before and during the financial crisis. How does the current value of the Ted spread compare to its highest values during the crisis? How does the current value of the Ted spread compare to its value at the beginning of 2007? (Note that the Ted spread is often quoted in basis points. One hundred basis points equals one percentage point.)

b. Has the Ted spread been relatively stable in recent months? In what range of values has the spread fluctuated?

c. What do you conclude about the willingness of banks to lend to one another now as compared to the beginning of 2007? as compared to the fall of 2008? Explain.

Further Readings

- There are already many good books on the crisis: among them Michael Lewis's *The Big Short* (W.W. Norton, 2010) and Gillian Tett's *Fool's Gold* (Free Press, 2009). Both books show how the financial system became increasingly risky until it finally collapsed. Both read like detective novels, with a lot of action and fascinating characters.

- *In Fed We Trust* (Crown Business, 2009), written in 2009 by David Wessel, the economics editor of the *Wall Street Journal*, describes how the Fed reacted to the crisis. It also makes for fascinating reading.

The Long Run

The next four chapters focus on the long run. In the long run, what dominates is not fluctuations, but growth. So now we need to ask: What determines growth?

Chapter 10

Chapter 10 looks at the facts of growth. It first documents the large increase in output that has taken place in rich countries over the past fifty years. Then, taking a wider look, it shows that on the scale of human history, such growth is a recent phenomenon. And it is not a universal phenomenon: Some countries are catching up, but many poor countries are suffering from no or low growth.

Chapter 11

Chapter 11 focuses on the role of capital accumulation in growth. It shows that capital accumulation cannot by itself sustain growth, but that it does affect the level of output. A higher saving rate typically leads to lower consumption initially, but to more consumption in the long run.

Chapter 12

Chapter 12 turns to technological progress. It shows how, in the long run, the growth rate of an economy is determined by the rate of technological progress. It then looks at the role of R&D in generating such progress. It returns to the facts of growth presented in Chapter 10, and shows how to interpret these facts in the light of the theories developed in Chapters 11 and 12.

Chapter 13

Chapter 13 looks at various issues raised by technological progress in the short, the medium, and the long run. Focusing on the short and the medium run, it discusses the relation between technological progress, unemployment, and wage inequality. Focusing on the long run, it discusses the role of institutions in sustaining technological progress and growth.

The Facts of Growth

Our perceptions of how the economy is doing are often dominated by year-to-year fluctuations in economic activity. A recession leads to gloom, and an expansion to optimism. But if we step back to get a look at activity over longer periods—say over many decades—the picture changes. Fluctuations fade. **Growth**—the steady increase in aggregate output over time—dominates the picture.

Figure 10-1, panels (a) and (b), shows the evolution of U.S. GDP and the evolution of U.S. GDP per person (both in 2000 dollars), respectively, since 1890. (The scale used to measure GDP on the vertical axis in Figure 10-1 is called a **logarithmic scale.** The defining characteristic of a logarithmic scale is that the same proportional increase in a variable is represented by the same distance on the vertical axis.)

◀ For more on log scales, see Appendix 2 at the end of the book.

The shaded years from 1929 to 1933 correspond to the large decrease in output during the Great Depression, and the other two shaded ranges correspond to the 1980–1982 recession—the largest postwar recession before the current crisis—and 2008–2010, the most recent crisis, the subject of much of the analysis in the rest of this book. Note how small these three episodes appear compared to the steady increase in output per person over the last 100 years. The cartoon makes the same point about growth and fluctuations, in an even more obvious way.

With this in mind, we now shift our focus from fluctuations to growth. Put another way, we turn from the study of the determination of output in the *short and medium run*—where fluctuations dominate—to the determination of output in the *long run*—where growth dominates. Our goal is to understand what determines growth, why some countries are growing while others are not, and why some countries are rich while many others are still poor.

Section 10-1 discusses a central measurement issue; namely how to measure the standard of living.

Section 10-2 looks at growth in the United States and other rich countries over the last fifty years.

Section 10-3 takes a broader look, across both time and space.

Section 10-4 then gives a primer on growth and introduces the framework that will be developed in the next three chapters. ●

Figure 10-1

Panel (a): U.S. GDP since 1890. Panel (b): U.S. GDP per person since 1890

Panel (a) shows the enormous increase in U.S. output since 1890, by a factor of 43. Panel (b) shows that the increase in output is not simply due to the large increase in U.S. population from 63 million to more than 300 million over this period. Output per person has risen by a factor of 9.

Source: 1890–1947: Historical Statistics of the United States. http://hsus.cambridge.org/ HSUSWeb/toc/hsusHome.do. 1948 to 2010: National Income and Product Accounts. Population estimates 1890 to 2010. From Louis Johnston and Samuel H. Williamson, "What Was the U.S. GDP Then?" Measuring Worth, 2011. http://www.measuringworth.org/ usgdp/

(a)

(b)

10-1 Measuring the Standard of Living

Output per person is also called output per capita ("capita" means "head" in Latin). And given that output ▶ and income are always equal, it is also called income per person, or income per capita.

The reason we care about growth is that we care about the **standard of living.** Looking across time, we want to know by how much the standard of living has increased. Looking across countries, we want to know how much higher the standard of living is in one country relative to another. Thus, the variable we want to focus on, and compare either over time or across countries, is **output per person**, rather than *output* itself.

A practical problem then arises: How do we compare output per person across countries? Countries use different currencies; thus output in each country is expressed in terms of its own currency. A natural solution is to use exchange rates: When

*"It's true, Caesar. Rome is declining, but I expect it
to pick up in the next quarter."*

comparing, say, the output per person of India to the output per person of the United States, we can compute Indian GDP per person in rupees, use the exchange rate to get Indian GDP per person in dollars, and compare it to the U.S. GDP per person in dollars. This simple approach will not do, however, for two reasons:

- First, exchange rates can vary a lot (more on this in Chapters 18 to 21). For example, the dollar increased and then decreased in the 1980s by roughly 50% vis-à-vis the currencies of the trading partners of the United States. But, surely, the standard of living in the United States did not increase by 50% and then decrease by 50% compared to the standard of living of its trading partners during the decade. Yet this is the conclusion we would reach if we were to compare GDP per person using exchange rates.

- The second reason goes beyond fluctuations in exchange rates. In 2010, GDP per person in India, using the current exchange rate, was $1,300 compared to $47,300 in the United States. Surely no one could live on $1,300 a year in the United States. But people live on it—admittedly, not very well—in India, where the prices of basic goods—those goods needed for subsistence—are much lower than in the United States. The level of consumption of the average person in India, who consumes mostly basic goods, is not 36 (47,300 divided by 1,300) times smaller than that of the average person in the United States. This point applies to other countries besides the United States and India: In general, the lower a country's output per person, the lower the prices of food and basic services in that country.

> Recall a similar discussion in Chapter 1 where we looked at output per person in China.

So, when we focus on comparing standards of living, we get more meaningful comparisons by correcting for the two effects we just discussed—variations in exchange rates, and systematic differences in prices across countries. The details of constructing these differences are complicated, but the principle is simple: The numbers for GDP—and hence for GDP per person— are constructed using a common set of prices for all countries. Such adjusted real GDP numbers, which you can think of as measures of **purchasing power** across time or across countries, are called **purchasing power parity** (PPP) numbers. Further discussion is given in the Focus box "The Construction of PPP Numbers."

The Construction of PPP Numbers

Consider two countries—let's call them the United States and Russia, although we are not attempting to fit the characteristics of those two countries very closely:

In the United States, annual consumption per person equals $20,000. People in the United States each buy two goods: Every year, they buy a new car for $10,000 and spend the rest on food. The price of a yearly bundle of food in the United States is $10,000.

In Russia, annual consumption per person equals 60,000 rubles. People there keep their cars for 15 years. The price of a car is 300,000 rubles, so individuals spend on average 20,000 rubles—300,000/15—a year on cars. They buy the same yearly bundle of food as their U.S. counterparts, at a price of 40,000 rubles.

Russian and U.S. cars are of identical quality, and so are Russian and U.S. food. (You may dispute the realism of these assumptions. Whether a car in country X is the same as a car in country Y is very much the type of problem confronting economists when constructing PPP measures.) The exchange rate is such that one dollar is equal to 30 rubles. What is consumption per person in Russia relative to consumption per person in the United States?

One way to answer is by taking consumption per person in Russia and converting it into dollars using the exchange rate. Using this method, Russian consumption per person in dollars is $2,000 (60,000 rubles divided by the exchange rate, 30 rubles to the dollar). According to these numbers, consumption per person in Russia is only 10% of U.S. consumption per person.

Does this answer make sense? True, Russians are poorer, but food is much cheaper in Russia. A U.S. consumer spending all of his 20,000 dollars on food would buy 2 bundles of food ($20,000/$10,000). A Russian consumer spending all of his 60,000 rubles on food would buy 1.5 bundles of food (60,000 rubles/40,000 rubles). In terms of food bundles, the difference looks much smaller between U.S. and Russian consumption per person. And given that one-half of consumption in the United States and two-thirds of consumption in Russia go to spending on food, this seems like a relevant computation.

Can we improve on our initial answer? Yes. One way is to use the same set of prices for both countries and then measure the quantities of each good consumed in each country using this common set of prices. Suppose we use U.S. prices. In terms of U.S. prices, annual consumption per person in the United States is obviously still $20,000. What is it in Russia? Every year, the average Russian buys approximately 0.07 car (one car every fifteen years) and one bundle of food. Using U.S. prices—specifically, $10,000 for a car and $10,000 for a bundle of food—gives Russian consumption per person as $[(0.07 \times \$10,000) + (1 \times \$10,000)] = [\$700 + \$10,000] = \$10,700$. So, using U.S. prices to compute consumption in both countries puts annual Russian consumption per person at $10,700/$20,000 = 53.5% of annual U.S. consumption per person, a better estimate of relative standards of living than we obtained using our first method (which put the number at only 10%).

This type of computation, namely the construction of variables across countries using a common set of prices, underlies PPP estimates. Rather than using U.S. dollar prices as in our example (why use U.S. rather than Russian or, for that matter, French prices?), these estimates use average prices across countries. These average prices are called *international dollar prices*. Many of the estimates we use in this chapter are the result of an ambitious project known as the "Penn World Tables." (Penn stands for the University of Pennsylvania, where the project is located.) Led by three economists—Irving Kravis, Robert Summers, and Alan Heston—over the course of more than 40 years, researchers working on the project have constructed PPP series not only for consumption (as we just did in our example), but more generally for GDP and its components, going back to 1950, for most countries in the world.

For more on the construction of PPP numbers, go to the Web site http://pwt.econ.upenn.edu/ associated with the Penn World Tables. (In the Penn tables, what is the ratio of Russian PPP GDP per person to U.S. PPP GDP per person?) The IMF and the World Bank also construct their own set of PPP numbers.

When comparing rich versus poor countries, the differences between PPP numbers and the numbers based on current exchange rates can be very large. Return to the comparison between India and the United States. We saw that, at current exchange rates, the ratio of GDP per person in the United States to GDP per person in India was 36. Using PPP numbers, the ratio is "only" 14. Although this is still a large difference, it is much smaller than the ratio we obtained using current exchange rates. Differences between PPP numbers and numbers based on current exchange rate are typically smaller when making comparisons among rich countries. If we were to compare using current exchange rates—GDP per person in the United States in 2010 was equal to 115% of the GDP per person in Germany. Based on PPP numbers, GDP per person in the United States is in fact equal to 129% of GDP per person in Germany. More generally, PPP numbers suggest that the United States still has the highest GDP per person among the world's major countries.

The bottom line: When comparing standard of living across countries, make sure to use PPP numbers.

Let me end this section with three remarks before we move on and look at growth:

- What matters for people's welfare is their consumption rather than their income. One might therefore want to use *consumption per person* rather than output per person as a measure of the standard of living. (This is indeed what we did in the Focus box, "The Construction of PPP Numbers.") Because the ratio of consumption to output is rather similar across countries, the ranking of countries is roughly the same, whether we use consumption per person or output per person.

- Thinking about the production side, we may be interested in differences in productivity rather than in differences in the standard of living across countries. In this case, the right measure is *output per worker*—or, even better, *output per hour worked* if the information about total hours worked is available—rather than output per person. Output per person and output per worker (or per hour) will differ to the extent that the ratio of the number of workers (or hours) to population differs across countries. Most of the aforementioned difference between output per person in the United States and in Germany comes, for example, from differences in hours worked per person rather than from differences in productivity. Put another way, German workers are about as productive as their U.S. counterparts. However, they work fewer hours, so their standard of living, measured by output per person, is lower. In exchange, however, they enjoy more leisure time.

- The reason we ultimately care about the standard of living is presumably that we care about happiness. We may therefore ask the obvious question: Does a higher standard of living lead to greater happiness? The answer is given in the Focus box "Does Money Buy Happiness?". The answer: a qualified yes.

10-2 Growth in Rich Countries since 1950

Let's start by looking, in this section, at growth in rich countries since 1950. In the next section, we shall look further back in time and across a wider range of countries.

Table 10-1 shows the evolution of *output per person* (GDP divided by population, measured at PPP prices) for France, Japan, the United Kingdom, and the United States, since 1950. We have chosen these four countries not only because they are some of the

Table 10-1 The Evolution of Output per Person in Four Rich Countries since 1950				
	Annual Growth Rate Output per Person (%)	Real Output per Person (2005 dollars)		
	1950–2009	1950	2009	2009/1950
France	2.5	7,112	30,821	4.3
Japan	3.9	3,118	31,958	10.2
United Kingdom	2.0	10,400	33,386	3.2
United States	1.9	13,183	41,102	3.1
Average	2.6	8,453	34,317	5.2

Notes: The data stop in 2009, the latest year (at this point) available in the Penn tables. The average in the last line is a simple unweighted average. *Source:* Alan Heston, Robert Summers, and Bettina Aten, Penn World Table Version 7.0, Center for International Comparisons of Production, Income and Prices at the University of Pennsylvania, May 2011

Does Money Lead to Happiness?

FOCUS

Does money lead to happiness? Or, put more accurately, does higher income per person lead to more happiness? The implicit assumption, when economists assess the performance of an economy by looking at its level of income per person or at its growth rate, is that this is indeed the case. Early examinations of data on the relation between income and self-reported measures of happiness suggested that this assumption may not be right. They yielded what is now known as the **Easterlin paradox** (so named for Richard Easterlin, who was one of the first economists to look systematically at the evidence):

■ Looking across countries, happiness in a country appeared to be higher, the higher the level of income per person. The relation, however, appeared to hold only in relatively poor countries. Looking at rich countries, say the set of OECD countries (look at Chapter 1 for the list), there appeared to be little relation between income per person and happiness.

■ Looking over time, average happiness in rich countries did not seem to increase very much, if at all, with income. (There were no reliable data for poor countries.) In other words, in rich countries, growth did not appear to increase happiness.

■ Looking across people within a given country, happiness appeared to be strongly correlated with income. Rich people were consistently happier than poor people. This was true in both poor and rich countries.

The first two facts suggested that, once basic needs are satisfied, higher income per person does not increase happiness. The third fact suggested that what was important was not the absolute level of income but the level of income relative to others.

If this interpretation is right, it has major implications for the way we think about the world and about economic policies. In rich countries, policies aimed at increasing income per person might be misdirected because what matters is the distribution of income rather than its average level. Globalization and the diffusion of information, to the extent that it makes people in poor countries compare themselves not to rich people in the same country but to people in richer countries, may actually decrease rather than increase happiness. So, as you can guess, these findings have led to an intense debate and further research. As new data sets have become available better evidence has accumulated. The state of knowledge and the remaining controversies are analyzed in a recent article by Betsey Stevenson and Justin Wolfers. Their conclusions are well summarized in Figure 1 below.

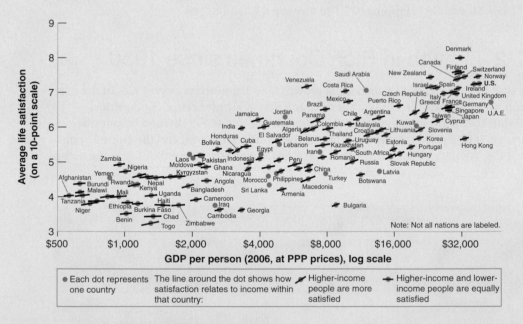

Figure 1 *Life Satisfaction and Income per Person*

Source: Betsey Stevenson and Justin Wolfers, Wharton School at the University of Pennsylvania.

The figure contains a lot of information. Let's go through it step by step.

The horizontal axis measures PPP GDP per person for 131 countries. The scale is a logarithmic scale, so a given size interval represents a given percentage increase in GDP. The vertical axis measures average life satisfaction in each country. The source for this variable is a 2006 Gallup World Poll survey, which asked about a thousand individuals in each country the following question:

> "Here is a ladder representing the "ladder of life." Let's suppose the top of the ladder represents the best possible life for you; and the bottom, the worst possible life for you. On which step of the ladder do you feel you personally stand at the present time?"

The ladder went from 0 to 10. The variable measured on the vertical axis is the average of the individual answers in each country.

Focus first on the dots representing each country, ignoring for the moment the lines that cross each dot. The visual impression is clear: There is a strong relation across countries between average income and average happiness. The index is around 4 in the poorest countries, around 8 in the richest. And, more importantly in view of the early Easterlin paradox, this relation appears to hold both for poor and rich countries.

Focus now on the lines through each dot. The slope of each line reflects the estimated relation between life satisfaction and income across individuals within each country. Note first that all the lines slope upward: This confirms the third leg of the Easterlin paradox: In each country, rich people are happier than poor people. Note also that the slopes of most of these lines are roughly similar to the slope of the relation across countries. This goes against the Easterlin paradox: Individual happiness increases with income, whether this is because the country is getting richer or because the individual becomes relatively richer within the country.

Stevenson and Wolfers draw a strong conclusion from their findings: While individual happiness surely depends on much more than income, it definitely increases with income. Thus, it is not a crime for economists to focus first on levels and growth rates of GDP per person. So, is the debate over? The answer is no. Even if we accept this interpretation of the evidence, clearly, many other aspects of the economy matter for welfare, income distribution surely being one of them. And not everybody is convinced by the evidence. In particular, the evidence on the relation between happiness and income per person over time within a country is not as clear as the evidence across countries or across individuals presented in Figure 1. Given the importance of the question, the debate will continue for some time.

Sources: Betsey Stevenson and Justin Wolfers, "Economic Growth and Subjective Well–Being: Reassessing the Easterlin Paradox," Brookings Papers on Economic Activity, Vol. 2008 (Spring 2008): 1–87.

For a view closer to the Easterlin paradox and a fascinating discussion of policy implications, read Richard Layard, *Happiness: Lessons from a New Science*, Penguin Books, 2005.

world's major economic powers, but because what has happened to them is broadly representative of what has happened in other advanced countries over the last half century or so.

Table 10-1 yields two main conclusions:

- There has been a large increase in output per person.
- There has been a convergence of output per person across countries.

Let's look at each of these points in turn.

The Large Increase in the Standard of Living since 1950

Look at the column on the far right of the table. Output per person has increased by a factor of 3.1 since 1950 in the United States, by a factor of 4.3 in France, and by a factor of 10.2 in Japan.

These numbers show what is sometimes called the **force of compounding**. In a different context, you probably have heard how saving even a little while you are young will build to a large amount by the time you retire. For example, if the interest rate is 3.9% a year, an investment of one dollar, with the proceeds reinvested every year, will grow to about 10 dollars ($[1 + 0.039]^{60}$) 60 years later. The same logic applies to growth rates. The average annual growth rate in Japan over the period 1950 to 2009 was equal to 3.9%. This high growth rate has led to an ten-fold increase in real output per person in Japan over the period.

Most of the increase in Japan took place before 1990. As we saw in Chapter 9, since then, Japan has been in a prolonged economic slump, with ◀ very low growth.

Clearly, a better understanding of growth, if it leads to the design of policies that stimulate growth, can have a very large effect on the standard of living. Suppose we could find a policy measure that permanently increased the growth rate by 1% per year.

$1.01^{40} - 1 = 1.48 - 1 = 48\%$. Unfortunately, policy measures with such magic results have proven difficult to discover!

This would lead, after 40 years, to a standard of living 48% higher than it would have been without the policy—a substantial difference.

The Convergence of Output per Person

The second and third columns of Table 10-1 show that the levels of output per person have converged (become closer) over time: The numbers for output per person are much more similar in 2009 than they were in 1950. Put another way, those countries that were behind have grown faster, reducing the gap between them and the United States.

In 1950, output per person in the United States was roughly twice the level of output per person in France and more than four times the level of output per person in Japan. From the perspective of Europe or Japan, the United States was seen as the land of plenty, where everything was bigger and better. Today these perceptions have faded, and the numbers explain why. Using PPP numbers, U.S. output per person is still the highest, but, in 2009, it was only 20% above average output per person in the other three countries, a much smaller difference than in the 1950s.

For the list of countries, see the appendix to Chapter 1.

The figure includes only those OECD members for which we have a reliable estimate of the level of output per person in 1950.

This **convergence** of levels of output per person across countries is not specific to the four countries we are looking at. It extends to the set of OECD countries. This is shown in Figure 10-2, which plots the average annual growth rate of output per person since 1950 against the initial level of output per person in 1950 for the set of countries that are members of the OECD today. There is a clear negative relation between the initial level of output per person and the growth rate since 1950: Countries that were behind in 1950 have typically grown faster. The relation is not perfect: Turkey, which had roughly the same low level of output per person as Japan in 1950, has had a growth rate equal to only about one-half that of Japan. But the relation is clearly there.

Some economists have pointed to a problem in graphs like Figure 10-2. By looking at the subset of countries that are members of the OECD today, what we have done in effect is to look at a club of economic winners: OECD membership is not officially based on economic success, but economic success is surely an important determinant of membership. But when you look at a club whose membership is based on economic success, you will find that those who came from behind had the fastest growth: This is

Figure 10-2

Growth Rate of GDP Per Person since 1950 versus GDP per Person in 1950; OECD Countries

Countries with lower levels of output per person in 1950 have typically grown faster.

Source: See Table 10-1.

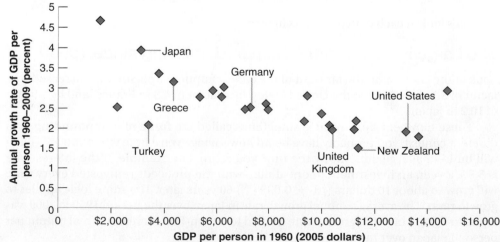

precisely why they made it to the club! The finding of convergence could come in part from the way we selected the countries in the first place.

So a better way of looking at convergence is to define the set of countries we look at not on the basis of where they are today—as we did in Figure 10-2 by taking today's OECD members—but on the basis of where they were in, say, 1950. For example, we can look at all countries that had an output per person of at least one-fourth of U.S. output per person in 1950, and then look for convergence within that group. It turns out that most of the countries in that group have indeed converged, and therefore convergence is not solely an OECD phenomenon. However, a few countries—Uruguay, Argentina, and Venezuela among them—have not converged. In 1950, those three countries had roughly the same output per person as France. In 2009, they had fallen far behind; their level of output per person stood only between one-fourth and one-half of the French level.

10-3 A Broader Look across Time and Space

In the previous section, we focused on growth over the last 50 years in rich countries. Let's now put this in context by looking at the evidence both over a much longer time span and a wider set of countries.

Looking across Two Millennia

Has output per person in the currently rich economies always grown at rates similar to the growth rates in Table 10-1? The answer is no. Estimates of growth are clearly harder to construct as we look further back in time. But there is agreement among economic historians about the main evolutions over the last 2,000 years.

From the end of the Roman Empire to roughly year 1500, there was essentially no growth of output per person in Europe: Most workers were employed in agriculture in which there was little technological progress. Because agriculture's share of output was so large, inventions with applications outside agriculture could only contribute little to overall production and output. Although there was some output growth, a roughly proportional increase in population led to roughly constant output per person.

This period of stagnation of output per person is often called the Malthusian era. Thomas Robert Malthus, an English economist, at the end of the eighteenth century, argued that this proportional increase in output and population was not a coincidence. Any increase in output, he argued, would lead to a decrease in mortality, leading to an increase in population until output per person was back to its initial level. Europe was in a **Malthusian trap**, unable to increase its output per person.

Eventually, Europe was able to escape this trap. From about 1500 to 1700, growth of output per person turned positive, but it was still small—only around 0.1% per year. It then increased to just 0.2% per year from 1700 to 1820. Starting with the Industrial Revolution, growth rates increased, but from 1820 to 1950 the growth rate of output per person in the United States was still only 1.5% per year. On the scale of human history, therefore, sustained growth of output per person—especially the high growth rates we have seen since 1950—is definitely a recent phenomenon.

Looking across Countries

We have seen how output per person has converged among OECD countries. But what about the other countries? Are the poorest countries also growing faster? Are they converging toward the United States, even if they are still far behind?

The answer is given in Figure 10-3, which plots the average annual growth rate of output per person since 1960 against output per person for the year 1960, for 76 countries.

The numbers for 1950 are missing for too many countries to use 1950 as the initial year, as we did in Figure 10-2.

The striking feature of Figure 10-3 is that there is no clear pattern: It is not the case that, in general, countries that were behind in 1960 have grown faster. Some have, but many have clearly not.

The cloud of points in Figure 10-3 hides, however, a number of interesting patterns that appear when we put countries into different groups. Note that we have used different symbols in the figure: The diamonds represent OECD countries; the squares represent African countries; the triangles represent Asian countries. Looking at patterns by groups yields three main conclusions:

1. The picture for the OECD countries (for the rich countries) is much the same as in Figure 10-2, which looked at a slightly longer period of time (from 1950 onward, rather than from 1960). Nearly all start at high levels of output per person (say, at least one-third of the U.S. level in 1960), and there is clear evidence of convergence.

   As we saw in Chapter 9, this fast growth came to an end in the 1990s, and Japan has ▶ remained in a slump since.

2. Convergence is also visible for many Asian countries: Most of the countries with very high growth rates over the period are in Asia. Japan was the first country to take off. Starting a decade later, in the 1960s, four countries—Singapore, Taiwan, Hong Kong, and South Korea, a group of countries sometimes called the **four tigers**—started catching up as well. In 1960, their average output per person was about 18% of the U.S.; by 2009, it had increased to 83% of U.S. output. More recently, the major story has been China—both because of its very high growth rates and because of its sheer size. Over the period, growth of output per person in China has been 4.4%. But, because it started very low, its output per person is still only about one-sixth of the U.S.

   Paradoxically, the two fastest growing countries in Figure 10-3 are Botswana and Equatorial Guinea, both in Africa. In both cases, however, high growth reflects primarily favorable natural resources—diamonds in Botswana, oil in Guinea.

3. The picture is different, however, for African countries. Most African countries (represented by squares) were very poor in 1960, and most have not done well over the period. Many have suffered from either internal or external conflicts. Eight of them have had negative growth of output per person—an absolute decline in their

Figure 10-3

Growth Rate of GDP per Person since 1960, versus GDP Per Person in 1960 (2005 dollars); 76 Countries

There is no clear relation between the growth rate of output since 1960 and the level of output per person in 1960.

Source: See Table 10-1.

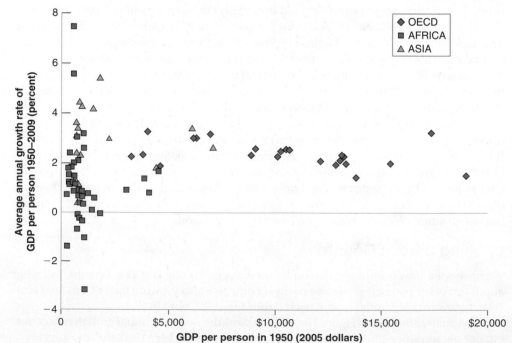

standard of living between 1960 and 2009. Growth averaged −1% in the Central African Republic and −0.7% in Niger. As a result, output per person in the Central African Republic in 2009 is 60% of its level in 1960. Some hope, however, comes from more recent numbers: Growth of output per person in Sub Saharan Africa, which averaged only 1.3% in the 1990s, was close to 5.0% in the 2000s.

Looking further back in time the following picture emerges. For much of the first millennium, and until the fifteenth century, China probably had the world's highest level of output per person. For a couple of centuries, leadership moved to the cities of northern Italy. But, until the nineteenth century, differences across countries were typically much smaller than they are today. Starting in the nineteenth century, a number of countries, first in Western Europe, then in North and South America, started growing faster than others. Since then, a number of other countries, most notably in Asia, have started growing fast and are converging. Many others, mainly in Africa, are not.

Our main focus, in this and the next chapter, will primarily be on growth in rich and emerging countries. We shall not take on some of the wider challenges raised by the facts we have just seen, such as why growth of output per person started in earnest in the nineteenth century or why Africa has remained so poor. Doing so would take us too far into economic history and development economics. But these facts put into perspective the two basic facts we discussed earlier when looking at the OECD: Neither ◀ growth nor convergence is a historical necessity.

The distinction between *growth theory* and *development economics* is fuzzy. A rough distinction: Growth theory takes many of the institutions of a country (for example, its legal system and its form of government) as given. Development economics asks what institutions are needed to sustain steady growth, and how they can be put in place.

10-4 Thinking About Growth: A Primer

To think about growth economists use a framework developed originally by Robert Solow, from the Massachusetts Institute of Technology (MIT) in the late 1950s. The framework has proven sturdy and useful, and we will use it here. This section provides ◀ an introduction. Chapters 11 and 12 will provide a more detailed analysis, first of the role of capital accumulation and then of the role of technological progress in the process of growth.

Solow's article, "A Contribution to the Theory of Economic Growth," Robert M. Solow, *The Quarterly Journal of Economics*, Vol. 70, No. 1. (Feb., 1956), pp. 65–94. Solow was awarded the Nobel Prize in 1987 for his work on growth.

The Aggregate Production Function

The starting point for any theory of growth must be an **aggregate production function**, a specification of the relation between aggregate output and the inputs in production.

The aggregate production function we introduced in Chapter 6 to study the determination of output in the short run and the medium run took a particularly simple form. Output was simply proportional to the amount of labor used by firms—more specifically, proportional to the number of workers employed by firms (equation (6.2)). So long as our focus was on fluctuations in output and employment, the assumption was acceptable. But now that our focus has shifted to growth this assumption will no longer do: It implies that output per worker is constant, ruling out growth (or at least growth of output per worker) altogether. It is time to relax it. From now on, we will assume that there are two inputs—capital and labor—and that the relation between aggregate output and the two inputs is given by:

$$Y = F(K, N) \tag{10.1}$$

As before, Y is aggregate output. K is capital—the sum of all the machines, plants, and office buildings in the economy. N is labor—the number of workers in the economy. The function F, which tells us how much output is produced for given quantities of capital and labor, is the *aggregate production function*.

The aggregate production function is

$$Y = F(K, N)$$

Aggregate output (Y) depends on the aggregate capital stock (K) and aggregate employment (N).

This way of thinking about aggregate production is an improvement on our treatment in Chapter 6. But it should be clear that it is still a dramatic simplification of reality. Surely, machines and office buildings play very different roles in production and should be treated as separate inputs. Surely, workers with Ph.D.'s are different from high-school dropouts; yet, by constructing the labor input as simply the *number* of workers in the economy, we treat all workers as identical. We will relax some of these simplifications later. For the time being, equation (10.1), which emphasizes the role of both labor and capital in production, will do.

The next step must be to think about where the aggregate production function F, which relates output to the two inputs, comes from. In other words, what determines how much output can be produced for given quantities of capital and labor? The answer: the **state of technology**. A country with a more advanced technology will produce more output from the same quantities of capital and labor than will an economy with a primitive technology.

The function F depends on the state of technology. The higher the state of technology, ▶ the higher $F(K, N)$ for a given K and a given N.

How should we define the *state of technology*? Should we think of it as the list of blueprints defining both the range of products that can be produced in the economy as well as the techniques available to produce them? Or should we think of it more broadly, including not only the list of blueprints, but also the way the economy is organized—from the internal organization of firms, to the system of laws and the quality of their enforcement, to the political system, and so on? In the next two chapters we will have in mind the narrower definition—the set of blueprints. In Chapter 13, however, we will consider the broader definition and return to what we know about the role of the other factors, from legal institutions to the quality of government.

Returns to Scale and Returns to Factors

Now that we have introduced the aggregate production function, the next question is: What restrictions can we reasonably impose on this function?

Consider first a thought experiment in which we double both the number of workers and the amount of capital in the economy. What do you expect will happen to output? A reasonable answer is that output will double as well: In effect, we have cloned the original economy, and the clone economy can produce output in the same way as the original economy. This property is called **constant returns to scale**: If the scale of operation is doubled—that is, if the quantities of capital and labor are doubled—then output will also double.

$$2Y = F(2K, 2N)$$

Or, more generally, for any number x (this will be useful below)

$$xY = F(xK, xN) \tag{10.2}$$

Constant returns to scale: $F(xK, xN) = xY$.

We have just looked at what happens to production when *both* capital and labor are increased. Let's now ask a different question. What should we expect to happen if *only one* of the two inputs in the economy—say capital—is increased?

Surely output will increase. That part is clear. But it is also reasonable to assume that the same increase in capital will lead to smaller and smaller increases in output as the level of capital increases. In other words, if there is little capital to start with, a little more capital will help a lot. If there is a lot of capital to start with, a little more capital may make little difference. Why? Think, for example, of a secretarial pool, composed of a given number of secretaries. Think of capital as computers. The introduction of the first computer will substantially increase the pool's production, because some of the more time-consuming tasks can now be done automatically by the computer. As the number of computers increases and more secretaries in the pool get their own

Output here is secretarial services. The two inputs are secretaries and computers. The production function re- ▶ lates secretarial services to the number of secretaries and the number of computers.

computers, production will further increase, although perhaps by less per additional computer than was the case when the first one was introduced. Once each and every secretary has a computer, increasing the number of computers further is unlikely to increase production very much, if at all. Additional computers might simply remain unused and left in their shipping boxes and lead to no increase in output.

We shall refer to the property that increases in capital lead to smaller and smaller increases in output as **decreasing returns to capital** (a property that will be familiar to those who have taken a course in microeconomics).

A similar argument applies to the other input, labor. Increases in labor, given capital, lead to smaller and smaller increases in output. (Return to our example, and think of what happens as you increase the number of secretaries for a given number of computers.) There are **decreasing returns to labor** as well.

Even under constant returns to scale, there are decreasing returns to each factor, keeping the other factor constant:

There are decreasing returns to capital: Given labor, increases in capital lead to smaller and smaller increases in output.

There are decreasing returns to labor: Given capital, increases in labor lead to smaller and smaller increases in output.

Output per Worker and Capital per Worker

The production function we have written down, together with the assumption of constant returns to scale, implies that there is a simple relation between *output per worker* and *capital per worker.*

To see this, set $x = 1/N$ in equation (10.2), so that

$$\frac{Y}{N} = F\left(\frac{K}{N}, \frac{N}{N}\right) = F\left(\frac{K}{N}, 1\right) \tag{10.3}$$

Note that Y/N is output per worker, K/N is capital per worker. So equation (10.3) tells us that the amount of output per worker depends on the amount of capital per worker. This relation between output per worker and capital per worker will play a central role in what follows, so let's look at it more closely.

This relation is drawn in Figure 10-4. Output per worker (Y/N) is measured on the vertical axis, and capital per worker (K/N) is measured on the horizontal axis. The relation between the two is given by the upward-sloping curve. As capital per worker increases, so does output per worker. Note that the curve is drawn so that increases in capital lead to smaller and smaller increases in output. This follows from the property that there are *decreasing returns to capital*: At point A, where capital per worker is low, an increase in capital per worker, represented by the horizontal distance AB, leads to an increase in output per worker equal to the vertical distance $A'B'$. At point C, where capital per worker is larger, the same increase in capital per worker, represented by the

Make sure you understand what is behind the algebra. Suppose capital and the number of workers both double. What happens to output per worker?

Figure 10-4

Output and Capital per Worker

Increases in capital per worker lead to smaller and smaller increases in output per worker.

Increases in capital per worker lead to smaller and smaller increases in output per worker as the level of capital per worker increases.

horizontal distance *CD* (where the distance *CD* is equal to the distance *AB*), leads to a much smaller increase in output per worker, only *C′D′*. This is just like our secretarial pool example, where additional computers had less and less impact on total output.

The Sources of Growth

We are now ready to return to our basic question: Where does growth come from? Why does output per worker—or output per person, if we assume the ratio of workers to the population as a whole remains constant over time—go up over time? Equation (10.3) gives a first answer:

- Increases in output per worker (Y/N) can come from increases in capital per worker (K/N). This is the relation we just looked at in Figure 10-4. As (K/N) increases—that is, as we move to the right on the horizontal axis—(Y/N) increases.

Increases in capital per worker: Movements along the production function.

- Or they can come from improvements in the state of technology that shift the production function, *F*, and lead to more output per worker *given* capital per worker. This is shown in Figure 10-5. An improvement in the state of technology shifts the

Improvements in the state of technology: Shifts (up) of the production function.

production function up, from $F(K/N, 1)$ to $F(K/N, 1)'$. For a given level of capital per worker, the improvement in technology leads to an increase in output per worker. For example, for the level of capital per worker corresponding to point *A*, output per worker, increases from *A′* to *B′*. (To go back to our secretarial pool example, a reallocation of tasks within the pool may lead to a better division of labor and an increase in the output per secretary.)

Hence, we can think of growth as coming from **capital accumulation** and from **technological progress**—the improvement in the state of technology. We will see, however, that these two factors play very different roles in the growth process:

- Capital accumulation *by itself* cannot sustain growth. A formal argument will have to wait until Chapter 11. But you can already see the intuition behind this from Figure 10-5. Because of decreasing returns to capital, sustaining a steady increase in output per worker will require larger and larger increases in the level of capital per worker. At some stage, the economy will be unwilling or unable to save and invest enough to further increase capital. At that stage, output per worker will stop growing.

   Does this mean that an economy's **saving rate**—the proportion of income that is saved—is irrelevant? No. It is true that a higher saving rate cannot permanently increase the *growth rate* of output. But a higher saving rate can sustain a higher

Figure 10-5

The Effects of an Improvement in the State of Technology

An improvement in technology shifts the production function up, leading to an increase in output per worker for a given level of capital per worker.

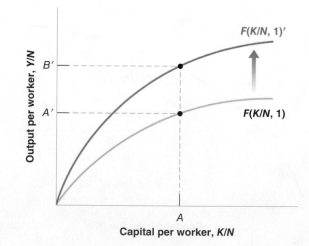

level of output. Let me state this in a slightly different way. Take two economies that differ only in their saving rates. The two economies will grow at the same rate, but, at any point in time, the economy with the higher saving rate will have a higher level of output per person than the other. How this happens, how much the saving rate affects the level of output, and whether or not a country like the United States (which has a very low saving rate) should try to increase its saving rate will be one of the topics we take up in Chapter 11.

■ Sustained growth requires sustained technological progress. This really follows from the previous proposition: Given that the two factors that can lead to an increase in output are capital accumulation and technological progress, if capital accumulation cannot sustain growth forever, then technological progress must be the key to growth. And it is. We will see in Chapter 12 that the economy's rate of growth of output per person is eventually determined by its rate of technological progress.

This is very important. It means that in the long run, an economy that sustains a higher rate of technological progress will eventually overtake all other economies. This, of course, raises yet another question: What determines the rate of technological progress? Recall the two definitions of the state of technology we discussed earlier: a narrow definition, namely the set of blueprints available to the economy; and a broader definition, which captures how the economy is organized, from the nature of institutions to the role of the government. What we know about the determinants of technological progress narrowly defined—the role of fundamental and applied research, the role of patent laws, the role of education and training—will be taken up in Chapter 12. The role of broader factors will be discussed in Chapter 13. ◄

Following up on the distinction introduced earlier between growth theory and development economics: Chapter 12 will deal with technological progress from the viewpoint of growth theory; Chapter 13 will come closer to development economics.

Summary

. . . .

■ Over long periods, fluctuations in output are dwarfed by growth— the steady increase of aggregate output over time.

■ Looking at growth in four rich countries (France, Japan, the United Kingdom, and the United States) since 1950, two main facts emerge:

1. All four countries have experienced strong growth and a large increase in the standard of living. Growth from 1950 to 2009 increased real output per person by a factor of 3.1 in the United States and by a factor of 10.2 in Japan.

2. The levels of output per person across the four countries have converged over time. Put another way, those countries that were behind have grown faster, reducing the gap between them and the current leader, the United States.

■ Looking at the evidence across a broader set of countries and a longer period, the following facts emerge:

1. On the scale of human history, sustained output growth is a recent phenomenon.

2. The convergence of levels of output per person is not a worldwide phenomenon. Many Asian countries are rapidly catching up, but most African countries have both low levels of output per person and low growth rates.

■ To think about growth, economists start from an aggregate production function relating aggregate output to two factors of production: capital and labor. How much output is produced given these inputs depends on the state of technology.

■ Under the assumption of constant returns, the aggregate production function implies that increases in output per worker can come either from increases in capital per worker or from improvements in the state of technology.

■ Capital accumulation by itself cannot permanently sustain growth of output per person. Nevertheless, how much a country saves is very important because the saving rate determines the *level* of output per person, if not its growth rate.

■ Sustained growth of output per person is ultimately due to technological progress. Perhaps the most important question in growth theory is what the determinants of technological progress are.

Key Terms

Questions and Problems

QUICK CHECK

All Quick Check questions and problems are available on MyEconLab.

1. Using the information in this chapter, label each of the following statements true, false, or uncertain. Explain briefly.

a. On a logarithmic scale, a variable that increases at 5% per year will move along an upward-sloping line with a slope of 0.05.

b. The price of food is higher in poor countries than it is in rich countries.

c. Evidence suggests that happiness in rich countries increases with output per person.

d. In virtually all the countries of the world, output per person is converging to the level of output per person in the United States.

e. For about 1,000 years after the fall of the Roman Empire, there was essentially no growth in output per person in Europe, because any increase in output led to a proportional increase in population.

f. Capital accumulation does not affect the level of output in the long run; only technological progress does.

g. The aggregate production function is a relation between output on one hand and labor and capital on the other.

2. Assume that the average consumer in Mexico and the average consumer in the United States buy the quantities and pay the prices indicated in the following table:

	Food		Transportation Services	
	Price	*Quantity*	*Price*	*Quantity*
Mexico	5 pesos	400	20 pesos	200
United States	$1	1,000	$2	2,000

a. Compute U.S. consumption per capita in dollars.

b. Compute Mexican consumption per capita in pesos.

c. Suppose that 1 dollar is worth 10 pesos. Compute Mexico's consumption per capita in dollars.

d. Using the purchasing power parity method and U.S. prices, compute Mexican consumption per capita in dollars.

e. Under each method, how much lower is the standard of living in Mexico than in the United States? Does the choice of method make a difference?

3. Consider the production function

$$Y = \sqrt{K}\sqrt{N}$$

a. Compute output when $K = 49$ and $N = 81$.

b. If both capital and labor double, what happens to output?

c. Is this production function characterized by constant returns to scale? Explain.

d. Write this production function as a relation between output per worker and capital per worker.

e. Let $K/N = 4$. What is Y/N? Now double K/N to 8. Does Y/N double as a result?

f. Does the relation between output per worker and capital per worker exhibit constant returns to scale?

g. Is your answer to (f) the same as your answer to (c)? Why or why not?

h. Plot the relation between output per worker and capital per worker. Does it have the same general shape as the relation in Figure 10-4? Explain.

DIG DEEPER

All Dig Deeper questions and problems are available on MyEconLab.

4. The growth rates of capital and output

Consider the production function given in problem 3. Assume that N is constant and equal to 1. Note that if $z = x^a$, then $g_z \approx a g_x$, where g_z and g_x are the growth rates of z and x.

a. Given the growth approximation here, derive the relation between the growth rate of output and the growth rate of capital.

b. Suppose we want to achieve output growth equal to 2% per year. What is the required rate of growth of capital?

c. In (b), what happens to the ratio of capital to output over time?

d. Is it possible to sustain output growth of 2% forever in this economy? Why or why not?

5. Between 1950 and 1973, France, Germany, and Japan all experienced growth rates that were at least two percentage points higher than those in the United States. Yet the most important technological advances of that period were made in the United States. How can this be?

EXPLORE FURTHER

6. Convergence between Japan and the United States since 1950

Go to the Web site containing the Penn World Table (pwt.econ.upenn.edu) and collect data on the annual growth rate of GDP per person for the United States and Japan from 1951 to the most recent year available. In addition, collect the numbers for real GDP per person (chained series) for the United States and Japan in 1973.

  a. Compute the average annual growth rates of GDP per person for the United States and Japan for three time periods: 1951 to 1973, 1974 to the most recent year available, and 1991 to the most recent year available. Did the level of real output per person in Japan tend to converge to the level of real output per person in the United States in each of these three periods? Explain.

  b. Suppose that in every year since 1973, Japan and the United States had each continued to have their average annual growth rates for the period 1951 to 1973. How would real GDP per person compare in Japan and the United States today (i.e., in the most recent year available in the Penn World Table)?

7. Convergence in two sets of countries

Go to the Web site containing the Penn World Table and collect data on real GDP per person (chained series) from 1951 to the most recent year available for the United States, France, Belgium, Italy, Argentina, Venezuela, Chad, and Madagascar.

  a. Define for each country for each year the ratio of its real GDP to that of the United States for that year (so that this ratio will be equal to 1 for the United States for all years).

  b. In one graph, plot the ratios for France, Belgium, and Italy over the period for which you have data. Does your graph support the notion of convergence among France, Belgium, Italy, with the US?

  c. Draw a graph with the ratios for Argentina, Venezuela, Chad, and Madagascar. Does your new graph support the notion of convergence among Argentina, Venezuela, Chad, Madagascar, with the United States?

8. Growth successes and failures

Go to the Web site containing the Penn World Table and collect data on real GDP per capita (chained series) for 1970 for all available countries. Do the same for a recent year of data, say one year before the most recent year available in the Penn World Table. (If you choose the most recent year available, the Penn World Table may not have the data for some countries relevant to this question.)

  a. Rank the countries according to GDP per person in 1970. List the countries with the 10 highest levels of GDP per person in 1970. Are there any surprises?

  b. Carry out the analysis in part (a) for the most recent year for which you collected data. Has the composition of the 10 richest countries changed since 1970?

  c. For each of the 10 countries you collected data for, divide the recent level of GDP per capita by the level in 1970. Which of these countries has had the greatest proportional increase in GDP per capita since 1970?

  d. Carry out the exercise in part (c) for all the countries for which you have data. Which country has had the highest proportional increase in GDP per capita since 1970? Which country had the smallest proportional increase? What fraction of countries has had negative growth since 1970?

  e. Do a brief Internet search on either the country from part (c) with the greatest increase in GDP per capita or the country from part (d) with the smallest increase. Can you ascertain any reasons for the economic success, or lack of it, for this country?

Further Readings

■ Brad deLong has a number of fascinating articles on growth on his Web page (http://econ161.berkeley.edu/). Read in particular "Berkeley Faculty Lunch Talk: Main Themes of Twentieth Century Economic History," which covers many of the themes of this chapter.

■ A broad presentation of facts about growth is given by Angus Maddison in *The World Economy. A Millenium Perspective* (Paris: OECD, 2001). The associated site www.theworldeconomy.org has a large number of facts and data on growth over the last two millenia.

■ Chapter 3 in *Productivity and American Leadership*, by William Baumol, Sue Anne Batey Blackman, and Edward Wolff (Cambridge, MA: MIT Press 1989), gives a vivid description of how life has been transformed by growth in the United States since the mid-1880s.

Saving, Capital Accumulation, and Output

ince 1970 the U.S. **saving rate**—the ratio of saving to GDP—has averaged only 17%, compared to 22% in Germany and 30% in Japan. Can this explain why the U.S. growth rate has been lower than in most OECD countries in the last 40 years? Would increasing the U.S. saving rate lead to sustained higher U.S. growth in the future?

We have already given the basic answer to these questions at the end of Chapter 10. The answer is no. Over long periods—an important qualification to which we will return—an economy's growth rate does not depend on its saving rate. It does not appear that lower U.S. growth in the last 50 years comes primarily from a low saving rate. Nor should we expect that an increase in the saving rate will lead to sustained higher U.S. growth.

This conclusion does not mean, however, that we should not be concerned about the low U.S. saving rate. Even if the saving rate does not permanently affect the growth rate, it does affect the level of output and the standard of living. An increase in the saving rate would lead to higher growth for some time and eventually to a higher standard of living in the United States.

This chapter focuses on the effects of the saving rate on the level and the growth rate of output.

Sections 11-1 and 11-2 look at the interactions between output and capital accumulation and the effects of the saving rate.

Section 11-3 plugs in numbers to give a better sense of the magnitudes involved.

Section 11-4 extends our discussion to take into account not only physical but also human capital.

11-1 Interactions between Output and Capital

At the center of the determination of output in the long run are two relations between output and capital:

- The amount of capital determines the amount of output being produced.
- The amount of output determines the amount of saving and, in turn, the amount of capital being accumulated over time.

Together, these two relations, which are represented in Figure 11-1, determine the evolution of output and capital over time. The green arrow captures the first relation, from capital to output. The blue and purple arrows capture the two parts of the second relation, from output to saving and investment, and from investment to the change in the capital stock. Let's look at each relation in turn.

The Effects of Capital on Output

We started discussing the first of these two relations, the effect of capital on output, in Section 10-3. There we introduced the aggregate production function and you saw that, under the assumption of constant returns to scale, we can write the following relation between output and capital per worker:

$$\frac{Y}{N} = F\left(\frac{K}{N}, 1\right)$$

Output per worker (Y/N) is an increasing function of capital per worker (K/N). Under the assumption of decreasing returns to capital, the effect of a given increase in capital per worker on output per worker decreases as the ratio of capital per worker gets larger. When capital per worker is already very high, further increases in capital per worker have only a small effect on output per worker.

To simplify notation, we will rewrite this relation between output and capital per worker simply as

$$\frac{Y}{N} = f\left(\frac{K}{N}\right)$$

where the function f represents the same relation between output and capital per worker as the function F:

$$f\left(\frac{K}{N}\right) \equiv F\left(\frac{K}{N}, 1\right)$$

In this chapter, we shall make two further assumptions:

- The first is that the size of the population, the participation rate, and the unemployment rate are all constant. This implies that employment, N, is also constant. To see why, go back to the relations we saw in Chapter 2 and again in Chapter 6, between population, the labor force, unemployment, and employment.

> Suppose, for example, the function F has the "double square root" form $F(K, N) = \sqrt{K}\sqrt{N}$, so
>
> $$Y = \sqrt{K}\sqrt{N}$$
>
> Divide both sides by N, so
>
> $$Y/N = \sqrt{K}\sqrt{N}/N$$
>
> Note $\sqrt{N}/N = \sqrt{N}/(\sqrt{N}\sqrt{N}) = 1/\sqrt{N}$. Using this result in the preceding equation leads to a model of income per person:
>
> $$Y/N = \sqrt{K}/\sqrt{N} = \sqrt{K/N}$$
>
> So, in this case, the function f giving the relation between output per worker and capital per worker is simply the square root function
>
> $$f(K/N) = \sqrt{K/N}$$

Figure 11-1

Capital, Output, and Saving/Investment

- The labor force is equal to population times the participation rate. So if population is constant and the participation rate is constant, the labor force is also constant.
- Employment, in turn, is equal to the labor force times 1 minus the unemployment rate. If, for example, the size of the labor force is 100 million and the unemployment rate is 5%, then employment is equal to 95 million (100 million times $(1 - 0.05)$). So, if the labor force is constant and the unemployment rate is constant, employment is also constant.

Under these assumptions, output per worker, output per person, and output itself all move proportionately. Although we will usually refer to movements in output or capital *per worker*, to lighten the text we shall sometimes just talk about movements in output or capital, leaving out the "per worker" or "per person" qualification.

In the United States in 2009, output per person (in 2005 PPP dollars) was $41,102; output per worker was much higher, at $81,172. (From these two numbers, can you derive the ratio of employment to population?)

The reason for assuming that N is constant is to make it easier to focus on how capital accumulation affects growth: If N is constant, the only factor of production that changes over time is capital. The assumption is not very realistic, however, so we will relax it in the next two chapters. In Chapter 12, we will allow for steady population and employment growth. In Chapter 13, we shall see how we can integrate our analysis of the long run—which ignores fluctuations in employment—with our earlier analysis of the short and medium runs—which focused precisely on these fluctuations in employment (and the associated fluctuations in output and unemployment). But both steps are better left to later.

- The second assumption is that there is no technological progress, so the production function f (or, equivalently, F) does not change over time.

Again, the reason for making this assumption—which is obviously contrary to reality—is to focus just on the role of capital accumulation. In Chapter 12, we shall introduce technological progress and see that the basic conclusions we derive here about the role of capital in growth also hold when there is technological progress. Again, this step is better left to later.

With these two assumptions, our first relation between output and capital per worker, from the production side, can be written as

$$\frac{Y_t}{N} = f\left(\frac{K_t}{N}\right) \tag{11.1}$$

where we have introduced time indexes for output and capital—but not for labor, N, which we assume to be constant and so does not need a time index.

In words: Higher capital per worker leads to higher output per worker.

From the production side: The level of capital per worker determines the level of output per worker.

The Effects of Output on Capital Accumulation

To derive the second relation between output and capital accumulation, we proceed in two steps.

First, we derive the relation between output and investment.

Then we derive the relation between investment and capital accumulation.

As we will see in Chapter 19, saving and investment need not be equal in an open economy. A country can save less than it invests and borrow the difference from the rest of the world. This is indeed the case for the United States today.

Output and Investment

To derive the relation between output and investment, we make three assumptions:

- We continue to assume that the economy is closed. As we saw in Chapter 3 (equation (3.10)), this means that investment, I, is equal to saving—the sum of private saving, S, and public saving, $T - G$.

$$I = S + (T - G)$$

■ To focus on the behavior of private saving, we assume that public saving, $T - G$, is equal to zero. (We shall later relax this assumption when we focus on the effects of fiscal policy on growth.) With this assumption, the previous equation becomes

$$I = S$$

Investment is equal to private saving.

■ We assume that private saving is proportional to income, so

$$S = sY$$

The parameter s is the saving rate. It has a value between zero and 1. This assumption captures two basic facts about saving: First, the saving rate does not appear to systematically increase or decrease as a country becomes richer. Second, richer countries do not appear to have systematically higher or lower saving rates than poorer ones.

Combining these two relations and introducing time indexes gives a simple relation between investment and output:

$$I_t = sY_t$$

Investment is proportional to output: The higher output is, the higher is saving and so the higher is investment.

Investment and Capital Accumulation

The second step relates investment, which is a flow (the new machines produced and new plants built during a given period), to capital, which is a stock (the existing machines and plants in the economy at a point in time).

Think of time as measured in years, so t denotes year t, $t + 1$ denotes year $t + 1$, and so on. Think of the capital stock as being measured at the beginning of each year, so K_t refers to the capital stock at the beginning of year t, K_{t+1} to the capital stock at the beginning of year $t + 1$, and so on.

Assume that capital depreciates at rate δ (the lowercase Greek letter delta) per year: That is, from one year to the next, a proportion δ of the capital stock breaks down and becomes useless. Equivalently, a proportion $(1 - \delta)$ of the capital stock remains intact from one year to the next.

The evolution of the capital stock is then given by

$$K_{t+1} = (1 - \delta)K_t + I_t$$

The capital stock at the beginning of year $t + 1$, K_{t+1}, is equal to the capital stock at the beginning of year t, which is still intact in year $t + 1$, $(1 - \delta)K_t$, plus the new capital stock put in place during year t (i.e., investment during year t, I_t).

We can now combine the relation between output and investment and the relation between investment and capital accumulation to obtain the second relation we need in order to think about growth: the relation from output to capital accumulation.

Replacing investment by its expression from above and dividing both sides by N (the number of workers in the economy) gives

$$\frac{K_{t+1}}{N} = (1 - \delta)\frac{K_t}{N} + s\frac{Y_t}{N}$$

In words: Capital per worker at the beginning of year $t + 1$ is equal to capital per worker at the beginning of year t, adjusted for depreciation, plus investment per worker during year t, which is equal to the saving rate times output per worker during year t.

Expanding the term $(1 - \delta)K_t/N$ to $K_t/N - \delta K_t/N$, moving K_t/N to the left, and reorganizing the right side,

$$\frac{K_{t+1}}{N} - \frac{K_t}{N} = s\frac{Y_t}{N} - \delta\frac{K_t}{N} \qquad (11.2)$$

In words: The change in the capital stock per worker—represented by the difference between the two terms on the left—is equal to saving per worker—represented by the first term on the right—minus depreciation—represented by the second term on the right. This equation gives us the second relation between output and capital per worker.

From the saving side: The level of output per worker determines the change in the level of capital per worker over time.

11-2 The Implications of Alternative Saving Rates

We have derived two relations:

- From the production side, we have seen in equation (11.1) how capital determines output.
- From the saving side, we have seen in equation (11.2) how output in turn determines capital accumulation.

We can now put the two relations together and see how they determine the behavior of output and capital over time.

Dynamics of Capital and Output

Replacing output per worker (Y_t/N) in equation (11.2) by its expression in terms of capital per worker from equation (11.1) gives

$$\frac{K_{t+1}}{N} - \frac{K_t}{N} = s\,f\!\left(\frac{K_t}{N}\right) - \delta\frac{K_t}{N} \qquad (11.3)$$

$$\text{change in capital} = \text{invesment} - \text{depreciation}$$
$$\text{from year } t \text{ to year } t + 1 \quad \text{during year } t \quad \text{during year } t$$

This relation describes what happens to capital per worker. The change in capital per worker from this year to next year depends on the difference between two terms:

- Investment per worker, the first term on the right. The level of capital per worker this year determines output per worker this year. Given the saving rate, output per worker determines the amount of saving per worker and thus the investment per worker this year.

  ◀ $K_t/N \Rightarrow f(K_t/N) \Rightarrow sf(K_t/N)$

- Depreciation per worker, the second term on the right. The capital stock per worker determines the amount of depreciation per worker this year.

  ◀ $K_t/N \Rightarrow \delta K_t/N$

If investment per worker exceeds depreciation per worker, the change in capital per worker is positive: Capital per worker increases.

If investment per worker is less than depreciation per worker, the change in capital per worker is negative: Capital per worker decreases.

Given capital per worker, output per worker is then given by equation (11.1):

$$\frac{Y_t}{N} = f\!\left(\frac{K_t}{N}\right)$$

Equations (11.3) and (11.1) contain all the information we need to understand the dynamics of capital and output over time. The easiest way to interpret them is to use a

Figure 11-2

Capital and Output Dynamics

When capital and output are low, investment exceeds depreciation and capital increases. When capital and output are high, investment is less than depreciation and capital decreases.

graph. We do this in Figure 11-2: Output per worker is measured on the vertical axis, and capital per worker is measured on the horizontal axis.

In Figure 11-2, look first at the curve representing output per worker, $f(K_t/N)$, as a function of capital per worker. The relation is the same as in Figure 10-4: Output per worker increases with capital per worker, but—because of decreasing returns to capital—the effect is smaller the higher the level of capital per worker.

Now look at the two curves representing the two components on the right of equation (11.3):

To make the graph easier to read, we have assumed an unrealistically high saving rate. (Can you tell roughly what value we have assumed for s? What would be a plausible value for s?) ▸

■ The relation representing investment per worker, $s f(K_t/N)$, has the same shape as the production function except that it is lower by a factor s (the saving rate). Suppose the level of capital per worker is equal to K_0/N in Figure 11-2. Output per worker is then given by the distance AB, and investment per worker is given by the vertical distance AC, which is equal to s times the vertical distance AB. Thus, just like output per worker, investment per worker increases with capital per worker, but by less and less as capital per worker increases. When capital per worker is already very high, the effect of a further increase in capital per worker on output per worker, and by implication on investment per worker, is very small.

■ The relation representing depreciation per worker, $\delta K_t/N$, is represented by a straight line. Depreciation per worker increases in proportion to capital per worker so the relation is represented by a straight line with slope equal to δ. At the level of capital per worker K_0/N, depreciation per worker is given by the vertical distance AD.

The change in capital per worker is given by the difference between investment per worker and depreciation per worker. At K_0/N, the difference is positive; investment per worker exceeds depreciation per worker by an amount represented by the vertical distance $CD = AC - AD$, so capital per worker increases. As we move to the right along the horizontal axis and look at higher and higher levels of capital per worker, investment increases by less and less, while depreciation keeps increasing in proportion to capital. For some level of capital per worker, K^*/N in Figure 11-2, investment is just enough to cover depreciation, and capital per worker remains constant. To the left of K^*/N, investment exceeds depreciation and capital per worker increases. This is indicated by the arrows pointing to the right along the curve representing the production function. To the right of K^*/N, depreciation exceeds investment, and capital per worker decreases. This is indicated by the arrows pointing to the left along the curve representing the production function.

When capital per worker is low, capital per worker and output per worker increase over time. When capital per worker is high, capital per worker and output per worker decrease over time. ▸

Characterizing the evolution of capital per worker and output per worker over time is now easy. Consider an economy that starts with a low level of capital per worker—say, K_0/N in Figure 11-2. Because investment exceeds depreciation at this point, capital per worker increases. And because output moves with capital, output per worker increases as well. Capital per worker eventually reaches K^*/N, the level at which investment is equal to depreciation. Once the economy has reached the level of capital per worker K^*/N, output per worker and capital per worker remain constant at Y^*/N and K^*/N, their long-run equilibrium levels.

Think, for example, of a country that loses part of its capital stock, say as a result of bombing during a war. The mechanism we have just seen suggests that, if the country has suffered larger capital losses than population losses, it will come out of the war with a low level of capital per worker; that is, at a point to the left of K^*/N. The country will then experience a large increase in both capital per worker and output per worker for some time. This describes well what happened after World War II to countries that had proportionally larger destructions of capital than losses of human lives (see the Focus box "Capital Accumulation and Growth in France in the Aftermath of World War II").

What does the model predict for post-war growth if a country suffers proportional losses in population and in capital? Do you find this answer convincing? What elements may be missing from the model?

If a country starts instead from a high level of capital per worker—that is, from a point to the right of K^*/N—then depreciation will exceed investment, and capital per worker and output per worker will decrease: The initial level of capital per worker is too high to be sustained given the saving rate. This decrease in capital per worker will continue until the economy again reaches the point where investment is equal to depreciation and capital per worker is equal to K^*/N. From then on, capital per worker and output per worker will remain constant.

Steady-State Capital and Output

Let's look more closely at the levels of output per worker and capital per worker to which the economy converges in the long run. The state in which output per worker and capital per worker are no longer changing is called the **steady state** of the economy. Setting the left side of equation (11.3) equal to zero (in steady state, by definition, the change in capital per worker is zero), the steady-state value of capital per worker, K^*/N, is given by

$$s f\left(\frac{K^*}{N}\right) = \delta \frac{K^*}{N} \qquad (11.4)$$

The steady-state value of capital per worker is such that the amount of saving per worker (the left side) is just sufficient to cover depreciation of the capital stock per worker (the right side of the equation).

Given steady-state capital per worker (K^*/N), the steady-state value of output per worker (Y^*/N) is given by the production function

K^*/N is the long-run level of capital per worker.

$$\frac{Y^*}{N} = f\left(\frac{K^*}{N}\right) \qquad (11.5)$$

We now have all the elements we need to discuss the effects of the saving rate on output per worker, both over time and in steady state.

The Saving Rate and Output

Let's return to the question we posed at the beginning of the chapter: How does the saving rate affect the growth rate of output per worker? Our analysis leads to a three-part answer:

1. *The saving rate has no effect on the long-run growth rate of output per worker, which is equal to zero.*

Capital Accumulation and Growth in France in the Aftermath of World War II

When World War II ended in 1945, France had suffered some of the heaviest losses of all European countries. The losses in lives were large. More than 550,000 people had died, out of a population of 42 million. Relatively speaking, though, the losses in capital were much larger: It is estimated that the French capital stock in 1945 was about 30% below its prewar value. A vivid picture of the destruction of capital is provided by the numbers in Table 1.

The model of growth we have just seen makes a clear prediction about what will happen to a country that loses a large part of its capital stock: The country will experience high capital accumulation and output growth for some time. In terms of Figure 11-2, a country with capital per worker initially far below K^*/N will grow rapidly as it converges to K^*/N and output per worker converges to Y^*/N.

This prediction fares well in the case of postwar France. There is plenty of anecdotal evidence that small increases in capital led to large increases in output. Minor repairs to a major bridge would lead to the reopening of the bridge. Reopening the bridge would significantly shorten the travel time between two cities, leading to much lower transport costs. The lower transport costs would then enable a plant to get much needed inputs, increase its production, and so on.

More convincing evidence, however, comes directly from actual aggregate output numbers. From 1946 to 1950, the annual growth rate of French real GDP was a very high 9.6% per year. This led to an increase in real GDP of about 60% over the course of five years.

Was all of the increase in French GDP due to capital accumulation? The answer is no. There were other forces at work in addition to the mechanism in our model. Much of the remaining capital stock in 1945 was old. Investment had been low in the 1930s (a decade dominated by the Great Depression) and nearly nonexistent during the war. A good portion of the postwar capital accumulation was associated with the introduction of more modern capital and the use of more modern production techniques. This was another reason for the high growth rates of the postwar period.

Source: Gilles Saint-Paul, "Economic Reconstruction in France, 1945–1958," in Rudiger Dornbusch, Willem Nolling, and Richard Layard, eds. *Postwar Economic Reconstruction and Lessons for the East Today* (Cambridge, MA: MIT Press, 1993).

Table 1 Proportion of the French Capital Stock Destroyed by the End of World War II

Railways	Tracks	6%	Rivers	Waterways	86%
	Stations	38%		Canal locks	11%
	Engines	21%		Barges	80%
	Hardware	60%	Buildings	(numbers)	
Roads	Cars	31%		Dwellings	1,229,000
	Trucks	40%		Industrial	246,000

This conclusion is rather obvious: We have seen that, eventually, the economy converges to a constant level of output per worker. In other words, in the long run, the growth rate of output is equal to zero, no matter what the saving rate is.

There is, however, a way of thinking about this conclusion that will be useful when we introduce technological progress in Chapter 12. Think of what would be needed to sustain a constant positive growth rate of output per worker in the long run. Capital per worker would have to increase. Not only that, but, because of decreasing returns to capital, it would have to increase faster than output per worker. This implies that each year the economy would have to save a larger and larger fraction of its output and dedicate it to capital accumulation. At some point, the fraction of output it would need to save would be greater than 1—something clearly impossible. This is why it is impossible, absent technological progress, to sustain a constant positive growth rate forever. In the long run, capital per worker must be constant, and so output per worker must also be constant.

Some economists argue that the high output growth achieved by the Soviet Union from 1950 to 1990 was the result of such a steady increase in the saving rate over time, which could not be sustained forever. Paul Krugman has used the term "Stalinist growth" to denote this type of growth—growth resulting from a higher and higher saving rate over time. ▶

Figure 11-3

The Effects of Different Saving Rates

A country with a higher saving rate achieves a higher steady-state level of output per worker.

2. Nonetheless, *the saving rate determines the level of output per worker in the long run*. Other things being equal, countries with a higher saving rate will achieve higher output per worker in the long run.

   Figure 11-3 illustrates this point. Consider two countries with the same production function, the same level of employment, and the same depreciation rate, but different saving rates, say s_0 and $s_1 > s_0$. Figure 11-3 draws their common production function, $f(K_t/N)$, and the functions showing saving/investment per worker as a function of capital per worker for each of the two countries, $s_0 f(K_t/N)$ and $s_1 f(K_t/N)$. In the long run, the country with saving rate s_0 will reach the level of capital per worker K_0/N and output per worker Y_0/N. The country with saving rate s_1 will reach the higher levels K_1/N and Y_1/N.

3. *An increase in the saving rate will lead to higher growth of output per worker for some time, but not forever.*

   This conclusion follows from the two propositions we just discussed. From the first, we know that an increase in the saving rate does not affect the long-run *growth rate of output per worker*, which remains equal to zero. From the second, we know that an increase in the saving rate leads to an increase in the long-run *level of output per worker*. It follows that, as output per worker increases to its new higher level in response to the increase in the saving rate, the economy will go through a period of positive growth. This period of growth will come to an end when the economy reaches its new steady state.

   We can use Figure 11-3 again to illustrate this point. Consider a country that has an initial saving rate of s_0. Assume that capital per worker is initially equal to K_0/N, with associated output per worker Y_0/N. Now consider the effects of an increase in the saving rate from s_0 to s_1. The function giving saving/investment per worker as a function of capital per worker shifts upward from $s_0 f(K_t/N)$ to $s_1 f(K_t/N)$.

   At the initial level of capital per worker, K_0/N, investment exceeds depreciation, so capital per worker increases. As capital per worker increases, so does output per worker, and the economy goes through a period of positive growth. When capital per worker eventually reaches K_1/N, however, investment is again equal to depreciation, and growth ends. From then on, the economy remains at K_1/N, with associated output per worker Y_1/N. The movement of output per worker is plotted

◄ Note that the first proposition is a statement about the growth rate of output per worker. The second proposition is a statement about the level of output per worker.

Figure 11-4

The Effects of an Increase in the Saving Rate on Output per Worker in an Economy Without Technological Progress

An increase in the saving rate leads to a period of higher growth until output reaches its new higher steady-state level.

against time in Figure 11-4. Output per worker is initially constant at level Y_0/N. After the increase in the saving rate, say, at time t, output per worker increases for some time until it reaches the higher level of output per worker Y_1/N and the growth rate returns to zero.

We have derived these three results under the assumption that there was no technological progress, and, therefore, no growth of output per worker in the long run. But, as we will see in Chapter 12, the three results extend to an economy in which there is technological progress. Let us briefly indicate how:

An economy in which there is technological progress has a positive growth rate of output per worker, even in the long run. This long-run growth rate is independent of the saving rate—the extension of the first result just discussed. The saving rate affects the level of output per worker, however—the extension of the second result. An increase in the saving rate leads to growth greater than steady-state growth rate for some time until the economy reaches its new higher path—the extension of our third result.

These three results are illustrated in Figure 11-5, which extends Figure 11-4 by plotting the effect an increase in the saving rate has on an economy with positive technological progress. The figure uses a logarithmic scale to measure output per worker: It follows that an economy in which output per worker grows at a constant rate is represented by a line with slope equal to that growth rate. At the initial

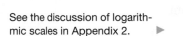

See the discussion of logarithmic scales in Appendix 2. ▶

Figure 11-5

The Effects of an Increase in the Saving Rate on Output per Worker in an Economy with Technological Progress

An increase in the saving rate leads to a period of higher growth until output reaches a new, higher path.

saving rate, s_0, the economy moves along AA. If, at time t, the saving rate increases to s_1, the economy experiences higher growth for some time until it reaches its new, higher path, BB. On path BB, the growth rate is again the same as before the increase in the saving rate (that is, the slope of BB is the same as the slope of AA).

The Saving Rate and Consumption

Governments can affect the saving rate in various ways. First, they can vary public saving. Given private saving, positive public saving—a budget surplus, in other words—leads to higher overall saving. Conversely, negative public saving—a budget deficit—leads to lower overall saving. Second, governments can use taxes to affect private saving. For example, they can give tax breaks to people who save, making it more attractive to save and thus increasing private saving.

Recall: Saving is the sum of private plus public saving. Recall also:

Public saving ⇔ Budget surplus;

Public dissaving ⇔ Budget deficit.

What saving rate should governments aim for? To think about the answer, we must shift our focus from the behavior of *output* to the behavior of *consumption*. The reason: What matters to people is not how much is produced, but how much they consume.

It is clear that an increase in saving must come initially at the expense of lower consumption (except when we think it helpful, we drop "per worker" in this subsection and just refer to consumption rather than consumption per worker, capital rather than capital per worker, and so on): A change in the saving rate this year has no effect on capital this year, and consequently no effect on output and income *this year*. So an increase in saving comes initially with an equal decrease in consumption.

Does an increase in saving lead to an increase in consumption in the long run? Not necessarily. Consumption may decrease, not only initially, but also in the long run. You may find this surprising. After all, we know from Figure 11-3 that an increase in the saving rate always leads to an increase in the level of *output* per worker. But output is not the same as consumption. To see why not, consider what happens for two extreme values of the saving rate:

Because we assume that employment is constant, we are ignoring the short run effect of an increase in the saving rate on output we focused on in Chapter 3. In the short run, not only does an increase in the saving rate reduce consumption given income, but it may also create a recession and decrease income further. We will return to a discussion of short-run and long-run effects of changes in saving at various points in the book. See, for example, Chapter 17 and Chapter 23.

- An economy in which the saving rate is (and has always been) zero is an economy in which capital is equal to zero. In this case, output is also equal to zero, and so is consumption. A saving rate equal to zero implies zero consumption in the long run.

- Now consider an economy in which the saving rate is equal to one: People save all their income. The level of capital, and thus output, in this economy will be very high. But because people save all of their income, consumption is equal to zero. What happens is that the economy is carrying an excessive amount of capital: Simply maintaining that level of output requires that all output be devoted to replacing depreciation! A saving rate equal to one also implies zero consumption in the long run.

These two extreme cases mean that there must be some value of the saving rate between zero and one that maximizes the steady-state level of consumption. Increases in the saving rate below this value lead to a decrease in consumption initially, but to an increase in consumption in the long run. Increases in the saving rate beyond this value decrease consumption not only initially, but also in the long run. This happens because the increase in capital associated with the increase in the saving rate leads to only a small increase in output—an increase that is too small to cover the increased depreciation: In other words, the economy carries too much capital. The level of capital associated with the value of the saving rate that yields the highest level of consumption in steady state is known as the **golden-rule level of capital**. Increases in capital beyond the golden-rule level reduce steady-state consumption.

Figure 11-6

The Effects of the Saving Rate on Steady-State Consumption per Worker

An increase in the saving rate leads to an increase, then to a decrease in steady-state consumption per worker.

This argument is illustrated in Figure 11-6, which plots consumption per worker in steady state (on the vertical axis) against the saving rate (on the horizontal axis). A saving rate equal to zero implies a capital stock per worker equal to zero, a level of output per worker equal to zero, and, by implication, a level of consumption per worker equal to zero. For s between zero and s_G (G for golden rule), a higher saving rate leads to higher capital per worker, higher output per worker, and higher consumption per worker. For s larger than s_G, increases in the saving rate still lead to higher values of capital per worker and output per worker; but they now lead to lower values of consumption per worker: This is because the increase in output is more than offset by the increase in depreciation due to the larger capital stock. For $s = 1$, consumption per worker is equal to zero. Capital per worker and output per worker are high, but all of the output is used just to replace depreciation, leaving nothing for consumption.

If an economy already has so much capital that it is operating beyond the golden rule, then increasing saving further will decrease consumption not only now, but also later. Is this a relevant worry? Do some countries actually have too much capital? The empirical evidence indicates that most OECD countries are actually far below their golden-rule level of capital. If they were to increase the saving rate, it would lead to higher consumption in the future—not lower consumption.

This means that, in practice, governments face a trade-off: An increase in the saving rate leads to lower consumption for some time, but higher consumption later. So what should governments do? How close to the golden rule should they try to get? That depends on how much weight they put on the welfare of current generations—who are more likely to lose from policies aimed at increasing the saving rate—versus the welfare of future generations—who are more likely to gain. Enter politics: Future generations do not vote. This means that governments are unlikely to ask current generations to make large sacrifices, which, in turn, means that capital is likely to stay far below its golden-rule level. These intergenerational issues are at the forefront of the current debate on Social Security reform in the United States. The Focus box "Social Security, Saving, and Capital Accumulation in the United States" explores this further.

11-3 Getting a Sense of Magnitudes

How big an impact does a change in the saving rate have on output in the long run? For how long and by how much does an increase in the saving rate affect growth? How far is the United States from the golden-rule level of capital? To get a better sense of the

Social Security, Saving, and Capital Accumulation in the United States

· ·

Social Security was introduced in the United States in 1935. The goal of the program was to make sure the elderly would have enough to live on. Over time, Social Security has become the largest government program in the United States. Benefits paid to retirees now exceed 4% of GDP. For two-thirds of retirees, Social Security benefits account for more than 50% of their income. There is little question that, on its own terms, the Social Security system has been a great success and has decreased poverty among the elderly. There is also little question that it has also led to a lower U.S. saving rate and therefore lower capital accumulation and lower output per person in the long run.

To understand why, we must take a theoretical detour. Think of an economy in which there is no social security system—one where workers have to save to provide for their own retirement. Now, introduce a social security system that collects taxes from workers and distributes benefits to the retirees. It can do so in one of two ways:

■ One way is by taxing workers, investing their contributions in financial assets, and paying back the principal plus the interest to the workers when they retire. Such a system is called a **fully funded social security system**: At any time, the system has funds equal to the accumulated contributions of workers, from which it will be able to pay out benefits to these workers when they retire.

■ The other way is by taxing workers and redistributing the tax contributions as benefits to the current retirees. Such a system is called a **pay-as-you-go social security system**: The system pays benefits out "as it goes," that is, as it collects them through contributions.

From the point of view of workers, the two systems may look broadly similar. In both cases, they pay contributions when they work and receive benefits when they retire. But there are two major differences:

First, what retirees receive is different in each case:

■ What they receive in a fully funded system depends on the rate of return on the financial assets held by the fund.

■ What they receive in a pay-as-you-go system depends on demographics—the ratio of retirees to workers—and on the evolution of the tax rate set by the system. When the population ages, and the ratio of retirees to workers increases, then either retirees receive less, or workers have to contribute more. This is very much the case in the United States today. Under current rules, benefits will increase from 4% of GDP today to 6% in 2030. Thus, either benefits will have to be reduced, in which case the rate of return to workers who contributed in the past will be low, or contributions will have to be increased, in which case this will decrease the

rate of return to workers who are contributing today, or, more likely, some combination of both will have to be implemented. We shall return to this issue in Chapter 23.

Second, and leaving aside the aging issue, the two systems have very different macroeconomic implications:

■ In the fully funded system, workers save less because they anticipate receiving benefits when they are old. But the Social Security system saves on their behalf, by investing their contributions in financial assets. The presence of a social security system changes the composition of overall saving: Private saving goes down, and public saving goes up. But, to a first approximation, it has no effect on total saving and therefore no effect on capital accumulation.

■ In the pay-as-you-go system, workers also save less because they again anticipate receiving benefits when they are old. But, now, the Social Security system does not save on their behalf. The decrease in private saving is not compensated by an increase in public saving. Total saving goes down, and so does capital accumulation.

Most actual social security systems are somewhere between pay-as-you-go and fully funded systems. When the U.S. system was set up in 1935, the intention was to partially fund it. But this did not happen: Rather than being invested, contributions from workers were used to pay benefits to the retirees, and this has been the case ever since. Today, because contributions have slightly exceeded benefits since the early 1980s, the Social Security has built a **social security trust fund**. But this trust fund is far smaller than the value of benefits promised to current contributors when they retire. The U.S. system is basically a pay-as-you-go system, and this has probably led to a lower U.S. saving rate over the last 70 years.

In this context, some economists and politicians have suggested that the United States should shift back to a fully funded system. One of their arguments is that the U.S. saving rate is indeed too low and that funding the Social Security system would increase it. Such a shift could be achieved by investing, from now on, tax contributions in financial assets rather than distributing them as benefits to retirees. Under such a shift, the Social Security system would steadily accumulate funds and would eventually become fully funded. Martin Feldstein, an economist at Harvard and an advocate of such a shift, has concluded that it could lead to a 34% increase of the capital stock in the long run.

How should we think about such a proposal? It would probably have been a good idea to fully fund the system at the start: The United States would have a higher saving rate. The U.S. capital stock would be higher, and output and consumption would also be higher. But we cannot rewrite history. The existing system has promised benefits to retirees and these promises have to be honored. This means that, under the proposal we just described, current workers would, in effect, have to contribute twice; once to fund the system and finance their own retirement, and then again to finance the benefits owed to current retirees. This would impose a disproportionate cost on current workers (and this would come on top of the problems coming from aging, which are likely to require larger contributions from workers in any case). The practical implication is that, if it is to happen, the move to a fully funded system will have to be very slow, so that the burden of adjustment does not fall too much on one generation relative to the others.

The debate is likely to be with us for some time. In assessing proposals from the administration or from Congress, ask yourself how they deal with the issue we just discussed. Take, for example, the proposal to allow workers, from now on, to make contributions to personal accounts instead of to the Social Security system, and to be able to draw from these accounts when they retire. By itself, this proposal would clearly increase private saving: Workers will be saving more. But its ultimate effect on saving depends on how the benefits already promised to current workers and retirees by the Social Security system are financed. If, as is the case under some proposals, these benefits are financed not through additional taxes but through debt finance, then the increase in private saving will be offset by an increase in deficits, an increase in public saving: The shift to personal accounts will not increase the U.S. saving rate. If, instead, these benefits are financed through higher taxes, then the U.S. saving rate will increase. But, in that case, current workers will have both to contribute to their personal accounts and pay the higher taxes. They will indeed pay twice.

To follow the debate on Social Security, look at the site run by the (nonpartisan) Concord Coalition (www.concordcoalition.org) and find the discussion related to Social Security.

answers to these questions, let's now make more specific assumptions, plug in some numbers, and see what we get.

Assume the production function is

$$Y = \sqrt{K}\sqrt{N} \tag{11.6}$$

Output equals the product of the square root of capital and the square root of labor. (A more general specification of the production function known as the Cobb-Douglas production function, and its implications for growth, is given in the appendix to this chapter.)

Dividing both sides by N (because we are interested in output per worker),

$$\frac{Y}{N} = \frac{\sqrt{K}\sqrt{N}}{N} = \frac{\sqrt{K}}{\sqrt{N}} = \sqrt{\frac{K}{N}}$$

▶ Check that this production function exhibits both constant returns to scale and decreasing returns to either capital or labor.

▶ The second equality follows from: $\sqrt{N}/N = \sqrt{N}/(\sqrt{N}\sqrt{N}) = 1/\sqrt{N}$.

Output per worker equals the square root of capital per worker. Put another way, the production function f relating output per worker to capital per worker is given by

$$f\left(\frac{K_t}{N}\right) = \sqrt{\frac{K_t}{N}}$$

Replacing $f(K_t/N)$ by $\sqrt{K_t/N}$ in equation (11.3),

$$\frac{K_{t+1}}{N} - \frac{K_t}{N} = s\sqrt{\frac{K_t}{N}} - \delta\frac{K_t}{N} \tag{11.7}$$

This equation describes the evolution of capital per worker over time. Let's look at what it implies.

The Effects of the Saving Rate on Steady-State Output

How big an impact does an increase in the saving rate have on the steady-state level of output per worker?

Start with equation (11.7). In steady state the amount of capital per worker is constant, so the left side of the equation equals zero. This implies

$$s \sqrt{\frac{K^*}{N}} = \delta \frac{K^*}{N}$$

(We have dropped time indexes, which are no longer needed because in steady state K/N is constant. The star is to remind you that we are looking at the steady-state value of capital.) Square both sides:

$$s^2 \frac{K^*}{N} = \delta^2 \left(\frac{K^*}{N}\right)^2$$

Divide both sides by (K/N) and reorganize:

$$\frac{K^*}{N} = \left(\frac{s}{\delta}\right)^2 \tag{11.8}$$

Steady-state capital per worker is equal to the square of the ratio of the saving rate to the depreciation rate.

From equations (11.6) and (11.8), steady-state output per worker is given by

$$\frac{Y^*}{N} = \sqrt{\frac{K^*}{N}} = \sqrt{\left(\frac{s}{\delta}\right)^2} = \frac{s}{\delta} \tag{11.9}$$

Steady-state output per worker is equal to the ratio of the saving rate to the depreciation rate.

A higher saving rate and a lower depreciation rate both lead to higher steady-state capital per worker (equation (11.8)) and higher steady-state output per worker (equation (11.9)). To see what this means, let's take a numerical example. Suppose the depreciation rate is 10% per year, and suppose the saving rate is also 10%. Then, from equations (11.8) and (11.9), steady-state capital per worker and output per worker are both equal to 1. Now suppose that the saving rate doubles, from 10% to 20%. It follows from equation (11.8) that in the new steady state, capital per worker increases from 1 to 4. And, from equation (11.9), output per worker doubles, from 1 to 2. Thus, doubling the saving rate leads, in the long run, to doubling the output per worker: This is a large effect.

The Dynamic Effects of an Increase in the Saving Rate

We have just seen that an increase in the saving rate leads to an increase in the steady-state level of output. But how long does it take for output to reach its new steady-state level? Put another way, by how much and for how long does an increase in the saving rate affect the growth rate?

To answer these questions, we must use equation (11.7) and solve it for capital per worker in year 0, in year 1, and so on.

Suppose that the saving rate, which had always been equal to 10%, increases in year 0 from 10% to 20% and remains at this higher value forever. In year 0, nothing happens to the capital stock (recall that it takes one year for higher saving and higher investment to show up in higher capital). So, capital per worker remains equal to the steady-state value associated with a saving rate of 0.1. From equation (11.8),

$$\frac{K_0}{N} = (0.1/0.1)^2 = 1^2 = 1$$

In year 1, equation (11.7) gives

$$\frac{K_1}{N} - \frac{K_0}{N} = s\sqrt{\frac{K_0}{N}} - \delta\frac{K_0}{N}$$

With a depreciation rate equal to 0.1 and a saving rate now equal to 0.2, this equation implies

$$\frac{K_1}{N} - 1 = [(0.2)(\sqrt{1})] - [(0.1)1]$$

so

$$\frac{K_1}{N} = 1.1$$

In the same way, we can solve for K_2/N, and so on. Once we have determined the values of capital per worker in year 0, year 1, and so on, we can then use equation (11.6) to solve for output per worker in year 0, year 1, and so on. The results of this computation are presented in Figure 11-7. Panel (a) plots the *level* of output per worker against time. (Y/N) increases over time from its initial value of 1 in year 0 to its steady-state value of 2 in the long run. Panel (b) gives the same information in a different way, plotting instead the *growth rate* of output per worker against time. As Panel (b) shows, growth of output

Figure 11-7

The Dynamic Effects of an Increase in the Saving Rate from 10% to 20% on the Level and the Growth Rate of Output per Worker

It takes a long time for output to adjust to its new higher level after an increase in the saving rate. Put another way, an increase in the saving rate leads to a long period of higher growth.

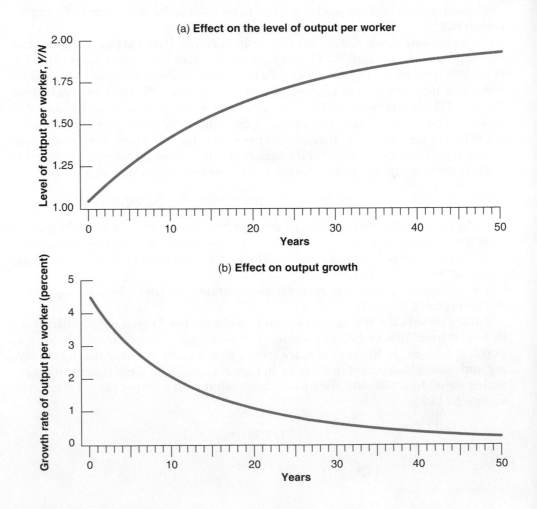

per worker is highest at the beginning and then decreases over time. As the economy reaches its new steady state, growth of output per worker returns to zero.

The difference between investment and depreciation is greatest at the beginning. This is why capital accumulation, and, in turn, output growth is highest at the beginning.

Figure 11-7 clearly shows that the adjustment to the new, higher, long-run equilibrium takes a long time. It is only 40% complete after 10 years, and 63% complete after 20 years. Put another way, the increase in the saving rate increases the growth rate of output per worker for a long time. The average annual growth rate is 3.1% for the first 10 years, and 1.5% for the next 10. Although the changes in the saving rate have no effect on growth in the long run, they do lead to higher growth for a long time.

To go back to the question raised at the beginning of the chapter, can the low saving/investment rate in the United States explain why the U.S. growth rate has been so low—relative to other OECD countries—since 1950? The answer would be yes if the United States had had a higher saving rate in the past, and *if this saving rate had fallen substantially in the last 50 years.* If this were the case, it could explain the period of lower growth in the United States in the last 50 years along the lines of the mechanism in Figure 11-7 (with the sign reversed, as we would be looking at a decrease—not an increase—in the saving rate). But this is not the case: The U.S. saving rate has been low for a long time. Low saving cannot explain the relative poor U.S. growth performance over the last 50 years.

The U.S. Saving Rate and the Golden Rule

What is the saving rate that would maximize steady-state consumption per worker? Recall that, in steady state, consumption is equal to what is left after enough is put aside to maintain a constant level of capital. More formally, in steady state, consumption per worker is equal to output per worker minus depreciation per worker:

$$\frac{C}{N} = \frac{Y}{N} - \delta\frac{K}{N}$$

Using equations (11.8) and (11.9) for the steady-state values of output per worker and capital per worker, consumption per worker is thus given by

$$\frac{C}{N} = \frac{s}{\delta} - \delta\left(\frac{s}{\delta}\right)^2 = \frac{s(1-s)}{\delta}$$

Using this equation, together with equations (11.8) and (11.9), Table 11-1 gives the steady-state values of capital per worker, output per worker, and consumption

Table 11-1	The Saving Rate and the Steady-State Levels of Capital, Output, and Consumption per Worker		
Saving Rate s	Capital per Worker K/N	Output per Worker Y/N	Consumption per Worker C/N
0.0	0.0	0.0	0.0
0.1	1.0	1.0	0.9
0.2	4.0	2.0	1.6
0.3	9.0	3.0	2.1
0.4	16.0	4.0	2.4
0.5	25.0	5.0	2.5
0.6	36.0	6.0	2.4
...	...	...	...
1.0	100.0	10.0	0.0

per worker for different values of the saving rate (and for a depreciation rate equal to 10%).

Steady-state consumption per worker is largest when *s* equals one-half. In other words, the golden-rule level of capital is associated with a saving rate of 50%. Below that level, increases in the saving rate lead to an increase in long-run consumption per worker. We saw earlier that the average U.S. saving rate since 1970 has been only 17%. So we can be quite confident that, at least in the United States, an increase in the saving rate would increase both output per worker and consumption per worker in the long run.

Check your understanding of the issues: Using the equations in this section, argue the pros and cons of policy measures aimed at increasing the U.S. saving rate.

11-4 Physical versus Human Capital

We have concentrated so far on physical capital—machines, plants, office buildings, and so on. But economies have another type of capital: the set of skills of the workers in the economy, or what economists call **human capital**. An economy with many highly skilled workers is likely to be much more productive than an economy in which most workers cannot read or write.

The increase in human capital has been as large as the increase in physical capital over the last two centuries. At the beginning of the Industrial Revolution, only 30% of the population of the countries that constitute the OECD today knew how to read. Today, the literacy rate in OECD countries is above 95%. Schooling was not compulsory prior to the Industrial Revolution. Today it is compulsory, usually until the age of 16. Still, there are large differences across countries. Today, in OECD countries, nearly 100% of children get a primary education, 90% get a secondary education, and 38% get a higher education. The corresponding numbers in poor countries, countries with GDP per person below $400, are 95%, 32%, and 4%, respectively.

Even this comparison may be misleading because the quality of education can be quite different across countries.

How should we think about the effect of human capital on output? How does the introduction of human capital change our earlier conclusions? These are the questions we take up in this last section.

Extending the Production Function

The most natural way of extending our analysis to allow for human capital is to modify the production function relation (11.1) to read

$$\frac{Y}{N} = f\left(\frac{K}{N}, \frac{H}{N}\right) \tag{11.10}$$

$$(+, +)$$

Note that we are using the same symbol, *H*, to denote the monetary base in Chapter 4, and human capital in this chapter. Both uses are traditional. Do not be confused.

The level of output per worker depends on both the level of physical capital per worker, K/N, and the level of human capital per worker, H/N. As before, an increase in capital per worker (K/N) leads to an increase in output per worker. And an increase in the average level of skill (H/N) also leads to more output per worker. More skilled workers can do more complex tasks; they can deal more easily with unexpected complications. All of this leads to higher output per worker.

We assumed earlier that increases in physical capital per worker increased output per worker, but that the effect became smaller as the level of capital per worker increased. We can make the same assumption for human capital per worker: Think of increases in H/N as coming from increases in the number of years of education. The evidence is that the returns to increasing the proportion of children acquiring a primary education are very large. At the very least, the ability to read and write allows people to use equipment that is more complicated but more productive. For rich countries, however, primary education—and, for that matter, secondary education—are no longer the relevant margin: Most children now get both. The relevant margin is now higher education. We are sure it will come as good news to you that the evidence shows that higher education increases people's skills, at least as measured by the increase in the wages of those who acquire it. But, to take an extreme example, it is not clear that forcing everyone to acquire an advanced college degree would increase aggregate output very much. Many people would end up overqualified and probably more frustrated rather than more productive.

We look at this evidence in Chapter 13.

How should we construct the measure for human capital, H? The answer is: very much the same way we construct the measure for physical capital, K. To construct K, we just add the values of the different pieces of capital, so that a machine that costs $2,000 gets twice the weight of a machine that costs $1,000. Similarly, we construct the measure of H such that workers who are paid twice as much get twice the weight. Take, for example, an economy with 100 workers, half of them unskilled and half of them skilled. Suppose the relative wage of the skilled workers is twice that of the unskilled workers. We can then construct H as $[(50 \times 1) + (50 \times 2)] = 150$. Human capital per worker, H/N, is then equal to $150/100 = 1.5$.

The rationale for using relative wages as weights is that they reflect relative marginal products. A worker who is paid three times as much as another is assumed to have a marginal product that is three times higher.

An issue, however, is whether or not relative wages accurately reflect relative marginal products. To take a controversial example: In the same job, with the same seniority, women still often earn less than men. Is it because their marginal product is lower? Should they be given a lower weight than men in the construction of human capital?

Human Capital, Physical Capital, and Output

How does the introduction of human capital change the analysis of the previous sections?

Our conclusions about *physical capital accumulation* remain valid: An increase in the saving rate increases steady-state physical capital per worker and therefore increases output per worker. But our conclusions now extend to *human capital accumulation* as well. An increase in how much society "saves" in the form of human capital—through education and on-the-job training—increases steady-state human capital per worker, which leads to an increase in output per worker. Our extended model gives us a richer picture of how of output per worker is determined. In the long run, it tells us that output per worker depends on both how much society saves and how much it spends on education.

What are the relative importance of human capital and physical capital in the determination of output per worker? A place to start is to compare how much is spent on formal education to how much is invested in physical capital. In the United States, spending on formal education is about 6.5% of GDP. This number includes both government expenditures on education and private expenditures by people on education. It is between one-third and one-half of the gross investment rate for physical capital (which is around 16%). But this comparison is only a first pass. Consider the following complications:

- Education, especially higher education, is partly consumption—done for its own sake—and partly investment. We should include only the investment part for our purposes. However, the 6.5% number in the preceding paragraph includes both.
- At least for post secondary education, the opportunity cost of a person's education is his or her forgone wages while acquiring the education. Spending on education should include not only the actual cost of education but also this opportunity cost. The 6.5% number does not include this opportunity cost.

How large is your opportunity cost relative to your tuition?

- Formal education is only a part of education. Much of what we learn comes from on-the-job training, formal or informal. Both the actual costs and the opportunity costs of on-the-job training should also be included. The 6.5% number does not include the costs associated with on-the-job training.
- We should compare investment rates net of depreciation. Depreciation of physical capital, especially of machines, is likely to be higher than depreciation of human capital. Skills deteriorate, but do so only slowly. And, unlike physical capital, they deteriorate less quickly the more they are used.

For all these reasons, it is difficult to come up with reliable numbers for investment in human capital. Recent studies conclude that investment in physical capital and in education play roughly similar roles in the determination of output. This implies that output per worker depends roughly equally on the amount of physical capital and the amount of human capital in the economy. Countries that save more and/or spend more on education can achieve substantially higher steady-state levels of output per worker.

Endogenous Growth

Note what the conclusion we just reached did say and did not say. It did say that a country that saves more or spends more on education will achieve a *higher level* of output per worker in steady state. It did not say that by saving or spending more on education a country can sustain permanently *higher growth* of output per worker.

This conclusion, however, has been challenged in the past two decades. Following the lead of Robert Lucas and Paul Romer, researchers have explored the possibility that the joint accumulation of physical capital and human capital might actually be enough to sustain growth. Given human capital, increases in physical capital will run into decreasing returns. And given physical capital, increases in human capital will also run into decreasing returns. But, these researchers have asked, what if both physical and human capital increase in tandem? Can't an economy grow forever just by steadily having more capital and more skilled workers?

We have mentioned Lucas once already in connection with the Lucas critique in Chapter 8. ▶

Models that generate steady growth even without technological progress are called **models of endogenous growth** to reflect the fact that in those models—in contrast to the model we saw in earlier sections of this chapter—the growth rate depends, even in the long run, on variables such as the saving rate and the rate of spending on education. The jury on this class of models is still out, but the indications so far are that the conclusions we drew earlier need to be qualified, not abandoned. The current consensus is as follows:

■ Output per worker depends on the level of both physical capital per worker and human capital per worker. Both forms of capital can be accumulated, one through physical investment, the other through education and training. Increasing either the saving rate and/or the fraction of output spent on education and training can lead to much higher levels of output per worker in the long run. However, given the rate of technological progress, such measures do not lead to a permanently higher growth rate.

■ Note the qualifier in the last proposition: *given the rate of technological progress*. But is technological progress unrelated to the level of human capital in the economy? Can't a better educated labor force lead to a higher rate of technological progress? These questions take us to the topic of the next chapter, the sources and the effects of technological progress.

Summary

• •

■ In the long run, the evolution of output is determined by two relations. (To make the reading of this summary easier, we shall omit "per worker" in what follows.) First, the level of output depends on the amount of capital. Second, capital accumulation depends on the level of output, which determines saving and investment.

■ These interactions between capital and output imply that, starting from any level of capital (and ignoring technological progress, the topic of Chapter 12), an economy converges in the long run to a *steady-state* (constant) level of capital. Associated with this level of capital is a steady-state level of output.

- The steady-state level of capital, and thus the steady-state level of output, depends positively on the saving rate. A higher saving rate leads to a higher steady-state level of output; during the transition to the new steady state, a higher saving rate leads to positive output growth. But (again ignoring technological progress) in the long run, the growth rate of output is equal to zero and so does not depend on the saving rate.

- An increase in the saving rate requires an initial decrease in consumption. In the long run, the increase in the saving rate may lead to an increase or a decrease in consumption, depending on whether the economy is below or above the *golden-rule level of capital*, the level of capital at which steady-state consumption is highest.

- Most countries have a level of capital below the golden-rule level. Thus, an increase in the saving rate leads to an initial

decrease in consumption followed by an increase in consumption in the long run. When considering whether or not to adopt policy measures aimed at changing a country's saving rate, policy makers must decide how much weight to put on the welfare of current generations versus the welfare of future generations.

- While most of the analysis of this chapter focuses on the effects of physical capital accumulation, output depends on the levels of both physical *and* human capital. Both forms of capital can be accumulated, one through investment, the other through education and training. Increasing the saving rate and/or the fraction of output spent on education and training can lead to large increases in output in the long run.

Key Terms

saving rate, 225

steady state, 231

golden-rule level of capital, 235

fully funded social security system, 237

pay-as-you-go social security system, 237

Social Security trust fund, 237

human capital, 242

models of endogenous growth, 244

Questions and Problems

QUICK CHECK

All Quick Check questions and problems are available on MyEconLab.

1. Using the information in this chapter, label each of the following statements true, false, or uncertain. Explain briefly.

a. The saving rate is always equal to the investment rate.

b. A higher investment rate can sustain higher growth of output forever.

c. If capital never depreciated, growth could go on forever.

d. The higher the saving rate, the higher consumption in steady state.

e. We should transform Social Security from a pay-as-you-go system to a fully funded system. This would increase consumption both now and in the future.

f. The U.S. capital stock is far below the golden-rule level. The government should give tax breaks for saving because the U.S. capital stock is far below the golden-rule level.

g. Education increases human capital and thus output. It follows that governments should subsidize education.

2. Consider the following statement: "The Solow model shows that the saving rate does not affect the growth rate in the long run, so we should stop worrying about the low U.S. saving rate. Increasing the saving rate wouldn't have any important effects on the economy." *Explain why you agree or disagree with this statement?*

3. In Chapter 3 we saw that an increase in the saving rate can lead to a recession in the short run (i.e., the paradox of saving). We examined the issue in the medium run in Problem 5 at at

the end of Chapter 7. We can now examine the long-run effects of an increase in saving.

Using the model presented in this chapter, what is the effect of an increase in the saving rate on output per worker likely to be after one decade? After five decades?

DIG DEEPER

All Dig Deeper questions and problems are available on MyEconLab.

4. Discuss how the level of output per person in the long run would likely be affected by each of the following changes:

a. The right to exclude saving from income when paying income taxes.

b. A higher rate of female participation in the labor market (but constant population).

5. Suppose the United States moved from the current pay-as-you-go Social Security system to a fully funded one, and financed the transition without additional government borrowing. How would the shift to a fully funded system affect the level and the rate of growth of output per worker in the long run?

6. Suppose that the production function is given by

$$Y = 0.5\sqrt{K}\sqrt{N}$$

a. Derive the steady-state levels of output per worker and capital per worker in terms of the saving rate, s, and the depreciation rate, δ.

b. Derive the equation for steady-state output per worker and steady-state consumption per worker in terms of s and δ.

c. Suppose that $\delta = 0.05$. With your favorite spreadsheet software, compute steady-state output per worker and steady-state consumption per worker for $s = 0$; $s = 0.1$; $s = 0.2$; ... ; $s = 1$. Explain the intuition behind your results.

d. Use your favorite spreadsheet software to graph the steady-state level of output per worker and the steady-state level of consumption per worker as a function of the saving rate (i.e., measure the saving rate on the horizontal axis of your graph and the corresponding values of output per worker and consumption per worker on the vertical axis).

e. Does the graph show that there is a value of s that maximizes output per worker? Does the graph show that there is a value of s that maximizes consumption per worker? If so, what is this value?

7. *The Cobb-Douglas production function and the steady state.*
    This problem is based on the material in the chapter appendix. Suppose that the economy's production function is given by

$$Y = K^{\alpha} N^{1-\alpha}$$

and assume that $\alpha = 1/3$.

a. Is this production function characterized by constant returns to scale? Explain.

b. Are there decreasing returns to capital?

c. Are there decreasing returns to labor?

d. Transform the production function into a relation between output per worker and capital per worker.

e. For a given saving rate, s, and depreciation rate, δ, give an expression for capital per worker in the steady state.

f. Give an expression for output per worker in the steady state.

g. Solve for the steady-state level of output per worker when $s = 0.32$ and $\delta = 0.08$.

h. Suppose that the depreciation rate remains constant at $\delta = 0.08$, while the saving rate is reduced by half, to $s = 0.16$. What is the new steady-state output per worker?

8. *Continuing with the logic from Problem 7, suppose that the economy's production function is given by $Y = K^{1/3}N^{2/3}$ and that both the saving rate, s, and the depreciation rate, δ, are equal to 0.10.*

a. What is the steady-state level of capital per worker?

b. What is the steady-state level of output per worker?

    Suppose that the economy is in steady state and that, in period t, the depreciation rate increases permanently from 0.10 to 0.20.

c. What will be the new steady-state levels of capital per worker and output per worker?

d. Compute the path of capital per worker and output per worker over the first three periods after the change in the depreciation rate.

9. *Deficits and the capital stock*
    For the production function, $Y = \sqrt{K}\sqrt{N}$ equation (11.8) gives the solution for the steady-state capital stock per worker.

a. Retrace the steps in the text that derive equation (11.8).

b. Suppose that the saving rate, s, is initially 15% per year, and the depreciation rate, δ, is 7.5%. What is the steady-state capital stock per worker? What is steady-state output per worker?

c. Suppose that there is a government deficit of 5% of GDP and that the government eliminates this deficit. Assume that private saving is unchanged so that total saving increases to 20%. What is the new steady-state capital stock per worker? What is the new steady-state output per worker? How does this compare to your answer to part (b)?

EXPLORE FURTHER

10. *U.S. saving*
    This question continues the logic of Problem 9 to explore the implications of the U.S. budget deficit for the long-run capital stock. The question assumes that the United States will have a budget deficit over the life of this edition of the text.

a. Go to the most recent *Economic Report of the President* (**www.gpoaccess.gov/eop/**). From Table B-32, get the numbers for gross national saving for the most recent year available. From Table B-1, get the number for U.S. GDP for the same year. What is the total saving rate, as a percentage of GDP? Using the depreciation rate and the logic from Problem 9, what would be the steady-state capital stock per worker? What would be steady-state output per worker?

b. In Table B-79 of the *Economic Report of the President*, get the number for the federal budget deficit as a percentage of GDP for the year corresponding to the data from part (a). Again using the reasoning from Problem 9, suppose that the federal budget deficit was eliminated and there was no change in private saving. What would be the effect on the long-run capital stock per worker? What would be the effect on long-run output per worker?

Further Readings

- The classic treatment of the relation between the saving rate and output is by Robert Solow, *Growth Theory: An Exposition* (New York: Oxford University Press, 1970).

- An easy-to-read discussion of whether and how to increase saving and improve education in the United States

is given in Memoranda 23 to 27 in *Memos to the President: A Guide through Macroeconomics for the Busy Policymaker*, by Charles Schultze (the Chairman of the Council of Economic Advisers during the Carter administration) (Washington D.C: Brookings Institution, 1992).

APPENDIX: The Cobb-Douglas Production Function and the Steady State

In 1928, Charles Cobb (a mathematician) and Paul Douglas (an economist, who went on to become a U.S. senator) concluded that the following production function gave a very good description of the relation between output, physical capital, and labor in the United States from 1899 to 1922:

$$Y = K^\alpha N^{1-\alpha} \qquad (11.A1)$$

with α being a number between zero and one. Their findings proved surprisingly robust. Even today, the production function (11.A1), now known as the **Cobb-Douglas production function**, still gives a good description of the relation between output, capital, and labor in the United States, and it has become a standard tool in the economist's toolbox. (Verify for yourself that it satisfies the two properties we discussed in the text: constant returns to scale and decreasing returns to capital and to labor.)

The purpose of this appendix is to characterize the steady state of an economy when the production function is given by (11.A1). (All you need to follow the steps is a knowledge of the properties of exponents).

Recall that, in steady state, saving per worker must be equal to depreciation per worker. Let's see what this implies.

■ To derive saving per worker, we must first derive the relation between output per worker and capital per worker implied by equation (11.A1). Divide both sides of equation (11.A1) by N:

$$Y/N = K^\alpha N^{1-\alpha}/N$$

Using the properties of exponents,

$$N^{1-\alpha}/N = N^{1-\alpha}N^{-1} = N^{-\alpha}$$

so, replacing the terms in N in the preceding equation, we get:

$$Y/N = K^\alpha N^{-\alpha} = (K/N)^\alpha$$

Output per worker, Y/N, is equal to the ratio of capital per worker, K/N, raised to the power α.

Saving per worker is equal to the saving rate times output per worker, so, using the previous equation, it is equal to

$$s(K^*/N)^\alpha$$

■ Depreciation per worker is equal to the depreciation rate times capital per worker:

$$\delta(K^*/N)$$

■ The steady-state level of capital, K^*, is determined by the condition that saving per worker be equal to depreciation per worker, so:

$$s(K^*/N)^\alpha = \delta(K^*/N)$$

To solve this expression for the steady-state level of capital per worker K^*/N, divide both sides by $(K^*/N)^\alpha$:

$$s = \delta(K^*/N)^{1-\alpha}$$

Divide both sides by δ, and change the order of the equality:

$$(K^*/N)^{1-\alpha} = s/\delta$$

Finally, raise both sides to the power $1/(1-\alpha)$:

$$(K^*/N) = (s/\delta)^{1/(1-\alpha)}$$

This gives us the steady-state level of capital per worker.

From the production function, the steady-state level of output per worker is then equal to

$$(Y^*/N) = K/N^\alpha = (s/\delta)^{\alpha/(1-\alpha)}$$

Let's see what this last equation implies.

■ In the text, we actually worked with a special case of an equation (11.A1), the case where $\alpha = 0.5$. (Taking a variable to the power 0.5 is the same as taking the square root of this variable.) If $\alpha = 0.5$, the preceding equation means

$$Y^*/N = s/\delta$$

Output per worker is equal to the ratio of the saving rate to the depreciation rate. This is the equation we discussed in the text. A doubling of the saving rate leads to a doubling in steady-state output per worker.

■ The empirical evidence suggests, however, that, if we think of K as physical capital, α is closer to one-third than to one-half. Assuming $\alpha = 1/3$, then $\alpha(1-\alpha) = (1/3)/(1-(1/3)) = (1/3)/(2/3) = 1/2$, and the equation for output per worker yields

$$Y^*/N = (s/\delta)^{1/2} = \sqrt{s/\delta}$$

This implies smaller effects of the saving rate on output per worker than was suggested by the computations in the text. A doubling of the saving rate, for example, means that output per worker increases by a factor of $\sqrt{2}$, or only about 1.4 (put another way, a 40% increase in output per worker).

■ There is, however, an interpretation of our model in which the appropriate value of α is close to 1/2, so the computations in the text are applicable. If, along the lines of Section 11-4, we take human capital into account as well as physical capital, then a value of α around 1/2 for the contribution of this broader definition of capital to output is, indeed, roughly appropriate. Thus, one interpretation of the numerical results in Section 11-3 is that they show the effects of a given saving rate, but that saving must be interpreted to include saving in both physical capital and in human capital (more machines and more education).

Key Term

Cobb-Douglas production function, 247

Technological Progress and Growth

T he conclusion in Chapter 11 that capital accumulation cannot by itself sustain growth has a straight-forward implication: Sustained growth *requires* technological progress. This chapter looks at the role of technological progress in growth.

Section 12-1 looks at the respective role of technological progress and capital accumulation in growth. It shows how, in steady state, the rate of growth of output per person is simply equal to the rate of technological progress. This does not mean, however, that the saving rate is irrelevant: The saving rate affects the level of output per person—but not its rate of growth.

Section 12-2 turns to the determinants of technological progress, focusing in particular on the role of research and development (R&D).

Section 12-3 returns to the facts of growth presented in Chapter 10 and interprets them in the light of what we have learned in this and the previous chapter. ●

12-1 Technological Progress and the Rate of Growth

In an economy in which there is both capital accumulation and technological progress, at what rate will output grow? To answer this question, we need to extend the model developed in Chapter 11 to allow for technological progress. To introduce technological progress into the picture, we must first revisit the aggregate production function.

Technological Progress and the Production Function

Technological progress has many dimensions:

- It can lead to larger quantities of output for given quantities of capital and labor: Think of a new type of lubricant that allows a machine to run at a higher speed, and to increase production.
- It can lead to better products: Think of the steady improvement in automobile safety and comfort over time.
- It can lead to new products: Think of the introduction of the CD or MP3 player, the fax machine, wireless communication technology in all its variants, flat screen monitors, and high-definition television.
- It can lead to a larger variety of products: Think of the steady increase in the number of breakfast cereals available at your local supermarket.

The average number of items carried by a supermarket increased from 2,200 in 1950 to 38,700 in 2010. To get a sense of what this means, see ▶ Robin Williams (who plays an immigrant from the Soviet Union) in the supermarket scene in the movie *Moscow on the Hudson.*

These dimensions are more similar than they appear. If we think of consumers as caring not about the goods themselves but about the services these goods provide, then they all have something in common: In each case, consumers receive more services. A better car provides more safety, a new product such as the fax machine or a new service such as wireless communication technology provides more communication services, and so on. If we think of output as the set of underlying services provided by the goods produced in the economy, we can think of technological progress as leading to increases in output for given amounts of capital and labor. We can then think of the **state of technology** as a variable that tells us how much output can be produced from given amounts of capital and labor at any time. If we denote the state of technology by A, we can rewrite the production function as

As you saw in the Focus box "Real GDP, Technological Progress, and the Price of Computers" in Chapter 2, ▶ thinking of products as providing a number of underlying services is the method used to construct the price index for computers.

$$Y = F(K, N, A)$$
$$(+, +, +)$$

This is our extended production function. Output depends on both capital and labor (K and N) and on the state of technology (A): Given capital and labor, an improvement in the state of technology, A, leads to an increase in output.

For simplicity, we shall ignore human capital here. We return ▶ to it later in the chapter.

It will be convenient to use a more restrictive form of the preceding equation, namely

$$Y = F(K, AN) \tag{12.1}$$

This equation states that production depends on capital and on labor multiplied by the state of technology. Introducing the state of technology in this way makes it easier to think about the effect of technological progress on the relation between output, capital, and labor. Equation (12.1) implies that we can think of technological progress in two equivalent ways:

- Technological progress *reduces* the number of workers needed to produce a given amount of output. Doubling A produces the same quantity of output with only half the original number of workers, N.

- Technological progress *increases* the output that can be produced with a given number of workers. We can think of AN as the amount of **effective labor** in the economy. If the state of technology A doubles, it is as if the economy had twice as many workers. In other words, we can think of output being produced by two factors: capital (K), and effective labor (AN).

What restrictions should we impose on the extended production function (12.1)? We can build directly here on our discussion in Chapter 11.

Again, it is reasonable to assume constant returns to scale: *For a given state of technology (A)*, doubling both the amount of capital (K) and the amount of labor (N) is likely to lead to a doubling of output

$$2Y = F(2K, 2AN)$$

More generally, for any number x,

$$xY = F(xK, xAN)$$

It is also reasonable to assume decreasing returns to each of the two factors—capital and effective labor. Given effective labor, an increase in capital is likely to increase output, but at a decreasing rate. Symmetrically, given capital, an increase in effective labor is likely to increase output, but at a decreasing rate.

It was convenient in Chapter 11 to think in terms of output *per worker* and capital *per worker*. That was because the steady state of the economy was a state where output *per worker* and capital *per worker* were constant. It is convenient here to look at output *per effective worker* and capital *per effective worker*. The reason is the same: As we shall soon see, in steady state, output *per effective worker* and capital *per effective worker* are constant.

To get a relation between output per effective worker and capital per effective worker, take $x = 1/AN$ in the preceding equation. This gives

$$\frac{Y}{AN} = F\left(\frac{K}{AN}, 1\right)$$

Or, if we define the function f so that $f(K/AN) \equiv F(K/AN, 1)$:

$$\frac{Y}{AN} = f\left(\frac{K}{AN}\right) \tag{12.2}$$

In words: *Output per effective worker* (the left side) is a function of *capital per effective worker* (the expression in the function on the right side).

The relation between output per effective worker and capital per effective worker is drawn in Figure 12-1. It looks very much the same as the relation we drew in Figure 11-2

AN is also sometimes called **labor in efficiency units**. The use of "efficiency" for "efficiency units" here and for "efficiency wages" in Chapter 6 is a coincidence: The two notions are unrelated.

Per worker: divided by the number of workers (N).
    Per effective worker: divided by the number of effective workers (AN)—the number of workers, N, times the state of technology, A.

Suppose that F has the "double square root" form:

$$Y = F(K, AN) = \sqrt{K}\sqrt{AN}$$

Then

$$\frac{Y}{AN} = \frac{\sqrt{K}\sqrt{AN}}{AN} = \frac{\sqrt{K}}{\sqrt{AN}}$$

So the function f is simply the square root function:

$$f\left(\frac{K}{AN}\right) = \sqrt{\frac{K}{AN}}$$

Figure 12-1

Output per Effective Worker versus Capital per Effective Worker

Because of decreasing returns to capital, increases in capital per effective worker lead to smaller and smaller increases in output per effective worker.

between output per worker and capital per worker in the absence of technological progress. There, increases in K/N led to increases in Y/N, but at a decreasing rate. Here, increases in K/AN lead to increases in Y/AN, but at a decreasing rate.

Interactions between Output and Capital

We now have the elements we need to think about the determinants of growth. Our analysis will parallel the analysis of Chapter 11. There we looked at the dynamics of *output per worker* and *capital per worker*. Here we look at the dynamics of *output per effective worker* and *capital per effective worker*.

In Chapter 11, we characterized the dynamics of output and capital per worker using Figure 11-2. In that figure, we drew three relations:

- The relation between output per worker and capital per worker.
- The relation between investment per worker and capital per worker.
- The relation between depreciation per worker—equivalently, the investment per worker needed to maintain a constant level of capital per worker—and capital per worker.

The dynamics of capital per worker and, by implication output per worker, were determined by the relation between investment per worker and depreciation per worker. Depending on whether investment per worker was greater or smaller than depreciation per worker, capital per worker increased or decreased over time, as did output per worker.

We shall follow the same approach in building Figure 12-2. The difference is that we focus on output, capital, and investment *per effective worker*, rather than per worker.

- The relation between output per effective worker and capital per effective worker was derived in Figure 12-1. This relation is repeated in Figure 12-2: Output per effective worker increases with capital per effective worker, but at a decreasing rate.
- Under the same assumptions as in Chapter 11—that investment is equal to private saving, and the private saving rate is constant—investment is given by

$$I = S = sY$$

Divide both sides by the number of effective workers, AN, to get

$$\frac{I}{AN} = s\frac{Y}{AN}$$

The simple key to understanding the results in this section: The results we derived for *output per worker* in Chapter 11 still hold in this chapter, but now for *output per effective worker*. For example, in Chapter 11, we saw that output per worker was constant in steady state. In this chapter, we shall see that output per effective worker is constant in steady state. And so on.

Figure 12-2

The Dynamics of Capital per Effective Worker and Output per Effective Worker

Capital per effective worker and output per effective worker converge to constant values in the long run.

Capital per effective worker, K/AN

Replacing output per effective worker, Y/AN, by its expression from equation (12.2) gives

$$\frac{I}{AN} = sf\left(\frac{K}{AN}\right)$$

The relation between investment per effective worker and capital per effective worker is drawn in Figure 12-2. It is equal to the upper curve—the relation between output per effective worker and capital per effective worker—multiplied by the saving rate, s. This gives us the lower curve.

■ Finally, we need to ask what level of investment per effective worker is needed to maintain a given level of capital per effective worker.

In Chapter 11, the answer was: For capital to be constant, investment had to be equal to the depreciation of the existing capital stock. Here, the answer is slightly more complicated. The reason is as follows: Now that we allow for technological progress (so A increases over time), the number of effective workers (AN) increases over time. Thus, maintaining the same ratio of capital to effective workers (K/AN) requires an increase in the capital stock (K) proportional to the increase in the number of effective workers (AN). Let's look at this condition more closely.

Let δ be the depreciation rate of capital. Let the rate of technological progress be equal to g_A. Let the rate of population growth be equal to g_N. If we assume that the ratio of employment to the total population remains constant, the number of workers (N) also grows at annual rate g_N. Together, these assumptions imply that the growth rate of effective labor (AN) equals $g_A + g_N$. For example: If the number of workers is growing at 1% per year and the rate of technological progress is 2% per year, then the growth rate of effective labor is equal to 3% per year. These assumptions imply that the level of investment needed to maintain a given level of capital per effective worker is therefore given by

$$I = \delta K + (g_A + g_N)K$$

Or, equivalently,

$$I = (\delta + g_A + g_N)K \tag{12.3}$$

An amount δK is needed just to keep the capital stock constant. If the depreciation rate is 10%, then investment must be equal to 10% of the capital stock just to maintain the same level of capital. And an additional amount $(g_A + g_N)K$ is needed to ensure that the capital stock increases at the same rate as effective labor. If effective labor increases at 3% per year, for example, then capital must increase by 3% per year to maintain the same level of capital per effective worker. Putting δK and $(g_A + g_N)K$ together in this example: If the depreciation rate is 10% and the growth rate of effective labor is 3%, then investment must equal 13% of the capital stock to maintain a constant level of capital per effective worker.

Dividing the previous expression by the number of effective workers to get the amount of investment per effective worker needed to maintain a constant level of capital per effective worker gives

$$\frac{I}{AN} = (\delta + g_A + g_N)\frac{K}{AN}$$

The level of investment per effective worker needed to maintain a given level of capital per effective worker is represented by the upward-sloping line, "Required investment" in Figure 12-2. The slope of the line equals $(\delta + g_A + g_N)$.

In Chapter 11, we assumed $g_A = 0$ and $g_N = 0$. Our focus in this chapter is on the implications of technological progress, $g_A > 0$. But, once we allow for technological progress, introducing population growth $g_N > 0$ is straightforward. Thus, we allow for both $g_A > 0$ and ◄ $g_N > 0$.

The growth rate of the product ◄ of two variables is the sum of the growth rates of the two variables. See Proposition 7 in Appendix 2 at the end of the book.

Dynamics of Capital and Output

We can now give a graphical description of the dynamics of capital per effective worker and output per effective worker.

Consider a given level of capital per effective worker, say $(K/AN)_0$ in Figure 12-2. At that level, output per effective worker equals the vertical distance AB. Investment per effective worker is equal to AC. The amount of investment required to maintain that level of capital per effective worker is equal to AD. Because actual investment exceeds the investment level required to maintain the existing level of capital per effective worker, K/AN increases.

Hence, starting from $(K/AN)_0$, the economy moves to the right, with the level of capital per effective worker increasing over time. This goes on until investment per effective worker is just sufficient to maintain the existing level of capital per effective worker, until capital per effective worker equals $(K/AN)^*$.

In the long run, capital per effective worker reaches a constant level, and so does output per effective worker. Put another way, the steady state of this economy is such that *capital per effective worker and output per effective worker are constant and equal to $(K/AN)^*$ and $(Y/AN)^*$, respectively.*

This implies that, in steady state, output (Y) is growing at the same rate as effective labor (AN) (so that the ratio of the two is constant). Because effective labor grows at rate $(g_A + g_N)$, output growth in steady state must also equal $(g_A + g_N)$. The same reasoning applies to capital. Because capital per effective worker is constant in steady state, capital is also growing at rate $(g_A + g_N)$.

Stated in terms of capital or output per effective worker, these results seem rather abstract. But it is straightforward to state them in a more intuitive way, and this gives us our first important conclusion:

In steady state, the growth rate of output equals the rate of population growth (g_N) plus the rate of technological progress (g_A). By implication, the growth rate of output is independent of the saving rate.

To strengthen your intuition, let's go back to the argument we used in Chapter 11 to show that, in the absence of technological progress and population growth, the economy could not sustain positive growth forever.

■ The argument went as follows: Suppose the economy tried to sustain positive output growth. Because of decreasing returns to capital, capital would have to grow faster than output. The economy would have to devote a larger and larger proportion of output to capital accumulation. At some point there would be no more output to devote to capital accumulation. Growth would come to an end.

■ Exactly the same logic is at work here. Effective labor grows at rate $(g_A + g_N)$. Suppose the economy tried to sustain output growth in excess of $(g_A + g_N)$. Because of decreasing returns to capital, capital would have to increase faster than output. The economy would have to devote a larger and larger proportion of output to capital accumulation. At some point this would prove impossible. Thus the economy cannot permanently grow faster than $(g_A + g_N)$.

We have focused on the behavior of aggregate output. To get a sense of what happens not to aggregate output, but rather to the standard of living over time, we must look instead at the behavior of output per worker (not output per *effective* worker). Because output grows at rate $(g_A + g_N)$ and the number of workers grows at rate g_N, output per worker grows at rate g_A. In other words, *when the economy is in steady state, output per worker grows at the rate of technological progress.*

Because output, capital, and effective labor all grow at the same rate $(g_A + g_N)$ in steady state, the steady state of this economy is also called a state of **balanced growth**:

Table 12-1 The Characteristics of Balanced Growth

		Growth Rate:
1	Capital per effective worker	0
2	Output per effective worker	0
3	Capital per worker	g_A
4	Output per worker	g_A
5	Labor	g_N
6	Capital	$g_A + g_N$
7	Output	$g_A + g_N$

In steady state, output and the two inputs, capital and effective labor, grow "in balance," at the same rate. The characteristics of balanced growth will be helpful later in the chapter and are summarized in Table 12-1.

On the balanced growth path (equivalently: in steady state; equivalently: in the long run):

- *Capital per effective worker* and *output per effective worker* are constant; this is the result we derived in Figure 12-2.
- Equivalently, *capital per worker* and *output per worker* are growing at the rate of technological progress, g_A.
- Or, in terms of labor, capital, and output: *Labor* is growing at the rate of population growth, g_N; *capital* and *output* are growing at a rate equal to the sum of population growth and the rate of technological progress, $(g_A + g_N)$.

The Effects of the Saving Rate

In steady state, the growth rate of output depends *only* on the rate of population growth and the rate of technological progress. Changes in the saving rate do not affect the steady-state growth rate. But changes in the saving rate do increase the steady-state level of output per effective worker.

This result is best seen in Figure 12-3, which shows the effect of an increase in the saving rate from s_0 to s_1. The increase in the saving rate shifts the investment relation up, from $s_0 f(K/AN)$ to $s_1 f(K/AN)$. It follows that the steady-state level of capital per

Figure 12-3

The Effects of an Increase in the Saving Rate: I

An increase in the saving rate leads to an increase in the steady-state levels of output per effective worker and capital per effective worker.

Figure 12-4

The Effects of an Increase in the Saving Rate: II

The increase in the saving rate leads to higher growth until the economy reaches its new, higher, balanced growth path.

Figure 12-4 is the same as Figure 11-5, which anticipated the derivation presented here. ▶ For a description of logarithmic scales, see Appendix 2 at the end of the book.

When a logarithmic scale is used, a variable growing at a constant rate moves along a straight line. The slope of the ▶ line is equal to the rate of growth of the variable.

effective worker increases from $(K/AN)_0$ to $(K/AN)_1$, with a corresponding increase in the level of output per effective worker from $(Y/AN)_0$ to $(Y/AN)_1$.

Following the increase in the saving rate, capital per effective worker and output per effective worker increase for some time as they converge to their new higher level. Figure 12-4 plots output against time. Output is measured on a logarithmic scale. The economy is initially on the balanced growth path AA: Output is growing at rate $(g_A + g_N)$—so the slope of AA is equal to $(g_A + g_N)$. After the increase in the saving rate at time t, output grows faster for some period of time. Eventually, output ends up at a higher level than it would have been without the increase in saving. But its growth rate returns to $g_A + g_N$. In the new steady state, the economy grows at the same rate, but on a higher growth path BB. BB, which is parallel to AA, also has a slope equal to $(g_A + g_N)$.

Let's summarize: In an economy with technological progress and population growth, output grows over time. In steady state, output *per effective worker* and capital *per effective worker* are constant. Put another way, output *per worker* and capital *per worker* grow at the rate of technological progress. Put yet another way, output and capital grow at the same rate as effective labor, and therefore at a rate equal to the growth rate of the number of workers plus the rate of technological progress. When the economy is in steady state, it is said to be on a balanced growth path.

The rate of output growth in steady state is independent of the saving rate. However, the saving rate affects the steady-state level of output per effective worker. And increases in the saving rate lead, for some time, to an increase in the growth rate above the steady-state growth rate.

12-2 The Determinants of Technological Progress

We have just seen that the growth rate of output per worker is ultimately determined by the rate of technological progress. This leads naturally to the next question: What determines the rate of technological progress? This is the question we take up in this section.

"Technological progress" brings to mind images of major discoveries: the invention of the microchip, the discovery of the structure of DNA, and so on. These discoveries suggest a process driven largely by scientific research and chance rather than by economic forces. But the truth is that most technological progress in modern economies is the result of a humdrum process: the outcome of firms' **research and development (R&D)**

activities. Industrial R&D expenditures account for between 2% and 3% of GDP in each of the four major rich countries we looked at in Chapter 10 (the United States, France, Japan, and the United Kingdom). About 75% of the roughly one million U.S. scientists and researchers working in R&D are employed by firms. U.S. firms' R&D spending equals more than 20% of their spending on gross investment, and more than 60% of their spending on net investment—gross investment less depreciation.

Firms spend on R&D for the same reason they buy new machines or build new plants: to increase profits. By increasing spending on R&D, a firm increases the probability that it will discover and develop a new product. (We shall use "product" as a generic term to denote new goods or new techniques of production.) If the new product is successful, the firm's profits will increase. There is, however, an important difference between purchasing a machine and spending more on R&D. The difference is that the outcome of R&D is fundamentally *ideas*. And, unlike a machine, an idea can potentially be used by many firms at the same time. A firm that has just acquired a new machine does not have to worry that another firm will use that particular machine. A firm that has discovered and developed a new product can make no such assumption.

This last point implies that the level of R&D spending depends not only on the **fertility of research**—how spending on R&D translates into new ideas and new products—but also on the **appropriability** of research results—the extent to which firms benefit from the results of their own R&D. Let's look at each aspect in turn.

The Fertility of the Research Process

If research is very fertile—that is, if R&D spending leads to many new products—then, other things being equal, firms will have strong incentives to spend on R&D; R&D spending and, by implication, technological progress will be high. The determinants of the fertility of research lie largely outside the realm of economics. Many factors interact here:

The fertility of research depends on the successful interaction between basic research (the search for general principles and results) and applied research and development (the application of these results to specific uses, and the development of new products). Basic research does not lead, by itself, to technological progress. But the success of applied research and development depends ultimately on basic research. Much of the computer industry's development can be traced to a few breakthroughs, from the invention of the transistor to the invention of the microchip.

Some countries appear more successful at basic research; other countries are more successful at applied research and development. Studies point to differences in the education system as one of the reasons why. For example, it is often argued that the French higher education system, with its strong emphasis on abstract thinking, produces researchers who are better at basic research than at applied research and development. Studies also point to the importance of a "culture of entrepreneurship," in which a big part of technological progress comes from the ability of entrepreneurs to organize the successful development and marketing of new products—a dimension where the United States appears better than most other countries.

It takes many years, and often many decades, for the full potential of major discoveries to be realized. The usual sequence is one in which a major discovery leads to the exploration of potential applications, then to the development of new products, and, finally, to the adoption of these new products. The Focus box "The Diffusion of New Technology: Hybrid Corn" shows the results of one of the first studies of this process of the diffusion of ideas. Closer to us is the example of personal computers. Twenty-five years after the commercial introduction of personal computers, it often seems as if we have just begun discovering their uses.

In Chapter 11, we looked at the role of human capital as an input in production: More educated people can use more complex machines, or handle more complex tasks. Here, we see a second role for human capital: Better researchers and scientists and, by implication, a higher rate of technological progress.

The Diffusion of New Technology: Hybrid Corn

New technologies are not developed or adopted overnight. One of the first studies of the diffusion of new technologies was carried out in 1957 by Zvi Griliches, a Harvard economist, who looked at the diffusion of hybrid corn in different states in the United States.

Hybrid corn is, in the words of Griliches, "the invention of a method of inventing." Producing hybrid corn entails crossing different strains of corn to develop a type of corn adapted to local conditions. The introduction of hybrid corn can increase the corn yield by up to 20%.

Although the idea of hybridization was first developed at the beginning of the twentieth century, the first commercial application did not take place until the 1930s in the United States. Figure 1 shows the rate at which hybrid corn was adopted in a number of U.S. states from 1932 to 1956.

The figure shows two dynamic processes at work. One is the process through which hybrid corns appropriate to each state were discovered. Hybrid corn became available in southern states (Texas and Alabama) more than 10 years after it had become available in northern states (Iowa, Wisconsin, and Kentucky). The other is the speed at which hybrid corn was adopted within each state. Within eight years of its introduction, practically all corn in Iowa was hybrid corn. The process was much slower in the South. More than 10 years after its introduction, hybrid corn accounted for only 60% of total acreage in Alabama.

Why was the speed of adoption higher in Iowa than in the South? Griliches's article showed that the reason was economic: The speed of adoption in each state was a function of the profitability of introducing hybrid corn. And profitability was higher in Iowa than in the southern states.

Source: Zvi Griliches, "Hybrid Corn: An Exploration in the Economics of Technological Change," Econometrica 1957 25 (No. 4): pp. 501–522.

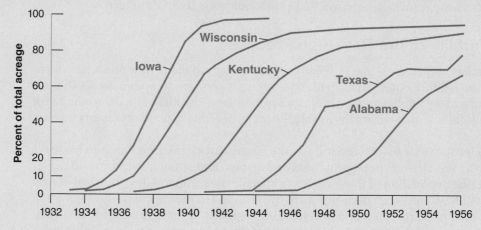

Figure 1 *Percentage of Total Corn Acreage Planted with Hybrid Seed, Selected U.S. States, 1932–1956*

An age-old worry is that research will become less and less fertile, that most major discoveries have already taken place and that technological progress will begin to slow down. This fear may come from thinking about mining, where higher-grade mines were exploited first, and where we have had to exploit increasingly lower-grade mines. But this is only an analogy, and so far there is no evidence that it is correct.

The Appropriability of Research Results

The second determinant of the level of R&D and of technological progress is the degree of *appropriability* of research results. If firms cannot appropriate the profits from the development of new products, they will not engage in R&D and technological progress will be slow. Many factors are also at work here:

The nature of the research process itself is important. For example, if it is widely believed that the discovery of a new product by one firm will quickly lead to the discovery of an even better product by another firm, there may be little payoff to being first. In other words, a highly fertile field of research may not generate high levels of R&D, because no company will find the investment worthwhile. This example is extreme, but revealing.

Even more important is the legal protection given to new products. Without such legal protection, profits from developing a new product are likely to be small. Except in rare cases where the product is based on a trade secret (such as Coca Cola), it will generally not take long for other firms to produce the same product, eliminating any advantage the innovating firm may have initially had. This is why countries have patent laws. **Patents** give a firm that has discovered a new product—usually a new technique or device—the right to exclude anyone else from the production or use of the new product for some time.

How should governments design patent laws? On the one hand, protection is needed to provide firms with the incentives to spend on R&D. On the other, once firms have discovered new products, it would be best for society if the knowledge embodied in those new products were made available to other firms and to people without restrictions. Take, for example, biogenetic research. Only the prospect of large profits is leading bio-engineering firms to embark on expensive research projects. Once a firm has found a new product, and the product can save many lives, it would clearly be best to make it available at cost to all potential users. But if such a policy was systematically followed, it would eliminate incentives for firms to do research in the first place. So, patent law must strike a difficult balance. Too little protection will lead to little R&D. Too much protection will make it difficult for new R&D to build on the results of past R&D, and may also lead to little R&D. (The difficulty of designing good patent or copyright laws is illustrated in the cartoon about cloning.)

This type of dilemma is known as "time inconsistency." We shall see other examples and discuss it at length in Chapter 22.

These issues go beyond patent laws. To take two controversial examples: What is the role of open-source software? Should students download music, movies, and even textbooks without making payments to the creators?

Countries that are less technologically advanced often have poorer patent protection. China, for example, is a country with poor enforcement of patent rights. Our discussion helps explain why. These countries are typically users rather than producers of new technologies. Much of their improvement in productivity comes not from inventions within the country, but from the adaptation of foreign technologies. In this case, the costs of weak patent protection are small, because there would be few domestic inventions anyway. But the benefits of low patent protection are clear: They allow domestic firms to use and adapt foreign technology without having to pay royalties to the foreign firms that developed the technology—which is good for the country.

12-3 The Facts of Growth Revisited

We can now use the theory we have developed in this and the previous chapter to interpret some of the facts we saw in Chapter 10.

Capital Accumulation versus Technological Progress in Rich Countries since 1985

Suppose we observe an economy with a high growth rate of output per worker over some period of time. Our theory implies this fast growth may come from two sources:

■ It may reflect a high rate of technological progress under balanced growth.
■ It may reflect instead the adjustment of capital per effective worker, K/AN, to a higher level. As we saw in Figure 12-4, such an adjustment leads to a period of higher growth, even if the rate of technological progress has not increased.

Can we tell how much of the growth comes from one source and how much comes from the other? Yes. If high growth reflects high balanced growth, output per worker should be growing at a rate *equal* to the rate of technological progress (see Table 10-1, line 4). If high growth reflects instead the adjustment to a higher level of capital per effective worker, this adjustment should be reflected in a growth rate of output per worker that *exceeds* the rate of technological progress.

Let's apply this approach to interpret the facts about growth in rich countries we saw in Table 10-1. This is done in Table 12-2, which gives, in column 1, the average rate of growth of output per worker $(g_Y - g_N)$ and, in column 2, the average rate of technological progress g_A, between 1985 and 2009 (2008 for Japan, and 2007 for the United Kingdom), for each of four countries—France, Japan, the United Kingdom, and the United States—we looked at in Table 10-1. (Note one difference between Tables 10-1

Table 12-2	Average Annual Rates of Growth of Output per Worker and Technological Progress in Four Rich Countries since 1985	
	Rate of Growth of Output per Worker (%) 1985–2009	Rate of Technological Progress (%) 1985–2009
France	1.9	1.6
Japan	1.8	2.1
United Kingdom	2.1	1.6
United States	1.9	1.3
Average	1.9	1.7

Source: Calculations from the OECD Productivity Statistics and 12-2: As suggested by the theory, Table 12-2 looks at the growth rate of output per worker, while Table 10-1, which was focusing on the standard of living, looked at the growth rate of output per person. The differences are small.) The rate of technological progress, g_A, is constructed using a method introduced by Robert Solow; the method and the details of construction are given in the appendix to this chapter.

Table 12-2 leads to two conclusions:

First, growth since 1985 has come from technological progress, not unusually high capital accumulation. This conclusion follows from the fact that, in all four countries, the growth rate of output per worker (column 1) has been roughly equal to the rate of technological progress (column 2). This is what we would expect when countries are growing along their balanced growth path.

In the United States, for example, the ratio of employment to population decreased slightly from 60.1% in 1985 to 59.3% in 2009. Thus output per person and output per worker grew at virtually the same rate over this period.

Note what this conclusion does not say. It does not say that capital accumulation was irrelevant. Capital accumulation was such as to allow these countries to maintain a roughly constant ratio of output to capital and achieve balanced growth. What it says is that, over the period, growth did not come from an unusual increase in capital accumulation (i.e., from an increase in the ratio of capital to output).

Second, convergence of output per worker between the United States and the other three countries comes from higher technological progress rather than from faster capital accumulation. France, Japan, and the United Kingdom all started behind the United States in 1985. In all three countries the rate of technological progress has been higher than in the United States.

What would have happened to the growth rate of output per worker if these countries had had the same rate of technological progress, but no capital accumulation, during the period?

This is an important conclusion. One can think, in general, of two sources of convergence between countries. First: Poorer countries are poorer because they have less capital to begin with. Over time, they accumulate capital faster than the others, generating convergence. Second: Poorer countries are poorer because they are less technologically advanced than the others. Thus, over time, they become more sophisticated, either by importing technology from advanced countries or developing their own. As technological levels converge, so does output per worker. The conclusion we can draw from Table 12-2 is that, in the case of rich countries, the more important source of convergence in this case is clearly the second one.

While the table only looks at four countries, a similar conclusion holds when we look at the set of all OECD countries. Countries that started behind in the 1950s after World War II converged mainly due to higher rates of technological progress since then.

Capital Accumulation versus Technological Progress in China

Going beyond growth in OECD countries, one of the striking facts of Chapter 10 was the high growth rates achieved by a number of Asian countries in the last three decades. Chapter 1 looked specifically at the high rate of growth in China. This raises again the same questions as those we just discussed: Do these high growth rates reflect fast technological progress, or do they reflect unusually high capital accumulation?

To answer the questions, we shall focus on China, because of its size and because of the astonishingly high output growth rate, nearly 10% since the late 1970s. Table 12-3

Table 12-3	Average Annual Rate of Growth of Output per Worker and Technological Progress in China, 1978–2007		
Period	Rate of Growth of Output (%)	Rate of Growth of Output per Worker (%)	Rate of Technological Progress (%)
1978–1995	10.2	8.6	7.8
1995–2007	9.9	9.4	6.0

Source: Barry Bosworth and Susan M. Collins, "Accounting for Growth: Comparing China and India," *Journal of Economic Perspectives*, 2008 22(No. 1): p. 49.

Warning: Chinese data for output, employment, and the capital stock (the latter is needed to construct g_A) are not as reliable as similar data for OECD countries. Thus, the numbers in the table should be seen as more tentative than the numbers in Table 12-2.

gives the average rate of growth, g_Y, the average rate of growth of output per worker, $g_Y - g_N$, and the average rate of technological progress, g_A, for two periods, 1978 to 1995 and 1995 to 2007.

Table 12-3 yields two conclusions: From the late 1970s to the mid-1990s, the rate of technological progress was close to the rate of growth of output per worker. China was roughly on a (very rapid) balanced growth path. Since 1995, however, while growth of output per worker has remained very high, the contribution of technological progress has decreased. Put another way, more recently, growth in China has come partly from unusually high capital accumulation—from an increase in the ratio of capital to output.

We can look at it another way. Recall, from Table 12-1, that under balanced growth, $g_K = g_Y = g_A + g_N$. To see what investment rate would be required if China had balanced growth, go back to equation (12.3) and divide both sides by output, Y, to get

$$\frac{I}{Y} = (\delta + g_A + g_N)\frac{K}{Y}$$

Let's plug in numbers for China for the period 1995–2007. The estimate of δ, the depreciation rate of capital in China, is 5% a year. As we just saw, the average value of g_A for the period was 6.0%. The average value of g_N, the rate of growth of employment, was 0.5%. The average value of the ratio of capital to output was 2.6. This implies a ratio of investment of output required to achieve balanced growth of $(5.0\% + 6.0\% + 0.5\%) \times 2.6 = 30\%$. The actual average ratio of investment to output for 1995–2007 was a much higher 39%. Thus, both rapid technological progress and unusually high capital accumulation explain high Chinese growth. If the rate of technological progress were to remain the same, this suggests that, as the ratio of capital to output stabilizes, the Chinese growth rate will decrease somewhat, closer to 6% than to 9.4%.

Where does the technological progress in China come from? A closer look at the data suggests two main channels. First, China has transferred labor from the countryside, where productivity is very low, to industry and services in the cities, where productivity is much higher. Second, China has imported the technology of more technologically advanced countries. It has, for example, encouraged the development of joint ventures between Chinese firms and foreign firms. Foreign firms have come with better technologies, and, over time, Chinese firms have learned how to use them.

This leads to a more general point: The nature of technological progress is likely to be different between more advanced and less advanced economies. The more advanced economies, being by definition at the **technological frontier**, need to develop new ideas, new processes, new products. They need to innovate. The countries that are behind can instead improve their level of technology by copying and adapting the new processes and products developed in the more advanced economies. They need to imitate. The farther behind a country is, the larger the role of imitation relative to innovation. As imitation is likely to be easier than innovation, this can explain why convergence, both within the OECD, and in the case of China and other countries, typically takes the form of **technological catch-up.** It raises, however, yet another question: If imitation is so easy, why is it that so many other countries do not seem to be able to do the same and grow? This points to the broader aspects of technology we discussed earlier in the chapter. Technology is more than just a set of blueprints. How efficiently these blueprints can be used and how productive an economy is depend on its institutions, on the quality of its government, and so on. We shall return to this issue in the next chapter.

Summary

- When we think about the implications of technological progress for growth, it is useful to think of technological progress as increasing the amount of effective labor available in the economy (that is, labor multiplied by the state of technology). We can then think of output as being produced with capital and effective labor.

- In steady state, output *per effective worker* and capital *per effective worker* are constant. Put another way, output *per worker* and capital *per worker* grow at the rate of technological progress. Put yet another way, output and capital grow at the same rate as effective labor, thus at a rate equal to the growth rate of the number of workers plus the rate of technological progress.

- When the economy is in steady state, it is said to be on a balanced growth path. Output, capital, and effective labor are all growing "in balance," that is, at the same rate.

- The rate of output growth in steady state is independent of the saving rate. However, the saving rate affects the steady-state level of output per effective worker. And increases in the saving rate will lead, for some time, to an increase in the growth rate above the steady-state growth rate.

- Technological progress depends on both (1) the fertility of research and development—how spending on R&D translates into new ideas and new products, and (2) the appropriability of the results of R&D—the extent to which firms benefit from the results of their R&D.

- When designing patent laws, governments must balance their desire to protect future discoveries and provide incentives for firms to do R&D with their desire to make existing discoveries available to potential users without restrictions.

- France, Japan, the United Kingdom, and the United States have experienced roughly balanced growth since 1950. Growth of output per worker has been roughly equal to the rate of technological progress. Growth in China is a combination of a high rate of technological progress and unusually high investment, leading to an increase in the ratio of capital to output.

Key Terms

state of technology, 250
effective labor, or labor in efficiency units, 251
balanced growth, 254
research and development (R&D), 256
fertility of research, 257

appropriability, 257
patents, 259
technology frontier, 262
technological catch-up, 262

Questions and Problems

QUICK CHECK
All Quick Check questions and problems are available on MyEconLab.

1. Using the information in this chapter, label each of the following statements true, false, or uncertain. Explain briefly.

a. Writing the production function in terms of capital and effective labor implies that as the level of technology increases by 10%, the number of workers required to achieve the same level of output decreases by 10%.

b. If the rate of technological progress increases, the investment rate (the ratio of investment to output) must increase in order to keep capital per effective worker constant.

c. In steady state, output per effective worker grows at the rate of population growth.

d. In steady state, output per worker grows at the rate of technological progress.

e. A higher saving rate implies a higher level of capital per effective worker in the steady state and thus a higher rate of growth of output per effective worker.

f. Even if the potential returns from R&D spending are identical to the potential returns from investing in a new machine, R&D spending is much riskier for firms than investing in new machines.

g. The fact that one cannot patent a theorem implies that private firms will not engage in basic research.

h. Because eventually we will know everything, growth will have to come to an end.

i. Technology has not played an important part in Chinese economic growth.

2. R&D and growth

a. Why is the amount of R&D spending important for growth? How do the appropriability and fertility of research affect the amount of R&D spending?

   How do each of the policy proposals listed in (b) through (e) affect the appropriability and fertility of research, R&D spending in the long run, and output in the long run?

b. An international treaty ensuring that each country's patents are legally protected all over the world.

c. Tax credits for each dollar of R&D spending.

d. A decrease in funding of government-sponsored conferences between universities and corporations.

e. The elimination of patents on breakthrough drugs, so the drugs can be sold at a low cost as soon as they become available.

3. *Sources of technological progress: Leaders versus followers.*
   a. Where does technological progress come from for the economic leaders of the world?
   b. Do developing countries have other alternatives to the sources of technological progress you mentioned in part (a)?
   c. Do you see any reasons developing countries may choose to have poor patent protection? Are there any dangers in such a policy (for developing countries)?

DIG DEEPER

All Dig Deeper questions and problems are available on MyEconLab.

4. *For each of the economic changes listed in (a) and (b), assess the likely impact on the growth rate and the level of output over the next five years and over the next five decades.*
   a. A permanent reduction in the rate of technological progress.
   b. A permanent reduction in the saving rate.

5. *Measurement error, inflation, and productivity growth*
   Suppose that there are only two goods produced in an economy: haircuts and banking services. Prices, quantities, and the number of workers occupied in the production of each good for year 1 and for year 2 are given below:

	Year 1			Year 2		
	P1	Q1	W1	P2	Q2	W2
Haircut	10	100	50	12	100	50
Banking	10	200	50	12	230	60

   a. What is nominal GDP in each year?
   b. Using year 1 prices, what is real GDP in year 2? What is the growth rate of real GDP?
   c. What is the rate of inflation using the GDP deflator?
   d. Using year 1 prices, what is real GDP per worker in year 1 and year 2? What is labor productivity growth between year 1 and year 2 for the whole economy?

   Now suppose that banking services in year 2 are not the same as banking services in year 1. Year 2 banking services include telebanking, which year 1 banking services did not include. The technology for telebanking was available in year 1, but the price of banking services with telebanking in year 1 was $13, and no one chose to purchase this package. However, in year 2, the price of banking services with telebanking was $12, and everyone chose to have this package (i.e., in year 2 no one chose to have the year 1 banking services package without telebanking). (Hint: Assume that there are now two types of banking services: those with telebanking and those without. Rewrite the preceding table but now with three goods: haircuts and the two types of banking services.)
   e. Using year 1 prices, what is real GDP for year 2? What is the growth rate of real GDP?
   f. What is the rate of inflation using the GDP deflator?
   g. What is labor productivity growth between year 1 and year 2 for the whole economy?

   h. Consider this statement: "If banking services are mismeasured—for example, by not taking into account the introduction of telebanking—we will overestimate inflation and underestimate productivity growth." Discuss this statement in light of your answers to parts (a) through (g).

6. *Suppose that the economy's production function is*

$$Y = \sqrt{K}\sqrt{AN}$$

   that the saving rate, s, is equal to 16%, and that the rate of depreciation, δ, is equal to 10%. Suppose further that the number of workers grows at 2% per year and that the rate of technological progress is 4% per year.
   a. Find the steady-state values of the variables listed in (i) through (v).
      i. The capital stock per effective worker
      ii. Output per effective worker
      iii. The growth rate of output per effective worker
      iv. The growth rate of output per worker
      v. The growth rate of output
   b. Suppose that the rate of technological progress doubles to 8% per year. Recompute the answers to part (a). Explain.
   c. Now suppose that the rate of technological progress is still equal to 4% per year, but the number of workers now grows at 6% per year. Recompute the answers to (a). Are people better off in (a) or in (c)? Explain.

7. *Discuss the potential role of each of the factors listed in (a) through (g) on the steady state level of output per worker. In each case, indicate whether the effect is through A, through K, through H, or through some combination of A, K, and H. A is the level of technology, K is the level of capital stock, H is the level of the Human capital stock.*
   a. Geographic location
   b. Education
   c. Protection of property rights
   d. Openness to trade
   e. Low tax rates
   f. Good public infrastructure
   g. Low population growth

EXPLORE FURTHER

8. *Growth accounting*
   The appendix to this chapter shows how data on output, capital, and labor can be used to construct estimates of the rate of growth of technological progress. We modify that approach in this problem to examine the growth of capital per worker.

$$Y = K^{1/3}(AN)^{2/3}$$

The function gives a good description of production in rich countries. Following the same steps as in the appendix, you can show that

$$(2/3)\,g_A = g_Y - (2/3)\,g_N - (1/3)\,g_K$$
$$= (g_Y - g_N) - (1/3)(g_K - g_N)$$

where g_y denotes the growth rate of Y.

a. What does the quantity $g_Y - g_N$ represent? What does the quantity $g_K - g_N$ represent?

b. Rearrange the preceding equation to solve for the growth rate of capital per worker.

c. Look at Table 12-2 in the chapter. Using your answer to part (b), substitute in the average annual growth rate of output per worker and the average annual rate of technological progress for the United States for the period 1985 to 2009 to obtain a crude measure of the average annual growth of capital per worker. (Strictly speaking, we should construct these measures individually for every year, but we limit ourselves to readily available data in this problem.) Do the same for the other countries listed in Table 12-2. How does the average growth of capital per worker compare across the countries in Table 12-2? Do the results make sense to you? Explain.

Further Readings

■ For more on growth, both theory and evidence, read Charles Jones, *Introduction to Economic Growth*, 2nd ed. (Norton, 2002). Jones's Web page, http://emlab.berkeley.edu/users/chad/, is a useful portal to the research on growth.

■ For more on patents, see *The Economist,* Special Report: Patents and Technology, October 20th, 2005.

■ For more on growth in two large, fast growing countries, read Barry Bosworth and Susan M. Collins, "Accounting for Growth: Comparing China and India," *Journal of Economic Perspectives*, 2008 22(No. 1): pp. 45–66.

On two issues we have not explored in the text:

■ Growth and global warming. Read the *Stern Review on the Economics of Climate Change*, 2006. You can find it at www.hm-treasury.gov.uk/independent_reviews/stern_review_economics_climate_change/stern_review_report.cfm (The report is very long. Read just the executive summary).

■ Growth and the environment. Read The Economist Survey on *The Global Environment; The Great Race*, July 4, 2002, and the update entitled "The Anthropocene: A Man-made World," May 26, 2011.

APPENDIX: Constructing a Measure of Technological Progress

In 1957, Robert Solow devised a way of constructing an estimate of technological progress. The method, which is still in use today, relies on one important assumption: that each factor of production is paid its marginal product.

Under this assumption, it is easy to compute the contribution of an increase in any factor of production to the increase in output. For example, if a worker is paid $30,000 a year, the assumption implies that her contribution to output is equal to $30,000. Now suppose that this worker increases the amount of hours she works by 10%. The increase in output coming from the increase in her hours will therefore be equal to $30,000 × 10%, or $3,000.

Let us write this more formally. Denote output by Y, labor by N, and the real wage by W/P. The symbol, Δ, means change in. Then, as we just established, the change in output is equal to the real wage multiplied by the change in labor.

$$\Delta Y = \frac{W}{P} \Delta N$$

Divide both sides of the equation by Y, divide and multiply the right side by N, and reorganize:

$$\frac{\Delta Y}{Y} = \frac{WN}{PY} \frac{\Delta N}{N}$$

Note that the first term on the right (WN/PY) is equal to the share of labor in output—the total wage bill in dollars divided by the value of output in dollars. Denote this share by α. Note that $\Delta Y/Y$ is the rate of growth of output, and denote it by g_Y. Note similarly that $\Delta N/N$ is the rate of change of the labor input, and denote it by g_N. Then the previous relation can be written as

$$g_Y = \alpha g_N$$

More generally, this reasoning implies that the part of output growth attributable to growth of the labor input is equal to α times g_N. If, for example, employment grows by 2% and the share of labor is 0.7, then the output growth due to the growth in employment is equal to 1.4% (0.7 times 2%).

Similarly, we can compute the part of output growth attributable to growth of the capital stock. Because there are only two factors of production, labor and capital, and because the share of labor is equal to α, the share of capital in income must be equal to $(1 - \alpha)$. If the growth rate of capital is equal to g_K, then the part of output growth attributable to growth of capital is equal to $(1 - \alpha)$ times g_K. If, for example, capital grows by 5%, and the share of capital is 0.3, then the output growth due to the growth of the capital stock is equal to 1.5% (0.3 times 5%).

Putting the contributions of labor and capital together, the growth in output attributable to growth in both labor and capital is equal to $(\alpha g_N + (1 - \alpha)g_K)$.

We can then measure the effects of technological progress by computing what Solow called the residual, the excess of actual growth of output g_Y over the growth attributable to growth of labor and the growth of capital $(\alpha g_N + (1 - \alpha)g_K)$.

$$\text{residual} \equiv g_Y - [\alpha g_N + (1 - \alpha)g_K]$$

This measure is called the **Solow residual**. It is easy to compute: All we need to know to compute it are the growth rate of output, g_Y, the growth rate of labor, g_N, and the growth rate of capital, g_K, together with the shares of labor, α, and capital, $(1 - \alpha)$.

To continue with our previous numerical examples: Suppose employment grows by 4%, the capital stock grows by 5%, and the share of labor is 0.7 (and so the share of capital is 0.3). Then the part of output growth attributable to growth of labor and growth of capital is equal to 2.9% (0.7 times 2% plus 0.3 times 5%). If output growth is equal, for example, to 4%, then the Solow residual is equal to 1.1% (4% minus 2.9%).

The Solow residual is sometimes called the **rate of growth of total factor productivity** (or **the rate of TFP growth,** for short). The use of "total factor productivity" is to distinguish it from the *rate of growth of labor productivity*, which is defined as $(g_Y - g_N)$, the rate of output growth minus the rate of labor growth.

The Solow residual is related to the rate of technological progress in a simple way. The residual is equal to the share of labor times the rate of technological progress:

$$\text{residual} = \alpha g_A$$

We shall not derive this result here. But the intuition for this relation comes from the fact that what matters in the production function $Y = F(K, AN)$ (equation (12.1)) is the product of the state of technology and labor, AN. We saw that to get the contribution of labor growth to output growth, we must multiply the growth rate of labor by its share. Because N and A enter the production function in the same way, it is clear that to get the contribution of technological progress to output growth, we must also multiply it by the share of labor.

If the Solow residual is equal to zero, so is technological progress. To construct an estimate of g_A, we must construct the Solow residual and then divide it by the share of labor. This is how the estimates of g_A presented in the text are constructed.

In the numerical example we saw earlier: The Solow residual is equal to 1.1%, and the share of labor is equal to 0.7. So, the rate of technological progress is equal to 1.6% (1.1% divided by 0.7).

Keep straight the definitions of productivity growth you have seen in this chapter:

- Labor productivity growth (equivalently: the rate of growth of output per worker): $g_Y - g_N$
- The rate of technological progress: g_A

In steady state, labor productivity growth $(g_Y - g_N)$ equals the rate of technological progress g_A. Outside of steady state, they need not be equal: An increase in the ratio of capital per effective worker due, for example, to an increase in the saving rate, will cause $g_Y - g_N$ to be higher than g_A for some time.

The original presentation of the ideas discussed in this appendix is found in Robert Solow, "Technical Change and the Aggregate Production Function," *Review of Economics and Statistics*, 1957, 312–320.

Key Terms

Solow residual, or rate of growth of total factor productivity, or rate of TFP growth, 266

Technological Progress: The Short, the Medium, and the Long Run

We spent much of Chapter 12 celebrating the merits of technological progress. In the long run, technological progress, we argued, is the key to increases in the standard of living. Popular discussions of technological progress are often more ambivalent. Technological progress is often blamed for higher unemployment, and for higher income inequality. Are these fears groundless? This is the first set of issues we take up in this chapter.

Section 13-1 looks at the short-run response of output and unemployment to increases in productivity.

Even if, in the long run, the adjustment to technological progress is through increases in output rather than increases in unemployment, the question remains: How long will this adjustment take? The section concludes that the answer is ambiguous: In the short run, increases in productivity sometimes decrease unemployment and sometimes increase it.

Section 13-2 looks at the medium-run response of output and unemployment to increases in productivity.

It concludes that neither the theory nor the evidence supports the fear that faster technological progress leads to more unemployment. If anything, the effect seems to go the other way: In the medium run, increases in productivity growth appear to be associated with lower unemployment.

Section 13-3 focuses on the distribution effects of technological progress.

Along with technological progress comes a complex process of job creation and job destruction. For those who lose their jobs, or for those who have skills that are no longer in demand, technological progress can indeed be a curse, not a blessing: As consumers, they benefit from the availability of new and cheaper goods. As workers, they may suffer from prolonged unemployment and have to settle for lower wages when taking a new job. Section 13-3 discusses these effects and looks at the evidence.

Another theme of Chapter 12 was that, for countries behind the technological frontier, technological progress is as much about imitation as it is about innovation. This makes it sound easy, and the experience of countries such as China reinforces this impression. But, if it is that easy, why are so many other countries unable to achieve sustained technological progress and growth? This is the second set of issues we take up in this chapter.

Section 13-4 discusses why some countries are able to achieve steady technological progress and others do not. In so doing, it looks at the role of institutions, from property rights to the efficiency of government, in sustaining growth. ●

13-1 Productivity, Output, and Unemployment in the Short Run

In Chapter 12, we represented technological progress as an increase in A, the *state of technology*, in the production function

$$Y = F(K, AN)$$

What matters for the issues we shall be discussing in this chapter is technological progress, not capital accumulation. So, for simplicity, we shall ignore capital for now and assume that output is produced according to the following production function:

$$Y = AN \tag{13.1}$$

Under this assumption, output is produced using only labor, N, and each worker produces A units of output. Increases in A represent technological progress.

A has two interpretations here. One is indeed as the state of technology. The other is as labor productivity (output per worker), which follows from the fact that $Y/N = A$. So, when referring to increases in A, we shall use *technological progress* or (labor) *productivity growth* interchangeably. We rewrite equation (13.1) as

$$N = Y/A \tag{13.2}$$

Employment is equal to output divided by productivity. Given output, the higher the level of productivity, the lower the level of employment. This naturally leads to the question: When productivity increases, does output increase enough to avoid a decrease in employment? In this section we look at the short-run responses of output, employment, and unemployment. In the next, we look at their medium-run responses and, in particular, at the relation between the natural rate of unemployment and the rate of technological progress.

"Output per worker" (Y/N) ▶ and "the state of technology" (A) are in general not the same. Recall from Chapter 12 that an increase in output per worker may come from an increase in capital per worker, even if the state of technology has not changed. They are the same here because, in writing the production function as equation (13.1), we ignore the role of capital in production.

Technological Progress, Aggregate Supply, and Aggregate Demand

The right model to use when thinking about the short- and medium-run responses of output to a change in productivity in the short run is the model that we developed in Chapter 7. Recall its basic structure:

■ Output is determined by the intersection of the aggregate supply curve and the aggregate demand curve.

■ The *aggregate supply* relation gives the price level for a given level of output. The aggregate supply curve is upward sloping: An increase in the level of output leads to an increase in the price level. Behind the scenes, the mechanism is: An increase in output leads to a decrease in unemployment. The decrease in unemployment leads to an increase in nominal wages, which in turn leads to an increase in prices—an increase in the price level.

■ The *aggregate demand* relation gives output for a given price level. The aggregate demand curve is downward sloping: An increase in the price level leads to a decrease in the demand for output. The mechanism behind the scenes is as follows: An increase in the price level leads to a decrease in the real money stock. The decrease in the real money stock leads in turn to an increase in the interest rate. The increase in the interest rate then leads to a decrease in the demand for goods, decreasing output.

The aggregate supply curve is drawn as *AS* in Figure 13-1. The aggregate demand curve is drawn as *AD*. The intersection of the aggregate supply curve and the aggregate demand curve gives the level of output *Y* consistent with equilibrium in labor, goods, and financial markets. Given the equilibrium level of output *Y*, the level of employment is determined by $N = Y/A$. The higher the level of productivity, the smaller the number of workers needed to produce a given level of output.

Suppose productivity increases from level *A* to level *A'*. What happens to output and to employment and unemployment in the short run? The answer depends on how the increase in productivity shifts the aggregate supply curve and the aggregate demand curve.

◄ *A* and *A'* refer to levels of productivity here, not points on the graph. (To avoid confusion, points in the graph are denoted by *B* and *B'*.)

Take the aggregate supply curve first. The effect of an increase in productivity is to decrease the amount of labor needed to produce a unit of output, reducing costs for firms. This leads firms to reduce the price they charge at any level of output. As a result, the aggregate supply curve shifts down, from *AS* to *AS'* in Figure 13-2.

Now take the aggregate demand curve. Does an increase in productivity increase or decrease the demand for goods at a given price level? There is no general answer because productivity increases do not appear in a vacuum; what happens to aggregate demand depends on what triggered the increase in productivity in the first place:

■ Take the case where productivity increases come from the widespread implementation of a major invention. It is easy to see how such a change may be associated with an increase in demand at a given price level. The prospect of higher growth in the future leads consumers to feel more optimistic about the future, so they increase their consumption given their current income. The prospect of higher profits in the future, as well as the need to put the new technology in place, may also lead to a boom in investment. In this case, the demand for goods increases at a given price level; the aggregate demand curve shifts to the right.

Recall our discussion of such ◄ major inventions in Chapter 12.

This argument points to the role of expectations in determining consumption and investment, something we ◄ have not yet studied, but will in Chapter 16.

■ Now take the case where productivity growth comes not from the introduction of new technologies but from the more efficient use of existing technologies. One of the

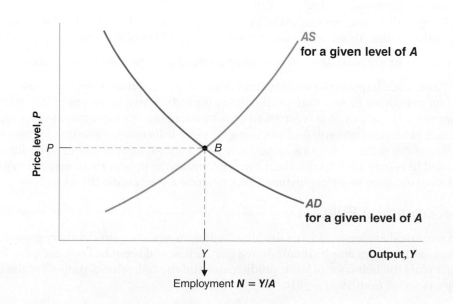

Figure 13-1

Aggregate Supply and Aggregate Demand for a Given Level of Productivity

The aggregate supply curve is upward sloping: An increase in output leads to an increase in the price level. The aggregate demand curve is downward sloping: An increase in the price level leads to a decrease in output.

Figure 13-2

The Effects of an Increase in Productivity on Output in the Short Run

An increase in productivity shifts the aggregate supply curve down. It has an ambiguous effect on the aggregate demand curve, which may shift either to the left or to the right. In this figure, we assume it shifts to the right.

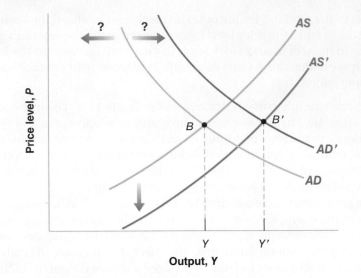

implications of increased international trade has been an increase in foreign competition. This competition has forced many firms to cut costs by reorganizing production and eliminating jobs (this is often called "downsizing"). When such reorganizations are the source of productivity growth, there is no presumption that aggregate demand will increase: Reorganization of production may require little or no new investment. Increased uncertainty and job security worries faced by workers might cause them to want to save more, and so to reduce consumption spending given their current income. In this case, aggregate demand may shift to the left rather than to the right.

Let's assume the more favorable case (more favorable from the point of view of output and employment), namely the case where the aggregate demand curve shifts to the right. When this happens, the increase in productivity shifts the aggregate supply curve down, from AS to AS', and shifts the aggregate demand curve to the right, from AD to AD'. These shifts are drawn in Figure 13-2. Both shifts contribute to an increase in equilibrium output, from Y to Y'. In this case, the increase in productivity unambiguously leads to an increase in output. In words: Lower costs and high demand combine to create an economic boom.

> Start from the production function $Y = AN$. From Proposition 7 in Appendix 2 at the end of the book, this relation implies that $g_Y = g_A + g_N$. Or equivalently: $g_N = g_Y - g_A$.

Even in this case, we cannot tell what happens to employment without having more information. To see why, note that equation (13.2) implies the following relation:

% change in employment = % change in output − % change in productivity

> The discussion has assumed that macroeconomic policy was given. But, by shifting the aggregate demand curve, fiscal policy and monetary policy can clearly affect the outcome. Suppose you were in charge of monetary policy in this economy, and there appears to be an increase in the rate of productivity growth: What level of output would you try to achieve? This was one of the questions the Fed faced in the 1990s.

Thus, what happens to employment depends on whether output increases proportionately more or less than productivity. If productivity increases by 2%, it takes an increase in output of at least 2% to avoid a decrease in employment—that is, an increase in unemployment. And without a lot more information about the slopes and the size of the shifts of the AS and AD curves, we cannot tell whether this condition is satisfied in Figure 13-2. In the short run, an increase in productivity may or may not lead to an increase in unemployment. Theory alone cannot settle the issue.

The Empirical Evidence

Can empirical evidence help us decide whether, in practice, productivity growth increases or decreases employment? At first glance, it would seem to. Look at Figure 13-3, which plots the behavior of labor productivity and the behavior of output for the U.S. business sector from 1960 to 2010.

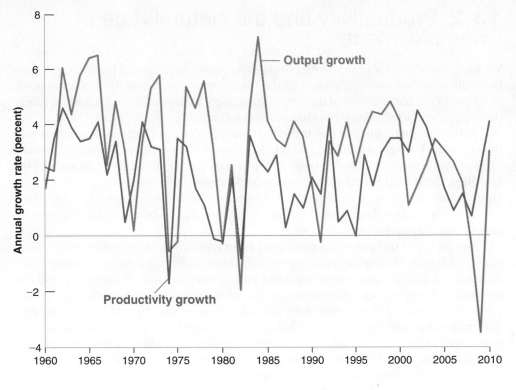

Figure 13-3

Labor Productivity and Output Growth. United States, since 1960

There is a strong positive relation between output growth and productivity growth. But the causality runs from output growth to productivity growth, not the other way around.

Source: Unemployment rate: Series UNRATE Federal Reserve Economic Data (FRED) http://research.stlouisfed.org/fred2/; Productivity growth; Series PRS84006092, U.S. Bureau of Labor Statistics

The figure shows a strong positive relation between year-to-year movements in output growth and productivity growth. Furthermore, the movements in output are typically larger than the movements in productivity. This would seem to imply that, when productivity growth is high, output increases by more than enough to avoid any adverse effect on employment. But this conclusion would be wrong. The reason is that, *in the short run*, the causal relation runs mostly the other way, from output growth to productivity growth. That is, in the short run, higher output growth leads to higher productivity growth, not the other way around.

The reason is that, in bad times, firms hoard labor—they keep more workers than is necessary for current production. When the demand for goods increases for any reason, firms respond partly by increasing employment and partly by having currently employed workers work harder. This is why increases in output lead to increases in productivity. And this is what we see in Figure 13-3: High output growth leads to higher productivity growth. This is not the relation we are after. Rather, we want to know what happens to output and unemployment when there is an *exogenous* change in productivity—a change in productivity that comes from a change in technology, not from the response of firms to movements in output. Figure 13-3 does not help us much here. And the conclusion from the research that has looked at the effects of exogenous movements in productivity growth on output is that the data give an answer just as ambiguous as the answer given by the theory:

◄ Correlation versus causality: If we see a positive correlation between output growth and productivity growth, should we conclude that high productivity growth leads to high output growth, or that high output growth leads to high productivity growth?

■ Sometimes increases in productivity lead to increases in output sufficient to maintain or even increase employment in the short run.

■ Sometimes they do not, and unemployment increases in the short run.

13-2 Productivity and the Natural Rate of Unemployment

We have looked so far at *short-run* effects of a change in productivity on output and, by implication, on unemployment. In the medium run, we know the economy tends to return to the natural level of unemployment. Now we must ask: Is the natural rate of unemployment itself affected by changes in productivity?

Since the beginning of the Industrial Revolution, workers have worried that technological progress would eliminate jobs and increase unemployment. In early nineteenth-century England, groups of workers in the textile industry, known as the Luddites, destroyed the new machines that they saw as a direct threat to their jobs. Similar movements took place in other countries. *"Saboteur"* comes from one of the ways French workers destroyed machines: by putting their sabots (their heavy wooden shoes) into the machines.

The theme of **technological unemployment** typically resurfaces whenever unemployment is high. During the Great Depression, a movement called the *technocracy movement* argued that high unemployment came from the introduction of machinery, and that things would only get worse if technological progress were allowed to continue. In the late 1990s, France passed a law reducing the normal workweek from 39 to 35 hours. One of the reasons invoked was that, because of technological progress, there was no longer enough work for all workers to have full-time jobs. Thus the proposed solution: Have each worker work fewer hours (at the same hourly wage) so that more of them could be employed.

In its crudest form, the argument that technological progress must lead to unemployment is obviously false. The very large improvements in the standard of living that advanced countries have enjoyed during the twentieth century have come with large *increases* in employment and no systematic increase in the unemployment rate. In the United States, output per person has increased by a factor of 9 since 1890 and, far from declining, employment has increased by a factor of 6 (reflecting a parallel increase in the size of the U.S. population). Nor, looking across countries, is there any evidence of a systematic positive relation between the unemployment rate and the level of productivity.

A more sophisticated version of the argument cannot, however, be dismissed so easily. Perhaps periods of unusually fast technological progress are associated with a higher natural rate of unemployment, periods of unusually slow progress associated with a lower natural rate of unemployment. To think about the issues, we can use the model we developed in Chapter 6.

Recall from Chapter 6 that we can think of this natural rate of unemployment (the natural rate, for short, in what follows) as being determined by two relations, the price-setting relation and the wage-setting relation. Our first step must be to think about how changes in productivity affect each of these two relations.

Price Setting and Wage Setting Revisited

Consider price setting first.

- From equation (13.1), each worker produces A units of output; put another way, producing 1 unit of output requires $1/A$ workers.
- If the nominal wage is equal to W, the nominal cost of producing 1 unit of output is therefore equal to $(1/A)W = W/A$.
- If firms set their price equal to $1 + m$ times cost (where m is the markup), the price level is given by:

$$\text{Price setting} \quad P = (1 + m)\frac{W}{A} \tag{13.3}$$

The only difference between this equation and equation (6.3) is the presence of the productivity term, A (which we had implicitly set to 1 in Chapter 6). An increase in productivity decreases costs, which decreases the price level given the nominal wage.

◀ Equation (6.3): $P = (1 + \mu)w$

Turn to wage setting. The evidence suggests that, other things being equal, wages are typically set to reflect the increase in productivity over time. If productivity has been growing at 2% per year on average for some time, then wage contracts will build in a wage increase of 2% per year. This suggests the following extension of our earlier wage-setting equation (6.1):

◀ Equation (6.1): $W = P^e F(u, z)$

$$\text{Wage setting} \qquad W = A^e P^e F(u, z) \qquad (13.4)$$

Look at the three terms on the right of equation (13.4).

■ Two of them, P^e and $F(u, z)$, should be familiar from equation (6.1). Workers care about real wages, not nominal wages, so wages depend on the (expected) price level, P^e. Wages depend (negatively) on the unemployment rate, u, and on institutional factors captured by the variable z.

■ The new term is A^e: Wages now also depend on the expected level of productivity, A^e. If workers and firms both expect productivity to increase, they will incorporate those expectations into the wages set in bargaining.

Think of workers and firms setting the wage so as to divide (expected) output between workers and firms according to their relative bargaining power. If both sides expect higher productivity and therefore higher output, this will be reflected in the bargained wage.

The Natural Rate of Unemployment

We can now characterize the natural rate. Recall that the natural rate is determined by the price-setting and wage-setting relations, and the additional condition that expectations be correct. In this case, this condition requires that expectations of *both* prices *and* productivity be correct, so $P^e = P$ *and* $A^e = A$.

The price-setting equation determines the real wage paid by firms. Reorganizing equation (13.3), we can write

$$\frac{W}{P} = \frac{A}{1 + m} \qquad (13.5)$$

The real wage paid by firms, W/P, increases one for one with productivity A: The higher the level of productivity, the lower the price set by firms given the nominal wage, and therefore the higher the real wage paid by firms.

This equation is represented in Figure 13-4. The real wage is measured on the vertical axis. The unemployment rate is measured on the horizontal axis. Equation (13.5) is represented by the lower horizontal line at $W/P = A/(1 + m)$: The real wage implied by price setting is independent of the unemployment rate.

Turn to the wage-setting equation. Under the condition that expectations are correct—so both $P^e = P$ and $A^e = A$—the wage-setting equation (13.4) becomes

$$\frac{W}{P} = A \, F(u, z) \qquad (13.6)$$

The real wage W/P implied by wage bargaining depends on both the level of productivity and the unemployment rate. For a given level of productivity, equation (13.6) is represented by the lower downward-sloping curve in Figure 13-4: The real wage implied by wage setting is a decreasing function of the unemployment rate.

Equilibrium in the labor market is given by point B, and the natural rate is equal to u_n. Let's now ask what happens to the natural rate in response to an increase in

The reason for using B rather than A to denote the equilibrium: We are already using the letter A to denote the level of ◀ productivity.

Figure 13-4

The Effects of an Increase in Productivity on the Natural Rate of Unemployment

An increase in productivity shifts both the wage and the price-setting curves by the same proportion and thus has no effect on the natural rate.

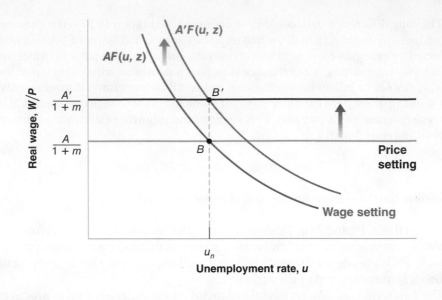

productivity. Suppose that A increases by 3%, so the new level of productivity A' equals 1.03 times A.

- From equation (13.5) we see that the real wage implied by price setting is now higher by 3%: The price setting line shifts up.
- From equation (13.6), we see that at a given unemployment rate, the real wage implied by wage setting is also higher by 3%: The wage-setting curve shifts up.
- Note that, at the initial unemployment rate u_n, both curves shift up by the same amount, namely 3% of the initial real wage. That is why the new equilibrium is at B', directly above B: The real wage is higher by 3%, and the natural rate remains the same.

The intuition for this result is straightforward. A 3% increase in productivity leads firms to reduce prices by 3% given wages, leading to a 3% increase in real wages. This increase exactly matches the increase in real wages from wage bargaining at the initial unemployment rate. Real wages increase by 3%, and the natural rate remains the same.

We have looked at a one-time increase in productivity, but the argument we have developed also applies to productivity growth. Suppose that productivity steadily increases, so that each year A increases by 3%. Then, each year, real wages will increase by 3%, and the natural rate will remain unchanged.

The Empirical Evidence

We have just derived two strong results: The natural rate should depend neither on the level of productivity nor on the rate of productivity growth. How do these two results fit the facts?

An obvious problem in answering this question is that we do not observe the natural rate. Because the actual unemployment rate moves around the natural rate, looking at the average unemployment rate over a decade should give us a good estimate of the natural rate for that decade. Looking at average productivity growth over a decade also takes care of another problem we discussed earlier: Although changes in labor hoarding can have a large effect on year-to-year changes in labor productivity, these changes in labor hoarding are unlikely to make much difference when we look at average productivity growth over a decade.

Figure 13-5 plots average U.S. labor productivity growth and the average unemployment rate during each decade since 1890. At first glance, there seems to be little relation between the two. But it is possible to argue that the decade of the Great Depression is so different that it should be left aside. If we ignore the 1930s (the decade of the Great Depression), then a relation—although not a very strong one—emerges

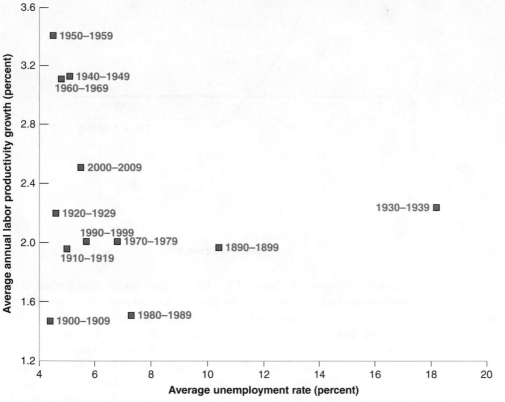

Figure 13-5

Productivity Growth and Unemployment. Averages by Decade, 1890–2009

There is little relation between the 10-year averages of productivity growth and the 10-year averages of the unemployment rate. If anything, higher productivity growth is associated with lower unemployment.

Source: Data prior to 1950: Historical Statistics of the United States. Data after 1950: See Figure 13-3.

between productivity growth and the unemployment rate. But it is the *opposite* of the relation predicted by those who believe in technological unemployment: Periods of *high productivity growth*, like the 1940s to the 1960s, have been associated with *a lower unemployment rate*. Periods of *low productivity growth*, such as the United States saw in the 1970s and 1980s, have been associated with *a higher unemployment rate*.

Can the theory we have developed be extended to explain this inverse relation in the medium run between productivity growth and unemployment? The answer is yes. To see why, we must look more closely at how expectations of productivity are formed.

Up to this point, we have looked at the rate of unemployment that prevails when *both* price expectations *and* expectations of productivity are correct. However, the evidence suggests that it takes a very long time for expectations of productivity to adjust to the reality of lower or higher productivity growth. When, for example, productivity growth slows down for any reason, it takes a long time for society, in general, and for workers, in particular, to adjust their expectations. In the meantime, workers keep asking for wage increases that are no longer consistent with the new lower rate of productivity growth.

To see what this implies, let's look at what happens to the unemployment rate when price expectations are correct (that is, $P^e = P$) but expectations of productivity (A^e) may not be (that is, A^e may not be equal to A). In this case, the relations implied by price setting and wage setting are

$$\text{Price setting} \qquad \frac{W}{P} = \frac{A}{1 + m}$$

$$\text{Wage setting} \qquad \frac{W}{P} = A^e \, F(u, z)$$

Figure 13-6

The Effects of a Decrease in Productivity Growth on the Unemployment Rate When Expectations of Productivity Growth Adjust Slowly

If it takes time for workers to adjust their expectations of productivity growth, a slow-down in productivity growth will lead to an increase in the natural rate for some time.

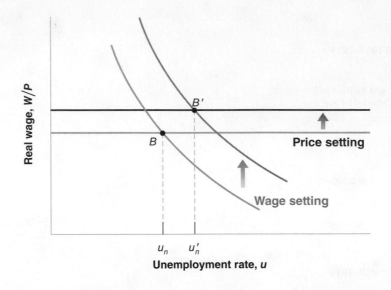

The price-setting relation shifts up by a factor A. The wage-setting relation shifts up by a factor A^e. If $A^e > A$, the ▶ price-setting relation shifts up by less than the wage-setting relation shifts up.

Some researchers indeed at- ▶ tribute some of the apparent decrease in the U.S. natural rate in the 2000s we saw in Chapter 8 to an unusually high rate of productivity growth. If they are right, this effect should eventually go away as workers' expectations adjust.

Suppose productivity growth declines: A increases more slowly than before. If expectations of productivity growth adjust slowly, then A^e will increase for some time by more than A does. What will then happen to unemployment is shown in Figure 13-6. If A^e increases by more than A, the wage-setting relation will shift up by more than the price-setting relation. The equilibrium will move from B to B', and the natural rate will increase from u_n to u'_n. The natural rate will remain higher until expectations of productivity have adjusted to the new reality—that is, until A^e and A are again equal. In words: After the slowdown in productivity growth, workers will ask for larger wage increases than firms are able to give. This will lead to a rise in unemployment. As workers eventually adjust their expectations, unemployment will fall back to its original level.

Let's summarize what we have seen in this and the preceding section:

There is not much support, either in theory or in the data, for the idea that faster productivity growth leads to higher unemployment.

- In the short run, there is no reason to expect, nor does there appear to be, a systematic relation between movements in productivity growth and movements in unemployment.
- In the medium run, if there is a relation between productivity growth and unemployment, it appears to be an inverse relation. Lower productivity growth leads to higher unemployment. Higher productivity growth leads to lower unemployment.

Given this evidence, where do fears of technological unemployment come from? They probably come from the dimension of technological progress we have neglected so far, **structural change**—the change in the structure of the economy induced by technological progress. For some workers—those with skills no longer in demand—structural change may indeed mean unemployment, or lower wages, or both. Let's now turn to that.

13-3 Technological Progress, Churning, and Distribution Effects

Technological progress is a process of structural change. This theme was central to the work of Joseph Schumpeter, a Harvard economist who, in the 1930s, emphasized that the process of growth was fundamentally a process of **creative destruction**. New goods are developed, making old ones obsolete. New techniques of production are introduced, requiring new skills and making some old skills less useful. The essence of this **churning** process is nicely reflected in the following quote from a past president of the Federal Reserve Bank of Dallas in his introduction to a report titled *The Churn*:

◄ *The Churn: The Paradox of Progress* (Dallas, TX: Federal Reserve Bank of Dallas, 1993).

> "My grandfather was a blacksmith, as was his father. My dad, however, was part of the evolutionary process of the churn. After quitting school in the seventh grade to work for the sawmill, he got the entrepreneurial itch. He rented a shed and opened a filling station to service the cars that had put his dad out of business. My dad was successful, so he bought some land on the top of a hill, and built a truck stop. Our truck stop was extremely successful until a new interstate went through 20 miles to the west. The churn replaced US 411 with Interstate 75, and my visions of the good life faded."

Many professions, from those of blacksmiths to harness makers, have vanished forever. For example, there were more than 11 million farm workers in the United States at the beginning of the last century; because of very high productivity growth in agriculture, there are less than a million today. By contrast, there are now more than 3 million truck, bus, and taxi drivers in the United States; there were none in 1900. Similarly, today, there are more than 1 million computer programmers; there were practically none in 1960. Even for those with the right skills, higher technological change increases uncertainty and the risk of unemployment: The firm in which they work may be replaced by a more efficient firm, the product their firm was selling may be replaced by another product. This tension between the benefits of technological progress for consumers (and, by implication, for firms and their shareholders) and the risks for workers is well captured in the cartoon below. The tension between the large gains for all of society from technological change and the large costs of that technological change to the workers who lose their jobs is explored in the Focus box "Job Destruction, Churning, and Earnings Losses."

Job Destruction, Churning, and Earnings Losses

Technological progress may be good for the economy, but it is tough on the workers who lose their jobs. This is documented in a study by Steve Davis and Till von Wachter (2011), who use records from the Social Security system between 1974 and 2008 to look at what happens to workers who lose their job as a result of a mass layoff.

Davis and von Wachter find all the firms with more than 50 workers where at least 30% of the workforce was laid off in one quarter, an event they call a mass layoff. Then they identify the laid-off workers who had been employed at that firm for at least 3 years. These are long-term employees. They compare the labor market experience of long-term employees who were laid off in a mass layoff to other similar workers in the labor force who did not separate in the layoff year or in the next two years. Finally, they compare the workers who experience a mass layoff in a recession to those who experience a mass layoff in an expansion.

Figure 1 summarizes their results. The year 0 is the year of the mass layoff. Years 1, 2, 3, and so on are the years after the mass layoff event. The negative years are the years prior to the layoff. If you have a job and are a long-term employee, your earnings rise relative to the rest of society prior to the mass layoff event. Having a long-term job at the same firm is good for an individual's wage growth. This is true in both recessions and expansions.

Look at what happens in the first year after the layoff: If you experience a mass layoff in a recession, your earnings fall by 40 percentage points relative to a worker who does not experience a mass layoff. If you are less unfortunate and you experience your mass layoff in an expansion, then the fall

in your relative earnings is only 25 percentage points. The conclusion: Mass layoffs cause enormous relative earnings declines whether they occur in a recession or an expansion.

Figure 1 makes another important point. The decline in relative earnings of workers who are part of a mass layoff persists for years after the layoff. Beyond 5 years or even up to 20 years after the mass layoff, workers who experienced a mass layoff suffer a relative earnings decline of about 20 percentage points if the mass layoff took place in a recession and about 10 percentage points in the mass layoff took place in an expansion. Thus the evidence is very strong that a mass layoff is associated with a very substantial decline in lifetime earnings.

It is not hard to explain why such earnings losses are likely, even if the size of the loss is surprising. The workers who have spent a considerable part of their career at the same firm have very specific skills, skills that are most useful in that firm or industry. The mass layoff, if due to technological change, renders those skills much less valuable than they were.

Other studies have found that in families that experience a mass layoff, the worker has a less stable employment path (more periods of unemployment), poorer health outcomes, and children who have a lower level of educational achievement and higher mortality when compared to the workers who have not experienced a mass layoff. These are additional personal costs associated with mass layoffs.

So, although technological change is the main source of growth in the long run, and clearly enables a higher standard of living for the average person in society, the workers who experience mass layoffs are the clear losers. It is not surprising that technological change can and does generate anxiety.

Figure 1 *Earnings Losses of Workers Who Experience a Mass Layoff*

Source: Steven J. Davis and Till M. von Wachter, "Recessions and the Cost of Job Loss," National Bureau of Economics Working Paper No. 17638.

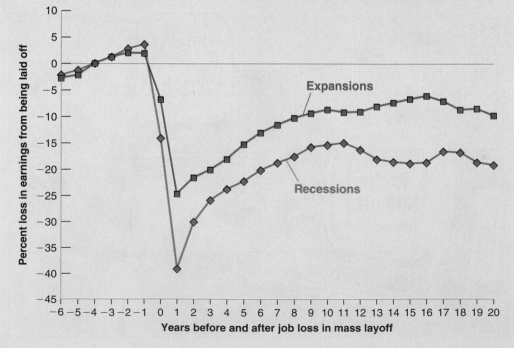

The Increase in Wage Inequality

For those in growing sectors, or those with the right skills, technological progress leads to new opportunities and higher wages. But for those in declining sectors, or those with skills that are no longer in demand, technological progress can mean the loss of their job, a period of unemployment, and possibly much lower wages. In the last 25 years in the United States, we have seen a large increase in wage inequality. Most economists believe that one of the main culprits behind this increase is technological change.

Figure 13-7 shows the evolution of relative wages for various groups of workers, by education level, from 1973 to 2007. The figure is based on information about individual workers from the Current Population Survey. Each of the lines in the figure shows the ◀ evolution of the wage of workers with a given level of education—"some high school," "high school diploma," "some college," "college degree," "advanced degree"—*relative to* the wage of workers who only have high school diplomas. All relative wages are further divided by their value in 1973, so the resulting wage series are all equal to one in 1973. The figure yields a very striking conclusion:

We described the CPS survey and some of its uses in Chapter 6.

Starting around the early 1980s, workers with low levels of education have seen their relative wage fall steadily over time, while workers with high levels of education have seen their relative wage rise steadily. At the bottom end of the education ladder, the relative wage of workers who have not completed high school has declined by 13%. This implies that, in many cases, these workers have seen a drop not only in their relative wage, but in their absolute real wages as well. At the top end of the education ladder, the relative wage of those with an advanced degree has increased by 25% since the early 1980s. In short, wage inequality has increased a lot in the United States over the last 30 years.

The Causes of Increased Wage Inequality

What are the causes of this increase in wage inequality? There is general agreement that the main factor behind the increase in the wage of high-skill relative to the wage of low-skill workers is a steady increase in the demand for high-skill workers relative to the demand for low-skill workers.

This trend in relative demand is not new; it was already present to some extent in the 1960s and 1970s. But it was offset then by a steady increase in the relative supply of high-skill

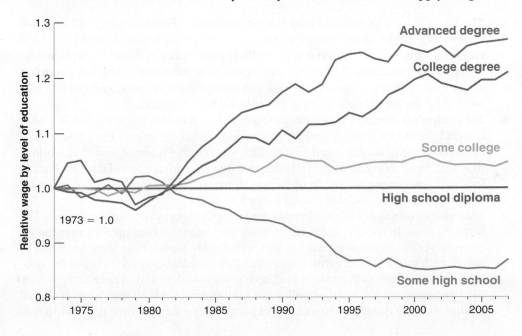

Figure 13-7

Evolution of Relative Wages, by Education Level, 1973–2007

Since the early 1980s, the relative wages of workers with a low education level have fallen; the relative wages of workers with a high education level have risen.

Source: Economic Policy Institute Datazone. www.epinet.org

workers: A steadily larger proportion of children finished high school, went to college, finished college, and so on. Since the early 1980s, relative supply has continued to increase, but not fast enough to match the continuing increase in relative demand. The result has been a steady increase in the relative wage of high-skill workers versus low-skill workers.

What explains this steady shift in relative demand?

Pursuing the effects of international trade would take us too far afield. For a more thorough discussion of who gains ▶ and who loses from trade, look at the textbook by Paul Krugman and Maurice Obstfeld, *International Economics*, 9th ed. (Harper Collins, 2012).

■ One line of argument focuses on the role of international trade. Those U.S. firms that employ higher proportions of low-skill workers, the argument goes, are increasingly driven out of markets by imports from similar firms in low-wage countries. Alternatively, to remain competitive, firms must relocate some of their production to low-wage countries. In both cases, the result is a steady decrease in the relative demand for low-skill workers in the United States. There are clear similarities between the effects of trade and the effects of technological progress: While both trade and technological progress are good for the economy as a whole, they lead nonetheless to structural change and make some workers worse off.

There is no question that trade is partly responsible for increased wage inequality. But a closer examination shows that trade accounts for only part of the shift in relative demand. The most telling fact countering explanations based solely on trade is that the shift in relative demand toward high-skill workers appears to be present even in those sectors that are not exposed to foreign competition.

■ The other line of argument focuses on **skill-biased technological progress**. New machines and new methods of production, the argument goes, require more high-skill workers today than in the past. The development of computers requires workers to be increasingly computer literate. The new methods of production require workers to be more flexible and better able to adapt to new tasks. Greater flexibility in turn requires more skills and more education. Unlike explanations based on trade, skill-biased technological progress can explain why the shift in relative demand appears to be present in nearly all sectors of the economy. At this point, most economists believe it is the dominant factor in explaining the increase in wage dispersion.

Does all this imply that the United States is condemned to steadily increasing wage inequality? Not necessarily. There are at least three reasons to think that the future may be different from the recent past:

Note that in Figure 13-7, ▶ wage differences have not increased further since 2000. It is, however, too early to know whether this is a change in trends.

■ The trend in relative demand may simply slow down. For example, it is likely that computers will become easier and easier to use in the future, even by low-skill workers. Computers may even replace high-skill workers, those workers whose skills involve primarily the ability to compute or to memorize. Paul Krugman has argued—only partly tongue in cheek—that accountants, lawyers, and doctors may be next on the list of professions to be replaced by computers.

■ Technological progress is not exogenous: This is a theme we explored in Chapter 12. How much firms spend on R&D and in what directions they direct their research depend on expected profits. The low relative wage of low-skill workers may lead firms to explore new technologies that take advantage of the presence of low-skill, low-wage workers. In other words, market forces may lead technological progress to become less skill biased in the future.

■ The relative supply of high-skill versus low-skill workers is also not exogenous. The large increase in the relative wage of more educated workers implies that the returns to acquiring more education and training are higher than they were one or two decades ago. Higher returns to training and education can increase the relative supply of high-skill workers and, as a result, work to stabilize relative wages. Many economists believe that policy has an important role to play here. It should ensure that the quality of primary and secondary education for the children of low-wage workers does not further deteriorate, and that those who want to acquire more education can borrow to pay for it.

13-4 Institutions, Technological Progress, and Growth

To end this chapter, and to end the core, we want to return to the issue raised at the end of the previous chapter: For poor countries, technological progress is more a process of imitation rather than a process of innovation. China and other Asian countries make it look easy. So, why are so many other countries unable to do the same? As we indicated in Chapter 12, this question takes us from *macroeconomics* to *development economics*, and it would take a textbook in development economics to do it justice. But it is too important a question to leave aside entirely here.

To get a sense of the issues, compare Kenya and the United States. In 2009, PPP GDP per person in Kenya was about 1/30th of PPP GDP per person in the United States. Part of the difference was due to a much lower level of capital per worker in Kenya. The other part of the difference was due to a much lower technological level in Kenya: It is estimated that A, the state of technology in Kenya, is about 1/13th of the U.S. level. Why is the state of technology in Kenya so low? Kenya potentially has access to most of the technological knowledge in the world. What prevents it from simply adopting much of the advanced countries' technology and quickly closing much of its technological gap with the United States?

One can think of a number of potential answers, ranging from Kenya's geography and climate to its culture. Most economists believe, however, that the main source of the problem, for poor countries in general and for Kenya in particular, lies in their poor institutions.

What institutions do economists have in mind? At a broad level, the protection of **property rights** may well be the most important. Few individuals are going to create firms, introduce new technologies, and invest if they expect that profits will be either appropriated by the state, extracted in bribes by corrupt bureaucrats, or stolen by other people in the economy. Figure 13-8 plots PPP GDP per person in 1995 (using a

Average Protection against Risk of Expropriation, 1985–1995

Figure 13-8

Protection from Expropriation and GDP per Person

There is a strong positive relation between the degree of protection from expropriation and the level of GDP per person.

Source: Daron Acemoglu, "Understanding Institutions," Lionel Robbins Lectures, 2004. London School of Economics. http://economics.mit.edu/files/1353

The Importance of Institutions: North and South Korea

Following the surrender of Japan in 1945, Korea formally acquired its independence but became divided at the 38th parallel into two zones of occupation, with Soviet armed forces occupying the North and U.S. armed forces occupying the South. Attempts by both sides to claim jurisdiction over all of Korea triggered the Korean War, which lasted from 1950 to 1953. At the armistice in 1953, Korea became formally divided into two countries, the Democratic People's Republic of North Korea in the North, and the Republic of Korea in the South.

An interesting feature of Korea before separation was its ethnic and linguistic homogeneity. The North and the South were inhabited by essentially the same people, with the same culture and the same religion. Economically, the two regions were also highly similar at the time of separation. PPP GDP per person, in 1996 dollars, was roughly the same, about $700 in both the North and South.

Yet, 50 years later, as shown in Figure 1, GDP per person was 10 times higher in South Korea than in North Korea—$12,000 versus $1,100! On the one hand, South Korea had joined the OECD, the club of rich countries. On the other, North Korea had seen its GDP per person

decrease by nearly two-thirds from its peak of $3,000 in the mid-1970s and was facing famine on a large scale. (The graph, taken from the work of Daron Acemoglu, stops in 1998. But, if anything, the difference between the two Koreas has become larger since then.)

What happened? Institutions and the organization of the economy were dramatically different during that period in the South and in the North. South Korea relied on a capitalist organization of the economy, with strong state intervention but also private ownership and legal protection of private producers. North Korea relied on central planning. Industries were quickly nationalized. Small firms and farms were forced to join large cooperatives, so they could be supervised by the state. There were no private property rights for individuals. The result was the decline of the industrial sector and the collapse of agriculture. The lesson is sad, but transparent: Institutions matter very much for growth.

Source: Daron Acemoglu, "Understanding Institutions," Lionel Robbins Lectures, 2004. London School of Economics. http://economics.mit.edu/files/1353

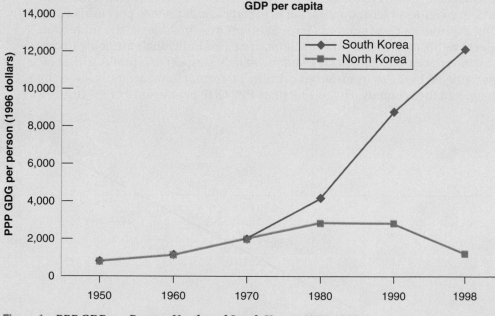

Figure 1 *PPP GDP per Person, North and South Korea, 1950–1998*

logarithmic scale) for 90 countries against an index measuring the degree of protection from expropriation; the index was constructed for each of these countries by an international business organization. The positive correlation between the two is striking (the figure also plots the regression line): Low protection is associated with a low GDP per person (at the extreme left of the figure are Zaire and Haiti); high protection

What is behind Chinese Growth?

From 1949—the year in which the People's Republic of China was established—to the late 1970s, China's economic system was based on central planning. Two major politico-economic reforms, the Great Leap Forward in 1958 and the Cultural Revolution in 1966, ended up as human and economic catastrophes. Output decreased by 20% from 1959 to 1962, and it is estimated that 25 million people died of famine during the same period. Output again decreased by more than 10% from 1966 to 1968.

After Chairman Mao's death in 1976, the new leaders decided to progressively introduce market mechanisms in the economy. In 1978, an agricultural reform was put in place, allowing farmers, after satisfying a quota due to the state, to sell their production in rural markets. Over time, farmers obtained increasing rights to the land, and today, state farms produce less than 1% of agricultural output. Outside of agriculture, and also starting in the late 1970s, state firms were given increasing autonomy over their production decisions, and market mechanisms and prices were introduced for an increasing number of goods. Private entrepreneurship was encouraged, often taking the form of Town and Village Enterprises, collective ventures guided by a profit motive. Tax advantages and special agreements were used to attract foreign investors.

The economic effects of these cumulative reforms have been dramatic: Average growth of output per worker has increased from 2.5% between 1952 and 1977, to more than 9% since then.

Is such high growth surprising? One could argue that it is not. Looking at the ten-fold difference in productivity between North and South Korea we saw in the previous Focus box, it is clear that central planning is a poor economic system. Thus, it would seem that, by moving from central planning to a market economy, countries could easily experience large increases in productivity. The answer is not so obvious, however, when one looks at the experience of the many countries that, since the late 1980s, have indeed moved away from central planning. In most Central European countries, this transition was typically associated initially with a 10 to 20% drop in GDP, and it took five years or more for output to exceed its pre-transition level. In Russia and in the new countries carved out of the Soviet Union, the drop was even larger and longer lasting. (Many transition countries now have strong growth, although their growth rates are far below that of China.)

In Central and Eastern Europe, the initial effect of transition was a collapse of the state sector, only partially compensated by slow growth of the new private sector. In China, the state sector has declined more slowly, and its decline has been more than compensated by strong private sector growth. This gives a proximate explanation for the difference between China and the other transition countries. But it still begs the question: How was China able to achieve this smoother transition?

Some observers offer a cultural explanation. They point to the Confucian tradition, based on the teachings of Confucius, which still dominates Chinese values and emphasizes hard work, respect of one's commitments, and trustworthiness among friends. All these traits, they argue, are the foundations of institutions that allow a market economy to perform well.

Some observers offer an historical explanation. They point to the fact that, in contrast to Russia, central planning in China lasted only for a few decades. Thus, when the shift back to a market economy took place, people still knew how such an economy functioned, and adapted easily to the new economic environment.

Most observers point to the strong rule of the communist party in the process. They point out that, in contrast to Central and Eastern Europe, the political system did not change, and the government was able to control the pace of transition. It was able to experiment along the way, to allow state firms to continue production while the private sector grew, and to guarantee property rights to foreign investors (in Figure 13-8, China has an index of property rights of 7.7, not far from its value in rich countries). With foreign investors has come the technology from rich countries, and, in time, the transfer of this knowledge to domestic firms. For political reasons, such a strategy was simply not open to governments in Central and Eastern Europe.

The limits of the Chinese strategy are clear. Property rights are still not well established. The banking system is still inefficient. So far, however, these problems have not stood in the way of growth.

For more on China's economy, read Gregory Chow, China's Economic Transformation, Blackwell Publishers, 2002.

For a comparison between transition in Eastern Europe and China, read Jan Svejnar, China in Light of the Performance of Central and East European Economies, IZA Discussion Paper 2791, May 2007.

---

is associated with a high GDP per person (at the extreme right are the United States, Luxembourg, Norway, Switzerland, and the Netherlands).

What does "protection of property rights" mean in practice? It means a good political system, in which those in charge cannot expropriate or seize the property of the citizens. It means a good judicial system, where disagreements can be resolved

Kenya's index is 6. Kenya is below the regression line, which means that Kenya has lower GDP per person than would be predicted based just on the index.

efficiently, rapidly, and fairly. Looking at an even finer degree of detail, it means laws against insider trading in the stock market, so people are willing to buy stocks and so provide financing to firms; it means clearly written and well-enforced patent laws, so firms have an incentive to do research and develop new products. It means good anti trust laws, so competitive markets do not turn into monopolies with few incentives to introduce new methods of production and new products. And the list obviously goes on. (A particularly dramatic example of the role of institutions is given in the Focus box "The Importance of Institutions: North and South Korea.)

This still leaves one essential question: Why don't poor countries adopt these good institutions? The answer is that it is hard! Good institutions are complex and difficult for poor countries to put in place. Surely, causality runs both ways in Figure 13-8: Low protection against expropriation leads to low GDP per person. But it is also the case that low GDP per person leads to worse protection against expropriation: Poor countries are often too poor to afford a good judicial system and to maintain a good police force, for example. Thus, improving institutions and starting a virtuous cycle of higher GDP per person and better institutions is often very difficult. The fast growing countries of Asia have succeeded. (The Focus box "What is behind Chinese Growth?" explores the case of China in more detail.) So far, much of Africa has been unable to start such a virtuous cycle.

Summary

- People often fear that technological progress destroys jobs and leads to higher unemployment. This fear was present during the Great Depression. Theory and evidence suggest these fears are largely unfounded. There is not much support, either in theory or in the data, for the idea that faster technological progress leads to higher unemployment.

- In the short run, there is no reason to expect, nor does there appear to be, a systematic relation between changes in productivity and movements in unemployment.

- If there is a relation between changes in productivity and movements in unemployment in the medium run, it appears to be an inverse relation: Lower productivity growth appears to lead to higher unemployment; higher productivity growth appears to lead to lower unemployment. An explanation is that it takes high unemployment to reconcile workers' wage expectations with lower productivity growth.

- Technological progress is not a smooth process in which all workers are winners. Rather, it is a process of structural change. Even if most people benefit from the increase in the average standard of living, there are losers as well. As new goods and new techniques of production are developed, old goods and old techniques of production become obsolete. Some workers find their skills in higher demand and benefit from technological progress. Others find their skills in lower demand and suffer unemployment and/or reductions in relative wages.

- Wage inequality has increased in the past 25 years in the United States. The real wage of low-skill workers has declined not only relative to the real wage of high-skill workers, but also in absolute terms. The two main causes are international trade and skill-biased technological progress.

- Sustained technological progress requires that the right institutions are in place. In particular, it requires well-established and well-protected property rights. Without good property rights, a country is likely to remain poor. But, in turn, a poor country may find it difficult to put in place good property rights.

Key Terms

technological unemployment, 272

structural change, 276

creative destruction, 276

churning, 277

skill-biased technological progress, 280

property rights, 281

Questions and Problems

QUICK CHECK

All Quick Check questions and problems are available on MyEconLab.

1. Using the information in this chapter, label each of the following statements true, false, or uncertain. Explain briefly.

a. The change in employment and output per person in the United States since 1900 lends support to the argument that technological progress leads to a steady increase in employment.

b. Workers benefit equally from the process of creative destruction.

c. In the past two decades, the real wages of low-skill U.S. workers have declined relative to the real wages of high-skill workers.

d. Technological progress leads to a decrease in employment if, and only if, the increase in output is smaller than the increase in productivity.

e. The "jobless recovery" after the recession of 2001 can be explained by unusually high productivity growth unaccompanied by a boom in aggregate demand.

f. The apparent decrease in the natural rate of unemployment in the United States in the second half of the 1990s can be explained by the fact that productivity growth was unexpectedly high during that period.

g. If we could stop technological progress, doing so would lead to a decrease in the natural rate of unemployment.

2. Suppose an economy is characterized by the equations below.

Price setting: $P = (1 + m)(W/A)$

Wage setting: $W = A^e P^e (1 - u)$

a. Solve for the unemployment rate if $P^e = P$ but A^e does not necessarily equal A. Explain the effects of (A^e/A) on the unemployment rate.

Now suppose that expectations of both prices and productivity are accurate.

b. Solve for the natural rate of unemployment if the markup (m) is equal to 5%.

c. Does the natural rate of unemployment depend on productivity? Explain.

3. Discuss the following statement: "Higher labor productivity allows firms to produce more goods with the same number of workers and thus to sell the goods at the same or even lower prices. That's why increases in labor productivity can permanently reduce the rate of unemployment without causing inflation".

4. How might policy changes in (a) through (d) affect the wage gap between low-skill and high-skill workers in the United States?

a. increased spending on computers in public schools.

b. restrictions on the number of foreign temporary agricultural workers allowed to enter the United States.

c. an increase in the number of public colleges.

d. tax credits in Central America for U.S. firms.

All Dig Deeper questions and problems are available on MyEconLab.

5. Technological progress, agriculture, and employment

Discuss the following statement: "Those who argue that technological progress does not reduce employment should look at agriculture. At the start of the last century, there were more than 11 million farm workers. Today, there are fewer than 1 million. If all sectors start having the productivity growth that took place in agriculture during the twentieth century, no one will be employed a century from now."

6. Productivity and the aggregate supply curve

Consider an economy in which production is given by

$$Y = AN$$

Assume that price setting and wage setting are described in the equations below.

Price setting: $P = (1 + m)(W/A)$

Wage setting: $W = A^e P^e (1 - u)$

Recall that the relation between employment, N, the labor force, L, and the unemployment rate, u, is given by

$$N = (1 - u)L$$

a. Derive the aggregate supply curve (that is, the relation between the price level and the level of output, given the markup, the actual and expected levels of productivity, the labor force, and the expected price level). Explain the role of each variable.

b. Show the effect of an equiproportional increase in A and A^e (so that A/A^e remains unchanged) on the position of the aggregate supply curve. Explain.

c. Suppose instead that actual productivity, A, increases, but expected productivity, A^e, does not change. Compare the results in this case to your conclusions in part (b). Explain the difference.

7. Technology and the labor market

In the appendix to Chapter 6, we learned how the wage-setting and price-setting equations could be expressed in terms of labor demand and labor supply. In this problem, we extend the analysis to account for technological change.
Consider the wage-setting equation

$$W/P = F(u, z)$$

as the equation corresponding to labor supply. Recall that for a given labor force, L, the unemployment rate, u, can be written as

$$u = 1 - N/L$$

where N is employment.

a. Substitute the expression for u into the wage-setting equation.

b. Using the relation you derived in part (a), graph the labor supply curve in a diagram with N on the horizontal axis and W/P, the real wage, on the vertical axis.

Now write the price setting equation as

$$P = (1 + m) MC$$

where MC is the marginal cost of production. To generalize somewhat our discussion in the text, we shall write

$$MC = W/MPL$$

where W is the wage and MPL is the marginal product of labor.

c. Substitute the expression for MC into the price-setting equation and solve for the real wage, W/P. The result is the labor demand relation, with W/P as a function of the MPL and the markup, m.

In the text, we assumed for simplicity that the MPL was constant for a given level of technology. Here, we assume that the MPL decreases with employment (again for a given level of technology), a more realistic assumption.

d. Assuming that the MPL decreases with employment, graph the labor demand relation you derived in part (c). Use the same diagram you drew for part (b).

e. What happens to the labor demand curve if the level of technology improves? (Hint: What happens to MPL when technology improves?) Explain. How is the real wage affected by an increase in the level of technology?

EXPLORE FURTHER

8. The churn

The Bureau of Labor Statistics presents a forecast of occupations with the largest job decline and the largest job growth. Examine the tables at **www.bls.gov/emp/emptab4.htm** (for the largest job decline) and **www.bls.gov/emp/emptab3.htm** (for the largest job growth).

a. Which occupations in decline can be linked to technological change? Which can be linked to foreign competition?

b. Which occupations that are forecast to grow can be linked to technological change? Which can be linked to demographic change—in particular, the aging of the U.S. population?

9. Real wages

The chapter has presented data on relative wages of high-skill and low-skill workers. In this question, we look at the evolution of real wages.

a. Based on the price-setting equation we use in the text, how should real wages change with technological progress? Explain. Has there been technological progress during the period from 1973 to the present?

b. Go to the Web site of the Economic Report of the President (**www.gpoaccess.gov/eop/**) and find Table B-47. Look at the data on average hourly earnings (in nonagricultural industries) in 1982–1984 dollars (i.e., real hourly earnings). How do real hourly earnings in 1973 compare to real hourly earnings in the latest year for which data are available?

c. Given the data on relative wages presented in the chapter, what do your results from part (b) suggest about the evolution of real wages of low-skill workers since 1973? What do your answers suggest about the strength of the relative decline in demand for low-skill workers?

d. What might be missing from this analysis of worker compensation? Do workers receive compensation in forms other than wages?

The Economic Policy Institute (EPI) publishes detailed information about the real wages of various classes of workers in its publication The State of Working America. *Sometimes, EPI makes data from* The State of Working America *available at* **www.stateofworkingamerica.org**.

Further Readings

- For more on the process of reallocation that characterizes modern economies, read *The Churn: The Paradox of Progress*, a report by the Federal Reserve Bank of Dallas, 1993.
- For a fascinating account on how computers are transforming the labor market, read *The New Division of Labor: How Computers Are Creating the Next Job Market*, by Frank Levy and Richard Murnane, (Princeton University Press, 2004).
- For more statistics on various dimensions of inequality in the United States, a very useful site is "The State of Working America," published by the Economic Policy Institute, at http://www.stateofworkingamerica.org/
- For the role of institutions in growth, read "Growth Theory Through the Lens of Development Economics," by Abhijit Banerjee and Esther Duflo, Chapter 7, *Handbook of Economic Growth*, (North Holland, 2005) (read sections 1 to 4).
- For more on institutions and growth, you can read the slides from the 2004 Lionel Robbins lectures "Understanding Institutions" given by Daron Acemoglu. These are found at http://economics.mit.edu/files/1353

Expectations

The next four chapters cover the first extension of the core. They look at the role of expectations in output fluctuations.

Chapter 14

Chapter 14 introduces two important concepts. The first is the distinction between the real interest rate and the nominal interest rate. It uses this distinction to discuss the Fisher hypothesis, the proposition that, in the medium run, nominal interest rates fully reflect inflation and money growth. The second is the concept of expected present discounted value, which plays a central role in the determination of asset prices and in consumption and investment decisions.

Chapter 15

Chapter 15 focuses on the role of expectations in financial markets. It first looks at the determination of bond prices and bond yields. It shows how we can learn about the course of expected future interest rates by looking at the yield curve. It then turns to stock prices and shows how they depend on expected future dividends and interest rates. Finally, it discusses whether stock prices always reflect fundamentals or may instead reflect bubbles or fads.

Chapter 16

Chapter 16 focuses on the role of expectations in consumption and investment decisions. The chapter shows how consumption depends partly on current income, partly on human wealth, and partly on financial wealth. It shows how investment depends partly on current cash flow and partly on the expected present value of future profits.

Chapter 17

Chapter 17 looks at the role of expectations in output fluctuations. Starting from the IS–LM model, it modifies the description of goods-market equilibrium (the IS relation) to reflect the effect of expectations on spending. It revisits the effects of monetary and fiscal policy on output. It shows for example, that, in contrast to the results derived in the core, a fiscal contraction can sometimes increase output, even in the short run.

Expectations:
The Basic Tools

The consumer who considers buying a new car must ask: Can I safely take a new car loan? How much of a wage raise can I expect over the next few years? Is another recession coming? How safe is my job?

The manager who observes an increase in current sales must ask: Is this a temporary boom that I should try to meet with the existing production capacity? Or is it likely to last, in which case I should order new machines?

The pension fund manager who observes a boom in the stock market must ask: Are stock prices going to increase further, or is the boom likely to fizzle? Does the increase in stock prices reflect expectations of firms' higher profits in the future? Do I share those expectations? Should I move some of my funds into or out of the stock market?

These examples make clear that many economic decisions depend not only on what is happening today but also on expectations of what will happen in the future. Indeed, some decisions should depend very little on what is happening today. For example, why should an increase in sales today—if it is not accompanied by expectations of continued higher sales in the future—cause a firm to alter its investment plans? The new machines may not be in operation before sales have returned to normal. By then, they may sit idle, gathering dust.

Until now, we have not paid systematic attention to the role of expectations. We discussed it informally for example, when discussing the effect of consumer confidence on consumption in Chapter 3, or the effects of the stock market decline on spending in Chapter 1. But it is time to do it more carefully. This is what we shall do in this and the next three chapters.

This chapter lays the groundwork and introduces two key concepts:

Section 14-1 introduces the first concept, the distinction between the *real* interest rate and the *nominal* interest rate.

Sections 14-2 and 14-3 then build on this distinction to revisit the effects of money growth on interest rates. They lead to a surprising but important result: Higher money growth leads to *lower* nominal interest rates in the short run, but to *higher* nominal interest rates in the medium run.

Section 14-4 introduces the second concept, *expected present discounted value*. ●

14-1 Nominal versus Real Interest Rates

At the time of this writing, the one-year T-bill rate is even lower, very close to zero. We shall return to this below. For our purposes, comparing 1981 and 2006 is the best way to make the point we want to make in this section.

In January 1981, the *one-year T-bill rate*—the interest rate on one-year government bonds—was 12.6%. In January 2006, the one-year T-bill rate was only 4.5%. Although most of us cannot borrow at the same interest rate as the government (this was clear in our discussion of the crisis in Chapter 9), the interest rates we faced as consumers were also substantially lower in 2006 than in 1981. It was much cheaper to borrow in 2006 than it was in 1981.

Or was it? In 1981, inflation was around 12%. In 2006, inflation was around 2%. This would seem relevant: The interest rate tells us how many dollars we shall have to pay in the future in exchange for having one more dollar today.

But we do not consume dollars. We consume goods.

When we borrow, what we really want to know is how many goods we will have to give up in the future in exchange for the goods we get today. Likewise, when we lend, we want to know how many goods—not how many dollars—we will get in the future for the goods we give up today. The presence of inflation makes this distinction important. What is the point of receiving high interest payments in the future if inflation between now and then is so high that we are unable to buy more goods in the future?

This is where the distinction between nominal interest rates and real interest rates comes in:

- Interest rates expressed in terms of dollars (or, more generally, in units of the national currency) are called **nominal interest rates**. The interest rates printed in the financial pages of newspapers are nominal interest rates. For example, when we say that the one-year T-bill rate is 4.5%, we mean that for every dollar the government borrows by issuing one-year T-bills, it promises to pay 1.045 dollars a year from now. More generally, if the nominal interest rate for year t is i_t, borrowing 1 dollar this year requires you to pay $1 + i_t$ dollars next year. (We shall use interchangeably "this year" for "today" and "next year" for "one year from today.")

Nominal interest rate: The interest rate in terms of dollars.

- Interest rates expressed *in terms of a basket of goods* are called **real interest rates**. If we denote the real interest rate for year t by r_t, then, by definition, borrowing the equivalent of one basket of goods this year requires you to pay the equivalent of $1 + r_t$ baskets of goods next year.

Real interest rate: The interest rate in terms of a basket of goods.

What is the relation between nominal and real interest rates? How do we go from nominal interest rates—which we do observe—to real interest rates—which we typically do not observe? The intuitive answer: We must adjust the nominal interest rate to take into account expected inflation.

Let's go through the step-by-step derivation:

Assume there is only one good in the economy, bread (we shall add jam and other goods later). Denote the one-year nominal interest rate, in terms of dollars, by i_t: If you borrow one dollar this year, you will have to repay $1 + i_t$ dollars next year. But you are not interested in dollars. What you really want to know is: If you borrow enough to eat one more pound of bread this year, how much will you have to repay, in terms of pounds of bread, next year?

Figure 14-1 helps us derive the answer. The top part repeats the definition of the one-year real interest rate. The bottom part shows how we can derive the one-year real interest rate from information about the one-year nominal interest rate and the price of bread.

- Start with the downward pointing arrow in the lower left of Figure 14-1. Suppose you want to eat one more pound of bread this year. If the price of a pound of bread this year is P_t dollars, to eat one more pound of bread, you must borrow P_t dollars.

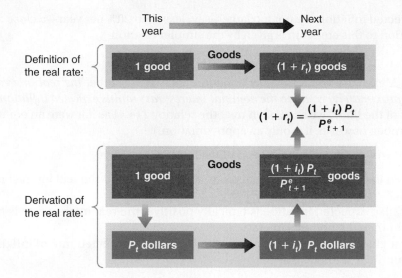

Figure 14-1

Definition and Derivation of the Real Interest Rate

- If i_t is the one-year nominal interest rate—the interest rate in terms of dollars—and if you borrow P_t dollars, you will have to repay $(1 + i_t)P_t$ dollars next year. This is represented by the arrow from left to right at the bottom of Figure 14-1.

- What you care about, however, is not dollars, but pounds of bread. Thus, the last step involves converting dollars back to pounds of bread next year. Let P_{t+1}^e be the price of bread you expect for next year. (The superscript *e* indicates that this is an expectation: You do not know yet what the price of bread will be next year.) How much you expect to repay next year, in terms of pounds of bread, is therefore equal to $(1 + i_t)P_t$ (the number of dollars you have to repay next year) divided by P_{t+1}^e (the price of bread in terms of dollars expected for next year), so $(1 + i_t)P_t/P_{t+1}^e$. ◄ This is represented by the arrow pointing up in the lower right of Figure 14-1.

Putting together what you see in both the top part and the bottom part of Figure 14-1, it follows that the one-year real interest rate, r_t, is given by:

$$1 + r_t = (1 + i_t)\frac{P_t}{P_{t+1}^e} \tag{14.1}$$

This relation looks intimidating. Two simple manipulations make it look friendlier:

- Denote expected inflation between t and $t + 1$ by π_{t+1}^e. Given that there is only one good—bread—the expected rate of inflation equals the expected change in the dollar price of bread between this year and next year, divided by the dollar price of bread this year:

$$\pi_{t+1}^e \equiv \frac{(P_{t+1}^e - P_t)}{P_t} \tag{14.2}$$

Using equation (14.2), rewrite P_t/P_{t+1}^e in equation (14.1) as $1/(1 + \pi_{t+1}^e)$. ◄ Replace in (14.1) to get

$$(1 + r_t) = \frac{1 + i_t}{1 + \pi_{t+1}^e} \tag{14.3}$$

One plus the real interest rate equals the ratio of one plus the nominal interest rate, divided by one plus the expected rate of inflation.

- Equation (14.3) gives us the *exact* relation of the real interest rate to the nominal interest rate and expected inflation. However, when the nominal interest rate and

If you have to pay \$10 next year and you expect the price of bread next year to be \$2 a loaf, you expect to have to repay the equivalent of $10/2 = 5$ loaves of bread next year. This is why we divide the dollar amount $(1 + i_t)P_t$ by the expected price of bread next year, P_{t+1}^e.

Add 1 to both sides in (14.2):

$$1 + \pi_{t+1}^e = 1 + \frac{(P_{t+1}^e - P_t)}{P_t}$$

Reorganize:

$$1 + \pi_{t+1}^e = \frac{P_{t+1}^e}{P_t}$$

Take the inverse on both sides:

$$\frac{1}{1 + \pi_{t+1}^e} = \frac{P_t}{P_{t+1}^e}$$

Replace in (14.1) and you get (14.3).

See Proposition 6, Appendix 2 at the end of the book. Suppose $i = 10\%$ and $\pi^e = 5\%$. The exact relation (14.3) gives $r_t = 4.8\%$. The approximation given by equation (14.4) gives 5%—close enough.

The approximation can be quite bad, however, when i and π^e are high. If $i = 100\%$ and $\pi^e = 80\%$. the exact relation gives $r = 11\%$; but the approximation gives $r = 20\%$—a big difference.

expected inflation are not too large—say, less than 20% per year—a close approximation to this equation is given by the simpler relation

$$r_t \approx i_t - \pi^e_{t+1} \qquad (14.4)$$

Make sure you remember equation (14.4). It says that *the real interest rate is (approximately) equal to the nominal interest rate minus expected inflation.* (In the rest of the book, we shall often treat the relation (14.4) as if it were an equality. Remember, however, it is only an approximation.)

Note some of the implications of equation (14.4):

- When expected inflation equals zero, the nominal and the real interest rates are equal.
- Because expected inflation is typically positive, the real interest rate is typically lower than the nominal interest rate.
- For a given nominal interest rate, the higher the expected rate of inflation, the lower the real interest rate.

The case where expected inflation happens to be equal to the nominal interest rate is worth looking at more closely. Suppose the nominal interest rate and expected inflation both equal 10%, and you are the borrower. For every dollar you borrow this year, you will have to repay 1.10 dollars next year. This looks expensive. But dollars will be worth 10% less in terms of bread next year. So, if you borrow the equivalent of one pound of bread, you will have to repay the equivalent of one pound of bread next year: The real cost of borrowing—the real interest rate—is equal to zero. Now suppose you are the lender: For every dollar you lend this year, you will receive 1.10 dollars next year. This looks attractive, but dollars next year will be worth 10% less in terms of bread. If you lend the equivalent of one pound of bread this year, you will get the equivalent of one pound of bread next year: Despite the 10% nominal interest rate, the real interest rate is equal to zero.

We have assumed so far that there is only one good—bread. But what we have done generalizes easily to many goods. All we need to do is to substitute the *price level*—the price of a basket of goods—for the price of bread in equation (14.1) or equation (14.3). If we use the consumer price index (the CPI) to measure the price level, the real interest rate tells us how much consumption we must give up next year to consume more today.

Nominal and Real Interest Rates in the United States since 1978

Let us return to the question at the start of this section. We can now restate it as follows: Was the *real interest rate* lower in 2006 than it was in 1981? More generally, what has happened to the real interest rate in the United States since the early 1980s?

The answer is shown in Figure 14-2, which plots both nominal and real interest rates since 1978. For each year, the nominal interest rate is the one-year T-bill rate at the beginning of the year. To construct the real interest rate, we need a measure of expected inflation—more precisely, the rate of inflation expected as of the beginning of each year. We use, for each year, the forecast of inflation for that year published at the end of the previous year by the OECD. For example, the forecast of inflation used to construct the real interest rate for 2006 is the forecast of inflation to occur over 2006 as published by the OECD in December 2005—2.2%.

Note that the real interest rate $(i - \pi^e)$ is based on *expected* inflation. If actual inflation turns out to be different from expected inflation, the realized real interest rate $(i - \pi)$ will be different from the real interest rate. For this reason, the

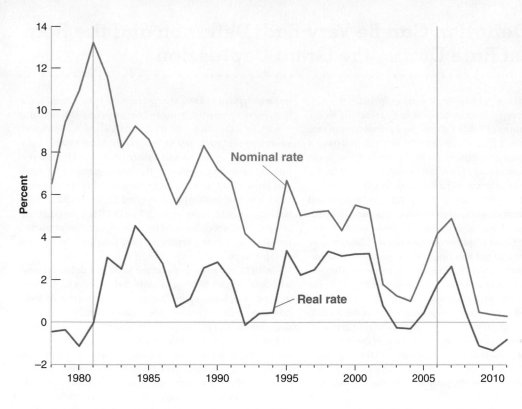

Figure 14-2

Nominal and Real One-Year T-Bill Rates in the United States since 1978

The nominal rate has declined considerably since the early 1980s but, because expected inflation has declined as well, the real rate has declined much less than the nominal rate.

Source: Nominal interest rate is the 1-year Treasury bill in December of the previous year: Series TB1YR, Federal Reserve Economic Data (FRED) http://research.stlouisfed.org/fred2/ (Series TB6MS in December 2001, 2002, 2003, and 2004.) Expected inflation is the 12-month forecast of inflation from the December OECD Economic Outlook from the previous year.

real interest rate is sometimes called the *ex-ante* real interest rate ("ex-ante" means "before the fact": here, before inflation is known). The realized real interest rate is called the *ex-post* real interest rate ("ex-post" means "after the fact": here, after inflation is known).

Figure 14-2 shows the importance of adjusting for inflation. Although the nominal interest was much lower in 2006 than it was in 1981, the real interest rate was actually *higher* in 2006 than it was in 1981: The real rate was about 2.0% in 2006 and about 0.0% in 1981. Put another way, despite the large decline in nominal interest rates, borrowing was actually more expensive in 2006 than it was 1981. This is due to the fact that inflation (and with it, expected inflation) has steadily declined since the early 1980s.

This answers the question we asked at the beginning of the section. Let's now turn to the situation in January 2011, the last observation in the figure. In January 2011, the nominal interest rate was a very low 0.3%; as we saw in Chapter 9, this is the result of the decision by the Fed to decrease the nominal interest rate in order to increase spending and help the recovery. Expected inflation was 1.1%, so the real interest rate was negative, equal to −0.8%. Such a low real interest rate should lead to higher spending, but, as we also saw in Chapter 9, this, by itself, is not enough to lead to a strong recovery. And, now that we have introduced the distinction between nominal and real interest rates, you can see why the Fed is worried. Not only can it not decrease the nominal rate further: The economy is in the liquidity trap. But, if under the pressure of high unemployment, inflation was going to decrease further and turn into deflation, the real interest rate would increase, making it even harder for the economy to recover. So far inflation has not become negative. But the worry is not unfounded: As examined in the ◀ See the discussion at the end Focus box "Why Deflation Can Be Very Bad: Deflation and the Real Interest Rate During the Great Depression," it happened during the Great Depression. We have to hope it will not happen again.

See the discussion at the end of Chapter 9.

Why Deflation Can Be Very Bad: Deflation and the Real Interest Rate During the Great Depression

After the collapse of the stock market in 1929, the U.S. economy plunged into an economic depression. As the first two columns of Table 1 show, the unemployment rate increased from 3.2% in 1929 to 24.9% in 1933, and output growth was strongly negative for four years in a row. From 1933 on, the economy recovered slowly, but by 1940, the unemployment rate was still a very high 14.6%.

The Great Depression has many elements in common with the current crisis: A large increase in asset prices before the crash—housing prices in this crisis, stock market prices in the Great Depression, and the amplification of the shock through the banking system. There are also important differences: As you can see by comparing the output growth and unemployment numbers in Table 1 to the numbers for the current crisis in Chapter 1, the decrease in output and the increase in unemployment were much larger then than they have been in the current crisis. In this box, we shall focus on just one aspect of the Great Depression, the evolution of the nominal and the real interest rates and the dangers of deflation. For a more general description of the Great Depression, see the references at the end of the box.

As you can see in the third column of the table, the Fed decreased the nominal interest rate, although it did this slowly. The nominal interest rate decreased from 5.3% in 1929 to 2.6% in 1933. At the same time, as shown in the fourth column, the decline in output and the increase in unemployment led to a sharp decrease in inflation. Inflation, equal to zero 1929, turned negative in 1930, reaching −9.2% in 1931, and −10.8% in 1932. If we make the assumption that expected deflation was equal to actual deflation in each year, we can construct a series for the real interest rate. This is done in the last column of the table and gives a hint for why output continued to decline until 1933. The real interest rate reached 12.3% in 1931, 14.8% in 1932, and still a very high 7.8% in 1933! It is no great surprise that, at those interest rates, both consumption and investment demand remained very low, and the depression got worse.

In 1933, the economy seemed to be in a deflation trap, with low activity leading to more deflation, a higher real interest rate, lower spending, and so on. Starting in 1934, however, deflation gave way to inflation, leading to a large decrease in the real interest rate, and the economy began to recover. Why, despite a very high unemployment rate, the U.S. economy was able to avoid further and further deflation remains a hotly debated issue in economics. Some point to a change in monetary policy, a very large increase in the money supply, leading to a change in inflation expectations. Others point to the policies of the New Deal, in particular the establishment of a minimum wage, thus limiting further wage decreases. Whatever the reason, this was the end of the deflation trap and the beginning of a long recovery.

Table 1	The Nominal Interest Rate, Inflation, and the Real Interest Rate, 1929–1933				
Year	Unemployment Rate (%)	Output Growth Rate (%)	One-Year Nominal Interest Rate (%) i	Inflation Rate (%) π	One-Year Real Interest Rate (%) r
1929	3.2	−9.8	5.3	0.0	5.3
1930	8.7	−7.6	4.4	−2.5	6.9
1931	15.9	−14.7	3.1	−9.2	12.3
1932	23.6	−1.8	4.0	−10.8	14.8
1933	24.9	9.1	2.6	−5.2	7.8

For more on the Great Depression:

Lester Chandler, *America's Greatest Depression* (Harper and Row, 1970), gives the basic facts. So does the book by John A. Garraty, *The Great Depression* (Harcourt Brace Jovanovich, 1986).
Did Monetary Forces Cause the Great Depression? (W.W. Norton, 1976), by Peter Temin, looks more specifically at the macroeconomic issues. So do the articles in a symposium on the Great Depression in the *Journal of Economic Perspectives*, Spring 1993.
For a look at the Great Depression in countries other than the United States, read Peter Temin's *Lessons from the Great Depression* (MIT Press, 1989).
A description of the Great Depression through the eyes of those who suffered through it is given in Studs Terkel, *Hard Times: An Oral History of the Great Depression in America* (Pantheon Books, 1970).

14-2 Nominal and Real Interest Rates, and the *IS–LM* Model

In the *IS–LM* model we developed in the core (Chapter 5), "the" interest rate came into play in two places: It affected investment in the *IS* relation, and it affected the choice between money and bonds in the *LM* relation. Which interest rate—nominal or real—were we talking about in each case?

- Take the *IS* relation first. Our discussion in Section 14-1 makes it clear that firms, in deciding how much investment to undertake, care about the *real interest rate*: Firms produce goods. They want to know how much they will have to repay, not in terms of dollars but in terms of goods. So what belongs in the *IS* relation is the real interest rate. Let r denote the real interest rate. The *IS* relation must therefore be modified to read:

$$Y = C(Y - T) + I(Y, r) + G \qquad (14.5)$$

> We shall ignore time subscripts here; they are not needed for this and the next section.

Investment spending, and thus the demand for goods, depends on the *real* interest rate.

> For the time being, we focus only on how the interest rate affects investment. In Chapter 16, you will see how the real interest rate affects both investment and consumption decisions. We also ignore the complications introduced in Chapter 9, such as the role of banks.

- Now turn to the *LM* relation. When we derived the *LM* relation, we assumed that the demand for money depended on the interest rate. But were we referring to the nominal interest rate or the real interest rate?

    The answer is: the *nominal interest rate*. Remember why the interest rate affects the demand for money. When people decide whether to hold money or bonds, they take into account the opportunity cost of holding money rather than bonds—the opportunity cost is what they give up by holding money rather than bonds. Money pays a zero nominal interest rate. Bonds pay a nominal interest rate of i. Hence, the opportunity cost of holding money is equal to the difference between the interest rate from holding bonds minus the interest from holding money, so $i - 0 = i$, which is just the nominal interest rate. Therefore, the *LM* relation is still given by

$$\frac{M}{P} = Y L(i)$$

Putting together the *IS* equation above with this equation and the relation between the real interest rate and the nominal interest rate, the extended *IS–LM* model is given by

$$\text{IS relation:} \quad Y = C(Y - T) + I(Y, r) + G$$

$$\text{LM relation:} \quad \frac{M}{P} = Y L(i)$$

$$\text{Real interest rate:} \quad r = i - \pi^e$$

Note an immediate implication of these three relations:

- The interest rate directly affected by monetary policy (the interest rate that enters the *LM* equation) is the nominal interest rate.

> Interest rate in the *LM* relation: Nominal interest rate, i.

- The interest rate that affects spending and output (the rate that enters the *IS* relation) is the real interest rate.

> Interest rate in the *IS* relation: Real interest rate, r.

- So, the effects of monetary policy on output depend therefore on how movements in the nominal interest rate translate into movements in the real interest rate. We saw an example of this complex relation in the Focus box on the Great Depression in the previous section. To explore the question further, the next section looks at how an increase in money growth affects the nominal interest rate and the real interest rate, both in the short run and in the medium run.

14-3 Money Growth, Inflation, Nominal and Real Interest Rates

"The Fed's decision to allow for higher money growth is the main factor behind the decline in interest rates in the last six months" (circa 1991).

The two economists were ▶
Alan Blinder, from Princeton,
and Janet Yellen, then from
Berkeley, now vice-chair of
the Fed. More on Alan Blinder
in a Focus box in Chapter 22.

"The nomination to the Board of the Federal Reserve of two left-leaning economists, both perceived to be soft on inflation, has led financial markets to worry about higher money growth, higher inflation, and higher interest rates in the future" (circa May 1994).

These two quotes are made up, but they are composites of what was written at the time. Which one is right? Does higher money growth lead to lower interest rates, or does higher money growth lead to higher interest rates? The answer: Both!

There are two keys to the answer: one, the distinction we just introduced between the real and the nominal interest rate; the other, the distinction between the short run and the medium run. As you shall see, the full answer is:

- Higher money growth leads to lower nominal interest rates in the short run but to higher nominal interest rates in the medium run.
- Higher money growth leads to lower real interest rates in the short run but has no effect on real interest rates in the medium run.

The purpose of this section is to develop this answer and explore its implications.

Revisiting the *IS–LM* Model

We have derived three equations—the *IS* relation, the *LM* relation, and the relation between the real and the nominal interest rate. It will be more convenient to reduce them to two equations. To do so, replace the real interest rate in the *IS* relation by the nominal interest rate minus expected inflation: $r = i - \pi^e$. This gives:

$$IS: \quad Y = C(Y - T) + I(Y, i - \pi^e) + G$$

$$LM: \quad \frac{M}{P} = YL(i)$$

These two equations are the same as in Chapter 5, with just one difference: Investment spending in the *IS* relation depends on the real interest rate, which is equal to the nominal interest rate minus expected inflation.

The associated *IS* and *LM* curves are drawn in Figure 14-3 for given values of P, M, G, and T and for a given expected rate of inflation, π^e.

- The *IS* curve is still downward sloping: For a given expected rate of inflation (π^e), the nominal interest rate and the real interest rate move together. So, a decrease in the nominal interest rate leads to an equal decrease in the real interest rate, leading to an increase in spending and in output.
- The *LM* curve is upward sloping: Given the money stock, an increase in output, which leads to an increase in the demand for money, requires an increase in the nominal interest rate.
- The equilibrium is at the intersection of the *IS* curve and the *LM* curve, point A, with output level Y_A, nominal interest rate i_A. Given the nominal interest rate, the real interest rate r_A is given by $r_A = i_A - \pi^e$.

Nominal and Real Interest Rates in the Short Run

Assume the economy is initially at the natural rate of output, so $Y_A = Y_n$. Now suppose the central bank increases the rate of growth of money. What happens to output, to the nominal interest rate, and to the real interest rate *in the short run*?

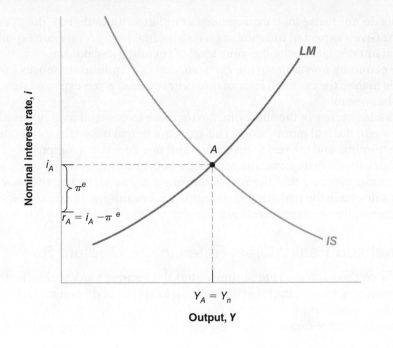

Figure 14-3

Equilibrium Output and Interest Rates

The equilibrium level of output and the equilibrium nominal interest rate are given by the intersection of the *IS* curve and the *LM* curve. The real interest rate equals the nominal interest rate minus expected inflation.

One of the lessons from our analysis of monetary policy in the core is that, in the short run, the faster increase in nominal money will not be matched by an equal increase in the price level. In other words, the higher rate of growth of nominal money will lead, in the short run, to an increase in the real money stock, (M/P). This is all we need to know for our purposes. What happens to output and to interest rates in the short run is shown in Figure 14-4.

The increase in the real money stock causes a shift in the *LM* curve down, from *LM* to *LM'*: For a given level of output, the increase in the real money stock leads to a decrease in the nominal interest rate. If we assume—as seems reasonable—that people

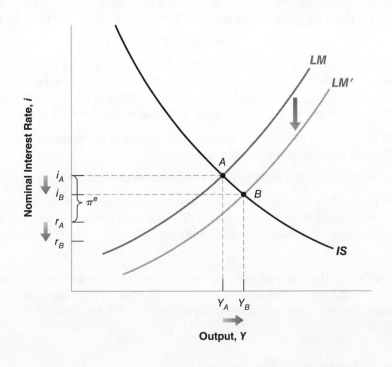

Figure 14-4

The Short-Run Effects of an Increase in Money Growth

An increase in money growth increases the real money stock in the short run. This increase in real money leads to an increase in output and decreases in both the nominal and real interest rates.

Can you tell what happens if, in addition, people revise their expectations of inflation upward?

and firms do not revise their expectations of inflation immediately, the *IS* curve does not shift: Given expected inflation, a given nominal interest rate corresponds to the same real interest rate and to the same level of spending and output.

In the short run, when the rate of money growth increases, M/P increases. Both i and r decrease and Y increases.

The economy moves down the *IS* curve, and the equilibrium moves from *A* to *B*. Output is higher, the nominal interest rate is lower, and, given expected inflation, so is the real interest rate.

Let's summarize: In the short run, the increase in nominal money growth leads to an increase in the real money stock. This increase in real money leads to a decrease in both the nominal and the real interest rates and to a decrease in output.

Go back to our first quote: The goal of the Fed, circa 1991, was precisely to achieve this outcome. Worried that the recession might deepen, the Fed increased money growth to decrease the real interest rate and increase output. (It worked, and reduced the length and depth of the recession.)

Nominal and Real Interest Rates in the Medium Run

Turn now to the *medium run*. Suppose that the central bank increases the rate of money growth permanently. What will happen to output and nominal and real interest rates in the medium run?

To answer this question, we can rely on two of the central propositions we derived in the core:

For a refresher, go back to Chapter 6, Section 6-5.

■ In the medium run, output returns to the natural level of output, Y_n. (We spent Chapters 10 to 13 looking at growth. For simplicity, here we will ignore output growth and assume that Y_n, the natural level of output, is constant over time.)

This has a straightforward implication for what happens to the real interest rate. To see why, return to the *IS* equation:

$$Y = C(Y - T) + I(Y, r) + G$$

One way of thinking about the *IS* relation is that it tells us, for given values of *G* and *T*, what real interest rate *r* is needed to sustain a given level of spending, and so a given level of output *Y*. If, for example, output is equal to the natural level of output Y_n, then, for given values of *G* and *T*, the real interest rate must be such that

$$Y_n = C(Y_n - T) + I(Y_n, r) + G$$

This is how it was called by Wicksell, a Swedish economist, at the turn of the twentieth century.

Since we used the word "natural" to denote the level of output in the medium run, let's similarly call this value of the real interest rate the **natural real interest rate** and denote it by r_n. Then our earlier proposition that, in the medium run, output returns to its natural level Y_n, has a direct implication for the real interest rate:

In the medium run, the real interest rate returns to the natural interest rate, r_n. It is independent of the rate of money growth.

For a refresher, go back to Chapter 8, Section 8-2.

■ In the medium run, the rate of inflation is equal to the rate of money growth.

These two propositions have a straightforward implication for what happens to the nominal interest rate in the medium run. To see why, recall the relation between the nominal interest rate and the real interest rate:

$$i = r + \pi^e$$

We saw that in the medium run, the real interest rate equals the natural interest rate, r_n. Also, in the medium run, expected inflation is equal to actual inflation (people cannot have incorrect expectations of inflation forever). It follows that

$$i = r_n + \pi$$

Now, because inflation is equal to money growth in the medium run, we get:

$$i = r_n + g_M$$

In the medium run, the nominal interest rate is equal to the natural real interest rate plus the rate of money growth. So, in the medium run, an increase in money growth leads to an equal increase in the nominal interest rate.

◄ This ignores output growth. If output is growing at rate g_Y, then the equation takes the form $i = r_n + g_M - g_Y$, where g_Y is the trend growth rate of output.

Let's summarize: In the medium run, money growth does not affect the real interest rate, but affects both inflation and the nominal interest rate one-for-one.

A permanent increase in nominal money growth of, say, 10%, is eventually reflected in a 10% increase in the inflation rate and a 10% increase in the nominal interest rate—leaving the real interest rate unchanged. This result—that, in the medium run, the nominal interest rate increases one-for-one with inflation—is known as the **Fisher effect**, or the **Fisher hypothesis**, after Irving Fisher, an economist at Yale University who first stated it and its logic at the beginning of the twentieth century.

◄ Irving Fisher, *The Rate of Interest* (New York: Macmillan 1906).

This result underlies the second quote we saw at the beginning of the section: If financial investors were worried that the appointment of new Board members at the Fed might lead to higher money growth, they were right to expect higher nominal interest rates in the future.

◄ In this case, their fears turned out to be unfounded. The Fed remained committed to low inflation. The issue, however, resurfaces regularly.

From the Short to the Medium Run

We have now seen how to reconcile the two quotes at the beginning of the section: An increase in monetary growth (a monetary expansion) leads to *a decrease* in nominal interest rates in the short run, but to *an increase* in nominal interest rates in the medium run.

What happens, however, between the short run and the medium run? A full characterization of the movements of the real interest rate and the nominal interest rate over time would take us beyond what we can do here. But the basic features of the adjustment process are easy to describe:

In the short run, the real interest rate and the nominal interest rate both go down. Why don't they stay down forever? Let us first state the answer in short: Because low interest rates lead to higher demand, which leads to higher output, which eventually leads to higher inflation; higher inflation leads in turn to a decrease in the real money stock and an increase in interest rates.

Now, the answer step by step:

■ So long as the real interest rate is below the natural real interest rate—that is, the value corresponding to the natural level of output—output is higher than the natural level of output, and unemployment is below its natural rate.

■ From the Phillips curve relation, we know that as long as unemployment is below the natural rate of unemployment, inflation increases.

■ As inflation increases, it eventually becomes higher than nominal money growth, leading to negative real money growth. When real money growth turns negative, the nominal interest rate starts increasing. And, given expected inflation, so does the real interest rate.

◄ Real money growth is nominal money growth minus inflation.
◄ Negative real money growth ⇔ Monetary contraction.

■ In medium run, the real interest rate increases back to its initial value. Output is then back to the natural level of output, unemployment is back to the natural rate of unemployment, and inflation is no longer changing. As the real interest rate converges back to its initial value, the nominal interest rate converges to a new higher value, equal to the real interest rate plus the new, higher, rate of nominal money growth.

Figure 14-5 summarizes these results by showing the adjustment over time of the real interest rate and the nominal interest rate to an increase in nominal money growth from, say, 0% to 10%, starting at time *t*. Before time *t*, both interest rates are constant

Figure 14-5

The Adjustment of the Real and the Nominal Interest Rates to an Increase in Money Growth

An increase in money growth leads initially to decreases in both the real and the nominal interest rates. Over time, however, the real interest rate returns to its initial value and the nominal interest rate rises to a new higher value, equal to the initial value plus the increase in money growth.

and equal to each other. The real interest rate is equal to r_n. The nominal interest rate is also equal to r_n (as inflation and expected inflation are equal to zero).

At time t, the rate of money growth increases from 0% to 10%. The increase in the rate of nominal money growth leads, for some time, to an increase in the real money stock and to a decrease in the nominal interest rate. As expected inflation increases, the decrease in the real interest rate is larger than the decrease of the nominal interest rate.

Eventually, the nominal interest rate and the real interest rate start increasing. In the medium run, the real interest rate returns to its initial value. Inflation and expected inflation converge to the new rate of money growth; in this case, 10%. The result is that the nominal interest rate rises to a value equal to the real interest rate plus 10%.

Evidence on the Fisher Hypothesis

There is plenty of evidence that a monetary expansion decreases nominal interest rates in the short run (see, for example, Chapter 5, Section 5-5). But how much evidence is there for the Fisher hypothesis, the proposition that, in the medium run, increases in inflation lead to one-for-one increases in nominal interest rates?

Economists have tried to answer this question by looking at two types of evidence. One is the relation between nominal interest rates and inflation *across countries*. Because the relation holds only in the medium run, we should not expect inflation and nominal interest rates to be close to each other in any one country at any one time, but the relation should hold on average. This approach is explored further in the Focus box "Nominal Interest Rates and Inflation across Latin America in the Early 1990s," which looks at Latin American countries during a period when they had high inflation and finds substantial support for the Fisher hypothesis.

The other type of evidence is the relation between the nominal interest rate and inflation over time in a given country. Again, the Fisher hypothesis does not imply that the two should move together from year to year. But it does suggest that the long swings in inflation should eventually be reflected in similar swings in the nominal interest rate. To see these long swings, we need to look at as long a period of time as we

Nominal Interest Rates and Inflation across Latin America in the Early 1990s

FOCUS

Figure 1 plots nominal interest rate–inflation pairs for eight Latin American countries (Argentina, Bolivia, Chile, Ecuador, Mexico, Peru, Uruguay, and Venezuela) for 1992 and for 1993—a period of high inflation in Latin America. Because the Brazilian numbers would dwarf those from other countries, they are not included in the figure. (In 1992, Brazil's annual inflation rate was 1,008% and its nominal interest rate was 1,560%. In 1993, inflation was 2,140% and the nominal interest rate was 3,240%!) The numbers for inflation refer to the rate of change of the consumer price index. The numbers for nominal interest rates refer to the "lending rate." The exact definition of the lending rate varies with each country, but you can think of it as corresponding to the prime interest rate in the United States—the rate charged to borrowers with the best credit rating.

Note the wide range of inflation rates, from 10% to about 100%. This is precisely why we have chosen to present numbers from Latin America in the early 1990s. With this much variation in inflation, we can learn a lot about the relation between nominal interest rates and inflation. And the figure indeed shows a clear relation between inflation and nominal interest rates. The line drawn in the figure plots what the nominal interest rate should be under the Fisher hypothesis, assuming an underlying real interest rate of 5%, so that $i = 5\% + \pi$. The slope of the line is one: Under the Fisher hypothesis, a 1% increase in inflation should be reflected in a 1% increase in the nominal interest rate.

As you can see, the line fits reasonably well, and roughly half of the points are above the line and the other half are below. The Fisher hypothesis appears roughly consistent with the cross-country evidence from Latin America in the early 1990s.

Figure 1 *Nominal Interest Rates and Inflation: Latin America, 1992–1993*

Source: IMF International Financial Statistics.

can. Figure 14-6 looks at the nominal interest rate and inflation in the United States since 1927. The nominal interest rate is the three-month Treasury bill rate, and inflation is the rate of change of the CPI.

Figure 14-6 has at least three interesting features:

■ The steady increase in inflation from the early 1960s to the early 1980s was associated with a roughly parallel increase in the nominal interest rate. The decrease in

Figure 14-6

The Treasury Bill Rate and Inflation in the United States since 1927

The increase in inflation from the early 1960s to the early 1980s was associated with an increase in the nominal interest rate. The decrease in inflation since the mid-1980s has been associated with a decrease in the nominal interest rate.

Source: Inflation from CPIAUNCS; three-month T-bill rate 1934–2010 Series TB3MS. Federal Reserve Economic Data (FRED) http://research.stlouisfed.org/fred2/. Prior to 1933, the interest rate is the three-month commercial paper rate, http://www.measuringworth.com/interestrates

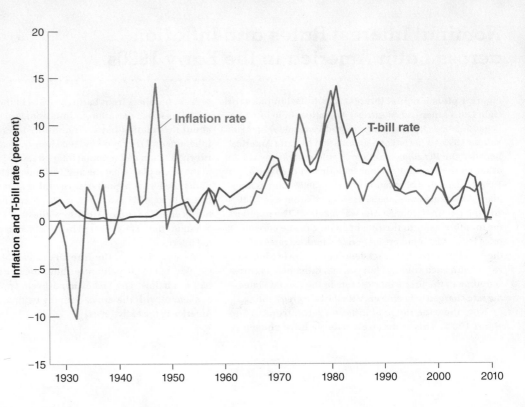

inflation since the mid-1980s has been associated with a decrease in the nominal interest rate. This evidence supports the Fisher hypothesis.

■ Evidence of the short-run effects that we discussed earlier is also easy to see. The nominal interest rate lagged behind the increase in inflation in the 1970s, while the disinflation of the early 1980s was associated with an initial *increase* in the nominal interest rate, followed by a much slower decline in the nominal interest rate than in inflation.

■ The other episode of inflation, during and after World War II, underscores the importance of the "medium run" qualifier in the Fisher hypothesis. During that period, inflation was high but short lived. And it was gone before it had time to be reflected in a higher nominal interest rate. The nominal interest rate remained very low throughout the 1940s.

▶ This was the result of a deliberate policy by the Fed to maintain a very low nominal interest rate with the goal of reducing interest payments on the large government debt created during World War II.

More careful studies confirm our basic conclusion. The Fisher hypothesis that, in the medium run, increases in inflation are reflected in a higher nominal interest rate, appears to fit the data quite well. But the adjustment takes a long time. The data confirm the conclusion reached by Milton Friedman, which we quoted in a Focus box in Chapter 8, that it typically takes a "couple of decades" for nominal interest rates to reflect the higher inflation rate.

14-4 Expected Present Discounted Values

Let us now turn to the second key concept introduced in this chapter, that of expected present discounted value.

To motivate our discussion, let's return to the example of the manager considering whether or not to buy a new machine. On the one hand, buying and installing the machine involves a cost today. On the other, the machine allows for higher production, higher sales, and higher profits in the future. The question facing the manager is whether the value of these expected profits is higher than the cost of buying and installing the machine. This is where the concept of expected present discounted value comes in handy: The **expected present discounted value** of a sequence of future payments is the value today of this expected sequence of payments. Once the manager has computed the expected present discounted value of the sequence of profits, her problem becomes simple. She compares two numbers, the expected present discounted value and the initial cost. If the value exceeds the cost, she should go ahead and buy the machine. If it does not, she should not.

As for the real interest rate, the practical problem is that expected present discounted values are not directly observable. They must be constructed from information on the sequence of expected payments and expected interest rates. Let's first look at the mechanics of construction.

Computing Expected Present Discounted Values

If the one-year nominal interest rate is i_t, lending one dollar this year implies getting back $1 + i_t$ dollars next year. Equivalently, borrowing one dollar this year implies paying back $1 + i_t$ dollars next year. In this sense, one dollar this year is worth $1 + i_t$ dollars next year. This relation is represented graphically in the first line of Figure 14-7.

Turn the argument around and ask: How much is one dollar *next year* worth this year? The answer, shown in the second line of Figure 14-7, is $1/(1 + i_t)$ dollars. Think of it this way: If you lend $1/(1 + i_t)$ dollars this year, you will receive $1/(1 + i_t)$ times $(1 + i_t) = 1$ dollar next year. Equivalently, if you borrow $1/(1 + i_t)$ dollars this year, you will have to repay exactly one dollar next year. So, one dollar next year is worth $1/(1 + i_t)$ dollars this year.

More formally, we say that $1/(1 + i_t)$ is the *present discounted value* of one dollar next year. The word "present" comes from the fact that we are looking at the value of a payment next year in terms of dollars *today*. The word "discounted" comes from the fact that the value next year is discounted, with $1/(1 + i_t)$ being the **discount factor** (The one-year nominal interest rate, i_t, is sometimes called the **discount rate**).

Because the nominal interest rate is always positive, the discount factor is always less than 1: A dollar next year is worth less than a dollar today. The higher the nominal interest rate, the lower the value today of a dollar received next year. If $i = 5$, the value this year of a dollar next year is $1/1.05 \approx 95$ cents. If $i = 10\%$ the value today of a dollar next year is $1/1.10 \approx 91$ cents.

◀ i_t: discount rate.
$1/(1 + i_t)$: discount factor.
If the discount rate goes up, the discount factor goes down.

Now apply the same logic to the value today of a dollar received *two years from now*. For the moment, assume that current and future one-year nominal interest rates are known with certainty. Let i_t be the nominal interest rate for this year, and i_{t+1} be the one-year nominal interest rate next year.

This year		Next year	2 years from now
\$1	→	\$$(1 + i_t)$	
\$$\dfrac{1}{1 + i_t}$	←	\$1	
\$1	→		\$$(1 + i_t)(1 + i_{t+1})$
\$$\dfrac{1}{(1 + i_t)(1 + i_{t+1})}$	←		\$1

Figure 14-7

Computing Present Discounted Values

If, today, you lend one dollar for two years, you will get $(1 + i_t)(1 + i_{t+1})$ dollars two years from now. Put another way, one dollar today is worth $(1 + i_t)(1 + i_{t+1})$ dollars two years from now. This relation is represented in the third line of Figure 14-7.

What is one dollar two years from now worth today? By the same logic as before, the answer is $1/(1 + i_t)(1 + i_{t+1})$ dollars: If you lend $1/(1 + i_t)(1 + i_{t+1})$ dollars this year, you will get exactly one dollar in two years. So: The *present discounted value of a dollar two years from now* is equal to $1/(1 + i_t)(1 + i_{t+1})$ dollars. This relation is shown in the last line of Figure 14-7. If, for example, the one-year nominal interest rate is the same this year and next and equal to 5%, so $i_t = i_{t+1} = 5$, then the present discounted value of a dollar in two years is equal to $1/(1.05)^2$ or about 91 cents today.

A General Formula

Having gone through these steps, it is easy to derive the present discounted value for the case where both payments and interest rates can change over time.

Consider a sequence of payments in dollars, starting today and continuing into the future. Assume for the moment that both future payments and future interest rates are known with certainty. Denote today's payment by $\$z_t$, the payment next year by $\$z_{t+1}$, the payment two years from today by $\$z_{t+2}$, and so on.

The present discounted value of this sequence of payments—that is, the value in today's dollars of the sequence of payments—which we shall call $\$V_t$ is given by

$$\$V_t = \$z_t + \frac{1}{(1 + i_t)} \$z_{t+1} + \frac{1}{(1 + i_t)(1 + i_{t+1})} \$z_{t+2} + \cdots$$

Each payment in the future is multiplied by its respective discount factor. The more distant the payment, the smaller the discount factor, and thus the smaller today's value of that distant payment. In other words, future payments are discounted more heavily, so their present discounted value is lower.

We have assumed that future payments and future interest rates were known with certainty. Actual decisions, however, have to be based on expectations of future payments rather than on actual values for these payments. In our earlier example, the manager cannot be sure of how much profit the new machine will actually bring; nor does she know what interest rates will be in the future. The best she can do is get the most accurate forecasts she can and then compute the *expected present discounted value* of profits based on these forecasts.

This statement ignores an important issue—risk. If people dislike risk, the value of an uncertain (and therefore risky) payment, now or in the future, will be lower than the value of a riskless payment, even if ▶ both have the same expected value. We ignore this effect here but briefly return to it in Chapter 15. For a full treatment, you would have to take a course in finance.

How do we compute the expected present discounted value when future payments and interest rates are uncertain? Basically in the same way as before, but by replacing the *known* future payments and *known* interest rates with *expected* future payments and *expected* interest rates. Formally: Denote expected payments next year by $\$z_{t+1}^e$, expected payments two years from now by $\$z_{t+2}^e$, and so on. Similarly, denote the expected one-year nominal interest rate next year by i_{t+1}^e, and so on (the one-year nominal interest rate this year, i_t, is known today, so it does not need a superscript e). The expected present discounted value of this expected sequence of payments is given by

$$\$V_t = \$z_t + \frac{1}{(1 + i_t)} \$z_{t+1}^e + \frac{1}{(1 + i_t)(1 + i_{t+1}^e)} \$z_{t+2}^e + \cdots \tag{14.6}$$

"Expected present discounted value" is a heavy expression to carry; instead, for short, we will often just use **present discounted value**, or even just **present value**. Also, it will be convenient to have a shorthand way of writing expressions like equation (14.6). To denote the present value of an expected sequence for $\$z$, we shall write $V(\$z_t)$, or just $V(\$z)$.

Using Present Values: Examples

Equation (14.6) has two important implications:

- The present value depends positively on today's actual payment and expected future payments. An increase in either today's z or any future z^e leads to an increase in the present value.

◀ $z or future z^e increase ⇒ $V increases.

- The present value depends negatively on current and expected future interest rates. An increase in either current i or in any future i^e leads to a decrease in the present value.

◀ i or future i^e increase ⇒ $V decreases.

Equation (14.6) is not simple, however, and so it will help to go through some examples.

Constant Interest Rates

To focus on the effects of the sequence of payments on the present value, assume that interest rates are expected to be constant over time, so that $i_t = i^e_{t+1} = \ldots$, and denote their common value by i. The present value formula—equation (14.6)—becomes

$$\$V_t = \$z_t + \frac{1}{(1+i)} \$z^e_{t+1} + \frac{1}{(1+i)^2} \$z^e_{t+2} + \cdots \tag{14.7}$$

In this case, the present value is a *weighted sum* of current and expected future payments, with weights that decline *geometrically* through time. The weight on a payment this year is 1, the weight on the payment n years from now is $(1/(1+i))^n$. With a positive interest rate, the weights get closer and closer to zero as we look further and further into the future. For example, with an interest rate equal to 10%, the weight on a payment 10 years from today is equal to $1/(1 + 0.10)^{10} = 0.386$, so that a payment of $1,000 in 10 years is worth $386 today. The weight on a payment in 30 years is $1/(1 + 0.10)^{30} = 0.057$, so that a payment of $1,000 thirty years from today is worth only $57 today!

◀ The weights correspond to the terms of a geometric series. See the discussion of geometric series in Appendix 2 at the end of the book.

Constant Interest Rates and Payments

In some cases, the sequence of payments for which we want to compute the present value is simple. For example, a typical fixed-rate, 30-year mortgage requires constant dollar payments over 30 years. Consider a sequence of equal payments—call them z without a time index—over n years, including this year. In this case, the present value formula in equation (14.7) simplifies to

$$\$V_t = \$z \left[1 + \frac{1}{(1+i)} + \cdots + \frac{1}{(1+i)^{n-1}} \right]$$

Because the terms in the expression in brackets represent a geometric series, we can compute the sum of the series and get

◀ By now, geometric series should not hold any secret, and you should have no problem deriving this relation. But if you do, see Appendix 2 at the end of the book.

$$\$V_t = \$z \frac{1 - [1/(1+i)^n]}{1 - [1/(1+i)]}$$

Suppose you have just won one million dollars from your state lottery and have been presented with a 6-foot $1,000,000 check on TV. Afterward, you are told that, to protect you from your worst spending instincts as well as from your many new "friends," the state will pay you the million dollars in equal yearly installments of $50,000 over the next 20 years. What is the present value of your prize today? Taking, for example, an interest rate of 6% per year, the preceding equation gives $V = \$50,000(0.688)/(0.057) =$ or about $608,000. Not bad, but winning the prize did not make you a millionaire.

◀ What is the present value if i equals 4%? 8%? (Answers: $706,000, $530,000)

Constant Interest Rates and Payments Forever

Most consols were bought back by the British government at the end of the nineteenth century and early twentieth century. A few are still around.

Let's go one step further and assume that payments are not only constant, but go on forever. Real-world examples are harder to come by for this case, but one example comes from nineteenth-century England, when the government issued *consols*, bonds paying a fixed yearly amount forever. Let $z be the constant payment. Assume that payments start next year, rather than right away as in the previous example (this makes for simpler algebra). From equation (14.7), we have

$$\$V_t = \frac{1}{(1 + i)} \$z + \frac{1}{(1 + i)^2} \$z + \cdots$$

$$= \frac{1}{(1 + i)} \left[1 + \frac{1}{(1 + i)} + \cdots \right] \$z$$

where the second line follows by factoring out $1/(1 + i)$. The reason for factoring out $1/(1 + i)$ should be clear from looking at the term in brackets: It is an infinite geometric sum, so we can use the property of geometric sums to rewrite the present value as

$$\$V_t = \frac{1}{1 + i} \frac{1}{(1 - (1/(1 + i)))} \$z$$

Or, simplifying (the steps are given in the application of Proposition 2 in Appendix 2 at the end of the book),

$$\$V_t = \frac{\$z}{i}$$

The present value of a constant sequence of payments $z is simply equal to the ratio of $z to the interest rate i. If, for example, the interest rate is expected to be 5% per year forever, the present value of a consol that promises $10 per year forever equals $10/0.05 = $200. If the interest rate increases and is now expected to be 10% per year forever, the present value of the consol decreases to $10/0.10 = $100.

Zero Interest Rates

Because of discounting, computing present discounted values typically requires the use of a calculator. There is, however, a case where computations simplify. This is the case where the interest rate is equal to zero: If $i = 0$, then $1/(1 + i)$ equals 1, and so does $(1/(1 + i)^n)$ for any power n. For that reason, the present discounted value of a sequence of expected payments is just the *sum* of those expected payments. Because the interest rate is in fact typically positive, assuming the interest rate is zero is only an approximation. But it is a very useful one for back-of-the-envelope computations.

Nominal versus Real Interest Rates, and Present Values

So far, we have computed the present value of a sequence of dollar payments by using interest rates in terms of dollars—nominal interest rates. Specifically, we have written equation (14.6):

$$\$V_t = \$z_t + \frac{1}{(1 + i_t)} \$z_{t+1}^e + \frac{1}{(1 + i_t)(1 + i_{t+1}^e)} \$z_{t+2}^e + \cdots$$

where $i_t, i_{t+1}^e, \ldots$ is the sequence of current and expected future nominal interest rates and $\$z_t, \$z_{t+1}^e, \$z_{t+2}^e, \ldots$ is the sequence of current and expected future dollar payments.

Suppose we want to compute instead the present value of a sequence of *real* payments—that is, payments in terms of a basket of goods rather than in terms of dollars. Following the same logic as before, we need to use the right interest rates for this case: namely interest rates in terms of the basket of goods— *real interest rates*. Specifically, we can write the present value of a sequence of real payments as

$$V_t = z_t + \frac{1}{(1 + r_t)} z_{t+1}^e + \frac{1}{(1 + r_t)(1 + r_{t+1}^e)} z_{t+2}^e + \cdots \qquad (14.8)$$

where $r_t, r_{t+1}^e, \ldots$ is the sequence of current and expected future real interest rates, $z_t, z_{t+1}^e, z_{t+2}^e, \ldots$ is the sequence of current and expected future real payments, and V_t is the real present value of future payments.

These two ways of writing the present value turn out to be equivalent. That is, the real value obtained by constructing $\$V_t$ using equation (14.6) and dividing by P_t, the price level, is equal to the real value V_t obtained from equation (14.8), so

$$\$V_t/P_t = V_t$$

> The proof is given in the appendix to this chapter. Go through it to test your understanding of the two tools introduced in this chapter: real interest rate versus nominal interest rate, and expected present values.

In words: We can compute the present value of a sequence of payments in two ways. One way is to compute it as the present value of the sequence of payments expressed in dollars, discounted using nominal interest rates, and then divided by the price level today. The other way is to compute it as the present value of the sequence of payments expressed in real terms, discounted using real interest rates. The two ways give the same answer.

Do we need both formulas? Yes. Which one is more helpful depends on the context:

Take bonds, for example. Bonds typically are claims to a sequence of nominal payments over a period of years. For example, a 10-year bond might promise to pay $50 each year for 10 years, plus a final payment of $1,000 in the last year. So when we look at the pricing of bonds in Chapter 15, we shall rely on equation (14.6) (which is expressed in terms of dollar payments) rather than on equation (14.8) (which is expressed in real terms).

But sometimes, we have a better sense of future expected real values than of future expected dollar values. You might not have a good idea of what your dollar income will be in 20 years: Its value depends very much on what happens to inflation between now and then. But you might be confident that your nominal income will increase by at least as much as inflation—in other words, that your real income will not decrease. In this case, using equation (14.6), which requires you to form expectations of future dollar income, will be difficult. However, using equation (14.8), which requires you to form expectations of future real income, may be easier. For this reason, when we discuss consumption and investment decisions in Chapter 16, we shall rely on equation (14.8) rather than equation (14.6).

We now have the tools we need to look at the role of expectations in the economy. This is what we do in the next three chapters.

Summary

- The nominal interest rate tells you how many dollars you need to repay in the future in exchange for one dollar today.
- The real interest rate tells you how many goods you need to repay in the future in exchange for one good today.
- The real interest rate is approximately equal to the nominal interest rate minus expected inflation.
- Investment decisions depend on the real interest rate. The choice between money and bonds depends on the nominal interest rate. Thus, the real interest rate enters the *IS* relation, while the nominal interest rate enters the *LM* relation.
- In the short run, an increase in money growth decreases both the nominal interest rate and the real interest rate.

  In the medium run, an increase in money growth has no effect on the real interest rate, but it increases the nominal interest rate one-for-one.

- The proposition that, in the medium run, changes in inflation are reflected one-for-one in changes in the nominal interest rate is known as the Fisher effect or the Fisher hypothesis. The empirical evidence suggests that, while it takes a long time, changes in inflation are eventually reflected in changes in the nominal interest rate.

- The expected present discounted value of a sequence of payments equals the value this year of the expected sequence of payments. It depends positively on current and future expected payments and negatively on current and future expected interest rates.

- When discounting a sequence of current and expected future nominal payments, one should use current and expected future nominal interest rates. In discounting a sequence of current and expected future real payments, one should use current and expected future real interest rates.

Key Terms

nominal interest rate, 292
real interest rate, 292
deflation trap, 296
natural interest rate, 300
Fisher effect, Fisher hypothesis, 301

expected present discounted value, 305
discount factor, 305
discount rate, 305
present discounted value, 306
present value, 306

Questions and Problems

QUICK CHECK
All Quick Check questions and problems are available on MyEconLab.

1. Using the information in this chapter, label each of the following statements true, false, or uncertain. Explain briefly.

a. As long as inflation remains roughly constant, the movements in the real interest rate are roughly equal to the movements in the nominal interest rate.

b. If inflation turns out to be higher than expected, the realized real cost of borrowing turns out to be lower than the real interest rate.

c. Looking across countries, the real interest rate is likely to vary much less than the nominal interest rate.

d. The real interest rate is equal to the nominal interest rate divided by the price level.

e. In the medium run, the real interest rate is not affected by money growth.

f. The Fisher effect states that in the medium run, the nominal interest rate is not affected by money growth.

g. The experience of Latin American countries in the early 1990s supports the Fisher hypothesis.

h. The value today of a nominal payment in the future cannot be greater than the nominal payment itself.

i. The real value today of a real payment in the future cannot be greater than the real payment itself.

2. For which of the problems listed in (a) through (c) would you want to use real payments and real interest rates, and for which would you want to use nominal payments and nominal interest rates to compute the expected present discounted value? In each case, explain why.

a. Estimating the present discounted value of the profits from an investment in a new machine.

b. Estimating the present value of a 20-year U.S. government bond.

c. Deciding whether to lease or buy a car.

3. Compute the real interest rate using the exact formula and the approximation formula for each set of assumptions listed in (a) through (c).

a. $i = 4\%$; $\pi^e = 2\%$

b. $i = 15\%$; $\pi^e = 11\%$

c. $i = 54\%$; $\pi^e = 46\%$

4. Nominal and real interest rates around the world

a. Can the nominal interest rate ever be negative? Explain.

b. Can the real interest rate ever be negative? Under what circumstances can it be negative? If so, why not just hold cash instead of bonds?

c. What are the effects of a negative real interest rate on borrowing and lending?

d. Find a recent issue of *The Economist* and look at the tables in the back (titled "Economic Indicators" and "Financial Indicators"). Use the three-month money market rate as the nominal interest rate, and the most recent three-month rate of change in consumer prices as the expected rate of inflation (both are in annual terms). Which countries have the lowest nominal interest rates? Which countries have the lowest real interest rates? Are these real interest rates close to being negative?

5. Regular IRAs versus Roth IRAs

You want to save $2,000 today for retirement in 40 years. You have to choose between the two plans listed in (i) and (ii).

i. Pay no taxes today, put the money in an interest-yielding account, and pay taxes equal to 25% of the total amount withdrawn at retirement. (In the United States, such an account is known as a regular individual retirement account, or IRA.)

ii. Pay taxes equivalent to 20% of the investment amount today, put the remainder in an interest-yielding account, and pay no taxes when you withdraw your funds at retirement. (In the United States, this is known as a Roth IRA.)

a. What is the expected present discounted value of each of these plans if the interest rate is 1%? 10%?

b. Which plan would you choose in each case?

6. *Approximating the price of long-term bonds*

The present value of an infinite stream of dollar payments of $z (that starts next year) is $z/i when the nominal interest rate, i, is constant. This formula gives the price of a consol—a bond paying a fixed nominal payment each year, forever. It is also a good approximation for the present discounted value of a stream of constant payments over long but not infinite periods, as long as i is constant. Let's examine how close the approximation is.

a. Suppose that $i = 10\%$. Let $\$z = 100$. What is the present value of the consol?

b. If $i = 10\%$, what is the expected present discounted value of a bond that pays $\$z$ over the next 10 years? 20 years? 30 years? 60 years? (*Hint*: Use the formula from the chapter but remember to adjust for the first payment.)

c. Repeat the calculations in (a) and (b) for $i = 2\%$ and $i = 5\%$.

7. *The Fisher hypothesis*

a. What is the Fisher hypothesis?

b. Does the experience of Latin American countries in the 1990s support or refute the Fisher hypothesis? Explain.

c. Look at the figure in the Focus box on Latin America. Note that the line drawn through the scatter of points does not go through the origin. Does the Fisher effect suggest that it should go through the origin? Explain.

d. Consider this statement: "If the Fisher hypothesis is true, then changes in the growth rate of the money stock translate one-for-one into changes in i, and the real interest rate is left unchanged. Thus, there is no room for monetary policy to affect real economic activity." Discuss.

DIG DEEPER

All Dig Deeper questions and problems are available on MyEconLab.

8. *When looking at the short run in Section 14-2, we showed how an increase in nominal money growth led to higher output, a lower nominal interest rate, and a lower real interest rate.*

The analysis in the text (as summarized in Figure 14-5) assumed that expected inflation, π^e, did not change in the short run. Let us now relax this assumption and assume that in the short run, both money growth and expected inflation increase.

a. Show how this effects the *IS* curve. Explain in words.

b. Show how this effects the *LM* curve. Explain in words.

c. How does this affect output and the nominal interest rate? Could the nominal interest rate end up higher—not lower—than before the change in money growth? Why?

d. Even if what happens to the nominal interest rate is ambiguous, can you tell what happens to the real interest rate? (*Hint*: What happens to output relative to Figure 14-4? What does this imply about what happens to the real interest rate?)

EXPLORE FURTHER

9. *Inflation-indexed bonds*

Some bonds issued by the U.S. Treasury make payments indexed to inflation. These inflation-indexed bonds compensate investors for inflation. Therefore, the current interest rates on these bonds are real interest rates—interest rates in terms of goods. These interest rates can be used, together with nominal interest rates, to provide a measure of expected inflation. Let's see how.

*Go to the Web site of the Federal Reserve Board and get the most recent statistical release listing interest rates (**www.federalreserve.gov/releases/h15/Current**). Find the current nominal interest rate on Treasury securities with a five-year maturity. Now find the current interest rate on "inflation-indexed" Treasury securities with a five-year maturity. What do you think participants in financial markets think the average inflation rate will be over the next five years?*

APPENDIX: Deriving the Expected Present Discounted Value Using Real or Nominal Interest Rates

This appendix shows that the two ways of expressing present discounted values, equations (14.6) and (14.8), are equivalent.

Equation (14.6) gives the present value as the sum of current and future expected *nominal payments*, discounted using current and future expected *nominal interest rates*:

$$\$V_t = \$z_t + \frac{1}{1 + i_t}\$z^e_{t+1}$$
$$+ \frac{1}{(1 + i_t)(1 + i^e_{t+1})}\$z^e_{t+2} + \cdots \quad (14.6)$$

Equation (14.8) gives the present value as the sum of current and future expected *real payments*, discounted using current and future expected *real interest rates*:

$$V_t = z_t + \frac{1}{1 + r_t}z^e_{t+1}$$
$$+ \frac{1}{(1 + r_t)(1 + r^e_{t+1})}z^e_{t+2} + \cdots \quad (14.8)$$

Divide both sides of equation (14.6) by the current price level, P_t. So:

$$\frac{\$V_t}{P_t} = \frac{\$z_t}{P_t} + \frac{1}{1 + i_t} \frac{\$z^e_{t+1}}{P_t}$$

$$+ \frac{1}{(1 + i_t)(1 + i^e_{t+1})} \frac{\$z^e_{t+2}}{P_t} + \cdots \quad (14.9)$$

Let's look at each term on the right side of equation (14.9) and show that it is equal to the corresponding term in equation (14.8):

■ Take the first term, $\$z_t/P_t$. Note $\$z_t/P_t = z_t$, the real value of the current payment. So, this term is the same as the first term on the right of equation (14.8).

■ Take the second term:

$$\frac{1}{1 + i_t} \frac{\$z^e_{t+1}}{P_t}$$

Multiply the numerator and the denominator by P^e_{t+1}, the price level expected for next year, to get:

$$\frac{1}{1 + i_t} \frac{P^e_{t+1}}{P_t} \frac{\$z^e_{t+1}}{P^e_{t+1}}$$

Note that the fraction on the right, $\$z^e_{t+1}/P^e_{t+1}$, is equal to z^e_{t+1}, the expected real payment at time $t + 1$. Note that the fraction in the middle, P^e_{t+1}/P_t, can be rewritten as $1 + [(P^e_{t+1} - P_t)/P_t]$. Using the definition of expected inflation as $(1 + \pi^e_{t+1})$ and the re-writing of the middle term, we arrive at:

$$\frac{(1 + \pi^e_{t+1})}{(1 + i_t)} z^e_{t+1}$$

Recall the relation among the real interest rate, the nominal interest rate, and expected inflation in equation (14.3) $(1 + r_t) = (1 + i_t)/(1 + \pi^e_{t+1})$. Using this relation in the previous equation gives:

$$\frac{1}{(1 + r_t)} z^e_{t+1}$$

This term is the same as the second term on the right side of equation (14.8).

■ The same method can be used to rewrite the other terms; make sure that you can derive the next one.

We have shown that the right sides of equations (14.8) and (14.9) are equal to each other. It follows that the terms on the left side are equal, so:

$$V_t = \frac{\$V_t}{P_t}$$

This says: The present value of current and future expected *real payments*, discounted using current and future expected *real interest rates* (the term on the left side), is equal to: The present value of current and future expected *nominal payments*, discounted using current and future expected *nominal interest rates*, divided by the current price level (the term on the left side).

Financial Markets and Expectations

Our focus throughout this chapter will be on the role expectations play in the determination of asset prices, from bonds, to stocks, to houses. There is a good reason this topic belongs in a macroeconomics textbook. As you will see, not only are these prices affected by current and expected future activity, but they in turn affect decisions that influence current economic activity. Understanding their determination is central to understanding fluctuations.

Section 15-1 looks at the determination of bond prices and bond yields. It shows how bond prices and yields depend on current and expected future short-term interest rates. It then shows how we can use the yield curve to learn about the expected course of future short–term interest rates.

Section 15-2 looks at the determination of stock prices. It shows how stock prices depend on current and expected future profits, as well as on current and expected future interest rates. It then discusses how movements in economic activity affect stock prices.

Section 15-3 looks more closely at two issues; first, the effect of perceptions of risk on asset prices; second, the relevance of fads and bubbles—episodes where asset prices (stock or house prices, in particular) appear to move for reasons unrelated to either current and expected future payments or interest rates.

15-1 Bond Prices and Bond Yields

Bonds differ in two basic dimensions:

- **Default risk**: The risk that the issuer of the bond (it could be a government or a company) will not pay back the full amount promised by the bond.
- **Maturity**: The length of time over which the bond promises to make payments to the holder of the bond. A bond that promises to make one payment of $1,000 in six months has a maturity of six months; a bond that promises to pay $100 per year for the next 20 years and a final payment of $1,000 at the end of those 20 years has a maturity of 20 years.

In this section, we shall leave risk aside and focus on maturity. Bonds of different maturities each have a price and an associated interest rate called the **yield to maturity**, or simply the **yield**. Yields on bonds with a short maturity, typically a year or less, are called *short-term interest rates*. Yields on bonds with a longer maturity are called *long-term interest rates*.

On any given day, we observe the yields on bonds of different maturities, and so we can trace graphically how the yield depends on the maturity of a bond. This relation between maturity and yield is called the **yield curve**, or the **term structure of interest rates** (the word "term" is synonymous with maturity). Figure 15-1 gives, for example, the term structure of U.S. government bonds on November 1, 2000, and the term structure of U.S. government bonds on June 1, 2001. The choice of the two dates is not accidental; why we chose them will become clear later.

Note that in Figure 15-1, on November 1, 2000, the yield curve was slightly downward-sloping, declining from a three-month interest rate of 6.2% to a 30-year interest rate of 5.8%. In other words, long-term interest rates were slightly lower than short-term interest rates. Note how, seven months later, on June 1, 2001, the yield curve was sharply upward sloping, increasing from a three-month interest rate of 3.5% to a 30-year interest rate of 5.7%. In other words, long-term interest rates were much higher than short-term interest rates.

Why was the yield curve downward sloping in November 2000 but upward sloping in June 2001? Put another way, why were long-term interest rates slightly lower than short-term interest rates in November 2000, but higher than short-term interest rates in June 2001? What were financial market participants thinking at each date? To answer these questions, and more generally to think about the determination of the

Do not worry: We am just introducing the terms here. They will be defined and explained later in this section as well as in the Focus box "The Vocabulary of Bond Markets." ▶

Term structure ≡ Yield curve. ▶

To find out what the yield ▶ curve for U.S bonds is at the time you read this chapter, go to yieldcurve.com and click on "yield curves." You will see the yield curves for both U.K. and U.S. bonds.

Figure 15-1

U.S. Yield Curves: November 1, 2000 and June 1, 2001

The yield curve, which was slightly downward sloping in November 2000, was sharply upward sloping seven months later.

Source: Series DGS1MO, DGS3MO, DGS6MO,DGS1,DGS2,DGS3,DGS5, DGS7,DGS10 DGS20,DGS30. Federal Reserve Economic Data (FRED) http://research.stlouisfed.org/fred2/)

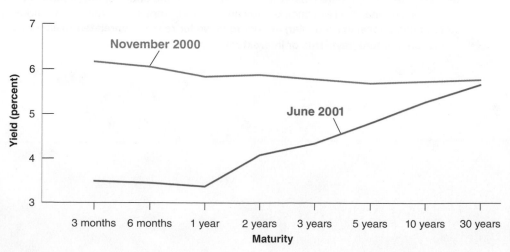

Expectations   **Extensions**

The Vocabulary of Bond Markets

Understanding the basic vocabulary of financial markets will help make them less mysterious. Here is a basic vocabulary review.

- Bonds are issued by governments or by firms. If issued by the government or government agencies, the bonds are called **government bonds**. If issued by firms (corporations), they are called **corporate bonds**.

- Bonds are rated for their default risk (the risk that they will not be repaid) by rating agencies. The two major rating agencies are the Standard and Poor's Corporation (S&P) and Moody's Investors Service. Moody's bond ratings range from Aaa for bonds with nearly no risk of default, to C for bonds where the default risk is high. In August 2011, Standard and Poor's downgraded U.S. government bonds from Aaa to AA+, reflecting their worry about the large budget deficits. This downgrade created a strong controversy. A lower rating typically implies that the bond has to pay a higher interest rate, or else investors will not buy it. The difference between the interest rate paid on a given bond and the interest rate paid on the bond with the highest (best) rating is called the **risk premium** associated with the given bond. Bonds with high default risk are sometimes called **junk bonds**.

- Bonds that promise a single payment at maturity are called **discount bonds**. The single payment is called the **face value** of the bond.

- Bonds that promise multiple payments before maturity and one payment at maturity are called **coupon bonds**. The payments before maturity are called **coupon payments**. The final payment is called the face value of the bond. The ratio of coupon payments to the face value is called the **coupon rate**. The **current yield** is the ratio of the coupon payment to the price of the bond.

  For example, a bond with coupon payments of $5 each year, a face value of $100, and a price of $80 has a coupon rate of 5% and a current yield of $5/80 = 0.0625 = 6.25\%$. From an economic viewpoint, neither the coupon rate nor the current yield are interesting measures. The correct measure of the interest rate on a bond is its yield to maturity, or simply **yield**; you can think of it as roughly the average interest rate paid by the bond over its life (the life of a bond is the amount of time left until the bond matures). We shall define the yield to maturity more precisely later in this chapter.

- U.S. government bonds range in maturity from a few days to 30 years. Bonds with a maturity of up to a year when they are issued are called **Treasury bills**, or **T-bills**. They are discount bonds, making only one payment at maturity. Bonds with a maturity of 1 to 10 years when they are issued are called **Treasury notes**. Bonds with a maturity of 10 or more years when they are issued are called **Treasury bonds**. Both Treasury notes and Treasury bonds are coupon bonds.

- Bonds are typically nominal bonds: They promise a sequence of fixed nominal payments—payments in terms of domestic currency. There are, however, other types of bonds. Among them are **indexed bonds**, bonds that promise payments adjusted for inflation rather than fixed nominal payments. Instead of promising to pay, say, 100 dollars in a year, a one-year indexed bond promises to pay $100(1 + \pi)$ dollars, whatever π, the rate of inflation that will take place over the coming year, turns out to be. Because they protect bondholders against the risk of inflation, indexed bonds are popular in many countries. They play a particularly important role in the United Kingdom, where, over the last 20 years, people have increasingly used them to save for retirement. By holding long-term indexed bonds, people can make sure that the payments they receive when they retire will be protected from inflation. Indexed bonds (called **Treasury Inflation Protected Securities**, or **TIPS** for short) were introduced in the United States in 1997.

---

yield curve and the relation between short-term interest rates and long-term interest rates, we proceed in two steps.

1. First, we derive *bond prices* for bonds of different maturities.

2. Second, we go from bond prices to *bond yields*, and examine the determinants of the yield curve and the relation between short-term and long-term interest rates.

Bond Prices as Present Values

In much of this section, we shall look at just two types of bonds, a bond that promises one payment of $100 in one year—a one-year bond—and a bond that promises one payment of $100 in two years—a two–year bond. Once you understand how their

Note that both bonds are *discount bonds* (see the Focus box "The Vocabulary of Bond Markets").

prices and yields are determined, it will be easy to generalize our results to bonds of any maturity. We shall do so later.

Let's start by deriving the prices of the two bonds.

■ Given that the one-year bond promises to pay $100 next year, it follows from Section 14-4 that its price, call it P_{1t}, must be equal to the present value of a payment of $100 next year. Let the current one-year nominal interest rate be i_{1t}. Note that we now denote the one-year interest rate in year t by i_{1t} rather than simply by i_t as we did in earlier chapters. This is to make it easier for you to remember that it is the *one-year* interest rate. So,

$$\$P_{1t} = \frac{\$100}{1 + i_{1t}} \tag{15.1}$$

We already saw this relation in Chapter 4, Section 4-2.

The price of the one-year bond varies inversely with the current one-year nominal interest rate.

■ Given that the two-year bond promises to pay $100 in two years, its price, call it P_{2t}, must be equal to the present value of $100 two years from now:

$$\$P_{2t} = \frac{\$100}{(1 + i_{1t})(1 + i_{1t+1}^e)} \tag{15.2}$$

where i_{1t} denotes the one-year interest rate this year and i_{1t+1}^e denotes the one-year rate expected by financial markets for next year. The price of the two-year bond depends inversely on both the current one-year rate and the one-year rate expected for next year.

Arbitrage and Bond Prices

Before further exploring the implications of equations (15.1) and (15.2), let us look at an alternative derivation of equation (15.2). This alternative derivation will introduce you to the important concept of **arbitrage**.

Suppose you have the choice between holding one-year bonds or two-year bonds and what you care about is how much you will have one year from today. Which bonds should you hold?

■ Suppose you hold one-year bonds. For every dollar you put in one-year bonds, you will get $(1 + i_{1t})$ dollars next year. This relation is represented in the first line of Figure 15-2.

■ Suppose you hold two-year bonds. Because the price of a two-year bond is P_{2t}, every dollar you put in two-year bonds buys you $\$1/\$P_{2t}$ bonds today.

When next year comes, the bond will have only one more year before maturity. Thus, one year from today, the two-year bond will now be a one-year bond. Therefore the price at which you can expect to sell it next year is $\$P_{1t+1}^e$, which is the expected price of a one-year bond next year.

So for every dollar you put in two-year bonds, you can expect to receive $\$1/\$P_{2t}$ times $\$P_{1t+1}^e$, or, equivalently, $\$P_{1t+1}^e/\$P_{2t}$ dollars next year. This is represented in the second line of Figure 15-2.

Which bonds should you hold? Suppose you, and other financial investors, care *only* about the expected return. (This assumption is known as the **expectations hypothesis**. It is a strong simplification: You, and other financial investors, are likely to care not only about the expected return, but also about the risk associated with holding each bond. If you hold a one-year bond, you know with certainty what you will get next year. If you hold a two-year bond, the price at which you will sell it next year is

316   Expectations   Extensions

uncertain; holding the two-year bond for one year is risky. We will disregard this for now but come back to it later.)

Under the assumption that you, and other financial investors, care only about expected return, it follows that the two bonds must offer the same expected one-year return. Suppose this condition was not satisfied. Suppose that, for example, the one-year return on one-year bonds was lower than the expected one-year return on two-year bonds. In this case, no one would want to hold the existing supply of one-year bonds, and the market for one-year bonds could not be in equilibrium. Only if the expected one-year return is the same on both bonds will financial investors be willing to hold both one-year bonds and two-year bonds.

If the two bonds offer the same expected one-year return, it follows from Figure 15-2 that

$$1 + i_{1t} = \frac{\$P^e_{1t+1}}{\$P_{2t}} \tag{15.3}$$

The left side of the equation gives the return per dollar from holding a one-year bond for one year; the right side gives the expected return per dollar from holding a two-year bond for one year. We shall call equations such as (15.3)—equations that state that the expected returns on two assets must be equal— *arbitrage* relations. Rewrite equation (15.3) as

$$\$P_{2t} = \frac{\$P^e_{1t+1}}{1 + i_{1t}} \tag{15.4}$$

Arbitrage implies that the price of a two-year bond today is the present value of the expected price of the bond next year. This raises the next question: What does the expected price of one-year bonds next year ($\$P^e_{1t+1}$) depend on?

The answer is straightforward. Just as the price of a one-year bond this year depends on this year's one-year interest rate, the price of a one-year bond next year will depend on the one-year interest rate next year. Writing equation (15.1) for next year (year $t + 1$) and denoting expectations in the usual way, we get

$$\$P^e_{1t+1} = \frac{\$100}{(1 + i^e_{1t+1})}$$

The price of the bond next year is expected to equal the final payment, $100, discounted by the one-year interest rate expected for next year.

Replacing $\$P^e_{1t+1}$ by $\$100/(1 + i^e_{1t+1})$ in equation (15.4) gives

$$\$P_{2t} = \frac{\$100}{(1 + i_{1t})(1 + i^e_{1t+1})} \tag{15.5}$$

This expression is the same as equation (15.2). What we have shown is that *arbitrage* between one- and two-year bonds implies that the price of two-year bonds is the *present value* of the payment in two years, namely $100, discounted using current and next year's expected one-year interest rates.

We use "arbitrage" to denote the proposition that expected returns on two assets must be equal. Some economists reserve "arbitrage" for the narrower proposition that *riskless* profit opportunities do not go unexploited.

The relation between arbitrage and present values: Arbitrage between bonds of different maturities implies that bond prices are equal to the expected present values of payments on these bonds.

From Bond Prices to Bond Yields

Having looked at bond prices, we now go on to bond yields. The basic point: Bond yields contain the same information about future expected interest rates as bond prices. They just do so in a much clearer way.

To begin, we need a definition of the yield to maturity: The *yield to maturity* on an *n*-year bond, or, equivalently, the **n-year interest rate**, is defined as that constant annual interest rate that makes the bond price today equal to the present value of future payments on the bond.

This definition is simpler than it sounds. Take, for example, the two-year bond we introduced earlier. Denote its yield by i_{2t}, where the subscript 2 is there to remind us that this is the *yield to maturity* on a two-year bond, or, equivalently, the two-year interest rate. Following the definition of the yield to maturity, this yield is the constant annual interest rate that would make the present value of $100 in two years equal to the price of the bond today. So, it satisfies the following relation:

$$\$P_{2t} = \frac{\$100}{(1 + i_{2t})^2} \tag{15.6}$$

Suppose the bond sells for $90 today. Then, the two-year interest rate i_{2t} is given by $\sqrt{100/90} - 1$, or 5.4%. In other words, holding the bond for two years—until maturity—yields an interest rate of 5.4% per year.

What is the relation of the two-year interest rate to the current one-year interest rate and the expected one-year interest rate? To answer this question, look at equation (15.6) and equation (15.5). Eliminating $\$P_{2t}$ between the two gives

$$\frac{\$100}{(1 + i_{2t})^2} = \frac{\$100}{(1 + i_{1t})(1 + i^e_{1t+1})}$$

Rearranging,

$$(1 + i_{2t})^2 = (1 + i_{1t})(1 + i^e_{1t+1})$$

This gives us the exact relation between the two-year interest rate i_{2t}, the current one-year interest rate i_{1t}, and next year's expected one-year interest rate i^e_{t+1}. A useful approximation to this relation is given by

$$i_{2t} \approx \frac{1}{2}(i_{1t} + i^e_{1t+1}) \tag{15.7}$$

Equation (15.7) simply says that *the two-year interest rate is (approximately) the average of the current one-year interest rate and next year's expected one-year interest rate.*

We have focused on the relation between the prices and yields of one-year and two-year bonds. But our results generalize to bonds of any maturity. For instance, we could have looked at bonds with maturities of less than a year. To take an example: The yield on a bond with a maturity of six months is (approximately) equal to the average of the current three-month interest rate and next quarter's expected three-month interest rate. Or, we could have looked instead at bonds with maturities longer than two years. For example, the yield on a 10-year bond is (approximately) equal to the average of the current one-year interest rate and the one-year interest rates expected for the next nine years.

The general principle is clear: Long-term interest rates reflect current and future expected short-term interest rates.

(margin note left of text, beside the $90 example):

$\$90 = \$100/(1 + i_{2t})^2 \Rightarrow$
$(1 + i_{2t})^2 = \$100/\$90 \Rightarrow$
$(1 + i_{2t}) = \sqrt{\$100/\$90} \Rightarrow$
$i_{2t} = 5.4\%$

(margin note): We used a similar approximation when we looked at the relation between the nominal interest rate and the real interest rate in Chapter 14. See Proposition 3 in Appendix 2.

Interpreting the Yield Curve

The relations we just derived tell us what we need to interpret the slope of the yield curve. By looking at yields for bonds of different maturities, we can infer what financial markets expect short-term interest rates will be in the future.

Suppose we want to find out for example what financial markets expect the one-year interest rate to be one year from now. All we need to do is to look at the yield on a two-year bond, i_{2t}, and the yield on a one-year bond, i_{1t}. From equation (15.7), multiplying both sides by 2 and reorganizing, we get

$$i_{1t+1}^e = 2i_{2t} - i_{1t} \tag{15.8}$$

The one-year interest rate expected for next year is equal to twice the yield on a two-year bond minus the current one-year interest rate. Take, for example, the yield curve for June 1, 2001 shown in Figure 15-1.

On June 1, 2001, the one-year interest rate, i_{1t}, was 3.4%, and the two-year interest rate, i_{2t}, was 4.1%. From equation (15.8), it follows that, on June 1, 2001, financial markets expected the one-year interest rate one year later—that is, the one-year interest rate on June 1, 2002—to equal $2 \times 4.1\% - 3.4\% = 4.8\%$—that is, 1.4% higher than the one-year interest rate on June 1, 2001. In words: On June 1, 2001, financial markets expected the one-year interest rate to be substantially higher one year later.

More generally: When the yield curve is upward sloping—that is, when long-term interest rates are higher than short-term interest rates—this tells us that financial markets expect short-term rates to be higher in the future. When the yield curve is downward sloping—that is, when long-term interest rates are lower than short-term interest rates—this tells us that financial markets expect short-term interest rates to be lower in the future.

The Yield Curve and Economic Activity

We can now return to the question: Why did the yield curve go from being downward sloping in November 2000 to being upward sloping in June 2001? Put another way, why did long-term interest rates go from being lower than short-term interest rates in November 2000 to much higher than short-term interest rates in June 2001?

First, the answer in short: Because an unexpected slowdown in economic activity in the first half of 2001 led to a sharp decline in short-term interest rates. And because, even as the slowdown was taking place, financial markets expected output to recover and expected short-term interest rates to return to higher levels in the future, leading long-term interest rates to fall by much less than short-term interest rates.

To go through the answer step by step, let's use the *IS–LM* model we developed in the core (Chapter 5). Think of the interest rate measured on the vertical axis as a short-term nominal interest rate. And to keep things simple, let's assume that expected inflation is equal to zero, so we do not have to worry about the distinction between the nominal and real interest rate we introduced in Chapter 14. This distinction is not central here.

Go back to November 2000. At that time, economic indicators suggested that, after many years of high growth, the U.S. economy had started to slow down. This slowdown was perceived as largely for the better: Most economists believed output was above the natural level of output (equivalently, that the unemployment rate was below the natural rate), so a mild slowdown was desirable. And the forecasts were indeed for a mild slowdown, or what was called a **soft landing** of output back to the natural level of output.

The economic situation at the time is represented in Figure 15-3. The U.S. economy was at a point such as *A*, with interest rate *i* and output *Y*. The level of output, *Y*,

We shall extend the *IS–LM* model in Chapter 17 to explicitly take into account what we have learned about the role of expectations on decisions. For the moment, the basic *IS–LM* model will do.

It would be easy (and more realistic) to allow for constant but positive (rather than zero) expected inflation. The conclusions would be the same.

You may want to reread the box on the 2001 recession in Chapter 5.

Figure 15-3

The U.S. Economy as of November 2000

In November 2000, the U.S. economy was operating above the natural level of output. Forecasts were for a "soft landing," a return of output to the natural level of output and a small decrease in interest rates.

was believed to be above the natural level of output Y_n. The forecasts were that the *IS* curve would gradually shift to the left, from *IS* to *IS'*, leading to a return of output to the natural level of output Y_n and a small decrease in the interest rate from *i* to *i'*. This small expected decrease in the interest rate was the reason why the yield curve was slightly downward sloping in November 2000.

Forecasts for a mild slowdown turned out, however, to be too optimistic. Beginning in late 2000, the economic situation was worse than had been forecast. What happened is represented in Figure 15-4. There were two major developments:

■ The adverse shift in spending was stronger than had been expected. Instead of shifting from *IS* to *IS'* as forecast (see Figure 15-3), the *IS* curve shifted by much more, from *IS* to *IS"* in Figure 15-4. Had monetary policy remained unchanged, the economy would have moved along the *LM* curve and the equilibrium would have moved from *A* to *B*, leading to a decrease in output and a decrease in the short-term interest rate.

■ There was more, however, at work. Realizing that the slowdown was stronger than it had anticipated, the Fed shifted in early 2001 to a policy of monetary

Figure 15-4

The U.S. Economy from November 2000 to June 2001

From November 2000 to June 2001, an adverse shift in spending, together with a monetary expansion, combined to lead to a decrease in the short-term interest rate.

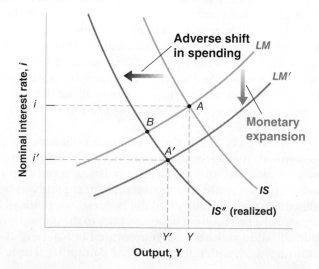

Expectations   **Extensions**

expansion, leading to a downward shift in the *LM* curve. As a result of this shift in the *LM* curve, the economy was, in June 2001, at a point like *A'*—rather than at point like *B*. Output was higher and the interest rate was lower than they would have been in the absence of the monetary expansion.

In words: The decline in short-term interest rates—and therefore the decline at the short-term end of the yield curve from November 1, 2000 to June 1, 2001—was the result of an unexpectedly large adverse shift in spending, combined with a strong response by the Fed aimed at limiting the size of the decrease in output. This still leaves one question. Why was the yield curve upward sloping in June 2001? Equivalently: Why were long-term interest rates higher than short-term interest rates?

To answer this question, we must look at what the markets *expected* to happen to the U.S. economy in the future, as of June 2001. This is represented in Figure 15-5. Financial markets expected two main developments:

■ They expected a pickup in spending—a shift of the *IS* curve to the right, from *IS* to *IS'*. The reasons: Some of the factors that had contributed to the adverse shift in the first half of 2001 were expected to turn more favorable. Investment spending was expected to rise. Also, the tax cut passed in May 2001, to be implemented over the rest of the year, was expected to lead to higher consumption spending.

■ They also expected that, once the *IS* curve started shifting to the right and output started to recover, the Fed would start shifting back to a tighter monetary policy. In terms of Figure 15-5, they expected the *LM* curve to shift up.

As a result of both shifts, financial markets expected the U.S. economy to move from point *A* to point *A'*; they expected both output to recover and short-term interest rates to increase. The anticipation of higher short-term interest rates was the reason why long-term interest rates remained high, and why the yield curve was upward sloping in June 2001.

Note that the yield curve in June 2001 was nearly flat for maturities up to one year. This tells us that financial markets did not expect interest rates to start rising until a year hence; that is, before June 2002. Did they turn out to be right? Not quite. The Fed did not increase the short-term interest rate until June 2004—fully two years later than financial markets had anticipated.

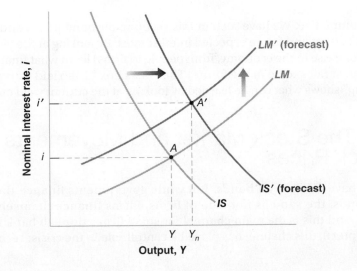

Figure 15-5

The Expected Path of the U.S. Economy as of June 2001

In June 2001, financial markets expected stronger spending and tighter monetary policy to lead to higher short-term interest rates in the future.

The Yield Curve and the Liquidity Trap

Figure 1 shows the yield curve as of July 2011. At the short end, the T-bill rate is nearly equal to zero: As we saw in Chapter 9, this reflects the fact that the Fed has decreased the nominal interest rate as far as it could, namely zero, and the U.S. economy is now in the liquidity trap. What the yield curve tells us is that financial markets expect this to remain the case for

many years: The one-year rate is equal to 0.10%, the two-year rate equal to 0.20%, the three-year rate is less than 1%. Only when we look at 10-year and 30-year horizons do the rates go up. In short: Financial markets believe that the U.S. economy will remain weak, and thus the Fed will keep the nominal interest rate very low for a long time to come.

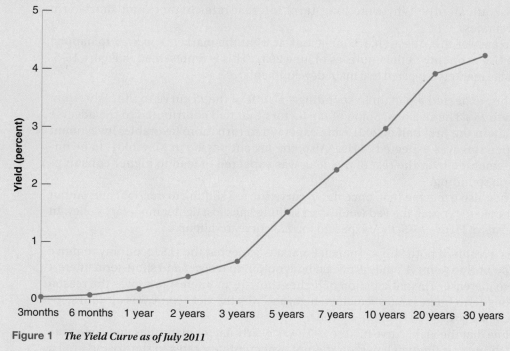

Figure 1 *The Yield Curve as of July 2011*

Source: Series DGS1MO, DGS3MO, DGS6MO, DGS1, DGS2, DGS3, DGS5, DGS7, DGS10, DGS20, DGS30. Federal Reserve Economic Data (FRED) http://research.stlouisfed.org/fred2/

Let's summarize. We have seen in this section how bond prices and bond yields depend on current and future expected interest rates. By looking at the yield curve, we (and everyone else in the economy, from people to firms) learn what financial markets expect interest rates to be in the future. The Focus box "The Yield Curve and the Liquidity Trap" shows what can be learned by looking at the current yield curve.

15-2 The Stock Market and Movements in Stock Prices

So far, we have focused on bonds. But while governments finance themselves by issuing bonds, the same is not true of firms. Firms finance themselves in three ways. First, and this is the main channel for small firms, through bank loans. As we saw in Chapter 9, this channel has played a central role in the crisis; second, through

Figure 15-6

Standard and Poor's Stock Price Index, in Real Terms, since 1970

Note the sharp fluctuations in stock prices since the mid 1990s.

Source: Calculated using series SP500 and CPIAUSCL, Federal Reserve Economic Data (FRED) http://research.stlouisfed.org/fred2/

debt finance—bonds and loans; and third, through **equity finance**, issuing **stocks**—or **shares**, as stocks are also called. Instead of paying predetermined amounts as bonds do, stocks pay **dividends** in an amount decided by the firm. Dividends are paid from the firm's profits. Typically dividends are less than profits, as firms retain some of their profits to finance their investment. But dividends move with profits: When profits increase, so do dividends.

Our focus in this section will be on the determination of stock prices. As a way of introducing the issues, let's look at the behavior of an index of U.S. stock prices, the *Standard & Poor's 500 Composite Index* (or the S&P index for short) since 1980. Movements in the S&P index measure movements in the average stock price of 500 large companies.

Figure 15-6 plots the real stock price index, constructed by dividing the S&P index by the CPI for each month and normalizing so the index is equal to 1 in 1970. The striking feature of the figure is obviously the sharp movements in the value of the index. Note how the index went up from 1.4 in 1995 to 4.0 in 2000, only to decline sharply to reach 2.1 in 2003. Note how, in the recent crisis, the index declined from 3.4 in 2007 to 1.7 in 2009, only to recover partly since then. What determines these sharp movement in stock prices; how do stock prices respond to changes in the economic environment and macroeconomic policy? These are the questions we take up in the this and the next section.

Another and better-known index is the *Dow Jones Industrial Index*, an index of stocks of industrial firms only and therefore less representative of the average price of stocks than is the S&P index. Similar indexes exist for other countries. The *Nikkei Index* reflects movements in stock prices in Tokyo, and the *FT* and *CAC40* indexes reflect stock price movements in London and Paris, respectively.

Stock Prices as Present Values

What determines the price of a stock that promises a sequence of dividends in the future? By now, we are sure the material in Chapter 14 has become second nature, and you already know the answer: The stock price must equal the present value of future expected dividends.

Figure 15-7

*Returns from Holding
One-Year Bonds or Stocks
for One Year*

Just as we did for bonds, let's derive this result from looking at the implications of arbitrage between one-year bonds and stocks. Suppose you face the choice of investing either in one-year bonds or in stocks for a year. What should you choose?

■ Suppose you decide to hold one-year bonds. Then, for every dollar you put in one-year bonds, you will get $(1 + i_{1t})$ dollars next year. This payoff is represented in the upper line of Figure 15-7.

■ Suppose you decide instead to hold stocks for a year. Let $\$Q_t$ be the price of the stock. Let $\$D_t$ denote the dividend this year, $\$D_{t+1}^e$ the expected dividend next year. Suppose we look at the price of the stock after the dividend has been paid this year—this price is known as the **ex-dividend price**—so that the first dividend to be paid after the purchase of the stock is next year's dividend. (This is just a matter of convention; we could alternatively look at the price before this year's dividend has been paid. What term would we have to add?)

Holding the stock for a year implies buying a stock today, receiving a dividend next year, and then selling the stock. As the price of a stock is $\$Q_t$, every dollar you put in stocks buys you $\$1/\$Q_t$ stocks. And for each stock you buy, you expect to receive $(\$D_{t+1}^e + \$Q_{t+1}^e)$, the sum of the expected dividend and the stock price next year. Therefore, for every dollar you put in stocks, you expect to receive $(\$D_{t+1}^e + \$Q_{t+1}^e)/\$Q_t$. This payoff is represented in the lower line of Figure 15-7.

> This ignores the fact that holding a stock is more risky than holding a bond. We take this up in the next section. ▶

Let's use the same arbitrage argument we used for bonds earlier. Assume financial investors care only about expected rates of return. Equilibrium then requires that the expected rate of return from holding stocks for one year be the same as the rate of return on one-year bonds:

$$\frac{(\$D_{t+1}^e + \$Q_{t+1}^e)}{\$Q_t} = 1 + i_{1t}$$

Rewrite this equation as

$$\$Q_t = \frac{\$D_{t+1}^e}{(1 + i_{1t})} + \frac{\$Q_{t+1}^e}{(1 + i_{1t})} \tag{15.9}$$

Arbitrage implies that the price of the stock today must be equal to the present value of the expected dividend plus the present value of the expected stock price next year.

The next step is to think about what determines $\$Q_{t+1}^e$, the expected stock price next year. Next year, financial investors will again face the choice between stocks and one-year bonds. Thus, the same arbitrage relation will hold. Writing the previous equation, but now for time $t + 1$, and taking expectations into account gives

$$\$Q_{t+1}^e = \frac{\$D_{t+2}^e}{(1 + i_{1t+1}^e)} + \frac{\$Q_{t+2}^e}{(1 + i_{1t+1}^e)}$$

The expected price next year is simply the present value next year of the sum of the expected dividend and price two years from now. Replacing the expected price $\$Q_{t+1}^e$ in equation (15.9) gives

$$\$Q_t = \frac{\$D_{t+1}^e}{(1 + i_{1t})} + \frac{\$D_{t+2}^e}{(1 + i_{1t})(1 + i_{1t+1}^e)} + \frac{\$Q_{t+2}^e}{(1 + i_{1t})(1 + i_{1t+1}^e)}$$

The stock price is the present value of the expected dividend next year, plus the present value of the expected dividend two years from now, plus the expected price two years from now.

If we replace the expected price in two years as the present value of the expected price and dividends in three years, and so on for n years, we get

$$\$Q_t = \frac{\$D_{t+1}^e}{(1 + i_{1t})} + \frac{\$D_{t+2}^e}{(1 + i_{1t})(1 + i_{1t+1}^e)} + \cdots + \frac{\$D_{t+n}^e}{(1 + i_{1t}) \cdots (1 + i_{1t+n-1}^e)}$$
$$+ \frac{\$Q_{t+n}^e}{(1 + i_{1t}) \cdots (1 + i_{1t+n-1}^e)} \tag{15.10}$$

Look at the last term in equation (15.10)—the present value of the expected price in n years. As long as people do not expect the stock price to explode in the future, then, as we keep replacing Q_{t+n}^e and n increases, this term will go to zero. To see why, suppose the interest rate is constant and equal to i. The last term becomes

$$\frac{\$Q_{t+n}^e}{(1 + i_{1t}) \cdots (1 + i_{1t+n-1}^e)} = \frac{\$Q_{t+n}^e}{(1 + i)^n}$$

Suppose further that people expect the price of the stock to converge to some value, call it $\$\overline{Q}$, in the far future. Then, the last term becomes

$$\frac{\$Q_{t+n}^e}{(1 + i)^n} = \frac{\$\overline{Q}}{(1 + i)^n}$$

If the interest rate is positive, this expression goes to zero as n becomes large. Equation (15.10) reduces to

$$\$Q_t = \frac{\$D_{t+1}^e}{(1 + i_{1t})} + \frac{\$D_{t+2}^e}{(1 + i_{1t})(1 + i_{1t+1}^e)} + \cdots + \frac{\$D_{t+n}^e}{(1 + i_{1t}) \cdots (1 + i_{1t+n-1}^e)} \tag{15.11}$$

The price of the stock is equal to the present value of the dividend next year, discounted using the current one-year interest rate, plus the present value of the dividend two years from now, discounted using both this year's one-year interest rate and the next–year's expected one-year interest rate, and so on.

Equation (15.11) gives the stock price as the present value of *nominal* dividends, discounted by *nominal* interest rates. From Chapter 14, we know we can rewrite this equation to express the *real* stock price as the present value of *real* dividends, discounted by *real* interest rates. So we can rewrite the real stock price as:

$$Q_t = \frac{D_{t+1}^e}{(1 + r_{1t})} + \frac{D_{t+2}^e}{(1 + r_{1t})(1 + r_{1t+1}^e)} + \cdots \tag{15.12}$$

Q_t and D_t, without a dollar sign, denote the real price and real dividends at time t. The real stock price is the present value of future real dividends, discounted by the sequence of one-year real interest rates.

This relation has two important implications:

■ Higher expected future real dividends lead to a higher real stock price.
■ Higher current and expected future one-year real interest rates lead to a lower real stock price.

Let's now see what light this relation sheds on movements in the stock market.

The Stock Market and Economic Activity

Figure 15-6 showed the large movements in stock prices over the last two decades. It is not unusual for the index to go up or down by 15% within a year. In 1997, the stock

A subtle point. The condition that people expect the price of the stock to converge to some value over time seems reasonable. Indeed, most of the time it is likely to be satisfied. When, however, prices are subject to rational bubbles (Section 15-3), this is when people are expecting large increases in the stock price in the future and this is when the condition that the expected stock price does not explode is not satisfied. This is why, when there are bubbles, the argument just given fails, and the stock price is no longer equal to the present value of expected dividends.

Two equivalent ways of writing the stock price:

The—nominal—stock price equals the expected present discounted value of future nominal dividends, discounted by current and future nominal interest rates.

The—real—stock price equals the expected present discounted value of future real dividends, discounted by current and future real interest rates.

market went up by 24% (in real terms); in 2008, it went down by 46%. Daily movements of 2% or more are not unusual. What causes these movements?

The first point to be made is that these movements should be, and they are for the most part, unpredictable. The reason why is best understood by thinking in terms of the choice people have between stocks and bonds. If it were widely believed that, a year from now, the price of a stock was going to be 20% higher than today's price, holding the stock for a year would be unusually attractive, much more attractive than holding short-term bonds. There would be a very large demand for the stock. Its price would increase *today* to the point where the expected return from holding the stock was back in line with the expected return on other assets. In other words, the expectation of a high stock price next year would lead to a high stock price today.

There is indeed a saying in economics that it is a sign of a *well-functioning stock market* that movements in stock prices are unpredictable. The saying is too strong: At any moment, a few financial investors might have better information or simply be better at reading the future. If they are only a few, they may not buy enough of the stock to bid its price all the way up today. Thus, they may get large expected returns. But the basic idea is nevertheless correct. The financial market gurus who regularly predict large imminent movements in the stock market are quacks. Major movements in stock prices cannot be predicted.

If movements in the stock market cannot be predicted, if they are the result of news, where does this leave us? We can still do two things:

- We can do Monday-morning quarterbacking, looking back and identifying the news to which the market reacted.
- We can ask "what if" questions. For example: What would happen to the stock market if the Fed were to embark on a more expansionary policy, or if consumers were to become more optimistic and increase spending?

Let us look at two "what if" questions using the *IS–LM* model. To simplify, let's assume, as we did earlier, that expected inflation equals zero, so that the real interest rate and the nominal interest rate are equal.

A Monetary Expansion and the Stock Market

Suppose the economy is in a recession and the Fed decides to adopt a more expansionary monetary policy. The increase in money shifts the *LM* curve down to LM′ in Figure 15-8, and equilibrium output moves from point A to point A′. How will the stock market react?

You may have heard the proposition that stock prices follow a random walk. This is a technical term, but with a simple interpretation: Something—it can be a molecule, or the price of an asset—follows a random walk if each step it takes is as likely to be up as it is to be down. Its movements are therefore unpredictable.

This assumes that the interest rate is positive to start with, so the economy is not in a liquidity trap.

Figure 15-8

An Expansionary Monetary Policy and the Stock Market

A monetary expansion decreases the interest rate and increases output. What it does to the stock market depends on whether or not financial markets anticipated the monetary expansion.

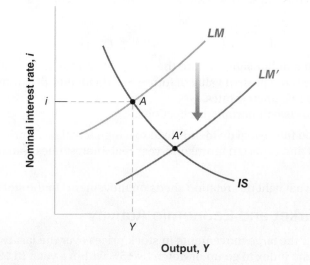

The answer depends on what participants in the stock market expected monetary policy to be before the Fed's move:

If they fully anticipated the expansionary policy, then the stock market will not react: Neither its expectations of future dividends nor its expectations of future interest rates are affected by a move it had already anticipated. Thus, in equation (15.11), nothing changes, and stock prices will remain the same.

Suppose instead that the Fed's move is at least partly unexpected. In this case, stock prices will increase. They increase for two reasons: First, a more expansionary monetary policy implies lower interest rates for some time. Second, it also implies higher output for some time (until the economy returns to the natural level of output), and therefore higher dividends. As equation (15.11) tells us, both lower interest rates and higher dividends—current and expected—will lead to an increase in stock prices.

An Increase in Consumer Spending and the Stock Market

Now consider an unexpected shift of the *IS* curve to the right, resulting, for example, from stronger-than-expected consumer spending. As a result of the shift, output in Figure 15-9(a) increases from *A* to *A'*.

Will stock prices go up? You might be tempted to say yes: A stronger economy means higher profits and higher dividends for some time. But this answer is incomplete, for at least two reasons.

First, the answer ignores the effect of higher activity on interest rates: The movement along the *LM* curve implies an increase in both output and interest rates. Higher

◄ On September 30, 1998 the Fed lowered the target federal funds rate by 0.5%. This decrease was expected by financial markets, though, so the Dow Jones index remained roughly unchanged (actually, going down 28 points for the day). Less than a month later, on October 15, 1998, the Fed lowered the target federal funds rate again, this time by 0.25%. In contrast to the September cut, this move by the Fed came as a complete surprise to financial markets. As a result, the Dow Jones index increased by 330 points on that day, an increase of more than 3%.

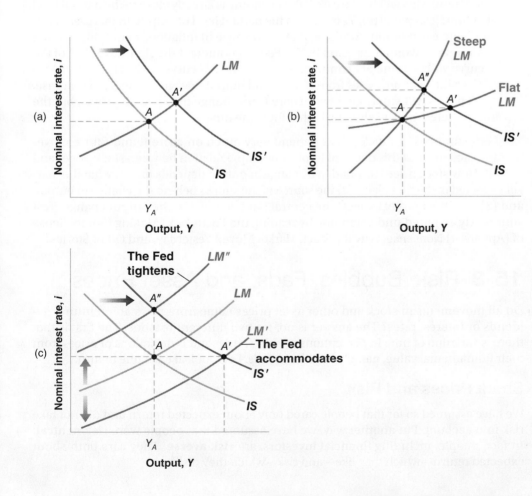

Figure 15-9

An Increase in Consumption Spending and the Stock Market

Panel (a) The increase in consumption spending leads to a higher interest rate and a higher level of output. What happens to the stock market depends on the slope of the LM curve and on the Fed's behavior:

Panel (b) If the LM curve is steep, the interest rate increases a lot, and output increases little. Stock prices go down. If the LM curve is flat, the interest rate increases little, and output increases a lot. Stock prices go up.

Panel (c) If the Fed accommodates, the interest rate does not increase, but output does. Stock prices go up. If the Fed decides instead to keep output constant, the interest rate increases, but output does not. Stock prices go down.

output leads to higher profits, and so higher stock prices. Higher interest rates lead to lower stock prices. Which of the two effects, higher profits or higher interest rates, dominates? The answer depends on the slope of the *LM* curve. This is shown in panel (b). A very flat *LM* curve leads to a movement from *A* to *A′*, with small increases in interest rates, large increases in output, and therefore an increase in stock prices. A very steep *LM* curve leads to a movement from *A* to *A″*, with large increases in interest rates, small increases in output, and therefore a decrease in stock prices.

Second, the answer ignores the effect of the shift in the *IS* curve on the Fed's behavior. In practice, this is the effect that financial investors often care about the most. After receiving the news of unexpectedly strong economic activity, the main question on Wall Street is: How will the Fed react?

- Will the Fed accommodate the shift in the *IS* curve; that is, increase the money supply in line with money demand so as to avoid an increase in the interest rate?

     Fed accommodation corresponds to a downward shift of the *LM* curve, from *LM* to *LM′* in panel (c). In this case, the economy will go from point *A* to point *A′*. Stock prices will increase, as output is expected to be higher and interest rates are not expected to increase.

- Will the Fed instead keep the same monetary policy, leaving the *LM* curve unchanged? In that case the economy will move along the *LM* curve. As we saw earlier, what happens to stock prices is ambiguous. Profits will be higher, but so will interest rates.

Another way of thinking about what happens is to think of the *LM* relation as an interest rate rule, as presented in the appendix to Chapter 5. Depending on how much the Fed increases the interest rate in response to the increase in output, the news will lead to an increase or a decrease in the stock market. ▶

- Or will the Fed worry that an increase in output above Y_A may lead to an increase in inflation? This will be the case if the economy is already close to the natural level of output; if, in panel (c), Y_A is close to the natural level of output. In this case, a further increase in output would lead to an increase in inflation, something that the Fed wants to avoid. A decision by the Fed to counteract the rightward shift of the *IS* curve with a monetary contraction causes the *LM* curve to shift up, from *LM* to *LM″*, so the economy goes from *A* to *A″* and output does not change. In that case, stock prices will surely go down: There is no change in expected profits, but the interest rate is now likely to be higher for some time.

Let's summarize: Stock prices depend very much on current and future movements in activity. But this does not imply any simple relation between stock prices and output. How stock prices respond to a change in output depends on: (1) what the market expected in the first place, (2) the source of the shocks behind the change in output, and (3) how the market expects the central bank to react to the output change. Test your newly acquired understanding by reading the Focus box "Making (Some) Sense of (Apparent) Nonsense: Why the Stock Market Moved Yesterday, and Other Stories".

15-3 Risk, Bubbles, Fads, and Asset Prices

Do all movements in stock and other asset prices come from news about future dividends or interest rates? The answer is no, for two different reasons. The first is that there is variation of time in perceptions of risk. The second is deviations of prices from their fundamental value, namely bubbles or fads. Let's look at each one in turn.

Stock Prices and Risk

We have assumed so far that people cared only about expected return and did not take risk into account. Put another way, we have assumed that people were **risk neutral**. In fact, people, including financial investors, are **risk averse**. They care both about expected return—which they like—and risk—which they dislike.

Making (Some) Sense of (Apparent) Nonsense: Why the Stock Market Moved Yesterday, and Other Stories

Here are some quotes from The Wall Street Journal from April 1997 to August 2001. Try to make sense of them, using what you've just learned. (And, if you have time, find your own quotes.)

■ **April 1997. Good news on the economy, leading to an increase in stock prices:**

"Bullish investors celebrated the release of market-friendly economic data by stampeding back into stock and bond markets, pushing the Dow Jones Industrial Average to its second-largest point gain ever and putting the blue-chip index within shooting distance of a record just weeks after it was reeling."

■ **December 1999. Good news on the economy, leading to a decrease in stock prices:**

"Good economic news was bad news for stocks and worse news for bonds. . . . The announcement of stronger-than-expected November retail-sales numbers wasn't welcome. Economic strength creates inflation fears and sharpens the risk that the Federal Reserve will raise interest rates again."

■ **September 1998. Bad news on the economy, leading to an decrease in stock prices:**

"Nasdaq stocks plummeted as worries about the strength of the U.S. economy and the profitability of U.S. corporations prompted widespread selling."

■ **August 2001. Bad news on the economy, leading to an increase in stock prices:**

"Investors shrugged off more gloomy economic news, and focused instead on their hope that the worst is now over for both the economy and the stock market. The optimism translated into another 2% gain for the Nasdaq Composite Index."

Most of **finance theory** is indeed concerned with how people make decisions when they are risk averse, and what risk aversion implies for asset prices. Exploring these issues would take us too far from our purpose. But we can nevertheless explore a simple extension of our framework, which captures the fact that people are risk averse and shows how to modify the arbitrage and the present value relations.

If people perceive stocks to be more risky than bonds, and people dislike risk, they are likely to require a *risk premium* to hold stocks rather than bonds. In the case of stocks, this risk premium is called the **equity premium**. Denote it by θ (the Greek lowercase letter theta). If θ is, for example, 5%, then people will hold stocks only if the expected rate of return on stocks exceeds the expected rate of return on short-term bonds by 5% a year.

In that case, the arbitrage equation between stocks and bonds becomes

$$\frac{\$D^e_{t+1} + \$Q^e_{t+1}}{\$Q_t} = 1 + i_{1t} + \theta$$

The only change is the presence of θ on the right side of the equation. Going through the same steps as before (replacing Q^e_{t+1} by its expression at time $t + 1$, and so on), the stock price equals

$$\$Q_t = \frac{\$D^e_{t+1}}{(1 + i_{1t} + \theta)} + \frac{\$D^e_{t+2}}{(1 + i_{1t} + \theta)(1 + i^e_{1t+1} + \theta)}$$

$$+ \cdots + \frac{\$D^e_{t+n}}{(1 + i_{1t} + \theta) \cdots (1 + i^e_{1t+n-1} + \theta)} \tag{15.13}$$

The stock price is still equal to the present value of expected future dividends. But the discount rate here equals the interest rate plus the equity premium. Note that the higher the premium, the lower the stock price. Over the last 100 years in the United States, the average equity premium has been equal to roughly 5%. But (in contrast to the assumption we made earlier, where we took θ to be constant) it is not constant. The equity premium appears, for example, to have decreased since the early 1950s, from around 7% to less than 3% today. And it may change quickly. Surely part of the stock market fall in 2008 was due not only to more pessimistic expectations of future dividends, but also to the large increase in uncertainty and the perception of higher risk by stock market participants.

Asset Prices, Fundamentals, and Bubbles

We have so far assumed that stock prices were always equal to their *fundamental value*, defined as the present value of expected dividends given in equation (15.11) (or equation (15.13) if we allow for a risk premium). Do stock prices always correspond to their fundamental value? Most economists doubt it. They point to Black October in 1929, when the U.S. stock market fell by 23% in two days, and to October 19, 1987, when the Dow Jones index fell by 22.6% in a single day. They point to the amazing rise in the Nikkei index (an index of Japanese stock prices) from around 13,000 in 1985 to around 35,000 in 1989, followed by a decline back to 16,000 in 1992. In each of these cases, they point to a lack of obvious news, or at least of news important enough to cause such enormous movements.

See the Focus box "Japan, The Liquidity Trap, and Fiscal Policy" in Chapter 9.

Instead, they argue that stock prices are not always equal to their **fundamental value**, defined as the present value of expected dividends given in equation (15.11), and that stocks are sometimes underpriced or overpriced. Overpricing eventually comes to an end, sometimes with a crash, as in October 1929, or with a long slide, as in the case of the Nikkei index.

Recall: Arbitrage is the condition that the expected rates of return on two financial assets be equal.

Under what conditions can such mispricing occur? The surprising answer is that it can occur even when investors are rational and when arbitrage holds. To see why, consider the case of a truly worthless stock (that is, the stock of a company that all financial investors know will never make profits and will never pay dividends). Putting D^e_{t+1}, D^e_{t+2}, and so on equal to zero in equation (15.11) yields a simple and unsurprising answer: The fundamental value of such a stock is equal to zero.

The example is obviously extreme. But it makes the point most simply.

Might you nevertheless be willing to pay a positive price for this stock? Maybe. You might if you expect the price at which you can sell the stock next year to be higher than this year's price. And the same applies to a buyer next year: He may well be willing to buy at a high price if he expects to sell at an even higher price in the following year. This process suggests that stock prices may increase just because investors expect them to.

Famous Bubbles: From Tulipmania in Seventeenth-Century Holland to Russia in 1994

Tulipmania in Holland

In the seventeenth century, tulips became increasingly popular in Western European gardens. A market developed in Holland for both rare and common forms of tulip bulbs.

An episode called the "tulip bubble" took place from 1634 to 1637. In 1634, the price of rare bulbs started increasing. The market went into a frenzy, with speculators buying tulip bulbs in anticipation of even higher prices later. For example, the price of a bulb called "Admiral Van de Eyck" increased from 1,500 guineas in 1634 to 7,500 guineas in 1637, equal to the price of a house at the time. There are stories about a sailor mistakenly eating bulbs, only to realize the cost of his "meal" later. In early 1637, prices increased faster. Even the price of some common bulbs exploded, rising by a factor of up to 20 in January. But, in February 1637, prices collapsed. A few years later, bulbs were trading for roughly 10% of their value at the peak of the bubble.

This account is taken from Peter Garber, "Tulipmania," Journal of Political Economy 1989, 97 (3): pp. 535–560.

The MMM Pyramid in Russia

In 1994 a Russian "financier," Sergei Mavrodi, created a company called MMM and proceeded to sell shares, promising shareholders a rate of return of at least 3,000% per year!

The company was an instant success. The price of MMM shares increased from 1,600 rubles (then worth $1) in February to 105,000 rubles (then worth $51) in July. And by July, according to the company claims, the number of shareholders had increased to 10 million.

The trouble was that the company was not involved in any type of production and held no assets, except for its 140 offices in Russia. The shares were intrinsically worthless. The company's initial success was based on a standard pyramid scheme, with MMM using the funds from the sale of new shares to pay the promised returns on the old shares. Despite repeated warnings by government officials, including Boris Yeltsin, that MMM was a scam and that the increase in the price of shares was a bubble, the promised returns were just too attractive to many Russian people, especially in the midst of a deep economic recession.

The scheme could work only as long as the number of new shareholders—and thus new funds to be distributed to existing shareholders—increased fast enough. By the end of July 1994, the company could no longer make good on its promises and the scheme collapsed. The company closed. Mavrodi tried to blackmail the government into paying the shareholders, claiming that not doing so would trigger a revolution or a civil war. The government refused, leading many shareholders to be angry at the government rather than at Mavrodi. Later on in the year, Mavrodi actually ran for Parliament, as a self-appointed defender of the shareholders who had lost their savings. He won!

Such movements in stock prices are called **rational speculative bubbles**: Financial investors might well be behaving rationally as the bubble inflates. Even those investors who hold the stock at the time of the crash, and therefore sustain a large loss, may also have been rational. They may have realized there was a chance of a crash, but also a chance that the bubble would continue and they could sell at an even higher price.

To make things simple, our example assumed the stock to be fundamentally worthless. But the argument is general and applies to stocks with a positive fundamental value as well. People might be willing to pay more than the fundamental value of a stock if they expect its price to further increase in the future. And the same argument applies to other assets, such as housing, gold, and paintings. Two such bubbles are described in the Focus box "Famous Bubbles: From Tulipmania in Seventeenth-Century Holland to Russia in 1994."

Are all deviations from fundamental values in financial markets rational bubbles? Probably not. The fact is that many financial investors are not rational. An increase in stock prices in the past, say due to a succession of good news, often creates excessive optimism. If investors simply extrapolate from past returns to predict future returns, a stock may become "hot" (high priced) for no reason other than its price has increased in the past. This is true not only of stocks, but also of houses (See the Focus box "The Increase in U.S. Housing Prices in the United States in the 2000s: Fundamentals or

In a speculative bubble, the price of a stock is higher than its fundamental value. Investors are willing to pay a high price for the stock, in the anticipation of being able to resell the stock at an even higher price.

The Increase in U.S. Housing Prices: Fundamentals or a Bubble?

Recall from Chapter 9 that the trigger behind the current crisis was a decline in housing prices starting in 2006 (see Figure 9-1 for the evolution of the housing price index). In retrospect, the large increase from 2000 on that preceded the decline is now widely interpreted as a bubble. But, in real time, as prices went up, there was little agreement as to what lay behind this increase.

Economists belonged to three camps:

The pessimists argued that the price increases could not be justified by fundamentals. In 2005, Robert Shiller said: "The home-price bubble feels like the stock-market mania in the fall of 1999, just before the stock bubble burst in early 2000, with all the hype, herd investing and absolute confidence in the inevitability of continuing price appreciation."

To understand his position, go back to the derivation of stock prices in the text. We saw that, absent bubbles, we can think of stock prices as depending on current and expected future interest rates, and current and expected future dividends. The same applies to house prices: Absent bubbles, we can think of house prices as depending on current and expected future interest rates, and current and expected rents. In that context, pessimists pointed out that the increase in house prices was not matched by a parallel increase in rents. You can see this in Figure 1, which plots the price–rent ratio (i.e., the ratio of an index of house prices to an index of rents) from 1987 to today (the index is set so its average value from 1987 to 1995 is 100). After remaining roughly constant from 1987 to 1995, the ratio then increased by nearly 60%, reaching a peak in 2006 and declining since then. Furthermore, Shiller pointed out, surveys of house buyers suggested extremely high expectations of continuing large increases in housing prices, often in excess of 10% a year, and thus of large capital gains. As we saw earlier, if assets are valued at their fundamental value, investors should not be expecting very large capital gains in the future.

The optimists argued that there were good reasons for the price–rent ratio to go up. First, as we saw in Figure 14-2, the real interest rate was decreasing, increasing the present value of rents. Second, the nominal interest rate was also decreasing, and this mattered because nominal, not real interest payments, are tax deductible. Third, the mortgage market was changing: More people were able to borrow and buy a house; people who borrowed were able to borrow a larger proportion of the value of the house. Both of these

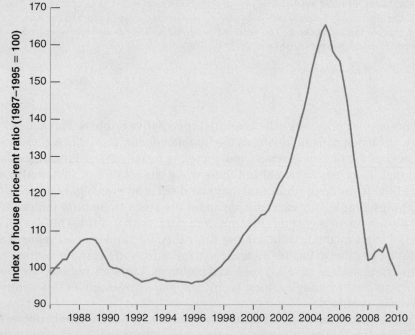

Figure 1   *The U.S. Housing Price–Rent Ratio since 1985.*

Source: Calculated using The Case-Shiller Home Price Indices (national series) downloaded from http://www.standardandpoors.com/indices/main/en/us and the rental component of the Consumer Price Index: series CUSR0000SEHA, Rent of Primary Residence, Bureau of Labor Statistics factors led to an increase in demand, and thus an increase in house prices. The optimists also pointed out that, every year since 2000, the pessimists had kept predicting the end of the bubble, and prices continued to increase: The pessimists were losing credibility.

The third group was by far the largest, and remained agnostic. (Harry Truman is reported to have said: "Give me a one-handed economist! All my economists say, On the one hand on the other.") They concluded that the increase in house prices reflected both improved fundamentals and bubbles, and that it was difficult to identify their relative importance.

What conclusions should you draw? That bubbles and fads are clearer in retrospect than while they are taking place. This makes the task of policy makers much harder: If they were sure it was a bubble, they should try to stop it before it gets too large and then bursts. But they can rarely be sure until it is too late.

Source: "Reasonable People Did Disagree: Optimism and Pessimism about the U.S. Housing Market before the Crash," Kristopher S. Gerardi, Christopher Foote, and Paul Willen, Federal Reserve Bank of Boston, September 10, 2010, available at www.bos.frb.org/economics/wp/index.htm

Bubble?") Such deviations of stock prices from their fundamental value are sometimes called **fads**. We are all aware of fads outside of the stock market; there are good reasons to believe they exist in the stock market as well.

We have focused in this chapter on how news about economic activity affects asset prices. But asset prices are more than just a sideshow. They affect economic activity, by influencing consumption and investment spending. There is little question, for example, that the decline in the stock market was one of the factors behind the 2001 recession. Most economists also believe that the stock market crash of 1929 was one of the sources of the Great Depression, and that the large decline in the Nikkei is one of the causes of the long Japanese slump in the 1990s. And, as we saw in Chapter 9, the decline in housing prices was the trigger for the current crisis. These interactions among asset prices, expectations, and economic activity are the topics of the next two chapters.

Summary

- Arbitrage between bonds of different maturities implies that the price of a bond is the present value of the payments on the bond, discounted using current and expected short-term interest rates over the life of the bond. Hence, higher current or expected short-term interest rates lead to lower bond prices.

- The yield to maturity on a bond is (approximately) equal to the average of current and expected short-term interest rates over the life of a bond.

- The slope of the yield curve—equivalently, the term structure—tells us what financial markets expect to happen to short-term interest rates in the future. A downward-sloping yield curve (when long-term interest rates are lower than short-term interest rates) implies that the market expects a decrease in short-term interest rates; an upward-sloping yield curve (when long-term interest rates are higher than short-term interest rates) implies that the market expects an increase in short-term rates.

- The fundamental value of a stock is the present value of expected future real dividends, discounted using current and future expected one-year real interest rates. In the absence

of bubbles or fads, the price of a stock is equal to its fundamental value.

- An increase in expected dividends leads to an increase in the fundamental value of stocks; an increase in current and expected one-year interest rates leads to a decrease in their fundamental value.

- Changes in output may or may not be associated with changes in stock prices in the same direction. Whether they are or not depends on (1) what the market expected in the first place, (2) the source of the shocks, and (3) how the market expects the central bank to react to the output change.

- Asset prices can be subject to bubbles and fads that cause the price to differ from its fundamental value. Bubbles are episodes in which financial investors buy an asset for a price higher than its fundamental value, anticipating to resell it at an even higher price. Fads are episodes in which, because of excessive optimism, financial investors are willing to pay more for an asset than its fundamental value.

Key Terms

Questions and Problems

QUICK CHECK

All Quick Check questions and problems are available on MyEconLab.

1. Using the information in this chapter, label each of the following statements true, false, or uncertain. Explain briefly.

a. Junk bonds are bonds nobody wants to hold.

b. The price of a one-year bond decreases when the nominal one-year interest rate increases.

c. Given the Fisher hypothesis, an upward-sloping yield curve may indicate that financial markets are worried about inflation in the future.

d. Long-term interest rates typically move more than short-term interest rates.

e. An equal increase in expected inflation and nominal interest rates at all maturities should have no effect on the stock market.

f. A monetary expansion will lead to an upward-sloping yield curve.

g. A rational investor should never pay a positive price for a stock that will never pay dividends.

h. The strong performance of the U.S. stock market in the 1990s reflects the strong performance of the U.S. economy during that period.

2. Determine the yield to maturity of each of the following bonds:

a. A discount bond with a face value of $1,000, a maturity of three years, and a price of $800.

b. A discount bond with a face value of $1,000, a maturity of four years, and a price of $800.

c. A discount bond with a face value of $1,000, a maturity of four years, and a price of $850.

3. Suppose that the annual interest rate this year is 5%, and financial market participants expect the annual interest rate to increase to 5.5% next year, to 6% two years from now, and to 6.5% three years from now. Determine the yield to maturity on each of the following bonds.

a. A one-year bond.

b. A two-year bond.

c. A three-year bond.

4. Using the IS–LM *model, determine the impact on stock prices of each of the policy changes described in (a) through (c). If the effect is ambiguous, explain what additional information would be needed to reach a conclusion.*

a. An unexpected expansionary monetary policy with no change in fiscal policy.

b. A fully expected expansionary monetary policy with no change in fiscal policy.

c. A fully expected expansionary monetary policy together with an unexpected expansionary fiscal policy.

DIG DEEPER

All Dig Deeper questions and problems are available on MyEconLab.

5. Money growth and the yield curve.

In Chapter 14, we examined the effects of an increase in the growth rate of money on interest rates and inflation.

a. Draw the path of the nominal interest rate following an increase in the growth rate of money. Suppose that the lowest point in the path is reached after one year and that the long-run values are achieved after three years.

b. Show the yield curve just after the increase in the growth rate of money, one year later, and three years later.

6. Interpreting the yield curve
a. Explain why an inverted (downward-sloping) yield curve may indicate that a recession is coming.
b. What does a steep yield curve imply about future inflation?

7. Stock prices and the risk premium
Suppose a share is expected to pay a dividend of $1,000 next year, and the real value of dividend payments is expected to increase by 3% per year forever.
a. What is the current price of the stock if the real interest rate is expected to remain constant at 5%? at 8%?
   Now suppose that people require a risk premium to hold stocks.
b. Redo the calculations in part (a) if the required risk premium is 8%.
c. Redo the calculations in part (a) if the required risk premium is 4%.
d. What do you expect would happen to stock prices if the risk premium decreased unexpectedly? Explain in words.

EXPLORE FURTHER
8. The yield curve after the crisis.
On November 3, 2010, The Fed Committee that sets the short-term interest rate said:

"The Committee will maintain the target range for the federal funds rate at 0 to 1/4 percent and continues to anticipate that economic conditions, including low rates of resource utilization, subdued inflation trends, and stable inflation expectations, are likely to warrant exceptionally low levels for the federal funds rate for an extended period."

Explain the shape of the yield curve that results from this statement.

9. The Volcker disinflation and the term structure
In the late 1970s, the U.S. inflation rate reached double digits. Paul Volcker was appointed chairman of the Federal Reserve Board in 1979. Volcker was considered the right person to lead the fight against inflation. In this problem, we will use yield curve data to judge whether the financial markets were indeed expecting Volcker to succeed in reducing the inflation rate.

Go to the data section of the Web site of the Federal Reserve Bank of St. Louis (**www.research.stlouisfed.org/fred2**). Go to "Consumer Price Indexes (CPI)" and download monthly data on the seasonally adjusted CPI for all urban consumers for the period 1970 to the latest available date. Import it into your favorite spreadsheet program. Similarly, under "Interest Rates" and then "Treasury Constant Maturity," find and download the monthly

series for "1-Year Treasury Constant Maturity Rate" and "30-Year Treasury Constant Maturity Rate" into your spreadsheet.
a. How can the Fed reduce inflation? How would this policy affect the nominal interest rate?
b. For each month, compute the annual rate of inflation as the percentage change in the CPI from last year to this year (i.e., over the preceding 12 months). In the same graph, plot the rate of inflation and the one-year interest rate from 1970 to the latest available date. When was the rate of inflation the highest?
c. For each month, compute the difference (called the *spread*) between the yield on the 30-year T-bond and the one-year T-bill. Plot it in the same graph with the one-year interest rate.
d. What does a declining spread imply about the expectations of financial market participants? As inflation was increasing in the late 1970s, what was happening to the one-year T-bill rate? Were financial market participants expecting that trend to continue?

In October 1979, the Fed announced several changes in its operating procedures that were widely interpreted as a commitment to fighting inflation.
e. Using the interest rate spread that you computed in part (c) for October 1979, do you find any evidence of such an interpretation by financial market participants? Explain.

In early 1980, it became obvious that the United States was falling into a sharp recession. The Fed switched to an expansionary monetary policy from April to July 1980 in order to boost the economy.
f. What was the effect of the policy switch on the one-year interest rate?
g. From April to July 1980, did financial markets expect the change in policy to last? Explain. Were financial market participants' expectations correct?

10. Use the data source found in Figure 15-1 and find the most recent information on the term structure of interest rates ranging from three months to 30 years. Term structure information can also be found in other places on the web.

Is the term structure upward sloping, downward sloping, or flat? Why do you think this would be?

11. Do a news search on the internet about the most recent Federal Open Market Committee (FOMC) meeting.
a. What did the FOMC decide about the interest rate?
b. What happened to stock prices on the day of the announcement?
c. To what degree do you think financial market participants were surprised by the FOMC's announcement? Explain.

Further Readings
· ·

■ There are many bad books written about the stock market. A good one, and one that is fun to read, is Burton Malkiel, *A Random Walk Down Wall Street,* (Norton, 2011) 10th edition.

■ An account of some historical bubbles is given by Peter Garber in "Famous First Bubbles," *Journal of Economic Perspectives,* Spring 1990, 4(2): pp. 35–54.

Expectations, Consumption, and Investment

Having looked at the role of expectations in financial markets, we now turn to the role expectations play in determining the two main components of spending—consumption and investment. This description of consumption and investment will be the main building block of the expanded *IS–LM* model we develop in Chapter 17.

Section 16-1 looks at consumption and shows how consumption decisions depend not only on a person's current income, but also on her expected future income and on financial wealth.

Section 16-2 turns to investment and shows how investment decisions depend on current and expected profits, and on current and expected real interest rates.

Section 16-3 looks at the movements in consumption and investment over time, and shows how to interpret those movements in light of what you learned in this chapter. ●

16-1 Consumption

How do people decide how much to consume and how much to save? In Chapter 3, we assumed that consumption depended only on current income. But, even then, it was clear that consumption depended on much more, particularly on expectations about the future. We now explore how those expectations affect the consumption decision.

The modern theory of consumption, on which this section is based, was developed independently in the 1950s by Milton Friedman of the University of Chicago, who called it the

Friedman received the Nobel Prize in economics in 1976; Modigliani received the Nobel Prize in economics in 1985.

From Chapter 3: Consumption spending accounts for 70.5% of total spending in the United States.

permanent income theory of consumption, and by Franco Modigliani of MIT, who called it the **life cycle theory of consumption**. Each chose his label carefully. Friedman's "permanent income" emphasized that consumers look beyond current income. Modigliani's "life cycle" emphasized that consumers' natural planning horizon is their entire lifetime.

The behavior of aggregate consumption has remained a hot area of research ever since, for two reasons: One is simply the sheer size of consumption as a component of GDP, and therefore the need to understand movements in consumption. The other is the increasing availability of large surveys of individual consumers, such as the Panel Study of Income Dynamics (PSID), described in the Focus box "Up Close and Personal: Learning from Panel Data Sets." These surveys, which were not available when Friedman and Modigliani developed their theories, have allowed economists to steadily improve their understanding of how consumers actually behave. This section summarizes what we know today.

The Very Foresighted Consumer

Let's start with an assumption that will surely—and rightly—strike you as extreme, but will serve as a convenient benchmark. We'll call it the theory of the *very foresighted consumer*. How would a very foresighted consumer decide how much to consume? He would proceed in two steps.

With a slight abuse of language, we shall use "housing wealth" to refer not only to housing, but also to the other goods that the consumer may own, from cars to paintings and so on.

- First, he would add up the value of the stocks and bonds he owns, the value of his checking and savings accounts, the value of the house he owns minus the mortgage still due, and so on. This would give him an idea of his **financial wealth** and his **housing wealth.**

  He would also estimate what his after-tax labor income was likely to be over his working life, and compute the present value of expected after-tax labor income. This would give him an estimate of what economists call his **human wealth**—to contrast it with his **nonhuman wealth**, defined as the sum of financial wealth and housing wealth.

Human wealth + Nonhuman wealth = Total wealth

- Adding his human wealth and nonhuman wealth, he would have an estimate of his **total wealth**. He would then decide how much to spend out of this total wealth. A reasonable assumption is that he would decide to spend a proportion of his total wealth such as to maintain roughly the same level of consumption each year throughout his life. If that level of consumption were higher than his current income, he would then borrow the difference. If it were lower than his current income, he would instead save the difference.

Let's write this formally. What we have described is a consumption decision of the form

$$C_t = C(\text{total wealth}_t) \tag{16.1}$$

where C_t is consumption at time t, and (total wealth$_t$) is the sum of nonhuman wealth (financial plus housing wealth) and human wealth at time t (the expected present value, as of time t, of current and future after-tax labor income).

This description contains much truth: Like the foresighted consumer, we surely do think about our wealth and our expected future labor income in deciding how much to consume today. But one cannot help thinking that it assumes too much computation and foresight on the part of the typical consumer.

To get a better sense of what this description implies and what is wrong with it, let's apply this decision process to the problem facing a typical U.S. college student.

An Example

Let's assume you are 19 years old, with three more years of college before you start your first job. You may be in debt today, having taken out a loan to go to college. You may own a car and a few other worldly possessions. For simplicity, let's assume your debt

Up Close and Personal: Learning from Panel Data Sets

Panel data sets are data sets that show the value of one or more variables for many individuals or many firms over time. We described one such survey, the Current Population Survey (*CPS*), in Chapter 6. Another is the *Panel Study of Income Dynamics (PSID)*.

The PSID was started in 1968, with approximately 4,800 families. Interviews of these families have been conducted every year since and still continue today. The survey has grown as new individuals have joined the original families surveyed, either by marriage or by birth. Each year, the survey asks people about their income, wage rate, number of hours worked, health, and food consumption. (The focus on food consumption is because one of the survey's initial aims was to better understand the living conditions of poor families. The survey would be more useful if it asked about all of consumption rather than food consumption. Unfortunately, it does not.)

By providing nearly four decades of information about individuals and their extended families, the survey has allowed economists to ask and answer questions for which there was previously only anecdotal evidence. Among the many questions for which the PSID has been used are:

- How much does (food) consumption respond to transitory movements in income—for example, to the loss of income from becoming unemployed?
- How much risk sharing is there within families? For example, when a family member becomes sick or unemployed, how much help does he or she get from other family members?
- How much do people care about staying geographically close to their families? When someone becomes unemployed, for example, how does the probability that he will migrate to another city depend on the number of his family members living in the city where he currently lives?

and your possessions roughly offset each other, so that your nonhuman wealth is equal to zero. Your only wealth therefore is your human wealth, the present value of your expected after-tax labor income.

You expect your starting annual salary in three years to be around $40,000 (in 2011 dollars) and to increase by an average of 3% per year in real terms, until your retirement at age 60. About 25% of your income will go to taxes.

Building on what we saw in Chapter 14, let's compute the present value of your labor income as the value of *real* expected after-tax labor income, discounted using *real* interest rates (equation (14.8)). Let Y_{Lt} denote real labor income in year t. Let T_t denote real taxes in year t. Let $V(Y_{Lt}^e - T_t^e)$ denote your human wealth; that is, the expected present value of your after-tax labor income—expected as of year t.

To make the computation simple, assume the real interest rate equals zero—so the expected present value is simply the sum of expected labor income over your working life and is therefore given by

$$V(Y_{Lt}^e - T_t^e) = (\$40,000)(0.75)\left[1 + (1.03) + (1.03)^2 + \cdots + (1.03)^{38}\right]$$

The first term ($40,000) is your initial level of labor income, in year 2000 dollars.

The second term (0.75) comes from the fact that, because of taxes, you keep only 75% of what you earn.

The third term $\left[1 + (1.03) + (1.03)^2 + \cdots + (1.03)^{38}\right]$ reflects the fact that you expect your real income to increase by 3% a year for 39 years (you will start earning income at age 22, and work until age 60).

Using the properties of geometric series to solve for the sum in brackets gives

$$V(Y_{Lt}^e - T_t^e) = (\$40,000)(0.75)(72.2) = \$2,166,000$$

Your wealth today, the expected value of your lifetime after-tax labor income, is around $2 million.

How much should you consume? You can expect to live about 16 years after you retire, so that your expected remaining life today is 58 years. If you want

You are welcome to use your own numbers and see where the computation takes you.

The computation of the consumption level you can sustain is made easier by our assumption that the real interest rate equals zero. In this case, if you consume one less good today, you can consume exactly one more good next year, and the condition you must satisfy is simply that the sum of consumption over your lifetime is equal to your wealth. So, if you want to consume a constant amount each year, you just need to divide your wealth by the remaining number of years you expect to live.

to consume the same amount every year, the constant level of consumption that you can afford equals your total wealth divided by your expected remaining life, or $2,166,000/58 = $37,344 a year. Given that your income until you get your first job is equal to zero, this implies you will have to borrow $37,344 a year for the next three years, and begin to save when you get your first job.

Toward a More Realistic Description

Your first reaction to this computation may be that this is a stark and slightly sinister way of summarizing your life prospects. You might find yourself more in agreement with the retirement plans described in this cartoon.

Your second reaction may be that while you agree with most of the ingredients that went into the computation, you surely do not intend to borrow $37,344 \times 3 = \$112,032$ over the next three years. For example:

1. You might not want to plan for constant consumption over your lifetime. Instead you may be quite happy to defer higher consumption until later. Student life usually does not leave much time for expensive activities. You may want to defer trips to the Galapágos Islands to later in life. You also have to think about the additional expenses that will come with having children, sending them to nursery school, summer camp, college, and so on.

2. You might find that the amount of computation and foresight involved in the computation we just went through far exceeds the amount you use in your own decisions. You may never have thought until now about exactly how much income you are going to earn, and for how many years. You might feel that most consumption decisions are made in a simpler, less forward-looking fashion.

3. The computation of total wealth is based on forecasts of what is expected to happen. But things can turn out better or worse. What happens if you are unlucky and you become unemployed or sick? How will you pay back what you borrowed? You might want to be prudent, making sure that you can adequately survive even the worst outcomes, and thus decide to borrow much less than $112,032.

4. Even if you decide to borrow $112,032, you might have a hard time finding a bank willing to lend it to you. Why? The bank may worry that you are taking on a commitment you will not be able to afford if times turn bad, and that you may not be able or willing to repay the loan.

These reasons, all good ones, suggest that to characterize consumers' actual behavior, we must modify the description we gave earlier. The last three reasons in particular suggest that consumption depends not only on total wealth but also on current income.

Take the second reason: You may, because it is a simple rule, decide to let your consumption follow your income and not think about what your wealth might be. In that case your consumption will depend on your current income, not on your wealth.

Now take the third reason: It implies that a safe rule may be to consume no more than your current income. This way, you do not run the risk of accumulating debt that you cannot repay if times were to turn bad.

Or take the fourth reason: It implies that you may have little choice anyway. Even if you wanted to consume more than your current income, you might be unable to do so because no bank will give you a loan.

If we want to allow for a direct effect of current income on consumption, what measure of current income should we use? A convenient measure is after-tax labor income, which we introduced when we defined human wealth. This leads to a consumption function of the form

$$C_t = C(\text{Total wealth}_t, \; Y_{Lt} - T_t) \tag{16.2}$$
$$(\qquad + \qquad , \qquad + \quad)$$

In words: Consumption is an increasing function of total wealth, and also an increasing function of current after-tax labor income. Total wealth is the sum of nonhuman wealth—financial wealth plus housing wealth—and human wealth—the present value of expected after-tax labor income.

How much does consumption depend on total wealth (and therefore on expectations of future income) and how much does it depend on current income? The evidence is that most consumers look forward, in the spirit of the theory developed by Modigliani and Friedman. (See the Focus box "Do People Save Enough for

Do People Save Enough for Retirement?

How carefully do people look forward when making consumption and saving decisions? One way to answer this question is to look at how much people save for retirement.

Table 1, taken from a study by Steven Venti, from Dartmouth, and David Wise, from Harvard, based on a panel data set called the Survey of Income and Program Participation, gives the basic numbers. The table shows the mean level and the composition of (total) wealth for people between 65 and 69 years in 1991—so, most of them retired.

The first three components of wealth capture the various sources of retirement income. The first is the present value of Social Security benefits. The second is the value of the retirement plans provided by employers. And the third is the value of personal retirement plans. The last three components include the other assets held by consumers, such as bonds and stocks, and housing.

A mean wealth of $314,000 is substantial (for comparison, U.S. per person personal consumption at the time of the study (1991) was $16,000). This level of mean wealth gives an image of forward-looking individuals making careful saving decisions and retiring with enough wealth to enjoy a comfortable retirement.

We must be careful, however: The high average may hide important differences across individuals. Some individuals may save a lot, others little. Another study, by Scholz, Seshadri, and Khitatrakun, from the University of Wisconsin, sheds light on this aspect. The study is based on another panel data set, called the *Health and Retirement Study*. The panel consists of 7,000 households whose heads of household were between 51 and 61 years at the time of the first interview in 1992, and who have been interviewed every two years since. The panel contains information about the level and the composition of wealth for each household, as well as on its labor income (if the individuals in the household have not yet retired). Based on this information, the authors construct a target level of wealth for each household (i.e., the wealth level that each household should have if it wants to maintain a roughly constant level of consumption after retirement). The authors then compare the actual wealth level to the target level, for each household.

The first conclusion of their study is similar to the conclusion reached by Venti and Wise: On average, people save enough for retirement. More specifically, the authors find that more than 80% of households have wealth above the target level. Put the other way around, only 20% of households have wealth below the target. But these numbers hide important differences across income levels:

Among those in the top half of the income distribution, more than 90% have wealth that exceeds the target, often by a large amount. This suggests that these households plan to leave bequests, and so save more than what is needed for retirement.

Among those in the bottom 20% of the income distribution, however, fewer than 70% have wealth above the target. For the 30% of households below the target, the difference between actual and target wealth is typically small. But the relatively large proportion of individuals with wealth below the target suggests that there are a number of individuals who, through bad planning or bad luck, do not save enough for retirement. For most of these individuals, nearly all their wealth comes from the present value of Social Security benefits (the first component of wealth in Table 1), and it is reasonable to think that the proportion of people with wealth below target would be even larger if Social Security did not exist. This is indeed what the Social Security system was designed to do: to make sure that people have enough to live on when they retire. In that regard, it appears to be a success.

Table 1 Mean Wealth of People, Age 65–69, in 1991 (in thousands of 1991 dollars)	
Social Security pension	100
Employer-provided pension	62
Personal retirement assets	11
Other financial assets	42
Home equity	65
Other equity	34
Total	314

Source: Venti and Wise, Table A1

Sources: John Scholz, Ananth Seshadri, and Surachai Khitatrakun, "Are Americans Saving 'Optimally' for Retirement?" *Journal of Political Economy*, 2006, 114 (4): pp. 607–643. Steven Venti and David Wise, "The Wealth of Cohorts: Retirement and Saving and the Changing Assets of Older Americans," in Sylvester Schieber and John B. Shoven (eds.), *Public Policy Toward Pensions* (MIT Press, 1997).

Retirement?") But some consumers, especially those who have temporarily low income and poor access to credit, are likely to consume their current income, regardless of what they expect will happen to them in the future. A worker who becomes unemployed and has no financial wealth may have a hard time borrowing to maintain her level of consumption, even if she is fairly confident that she will soon find another job. Consumers who are richer and have easier access to credit are more likely to give more weight to the expected future and to try to maintain roughly constant consumption over time.

Putting Things Together: Current Income, Expectations, and Consumption

Let's go back to what motivates this chapter—the importance of expectations in the determination of spending. Note first that, with consumption behavior described by equation (16.2), expectations affect consumption in two ways:

■ Expectations affect consumption directly through *human wealth*: To compute their human wealth, consumers have to form their own expectations about future labor income, real interest rates, and taxes.

■ Expectations affect consumption indirectly, through *nonhuman wealth*—stocks, bonds, and housing. Consumers do not need to do any computation here and can just take the value of these assets as given. As you saw in Chapter 15, the computation is in effect done for them by participants in financial markets: The price of their stocks, for example, itself depends on expectations of future dividends and ◄ interest rates.

This dependence of consumption on expectations has in turn two main implications for the relation between consumption and income:

■ *Consumption is likely to respond less than one-for-one to fluctuations in current income.* When deciding how much to consume, a consumer looks at more than her current income. If she concludes that the decrease in her income is permanent, she is likely to decrease consumption one-for-one with the decrease in income. But if she concludes that the decrease in her current income ◄ is transitory, she will adjust her consumption by less. In a recession, consumption adjusts less than one-for-one to decreases in income. This is because consumers know that recessions typically do not last for more than a few quarters, and that the economy will eventually return to the natural level of output. The same is true in expansions. Faced with an unusually rapid increase in income, consumers are unlikely to increase consumption by as much as income. They are likely to assume that the boom is transitory and that things will return to normal.

■ *Consumption may move even if current income does not change.* The election of a charismatic president who articulates the vision of an exciting future may lead people to become more optimistic about the future in general, and about their own future income in particular, leading them to increase consumption even if their current income does not change. Other events may have the opposite effect.

The effects of the crisis are particularly striking in this respect. Figure 16-1 shows, using data from a survey of consumers, the evolution of expectations about family income growth over the following year, for each year since 1990. Note how expectations remained relatively stable until 2008, and how they have dropped ◄ since then, from 2–3% down to close to 0%. The drop at the start of the crisis is not surprising: As they saw output falling, it was normal for consumers to expect a drop in income over the following year. This also occurred in the previous two

How expectations of higher output in the future affect consumption today:

Expected future output increases
⇒ Expected future labor income increases
⇒ Human wealth increases
⇒ Consumption increases

Expected future output increases
⇒ Expected future dividends increase
⇒ Stock prices increase
⇒ Nonhuman wealth increases
⇒ Consumption increases

Go back to the two consumption functions we used in the core:

Looking at the short run (Chapter 3), we assumed $C = c_0 + c_1 Y$ (ignoring taxes here). This implied that, when income increased, consumption increased less than proportionately with income (C/Y went down). This was appropriate because our focus was on fluctuations, on transitory movements in income.

Looking at the long run (Chapter 10), we assumed that $S = sY$, or, equivalently $C = (1 - s)Y$. This implied that, when income increased, consumption increased proportionately with income (C/Y remained the same). This was appropriate because our focus was on permanent—long-run—movements in income.

What does this suggest is going to happen to the saving ◄ rate in a recession?

Figure 16-1

Expected Change in Family Income since 1990

Expectations of income growth fell in the initial phases of all three recessions. However, the fall in expected income growth in 2008 was very large and very persistent. This crisis was different.

Source: Surveys of Consumers, Thomson Reuters and University of Michigan, http://www.sca.isr.umich.edu/ main.php

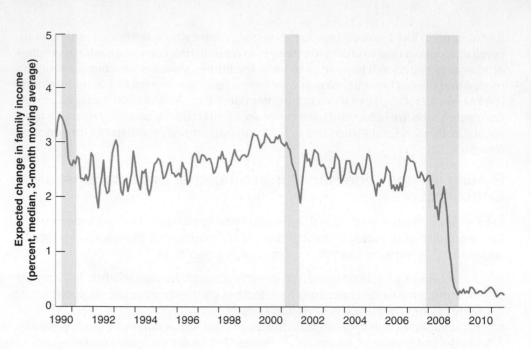

recessions. What was different about the crisis, both more striking and more worrisome, is how expectations of income growth did not recover from their fall. Consumers continued to be pessimistic about their income prospects. This is leading them to limit their consumption, which in turn is leading to a slow and painful recovery from the crisis.

16-2 Investment

How do firms make investment decisions? In our first pass at the answer in the core (Chapter 5), we took investment to depend on the current interest rate and the current level of sales. We refined that answer in Chapter 14 by pointing out that what mattered was the real interest rate, not the nominal interest rate. It should now be clear that investment decisions, just as consumption decisions, depend on more than current sales and the current real interest rate. They also depend very much on expectations of the future. We now explore how those expectations affect investment decisions.

Just like the basic theory of consumption, the basic theory of investment is straightforward. A firm deciding whether to invest—say, whether to buy a new machine—must make a simple comparison. The firm must first compute the present value of profits it can expect from having this additional machine. It must then compare the present value of profits to the cost of buying the machine. If the present value exceeds the cost, the firm should buy the machine—invest; if the present value is less than the cost, then the firm should not buy the machine—not invest. This, in a nutshell, is the theory of investment. Let's look at it in more detail.

Investment and Expectations of Profit

Let's go through the steps a firm must take to determine whether to buy a new machine. (Although we refer to a machine, the same reasoning applies to the other components of investment—the building of a new factory, the renovation of an office complex, and so on.)

Depreciation

To compute the present value of expected profits, the firm must first estimate how long the machine will last. Most machines are like cars. They can last nearly forever; but as time passes they become more and more expensive to maintain and less and less reliable.

◀ Look at cars in Cuba.

Assume a machine loses its usefulness at rate δ (the Greek lowercase letter delta) per year. A machine that is new this year is worth only $(1 - \delta)$ machines next year, $(1 - \delta)^2$ machines in two years, and so on. The *depreciation rate*, δ, measures how much usefulness the machine loses from one year to the next. What are reasonable values for δ? This is a question that the statisticians in charge of measuring the U.S. capital stock have had to answer. Based on their studies of depreciation of specific machines and buildings, they use numbers between 4% and 15% for machines, and between 2% and 4% for buildings and factories.

If the firm has a large number of machines, we can think of δ ◀ as the proportion of machines that die every year (think of lightbulbs—which work perfectly until they die). If the firm starts the year with K working machines and does not buy new ones, it will have only $K(1 - \delta)$ machines left one year later, and so on.

The Present Value of Expected Profits

The firm must then compute the present value of expected profits.

To capture the fact that it takes some time to put machines in place (and even more time to build a factory or an office building), let's assume that a machine bought in year t becomes operational—and starts depreciating—only one year later, in year $t + 1$. Denote profit per machine in real terms by Π.

This is an uppercase Greek pi as opposed to the lowercase ◀ Greek pi, which we use to denote inflation.

If the firm buys a machine in year t, the machine will generate its first profit in year $t + 1$; denote this expected profit by Π^e_{t+1}. The present value, in year t, of this expected profit in year $t + 1$, is given by

$$\frac{1}{1 + r_t} \Pi^e_{t+1}$$

This term is represented by the arrow pointing left in the upper line of Figure 16-2. Because we are measuring profit in real terms, we are using real interest rates to discount future profits. This is one of the lessons we learned in Chapter 14.

Denote expected profit per machine in year $t + 2$ by Π^e_{t+2}. Because of depreciation, only $(1 - \delta)$ of the machine is left in year $t + 2$, so the expected profit from the machine is equal to $(1 - \delta)\Pi^e_{t+2}$. The present value of this expected profit as of year t is equal to

$$\frac{1}{(1 + r_t)(1 + r^e_{t+1})} (1 - \delta) \Pi^e_{t+2}$$

This computation is represented by the arrow pointing left in the lower line of Figure 16-2.

The same reasoning applies to expected profits in the following years. Putting the pieces together gives us *the present value of expected profits* from buying the machine in year t, which we shall call $V(\Pi^e_t)$:

$$V(\Pi^e_t) = \frac{1}{1 + r_t} \Pi^e_{t+1} + \frac{1}{(1 + r_t)(1 + r^e_{t+1})} (1 - \delta) \Pi^e_{t+2} + \cdots \qquad (16.3)$$

Present value in Year t	Expected profit in:	
	Year $t + 1$	Year $t + 2$ ...
$\frac{1}{1 + r_t} \Pi^e_{t+1}$	Π^e_{t+1}	
$\frac{1}{(1 + r_t)(1 + r^e_{t+1})} (1 - \delta)\Pi^e_{t+2}$		$(1 - \delta)\Pi^e_{t+2}$

Figure 16-2

Computing the Present Value of Expected Profits

The expected present value is equal to the discounted value of expected profit next year, plus the discounted value of expected profit two years from now (taking into account the depreciation of the machine), and so on.

The Investment Decision

The firm must then decide whether or not to buy the machine. This decision depends on the relation between the present value of expected profits and the price of the machine. To simplify notation, let's assume the real price of a machine—that is, the machine's price in terms of the basket of goods produced in the economy—equals 1. What the firm must then do is to compare the present value of profits to 1.

If the present value is less than 1, the firm should not buy the machine: If it did, it would be paying more for the machine than it expects to get back in profits later. If the present value exceeds 1, the firm has an incentive to buy the new machine.

Let's now go from this one-firm one-machine example to investment in the economy as a whole.

Let I_t denote aggregate investment.

Denote profit per machine, or, more generally, profit per unit of capital (where capital includes machines, factories, office buildings, and so on) for the economy as a whole by Π_t.

Denote the expected present value of profit per unit of capital by $V(\Pi_t^e)$, as defined as in equation (16.3).

Our discussion suggests an investment function of the form

$$I_t = I\,[\,V(\Pi_t^e)\,] \qquad (16.4)$$
$$(\quad + \quad)$$

In words: Investment depends positively on the expected present value of future profits (per unit of capital). The higher the expected profits, the higher the expected present value and the higher the level of investment. The higher expected real interest rates, the lower the expected present value, and thus the lower the level of investment.

Tobin received the Nobel Prize in economics in 1981. ▶

If the present value computation the firm has to make strikes you as quite similar to the present value computation we saw in Chapter 15 for the fundamental value of a stock, you are right. This relation was first explored by James Tobin, from Yale University, who argued that, for this reason, there should indeed be a tight relation between investment and the value of the stock market. His argument and the evidence are presented in the Focus box "Investment and the Stock Market."

A Convenient Special Case

Before exploring further implications and extensions of equation (16.4), it is useful to go through a special case where the relation among investment, profit, and interest rates becomes very simple.

Suppose firms expect both future profits (per unit of capital) and future interest rates to remain at the same level as today, so that

$$\Pi_{t+1}^e = \Pi_{t+2}^e = \cdots = \Pi_t$$

and

$$r_{t+1}^e = r_{t+2}^e = \cdots = r_t$$

Economists call such expectations—expectations that the future will be like the present— **static expectations**. Under these two assumptions, equation (16.3) becomes

$$V(\Pi_t^e) = \frac{\Pi_t}{r_t + \delta} \qquad (16.5)$$

Expectations   **Extensions**

Investment and the Stock Market

FOCUS

Suppose a firm has 100 machines and 100 shares outstanding—one share per machine. Suppose the price per share is $2, and the purchase price of a machine is only $1. Obviously the firm should invest—buy a new machine—and finance it by issuing a share: Each machine costs the firm $1 to purchase, but stock market participants are willing to pay $2 for a share corresponding to this machine when it is installed in the firm.

This is an example of a more general argument made by Tobin that there should be a tight relation between the stock market and investment. When deciding whether or not to invest, he argued, firms might not need to go through the type of complicated computation you saw in the text. In effect, the stock price tells firms how much the stock market values each unit of capital already in place. The firm then has a simple problem: Compare the purchase price of an additional unit of capital to the price the stock market is willing to pay for it. *If the stock market value exceeds the purchase price, the firm should buy the machine; otherwise, it should not.*

Tobin then constructed a variable corresponding to the value of a unit of capital in place relative to its purchase price and looked at how closely it moved with investment. He used the symbol "q" to denote the variable, and the variable has become known as Tobin's q. Its construction is as follows.

1. Take the total value of U.S. corporations, as assessed by financial markets. That is, compute the sum of their stock market value (the price of a share times the number of shares). Compute also the total value of their bonds outstanding (firms finance themselves not only through stocks but also through bonds). Add together the value of stocks and bonds. Subtract the firms' financial assets, the value of the cash, bank accounts, and any bonds the firms might hold.
2. Divide this total value by the value of the capital stock of U.S. corporations at replacement cost (the price firms would have to pay to replace their machines, their plants, and so on).

The ratio gives us, in effect, the value of a unit of capital in place relative to its current purchase price. This ratio is Tobin's q. Intuitively, the higher q, the higher the value of capital relative to its current purchase price, and the higher investment should be. (In the example at the start of the box, Tobin's q is equal to 2, so the firm should definitely invest.)

How tight is the relation between Tobin's q and investment? The answer is given in Figure 1, which plots two variables for each year from 1960 to 2010 for the United States.

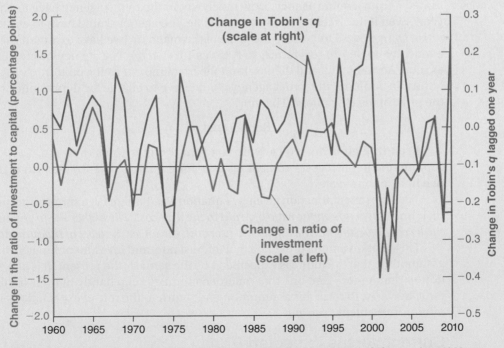

Figure 1 *Tobin's q versus the Ratio of Investment to Capital. Annual Rates of Change, since 1960*

Source: Flow of Funds Accounts Nonfarm Nonfinancial Corporate Business. Investment (line 12, Table F102). Capital measured by Nonfinancial assets (line 2, Table B102). Numerator of q: Market value of Equity (line 35) + [Financial Liabilities (line 21) − (Financial Assets (Total assets (line 1) − Nonfinancial assets (line 2))] all Table B102. Denominator of q: Nonfinancial assets (line 2, Table B102).

The present value of expected profits is simply the ratio of the profit rate—that is, profit per unit of capital—to the sum of the real interest rate and the depreciation rate. (The derivation is given in the appendix to this chapter.)

Replacing (16.5) in equation (16.4), investment is

$$I_t = I\left(\frac{\Pi_t}{r_t + \delta} \right) \tag{16.6}$$

Investment is a function of the ratio of the profit rate to the sum of the interest rate and the depreciation rate.

The sum of the real interest rate and the depreciation rate is called the **user cost** or the **rental cost** of capital. To see why, suppose the firm, instead of buying the machine, rented it from a rental agency. How much would the rental agency have to charge per year? Even if the machine did not depreciate, the agency would have to ask for an interest charge equal to r_t times the price of the machine (we have assumed the price of a machine to be 1 in real terms, so r_t times 1 is just r_t): The agency has to get at least as much from buying and then renting the machine out as it would from, say, buying bonds. In addition, the rental agency would have to charge for depreciation, δ, times the price of the machine, 1. Therefore:

$$\text{Rental cost} = (r_t + \delta)$$

> Such arrangements exist. For example, many firms lease cars and trucks from leasing companies.

Even though firms typically do not rent the machines they use, $(r_t + \delta)$ still captures the implicit cost—sometimes called the *shadow cost*—to the firm of using the machine for one year.

The investment function given by equation (16.6) then has a simple interpretation: *Investment depends on the ratio of profit to the user cost. The higher the profit, the higher the level of investment. The higher the user cost, the lower the level of investment.*

This relation among profit, the real interest rate, and investment hinges on a strong assumption: that the future is expected to be the same as the present. It is a useful relation to remember—and one that macroeconomists keep handy in their toolbox. It is time, however, to relax this assumption and return to the role of expectations in determining investment decisions.

Current versus Expected Profit

The theory we have developed implies that investment should be forward looking and should depend primarily on *expected future profits*. (Under our assumption that it takes a year for investment to generate profits, current profit does not even appear in equation (16.3).) One striking empirical fact about investment, however, is how strongly it moves with fluctuations in *current profit*.

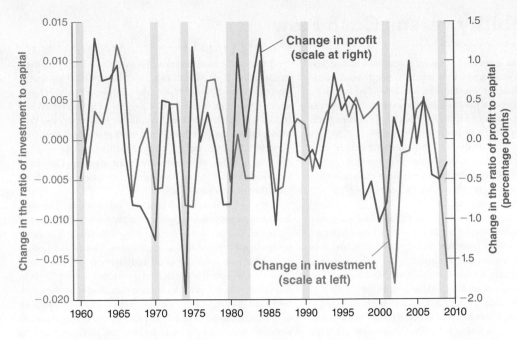

Investment and profit move very much together.

Source: Gross investment, Flow of funds variable FA105013005.A; Capital Stock Table 4.1, Bureau of Economic Analysis; Profit is constructed from After-tax profits and Net interest of nonfinancial corporations, Table B14, Economic Report of the President.

This relation is shown in Figure 16-3, which plots yearly changes in investment and profit since 1960 for the U.S. economy. Profit is constructed as the ratio of the sum of *after-tax profits plus interest payments paid by U.S. nonfinancial corporations*, divided by their capital stock. Investment is constructed as the ratio of investment by U.S. nonfinancial corporations to their capital stock. The shaded areas in the figure represent years in which there was a recession—a decline in output for at least two consecutive quarters of the year.

There is a clear positive relation between changes in investment and changes in current profit in Figure 16-3. Is this relation inconsistent with the theory we have just developed, which holds that investment should be related to the present value of expected future profits rather than to current profit? Not necessarily: If firms expect future profits to move very much like current profit, then the present value of those future profits will move very much like current profit, and so will investment.

Economists who have looked at the question more closely have concluded, however, that the effect of current profit on investment is stronger than would be predicted by the theory we have developed so far. How they have gathered some of the evidence is described in the Focus box "Profitability versus Cash Flow." On the one hand, some firms with highly profitable investment projects but low current profits appear to be investing too little. On the other hand, some firms that have high current profit appear sometimes to invest in projects of doubtful profitability. In short, current profit appears to affect investment, even after controlling for the expected present value of profits.

Why does current profit play a role in the investment decision? The answer lurks in Section 16-1, where we discussed why consumption depends directly on current income; some of the reasons we used to explain the behavior of consumers also apply to firms:

■ If its current profit is low, a firm that wants to buy new machines can get the funds it needs only by borrowing. It may be reluctant to borrow: Although expected profits might look good, things may turn bad, leaving the firm unable to repay the debt. But if current profit is high, the firm might be able to finance its investment just by retaining some of its earnings and without having to borrow. The bottom line is that higher current profit may lead the firm to invest more.

Profitability versus Cash Flow

How much does investment depend on the expected present value of future profits, and how much does it depend on current profit? In other words: Which is more important for investment decisions: profitability (the expected present discounted value of future profits) or **cash flow** (current profit, the net flow of cash the firm is receiving now)?

The difficulty in answering this question is that, most of the time, cash flow and profitability move together. Firms that do well typically have both large cash flows and good future prospects. Firms that suffer losses often also have poor future prospects.

The best way to isolate the effects of cash flow and profitability on investment is to identify times or events when cash flow and profitability move in different directions, and then look at what happens to investment. This is the approach taken by Owen Lamont, an economist at Yale University. An example will help you understand Lamont's strategy:

Think of two firms, A and B. Both firms are involved in steel production. Firm B is also involved in oil exploration.

Suppose there is a sharp drop in the price of oil, leading to losses in oil exploration. This shock decreases firm B's cash flow. If the losses in oil exploration are large enough to offset the profits from steel production, firm B might even show an overall loss.

The question we can now ask is: As a result of the drop in the price of oil, will firm B invest less in its steel operation than firm A does? If only the profitability of steel production matters, there is no reason for firm B to invest less in its steel operation than firm A. But if current cash flow also matters, the fact that firm B has a lower cash flow may prevent it from investing as much as firm A in its steel operation. Looking at investment in the steel operations of the two firms can tell us how much investment depends on cash flow versus profitability.

This is the empirical strategy followed by Lamont. He focused on what happened in 1986 when the price of oil in the United States dropped by 50%, leading to large losses in oil-related activities. He then looked at whether firms that had substantial oil activities cut investment in their nonoil activities relatively more than other firms in the same non-oil activities. He concluded that they did. He found that for every $1 decrease in cash flow due to the decrease in the price of oil, investment spending in nonoil activities was reduced by 10 to 20 cents. In short: Current cash flow matters.

Source: Owen Lamont, "Cash Flow and Investment: Evidence from Internal Capital Markets," *Journal of Finance* 1997 52 (1): pp. 83-109.

- Even if the firm wants to invest, it might have difficulty borrowing. Potential lenders may not be convinced the project is as good as the firm says it is, and they may worry the firm will be unable to repay. If the firm has large current profits, it does not have to borrow and so does not need to convince potential lenders. It can proceed and invest as it pleases, and is more likely to do so.

In summary: To fit the investment behavior we observe in practice, the investment equation is better specified as

$$I_t = I\,[\,V(\Pi_t^e),\,\Pi_t\,] \qquad (16.7)$$
$$(\ +\ ,\ +\ )$$

In words: Investment depends both on the expected present value of future profits and on the current level of profit.

Profit and Sales

Let's take stock of where we are. We have argued that investment depends on both current and expected profit or, more specifically, current and expected profit per unit of capital. We need to take one last step: What determines profit per unit of capital? Answer: Primarily two factors: (1) the level of sales, and (2) the existing capital stock. If sales are low relative to the capital stock, profits per unit of capital are likely to be low as well.

Let's write this more formally. Ignore the distinction between sales and output, and let Y_t denote output—equivalently, sales. Let K_t denote the capital stock at time t. Our discussion suggests the following relation:

$$\Pi_t = \Pi\left(\frac{Y_t}{K_t}\right) \tag{16.8}$$
$$(\ +\ )$$

Profit per unit of capital is an increasing function of the ratio of sales to the capital stock. For a given capital stock, the higher the sales, the higher the profit per unit of capital. For given sales, the higher the capital stock, the lower the profit per unit of capital.

How well does this relation hold in practice? Figure 16-4 plots yearly changes in profit per unit of capital (measured on the right vertical axis) and changes in the ratio of output to capital (measured on the left vertical axis) for the United States since 1960. As in Figure 16-3, profit per unit of capital is defined as the sum of after-tax profits plus interest payments by U.S. nonfinancial corporations, divided by their capital stock measured at replacement cost. The ratio of output to capital is constructed as the ratio of GDP to the aggregate capital stock.

Figure 16-4 shows that there is a tight relation between changes in profit per unit of capital and changes in the ratio of output to capital. Given that most of the year-to-year changes in the ratio of output to capital come from movements in output, and most of the year-to-year changes in profit per unit of capital come from movements in profit (capital moves slowly over time; the reason is that capital is large compared to yearly investment, so even large movements in investment lead to small changes in the capital stock), we can state the relation as follows: Profit decreases in recessions (shaded areas are periods of recession), and increases in expansions.

Why is this relation between output and profit relevant here? Because it implies a link between *current output and expected future output*, on the one hand, and *investment*, on the other: Current output affects current profit, expected future output affects expected future profit, and current and expected future profits affect investment.

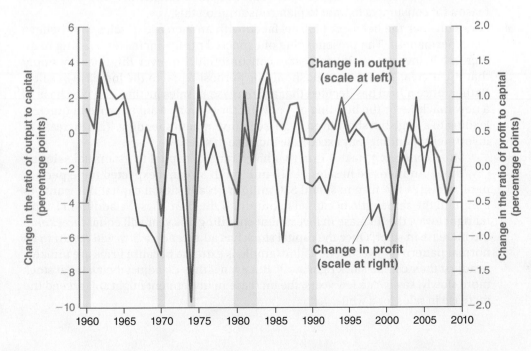

Figure 16-4

Changes in Profit per Unit of Capital versus Changes in the Ratio of Output to Capital in the United States, since 1960

Profit per unit of capital and the ratio of output to capital move largely together.

Source: Capital stock: Table 4.1, Bureau of Economic Analysis; profit is constructed from After-Tax Profits and Net Interest of Nonfinancial Corporations, Table B14, Economic Report of the President. Output of the nonfinancial corporate sector is measured by gross value added using Table B14, Economic Report of the President.

High expected output ⇒
High expected profit ⇒
High investment today.

For example, the anticipation of a long, sustained economic expansion leads firms to expect high profits, now and for some time in the future. These expectations in turn ▶ lead to higher investment. The effect of current and expected output on investment, together with the effect of investment back on demand and output, will play a crucial role when we return to the determination of output in Chapter 17.

16-3 The Volatility of Consumption and Investment

You will surely have noticed the similarities between our treatment of consumption and of investment behavior in Sections 16-1 and 16-2:

■ Whether consumers perceive current movements in income to be transitory or permanent affects their consumption decision. The more transitory they expect a current increase in income to be, the less they will increase their consumption.

■ In the same way, whether firms perceive current movements in sales to be transitory or permanent affects their investment decisions. The more transitory they expect a current increase in sales to be, the less they revise their assessment of the present value of profits, and thus the less likely they are to buy new machines or build new factories. This is why, for example, the boom in sales that happens every year between Thanksgiving and Christmas does not lead to a boom in investment every December. Firms understand that this boom is transitory.

In the United States, retail sales are 24% higher on average in December than in ▶ other months. In France and Italy, sales are 60% higher in December.

But there are also important differences between consumption decisions and investment decisions:

■ The theory of consumption we developed earlier implies that when faced with an increase in income consumers perceive as permanent, they respond with *at most* an equal increase in consumption. The permanent nature of the increase in income implies that they can afford to increase consumption now and in the future by the same amount as the increase in income. Increasing consumption more than one-for-one would require cuts in consumption later, and there is no reason for consumers to want to plan consumption this way.

■ Now consider the behavior of firms faced with an increase in sales they believe to be permanent. The present value of expected profits increases, leading to an increase in investment. In contrast to consumption, however, this does not imply that the increase in investment should be at most equal to the increase in sales. Rather, once a firm has decided that an increase in sales justifies the purchase of a new machine or the building of a new factory, it may want to proceed quickly, leading to a large but short-lived increase in investment spending. This increase in investment spending may exceed the increase in sales.

More concretely, take a firm that has a ratio of capital to its annual sales of, say, three. An increase in sales of $10 million this year, if expected to be permanent, requires the firm to spend $30 million on additional capital if it wants to maintain the same ratio of capital to output. If the firm buys the additional capital right away, the increase in investment spending this year will equal *three times* the increase in sales. Once the capital stock has adjusted, the firm will return to its normal pattern of investment. This example is extreme because firms are unlikely to adjust their capital stock right away. But even if they do adjust their capital stock more slowly, say over a few years, the increase in investment might still exceed the increase in sales for a while.

We can tell the same story in terms of equation (16.8). Because we make no distinction here between output and sales, the initial increase in sales leads to an equal increase in output, Y, so that Y/K—the ratio of the firm's output to its existing capital stock—also increases. The result is higher profit, which leads the firm to undertake more investment. Over time, the higher level of investment leads to a higher capital stock, K, so that Y/K decreases back to normal. Profit per unit of capital returns to normal, and so does investment. Thus, in response to a permanent increase in sales, investment may increase a lot initially, and then return to normal over time.

These differences suggest that investment should be more volatile than consumption. How much more? The answer is given in Figure 16-5, which plots yearly rates of change in U.S. consumption and investment since 1960. The shaded areas are years during which the U.S. economy was in recession. To make the figure easier to interpret, both rates of change are plotted as deviations from the average rate of change, so that they are, on average, equal to zero.

Figure 16-5 yields three conclusions:

- Consumption and investment usually move together: Recessions, for example, are typically associated with decreases in *both* investment and consumption. Given our discussion, which has emphasized that consumption and investment depend largely on the same determinants, this should not come as a surprise.
- Investment is much more volatile than consumption. Relative movements in investment range from −29% to 26%, while relative movements in consumption range only from −5% to 3%.
- Because, however, the level of investment is much smaller than the level of consumption (recall that investment accounts for about 15% of GDP, versus 70% for consumption), changes in investment from one year to the next end up being of the same overall magnitude as changes in consumption. In other words, both components contribute roughly equally to fluctuations in output over time.

Relative movements in *I* are larger than relative movements in *C*. But because *I* accounts only for 15% of GDP and *C* accounts for 70%, movements in *I* and *C* are of roughly equal magnitude.

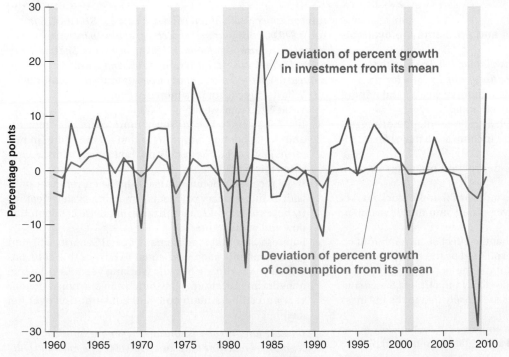

Deviation of percent growth in investment from its mean

Deviation of percent growth of consumption from its mean

Figure 16-5

Rates of Change of Consumption and Investment, in the United States, since 1960

Relative movements in investment are much larger than relative movements in consumption.

Source: Series PCECC96, GDPIC96 Federal Reserve Economic Data (FRED) http://research.stlouisfed.org/fred2/

Summary

- Consumption depends on both wealth and current income. Wealth is the sum of nonhuman wealth (financial wealth and housing wealth) and human wealth (the present value of expected after-tax labor income).

- The response of consumption to changes in income depends on whether consumers perceive these changes as transitory or permanent.

- Consumption is likely to respond less than one-for-one to movements in income. Consumption might move even if current income does not change.

- Investment depends on both current profit and the present value of expected future profits.

- Under the simplifying assumption that firms expect profits and interest rates to be the same in the future as they are today, we can think of investment as depending on the ratio of profit to the user cost of capital, where the user cost is the sum of the real interest rate and the depreciation rate.

- Movements in profit are closely related to movements in output. Hence, we can think of investment as depending indirectly on current and expected future output movements. Firms that anticipate a long output expansion, and thus a long sequence of high profits, will invest. Movements in output that are not expected to last will have a small effect on investment.

- Investment is much more volatile than consumption. But because investment accounts only for 15% of GDP and consumption accounts for 70%, movements in investment and consumption are of roughly equal importance in accounting for movements in aggregate output.

Key Terms

permanent income theory of consumption, 338
life cycle theory of consumption, 338
financial wealth, 338
housing wealth, 338
human wealth, 338
nonhuman wealth, 338
total wealth, 338

panel data sets, 339
static expectations, 346
Tobin's q, 347
user cost of capital, or rental cost of capital, 348
profitability, 350
cash flow, 350

Questions and Problems

QUICK CHECK
All Quick Check questions and problems are available on MyEconLab.

1. Using the information in this chapter, label each of the following statements true, false, or uncertain. Explain briefly.

a. For a typical college student, human wealth and nonhuman wealth are approximately equal.

b. Natural experiments, such as retirement, do not suggest that expectations of future income are a major factor affecting consumption.

c. Buildings and factories depreciate much faster than machines.

d. A high value for Tobin's q indicates that the stock market believes that capital is overvalued, and thus investment should be lower.

e. Economists have found that the effect of current profit on investment can be fully explained by the effect of current profit on expectations of future profits.

f. Data from the past three decades in the United States suggest that corporate profits are closely tied to the business cycle.

g. Changes in consumption and investment typically occur in the same direction and at roughly the same magnitude.

2. A consumer has nonhuman wealth equal to $100,000. She earns $40,000 this year and expects her salary to increase by 5% in real terms each year for the following two years. She will then retire. The real interest rate is equal to 0% and is expected to remain at 0% in the future. Labor income is taxed at a rate of 25%.

a. What is this consumer's human wealth?

b. What is her total wealth?

c. If she expects to live for seven more years after retiring, and wants her consumption to remain the same (in real terms) every year from now on, how much can she consume this year?

d. If she received a bonus of $20,000 in the current year only, with all future salary payments remaining as stated earlier, by how much could this consumer increase consumption now and in the future?

e. Suppose now that at retirement, Social Security will start paying benefits each year equal to 60% of this consumer's earnings during her last working year. Assume that benefits are not taxed. How much can she consume this year and still maintain constant consumption over her lifetime?

3. A pretzel manufacturer is considering buying another pretzel-making machine that costs $100,000. The machine will depreciate by 8% per year. It will generate real profits equal to $18,000 next year, $18,000 (1 – 8%) two years from now (that is, the same real profits but adjusted for depreciation), $18,000 (1 – 8%)² three years from now, and so on. Determine whether the manufacturer should buy the machine if the real interest rate is assumed to remain constant at each rate in (a) through (c).

  a. 5%   b. 10%   c. 15%

4. Suppose that at age 22, you have just finished college and have been offered a job with a starting salary of $40,000. Your salary will remain constant in real terms. However, you have also been admitted to a professional school. The school can be completed in two years. Upon graduation, you expect your starting salary to be 10% higher in real terms and to remain constant in real terms thereafter. The tax rate on labor income is 40%.

  a. If the real interest rate is zero and you expect to retire at age 60 (i.e., if you do not go to professional school, you expect to work for 38 years total), what is the maximum you should be willing to pay in tuition to attend this professional school?

  b. What is your answer to part (a) if you expect to pay 30% in taxes?

DIG DEEPER

All Dig Deeper questions and problems are available on MyEconLab.

5. Individual saving and aggregate capital accumulation

  Suppose that every consumer is born with zero financial wealth and lives for three periods: youth, middle age, and old age. Consumers work in the first two periods and retire in the last one. Their income is $5 in the first period, $25 in the second, and $0 in the last one. Inflation and expected inflation are equal to zero, and so is the real interest rate.

  a. What is the present discounted value of labor income at the beginning of life? What is the highest sustainable level of consumption such that consumption is equal in all three periods?

  b. For each age group, what is the amount of saving that allows consumers to maintain the constant level of consumption you found in part (a)? (Hint: Saving can be a negative number if the consumer needs to borrow in order to maintain a certain level of consumption.)

  c. Suppose there are n people born each period. What is total saving in the economy? (Hint: Add up the saving of each age group. Remember that some age groups may have negative saving.) Explain.

  d. What is total financial wealth in the economy? (Hint: Compute the financial wealth of people at the beginning of the first period of life, the beginning of the second period, and the beginning of the third period. Add the three numbers. Remember that people can be in debt, so financial wealth can be negative.)

6. Borrowing constraints and aggregate capital accumulation

  Continue with the setup from Problem 5, but suppose now that borrowing restrictions do not allow young consumers to borrow. If we call the sum of income and total financial wealth "cash on hand," then the borrowing restriction means that consumers cannot consume more than their cash on hand. In each age group, consumers compute their total wealth and then determine their desired level of consumption as the highest level that allows their consumption to be equal in all three periods. However, if at any time, desired consumption exceeds cash on hand, then consumers are constrained to consume exactly their cash on hand.

  a. Calculate consumption in each period of life. Compare this answer to your answer to part (a) of Problem 5, and explain any differences.

  b. Calculate total saving for the economy. Compare this answer to your answer to part (c) of Problem 5, and explain any differences.

  c. Derive total financial wealth for the economy. Compare this answer to your answer to part (d) of Problem 5, and explain any differences.

  d. Consider the following statement: "Financial liberalization may be good for individual consumers, but it is bad for overall capital accumulation." Discuss.

7. Saving with uncertain future income.

  Consider a consumer who lives for three periods: youth, middle age, and old age. When young, the consumer earns $20,000 in labor income. Earnings during middle age are uncertain; there is a 50% chance that the consumer will earn $40,000 and a 50% chance that the consumer will earn $100,000. When old, the consumer spends savings accumulated during the previous periods. Assume that inflation, expected inflation, and the real interest rate equal zero. Ignore taxes for this problem.

  a. What is the expected value of earnings in the middle period of life? Given this number, what is the present discounted value of expected lifetime labor earnings? If the consumer wishes to maintain constant expected consumption over her lifetime, how much will she consume in each period? How much will she save in each period?

  b. Now suppose the consumer wishes, above all else, to maintain a minimum consumption level of $20,000 in each period of her life. To do so, she must consider the worst outcome. If earnings during middle age turn out to be $40,000, how much should the consumer spend when she is young to guarantee consumption of at least $20,000 in each period? How does this level of consumption compare to the level you obtained for the young period in part (a)?

  c. Given your answer in part (b), suppose that the consumer's earnings during middle age turn out to be $100,000. How much will she spend in each period of life? Will consumption be constant over the consumer's lifetime? (Hint: When the consumer reaches middle age, she will try to maintain constant consumption for the last two periods of life, as long as she can consume at least $20,000 in each period.)

  d. What effect does uncertainty about future labor income have on saving (or borrowing) by young consumers?

EXPLORE FURTHER

8. The movements of consumption and investment

  Go to the latest Economic Report of the President (**www. gpoaccess.gov/eop/**) and find Table B-2 ("Real GDP") in the Statistical Appendix. Note that you can download the statistical appendix separately in a spreadsheet which will be easier to work with. Retrieve annual data for the years 1959 to the most recent date available for personal consumption expenditures and gross private domestic investment. Note that the data are in real terms.

a. On average, how much larger is consumption than investment?

b. Compute the change in the levels of consumption and investment from one year to the next, and graph them for the period 1959 to the latest available date. Are the year-to-year changes in consumption and investment of similar magnitude?

c. What do your answers in parts (a) and (b) imply about the average annual percentage changes of consumption and investment? Is this implication consistent with Figure 16-5?

9. *Consumer confidence, disposable income, and recessions*

*Go to the Web site of the University of Michigan Survey of Consumers (*__www.sca.isr.umich.edu__*) and download data on the annual Index of Consumer Sentiment from 1960 to the present day. We will use this data series as our measure of consumer confidence. Now, go to the Web site of the Economic Report of the President and download data from Table B-31 on the level of Disposable Personal Income per capita in Chained (2005) dollars. You will need to convert this series into an annual growth rate.*

a. Before you look at the data, can you think of any reasons to expect consumer confidence to be related to disposable income? Can you think of reasons why consumer confidence would be unrelated to disposable income?

b. Explain why, in the analysis of consumption, we would want to an income measure in per capita (often called per person elsewhere in the text).

c. Plot the level of the index of consumer sentiment against the growth rate of disposable income per person. Is the relationship positive?

d. Plot the change in the index of consumer sentiment against the growth rate of disposable income per person. Focus on the portion of the graph where the change in disposable income is zero. Is the value of the level of consumer sentiment the same when income is not changing? Relate your answer to part (a).

e. Now find every year where the growth in disposable income per person is negative. Does the index of consumer sentiment rise or fall in that quarter?

f. Focus in on the crisis years 2008 and 2009. How does the fall in consumer sentiment from 2007 to 2008 compare to the usual variation in consumer sentiment? Why? (*Hint*: The bankruptcy of Lehmann Brothers occurred in September 2008.) Although disposable income per person fell from 2008 to 2009, what happened to the level of consumer sentiment?

APPENDIX: Derivation of the Expected Present Value of Profits under Static Expectations

You saw in the text (equation (16.3)) that the expected present value of profits is given by

$$V\left(\Pi_t^e\right) = \frac{1}{1 + r_t}\,\Pi_{t+1}^e + \frac{1}{(1 + r_t)(1 + r_{t+1}^e)}\,(1 - \delta)\,\Pi_{t+2}^e + \cdots$$

If firms expect both future profits (per unit of capital) and future interest rates to remain at the same level as today, so that $\Pi_{t+1}^e = \Pi_{t+2}^e = \cdots = \Pi_t$ and $r_{t+1}^e = r_{t+2}^e = \cdots = r_t$, the equation becomes

$$V(\Pi_t^e) = \frac{1}{1 + r_t}\,\Pi_t + \frac{1}{(1 + r_t)^2}\,(1 - \delta)\,\Pi_t + \cdots$$

Factoring out $[1/(1 + r_t)]\Pi_t$,

$$V(\Pi_t^e) = \frac{1}{1 + r_t}\,\Pi_t\left(1 + \frac{1 - \delta}{1 + r_t} + \cdots\right) \qquad (16.A1)$$

The term in parentheses in this equation is a geometric series, a series of the form $1 + x + x^2 + \ldots$ So, from Proposition 2 in Appendix 2 at the end of the book,

$$(1 + x + x^2 + \cdots) = \frac{1}{1 - x}$$

Here x equals $(1 - \delta)/(1 + r_t)$, so

$$\left(1 + \frac{1 - \delta}{1 + r_t} + \left(\frac{1 - \delta}{1 + r_t}\right)^2 + \cdots\right)$$

$$= \frac{1}{1 - (1 - \delta)/(1 + r_t)} = \frac{1 + r_t}{r_t + \delta}$$

Replacing the term in parentheses in equation (16.A1) with the expression above and manipulating gives:

$$V(\Pi_t^e) = \frac{1}{1 + r_t}\frac{1 + r_t}{r_t + \delta}\,\Pi_t$$

Simplifying gives equation (16.5) in the text:

$$V(\Pi_t^e) = \frac{\Pi_t}{(r_t + \delta)}$$

Expectations, Output, and Policy

I n Chapter 15, we saw how expectations affected asset prices, from bonds to stocks to houses. In Chapter 16, we saw how expectations affected consumption decisions and investment decisions. In this chapter we put the pieces together and take another look at the effects of monetary and fiscal policy.

Section 17-1 draws the major implication of what we have learned, namely that expectations of both future output and future interest rates affect current spending, and therefore current output.

Section 17-2 looks at monetary policy. It shows how the effects of monetary policy depend crucially on how expectations respond to policy: Conventional monetary policy directly affects only the short-term interest rate. What happens to spending and output then depends on how changes in the short-term interest rate lead people and firms to change their expectations of future interest rates and future income, and, by implication, lead them to change their decisions.

Section 17-3 turns to fiscal policy. It shows how, in sharp contrast to the simple model you saw back in the core, a fiscal contraction may, under some circumstances, lead to an increase in output, even in the short run. Again, how expectations respond to policy is at the center of the story. ●

17-1 Expectations and Decisions: Taking Stock

Let's start by reviewing what we have learned, and then discuss how we should modify the characterization of goods and financial markets—the *IS–LM* model—we developed in the core.

Expectations, Consumption, and Investment Decisions

The theme of Chapter 16 was that both consumption and investment decisions depend very much on expectations of future income and interest rates. The channels through which expectations affect consumption and investment spending are summarized in Figure 17-1.

Note the many channels through which expected future variables affect current decisions, both directly and through asset prices:

- An increase in current and expected future after-tax real labor income and/or a decrease in current and expected future real interest rates increase human wealth (the expected present discounted value of after-tax real labor income), which in turn leads to an increase in consumption.
- An increase in current and expected future real dividends and/or a decrease in current and expected future real interest rates increase stock prices, which leads to an increase in non-human wealth and, in turn, to an increase in consumption.
- A decrease in current and expected future nominal interest rates leads to an increase in bond prices, which leads to an increase in non-human wealth and, in turn, to an increase in consumption.
- An increase in current and expected future real after-tax profits and/or a decrease in current and expected future real interest rates increase the present value of real after-tax profits, which leads, in turn, to an increase in investment.

Note that in the case of bonds, it is nominal rather than real interest rates that matter, because bonds are claims to dollars rather than goods in the future.

Expectations and the *IS* Relation

A model that gave a detailed treatment of consumption and investment along the lines suggested in Figure 17-1 would be very complicated. It can be done—and indeed it is done in the large empirical models that macroeconomists build to understand the economy and analyze policy; but this is not the place for such complications. We want to capture the essence of what you have learned so far, how consumption and investment depend on expectations of the future—without getting lost in the details.

Figure 17-1

Expectations and Spending: The Channels

Expectations affect consumption and investment decisions, both directly and through asset prices.

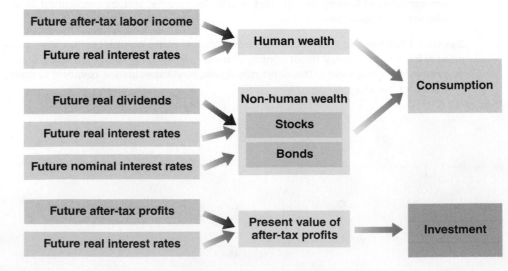

To do so, let's make a major simplification. Let us reduce the present and the future to only two periods: (1) a *current* period, which you can think of as the current year, and (2) a *future* period, which you can think of as all future years lumped together. This way we do not have to keep track of expectations about each future year.

This way of dividing time between "today" and "later" is the way many of us organize our own lives: Think of "things to do today" versus "things that can wait."

Having made this assumption, the question becomes: How should we write the *IS* relation for the current period? Earlier, we wrote the following equation for the *IS* relation:

$$Y = C(Y - T) + I(Y, r) + G$$

See equation (14.5) in Chapter 14, which itself extended equation (5.2) in Chapter 5 to allow for a distinction between the real and the nominal interest rate.

We assumed that consumption depended only on current income, and that investment depended only on current output and the current real interest rate. We now want to modify this to take into account how expectations affect both consumption and investment. We proceed in two steps:

First, we simply rewrite the equation in more compact form, but without changing its content. For that purpose, let's define aggregate private spending as the sum of consumption and investment spending:

$$A(Y, T, r) \equiv C(Y - T) + I(Y, r)$$

The reason for doing so is to group together the two components of demand, C and I, which both depend on expectations. We continue to treat G, government spending, as exogenous—unexplained within our model.

where *A* stands for **aggregate private spending**, or, simply, *private spending*. With this notation we can rewrite the *IS* relation as

$$Y = A(Y, T, r) + G \qquad (17.1)$$
$$(+, -, -)$$

The properties of aggregate private spending, *A*, follow from the properties of consumption and investment that we derived in earlier chapters:

- Aggregate private spending is an increasing function of income *Y*: Higher income (equivalently, output) increases consumption and investment.
- Aggregate private spending is a decreasing function of taxes *T*: Higher taxes decrease consumption.
- Aggregate private spending is a decreasing function of the real interest rate *r*: A higher real interest rate decreases investment.

The first step only simplified notation. The second step is to extend equation (17.1) to take into account the role of expectations. The natural extension is to allow spending to depend not only on current variables but also on their expected values in the future period:

$$Y = A(Y, T, r, Y'^e, T'^e, r'^e) + G \qquad (17.2)$$
$$(+, -, -, +, \quad -, \quad -)$$

Notation:
Primes stand for values of the variables in the future period. The superscript e stands for "expected."

Primes denote future values and the superscript e denotes an expectation, so Y'^e, T'^e, and r'^e denote future expected income, future expected taxes, and the future expected real interest rate, respectively. The notation is a bit heavy, but what it captures is straightforward:

- Increases in either current or expected future income increase private spending.
- Increases in either current or expected future taxes decrease private spending.
- Increases in either the current or expected future real interest rate decrease private spending.

Y or Y'^e increase $\Rightarrow$ A increases
T or T'^e increase $\Rightarrow$ A decreases
r or r'^e increase $\Rightarrow$ A decreases

With the goods market equilibrium now given by equation (17.2), Figure 17-2 shows the new *IS* curve for the current period. As usual, to draw the curve, we take all variables other than current output, *Y*, and the current real interest rate, *r*, as given.

Figure 17-2

The New IS Curve

Given expectations, a decrease in the real interest rate leads to a small increase in output: The *IS* curve is steeply downward sloping. Increases in government spending, or in expected future output, shift the *IS* curve to the right. Increases in taxes, in expected future taxes, or in the expected future real interest rate shift the *IS* curve to the left.

$\Delta T > 0$, or
$\Delta T'^e > 0$, or
$\Delta r'^e > 0$

$\Delta G > 0$, or
$\Delta Y'^e > 0$, or
$\Delta r'^e < 0$, or
$\Delta T'^e > 0$

Current interest rate, r

Current output, Y

Thus, the *IS* curve is drawn for given values of current and future expected taxes, T and T'^e, for given values of expected future output, Y'^e, and for given values of the expected future real interest rate, r'^e.

The new *IS* curve, based on equation (17.2), is still downward sloping, for the same reason as in Chapter 5: A decrease in the current interest rate leads to an increase in spending. This increase in spending leads, through a multiplier effect, to an increase in output. We can say more, however: The new *IS* curve is much steeper than the *IS* curve we drew in earlier chapters. Put another way, *everything else the same*, a large decrease in the current interest rate is likely to have only a small effect on equilibrium output.

To see why the effect is small, take point A on the *IS* curve in Figure 17-2, and consider the effects of a decrease in the real interest rate, from r_A to r_B. The effect of the decrease in the real interest rate on output depends on the strength of two effects: the effect of the real interest rate on spending given income, and the size of the multiplier. Let's examine each one.

■ A decrease in the current real interest rate, *given unchanged expectations of the future real interest rate*, does not have much effect on spending. We saw why in the previous chapters: A change in only the current real interest rate does not lead to large changes in present values, and therefore does not lead to large changes in spending. For example, firms are not likely to change their investment plans very much in response to a decrease in the current real interest rate if they do not expect future real interest rates to be lower as well.

■ The multiplier is likely to be small. Recall that the size of the multiplier depends on the size of the effect a change in current income (output) has on spending. But a change in current income, *given unchanged expectations of future income*, is unlikely to have a large effect on spending. The reason: Changes in income that are not expected to last have only a limited effect on either consumption or investment. Consumers who expect their income to be higher only for a year will

Suppose you have a 30-year loan, and the one-year interest rate goes down from 5% to 2%. All future one-year rates remain the same. By how much will the 30-year interest rate come down? (Answer: from 5% to 4.9%. To see why, extend equation (15.7) to the 30-year yield: The 30-year yield is the average of the 30 one-year rates.)

increase consumption, but by much less than the increase in their income. Firms that expect sales to be higher only for a year are unlikely to change their investment plans much, if at all.

◄ Suppose the firm where you work decides to give all employees a one-time bonus of $10,000. You do not expect it to happen again. By how much will you increase your consumption this year? (If you need to, look at the discussion of consumption behavior in Chapter 16.)

Putting things together, a large decrease in the current real interest rate—from r_A to r_B in Figure 17-2—leads to only a small increase in output, from Y_A to Y_B. Put another way: The *IS* curve, which goes through points *A* and *B*, is steeply downward sloping.

A change in any variable in equation (17.2) other than Y and r shifts the *IS* curve:

- Changes in current taxes (T) or in current government spending (G) shift the *IS* curve.
  An increase in current government spending increases spending at a given interest rate, shifting the *IS* curve to the right; an increase in taxes shifts the *IS* curve to the left. These shifts are represented in Figure 17-2.
- Changes in expected future variables also shift the *IS* curve.
  An increase in expected future output, Y'^e, shifts the *IS* curve to the right: Higher expected future income leads consumers to feel wealthier and spend more; higher expected future output implies higher expected profits, leading firms to invest more. Higher spending by consumers and firms leads, through the multiplier effect, to higher output. By a similar argument, an increase in expected future taxes leads consumers to decrease their current spending and shifts the *IS* curve to the left. And an increase in the expected future real interest rate decreases current spending, also leading to a decrease in output, shifting the *IS* curve to the left. These shifts are also represented in Figure 17-2.

The *LM* Relation Revisited

The *LM* relation we derived in Chapter 4 and have used until now was given by

$$\frac{M}{P} = Y\,L(i) \tag{17.3}$$

where M/P is the supply of money and $YL(i)$ is the demand for money. Equilibrium in financial markets requires that the supply of money be equal to the demand for money. The demand for money depends on real income and on the short-term nominal interest rate—the opportunity cost of holding money. We derived this demand for money before thinking about expectations. Now that we have introduced them, the question is whether we should modify equation (17.3). The answer—we are sure this will be good news—is: no.

Think of your own demand for money. How much money you want to hold today depends on your *current* level of transactions, not on the level of transactions you expect next year or the year after; there will be ample time for you to adjust your money balances to your transaction level if and when it changes in the future. And the opportunity cost of holding money today depends on the *current* nominal interest rate, not on the expected nominal interest rate next year or the year after. If short-term interest rates were to increase in the future, increasing the opportunity cost of holding money then, the time to reduce your money balances would be then, not now.

So, in contrast to the consumption decision, the decision about how much money to hold is myopic, depending primarily on current income and the current short-term nominal interest rate. We can still think of the demand for money as depending on the current level of output and the current nominal interest rate, and use equation (17.3) to describe the determination of the nominal interest rate in the current period.

Let's summarize:

We have seen that expectations about the future play a major role in spending decisions. This implies that expectations enter the *IS* relation: Private spending depends not only on current output and the current real interest rate, but also on expected future output and the expected future real interest rate.

In contrast, the decision about how much money to hold is largely myopic: The two variables entering the *LM* relation are still current income and the current nominal interest rate.

17-2 Monetary Policy, Expectations, and Output

Other distinctions may also be relevant. For example, we saw in Chapter 9 how, during the initial part of the crisis, the interest rates charged by banks increased a lot relative to the ▶ rates on government bonds. We leave these aside here.

We leave aside "unconventional" policies such as quantitative easing (see Chapter 9) ▶ here, but return to the issue below.

In the basic *IS–LM* model we developed in Chapter 5, there was only one interest rate, *i*, which entered both the *IS* relation and the *LM* relation. When the Fed expanded the money supply, "the" interest rate went down, and spending increased. From the previous three chapters, you have learned that there are in fact many interest rates, and that we must keep at least two distinctions in mind:

1. The distinction between the nominal interest rate and the real interest rate.

2. The distinction between current and expected future interest rates.

The interest rate that enters the *LM* relation, which is the interest rate that the Fed affects directly, is the *current nominal interest rate*. In contrast, spending in the *IS* relation depends on both *current and expected future real interest rates*. Economists sometimes state this distinction even more starkly by saying that, while the Fed controls the *short-term nominal interest rate*, what matters for spending and output is the *long-term real interest rate*. Let's look at this distinction more closely.

From the Short Nominal Rate to Current and Expected Real Rates

Expected current inflation: inflation expected, as of today, ▶ for the current period (the current year).

- Recall from Chapter 14 that the real interest rate is approximately equal to the nominal interest rate minus expected current inflation:

$$r = i - \pi^e$$

Expected future inflation: inflation expected, as of today, ▶ for the future period (all future years).

- Similarly, the expected future real interest rate is approximately equal to the expected future nominal interest rate minus expected future inflation.

$$r'^e = i'^e - \pi'^e$$

When the Fed increases the money supply—decreasing the current nominal interest rate *i*—the effects on the current and the expected future real interest rates depend, therefore, on two factors:

We explored the role of changing expectations of inflation on the relation between the nominal interest rate and the real interest rate in Chapter 14. Leaving changes in expected inflation aside will keep the analysis simpler here. You have, however, all the elements you need to think through what would happen if ▶ we also allowed expectations of current inflation and future inflation to adjust. How would these expectations adjust? Would this lead to a larger or a smaller effect on output in the current period?

- Whether the increase in the money supply leads financial markets to revise their expectations of the future nominal interest rate, i'^e.
- Whether the increase in the money supply leads financial markets to revise their expectations of both current and future inflation, π^e and π'^e. If, for example, the change in money leads financial markets to expect more inflation in the future—so π'^e increases—the expected future real interest rate, r'^e, will decrease by more than the expected future nominal interest rate, i'^e.

To keep things simple, we shall ignore here the second factor—the role of changing expectations of inflation—and focus on the first, the role of changing expectations of the future nominal interest rate. Thus we shall assume that expected current inflation and expected future inflation are both equal to zero. In this case, we do not need to distinguish between the nominal interest rate and the real interest rate, as they are equal, and we can use the same letter to denote both. Let *r* denote the current real (and nominal) interest rate, and r'^e denote the expected future real (and nominal) interest rate.

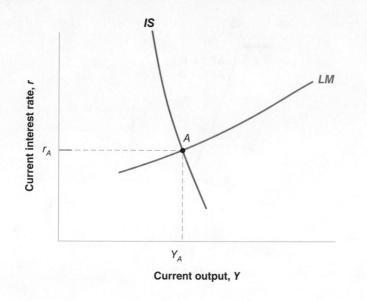

Figure 17-3

The New **IS–LM**

The *IS* curve is steeply downward sloping: Other things being equal, a change in the current interest rate has a small effect on output. The *LM* curve is upward sloping. The equilibrium is at the intersection of the *IS* and *LM* curves. In this diagram, I have assumed the expected rate of inflation is zero in both the current year and in the future.

With this simplification, we can rewrite the *IS* and *LM* relations in equations (17.2) and (17.3) as:

$$IS: \quad Y = A(Y, T, r, Y'^e, T'^e, r'^e) + G \tag{17.4}$$

$$LM: \quad \frac{M}{P} = Y L(r) \tag{17.5}$$

◀ The *IS* relation is the same as equation (17.2). The *LM* relation is now in terms of the real interest rate—which, here, is equal to the nominal interest rate.

The corresponding *IS* and *LM* curves are drawn in Figure 17-3. The vertical axis measures the current interest rate *r*; the horizontal axis measures current output *Y*. The *IS* curve is steeply downward sloping. We saw the reason why earlier: For given expectations, a change in the current interest rate has a limited effect on spending, and the multiplier is small. The *LM* curve is upward sloping. An increase in income leads to an increase in the demand for money; given the supply of money, the result is an increase in the interest rate. Equilibrium in goods and financial markets implies that the economy is at point *A*, on both the *IS* and the *LM* curves.

◀ There is no need to distinguish here between the real interest rate and the nominal interest rate: Given zero expected inflation, they are the same.

Monetary Policy Revisited

Now suppose the economy is in recession, and the Fed decides to increase the money supply.

Assume first that this expansionary monetary policy does not change expectations of either the future interest rate or future output. In Figure 17-4, the *LM* shifts down, from *LM* to *LM″*. (Because I have already used primes to denote future values of the variables, we shall use double primes, such as in *LM″*, to denote shifts in curves in this chapter.) The equilibrium moves from point *A* to point *B*, with higher output and a lower interest rate. The steep *IS* curve, however, implies that the increase in the money supply has only a small effect on output: Changes in the current interest rate, unaccompanied by changes in expectations, have only a small effect on spending, and in turn a small effect on output.

Is it reasonable, however, to assume that expectations are unaffected by an expansionary monetary policy? Isn't it likely that, as the Fed lowers the current interest rate, financial markets now anticipate lower interest rates in the future as well, along with higher future output stimulated by this lower future interest rate? What happens if they do? At a given current interest rate, prospects of a lower future interest rate and

Given expectations, an increase in the money supply leads to a shift in the *LM* curve and a movement down ◀ the steep *IS* curve. The result is a large decrease in *r*, a small increase in *Y*.

Figure 17-4

The Effects of an Expansionary Monetary Policy

The effects of monetary policy on output depend very much on whether and how monetary policy affects expectations.

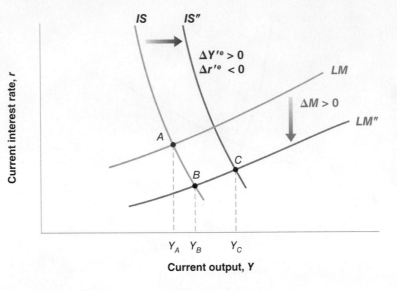

If the increase in money leads to an increase in Y'^e and a decrease in r'^e, the *IS* curve shifts to the right, leading to a larger increase in Y.

This is why central banks often argue that their task is not only to adjust the interest rate but also to "manage expectations," so as to lead to predictable effects of changes in this interest rate on the economy. More on this in Chapters 22 and 24.

of higher future output both increase spending and output; they shift the *IS* curve to the right, from *IS* to *IS"*. The new equilibrium is given by point *C*. Thus, while the direct effect of the monetary expansion on output is limited, the full effect, once changes in expectations are taken into account, is much larger.

You have just learned an important lesson. The effects of monetary policy—the effects of any type of macroeconomic policy for that matter—depend crucially on its effect on expectations:

- If a monetary expansion leads financial investors, firms, and consumers to revise their expectations of future interest rates and output, then the effects of the monetary expansion on output may be very large.
- But if expectations remain unchanged, the effects of the monetary expansion on output will be small.

The role of expectations is even more central in a case we have left aside, namely the case where the economy is in the liquidity trap and the short-term rate is already equal to zero. The discussion of how monetary policy may still work in this case is-taken up in the Focus box "The Liquidity Trap, Quantitative Easing, and the Role of Expectations."

We can link this to our discussion to our earlier discussion in Chapter 15, about the effects of changes in monetary policy on the stock market. Many of the same issues were present there. If, when the change in monetary policy takes place, it comes as no surprise to investors, firms, and consumers, then expectations will not change. The stock market will react only a little, if at all. And demand and output will change only a little, if at all. But, if the change comes as a surprise and is expected to last, expectations of future output will go up, expectations of future interest rates will come down, the stock market will boom, and output will increase.

At this stage, you may have become very skeptical that macroeconomists can say much about the effects of policy, or the effects of other shocks: If the effects depend so much on what happens to expectations, can macroeconomists have any hope of predicting what will happen? The answer is yes.

Saying that the effect of a particular policy depends on its effect on expectations is not the same as saying that anything can happen. Expectations are not arbitrary. The manager of a mutual fund who must decide whether to invest in stocks or bonds, the firm thinking about whether or not to build a new plant, the

The Liquidity Trap, Quantitative Easing, and the Role of Expectations

At the time of this writing, the scope for conventional monetary policy, namely a reduction in the nominal short-term interest rate, has simply disappeared: Since the end of 2008, the nominal short-term interest rate is close to zero, and the U.S. economy has been in a liquidity trap. This has led the Fed, as well as other central banks, to explore unconventional policies. These come by the name of "quantitative easing" or "credit easing." We briefly talked about them in Chapter 9. We look at them more closely here.

First, the semantics: Economists typically refer to "quantitative easing" to denote operations in which, while at the zero interest rate bound, the central bank continues to increase the money supply through open market operations, either by buying more T-bills or by buying longer-maturity government bonds. The purpose of quantitative easing is to increase the money supply. Economists apply the term "credit easing" to operations where the central bank buys a specific type of asset; for example, mortgage-based securities, or even stocks. The focus is then not so much on the increase in the money supply, but on the effects on the price or the interest rate on the specific asset being bought.

Why should such operations have any effect? After all, we saw in Chapter 9 how, at least under the assumptions we made there, an increase in the money supply had no effect on the short-term nominal interest rate. As both bonds and money paid the same nominal interest rate, namely zero, people willingly held more money and less bonds in response to an open market operation, leaving the nominal interest rate unchanged and equal to zero. As we saw in Chapter 15, so long as expectations of future interest rates were unchanged, arbitrage between short- and long-term bonds implied that interest rates on longer-term bonds also would not change. Nor would stock prices or other asset prices.

This simple argument is why many economists are skeptical that these unconventional policies can do much to increase spending and output. But you can see that there are a number of qualifiers in the previous paragraph. If some of the assumptions we stated there are not correct, these policies may have an effect. Economists have identified three channels through which quantitative or credit easing may affect the economy:

■ Arbitrage may not hold. Investors may, for example, think that an asset is so risky that they do not want to hold it at all. Or, and this happened during the crisis, investors may be short of funds and may have to sell the asset, even if they wanted to keep it. This is known as a case of fire sales. In this case, by doing credit easing, (i.e., by buying the asset), the central bank can replace these investors, increase the price of the asset,

and decrease the associated interest rate. Or, to take another example, if banks, for the reasons we saw in Chapter 9, suddenly lose some of their funding and are forced in turn to ration loans and turn down some borrowers, the central bank may be able to finance some of the borrowers. In short, when arbitrage fails, credit easing can work.

■ Quantitative easing may affect expectations of future nominal interest rates. As this chapter makes clear, given inflation expectations, what matters is not so much the current nominal interest rate as future nominal interest rates. If the increase in the money supply is taken as a signal by markets that the central bank will continue to follow a very expansionary monetary policy in the future, and thus keep nominal interest rates low for a long time, this will increase spending today.

■ Quantitative easing may affect expectations of inflation. In the strange world of the liquidity trap, higher expected inflation is good, as it leads to lower current and future expected real interest rates. Thus, if the large increase in the money supply leads people to expect more inflation in the future, this will also increase spending today.

None of these channels is a sure thing. The first is more likely to work during the acute phase of the crisis, when perceptions of risk are high and some investors have to sell assets in a hurry. The other two work through expectations and are far from mechanical. If expectations of either future nominal interest rates or of inflation do not move, easing will have no effect on spending, and in turn no effect on output.

What does the evidence suggest? To answer, we can look at what has happened in the United States during the crisis. Once the room for conventional monetary policy was exhausted, the Fed decided to use both credit and quantitative easing. In November 2008, it started a program known as **Quantitative Easing I, or QEI** for short, in which it purchased large amounts of mortgage-based securities. (A more appropriate name for the program would be Credit Easing I, as the purpose was clearly to decrease the interest rate on those particular assets, assets that private investors no longer wanted to hold.) In August 2010, in what is known as **Quantitative Easing II, or QEII**, the Fed started purchasing long-term government bonds, further increasing the money supply. Figure 1 shows the size and the composition of the assets held by the Fed since 2007. The yellow surface shows the holdings of mortgage-based securities and a few other assets; the blue surface represents the holdings of long-term government bonds (the green surface corresponds to loans to bank and nonbank financial institutions during the acute phase of the crisis, something we discussed in Chapter 9). You can see how, as a result of these purchases, central bank money has more than tripled in size, from roughly 6% of GDP in 2007 to nearly 20% of GDP in 2011! Has this massive increase had an effect on interest rates, either on MBS securities or on long-term bonds? Most of the research concludes that it has, but that the effects have been relatively modest, perhaps on the order of a decrease of 0.5% for the interest rate on long-term bonds. The effect on inflation expectations is harder to assess, but the good news is that expected inflation has remained positive, avoiding the deflation spiral that took place during the Great Depression (see the Focus box "Why Deflation Can Be Very Bad: Deflation and the Real Interest Rate in the Great Depression" in Chapter 14).

Figure 1   *The Asset Portfolio of the Fed since 2007*

consumer thinking about how much she should save for retirement, all give a lot of thought to what might happen in the future. We can think of each of them as forming expectations about the future by assessing the likely course of future expected policy and then working out the implications for future activity. If they do not do it themselves (surely most of us do not spend our time solving macroeconomic models before making decisions), they do so indirectly by watching TV and reading newsletters and newspapers or finding public information on the Web, all of which in turn rely on the forecasts of public and private forecasters. Economists refer to expectations formed in this forward-looking manner as **rational expectations**. The introduction of the assumption of rational expectations is one of the important developments in macroeconomics in the last 35 years. It has largely shaped the way macroeconomists think about policy. It is discussed further in the Focus box "Rational Expectations."

We could go back and think about the implications of rational expectations in the case of the monetary expansion we have just studied. It will be more fun to do this in the context of a change in fiscal policy, and this is what we now turn to.

Rational Expectations

Most macroeconomists today routinely solve their models under the assumption of rational expectations. This was not always the case. The last 40 years in macroeconomic research are often called the "rational expectations" revolution.

The importance of expectations is an old theme in macroeconomics. But until the early 1970s, macroeconomists thought of expectations in one of two ways:

- One was as animal spirits (from an expression Keynes introduced in the *General Theory* to refer to movements in investment that could not be explained by movements in current variables). In other words, shifts in expectations were considered important but were left unexplained.

- The other was as the result of simple, backward-looking rules. For example, people were often assumed to have *static expectations*; that is, to expect the future to be like the present (we used this assumption when discussing the Phillips curve in Chapter 8 and when exploring investment decisions in Chapter 16). Or people were assumed to have **adaptive expectations**: If, for example, their forecast of a given variable in a given period turned out to be too low, people were assumed to "adapt" by raising their expectation for the value of the variable for the following period. For example, seeing an inflation rate higher than they had expected led people to revise upward their forecast of inflation in the future.

In the early 1970s, a group of macroeconomists led by Robert Lucas (at Chicago) and Thomas Sargent (at Minnesota) argued that these assumptions did not reflect the way people form expectations. (Robert Lucas received the Nobel Prize in 1995; Thomas Sargent received the Nobel Prize in 2011.) They argued that, in thinking about the effects of alternative policies, economists should assume that people have rational expectations, that people look into the future and do the best job they can in predicting it. This is not the same as assuming that people know the future, but rather that they use the information they have in the best possible way.

Using the popular macroeconomic models of the time, Lucas and Sargent showed how replacing traditional assumptions about expectations formation by the assumption of rational expectations could fundamentally alter the results. We saw, for example, in Chapter 8 how Lucas challenged the notion that disinflation necessarily required an increase in unemployment for some time. Under rational expectations, he argued, a credible disinflation policy might be able to decrease inflation without any increase in unemployment. More generally, Lucas and Sargent's research showed the need for a complete rethinking of macroeconomic models under the assumption of rational expectations, and this is what happened over the next two decades.

Most macroeconomists today use rational expectations as a working assumption in their models and analyses of policy. This is not because they believe that people always have rational expectations. Surely there are times when people, firms, or financial market participants lose sight of reality and become too optimistic or too pessimistic. (Recall our discussion of bubbles and fads in Chapter 15.) But these are more the exception than the rule, and it is not clear that economists can say much about those times anyway. When thinking about the likely effects of a particular economic policy, the best assumption to make seems to be that financial markets, people, and firms will do the best they can to work out the implications of that policy. Designing a policy on the assumption that people will make systematic mistakes in responding to it is unwise.

Why did it take until the 1970s for rational expectations to become a standard assumption in macroeconomics? Largely because of technical problems. Under rational expectations, what happens today depends on expectations of what will happen in the future. But what happens in the future also depends on what happens today. Solving such models is hard. The success of Lucas and Sargent in convincing most macroeconomists to use rational expectations comes not only from the strength of their case, but also from showing how it could actually be done. Much progress has been made since in developing solution methods for larger and larger models. Today, a number of large macroeconometric models are solved under the assumption of rational expectations. (The simulation of the Taylor model presented in the box on monetary policy in Chapter 7 was derived under rational expectations. You will see another example in Chapter 22.)

17-3 Deficit Reduction, Expectations, and Output

Recall the conclusions we reached in the core about the effects of a budget deficit reduction:

- In the long run, a reduction in the budget deficit is good for the economy: In the medium run, a lower budget deficit implies higher saving and higher investment. In the long run, higher investment translates into higher capital and thus higher output.

We discussed the short- and medium-run effects of ▶ changes in fiscal policy in Section 7-5. We discussed the long-run effects of changes in fiscal policy in Section 11-2.

■ In the short run, however, a reduction in the budget deficit, unless it is offset by a monetary expansion, leads to lower spending and to a contraction in output.

It is this adverse short-run effect that—in addition to the unpopularity of increases in taxes or reductions in government programs in the first place—often deters governments from tackling their budget deficits: Why take the risk of a recession now for benefits that will accrue only in the future?

In the recent past, however, a number of economists have argued that, under some conditions, a deficit reduction might actually increase output even in the *short run*. Their argument: If people take into account the future beneficial effects of deficit reduction, their expectations about the future might improve enough so as to lead to an increase—rather than a decrease—in current spending, thereby increasing current output. This section explores their argument. The Focus box "Can a Budget Deficit Reduction Lead to an Output Expansion? Ireland in the 1980s" reviews some of the supporting evidence.

Assume the economy is described by equation (17.4) for the *IS* relation and equation (17.5) for the *LM* relation. Now suppose the government announces a program to reduce the deficit, through decreases both in current spending G and in future spending, G'^e. What will happen to output *this period*?

The Role of Expectations about the Future

Suppose first that expectations of future output (Y'^e) and of the future interest rate (r'^e) do not change. Then we get the standard answer: The decrease in government spending in the current period leads to a shift of the *IS* curve to the left, and so to a decrease in output.

The crucial question therefore is what happens to expectations. To answer, let us go back to what we learned in the core about the effects of a deficit reduction in the medium run and the long run:

■ In the medium run, a deficit reduction has no effect on output. It leads, however, to a lower interest rate and to higher investment. These were two of the main lessons of Chapter 7.

Let's review the logic behind each:

Recall that, when we look at the medium run, we ignore the effects of capital accumulation on output. So, in the medium run, the natural level of output depends on the level of productivity (taken as given) and on the natural level of employment. The natural level of employment depends in turn on the natural rate of unemployment. If spending by the government on goods and services does not affect the natural rate of unemployment—and there is no obvious reason why it should—then changes in spending will not affect the natural level of output. Therefore, a deficit reduction has no effect on the level of output in the medium run.

In the medium run: Output, Y, does not change, Investment, ▶ I, is higher.

Now recall that output must be equal to spending, and that spending is the sum of public spending and private spending. Given that output is unchanged and that public spending is lower, private spending must therefore be higher. Higher private spending requires a lower equilibrium interest rate: The lower interest rate leads to higher investment, and thus to higher private spending, which offsets the decrease in public spending and output unchanged.

In the long run: I increases ⟹ K increases ⟹ Y increases. ▶

■ In the long run—that is, taking into account the effects of capital accumulation on output—higher investment leads to a higher capital stock, and, therefore, a higher level of output.

This was the main lesson of Chapter 11. The higher the proportion of output saved (or invested; investment and saving must be equal for the goods market to be in equilibrium in a closed economy), the higher the capital stock, and thus the higher the level of output in the long run.

We can think of our *future period* as including both the medium and the long run. If people, firms, and financial market participants have *rational expectations*, then, in response to the announcement of a deficit reduction, they will expect these developments to take place in the future. Thus, they will revise their expectation of future output (Y'^e) up, and their expectation of the future interest rate (r'^e) down.

Back to the Current Period

We can now return to the question of what happens *this period* in response to the announcement and start of the deficit reduction program. Figure 17-5 draws the *IS* and *LM* curves for the current period. In response to the announcement of the deficit reduction, there are now three factors shifting the *IS* curve:

- Current government spending (G) goes down, leading the *IS* curve to shift to the left. At a given interest rate, the decrease in government spending leads to a decrease in total spending and so a decrease in output. This is the standard effect of a reduction in government spending, and the only one taken into account in the basic *IS–LM* model.
- Expected future output (Y'^e) goes up, leading the *IS* curve to shift to the right. At a given interest rate, the increase in expected future output leads to an increase in private spending, increasing output.
- The expected future interest rate (r'^e) goes down, leading the *IS* curve to shift to the right. At a given current interest rate, a decrease in the future interest rate stimulates spending and increases output.

What is the net effect of these three shifts in the *IS* curve? Can the effect of expectations on consumption and investment spending offset the decrease in government spending? Without much more information about the exact form of the *IS* and *LM* relations and about the details of the deficit reduction program, we cannot tell which shifts will dominate, and whether output will go up or down. But our analysis tells us that both cases are possible—that output may go up in response to the deficit reduction. And it gives us a few hints as to when this might happen:

- Note that the smaller the decrease in current government spending (G), the smaller the adverse effect on spending today. Note also that the larger the decrease

The way this is likely to happen: Forecasts by economists will show that these lower deficits are likely to lead to higher output and lower interest rates in the future. In response to these forecasts, long-term interest rates will decrease and ◄ the stock market will increase. People and firms, reading these forecasts and looking at bond and stock prices, will revise their spending plans and increase spending.

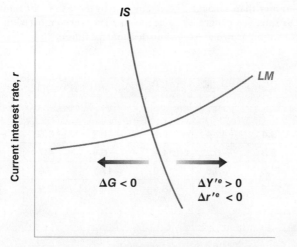

Figure 17-5

The Effects of a Deficit Reduction on Current Output

When account is taken of its effect on expectations, the decrease in government spending need not lead to a decrease in output.

Can a Budget Deficit Reduction Lead to an Output Expansion? Ireland in the 1980s

Ireland went through two major deficit reduction programs in the 1980s:

1. The first program was started in 1982. In 1981, the budget deficit had reached a very high 13% of GDP. Government debt, the result of the accumulation of current and past deficits, was 77% of GDP, also a very high level. The Irish government clearly had to regain control of its finances. Over the next three years, it embarked on a program of deficit reduction, based mostly on tax increases. This was an ambitious program: Had output continued to grow at its normal growth rate, the program would have reduced the deficit by 5% of GDP.

   The results, however, were dismal. As shown in line 2 of Table 1, output growth was low in 1982, and negative in 1983. Low output growth was associated with a major increase in unemployment, from 9.5% in 1981 to 15% in 1984 (line 3). Because of low output growth, tax revenues—which depend on the level of economic activity—were lower than anticipated. The actual deficit reduction from 1981 to 1984, shown in line 1, was only of 3.5% of GDP. And the result of continuing high deficits and low GDP growth was a further increase in the ratio of debt to GDP to 97% in 1984.

2. A second attempt to reduce budget deficits was made starting in February 1987. At the time, things were still very bad. The 1986 deficit was 10.7% of GDP; debt stood at 116% of GDP, a record high in Europe at the time. This new program of deficit reduction was different from the first. It was focused more on reducing the role of government and cutting government spending than on increasing taxes. The tax increases in the program were achieved through a tax reform widening the tax base—increasing the number of households paying taxes—rather than through an increase in the marginal tax rate. The program was again very ambitious: Had output grown at its normal rate, the reduction in the deficit would have been 6.4% of GDP.

   The results of the second program could not have been more different from the results of the first. 1987 to 1989 were years of strong growth, with average GDP growth exceeding 5%. The unemployment rate was reduced by almost 2%. Because of strong output growth, tax revenues were higher than anticipated, and the deficit was reduced by nearly 9% of GDP.

A number of economists have argued that the striking difference between the results of the two programs can be traced to the different reaction of expectations in each case. The first program, they argue, focused on tax increases and did not change what many people saw as too large a role of government in the economy. The second program, with its focus on cuts in spending and on tax reform, had a much more positive impact on expectations, and so a positive impact on spending and output.

Are these economists right? One variable, the household saving rate— defined as disposable income minus consumption, divided by disposable income—strongly suggests that expectations are an important part of the story. To interpret the behavior of the saving rate, recall the lessons from Chapter 16 about consumption behavior. When disposable income grows unusually slowly or goes down—as it does in a recession—consumption typically slows down or declines by less than disposable income because people expect things to improve in the future. Put another way, when the growth of disposable income is unusually low, the saving rate typically comes down. Now look (in line 4) at what happened from 1981 to 1984: Despite low growth throughout the period and a recession in 1983, the household saving rate actually increased slightly during the period. Put another way, people reduced their consumption by more than the reduction in their disposable income: The reason must be that they were very pessimistic about the future.

		1981	1982	1983	1984	1986	1987	1988	1989
1	Budget deficit (% of GDP)	−13.0	−13.4	−11.4	−9.5	−10.7	−8.6	−4.5	−1.8
2	Output growth rate (%)	3.3	2.3	−0.2	4.4	−0.4	4.7	5.2	5.8
3	Unemployment rate (%)	9.5	11.0	13.5	15.0	17.1	16.9	16.3	15.1
4	Household saving rate (% of disposable income)	17.9	19.6	18.1	18.4	15.7	12.9	11.0	12.6

Table 1 Fiscal and Other Macroeconomic Indicators, Ireland, 1981 to 1984, and 1986 to 1989

Source: OECD Economic Outlook, June 1998

Now turn to the period 1986 to 1989. During that period, economic growth was unusually strong. By the same argument as in the previous paragraph, we would have expected consumption to increase less strongly, and thus the saving rate to increase. Instead, the saving rate dropped sharply, from 15.7% in 1986 to 12.6% in 1989. Consumers must have become much more optimistic about the future to increase their consumption by more than the increase in their disposable income.

The next question is whether this difference in the adjustment of expectations over the two episodes can be attributed fully to the differences in the two fiscal programs. The answer is surely no. Ireland was changing in many ways at the time of the second fiscal program. Productivity was increasing much faster than real wages, reducing the cost of labor for firms. Attracted by tax breaks, low labor costs, and an educated labor force, many foreign firms were relocating to Ireland and building new plants: These factors played a major role in the expansion of the late 1980s. Irish growth was then very strong, usually more than 5% per year from 1990 to the time of the crisis in 2007. Surely, this long expansion is due to many factors. Nevertheless, the change in fiscal policy in 1987 probably played an important role in convincing people, firms—including foreign firms—and financial markets, that the government was regaining control of its finances. And the fact remains that the substantial deficit reduction of 1987–1989 was accompanied by a strong output expansion, not by the recession predicted by the basic *IS–LM* model.

For a more detailed discussion, look at Francesco Giavazzi and Marco Pagano, "Can Severe Fiscal Contractions Be Expansionary? Tales of Two Small European Countries," NBER Macroeconomics Annual, (MIT Press, 1990), Olivier Jean Blanchard and Stanley Fischer, editors.

For a more systematic look at whether and when fiscal consolidations have been expansionary (and a mostly negative answer), see "Will It Hurt? Macroeconomic Effects of Fiscal Consolidation," Chapter 3, World Economic Outlook, International Monetary Fund, October 2010.

in expected future government spending (G'^e), the larger the effect on expected future output and interest rates, thus the larger the favorable effect on spending today. This suggests that **backloading** the deficit reduction program toward the future, with small cuts today and larger cuts in the future is more likely to lead to an increase in output.

■ On the other hand, backloading raises other issues. Announcing the need for painful cuts in spending, and then leaving them to the future, is likely to decrease the program's **credibility**—the perceived probability that the government will do what it has promised when the time comes to do it.

■ The government must play a delicate balancing act: enough cuts in the current period to show a commitment to deficit reduction; enough cuts left to the future to reduce the adverse effects on the economy in the short-run.

More generally, our analysis suggests that anything in a deficit reduction program that improves expectations of how the future will look is likely to make the short-run effects of deficit reduction less painful. We will give you two examples.

■ Measures that are perceived by firms and financial markets as reducing some of the distortions in the economy may improve expectations, and make it more likely that output increases in the short run. Take for example unemployment benefits. You saw in Chapter 6 that lower unemployment benefits lead to a decline in the natural rate of unemployment, resulting in a higher natural level of output. So, a reform of the social insurance system, which includes a reduction in the generosity of unemployment benefits, is likely to have two effects on spending and thus on output in the short run:

One is an adverse effect on the consumption of the unemployed: Lower unemployment benefits will reduce their income and their consumption. The other is a positive effect on spending through expectations: The anticipation of higher output in the future may lead to both higher consumption and higher investment.

If the second effect dominates, the outcome might be an increase in overall spending, increasing output not only in the medium run but also in the short run. (An important caveat: Even if a reduction in unemployment benefits increases output, this surely does not imply that unemployment benefits should be eliminated. Even if aggregate income goes up, we must worry about the effects on the distribution of income: The consumption of the unemployed goes down, and the pain associated with being unemployed goes up.)

■ Or take an economy where the government has, in effect, lost control of its budget: Government spending is high, tax revenues are low, and the deficit is very large. In such an environment, a credible deficit reduction program is also more likely to increase output in the short run. Before the announcement of the program, people may have expected major political and economic troubles in the future. The announcement of a program of deficit reduction may well reassure them that the government has regained control, and that the future is less bleak than they anticipated. This decrease in pessimism about the future may lead to an increase in spending and output, even if taxes are increased as part of the deficit reduction program.

Let's summarize:

A program of deficit reduction may increase output even in the short run. Whether it does or does not depends on many factors, in particular:

■ The credibility of the program: Will spending be cut or taxes increased in the future as announced?

■ The timing of the program: How large are spending cuts in the future relative to current spending cuts?

■ The composition of the program: Does the program remove some of the distortions in the economy?

■ The state of government finances in the first place: How large is the initial deficit? Is this a "last chance" program? What will happen if it fails?

Note how far we have moved from the results of Chapter 3, where, by choosing spending and taxes wisely, the government could achieve any level of output it wanted. Here, even the direction of the effect of a deficit reduction on output is ambiguous.

More on current fiscal policy issues in Chapter 23.

This gives you a sense of both the importance of expectations in determining the outcome, and of the complexities involved in the use of fiscal policy in such a context. And it is far more than an illustrative example. At the time of this writing, it is at the center of macroeconomic policy discussions As we have seen, the crisis has led to large increases in government debt and large budget deficits throughout advanced countries. Nearly all governments must now embark on a path of fiscal consolidation—of budget deficit reduction. At what rate should they proceed, and whether they can hope that fiscal consolidation, if done right, will be expansionary rather than contractionary, are crucial issues. The analysis we have just gone through suggests the following conclusion:

■ There should be a clear, politically credible plan for how fiscal consolidation will be carried out. The more credible the plan, the more people are convinced that fiscal consolidation will be effectively carried out in the medium and long terms, the smaller the need for fiscal consolidation today, and thus the smaller the direct adverse effects of deficit reduction today.

At the time of writing, the interest rate on Italian and Spanish government debts are around 7%, nearly 6% higher than the interest rate on German government debt, which is considered safe.

■ In most cases, governments should not expect miracles, and fiscal consolidation is likely to lead to lower growth in the short run. In a few cases, however, where financial markets are very worried about the fiscal situation, and where, as a result, the interest rate on government debt is already very high, such as in Italy and Spain, it may be that the decrease in the interest rate that would follow from a credible fiscal consolidation may offset the adverse direct effects.

Summary

- Spending in the goods market depends on current and expected future output and on current and expected future real interest rates.

- Expectations affect demand and, in turn, affect output: Changes in expected future output or in the expected future real interest rate lead to changes in spending and in output today.

- By implication, the effects of fiscal and monetary policy on spending and output depend on how the policy affects expectations of future output and real interest rates.

- Rational expectations is the assumption that people, firms, and participants in financial markets form expectations of the future by assessing the course of future expected policy and then working out the implications for future output, future interest rates, and so on. Although it is clear that most people do not go through this exercise themselves, we can think of them as doing so indirectly by relying on the predictions of public and private forecasters.

- Although there are surely cases in which people, firms, or financial investors do not have rational expectations, the assumption of rational expectations seems to be the best benchmark to evaluate the potential effects of alternative policies. Designing a policy on the assumption that people will make systematic mistakes in responding to it would be unwise.

- Changes in the money supply affect the short-term nominal interest rate. Spending, however, depends instead on current and expected future real interest rates. Thus, the effect of monetary policy on activity depends crucially on whether and how changes in the short-term nominal interest rate lead to changes in current and expected future real interest rates.

- A budget deficit reduction may lead to an increase rather than a decrease in output. This is because expectations of higher output and lower interest rates in the future may lead to an increase in spending that more than offsets the reduction in spending coming from the direct effect of the deficit reduction on total spending.

Key Terms

aggregate private spending, or private spending, 359
fire sales, 365
Quantitative Easing I and II (QEI, QEII), 365
rational expectations, 366

animal spirits, 367
adaptive expectations, 367
backloading, 371
credibility, 371

Questions and Problems

QUICK CHECK

All Quick Check questions and problems are available on MyEconLab.

1. Using the information in this chapter, label each of the following statements true, false, or uncertain. Explain briefly.

  a. Changes in the current one-year real interest rate are likely to have a much larger effect on spending than changes in expected future one-year real interest rates.

  b. The introduction of expectations in the goods market model makes the *IS* curve flatter, although it is still downward sloping.

  c. Current money demand depends on current and expected future nominal interest rates.

  d. The rational expectations assumption implies that consumers take into account the effects of future fiscal policy on output.

  e. Expected future fiscal policy affects expected future economic activity but not current economic activity.

  f. Depending on its effect on expectations, a fiscal contraction may actually lead to an economic expansion.

  g. Ireland's experience with deficit reduction programs in 1982 and 1987 provides strong evidence against the hypothesis that deficit reduction can lead to an output expansion.

2. During the late 1990s, many observers claimed that the United States had transformed into a New Economy, and this justified the very high values for stock prices observed at the time.

  a. Discuss how the belief in the New Economy, combined with the increase in stock prices, affected consumption spending.

  b. Stock prices subsequently decreased. Discuss how this might have affected consumption.

3. For each of the changes in expectations in (a) through (d), determine whether there is a shift in the IS *curve, the* LM *curve, both curves, or neither. In each case, assume that expected current and future inflation are equal to zero and that no other exogenous variable is changing.*

  a. a decrease in the expected future real interest rate.

  b. an increase in the current money supply.

  c. an increase in expected future taxes.

  d. a decrease in expected future income.

4. Consider the following statement. "The rational expectations assumption is unrealistic because, essentially, it amounts to the assumption that every consumer has perfect knowledge of the economy." Discuss.

5. A new president, who promised during the campaign that she would cut taxes, has just been elected. People trust that she will keep her promise, but expect that the tax cuts will be implemented only in the future. Determine the impact of the election on current output, the current interest rate, and current private spending under each of the assumptions in (a) through (c). In each case, indicate what you think will happen to Y'^e, r'^e, and T'^e, and then how these changes in expectations affect output today.

   a. The Fed will not change its policy.
   b. The Fed will act to prevent any change in future output.
   c. The Fed will act to prevent any change in the future interest rate.

DIG DEEPER

All Dig Deeper questions and problems are available on MyEconLab.

6. *The Clinton deficit reduction package*

   In 1992, the U.S. deficit was $290 billion. During the presidential campaign, the large deficit emerged as a major issue. When President Clinton won the election, deficit reduction was the first item on the new administration's agenda.

   a. What does deficit reduction imply for the medium run and the long run? What are the advantages of reducing the deficit?

   In the final version passed by Congress in August 1993, the deficit reduction package included a reduction of $20 billion in its first year, increasing gradually to $131 billion four years later.

   b. Why was the deficit reduction package backloaded? What are the advantages and disadvantages of this approach to deficit reduction?

   In February 1993, President Clinton presented the budget in his State of the Union address. He asked Alan Greenspan, the Fed chairman, to sit next to First Lady Hillary Clinton during the delivery of the address.

   c. What was the purpose of this symbolic gesture? How can the Fed's decision to use expansionary monetary policy in the future affect the short-run response of the economy?

7. *A new Federal Reserve chairman*

   Suppose, in a hypothetical economy, that the chairman of the Fed unexpectedly announces that he will retire in one year. At the same time, the president announces her nominee to replace the retiring Fed chair. Financial market participants expect the nominee to be confirmed by Congress. They also believe that the nominee will conduct a more contractionary monetary policy in the future. In other words, market participants expect the money supply to decline in the future.

   a. Consider the present to be the last year of the current Fed chair's term and the future to be the time after that. Given that monetary policy will be more contractionary in the future, what will happen to future interest rates and future output (at least for a while, before output returns to its natural level)? Given that these changes in future output and future interest rates are predicted, what will happen to output and the interest rate in the present? What will happen to the yield curve on the day of the announcement that the current Fed chair will retire in one year?

   Now suppose that instead of making an unexpected announcement, the Fed chair is required by law to retire in one year (there are limits on the term of the Fed chair), and financial market participants have been aware of this for some time. Suppose, as in part (a), that the President nominates a replacement who is expected to conduct a more contractionary monetary policy than the current Fed chair.

   b. Suppose financial market participants are not surprised by the President's choice. In other words, market participants had correctly predicted who the President would choose as nominee. Under these circumstances, is the announcement of the nominee likely to have any effect on the yield curve?

   c. Suppose instead that the identity of the nominee is a surprise and that financial market participants had expected the nominee to be someone who favored an even more contractionary policy than the actual nominee. Under these circumstances, what is likely to happen to the yield curve on the day of the announcement? (*Hint:* Be careful. Compared to what was expected, is the actual nominee expected to follow a more contractionary or more expansionary policy?)

   d. On October 24, 2005, Ben Bernanke was nominated to succeed Alan Greenspan as chairman of the Federal Reserve. Do an internet search and try to learn what happened in financial markets on the day the nomination was announced. Were financial market participants surprised by the choice? If so, was Bernanke believed to favor policies that would lead to higher or lower interest rates (as compared to the expected nominee) over the next three to five years? (You may also do a yield curve analysis of the kind described in Problem 8 for the period around Bernanke's nomination. If you do this, use one-year and five-year interest rates.)

EXPLORE FURTHER

8. *Deficits and interest rates*

   Go back and look again at Figure 1-4. There was a dramatic change in the U.S. budget position after 2000 (from a surplus to a large and continuing deficit). This change took place well before the crisis and the election of President Obama. The change reinvigorated the debate about the effect of fiscal policy on interest rates. This problem asks you to review theory and evidence on this topic.

   a. Review what theory predicts about fiscal policy and interest rates. Suppose there is an increase in government spending and a decrease in taxes. Use an *IS–LM* diagram to show what will happen to the nominal interest rate in the short run and the medium run. Assuming that there is no change in monetary policy, what does the *IS–LM* model predict will happen to the yield curve immediately after an increase in government spending and a decrease in taxes?

   During the first term of the G. W. Bush administration, the actual and projected federal budget deficits increased dramatically. Part of the increase in the deficit can be attributed to the recession of 2001. However, deficits and projected deficits continued to increase even after the recession had ended.

The following table provides budget projections produced by the Congressional Budget Office (CBO) over the period August 2002 to January 2004. These projections are for the total federal budget deficit, so they include Social Security, which was running a surplus over the period. In addition, each projection assumes that current policy (as of the date of the forecast) continues into the future.

Date of Forecast	Projected Five-Year Deficit (as a % of GDP, negative number indicates a deficit)
August 2002	− 0.4
January 2003	− 0.2
August 2003	− 2.3
January 2004	− 2.3

b. Go to the web site of the Federal Reserve Bank of St. Louis (**research.stlouisfed.org/fred2/**). Under "Interest Rates" and then "Treasury Constant Maturity," obtain the data for "3-Month Constant Maturity Treasury Yield" and "5-Year Constant Maturity Treasury Yield" for each of the months in the table shown here. For each month, subtract the three-month yield from the five-year yield to obtain the interest rate spread. What happened to the interest rate spread as the budget picture worsened over the sample period? Is this result consistent with your answer to part (a)?

The analysis you carried out in this problem is an extension of work by William C. Gale and Peter R. Orszag. See "The Economic Effects of Long-Term Fiscal Discipline," Brookings Institution, December 17, 2002. Figure 5 in this paper relates interest rate spreads to CBO five-year projected budget deficits from 1982 to 2002.

The Open Economy

The next four chapters cover the second extension of the core. They look at the implications of openness—the fact that most economies trade both goods and assets with the rest of the world.

Chapter 18

Chapter 18 discusses the implications of openness in goods markets and financial markets. Openness in goods markets allows people to choose between domestic goods and foreign goods. An important determinant of their decisions is the real exchange rate—the relative price of domestic goods in terms of foreign goods. Openness in financial markets allows people to choose between domestic assets and foreign assets. This imposes a tight relation between the exchange rate, both current and expected, and domestic and foreign interest rates—a relation known as the interest parity condition.

Chapter 19

Chapter 19 focuses on equilibrium in the goods market in an open economy. It shows how the demand for domestic goods now depends on the real exchange rate. It shows how fiscal policy affects both output and the trade balance. It discusses the conditions under which a real depreciation improves the trade balance, and increases output.

Chapter **20**

Chapter 20 characterizes goods and financial markets' equilibrium in an open economy. In other words, it gives an open economy version of the *IS–LM* model we saw in the core. It shows how, under flexible exchange rates, monetary policy affects output not only through its effect on the interest rate but also through its effect on the exchange rate. It shows how fixing the exchange rate also implies giving up the ability to change the interest rate.

Chapter **21**

Chapter 21 looks at the properties of different exchange rate regimes. It first shows how, in the medium run, the real exchange rate can adjust even under a fixed exchange rate regime. It then looks at exchange rate crises under fixed exchange rates, and at movements in exchange rates under flexible exchange rates. It ends by discussing the pros and cons of various exchange rate regimes, including the adoption of a common currency such as the euro.

Openness in Goods and Financial Markets

W e have assumed until now that the economy we looked at was *closed*—that it did not interact with the rest of the world. We had to start this way, to keep things simple and to build up intuition for the basic macroeconomic mechanisms. Figure 18-1 shows how bad, in fact, that this assumption is. The figure plots the growth rates for advanced and emerging economies since 2005. What is striking is how the growth rates have moved together: Despite the fact that the crisis originated in the United States, the outcome was a worldwide recession, with negative growth both in advanced and in emerging economies. It is therefore time to relax this assumption. Understanding the macroeconomic implications of openness will occupy us for this and the next three chapters.

"Openness" has three distinct dimensions:

1. **Openness in goods markets**—the ability of consumers and firms to choose between domestic goods and foreign goods. In no country is this choice completely free of restrictions: Even the countries most committed to free trade have **tariffs**—taxes on imported goods—and **quotas**—restrictions on the quantity of goods that can be imported—on at least some foreign goods. At the same time, in most countries, average tariffs are low and getting lower.

2. **Openness in financial markets**—the ability of financial investors to choose between domestic assets and foreign assets. Until recently even some of the richest countries in the world, such as France and Italy, had **capital controls**—restrictions on the foreign assets their domestic residents could hold and the domestic assets foreigners could hold. These restrictions have largely disappeared. As a result, world financial markets are becoming more and more closely integrated.

3. **Openness in factor markets**—the ability of firms to choose where to locate production, and of workers to choose where to work. Here also trends are clear. Multinational companies operate plants in many countries and move their operations around the world to take advantage of low costs. Much of the debate about the **North American Free Trade Agreement (NAFTA)** signed in 1993 by the United States, Canada, and Mexico centered on how it would affect the relocation of U.S. firms to Mexico. Similar fears now center around China. And immigration from low-wage countries is a hot political issue in countries from Germany to the United States.

In the short run and in the medium run—the focus of this and the next three chapters—openness in factor markets plays much less of a role than openness in either goods markets or financial markets. Thus, we shall ignore openness in factor markets and focus on the implications of the first two dimensions of openness here.

Figure 18-1

Growth in Advanced and Emerging Economies since 2005

The crisis started in the United States, but it affected nearly all countries in the world.

Source: World Economic Outlook Database

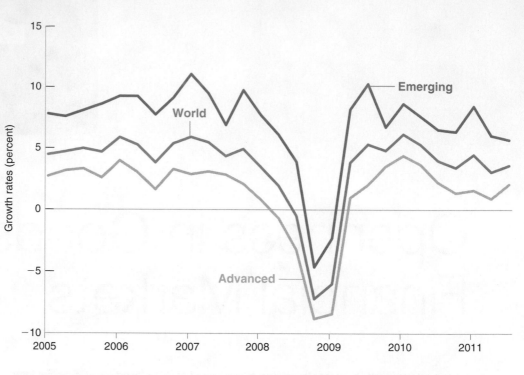

Section 18-1 looks at openness in the goods market, the determinants of the choice between domestic goods and foreign goods, and the role of the real exchange rate.

Section 18-2 looks at openness in financial markets, the determinants of the choice between domestic assets and foreign assets, and the role of interest rates and exchange rates.

Section 18-3 gives a map to the next three chapters.

18-1 Openness in Goods Markets

Let's start by looking at how much the United States sells to and buys from the rest of the world. Then, we shall be better able to think about the choice between domestic goods and foreign goods, and the role of the relative price of domestic goods in terms of foreign goods—the real exchange rate.

Exports and Imports

Figure 18-2 plots the evolution of U.S. exports and U.S. imports, as ratios to GDP, since 1960 ("U.S. exports" means exports *from* the United States; "U.S. imports" means imports *to* the United States). The figure suggests two main conclusions.

From Chapter 3: The trade balance is the difference between exports and imports:

If exports exceed imports, there is a trade surplus (equivalently, a positive trade balance).

If imports exceed exports, there is a trade deficit (equivalently, a negative trade balance).

■ The U.S. economy is becoming more open over time. Exports and imports, which were equal to 5% of GDP in the early 1960s, are now equal to about 14.5% of GDP (13% for exports, 16% for imports). In other words, the United States trades more than twice as much (relative to its GDP) with the rest of the world than it did 50 years ago.

■ Although imports and exports have followed the same upward trend, since the early 1980s imports have consistently exceeded exports. Put another way, for the last 30 years, the United States has consistently run a trade deficit. For four years in a row in the mid-2000s, the ratio of the trade deficit to GDP exceeded 5% of GDP. While it has decreased since the beginning of the crisis, it remains large today.

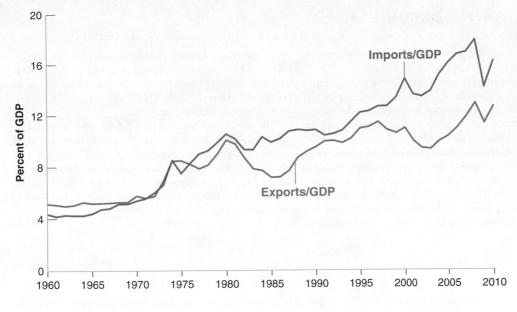

Figure 18-2

U.S. Exports and Imports as Ratios of GDP since 1960

Since 1960, exports and imports have more than doubled in relation to GDP. The United States has become a much more open economy.

Source: Series GDP, EXPGS, IMPGS. Federal Reserve Economic Data (FRED) http://research.stlouis-fed.org/fred2/

Understanding the sources and implications of this large deficit is a central issue in macroeconomics today and one to which we shall return later.

Given all the talk in the media about *globalization,* a volume of trade (measured by the average of the ratios of exports and imports to GDP) around 14.4% of GDP might strike you as small. However, the volume of trade is not necessarily a good measure of openness. Many firms are exposed to foreign competition but, by being competitive and keeping their prices low enough, these firms are able to retain their domestic market share and limit imports. This suggests that a better index of openness than export or import ratios is the proportion of aggregate output composed of **tradable goods**—goods that compete with ◄ foreign goods in either domestic markets or foreign markets. Estimates are that tradable goods represent about 60% of aggregate output in the United States today.

Tradable goods: cars, computers, etc. Nontradable goods: housing, most medical services, haircuts, etc.

With exports around 13% of GDP, it is true that the United States has one of the smallest ratios of exports to GDP among the rich countries of the world. Table 18-1 gives ratios for a number of OECD countries.

For more on the OECD and for ◄ the list of member countries, see Chapter 1.

The United States is at the low end of the range of export ratios. Japan's ratio is about the same, the United Kingdom's twice as large, and Germany's three times as large. And the smaller European countries have very large ratios, from 54% in Switzerland to 81% in Belgium. (Belgium's 81% ratio of exports to GDP raises an odd possibility: Can a country have exports larger than its GDP; in other words, can a country have an export ratio greater than one? The answer is: yes. The reason why is given in the Focus box "Can Exports Exceed GDP?")

Table 18-1 Ratios of Exports to GDP for Selected OECD Countries, 2010

Country	Export Ratio	Country	Export Ratio
United States	13%	Switzerland	54%
Japan	15%	Austria	55%
United Kingdom	30%	Netherlands	78%
Germany	46%	Belgium	81%

Source: OECD Economic Outlook Database

Can Exports Exceed GDP?

Can a country have exports larger than its GDP—that is, can it have an export ratio greater than one?

It would seem that the answer must be no: A country cannot export more than it produces, so that the export ratio must be less than one. Not so. The key to the answer is to realize that exports and imports may include exports and imports of intermediate goods.

Take, for example, a country that imports intermediate goods for $1 billion. Suppose it then transforms them into final goods using only labor. Say labor is paid $200 million and that there are no profits. The value of these final goods is thus equal to $1,200 million. Assume that $1 billion worth of final goods is exported and the rest, $200 million, is consumed domestically.

Exports and imports therefore both equal $1 billion. What is GDP in this economy? Remember that GDP is value added in the economy (see Chapter 2). So, in this example, GDP equals $200 million, and the ratio of exports to GDP equals $1,000/$200 = 5.

Hence, exports can exceed GDP. This is actually the case for a number of small countries where most economic activity is organized around a harbor and import–export activities. This is even the case for small countries such as Singapore, where manufacturing plays an important role. In 2010, the ratio of exports to GDP in Singapore was 211%!

Do these numbers indicate that the United States has more trade barriers than, say, the United Kingdom or Belgium? No. The main factors behind these differences are geography and size. Distance from other markets explains a part of the lower Japanese ratio. Size also matters: The smaller the country, the more it must specialize in producing and exporting only a few products and rely on imports for the other products. Belgium can hardly afford to produce the range of goods produced by the United States, a country roughly 40 times its economic size.

> Iceland is both isolated and small. What would you expect its export ratio to be? (Answer: ▶ 56% in 2010).

The Choice between Domestic Goods and Foreign Goods

How does openness in goods markets force us to rethink the way we look at equilibrium in the *goods market*?

> In a closed economy, people face one decision:
> Save, or buy (consume).
> In an open economy, they ▶ face two decisions:
> Save, or buy.
> Buy domestic, or buy foreign.

Until now, when we were thinking about consumers' decisions in the goods market, we focused on their decision to save or to consume. When goods markets are open, domestic consumers face a second decision: whether to buy domestic goods or to buy foreign goods. Indeed, all buyers—including domestic and foreign firms and governments—face the same decision. This decision has a direct effect on domestic output: If buyers decide to buy more domestic goods, the demand for domestic goods increases, and so does domestic output. If they decide to buy more foreign goods, then foreign output increases instead of domestic output.

Central to this second decision (to buy domestic goods or foreign goods) is the price of domestic goods relative to foreign goods. We call this relative price the **real exchange rate**. The real exchange rate is not directly observable, and you will not find it in the newspapers. What you will find in newspapers are *nominal exchange rates*, the relative prices of currencies. So we start by looking at nominal exchange rates and then see how we can use them to construct real exchange rates.

Nominal Exchange Rates

Nominal exchange rates between two currencies can be quoted in one of two ways:

- As the price of the domestic currency in terms of the foreign currency. If, for example, we look at the United States and the United Kingdom, and think of the dollar as the domestic currency and the pound as the foreign currency, we can express the nominal exchange rate as the price of a dollar in terms of pounds. In September 2011, the exchange rate defined this way was 0.61. In other words, one dollar was worth 0.61 pounds.

■ As the price of the foreign currency in terms of the domestic currency. Continuing with the same example, we can express the nominal exchange rate as the price of a pound in terms of dollars. In September 2011, the exchange rate defined this way was 1.63. In other words, one pound was worth 1.63 dollars.

Warning. There is unfortunately no agreed upon rule among economists or among newspapers as to which of the two definitions to use. You will encounter both. Always check which definition is used.

Either definition is fine; the important thing is to remain consistent. In this book, we shall adopt the first definition: we shall define the **nominal exchange rate** as *the price of the domestic currency in terms of foreign currency*, and denote it by *E*. When looking, for example, at the exchange rate between the United States and the United Kingdom (from the viewpoint of the United States, so the dollar is the domestic currency), *E* will denote the price of a dollar in terms of pounds (so, for example, *E* was 0.61 in September 2011).

E: Nominal exchange rate— Price of domestic currency in terms of foreign currency. (From the point of view of the United States looking at the United Kingdom, the price of a dollar in terms of pounds.)

Exchange rates between the dollar and most foreign currencies change every day—indeed every minute of the day. These changes are called *nominal appreciations* or *nominal depreciations*—appreciations or depreciations for short.

■ An **appreciation** of the domestic currency is an increase in the price of the domestic currency in terms of a foreign currency. Given our definition of the exchange rate, an appreciation corresponds to an *increase* in the exchange rate.

■ A **depreciation** of the domestic currency is a decrease in the price of the domestic currency in terms of a foreign currency. So, given our definition of the exchange rate, a depreciation of the domestic currency corresponds to a decrease in the exchange rate, *E*.

Appreciation of the domestic currency ⇔ Increase in the price of the domestic currency in terms of foreign currency ⇔ Increase in the exchange rate.

Depreciation of the domestic currency ⇔ Decrease in the price of the domestic currency in terms of foreign currency ⇔ Decrease in the exchange rate.

You may have encountered two other words to denote movements in exchange rates: "revaluations" and "devaluations." These two terms are used when countries operate under **fixed exchange rates**—a system in which two or more countries maintain a constant exchange rate between their currencies. Under such a system, increases in the exchange rate—which are infrequent by definition—are called **revaluations** (rather than appreciations). Decreases in the exchange rate are called **devaluations** (rather than depreciations).

We shall discuss fixed exchange rates in Chapter 21.

Figure 18-3 plots the nominal exchange rate between the dollar and the pound since 1970. Note the two main characteristics of the figure:

■ *The trend increase in the exchange rate.* In 1970, a dollar was worth only 0.41 pounds. In 2011, a dollar was worth 0.61 pounds. Put another way, there was an appreciation of the dollar relative to the pound over the period.

■ *The large fluctuations in the exchange rate.* In the 1980s, a sharp appreciation, in which the dollar more than doubled in value relative to the pound, was followed by a nearly equally sharp depreciation. In the 2000s, a large depreciation was followed by a large appreciation as the crisis started, and a smaller depreciation since then.

If we are interested, however, in the choice between domestic goods and foreign goods, the nominal exchange rate gives us only part of the information we need. Figure 18-3, for example, tells us only about movements in the relative price of the two currencies, the dollar and the pound. To U.S. tourists thinking of visiting the United Kingdom, the question is not only how many pounds they will get in exchange for their dollars but how much goods will cost in the United Kingdom relative to how much they cost in the United States. This takes us to our next step—the construction of real exchange rates.

From Nominal to Real Exchange Rates

How can we construct the real exchange rate between the United States and the United Kingdom—the price of U.S. goods in terms of British goods?

Suppose the United States produced only one good, a Cadillac luxury sedan, and the United Kingdom also produced only one good, a Jaguar luxury sedan. (This is one of those "Suppose" statements that run completely against the facts, but we shall become

Figure 18-3

The Nominal Exchange Rate between the Dollar and the Pound since 1971

Although the dollar has appreciated relative to the pound over the past four decades, this appreciation has come with large swings in the nominal exchange rate between the two currencies.

Source: Variable EXUSUK, Federal Reserve Economic Data (FRED) http://research.stlouisfed.org/fred2/

more realistic shortly.) Constructing the real exchange rate, the price of the U.S. goods (Cadillacs) in terms of British goods (Jaguars) would be straightforward. We would express both goods in terms of the same currency and then compute their relative price.

Suppose, for example, we expressed both goods in terms of pounds. Then

▶ *Check that, if we expressed both in terms of dollars instead, we would get the same result for the real exchange rate.*

- The first step would be to take the price of a Cadillac in dollars and convert it to a price in pounds. The price of a Cadillac in the United States is $40,000. The dollar is worth, say, 0.60 pounds, so the price of a Cadillac in pounds is 40,000 dollars times 0.60 = £24,000.

- The second step would be to compute the ratio of the price of the Cadillac in pounds to the price of the Jaguar in pounds. The price of a Jaguar in the United Kingdom is £30,000. So the price of a Cadillac in terms of Jaguars—that is, the real exchange rate between the United States and the United Kingdom—would be £24,000/£30,000 = 0.80. A Cadillac would be 20% cheaper than a Jaguar.

This example is straightforward, but how do we generalize it? The United States and the United Kingdom produce more than Cadillacs and Jaguars, and we want to construct a real exchange rate that reflects the relative price of *all* the goods produced in the United States in terms of *all* the goods produced in the United Kingdom.

The computation we just went through tells us how to proceed. Rather than using the price of a Jaguar and the price of a Cadillac, we must use a price index for all goods produced in the United Kingdom and a price index for all goods produced in the United States. This is exactly what the GDP deflators we introduced in Chapter 2 do: They are, by definition, price indexes for the set of final goods and services produced in the economy.

Let P be the GDP deflator for the United States, P^* be the GDP deflator for the United Kingdom (as a rule, we shall denote foreign variables by a star), and E be the dollar–pound nominal exchange rate. Figure 18-4 goes through the steps needed to construct the real exchange rate.

Figure 18-4

The Construction of the Real Exchange Rate

- The price of U.S. goods in dollars is P. Multiplying it by the exchange rate, E—the price of dollars in terms of pounds—gives us the price of U.S. goods in pounds, EP.
- The price of British goods in pounds is P^*. The *real exchange rate*, the price of U.S. goods in terms of British goods, which we shall call ϵ (the Greek lowercase epsilon), is thus given by

$$\epsilon = \frac{E\,P}{P^*} \qquad (18.1)$$

◄ ϵ: Real exchange rate—Price of domestic goods in terms of foreign goods. (For example, from the point of view of the U.S. looking at the United Kingdom, the price of U.S. goods in terms of British goods.)

The real exchange rate is constructed by multiplying the domestic price level by the nominal exchange rate and then dividing by the foreign price level—a straightforward extension of the computation we made in our Cadillac/Jaguar example.

Note, however, an important difference between our Cadillac/Jaguar example and this more general computation:

Unlike the price of Cadillacs in terms of Jaguars, the real exchange rate is an index number: that is, its level is arbitrary, and therefore uninformative. It is uninformative because the GDP deflators used to construct the real exchange rate are themselves index numbers; as we saw in Chapter 2, they are equal to 1 (or 100) in whatever year is chosen as the base year.

But all is not lost. Although the level of the real exchange rate is uninformative, the rate of change of the real exchange rate is informative: If, for example, the real exchange rate between the United States and the United Kingdom increases by 10%, this tells us U.S. goods are now 10% more expensive relative to British goods than they were before.

Like nominal exchange rates, real exchange rates move over time. These changes are called real appreciations or real depreciations:

- An increase in the real exchange rate—that is, an increase in the relative price of domestic goods in terms of foreign goods—is called a **real appreciation**.
- A decrease in the real exchange rate—that is, a decrease in the relative price of domestic goods in terms of foreign goods—is called a **real depreciation**.

◄ Real appreciation ⇔ Increase in the price of the domestic goods in terms of foreign goods ⇔ Increase in the real exchange rate.

◄ Real depreciation ⇔ Decrease in the price of the domestic goods in terms of foreign goods ⇔ Decrease in the real exchange rate.

Figure 18-5 plots the evolution of the real exchange rate between the United States and the United Kingdom since 1970, constructed using equation (18.1). For convenience, it also reproduces the evolution of the nominal exchange rate from Figure 18-3. The GDP deflators have both been set equal to 1 in the year 2000, so the nominal exchange rate and the real exchange rate are equal in that year by construction.

You should take two lessons from Figure 18-5:

- The nominal and the real exchange rate can move in opposite directions. Note how, from 1970 to 1980, while the nominal exchange rate went up, the real exchange rate actually went down.

Figure 18-5

Real and Nominal Exchange Rates between the United States and the United Kingdom since 1971

Except for the difference in trend reflecting higher average inflation in the United Kingdom than in the United States until the early 1990s, the nominal and the real exchange rates have moved largely together.

Source: Series GDPDEF, GBRGDP-DEFQISMEI and EXUSUK from Federal Reserve Economic Data (FRED) http://research.stlouisfed.org/fred2/

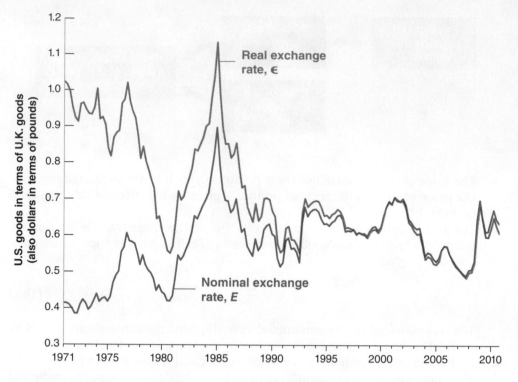

How do we reconcile the fact that there was both a nominal appreciation (of the dollar relative to the pound) and a real depreciation (of U.S. goods relative to British goods) during the period? To see why, return to the definition of the real exchange rate, a slightly rewritten version of (18.1):

$$\epsilon = E\frac{P}{P^*}$$

Two things happened in the 1971s:

First, E increased: The dollar went up in terms of pounds—this is the nominal appreciation we saw earlier.

Second, P/P^* decreased. The price level increased less in the United States than in the United Kingdom. Put another way, over the period, average inflation was lower in the United States than in the United Kingdom.

The resulting decrease in P/P^* was larger than the increase in E, leading to a decrease in ϵ, a real depreciation—a decrease in the relative price of domestic goods in terms of foreign goods.

To get a better understanding of what happened, let's go back to our U.S tourists thinking about visiting the United Kingdom, circa 1980. They would find that they could buy more pounds per dollar than in 1971 (E had increased). Did this imply their trip would be cheaper? No: When they arrived in the United Kingdom, they would discover that the prices of goods in the United Kingdom had increased much more than the prices of goods in the United States (P^* has increased more than P, so P/P^* has declined), and this more than canceled the increase in the value of the dollar in terms of pounds. They would find that their trip was actually more expensive (in terms of U.S. goods) than it would have been 10 years earlier.

There is a general lesson here. Over long periods of time, differences in inflation rates across countries can lead to very different movements in nominal exchange rates and real exchange rates. We shall return to this issue in Chapter 21.

Can there be a real appreciation with no nominal appreciation?

Can there be a nominal appreciation with no real appreciation? (The answers to both questions: yes.) ▶

- The large fluctuations in the nominal exchange rate we saw in Figure 18-3 also show up in the real exchange rate.

This not surprising: Year-to-year movements in the price ratio P/P^* are typically small compared to the often sharp movements in the nominal exchange rate E. Thus, from year to year, or even over the course of a few years, movements in the real exchange rate (ϵ) tend to be driven mostly by movements in the nominal exchange rate E. Note that, since the early 1990s, the nominal exchange rate and the real exchange rate have moved nearly together. This reflects the fact that, since the early 1990s, inflation rates have been very similar—and low—in both countries.

If inflation rates were exactly equal, P/P^* would be constant, and ϵ and E would move exactly together.

From Bilateral to Multilateral Exchange Rates

We need to take one last step. We have so far concentrated on the exchange rate between the United States and the United Kingdom. But the United Kingdom is just one of many countries the United States trades with. Table 18-2 shows the geographic composition of U.S. trade for both exports and imports.

The main message of the table is that the United States does most of its trade with three sets of countries. The first includes its neighbors to the North and to the South, Canada and Mexico: Trade with Canada and Mexico accounts for 26% of U.S. exports and 24% of U.S. imports. The second includes the countries of Western Europe, which account for 23% of U.S. exports and 20% of U.S. imports. The third includes the Asian countries, including Japan and China, which together account for 29% of U.S. exports and 38% of U.S. imports.

How do we go from **bilateral exchange rates**, like the real exchange rate between the United States and the United Kingdom we focused on earlier, to **multilateral exchange rates** that reflect this composition of trade? The principle we want to use is simple, even if the details of construction are complicated. We want the weight of a given country to incorporate not only how much the country trades with the United States but also how much it competes with the United States in other countries. (Why not just look at trade shares between the United States and each individual country? Take two countries, the United States and country A. Suppose the United States and country A do not trade with each other—so trade shares are equal to zero—but they are both exporting to another country, call it country B. The real exchange rate between the United States and country A will matter very much for how much the United States exports to country B and thus to the U.S. export performance.) The variable constructed in this way is called the **multilateral real U.S. exchange rate**, or the U.S. real exchange rate for short.

"Bi" means two. "Multi" means many.

These are all equivalent names for the relative price of U.S. goods in terms of foreign goods:

- The **multilateral real U.S. exchange rate**.
- The U.S. **trade-weighted real exchange rate**.
- The U.S. **effective real exchange rate**.

Table 18-2 The Country Composition of U.S. Exports and Imports, 2010

	Percent of Exports to	Percent of Imports from
Canada	16	13
Mexico	10	11
European Union	23	20
China	7	17
Japan	6	7
Rest of Asia and Pacific	16	14
Others	22	18

Source: Survey of Current Business, August 2011, Tables F2 and F3

Figure 18-6

The U.S. Multilateral Real Exchange Rate, since 1973

Since 1973 there have been two large real appreciations of the U.S. dollar and two large real depreciations.

Source: Price-Adjusted Broad Dollar Index—Monthly Index, Federal Reserve Board. www. federalreserve.gov/releases/h10/summary/

The figure begins in 1973 because this multilateral real exchange rate, which is constructed by the Federal Reserve Board, is only available back as far as 1973.

Figure 18-6 shows the evolution of this multilateral real exchange rate, the price of U.S goods in terms of foreign goods, since 1973. Like the bilateral real exchange rates we saw a few pages earlier, it is an index number and its level is arbitrary. You should note two things about Figure 18-6: first, a trend real depreciation since 1973 (in contrast to the trend nominal appreciation vis à vis the pound in Figure 18-3): second, and more strikingly, the large swings in the multilateral real exchange rate in the 1980s and, to a lesser extent, in the 2000s. These swings are so striking that they have been given various names, from the "dollar cycle" to the more graphic "dance of the dollar." In the coming chapters, we shall examine where these swings come from and their effects on the trade deficit and economic activity.

18-2 Openness in Financial Markets

Openness in financial markets allows financial investors to hold both domestic assets and foreign assets, to diversify their portfolios, to speculate on movements in foreign interest rates versus domestic interest rates, on movements in exchange rates, and so on.

Diversify and speculate they do. Given that buying or selling foreign assets implies buying or selling foreign currency—sometimes called **foreign exchange**—the volume of transactions in foreign exchange markets gives us a sense of the importance of international financial transactions. In 2010, for example, the recorded *daily* volume of foreign exchange transactions in the world was $4 trillion, of which 85%—about $3.4 trillion—involved U.S. dollars on one side of the transaction.

To get a sense of the magnitude of these numbers, the sum of U.S. exports and imports in 2010 totaled $4.1 trillion for the year, or about $11 billion a day. Suppose the only dollar transactions in foreign–exchange markets had been, on one side, by U.S.

exporters selling their foreign currency earnings, and on the other side by U.S. importers buying the foreign currency they needed to buy foreign goods. Then the volume of transactions involving dollars in foreign exchange markets would have been $11 billion a day, or about 0.3% of the actual daily total volume of dollar transactions ($3.40 trillion) involving dollars in foreign exchange markets. This computation tells us that most of the transactions are associated not with trade, but with purchases and sales of financial assets. Moreover, the volume of transactions in foreign exchange markets is not only high but also rapidly increasing. The volume of foreign exchange transactions has more than quadrupled since 2001. Again, this increase in activity reflects mostly an increase in financial transactions rather than an increase in trade.

Daily volume of foreign exchange transactions with dollars on one side of the transaction: $3.4 trillion. Daily volume of trade of the United States with the rest of the world: $11 billion (0.3% of the volume of foreign exchange transactions).

For a country as a whole, openness in financial markets has another important implication: It allows the country to run trade surpluses and trade deficits. Recall that a country running a trade deficit is buying more from the rest of the world than it is selling to the rest of the world. In order to pay for the difference between what it buys and what it sells, the country must borrow from the rest of the world. It borrows by making it attractive for foreign financial investors to increase their holdings of domestic assets—in effect, to lend to the country.

Let's start by looking more closely at the relation between trade flows and financial flows. When this is done, we shall then look at the determinants of these financial flows.

The Balance of Payments

A country's transactions with the rest of the world, including both trade flows and financial flows, are summarized by a set of accounts called the **balance of payments**. Table 18-3 presents the U.S. balance of payments for 2010. The table has two parts, separated by a line. Transactions are referred to either as **above the line** or **below the line**.

The Current Account
The transactions above the line record payments to and from the rest of the world. They are called **current account** transactions.

■ The first two lines record the exports and imports of goods and services. Exports lead to payments from the rest of the world, imports to payments to the rest of the

Table 18-3 The U.S. Balance of Payments, 2010, in Billions of U.S. Dollars		
Current Account		
Exports	1838	
Imports	2338	
Trade balance (deficit = −) (1)		−500
Income received	663	
Income paid	498	
Net income (2)		165
Net transfers received (3)		−136
Current account balance (deficit = −) (1) + (2) + (3)		−471
Capital Account		
Increase in foreign holdings of U.S. assets (4)	1260	
Increase in U.S. holdings of foreign assets (5)	1005	
Capital account balance (deficit = −) (4) − (5)		255
Statistical discrepancy		216
Source: Survey of Current Business, August 2011, Table F2		

world. The difference between exports and imports is the *trade balance*. In 2010, imports exceeded exports, leading to a U.S. *trade deficit* of $500 billion—roughly 3.4% of U.S. GDP.

■ Exports and imports are not the only sources of payments to and from the rest of the world. U.S. residents receive income on their holdings of foreign assets, and foreign residents receive income on their holdings of U.S. assets. In 2010, income received from the rest of the world was $663 billion, and income paid to foreigners was $498 billion, for a net **income balance** of $165 billion.

■ Finally, countries give and receive foreign aid; the net value of these payments is recorded as **net transfers received**. These net transfers amounted in 2010 to –$136 billion. This negative amount reflects the fact that, in 2010, the United States was—as it has traditionally been—a net donor of foreign aid.

The sum of net payments to and from the rest of the world is called the **current account balance.** If net payments from the rest of the world are positive, the country is running a **current account surplus**; if they are negative, the country is running a **current account deficit**. Adding all payments to and from the rest of the world, net payments from the United States to the rest of the world were equal in 2010 to $-\$500 + \$165 - \$136 = -\$471$ billion. Put another way, in 2010, the United States ran a current account deficit of $471 billion—roughly 3.2% of its GDP.

The Capital Account

The fact that the United States had a current account deficit of $471 billion in 2010 implies that it had to borrow $471 billion from the rest of the world—or, equivalently, that net foreign holdings of U.S. assets had to increase by $471 billion. The numbers below the line describe how this was achieved. Transactions below the line are called **capital account** transactions.

The increase in foreign holdings of U.S. assets was $1,260 billion: Foreign investors, be they foreign private investors, foreign governments, or foreign central banks, bought $1,260 billion worth of U.S. stocks, U.S. bonds, and other U.S. assets. At the same time, there was an increase in U.S. holdings of foreign assets of $1,005 billion: U.S. investors, private and public, bought $1,005 billion worth of foreign stocks, bonds, and other assets. The result was an increase in net U.S foreign indebtedness (the increase in foreign holdings of U.S. assets, minus the increase in U.S. holdings of foreign assets), also called **net capital flows** to the United States, of $1260 – $1005 = $255 billion. Another name for net capital flows is the **capital account balance**: Positive net capital flows are called a **capital account surplus**; negative net capital flows are called a **capital account deficit.** So, put another way, in 2010, the United States ran a capital account surplus of $255 billion.

Shouldn't net capital flows (equivalently, the capital account surplus) be exactly equal to the current account deficit (which we saw earlier was equal to $471 billion in 2010)?

In principle, yes. In practice, no.

The numbers for current and capital account transactions are constructed using different sources; although they should give the same answers, they typically do not. In 2010, the difference between the two—called the **statistical discrepancy**—was $216 billion, about 45% of the current account balance. This is yet another reminder that, even for a rich country such as the United States, economic data are far from perfect. (This problem of measurement manifests itself in another way as well. The sum of the current account deficits of all the countries in the world should be equal to zero: One country's deficit should show up as a surplus for the other countries taken as a whole. However, this is not the case in the data: If we just add the published current account

Can a country have:
    A trade deficit and no current account deficit?
    A current account deficit ▶ and no trade deficit?
(The answer to both questions: yes.)

In the same way that if you spend more than you earn, you ▶ have to finance the difference.

A country that runs a current account deficit must finance it through positive net capital ▶ flows. Equivalently, it must run a capital account surplus.

deficits of all the countries in the world, it would appear that the world is running a large current account deficit!)

Now that we have looked at the current account, we can return to an issue we touched on in Chapter 2, the difference between GDP, the measure of output we have used so far, and GNP, another measure of aggregate output.

GDP measures value added domestically. GNP measures the value added by domestic factors of production. When the economy is closed, the two measures are the same. When the economy is open, however, they can differ: Some of the income from domestic production goes to foreigners; and domestic residents receive some foreign income. Thus, to go from GDP to GNP, one must start from GDP, add income received from the rest of the world, and subtract income paid to the rest of the world. Put another way, GNP is equal to GDP plus net payments from the rest of the world. More formally, denoting these net income payments by NI,

$$GNP = GDP + NI$$

In most countries, the difference between the GNP and GDP is small (relative to GDP). For example, in the United States, you can see from Table 18-3 that net income payments were equal to $165 billion: GNP exceeded GDP by $165 billion, or about 1% of GDP. For some countries, however, the difference can be large. This is explored in the Focus box "GDP versus GNP: The Example of Kuwait."

The Choice between Domestic and Foreign Assets

Openness in financial markets implies that people (or financial institutions that act on their behalf) face a new financial decision: whether to hold domestic assets or foreign assets.

It would appear that we actually have to think about at least *two* new decisions, the choice of holding domestic *money* versus foreign *money*, and the choice of holding domestic *interest-paying assets* versus foreign *interest-paying assets*. But remember why people hold money: to engage in transactions. For someone who lives in the United States and whose transactions are mostly or fully in dollars, there is little point in holding foreign currency: Foreign currency cannot be used for transactions in the United States, and if the goal is to hold foreign assets, holding foreign currency is clearly less desirable than holding foreign bonds, which pay interest. This leaves us with only one new choice to think about, the choice between domestic interest–paying assets and foreign interest–paying assets.

Let's think of these assets for now as domestic one-year bonds and foreign one-year bonds. Consider, for example, the choice between U.S. one-year bonds and U.K. one-year bonds, from the point of view of a U.S. investor.

■ Suppose you decide to hold U.S. bonds.

Let i_t be the one-year U.S. nominal interest rate. Then, as Figure 18-7 shows, for every dollar you put in U.S. bonds, you will get $(1 + i_t)$ dollars next year. (This is represented by the arrow pointing to the right at the top of the figure.)

■ Suppose you decide instead to hold U.K. bonds.

To buy U.K. bonds, you must first buy pounds. Let E_t be the nominal exchange rate between the dollar and the pound. For every dollar, you get E_t pounds. (This is represented by the arrow pointing downward in the figure.)

Let i_t^* denote the one-year nominal interest rate on U.K. bonds (in pounds). When next year comes, you will have $E_t(1 + i_t^*)$ pounds. (This is represented by the arrow pointing to the right at the bottom of the figure.)

Some economists speculate that the explanation lies in unrecorded trade with Martians. Most others believe that mismeasurement is the explanation.

Two qualifications, from Chapter 4:
Foreigners involved in illegal activities often hold dollars, because dollars can be exchanged easily and cannot be traced.
In times of very high inflation, people sometimes switch to a foreign currency, often the dollar, for use even in some domestic transactions.

GDP versus GNP: The Example of Kuwait

When oil was discovered in Kuwait, Kuwait's government decided that a portion of oil revenues would be saved and invested abroad rather than spent, so as to provide future Kuwaiti generations with income when oil revenues came to an end. Kuwait ran a large current account surplus, steadily accumulating large foreign assets. As a result, it has large holdings of foreign assets and receives substantial income from the rest of the world. Table 1 gives GDP, GNP, and net investment income for Kuwait, from 1989 to 1994 (you will see the reason for the choice of dates below).

Note how much larger GNP was compared to GDP throughout the period. Net income from abroad was 34% of GDP in 1989. But note also how net factor payments decreased after 1989. This is because Kuwait had to pay its allies for part of the cost of the 1990–1991 Gulf War and also had to pay for reconstruction after the war. It did so by running a current account deficit—that is, by decreasing its net holdings of foreign assets. This in turn led to a decrease in the income it earned from

foreign assets and, by implication, a decrease in its net factor payments.

Since the Gulf War, Kuwait has rebuilt a sizable net foreign asset position. Net income from abroad was 37% of GDP in 2010.

Table 1	GDP, GNP, and Net Income in Kuwait, 1989–1994		
Year	GDP	GNP	Net Income (NI)
1989	7143	9616	2473
1990	5328	7560	2232
1991	3131	4669	1538
1992	5826	7364	1538
1993	7231	8386	1151
1994	7380	8321	941

Source: *International Financial Statistics, IMF.* All numbers are in millions of Kuwaiti dinars. 1 dinar = \$3.6 (2011)

You will then have to convert your pounds back into dollars. If you expect the nominal exchange rate next year to be E_{t+1}^e, each pound will be worth $(1/E_{t+1}^e)$ dollars. So you can expect to have $E_t(1 + i_t^*)(1/E_{t+1}^e)$ dollars next year for every dollar you invest now. (This is represented by the arrow pointing upward in the figure.)

We shall look at the expression we just derived in more detail soon. But note its basic implication already: In assessing the attractiveness of U.K. versus U.S. bonds, you cannot look just at the U.K. interest rate and the U.S. interest rate; you must also assess what you think will happen to the dollar/pound exchange rate between this year and next.

Let's now make the same assumption we made in Chapter 15 when discussing the choice between short-term bonds and long-term bonds, or between bonds and stocks. Let's assume that you and other financial investors care only about the expected rate of return and therefore want to hold only the asset with the highest expected rate of return. In this case, if both U.K. bonds and U.S. bonds are to be held, they must have

Figure 18-7

Expected Returns from Holding One-Year U.S. Bonds vs. One-Year U.K. Bonds

the same expected rate of return. In other words, because of arbitrage, the following relation must hold:

$$(1 + i_t) = (E_t)(1 + i_t^*)\left(\frac{1}{E_{t+1}^e}\right)$$

Reorganizing,

$$(1 + i_t) = (1 + i_t^*)\left(\frac{E_t}{E_{t+1}^e}\right) \tag{18.2}$$

Equation (18.2) is called the **uncovered interest parity** relation, or simply the **interest parity condition**.

The assumption that financial investors will hold only the bonds with the highest expected rate of return is obviously too strong, for two reasons:

- It ignores transaction costs: Going in and out of U.K. bonds requires three separate transactions, each with a transaction cost.
- It ignores risk: The exchange rate a year from now is uncertain; holding U.K. bonds is therefore more risky, in terms of dollars, than holding U.S. bonds.

But as a characterization of capital movements among the major world financial markets (New York, Frankfurt, London, and Tokyo), the assumption is not far off. Small changes in interest rates and rumors of impending appreciation or depreciation can lead to movements of billions of dollars within minutes. For the rich countries of the world, the arbitrage assumption in equation (18.2) is a good approximation of reality. Other countries whose capital markets are smaller and less developed, or countries that have various forms of capital controls, have more leeway in choosing their domestic interest rate than is implied by equation (18.2). We shall return to this issue at the end of Chapter 20.

Interest Rates and Exchange Rates

Let's get a better sense of what the interest parity condition implies. First rewrite E_t/E_{t+1}^e as $1/(1 + (E_{t+1}^e - E_t)/E_t)$. Replacing in equation (18.2) gives

$$(1 + i_t) = \frac{(1 + i_t^*)}{[1 + (E_{t+1}^e - E_t)/E_t]} \tag{18.3}$$

This gives us a relation between the domestic nominal interest rate, i_t, the foreign nominal interest rate, i_t^*, and the expected rate of appreciation of the domestic currency, $(E_{t+1}^e - E_t)/E_t$. As long as interest rates or the expected rate of depreciation are not too large—say below 20% a year—a good approximation to this equation is given by

$$i_t \approx i_t^* - \frac{E_{t+1}^e - E_t}{E_t} \tag{18.4}$$

This is the form of the *interest parity condition* you must remember: Arbitrage by investors implies that *the domestic interest rate must be equal to the foreign interest rate minus the expected appreciation rate of the domestic currency.*

Note that the expected appreciation rate of the domestic currency is also the expected depreciation rate of the foreign currency. So equation (18.4) can be equivalently stated as saying that *the domestic interest rate must be equal to the foreign interest rate minus the expected depreciation rate of the foreign currency.*

The word *uncovered* is to disinguish this relation from another relation called the *covered interest parity condition*. The covered interest parity condition is derived by looking at the following choice:

◄ Buy and hold U.S. bonds for one year. Or buy pounds today, buy one-year U.K. bonds with the proceeds, and agree to sell the pounds for dollars a year ahead at a predetermined price, called the *forward exchange rate*.

The rate of return on these two alternatives, which can both be realized at *no risk today*, must be the same. The covered interest parity condition is a *riskless arbitrage* condition.

Whether holding U.K. bonds or U.S. bonds is more risky ◄ actually depends on which investors we are looking at. Holding U.K. bonds is more risky from the point of view of U.S. investors. Holding U.S. bonds is more risky from the point of view of British investors. (Why?)

This follows from Proposition ◄ 3 in Appendix 2 at the end of the book.

If the dollar is expected to appreciate by 3% relative to the ◄ pound, then the pound is expected to depreciate by 3% relative to the dollar.

Buying Brazilian Bonds

Put yourself back in September 1993 (the very high interest rate in Brazil at the time helps make the point we want to get across here). Brazilian bonds are paying a monthly interest rate of 36.9%. This seems very attractive compared to the annual rate of 3% on U.S. bonds—corresponding to a monthly interest rate of about 0.2%. Shouldn't you buy Brazilian bonds?

The discussion in this chapter tells you that, to decide, you need one more crucial element, the expected rate of depreciation of the cruzeiro (the name of the Brazilian currency at the time; the currency is now called the real) in terms of dollars.

You need this information because, as we saw in equation (18.4), the return in dollars from investing in Brazilian bonds for a month is equal to one plus the Brazilian interest rate, divided by one plus the expected rate of depreciation of the cruzeiro relative to the dollar:

$$\frac{1 + i_t^*}{[1 + (E_{t+1}^e - E_t)/E_t]}$$

What rate of depreciation of the cruzeiro should you expect over the coming month? A reasonable first pass is to expect the rate of depreciation during the coming month to be equal to the rate of depreciation during last month. The dollar was worth 100,000 cruzeiros at the end of July 1993 and worth 134,600 cruzeiros at the end of August 1993, so the rate of appreciation of the dollar relative to the cruzeiro—equivalently, the rate of depreciation of the cruzeiro relative to the dollar—in August was 34.6%. If depreciation is expected to continue at the same rate in September as it did in August, the expected return from investing in Brazilian bonds for one month is

$$\frac{1.369}{1.346} = 1.017$$

The expected rate of return in dollars from holding Brazilian bonds is only $(1.017 - 1) = 1.6\%$ per month, not the 36.9% per month that initially looked so attractive. Note that 1.6% per month is still much higher than the monthly interest rate on U.S. bonds (about 0.2%). But think of the risk and the transaction costs—all the elements we ignored when we wrote the arbitrage condition. When these are taken into account, you may well decide to keep your funds out of Brazil.

Let's apply this equation to U.S. bonds versus U.K. bonds. Suppose the one-year nominal interest rate is 2.0% in the United States and 5.0% in the United Kingdom. Should you hold U.K. bonds or U.S. bonds? The answer:

■ It depends whether you expect the pound to depreciate relative to the dollar over the coming year by more or less than the difference between the U.S. interest rate and the U.K. interest rate, or 3.0% in this case (5.0% − 2.0%).

■ If you expect the pound to depreciate by more than 3.0%, then, despite the fact that the interest rate is higher in the United Kingdom than in the United States, investing in U.K. bonds is less attractive than investing in U.S. bonds. By holding U.K. bonds, you will get higher interest payments next year, but the pound will be worth less in terms of dollars next year, making investing in U.K. bonds less attractive than investing in U.S. bonds.

■ If you expect the pound to depreciate by less than 3.0% or even to appreciate, then the reverse holds, and U.K bonds are more attractive than U.S. bonds.

Looking at it another way: If the uncovered interest parity condition holds, and the U.S. one-year interest rate is 3% lower than the U.K. interest rate, it must be that financial investors are expecting, on average, an appreciation of the dollar relative to the pound over the coming year of about 3%, and this is why they are willing to hold U.S. bonds despite their lower interest rate. (Another—and more striking—example is provided in the Focus box "Buying Brazilian Bonds").

The arbitrage relation between interest rates and exchange rates, either in the form of equation (18.2) or equation (18.4), will play a central role in the following chapters. It suggests that, unless countries are willing to tolerate large movements in their exchange

Figure 18-8

Three-Month Nominal Interest Rates in the United States and in the United Kingdom since 1970

U.S. and U.K. nominal interest rates have largely moved together over the last 40 years.

Source: U.S. 3-Month Treasury Bill Rate Series DTB3(1); Federal Reserve Economic Data (FRED) http://research.stlouisfed.org/fred2/; U.K. 3-Month Treasury Bill Rate Series IUQAAJNB, Bank of England Web site.

rate, domestic and foreign interest rates are likely to move very much together. Take the extreme case of two countries that commit to maintaining their bilateral exchange rates at a fixed value. If markets have faith in this commitment, they will expect the exchange rate to remain constant, and the expected depreciation will be equal to zero. In this case, the arbitrage condition implies that interest rates in the two countries will have to move exactly together. Most of the time, as we shall see, governments do not make such absolute commitments to maintain the exchange rate, but they often do try to avoid large movements in the exchange rate. This puts sharp limits on how much they can allow their interest rate to deviate from interest rates elsewhere in the world.

> If $E_{t+1}^e = E_t$, then the interest parity condition implies $i_t = i_t^*$.

How much do nominal interest rates actually move together in major countries? Figure 18-8 plots the three-month nominal interest rate in the United States and the three-month nominal interest rate in the United Kingdom (both expressed at annual rates), since 1970. The figure shows that the movements are related but not identical. Interest rates were very high in both countries in the early 1980s, and high again—although much more so in the United Kingdom than in the United States—in the late 1980s. They have been low in both countries since the mid-1990s. At the same time, differences between the two have sometimes been quite large: In 1990, for example, the U.K. interest rate was nearly 7% higher than the U.S. interest rate. In the coming chapters, we shall return to why such differences emerge and what their implications may be.

> Meanwhile, do the following: Look at the back pages of a recent issue of *The Economist* for short-term interest rates in different countries relative to the United States. Assume uncovered interest parity holds. Which currencies are expected to appreciate against the dollar?

18-3 Conclusions and a Look Ahead

We have now set the stage for the study of the open economy:

- Openness in goods markets allows people and firms to choose between domestic goods and foreign goods. This choice depends primarily on the *real exchange rate*—the relative price of domestic goods in terms of foreign goods.

- Openness in financial markets allows investors to choose between domestic assets and foreign assets. This choice depends primarily on their relative rates of return, which depend on domestic interest rates and foreign interest rates, and on the expected rate of appreciation of the domestic currency.

In the next chapter, Chapter 19, we look at the implications of openness in goods markets. In Chapter 20, we further explore openness in financial markets. In Chapter 21, we discuss the pros and cons of different exchange rate regimes.

Summary

- Openness in goods markets allows people and firms to choose between domestic goods and foreign goods. Openness in financial markets allows financial investors to hold domestic financial assets or foreign financial assets.

- The nominal exchange rate is the price of the domestic currency in terms of foreign currency. From the viewpoint of the United States, the nominal exchange rate between the United States and the United Kingdom is the price of a dollar in terms of pounds.

- A nominal appreciation (an appreciation, for short) is an increase in the price of the domestic currency in terms of foreign currency. In other words, it corresponds to an increase in the exchange rate. A nominal depreciation (a depreciation, for short) is a decrease in the price of the domestic currency in terms of foreign currency. It corresponds to a decrease in the exchange rate.

- The real exchange rate is the relative price of domestic goods in terms of foreign goods. It is equal to the nominal exchange rate times the domestic price level divided by the foreign price level.

- A real appreciation is an increase in the relative price of domestic goods in terms of foreign goods (i.e., an increase in the real exchange rate). A real depreciation is a decrease in the relative price of domestic goods in terms of foreign goods (i.e., a decrease in the real exchange rate).

- The multilateral real exchange rate, or real exchange rate for short, is a weighted average of bilateral real exchange rates, with the weight for each foreign country equal to its share in trade.

- The balance of payments records a country's transactions with the rest of the world. The current account balance is equal to the sum of the trade balance, net income, and net transfers the country receives from the rest of the world. The capital account balance is equal to capital flows from the rest of the world minus capital flows to the rest of the world.

- The current account and the capital account are mirror images of each other. Leaving aside statistical problems, the current account plus the capital account must sum to zero. A current account deficit is financed by net capital flows from the rest of the world, thus by a capital account surplus. Similarly, a current account surplus corresponds to a capital account deficit.

- Uncovered interest parity, or interest parity for short, is an arbitrage condition stating that the expected rates of return in terms of domestic currency on domestic bonds and foreign bonds must be equal. Interest parity implies that the domestic interest rate approximately equals the foreign interest rate minus the expected appreciation rate of the domestic currency.

Key Terms

openness in goods markets, 379
tariffs, 379
quotas, 379
openness in financial markets, 379
capital controls, 379
openness in factor markets, 379
North American Free Trade Agreement (NAFTA), 379
tradable goods, 381
real exchange rate, 382
nominal exchange rate, 383
appreciation (nominal), 383

depreciation (nominal), 383
fixed exchange rates, 383
revaluation, 383
devaluation, 383
real appreciation, 385
real depreciation, 385
bilateral exchange rate, 387
multilateral exchange rate, 387
multilateral real U.S. exchange rate, 387
trade-weighted real exchange rate, 387
effective real exchange rate, 387

Questions and Problems

QUICK CHECK

**All Quick Check questions and problems are available
on** MyEconLab.

1. Using the information in this chapter, label each of the following statements true, false, or uncertain. Explain briefly.

  a. If there are no statistical discrepancies, countries with current account deficits must receive net capital inflows.

  b. While the export ratio can be larger than one—as it is in Singapore—the same cannot be true of the ratio of imports to GDP.

  c. That a rich country like Japan has such a small ratio of imports to GDP is clear evidence of an unfair playing field for U.S. exporters to Japan.

  d. Uncovered interest parity implies that interest rates must be the same across countries.

  e. If the dollar is expected to appreciate against the yen, uncovered interest parity implies that the U.S. nominal interest rate will be greater than the Japanese nominal interest rate.

  f. Given the definition of the exchange rate adopted in this chapter, if the dollar is the domestic currency and the euro the foreign currency, a nominal exchange rate of 0.75 means that 0.75 dollars is worth 0.75 euros.

  g. A real appreciation means that domestic goods become less expensive relative to foreign goods.

2. Consider two fictional economies, one called the domestic country and the other the foreign country. Given the transactions listed in (a) through (g), construct the balance of payments for each country. If necessary, include a statistical discrepancy.

  a. The domestic country purchased $100 in oil from the foreign country.

  b. Foreign tourists spent $25 on domestic ski slopes.

  c. Foreign investors were paid $15 in dividends from their holdings of domestic equities.

  d. Domestic residents gave $25 to foreign charities.

  e. Domestic businesses borrowed $65 from foreign banks.

  f. Foreign investors purchased $15 of domestic government bonds.

  g. Domestic investors sold $50 of their holdings of foreign government bonds.

3. Consider two bonds, one issued in euros (€) in Germany, and one issued in dollars ($) in the United States. Assume that both government securities are one-year bonds—paying the
face value of the bond one year from now. The exchange rate, E, stands at 1 dollar = 0.75 euro.

The face values and prices on the two bonds are given by

	Face Value	Price
United States	$10,000	$9,615.38
Germany	€10,000	€9,433.96

  a. Compute the nominal interest rate on each of the bonds.

  b. Compute the expected exchange rate next year consistent with uncovered interest parity.

  c. If you expect the dollar to depreciate relative to the euro, which bond should you buy?

  d. Assume that you are a U.S. investor. You exchange dollars for euros and purchase the German bond. One year from now, it turns out that the exchange rate, E, is actually 0.72 (1 dollar = 0.72 euro). What is your realized rate of return in dollars compared to the realized rate of return you would have made had you held the U.S. bond?

  e. Are the differences in rates of return in (d) consistent with the uncovered interest parity condition? Why or why not?

DIG DEEPER

**All Dig Deeper questions and problems are available
on** MyEconLab.

4. Consider a world with three equal-sized economies (A, B, and C) and three goods (clothes, cars, and computers). Assume that consumers in all three economies want to spend an equal amount on all three goods.

  The value of production of each good in the three economies is given below.

	A	B	C
Clothes	10	0	5
Cars	5	10	0
Computers	0	5	10

  a. What is GDP in each economy? If the total value of GDP is consumed and no country borrows from abroad, how much will consumers in each economy spend on each of the goods?

b. If no country borrows from abroad, what will be the trade balance in each country? What will be the pattern of trade in this world (i.e., which good will each country export and to whom)?

c. Given your answer to part (b), will country A have a zero trade balance with country B? with country C? Will any country have a zero trade balance with any other country?

d. The United States has a large trade deficit. It has a trade deficit with each of its major trading partners, but the deficit is much larger with some countries (e.g., China) than with others. Suppose the United States eliminates its overall trade deficit (with the world as a whole). Do you expect it to have a zero trade balance with every one of its trading partners? Does the especially large trade deficit with China necessarily indicate that China does not allow U.S. goods to compete on an equal basis with Chinese goods?

5. *The exchange rate and the labor market*
   Suppose the domestic currency depreciates (E falls).
   Assume that P and P* remain constant.

   a. How does the nominal depreciation affect the relative price of domestic goods (i.e., the real exchange rate)? Given your answer, what effect would a nominal depreciation likely have on (world) demand for domestic goods? on the domestic unemployment rate?

   b. Given the foreign price level, P^*, what is the price of foreign goods in terms of domestic currency? How does a nominal depreciation affect the price of foreign goods in terms of domestic currency? How does a nominal depreciation affect the domestic consumer price index? (*Hint*: Remember that domestic consumers buy foreign goods (imports) as well as domestic goods.)

   c. If the nominal wage remains constant, how does a nominal depreciation affect the real wage?

   d. Comment on the following statement. "A depreciating currency puts domestic labor on sale."

EXPLORE FURTHER

6. *Retrieve the nominal exchange rates between Japan and the United States from the Federal Reserve Bank of St. Louis FRED data site. It is series AEXJPUS.*

   a. Plot the yen versus the dollar since 1971. During which times period(s) did the yen appreciate? During which period(s) did the yen depreciate?

   b. Given the current Japanese slump (although there are some encouraging signs at the time of this writing), one

way of increasing demand would be to make Japanese goods more attractive. Does this require an appreciation or a depreciation of the yen?

   c. What has happened to the yen during the past few years? Has it appreciated or depreciated? Is this good or bad for Japan?

7. *Retrieve the most recent World Economic Outlook (WEO) from the web site of the International Monetary Fund (**www.imf.org**). In the Statistical Appendix, find the table titled "Balances on Current Account," which lists current account balances around the world. Use the data for the most recent year available to answer parts (a) through (c).*

   a. Note the sum of current account balances around the world. As noted in the chapter, the sum of current account balances should equal zero. What does this sum actually equal? Why does this sum indicate some mismeasurement (i.e., if the sum were correct, what would it imply)?

   b. Which regions of the world are borrowing and which are lending?

   c. Compare the U.S. current account balance to the current account balances of the other advanced economies. Is the United States borrowing only from advanced economies?

   d. The statistical tables in the WEO typically project data for two years into the future. Look at the projected data on current account balances. Do your answers to parts (b) and (c) seem likely to change in the near future?

8. *Saving and investment throughout the world*
   *Retrieve the most recent World Economic Outlook (WEO) from the web site of the International Monetary Fund (**www.imf.org**). In the Statistical Appendix, find the table titled "Summary of Sources and Uses of World Saving," which lists saving and investment (as a percentage of GDP) around the world. Use the data for the most recent year available to answer parts (a) and (b).*

   a. Does world saving equal investment? (You may ignore small statistical discrepancies.) Offer some intuition for your answer.

   b. How does U.S. saving compare to U.S. investment? How is the United States able to finance its investment? (*We explain this explicitly in the next chapter, but your intuition should help you figure it out now.*)

   c. The same publication has a table entitled "Table B14. Advanced Economies: Current Account Transactions." The Advanced countries are the United States, Germany, France, Italy, Spain, Japan, the United Kingdom, and Canada. Use this table to list the countries in which GNP is larger than GDP.

Further Readings

- If you want to learn more about international trade and international economics, a very good textbook is by Paul Krugman and Maurice Obstfeld, *International Economics, Theory and Policy*, 9th ed. (Pearson Addison Wesley, 2010).

- If you want to know current exchange rates between nearly any pair of currencies in the world, look at the "currency converter" on http://www.oanda.com.

The Goods Market in an Open Economy

I n 2009, countries around the world worried about the risk of a recession in the United States. But their worries were not so much for the United States as they were for themselves. To them, a U.S. recession meant lower exports to the United States, a deterioration of their trade position, and weaker growth at home.

Were their worries justified? Figure 18-1 from the previous chapter certainly suggested they were. The U.S. recession clearly led to a world recession. To understand what happened, we must expand the treatment of the goods market in Chapter 3 of the core and account for openness in the analysis of goods markets. This is what we do in this chapter.

Section 19-1 characterizes equilibrium in the goods market for an open economy.

Sections 19-2 and 19-3 show the effects of domestic shocks and foreign shocks on the domestic economy's output and trade balance.

Sections 19-4 and 19-5 look at the effects of a real depreciation on output and the trade balance.

Section 19-6 gives an alternative description of the equilibrium that shows the close connection among saving, investment, and the trade balance. ●

19-1 The *IS* Relation in the Open Economy

"The domestic demand for goods" and "The demand for domestic goods" sound close but are not the same. Part of ▶ domestic demand falls on foreign goods. Part of foreign demand falls on domestic goods.

When we were assuming the economy was closed to trade, there was no need to distinguish between the *domestic demand for goods* and the *demand for domestic goods*: They were clearly the same thing. Now, we must distinguish between the two: Some domestic demand falls on foreign goods, and some of the demand for domestic goods comes from foreigners. Let's look at this distinction more closely.

The Demand for Domestic Goods

In an open economy, the **demand for domestic goods**, Z is given by

$$Z \equiv C + I + G - IM/\epsilon + X \tag{19.1}$$

The first three terms—consumption, C, investment, I, and government spending, G—constitute the **domestic demand for goods**. If the economy were closed, $C + I + G$ would also be the demand for domestic goods. This is why, until now, we have only looked at $C + I + G$. But now we have to make two adjustments:

- First, we must subtract imports—that part of the domestic demand that falls on foreign goods rather than on domestic goods.

  We must be careful here: Foreign goods are different from domestic goods, so we cannot just subtract the quantity of imports, IM. If we were to do so, we would be subtracting apples (foreign goods) from oranges (domestic goods). We must first express the value of imports in terms of domestic goods. This is what IM/ϵ in equation (19.1) stands for: Recall from Chapter 18 that ϵ, the real exchange rate, is defined as the price of domestic goods in terms of foreign goods. Equivalently, $1/\epsilon$ is the price of foreign goods in terms of domestic goods. So $IM(1/\epsilon)$—or, equivalently, IM/ϵ—is the value of imports in terms of domestic goods.

In Chapter 3, we ignored the real exchange rate and subtracted *IM*, not *IM*/ϵ. But this was cheating; we did not want to have to talk about the real exchange rate—and compli- ▶ cate matters—so early in the book.

- Second, we must add exports—that part of the demand for domestic goods that comes from abroad. This is captured by the term X in equation (19.1).

Domestic demand for goods ▶ $C + I + G$
   $-$ Domestic demand for foreign goods (imports), IM/ϵ
   $+$ Foreign demand for domestic goods (exports), $X =$ Demand for domestic goods $C + I + G - IM/\epsilon + X$

The Determinants of *C*, *I*, and *G*

Having listed the five components of demand, our next task is to specify their determinants. Let's start with the first three: C, I, and G. Now that we are assuming the economy is open, how should we modify our earlier descriptions of consumption, investment, and government spending? The answer: not very much, if at all. How much consumers decide to spend still depends on their income and their wealth. While the real exchange rate surely affects the *composition* of consumption spending between domestic goods and foreign goods, there is no obvious reason why it should affect the overall *level* of consumption. The same is true of investment: The real exchange rate may affect whether firms buy domestic machines or foreign machines, but it should not affect total investment.

This is good news because it implies that we can use the descriptions of consumption, investment, and government spending that we developed earlier. Therefore,

$$\text{Domestic demand:} \quad C + I + G = C(Y - T) + I(Y, r) + G$$
$$(+) \qquad (+, -)$$

We again cheat a bit here. Income should include not only domestic income but also net income and transfers from abroad. For simplicity, we ignore ▶ these two additional terms here.

We assume that consumption depends positively on disposable income, $Y - T$, and that investment depends positively on production, Y, and negatively on the real interest rate, r. We continue to take government spending, G, as given. We leave aside the refinements introduced in Chapters 14 to 17, where we looked at how expectations affect spending. We want to take things one step at a time to understand the effects of opening the economy; we shall reintroduce some of those refinements later.

The Determinants of Imports

Imports are the part of domestic demand that falls on foreign goods. What do they depend on? They clearly depend on domestic income: Higher domestic income leads to a higher domestic demand for all goods, both domestic and foreign. So a higher domestic income leads to higher imports. They also clearly depend on the real exchange ◄ rate—the price of domestic goods in terms of foreign goods: The more expensive domestic goods are relative to foreign goods—equivalently, the cheaper foreign goods are relative to domestic goods— the higher is the domestic demand for foreign goods. So a higher real exchange rate leads to higher imports. Thus, we write imports as

$$IM = IM(Y, \epsilon) \tag{19.2}$$
$$(+, +)$$

Recall the discussion at the start of this chapter. Countries in the rest of the world worry about a U.S. recession. The reason: A U.S. recession means a decrease in the U.S. demand for foreign goods.

- An increase in domestic income, Y (equivalently, an increase in domestic output—income and output are still equal in an open economy) leads to an increase in imports. This positive effect of income on imports is captured by the positive sign under Y in equation (19.2).
- An increase in the real exchange rate, ϵ, leads to an increase in imports, IM. This positive effect of the real exchange rate on imports is captured by the positive sign under ϵ in equation (19.2). (As ϵ goes up, note that IM goes up, but $1/\epsilon$ goes down, so what happens to IM/ϵ, the *value* of imports in terms of domestic goods, is ambiguous. We will return to this point shortly.)

The Determinants of Exports

Exports are the part of foreign demand that falls on domestic goods. What do they depend on? They depend on foreign income: Higher foreign income means higher foreign demand for all goods, both foreign and domestic. So higher foreign income leads to higher exports. They depend also on the real exchange rate: The higher the price of domestic goods in terms of foreign goods, the lower the foreign demand for domestic goods. In other words, the higher the real exchange rate, the lower are exports.

Let Y^* denote foreign income (equivalently, foreign output). We therefore write ◄ exports as

Recall that asterisks refer to foreign variables.

$$X = X(Y^*, \epsilon) \tag{19.3}$$
$$(+, -)$$

- An increase in foreign income, Y^*, leads to an increase in exports.
- An increase in the real exchange rate, ϵ, leads to a decrease in exports.

Putting the Components Together

Figure 19-1 puts together what we have learned so far. It plots the various components of demand against output, keeping constant all other variables (the interest rate, taxes, government spending, foreign output, and the real exchange rate) that affect demand.

In Figure 19-1(a), the line DD plots domestic demand, $C + I + G$, as a function of output, Y. This relation between demand and output is familiar from Chapter 3. Under our standard assumptions, the slope of the relation between demand and output is positive but less than one: An increase in output—equivalently, an increase in income—increases demand but less than one-for-one. (In the absence of good reasons

Figure 19-1

The Demand for Domestic Goods and Net Exports

The domestic demand for goods is an increasing function of income (output). (Panel a)

The demand for domestic goods is obtained by subtracting the value of imports from domestic demand and then adding exports. (Panels b and c)

The trade balance is a decreasing function of output. (Panel d)

to the contrary, we draw the relation between demand and output, and the other relations in this chapter, as lines rather than curves. This is purely for convenience, and none of the discussions that follow depend on this assumption.)

To arrive at the demand for domestic goods, we must first *subtract imports*. This is done in Figure 19-1(b) and it gives us the line *AA*. The line *AA* represents the domestic demand for domestic goods. The distance between *DD* and *AA* equals the value of imports, IM/ϵ. Because the quantity of imports increases with income, the distance between the two lines increases with income. We can establish two facts about line AA, which will be useful later in the chapter:

■ AA is flatter than DD: As income increases, some of the additional domestic demand falls on foreign goods rather than on domestic goods. In other words, as income increases, the domestic demand for domestic goods increases less than total domestic demand.
■ As long as some of the additional demand falls on domestic goods, AA has a positive slope: An increase in income leads to some increase in the demand for domestic goods.

Finally, we must *add exports*. This is done in Figure 19-1(c) and it gives us the line ZZ, which is above AA. The line ZZ represents the demand for domestic goods. The distance between ZZ and AA equals exports. Because exports do not depend on domestic income (they depend on foreign income), the distance between ZZ and AA is constant, which is why the two lines are parallel. Because AA is flatter than DD, ZZ is also flatter than DD.

From the information in Figure 19-1(c) we can characterize the behavior of net exports—the difference between exports and imports $(X - IM/\epsilon)$—as a function of output. At output level Y, for example, exports are given by the distance AC and imports by the distance AB, so net exports are given by the distance BC.

This relation between net exports and output is represented as the line NX (for Net eXports) in Figure 19-1(d). Net exports are a decreasing function of output: As output increases, imports increase and exports are unaffected, so net exports decrease. Call Y_{TB} (TB for trade balance) the level of output at which the value of imports equals the value of exports, so that net exports are equal to zero. Levels of output above Y_{TB} lead to higher imports and to a trade deficit. Levels of output below Y_{TB} lead to lower imports and to a trade surplus.

19-2 Equilibrium Output and the Trade Balance

The goods market is in equilibrium when domestic output equals the demand—both domestic and foreign—for domestic goods:

$$Y = Z$$

Collecting the relations we derived for the components of the demand for domestic goods, Z, we get

$$Y = C(Y - T) + I(Y, r) + G - IM(Y, \epsilon)/\epsilon + X(Y^*, \epsilon) \qquad (19.4)$$

This equilibrium condition determines output as a function of all the variables we take as given, from taxes to the real exchange rate to foreign output. This is not a simple relation; Figure 19-2 represents it graphically, in a more user-friendly way.

In Figure 19-2(a), demand is measured on the vertical axis, output (equivalently production or income) on the horizontal axis. The line ZZ plots demand as a function of output; this line just replicates the line ZZ in Figure 19-1; ZZ is upward sloping, but with slope less than 1.

Equilibrium output is at the point where demand equals output, at the intersection of the line ZZ and the 45-degree line: point A in Figure 19-2(a), with associated output level Y.

Figure 19-2(b) replicates Figure 19-1(d), drawing net exports as a decreasing function of output. There is in general no reason why the equilibrium level of output, Y, should be the same as the level of output at which trade is balanced, Y_{TB}. As we have

For a given real exchange rate ϵ, IM/ϵ—the value of imports in terms of domestic goods—moves exactly with IM—the quantity of imports.

Recall that *net exports* is synonymous with trade balance. Positive net exports correspond to a trade surplus, whereas negative net exports correspond to a trade deficit.

The equilibrium level of output is given by the condition $Y = Z$. The level of output at which there is trade balance is given by the condition $X = IM/\epsilon$. These are two different conditions.

Figure 19-2

Equilibrium Output and Net Exports

The goods market is in equilibrium when domestic output is equal to the demand for domestic goods. At the equilibrium level of output, the trade balance may show a deficit or a surplus.

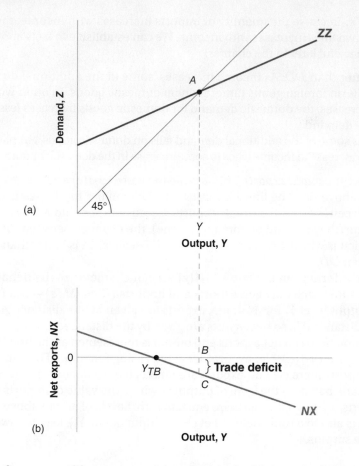

(a)

(b)

drawn the figure, equilibrium output is associated with a trade deficit, equal to the distance BC. Note that we could have drawn it differently, so equilibrium output was associated instead with a trade surplus.

We now have the tools needed to answer the questions we asked at the beginning of this chapter.

19-3 Increases in Demand, Domestic or Foreign

How do changes in demand affect output in an open economy? Let's start with an old favorite—an increase in government spending—then turn to a new exercise, the effects of an increase in foreign demand.

Increases in Domestic Demand

As in the core, we start with the goods market; the conclusions we derive here will still largely be correct when we introduce financial markets and labor markets later on.

Suppose the economy is in a recession and the government decides to increase government spending in order to increase domestic demand and output. What will be the effects on output and on the trade balance?

The answer is given in Figure 19-3. Before the increase in government spending, demand is given by ZZ in Figure 19-3(a), and the equilibrium is at point A, where output equals Y. Let's assume that trade is initially balanced—even though, as we have seen, there is no reason why this should be true in general. So, in Figure 19-3(b), $Y = Y_{TB}$.

What happens if the government increases spending by ΔG? At any level of output, demand is higher by ΔG, shifting the demand relation up by ΔG from ZZ to ZZ'. The equilibrium point moves from A to A', and output increases from Y to Y'. The

Figure 19-3

The Effects of an Increase in Government Spending

An increase in government spending leads to an increase in output and to a trade deficit.

increase in output is larger than the increase in government spending: There is a multiplier effect.

So far, the story sounds the same as the story for a closed economy in Chapter 3. However, there are two important differences:

- There is now an effect on the trade balance. Because government spending enters neither the exports relation nor the imports relation directly, the relation between net exports and output in Figure 19-3(b) does not shift. So the increase in output from Y to Y' leads to a *trade deficit* equal to BC: Imports go up, and exports do not change.

- Not only does government spending now generate a trade deficit, but the effect of government spending on output is smaller than it would be in a closed economy. Recall from Chapter 3 that the smaller the slope of the demand relation, the smaller the multiplier (for example, if ZZ were horizontal, the multiplier would be 1). And recall from Figure 19-1 that the demand relation, ZZ, is flatter than the demand relation in the closed economy, DD. This means the *multiplier is smaller in the open economy.*

The trade deficit and the smaller multiplier have the same cause: Because the economy is open, an increase in demand now falls not only on domestic goods, but also on foreign goods. So, when income increases, the effect on the demand for domestic goods is smaller than it would be in a closed economy, leading to a smaller multiplier. And, because some of the increase in demand falls on imports—and exports are unchanged—the result is a trade deficit.

◄ Starting from trade balance, an increase in government spending leads to a trade deficit.

◄ An increase in government spending increases output. The multiplier is smaller than in a closed economy.

◄ The smaller multiplier and the trade deficit have the same cause: Some domestic demand falls on foreign goods.

These two implications are important. In an open economy, an increase in domestic demand has a smaller effect on output than in a closed economy, and an adverse effect on the trade balance. Indeed, the more open the economy, the smaller the effect on output and the larger the adverse effect on the trade balance. Take Belgium, for example. As we saw in Chapter 18, Belgium's ratio of exports to GDP is very high. It is also true that Belgium's ratio of imports to GDP is very high. When domestic demand increases in Belgium, much of the increase in demand is likely to result in an increase in the demand for foreign goods rather than an increase in the demand for domestic goods. The effect of an increase in government spending is therefore likely to be a large increase in Belgium's trade deficit and only a small increase in its output, making domestic demand expansion a rather unattractive policy for Belgium. Even for the United States, which has a much lower import ratio, an increase in demand will be associated with a worsening of the trade balance.

Increases in Foreign Demand

Consider now an increase in foreign output, that is, an increase in Y^*. This could be due to an increase in foreign government spending, G^*—the policy change we just analyzed, but now taking place abroad. But we do not need to know where the increase in Y^* comes from to analyze its effects on the U.S. economy.

Figure 19-4 shows the effects of an increase in foreign activity on domestic output and the trade balance. The initial demand for domestic goods is given by ZZ in

Figure 19-4

The Effects of an Increase in Foreign Demand

An increase in foreign demand leads to an increase in output and to a trade surplus.

Figure 19-4(a). The equilibrium is at point A, with output level Y. Let's again assume trade is balanced, so that in Figure 19-4(b) the net exports associated with Y equal zero ($Y = Y_{TB}$).

It will be useful below to refer to the line that shows the *domestic demand for goods* $C + I + G$ as a function of income. This line is drawn as DD. Recall from Figure 19-1 that DD is steeper than ZZ. The difference between ZZ and DD equal net exports, so that if trade is balanced at point A, then ZZ and DD intersect at point A.

Now consider the effects of an increase in foreign output, ΔY^* (for the moment, ignore the line DD; we only need it later). Higher foreign output means higher foreign demand, including higher foreign demand for U.S. goods. So the direct effect of the increase in foreign output is an increase in U.S. exports by some amount, which we shall denote by ΔX.

- For a given level of output, this increase in exports leads to an increase in the demand for U.S. goods by ΔX, so the line showing the demand for domestic goods as a function of output shifts up by ΔX, from ZZ to ZZ'.
- For a given level of output, net exports go up by ΔX. So the line showing net exports as a function of output in Figure 19-4(b) also shifts up by ΔX, from NX to NX'.

The new equilibrium is at point A' in Figure 19-4(a), with output level Y'. The increase in foreign output leads to an increase in domestic output. The channel is clear: Higher foreign output leads to higher exports of domestic goods, which increases domestic output and the domestic demand for goods through the multiplier.

What happens to the trade balance? We know that exports go up. But could it be that the increase in domestic output leads to such a large increase in imports that the trade balance actually deteriorates? No: The trade balance must improve. To see why, note that, when foreign demand increases, the demand for domestic goods shifts up from ZZ to ZZ'; but the line DD, which gives the *domestic demand for goods* as a function of output, does not shift. At the new equilibrium level of output Y', domestic demand is given by the distance DC, and the demand for domestic goods is given by DA'. Net exports are therefore given by the distance CA' —which, because DD is necessarily below ZZ', is necessarily positive. Thus, while imports increase, the increase does not offset the increase in exports, and the trade balance improves.

◄ DD is the domestic demand for goods. ZZ is the demand for domestic goods. The difference between the two is equal to the trade deficit.

Y^* directly affects exports and so enters the relation between the demand for domestic goods and output. An increase in Y^* shifts ZZ up.

Y^* does not affect domestic consumption, domestic investment, or domestic government spending directly, and so it does not enter the relation between the domestic demand for goods and output. An increase in Y^* does not shift DD.

◄ An increase in foreign output increases domestic output and improves the trade balance.

Fiscal Policy Revisited

We have derived two basic results so far:

- An increase in domestic demand leads to an increase in domestic output but leads also to a deterioration of the trade balance. (We looked at an increase in government spending, but the results would have been the same for a decrease in taxes, an increase in consumer spending, and so on.)
- An increase in foreign demand (which could come from the same types of changes taking place abroad) leads to an increase in domestic output and an improvement in the trade balance.

These results, in turn, have two important implications. Both have been in evidence in the crisis.

First, and most obviously, they imply that shocks to demand in one country affect all other countries. The stronger the trade links between countries, the stronger the interactions, and the more countries will move together. This is what we saw in Figure 18-1:

While the crisis started in the United States, it quickly affected the rest of the world. Trade links were not the only reason; financial links also played a central role. But the evidence points to a strong effect of trade, starting with a decrease in exports from other countries to the United States.

Second, these interactions complicate the task of policy makers, especially in the case of fiscal policy. Let's explore this argument more closely.

Start with the following observation: Governments do not like to run trade deficits, and for good reasons. The main reason: A country that consistently runs a trade deficit accumulates debt vis à vis the rest of the world, and therefore has to pay steadily higher interest payments to the rest of the world. Thus, it is no wonder that countries prefer increases in foreign demand (which improve the trade balance) to increases in domestic demand (which worsen the trade balance).

But these preferences can have disastrous implications. Consider a group of countries, all doing a large amount of trade with each other, so that an increase in demand in any one country falls largely on the goods produced in the other countries. Suppose all these countries are in recession and each has roughly balanced trade to start. In this case, each country might be very reluctant to take measures to increase domestic demand. Were it to do so, the result might be a small increase in output but also a large trade deficit. Instead, each country might just wait for the other countries to increase their demand. This way, it gets the best of both worlds, higher output and an improvement in its trade balance. But if all the countries wait, nothing will happen and the recession may last a long time.

Is there a way out? There is—at least in theory. If all countries coordinate their macroeconomic policies so as to increase domestic demand simultaneously, each can increase demand and output without increasing its trade deficit (vis à vis the others; their combined trade deficit with respect to the rest of the world will still increase). The reason is clear: The coordinated increase in demand leads to increases in both exports and imports in each country. It is still true that domestic demand expansion leads to larger imports; but this increase in imports is offset by the increase in exports, which comes from the foreign demand expansions.

In practice, however, **policy coordination** is not so easy to achieve:

Some countries might have to do more than others and may not want to do so: Suppose that only some countries are in recession. Countries that are not in a recession will be reluctant to increase their own demand; but if they do not, the countries that expand will run a trade deficit vis á vis countries that do not. Or suppose some countries are already running a large budget deficit. These countries will not want to cut taxes or further increase spending as this would further increase their deficits. They will ask other countries to take on more of the adjustment. Those other countries may be reluctant to do so.

Countries have a strong incentive to promise to coordinate and then not deliver on that promise: Once all countries have agreed, say, to an increase in spending, each country has an incentive not to deliver, so as to benefit from the increase in demand elsewhere and thereby improve its trade position. But if each country cheats, or does not do everything it promised, there will be insufficient demand expansion to get out of the recession.

The result is that, despite declarations by governments at international meetings, coordination often fizzles. Only when things are really bad, does coordination appear to take hold. This was the case in 2009 and is explored in the Focus box "The G20 and the 2009 Fiscal Stimulus."

The G20 and the 2009 Fiscal Stimulus

In November 2008, the leaders of the **G20** met in an emergency meeting in Washington. The G20, a group of ministers of finance and central bank governors from 20 countries, including both the major advanced and the major emerging countries in the world, had been created in 1999 but had not played a major role until the crisis. With mounting evidence that the crisis was going to be both deep and widespread, the group met to coordinate their responses in terms of both macroeconomic and financial policies.

On the macroeconomic front, it had become clear that monetary policy would not be enough, and so the focus turned to fiscal policy. The decrease in output was going to lead to a decrease in revenues, and thus an increase in budget deficits. Dominique Strauss-Kahn, the then managing director of the International Monetary Fund, argued that further fiscal actions were needed and suggested taking additional discretionary measures—either decreases in taxes or increases in spending—adding up to roughly 2% of GDP on average for each country. Here is what he said:

"The fiscal stimulus is now essential to restore global growth. Each country's fiscal stimulus can be twice as effective in raising domestic output growth if its major trading partners also have a stimulus package."

He noted that some countries had more room for maneuver than others. "We believe that those countries— advanced and emerging economies—with the strongest fiscal policy frameworks, the best ability to finance fiscal expansion, and the most clearly sustainable debt should take the lead."

Over the next few months, most countries indeed adopted discretionary measures, aimed at either increasing private or public spending. For the G20 as a whole, discretionary measures added up to about 2.3% of GDP in 2009. Some countries, with less fiscal room, such as Italy, did less. Some countries, such as the United States or France, did more.

Was this fiscal stimulus successful? Some have argued that it was not: After all, the world economy had large negative growth in 2009. The issue here is one of counterfactuals. What would have happened in the absence of the stimulus? Many believe that, absent the fiscal stimulus, growth would have been even more negative, perhaps catastrophically so. Counterfactuals are hard to prove or disprove, and thus the controversy is likely to go on. (On the issue of counterfactuals and the difference between economists and politicians, politicians, following is a very nice quote from U.S. congressman Barney Frank: "Not for the first time, as an elected official, I envy economists. Economists have available to them, in an analytical approach, the counterfactual. Economists can explain that a given decision was the best one that could be made, because they can show what would have happened in the counterfactual situation. They can contrast what happened to what would have happened. No one has ever gotten reelected where the bumper sticker said, 'It would have been worse without me.' You probably can get tenure with that. But you can't win office.")

Was this fiscal stimulus dangerous? Some have argued that it has led to a large increase in debt, which is now forcing governments to adjust, leading to a fiscal contraction and making recovery more difficult (we discussed this in Chapter 9 and will return to it in Chapter 23). This argument is largely misplaced. Most of the increase in debt does not come from the discretionary measures that were taken, but from the decrease in revenues that came from the decrease in output during the crisis. And a number of countries were running large deficits before the crisis. It remains true, however, that this large increase in debt is now making it more difficult to use fiscal policy to help the recovery.

For more discussion at the time, see "Financial Crisis Response: IMF Spells Out Need for Global Fiscal Stimulus," in *IMF Survey Magazine* Online, December 29, 2008. (http://www.imf.org/external/pubs/ft/survey/so/2008/int122908a.htm)

19-4 Depreciation, the Trade Balance, and Output

Suppose the U.S. government takes policy measures that lead to a depreciation of the dollar—a decrease in the nominal exchange rate. (We shall see in Chapter 20 how it can do this by using monetary policy. For the moment we will assume the government can simply choose the exchange rate.)

Recall that the real exchange rate is given by

$$\epsilon \equiv \frac{E\,P}{P^*}$$

The real exchange rate, ϵ (the price of domestic goods in terms of foreign goods) is equal to the nominal exchange rate, E (the price of domestic currency in terms of foreign currency) times the domestic price level, P, divided by the foreign price level, P^*.

Given P and P^*, E increases $\Rightarrow \epsilon \equiv EP/P^*$ increases.

A look ahead: In Chapter 21, we shall look at the effects of a nominal depreciation when we allow the price level to adjust over time. You will see that a nominal depreciation leads to a real depreciation in the short run but not in the medium run.

More concretely, if the dollar depreciates vis à vis the yen by 10%:

U.S. goods will be cheaper in Japan, leading to a larger quantity of U.S. exports to Japan.

Japanese goods will be more expensive in the United States, leading to a smaller quantity of imports of Japanese goods to the United States.

Japanese goods will be more expensive, leading to a higher import bill for a given quantity of imports of Japanese goods to the United States.

It is named after the two economists, Alfred Marshall and Abba Lerner, who were the first to derive it.

Marshall-Lerner condition: Given output, a real depreciation leads to an increase in net exports.

In the short run, we can take the two price levels P and P^* as given. This implies that the nominal depreciation is reflected one for one in a real depreciation. More concretely, if the dollar depreciates vis à vis the yen by 10% (a 10% nominal depreciation), and if the price levels in Japan and the United States do not change, U.S. goods will be 10% cheaper compared to Japanese goods (a 10% real depreciation).

Let's now ask how this real depreciation will affect the U.S. trade balance and U.S. output.

Depreciation and the Trade Balance: The Marshall-Lerner Condition

Return to the definition of net exports:

$$NX \equiv X - IM/\epsilon$$

Replace X and IM by their expressions from equations (19.2) and (19.3):

$$NX = X(Y^*, \epsilon) - IM(Y, \epsilon)/\epsilon$$

As the real exchange rate ϵ enters the right side of the equation in three places, this makes it clear that the real depreciation affects the trade balance through three separate channels:

- *Exports, X, increase.* The real depreciation makes U.S. goods relatively less expensive abroad. This leads to an increase in foreign demand for U.S. goods—an increase in U.S. exports.
- *Imports, IM, decrease.* The real depreciation makes foreign goods relatively more expensive in the United States. This leads to a shift in domestic demand toward domestic goods and to a decrease in the quantity of imports.
- *The relative price of foreign goods in terms of domestic goods, $1/\epsilon$, increases.* This increases the import bill, IM/ϵ. The same quantity of imports now costs more to buy (in terms of domestic goods).

For the trade balance to improve following a depreciation, exports must increase enough and imports must decrease enough to compensate for the increase in the price of imports. The condition under which a real depreciation leads to an increase in net exports is known as the **Marshall-Lerner condition**. (It is derived formally in the appendix, called "Derivation of the Marshall Lerner Condition," at the end of this chapter.) It turns out—with a complication we will state when we introduce dynamics later in this chapter—that this condition is satisfied in reality. So, for the rest of this book, we shall assume that a real depreciation—a decrease in ϵ—leads to an increase in net exports—an increase in NX.

The Effects of a Depreciation

We have looked so far at the *direct* effects of a depreciation on the trade balance—that is, the effects *given U.S. and foreign output.* But the effects do not end there. The change in net exports changes domestic output, which affects net exports further.

Because the effects of a real depreciation are very much like those of an increase in foreign output, we can use Figure 19-4, the same figure that we used earlier to show the effects of an increase in foreign output.

Just like an increase in foreign output, a depreciation leads to an increase in net exports (assuming, as we do, that the Marshall-Lerner condition holds), at any level of output. Both the demand relation (ZZ in Figure 19-4(a)) and the net exports relation (NX in Figure 19-4(b)) shift up. The equilibrium moves from A to A', and output increases from Y to Y'. By the same argument we used earlier, the trade balance improves: The increase in imports induced by the increase in output is smaller than the direct improvement in the trade balance induced by the depreciation.

Let's summarize: *The depreciation leads to a shift in demand, both foreign and domestic, toward domestic goods. This shift in demand leads, in turn, to both an increase in domestic output and an improvement in the trade balance.*

Although a depreciation and an increase in foreign output have the same effect on domestic output and the trade balance, there is a subtle but important difference between the two. A depreciation works by making foreign goods relatively more expensive. But this means that given their income, people—who now have to pay more to buy foreign goods because of the depreciation—are worse off. This mechanism is strongly felt in countries that go through a large depreciation. Governments trying to achieve a large depreciation often find themselves with strikes and riots in the streets, as people react to the much higher prices of imported goods. This was the case in Mexico, for example, where the large depreciation of the peso in 1994–1995—from 29 cents per peso in November 1994 to 17 cents per peso in May 1995—led to a large decline in workers' living standards and to social unrest.

There is an alternative to riots—asking for and obtaining an increase in wages. But, if wages increase, the prices of domestic goods will follow and increase as well, leading to a smaller real depreciation. To discuss this mechanism, we need to look at the supply side in more detail than we have done so far. We return to the dynamics of depreciation, wage, and price movements in Chapter 21.

Combining Exchange Rate and Fiscal Policies

Suppose output is at its natural level, but the economy is running a large trade deficit. The government would like to reduce the trade deficit while leaving output unchanged. What should it do?

A depreciation alone will not do: It will reduce the trade deficit, but it will also increase output. Nor will a fiscal contraction: It will reduce the trade deficit, but it will decrease output. What should the government do? The answer: Use the right combination of depreciation and fiscal contraction. Figure 19-5 shows what this combination should be.

Suppose the initial equilibrium in Figure 19-5(a) is at A, associated with output Y. At this level of output, there is a trade deficit, given by the distance BC in Figure 19-5(b). If the government wants to eliminate the trade deficit without changing output, it must do two things:

- It must achieve a depreciation sufficient to eliminate the trade deficit at the initial level of output. So the depreciation must be such as to shift the net exports relation from NX to NX' in Figure 19-5(b). The problem is that this depreciation, and the associated increase in net exports, also shifts the demand relation in Figure 19-5(a) from ZZ to ZZ'. In the absence of other measures, the equilibrium would move from A to A', and output would increase from Y to Y'.
- In order to avoid the increase in output, the government must reduce government spending so as to shift ZZ' back to ZZ. This combination of a depreciation and a fiscal contraction leads to the same level of output and an improved trade balance.

There is a general point behind this example. To the extent that governments care about *both* the level of output and the trade balance, they have to use *both* fiscal policy and exchange rate policies. We just saw one such combination. Table 19-1 gives you others, depending on the initial output and trade situation. Take, for example, the box in the top right corner of the table: Initial output is too low (put

A general lesson: If you want to achieve two targets (here, output and trade balance), you better have two instruments (here, fiscal policy and the exchange rate).

Figure 19-5

Reducing the Trade Deficit without Changing Output

To reduce the trade deficit without changing output, the government must both achieve a depreciation and decrease government spending.

another way, unemployment is too high), and the economy has a trade deficit. A depreciation will help on both the trade and the output fronts: It reduces the trade deficit and increases output. But there is no reason for the depreciation to achieve both the correct increase in output and the elimination of the trade deficit. Depending on the initial situation and the relative effects of the depreciation on output and the trade balance, the government may need to complement the depreciation with either an increase or a decrease in government spending. This ambiguity is captured by the question mark in the box. Make sure that you understand the logic behind each of the other three boxes.

Table 19-1	Exchange Rate and Fiscal Policy Combinations	
Initial Conditions	**Trade Surplus**	**Trade Deficit**
Low output	$\epsilon ? \, G\uparrow$	$\epsilon\downarrow G?$
High output	$\epsilon\uparrow G?$	$\epsilon ? G\downarrow$

19-5 Looking at Dynamics: The J-Curve

We have ignored dynamics so far in this chapter. It is time to reintroduce them. The dynamics of consumption, investment, sales, and production we discussed in Chapter 3 are as relevant to the open economy as they are to the closed economy. But there are additional dynamic effects as well, which come from the dynamics of exports and imports. We focus on these effects here.

Return to the effects of the exchange rate on the trade balance. We argued earlier that a depreciation leads to an increase in exports and to a decrease in imports. But this does not happen overnight. Think of the dynamic effects of, say, a 10% dollar depreciation.

In the first few months following the depreciation, the effect of the depreciation is likely to be reflected much more in prices than in quantities. The price of imports in the United States goes up, and the price of U.S. exports abroad goes down. But the quantity of imports and exports is likely to adjust only slowly: It takes a while for consumers to realize that relative prices have changed, it takes a while for firms to shift to cheaper suppliers, and so on. So a depreciation may well lead to an initial deterioration of the trade balance; ϵ decreases, but neither X nor IM adjusts very much initially, leading to a decline in net exports ($X - IM/\epsilon$).

As time passes, the effects of the change in the relative prices of both exports and imports become stronger. Cheaper U.S. goods cause U.S. consumers and firms to decrease their demand for foreign goods: U.S. imports decrease. Cheaper U.S. goods abroad lead foreign consumers and firms to increase their demand for U.S. goods: U.S. exports increase. If the Marshall-Lerner condition eventually holds—and we have argued that it does—the response of exports and imports eventually becomes stronger than the adverse price effect, and the eventual effect of the depreciation is an improvement of the trade balance.

Figure 19-6 captures this adjustment by plotting the evolution of the trade balance against time in response to a real depreciation. The pre-depreciation trade deficit is *OA*. The depreciation initially *increases* the trade deficit to *OB*: ϵ decreases, but neither *IM* nor *X* changes right away. Over time, however, exports increase and imports decrease, reducing the trade deficit. Eventually (if the Marshall-Lerner condition is satisfied), the trade balance improves beyond its initial level; this is what happens from point *C* on in the figure. Economists refer to this adjustment process as the **J-curve**, because—admittedly, with a bit of imagination—the curve in the figure resembles a "J": first down, then up.

And even these prices may adjust slowly: Consider a dollar depreciation. If you are an exporter to the United States, you may want to increase your price less than implied by the exchange rate. In other words, you may decrease your markup in order to remain competitive with your U.S. competitors. If you are a U.S. exporter, you may decrease your price abroad by less than implied by the exchange rate. In other words, you may increase your markup.

The response of the trade balance to the real exchange rate:

Initially: X, IM unchanged, ϵ decreases $\Rightarrow$ ($X - IM/\epsilon$) decreases.
Eventually: X increases, IM decreases, ϵ decreases $\Rightarrow$ ($X - IM/\epsilon$) increases.

Figure 19-6

The J-Curve

A real depreciation leads initially to a deterioration and then to an improvement of the trade balance.

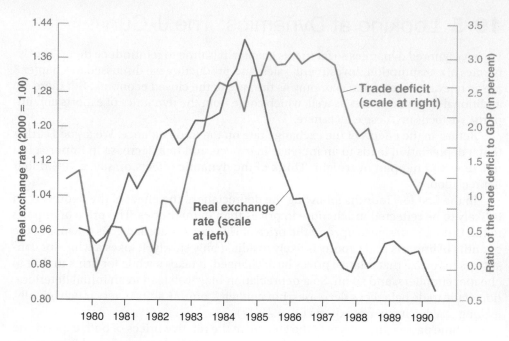

Figure 19-7

The Real Exchange Rate and the Ratio of the Trade Deficit to GDP: United States, 1980–1990

The large real appreciation and subsequent real depreciation from 1980 to 1990 were mirrored, with a lag, by an increase and then a decrease in the trade deficit.

Source: See Figures 18-1 and 18-5

The delays in 1985–1988 were unusually long, prompting some economists at the time to question whether there was still a relation between the real ▶ exchange rate and the trade balance. In retrospect, the relation was still there—the delays were just longer than usual.

The importance of the dynamic effects of the real exchange rate on the trade balance were seen in the United States in the mid-1980s: Figure 19-7 plots the U.S. trade deficit against the U.S. real exchange rate from 1980 to 1990. As we saw in the last chapter, the period from 1980 to 1985 was one of sharp real appreciation, and the period from 1985 to 1988 one of sharp real depreciation. Turning to the trade deficit, which is expressed as a proportion of GDP, two facts are clear:

1. Movements in the real exchange rate were reflected in parallel movements in net exports. The appreciation was associated with a large increase in the trade deficit, and the later depreciation was associated with a large decrease in the trade balance.

2. There were, however, substantial lags in the response of the trade balance to changes in the real exchange rate. Note how from 1981 to 1983, the trade deficit remained small while the dollar was appreciating. And note how the steady depreciation of the dollar from 1985 onward was not immediately reflected in an improvement in the trade balance before 1987: The dynamics of the J-curve were very much at work during both episodes.

In general, the econometric evidence on the dynamic relation among exports, imports, and the real exchange rate suggests that in all OECD countries, a real depreciation eventually leads to a trade balance improvement. But it also suggests that this process takes some time, typically between six months and a year. These lags have implications not only for the effects of a depreciation on the trade balance, but also for the effects of a depreciation on output. If a depreciation initially decreases net exports, it also initially exerts a contractionary effect on output. Thus, if a government relies on a depreciation both to improve the trade balance and to expand domestic output, the effects will go the "wrong" way for a while.

19-6 Saving, Investment, and the Current Account Balance

You saw in Chapter 3 how we could rewrite the condition for equilibrium in the goods market as the condition that investment was equal to saving—the sum of private saving and public saving. We can now derive the corresponding condition for the open economy, and you will see how useful this alternative way of looking at the equilibrium can be.

Start from our equilibrium condition

$$Y = C + I + G - IM/\epsilon + X$$

Move consumption, C, from the right side to the left side of the equation, subtract taxes, T, from both sides, denote net exports $- IM/\epsilon + X$ by NX to get

$$Y - T - C = I + (G - T) + NX$$

Recall that, in an open economy, the income of domestic residents is equal to output, Y, plus net income from abroad, NI, plus net transfers received. Denote these transfers by NT, and add NI and NT to both sides of the equation:

$$(Y + NI + NT - T) - C = I + (G - T) + (NX + NI + NT)$$

Note that the term in parentheses on left side is equal to disposable income, so the left side is equal to disposable income minus consumption (i.e., saving S). Note that the sum of net exports, net income from abroad, and net transfers on the right side is equal to the current account. Denote the current account by CA and rewrite the previous equation as:

$$S = I + (G - T) + CA$$

Reorganize the equation to read:

$$CA = S + (T - G) - I \tag{19.5}$$

The current account balance is equal to saving—the sum of private saving and public saving—minus investment. A current account surplus implies that the country is saving more than it invests. A current account deficit implies that the country is saving less than it invests.

One way of getting more intuition for this relation is to go back to the discussion of the current account and the capital account in Chapter 18. There we saw that a current account surplus implies net lending from the country to the rest of the world, and a current account deficit implies net borrowing by the country from the rest of the world. So, consider a country that invests more than it saves, so that $S + (T - G) - I$ is negative. That country must be borrowing the difference from the rest of the world; it must therefore be running a current account deficit. Symmetrically, a country that lends to the rest of the world is a country that saves more than it invests.

Note some of the things that equation (19.5) says:

- An increase in investment must be reflected in either an increase in private saving or public saving, or in a deterioration of the current account balance—a smaller current account surplus, or a larger current account deficit, depending on whether the current account is initially in surplus or in deficit.
- A deterioration in the government budget balance—either a smaller budget surplus or a larger budget deficit—must be reflected in an increase in either private saving, or in a decrease in investment, or else in a deterioration of the current account balance.
- A country with a high saving rate (private plus government) must have either a high investment rate or a large current account surplus.

Getting there involves some manipulations, but do not worry: The end result is intuitive.

Commentators often do not make a distinction between the trade balance and the current account balance. This is not necessarily a major crime: Because net income and net transfers typically move slowly over time, the trade and the current account balances typically move closely together.

The U.S. Current Account Deficit: Origins and Implications

Equation (19.5) tells us that we can look at the current account deficit as the difference between investment and saving. With this in mind, Figure 1 plots investment and saving as ratios to GDP for the United States since 1980; the difference between the two gives the ratio of the current account deficit to GDP. As you can see, the United States has consistently run a current account deficit since 1980. The deficit reached 5% of GDP in the mid-2000s. It is now a little smaller, at around 3%.

A current account deficit can reflect high investment; this can be seen as good news, indicating the country is borrowing abroad to increase its capital and, by implication, its output in the future. Or it can be due to low saving; this can be seen as bad news, indicating that the country is borrowing from abroad to finance consumption and may have a tough time repaying the debt in the future. Figure 1 suggests that, in the case of the United States, the cause of the deficit is low saving, not high investment. The trend evolutions are clear. The ratio of U.S. saving to GDP has declined from 20% in 1980 to 15% just before the crisis, and to 12% in 2010. The ratio of investment to GDP has also declined, although by less, from 22% in 1980 to 20% just before the crisis, and to 15% in 2010.

Looking at the Components of Saving

The next step is to ask what lies behind this trend decrease in U.S. saving. Think of saving as the sum of saving by households, saving by corporations—retained earnings—and saving by the government. All three are plotted in Figure 2, again as ratios to GDP. Leaving aside for the moment the current crisis, the years since 2007, Figure 2 suggests the need to distinguish among three periods:

- A first period, from 1980 to 1992, characterized by a slow but steady decrease in household saving and negative but stable government saving. (Government saving is not exactly the same as the budget surplus: The budget surplus is equal to government saving minus government investment. Put another way, government saving is equal to the budget surplus plus government investment. In 2010, government investment was roughly equal to 2.5% of U.S. GDP.)

- A second period, from 1992 to 2000, characterized by a further slow and steady decrease in household saving, but now more than offset by a steady increase in government saving, from −2% of GDP in 1992 to nearly 5% of GDP in 2000. This reflects the improvement in the budget under the Clinton administration, which we briefly discussed in Chapter 5. The result was, as we saw in Figure 1, a steady reduction in the current account deficit, the gap between investment and savings.

- A third period, from 2000 to the crisis, characterized by low but stable household saving, but a steady decrease in government saving, reflecting what has become known as the "Bush tax cuts." We discussed them in a Focus box, "The U.S. Recession of 2001," in Chapter 5.

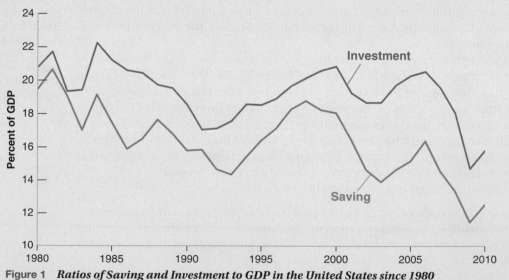

Figure 1 *Ratios of Saving and Investment to GDP in the United States since 1980*

Since the 1980s, the United States has run a current account deficit. This deficit reflects low saving rather than high investment.

Source: NIPA Table 5-1. Saving and Investment by Sector

These tax cuts, initially aimed at fighting the 2001 recession, remained on the books after the recession was over and led to increasing budget deficits, even before the crisis.

Investment, Saving, and the Crisis

Let's now turn to the crisis, the years since 2007. Figure 1 shows how much saving and investment have declined, with the decline in investment being larger than the decline in saving, leading to a reduction in the current account deficit. Figure 2 shows that behind the decline in saving are very different evolutions of household and corporate saving, on the one hand, and government saving, on the other. Both household and corporate saving have increased substantially (in the case of household saving reversing the long downward trend). But, more than offsetting this increase in private saving, government saving has dramatically decreased, down to −7% of GDP in 2010.

The easiest way to think about why this has happened is to think back in terms of equation (19.1) (recall that equations (19.1) and (19.5) are equivalent but often give two useful ways of thinking about the evolution of saving, investment, the trade deficit, and the current account deficit.). As we have seen, the crisis has led consumers and firms to be much less optimistic about the future. Consumers have decided to save more, to consume less. Firms have decided to invest less. In order, however, to limit the decrease in demand and thus in output, the U.S. government has increased spending and decreased taxes, leading to a large decrease in government saving and the dramatic increase in the budget deficit we have discussed throughout the book. The results of these changes in behavior during the crisis period have thus been higher private saving, lower government saving, lower investment, and a small decrease in the current account deficit.

What Should and Will Happen Next?

Should the United States reduce its current account deficit?

Even before the crisis, most economists argued that it should. They argued that the current account deficit reflected insufficient saving, both on the part of households and on the part of the government. The low household saving rate was widely seen as reflecting excessively optimistic expectations about the future. Low saving by the government and the increasing budget deficits in the 2000s were seen as dangerous, reflecting a failure of the political system to balance the budget (more on this in Chapter 22). The argument was therefore: Take measures to increase household saving, and decrease budget deficits. To the extent that these lead to a decrease in domestic demand, the argument was to offset this decrease by an increase in net exports, or, put another way, through a decrease in the trade deficit. And to do so, allow for the dollar to depreciate so as to increase exports and decrease imports.

If anything, the crisis has made the need to decrease the current account deficit more urgent. As a result of the crisis, consumption and investment have decreased. In order to sustain demand, the government has relied on monetary and fiscal policy. As we have seen, conventional

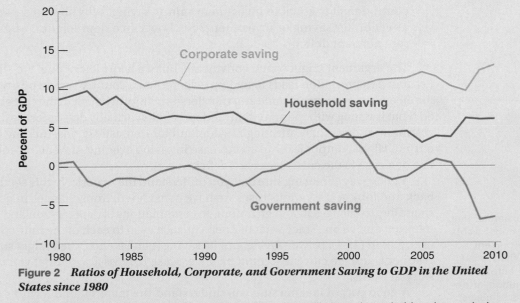

Figure 2 *Ratios of Household, Corporate, and Government Saving to GDP in the United States since 1980*

The decrease in U.S. saving reflects a combination of steadily lower household saving, and, since 2000, lower government saving as well.

Source: NIPA Table 5-1, Saving and Investment by Sector

monetary policy can no longer be used. The fiscal expansion has led to large deficits, and the government must now reduce them. Thus, if the recovery is to continue, another source of demand must come. From equation (19.1), it is clear that the only source of demand left is net exports. In other words, in order to sustain the recovery, the United States must reduce its trade deficit and, by implication, its current account deficit.

How can this be done? From Section 19-4, the answer would seem to be simple. What is needed is a dollar depreciation, which would increase exports and decrease imports. So the question is why this is not happening. A full discussion will have to wait until the next chapter, when

we look at the link between financial decisions and the exchange rate. But, in short, the answer is that there is a high demand for U.S. assets on the part of foreign investors. Thus, they have been willing to finance the U.S. current account deficit, and there has been little downward pressure on the dollar. Whether this remains the case in the future is, at this stage, an open question.

References. In 2011, the G20 asked the IMF for an assessment of the causes of current account deficits in a number of countries, including the United States, Germany, and China. You can find the reports at http://www.imf.org/external/np/g20/map2011.htm. This box is largely based on the United States report.

Note also, however, what equation (19.5) *does not say*. It does not say, for example, whether a government budget deficit will lead to a current account deficit, or, instead, to an increase in private saving, or to a decrease in investment. To find out what happens in response to a budget deficit, we must explicitly solve for what happens to output and its components using the assumptions that we have made about consumption, investment, exports, and imports. That is, we need to do the complete analysis laid out in this chapter. Using only equation (19.5) can, if you are not careful, be very misleading. To see how misleading, consider, for example, the following argument (which is so common that you may have read something similar in newspapers):

"It is clear the United States cannot reduce its large current account deficit through a depreciation." Look at equation (19.5): It shows that the current account deficit is equal to investment minus saving. Why should a depreciation affect either saving or investment? So, how can a depreciation affect the current account deficit?

The argument might sound convincing, but we know it is wrong. We showed earlier that a depreciation leads to an improvement in a country's trade position and, by implication—given net income and transfers—an improvement in the current account. So what is wrong with the argument? A depreciation actually does affect saving and investment: It does so by affecting the demand for domestic goods, thereby increasing output. Higher output leads to an increase in saving over investment, or, equivalently, to a decrease in the current account deficit.

A good way of making sure that you understand the material in this section is to go back and look at the various cases we have considered, from changes in government spending, to changes in foreign output, to combinations of depreciation and fiscal contraction, and so on. Trace what happens in each case to each of the four components of equation (19.5): private saving, public saving (equivalently, the budget surplus), investment, and the current account balance. Make sure, as always, that you can tell the story in words.

A good way of making sure you understand the material in the whole chapter is to read the Focus box on the U.S. Current Account Deficit. It will show you how the concepts we have developed in this chapter can be used to understand the origins and implications of one of the main issues facing U.S. policy makers.

Suppose, for example, that the U.S. government wants to reduce the current account deficit without changing the level of output, so it uses a combination of depreciation and fiscal contraction. What happens to private saving, public saving, and investment?

Summary

- In an open economy, the demand for domestic goods is equal to the domestic demand for goods (consumption, plus investment, plus government spending) minus the value of imports (in terms of domestic goods), plus exports.

- In an open economy, an increase in domestic demand leads to a smaller increase in output than it would in a closed economy because some of the additional demand falls on imports. For the same reason, an increase in domestic demand also leads to a deterioration of the trade balance.

- An increase in foreign demand leads, as a result of increased exports, to both an increase in domestic output and an improvement of the trade balance.

- Because increases in foreign demand improve the trade balance and increases in domestic demand worsen the trade balance, countries might be tempted to wait for increases in foreign demand to move them out of a recession. When a group of countries is in recession, coordination can, in principle, help their recovery.

- If the Marshall-Lerner condition is satisfied—and the empirical evidence indicates that it is—a real depreciation leads to an improvement in net exports.

- A real depreciation leads first to a deterioration of the trade balance, and then to an improvement. This adjustment process is known as the J-curve.

- The condition for equilibrium in the goods market can be rewritten as the condition that saving (public and private) minus investment must be equal to the current account balance. A current account surplus corresponds to an excess of saving over investment. A current account deficit usually corresponds to an excess of investment over saving.

Key Terms

demand for domestic goods, 400
domestic demand for goods, 400
policy coordination, 408

G20, 409
Marshall-Lerner condition, 410
J-curve, 413

Questions and Problems

QUICK CHECK
All Quick Check questions and problems are available on MyEconLab.

1. Using the information in this chapter, label each of the following statements true, false, or uncertain. Explain briefly.

  a. The current U.S. trade deficit is the result of unusually high investment, not the result of a decline in national saving.
  b. The national income identity implies that budget deficits cause trade deficits.
  c. Opening the economy to trade tends to increase the multiplier because an increase in expenditure leads to more exports.
  d. If the trade deficit is equal to zero, then the domestic demand for goods and the demand for domestic goods are equal.
  e. A real depreciation leads to an immediate improvement in the trade balance.
  f. A small open economy can reduce its trade deficit through fiscal contraction at a smaller cost in output than can a large open economy.
  g. The current high U.S. trade deficit is solely the result of a real appreciation of U.S. goods between 1995 and 2002.
  h. In the United States, GDP is larger than GNP.

2. Real and nominal exchange rates and inflation

Using the definition of the real exchange rate (and Propositions 7 and 8 in Appendix 2 at the end of the book), you can show that

$$\frac{(\epsilon_t - \epsilon_{t-1})}{\epsilon_{t-1}} = \frac{(E_t - E_{t-1})}{E_{t-1}} + \pi_t - \pi_t^*$$

In words, the percentage real appreciation equals the percentage nominal appreciation plus the difference between domestic and foreign inflation.

  a. If domestic inflation is higher than foreign inflation, but the domestic country has a fixed exchange rate, what happens to the real exchange rate over time? Assume that the Marshall-Lerner condition holds. What happens to the trade balance over time? Explain in words.
  b. Suppose the real exchange rate is constant—say, at the level required for net exports (or the current account) to equal zero. In this case, if domestic inflation is higher than foreign inflation, what must happen over time to maintain a trade balance of zero?

3. A European recession and the U.S. economy

  a. In 2010, European Union spending on U.S. goods accounted for 23% of U.S. exports (see Table 18-2), and U.S.

exports amounted to 13% of U.S. GDP (see Table 18-1). What was the share of European Union spending on U.S. goods relative to U.S. GDP?

b. Assume that the multiplier in the United States is 2 and that a major slump in Europe would reduce output and imports from the U.S. by 5% (relative to its normal level). Given your answer to part (a), what is the impact on U.S. GDP of the European slump?

c. If the European slump also leads to a slowdown of the other economies that import goods from the United States, the effect could be larger. To put a bound to the size of the effect, assume that U.S. exports decrease by 5% (as a result of changes in foreign output) in one year. What is the impact of a 5% drop in exports on U.S. GDP?

d. Comment on this statement. "Unless Europe can avoid a major slump following the problems with sovereign debt and the Euro, U.S. growth will grind to a halt."

4. Reproduce the results in Table 19-1.

DIG DEEPER

All Dig Deeper questions and problems are available on MyEconLab.

5. *Net exports and foreign demand*
   a. Suppose there is an increase in foreign output. Show the effect on the domestic economy (i.e., replicate Figure 19-4). What is the effect on domestic output? On domestic net exports?

   b. If the interest rate remains constant, what will happen to domestic investment? If taxes are fixed, what will happen to the domestic budget deficit?

   c. Using equation (19.5), what must happen to private saving? Explain.

   d. Foreign output does not appear in equation (19.5), yet it evidently affects net exports. Explain how this is possible.

6. *Eliminating a trade deficit*
   a. Consider an economy with a trade deficit ($NX < 0$) and with output equal to its natural level. Suppose that, even though output may deviate from its natural level in the short run, it returns to its natural level in the medium run. Assume that the natural level is unaffected by the real exchange rate. What must happen to the real exchange rate over the medium run to eliminate the trade deficit (i.e., to increase NX to 0)?

   b. Now write down the national income identity. Assume again that output returns to its natural level in the medium run. If NX increases to 0, what must happen to domestic demand ($C + I + G$) in the medium run? What government policies are available to reduce domestic demand in the medium run? Identify which components of domestic demand each of these policies affect.

7. *Multipliers, openness, and fiscal policy*
   Consider an open economy characterized by the equations below.

$$C = c_0 + c_1(Y - T)$$
$$I = d_0 + d_1 Y$$
$$IM = m_1 Y$$
$$X = x_1 Y^*$$

The parameters m_1 and x_1 are the propensities to import and export. Assume that the real exchange rate is fixed at a value of 1 and treat foreign income, Y^*, as fixed. Also assume that taxes are fixed and that government purchases are exogenous (i.e., decided by the government). We explore the effectiveness of changes in G under alternative assumptions about the propensity to import.

a. Write the equilibrium condition in the market for domestic goods and solve for Y.

b. Suppose government purchases increase by one unit. What is the effect on output? (Assume that $0 < m_1 < c_1 + d_1 < 1$. Explain why.)

c. How do net exports change when government purchases increase by one unit?

Now consider two economies, one with $m_1 = 0.5$ and the other with $m_1 = 0.1$. Each economy is characterized by $(c_1 + d_1) = 0.6$.

d. Suppose one of the economies is much larger than the other. Which economy do you expect to have the larger value of m_1? Explain.

e. Calculate your answers to parts (b) and (c) for each economy by substituting the appropriate parameter values.

f. In which economy will fiscal policy have a larger effect on output? In which economy will fiscal policy have a larger effect on net exports?

8. *Policy coordination and the world economy*
   Consider an open economy in which the real exchange rate is fixed and equal to one. Consumption, investment, government spending, and taxes are given by

$$C = 10 + 0.8(Y - T), I = 10, G = 10, \text{ and } T = 10$$

Imports and exports are given by

$$IM = 0.3Y \text{ and } X = 0.3 Y^*$$

where Y^* denotes foreign output.

a. Solve for equilibrium output in the domestic economy, given Y^*. What is the multiplier in this economy? If we were to close the economy—so exports and imports were identically equal to zero—what would the multiplier be? Why would the multiplier be different in a closed economy?

b. Assume that the foreign economy is characterized by the same equations as the domestic economy (with asterisks reversed). Use the two sets of equations to solve for the equilibrium output of each country. [*Hint:* Use the equations for the foreign economy to solve for Y^* as a function of Y and substitute this solution for Y^* in part (a).] What is the multiplier for each country now? Why is it different from the open economy multiplier in part (a)?

c. Assume that the domestic government, G, has a target level of output of 125. Assuming that the foreign government does not change G^*, what is the increase in G necessary to achieve the target output in the domestic economy? Solve for net exports and the budget deficit in each country.

d. Suppose each government has a target level of output of 125 and that each government increases government spending by the same amount. What is the common increase in G and G^* necessary to achieve the target output in both countries? Solve for net exports and the budget deficit in each country.

e. Why is fiscal coordination, such as the common increase in G and G^* in part (d), difficult to achieve in practice?

EXPLORE FURTHER

9. *The U.S. trade deficit, current account deficit,and investment*

a. Define national saving as private saving plus the government surplus—i.e., as $S + T - G$. Now, using equation (19.5), describe the relation among the current account deficit, net investment income, and the difference between national saving and domestic investment.

b. Go to the statistical tables of the most recent *Economic Report of the President* (**www.gpoaccess.gov/eop/**). In Table B-1, "Gross Domestic Product," retrieve annual data for GDP, gross domestic investment, and net exports from 1980 to the most recent year available. Divide gross domestic investment and net exports by GDP for each year to express their values as a percentage of GDP.

c. The trade surplus in 1980 was roughly zero. Subtract the value of net exports (as a percentage of GDP) in 1981 from the value of net exports (as a percentage of GDP) in the most recent year available. Do the same for gross domestic investment. Has the decline in net exports been matched by an equivalent increase in investment? What do your

calculations imply about the change in national saving between 1981 and the present?

d. When the United States began experiencing trade deficits during the 1980s, some officials in the Reagan administration argued that the trade deficits reflected attractive investment opportunities in the United States. Consider three time periods: 1981 to 1990, 1990 to 2000, and 2000 to the present. Apply the analysis of part (c) to each of these time periods (i.e., calculate the change in net exports and gross domestic investment as a percentage of GDP). How does the change in net exports from the 1980 values compare to the change in investment during each period? How did national saving change during each period?

e. Is a trade deficit more worrisome when not accompanied by a corresponding increase in investment? Explain your answer.

f. The question above focuses on the trade deficit rather than the current account deficit. How does net investment income (NI) relate to the difference between the trade deficit and the current account deficit in the United States? Find Table B-103 "U.S. International Transactions" from the Economic Report of the President. Use your work in part (b) to calculate NI as a percent of GDP. Is this value rising or falling over time? What is the implication of such changes?

Further Readings

■ A good discussion of the relation among trade deficits, current account deficits, budget deficits, private saving, and investment is given in Barry Bosworth's *Saving and Investment in a Global Economy* (Brookings Institution, 1993).

■ One view on likely future of the dollar is found in Martin Feldstein, "Why the Dollar Will Weaken Further," *The International Economy* 2011 79 (Summer): pp. 14–17.

APPENDIX: Derivation of the Marshall-Lerner Condition

Start from the definition of net exports

$$NX \equiv X - IM/\epsilon$$

Assume trade to be initially balanced, so that $NX = 0$ and $X = IM/\epsilon$, or, equivalently, $\epsilon X = IM$. The Marshall-Lerner condition is the condition under which a real depreciation, a decrease in ϵ, leads to an increase in net exports.

To derive this condition, first multiply both sides of the equation above by ϵ to get

$$\epsilon NX = \epsilon X - IM$$

Now consider a change in the real exchange rate of $\Delta\epsilon$. The effect of the change in the real exchange rate on the left

side of the equation is given by $(\Delta\epsilon)NX + \epsilon(\Delta NX)$. Note that, if trade is initially balanced, $NX = 0$, so the first term in this expression is equal to zero, and the effect of the change on the left side is simply given by $\epsilon(\Delta NX)$. The effect of the change in the real exchange rate on the right side of the equation is given by $(\Delta\epsilon)X + \epsilon(\Delta X) - (\Delta IM)$. Putting the two sides together gives

$$\epsilon(\Delta NX) = (\Delta\epsilon)X + \epsilon(\Delta X) - (\Delta IM)$$

Divide both sides by ϵX to get:

$$\frac{\epsilon(\Delta NX)}{\epsilon X} = \frac{(\Delta\epsilon)X}{\epsilon X} + \frac{\epsilon(\Delta X)}{\epsilon X} - \frac{\Delta(IM)}{\epsilon X}$$

Chapter 19   The Goods Market in an Open Economy   **421**

Simplify, and use the fact that, if trade is initially balanced, $\epsilon X = IM$ to replace ϵX by IM in the last term on the right. This gives

$$\frac{\Delta NX}{X} = \frac{\Delta \epsilon}{\epsilon} + \frac{\Delta X}{X} - \frac{\Delta IM}{IM}$$

The change in the trade balance (as a ratio to exports) in response to a real depreciation is equal to the sum of three terms:

■ The first term is equal to the proportional change in the real exchange rate. It is negative if there is a real depreciation.
■ The second term is equal to the proportional change in exports. It is positive if there is a real depreciation.

■ The third term is equal to minus the proportional change in the imports. It is positive if there is a real depreciation.

The Marshall-Lerner condition is the condition that the sum of these three terms be positive. If it is satisfied, a real depreciation leads to an improvement in the trade balance.

A numerical example will help here. Suppose that a 1% depreciation leads to a proportional increase in exports of 0.9%, and to a proportional decrease in imports of 0.8%. (Econometric evidence on the relation of exports and imports to the real exchange rate suggest that these are indeed reasonable numbers.) In this case, the right-hand side of the equation is equal to $-1\% + 0.9\% - (-0.8\%) = 0.7\%$. Thus, the trade balance improves: The Marshall-Lerner condition is satisfied.

Output, the Interest Rate, and the Exchange Rate

I n Chapter 19, we treated the exchange rate as one of the policy instruments available to the government. But the exchange rate is not a policy instrument. Rather, it is determined in the foreign exchange market—a market where, as you saw in Chapter 18, there is an enormous amount of trading. This fact raises two obvious questions: What determines the exchange rate? How can policy makers affect it?

These questions motivate this chapter. More generally, we examine the implications of equilibrium in both the goods market and financial markets, including the foreign exchange market. This allows us to characterize the joint movements of output, the interest rate, and the exchange rate in an open economy. The model we develop is an extension to the open economy of the *IS–LM* model you first saw in Chapter 5 and is known as the **Mundell-Fleming model**—after the two economists, Robert Mundell and Marcus Fleming, who first put it together in the 1960s. (The model presented here retains the spirit of the original Mundell-Fleming model but differs in its details.)

Section 20-1 looks at equilibrium in the goods market.

Section 20-2 looks at equilibrium in financial markets, including the foreign exchange market.

Section 20-3 puts the two equilibrium conditions together and looks at the determination of output, the interest rate, and the exchange rate.

Section 20-4 looks at the role of policy under flexible exchange rates.

Section 20-5 looks at the role of policy under fixed exchange rates. ●

20-1 Equilibrium in the Goods Market

Equilibrium in the goods market was the focus of Chapter 19, where we derived the equilibrium condition (equation (19.4)):

$$Y = C(Y - T) + I(Y, r) + G - IM(Y, \epsilon)/\epsilon + X(Y^*, \epsilon)$$
$$(+) \qquad (+, -) \qquad\qquad (+, +) \qquad (+, -)$$

Goods market equilibrium (*IS*): Output = Demand for domestic goods.

For the goods market to be in equilibrium, output (the left side of the equation) must be equal to the demand for domestic goods (the right side of the equation). The demand for domestic goods is equal to consumption, C, plus investment, I, plus government spending, G, minus the value of imports, IM/ϵ, plus exports, X.

- Consumption, C, depends positively on disposable income $Y - T$.
- Investment, I, depends positively on output, Y, and negatively on the real interest rate, r.
- Government spending, G, is taken as given.
- The quantity of imports, IM, depends positively on both output, Y, and the real exchange rate, ϵ. The value of imports in terms of domestic goods is equal to the quantity of imports divided by the real exchange rate.
- Exports, X, depend positively on foreign output, Y^*, and negatively on the real exchange rate, ϵ.

It will be convenient in what follows to regroup the last two terms under "net exports," defined as exports minus the value of imports:

$$NX(Y, Y^*, \epsilon) \equiv X(Y^*, \epsilon) - IM(Y, \epsilon)/\epsilon$$

It follows from our assumptions about imports and exports that net exports, NX, depend on domestic output, Y, foreign output, Y^*, and the real exchange rate ϵ: An increase in domestic output increases imports, thus decreasing net exports. An increase in foreign output increases exports, thus increasing net exports. An increase in the real exchange rate leads to a decrease in net exports.

We shall assume, throughout the chapter, that the Marshall-Lerner condition holds. Under this condition, an increase in the real exchange rate—a real appreciation—leads to a decrease in net exports (see Chapter 19).

Using this definition of net exports, we can rewrite the equilibrium condition as

$$Y = C(Y - T) + I(Y, r) + G + NX(Y, Y^*, \epsilon) \qquad (20.1)$$
$$(+) \qquad (+, -) \qquad\qquad (-, +, -)$$

For our purposes, the main implication of equation (20.1) is that both the real interest rate and the real exchange rate affect demand, and in turn equilibrium output:

- An increase in the real interest rate leads to a decrease in investment spending, and, as a result, to a decrease in the demand for domestic goods. This leads, through the multiplier, to a decrease in output.
- An increase in the real exchange rate leads to a shift in demand toward foreign goods, and, as a result, to a decrease in net exports. The decrease in net exports decreases the demand for domestic goods. This leads, through the multiplier, to a decrease in output.

For the remainder of the chapter, we shall simplify equation (20.1) in two ways:

- Given our focus on the short run, we assumed in our previous treatment of the *IS–LM* model that the (domestic) price level was given. We shall make the same assumption here and extend this assumption to the foreign price level, so the real exchange rate ($\epsilon \equiv EP/P^*$) and the nominal exchange rate, E, move together. A decrease in the nominal exchange rate—a nominal depreciation—leads, one-for-one, to a decrease in the real exchange rate—a real depreciation. Conversely, an increase in the nominal exchange rate—a nominal appreciation—leads, one-for-one, to an increase in the real exchange rate—a real appreciation. If, for notational convenience, we choose P and P^* so that $P/P^* = 1$ (and we can do so because both are index numbers), then $\epsilon = E$ and we can replace ϵ by E in equation (20.1).

◀ First simplification: $P = P^* = 1$, so $\epsilon = E$.

- Because we take the domestic price level as given, there is no inflation, neither actual nor expected. Therefore, the nominal interest rate and the real interest rate are the same, and we can replace the real interest rate, r, in equation (20.1) by the nominal interest rate, i.

Second simplification: $\pi^e = 0$, ◀ so $r = i$.

With these two simplifications, equation (20.1) becomes

$$Y = C(Y - T) + I(Y, i) + G + NX(Y, Y^*, E) \qquad (20.2)$$
$$ (+) \qquad (+, -) \qquad\qquad (-, +, -)$$

In words: Goods market equilibrium implies that output depends negatively on both the nominal interest rate and the nominal exchange rate.

20-2 Equilibrium in Financial Markets

When we looked at financial markets in the *IS–LM* model, we assumed that people chose only between two financial assets, money and bonds. Now that we look at a financially open economy, we must also take into account the fact that people have a choice between domestic bonds and foreign bonds. Let's consider each choice in turn.

◀ We leave aside the other choices—between short-term and long-term bonds and between short-term bonds and stocks—which were the focus of Chapter 15.

Money versus Bonds

When we looked at the determination of the interest rate in the *IS–LM* model in Chapter 5, we wrote the condition that the supply of money be equal to the demand for money as

$$\frac{M}{P} = Y L(i) \qquad (20.3)$$

We took the real supply of money (the left side of equation (20.3)) as given. We assumed that the real demand for money (the right side of equation (20.3)) depended on the level of transactions in the economy, measured by real output, Y, and on the opportunity cost of holding money rather than bonds; that is, the nominal interest rate on bonds, i.

How should we change this characterization now that the economy is open? You will like the answer: not very much, if at all.

In an open economy, the demand for domestic money is still mostly a demand by domestic residents. There is not much reason for, say, the residents of Japan to hold euro currency or euro demand deposits. Transactions in Japan require payment in yens, not in euros. If residents of Japan want to hold euro-denominated assets, they are better off holding euro bonds, which at least pay a positive interest rate. And the demand for money by domestic residents in any country still depends on the same factors as in Chapter 4: their level of transactions, which we measure by domestic real output, and the opportunity cost of holding money, the nominal interest rate on bonds.

A qualification from Chapter 4, with respect to the demand for U.S. currency: A good proportion of U.S. currency is actually held abroad. The two major reasons: (1) the dollars used for illegal transactions abroad, and (2) dollars used for domestic transactions in countries with very high inflation. We shall ignore this qual-◀ ification here.

Therefore, we can still use equation (20.3) to think about the determination of the nominal interest rate in an open economy. The interest rate must be such that the supply of money and the demand for money are equal. An increase in the money supply leads to a decrease in the interest rate. An increase in money demand, say as a result of an increase in output, leads to an increase in the interest rate.

Financial market equilibrium (*LM*):
◀ Supply of money = Demand for money.

Domestic Bonds versus Foreign Bonds

As we look at the choice between domestic bonds and foreign bonds, we shall rely on the assumption we introduced in Chapter 19: Financial investors, domestic or foreign, go for the highest expected rate of return. This implies that, in equilibrium, both domestic bonds and foreign bonds must have the same expected rate of return; otherwise, investors would be willing to hold only one or the other, but not both, and this could not be an equilibrium. (Like most economic relations, this relation is only an approximation to reality and does not always hold. More on this in the Focus box "Sudden Stops, Safe Havens, and the Limits of the Interest Parity Condition.")

As we saw in Chapter 18 (equation (18.2)), this assumption implies that the following arbitrage relation—the *interest parity condition*—must hold:

$$(1 + i_t) = (1 + i_t^*) \left(\frac{E_t}{E_{t+1}^e} \right)$$

The presence of E_t comes from the fact that, in order to buy the foreign bond, you must first exchange domestic currency for foreign currency. The presence of E_{t+1}^e ▶ comes from the fact that, in order to bring the funds back next period, you will have to exchange foreign currency for domestic currency.

where i_t is the domestic interest rate, i_t^* is the foreign interest rate, E_t is the current exchange rate, and E_{t+1}^e is the future expected exchange rate. The left side of the equation gives the return, in terms of domestic currency, from holding domestic bonds. The right side of the equation gives the expected return, also in terms of domestic currency, from holding foreign bonds. In equilibrium, the two expected returns must be equal.

Multiply both sides by E_{t+1}^e and reorganize to get

$$E_t = \frac{1 + i_t}{1 + i_t^*} E_{t+1}^e \tag{20.4}$$

For now, we shall take the expected future exchange rate as given and denote it as $\overline{E}^e$ (we shall relax this assumption in Chapter 21). Under this assumption, and dropping time indexes, the interest parity condition becomes

$$E = \frac{1 + i}{1 + i^*} \overline{E}^e \tag{20.5}$$

This relation tells us that the current exchange rate depends on the domestic interest rate, on the foreign interest rate, and on the expected future exchange rate:

- An increase in the domestic interest rate leads to an increase in the exchange rate.
- An increase in the foreign interest rate leads to a decrease in the exchange rate.
- An increase in the expected future exchange rate leads to an increase in the current exchange rate.

This relation plays a central role in the real world and will play a central role in this chapter. To understand the relation further, consider the following example.

Consider financial investors—investors, for short—choosing between U.S. bonds and Japanese bonds. Suppose that the one-year interest rate on U.S. bonds is 2%, and the one-year interest rate on Japanese bonds is also 2%. Suppose that the current exchange rate is 100 (one dollar is worth 100 yens), and the expected exchange rate a year from now is also 100. Under these assumptions, both U.S. and Japanese bonds have the same expected return in dollars, and the interest parity condition holds.

Suppose now that investors now expect the exchange rate to be 10% higher a year from now, so E^e is now equal to 110. At an unchanged current exchange rate, U.S. bonds are now much more attractive than Japanese bonds: U.S. bonds offer an interest rate of 2% in dollars. Japanese bonds still offer an interest rate of 2% in yens, but the yen a year from today are now expected to be worth 10% less in terms of dollars. In terms

Sudden Stops, Safe Havens, and the Limits to the Interest Parity Condition

The interest parity condition assumes that financial investors care only about expected returns. As we discussed in Chapter 15, investors care not only about expected returns, but also about risk and about liquidity—how easy it is to buy or sell the asset. Much of the time, we can ignore these other factors. Sometimes, however, these factors

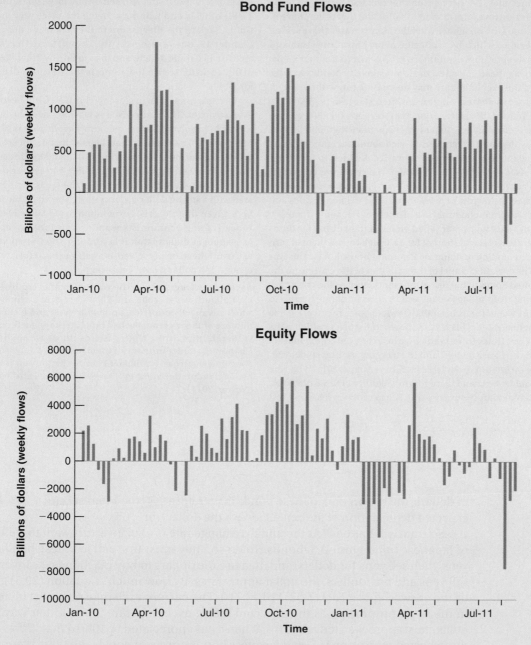

Figure 1 *The Volatility of Capital Flows to Emerging Countries since January 2010*

Capital flows have been very volatile during the crisis, reflecting mostly changes in perceived uncertainty.

Source: International Monetary Fund

play a big role in investors' decisions and in determining exchange rate movements.

This is an issue that many emerging countries know well. Perceptions of risk play an important role in the decision of large foreign investors, such as pension funds, to invest or not invest in their country. Sometimes, the perception that risk has decreased leads many foreign investors to simultaneously buy assets in the country. Sometimes, the perception that risk has increased leads the same investors to want to sell all the assets they have in the country, no matter what the interest rate. These selling episodes, which have affected many Latin American and Asian emerging economies, are known as **sudden stops**. During these episodes, the interest parity condition fails, and the exchange rate may decrease a lot, without much change in domestic or foreign interest rates.

Indeed, the start of the crisis in 2008 and 2009 was associated with large capital movements which had little to do with expected returns. Worried about uncertainty, many investors from advanced countries decided to take their funds home, where they felt safer. The result was large capital outflows from a number of emerging countries, leading to strong downward pressure on their exchange rates and serious financial problems: For example, some domestic banks that had so far relied on foreign investors for funds found themselves short of funds, which forced them in turn to cut lending to domestic firms and households. This was an important channel of transmission of the crisis from the United States to the rest of the world. And, as the crisis continues, continuing fluctuations in uncertainty are leading to large fluctuations in capital flows, despite relatively stable interest rates. This is best shown in Figure 1, which plots the net flows from funds that invest in emerging market bonds (figure on top) and in emerging market stocks (figure on bottom) from January 2010 to August 2011. What you should take from Figure 1 is the volatility of these net flows: This volatility is not primarily due to movements in interest rates, either in advanced or in emerging countries, but to fluctuations in perceived uncertainty.

A symmetrical phenomenon is at play in some advanced countries. Because of their characteristics, some countries are seen as particularly attractive by investors. This is the case for the United States.

Even in normal times, there is a large foreign demand for U.S. T-bills. The reason is the size and the liquidity of U.S. T-bill market: One can sell or buy large quantities of T-bills quickly and without moving the price very much. Going back to the discussion of the U.S. trade deficit in Chapter 19, one reason why the United States has been able to run a trade deficit, and thus to borrow from the rest of the world for such a long time, is the very high demand for T-bills.

In crisis times, the preference for U.S. T-bill becomes even stronger. The United States is widely seen by investors as being a **safe haven**, a country in which it is safe to move funds. The result is that times of higher uncertainty are often associated with a stronger demand for U.S. assets and thus upward pressure on the dollar. You can see this in Figure 18-6, where the beginning of the crisis was associated with a strong dollar appreciation. There is some irony here, given that the crisis originated in the United States. Indeed, some economists wonder how long, given the large budget deficits that it is running, the United States will continue to be perceived as a safe haven. If this were to change, the dollar would depreciate.

Further reading: Among the countries affected by large capital outflows in 2008 and 2009 were also a number of small advanced countries, notably Ireland and Iceland. A number of these countries had built up the same financial vulnerabilities as the United States (those we studied in Chapter 9), and a number of them suffered badly. A very good and easy read is Michael Lewis's chapters on Ireland and Iceland in Boomerang: Travels in a New Third World, (Norton 2011).

of dollars, the return on Japanese bonds is therefore 2% (the interest rate) −10% (the expected depreciation of the yen relative to the dollar), or −8%.

So what will happen? At the initial exchange rate of 100, investors want to shift out of Japanese bonds into U.S. bonds. To do so, they must first sell Japanese bonds for yens, then sell yens for dollars, and then use the dollars to buy U.S. bonds. As investors sell yens and buy dollars, the dollar appreciates. By how much? Equation (20.5) gives us the answer: $E = (1.02/1.02)110 = 110$. The current exchange rate must increase in the same proportion as the expected future exchange rate. Put another way, the dollar must appreciate today by 10%. When it has appreciated by 10% so $E = \bar{E}^e = 110$, the expected returns on U.S. and Japanese bonds are again equal, and there is equilibrium in the foreign exchange market.

Suppose instead that, as a result of a U.S. monetary contraction, the U.S. interest rate increases from 2% to 5%. Assume that the Japanese interest rate remains unchanged at 2%, and that the expected future exchange rate remains unchanged at 100.

At an unchanged current exchange rate, U.S. bonds are now again much more attractive than Japanese bonds. U.S. bonds yield a return of 5% in dollars. Japanese bonds give a return of 2% in yens, and—because the exchange rate is expected to be the same next year as it is today—an expected return of 5% in dollars as well.

So what will happen? Again, at the initial exchange rate of 100, investors want to shift out of Japanese bonds into U.S. bonds. As they do so, they sell yens for dollars, and the dollar appreciates. By how much? Equation (20.5) gives the answer: $E = (1.05/1.02)100 \approx 103$. The current exchange rate increases by approximately 3%.

Why 3%? Think of what happens when the dollar appreciates. If, as we have assumed, investors do not change their expectation of the future exchange rate, then the more the dollar appreciates today, the more investors expect it to depreciate in the future (as it is expected to return to the same value in the future). When the dollar has appreciated by 3% today, investors expect it to depreciate by 3% during the coming year. Equivalently, they expect the yen to appreciate relative to the dollar by 3% over the coming year. The expected rate of return in dollars from holding Japanese bonds is therefore 2% (the interest rate in yens) + 3% (the expected yen appreciation), or 5%. This expected rate of return is the same as the rate of return on holding U.S. bonds, so there is equilibrium in the foreign exchange market.

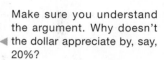
◀ Make sure you understand the argument. Why doesn't the dollar appreciate by, say, 20%?

Note that our argument relies heavily on the assumption that, when the interest rate changes, the expected exchange rate remains unchanged. This implies that an appreciation today leads to an expected depreciation in the future—because the exchange rate is expected to return to the same, unchanged, value. We shall relax the assumption that the future exchange rate is fixed in Chapter 21. But the basic conclusion will remain: *An increase in the domestic interest rate relative to the foreign interest rate leads to an appreciation.*

Figure 20-1 plots the relation between the domestic interest rate, i, and the exchange rate, E, implied by equation (20.5)—the interest parity relation. The relation is drawn for a given expected future exchange rate, $\overline{E}^e$, and a given foreign interest rate, i^*, and is represented by an upward-sloping line: The higher the domestic interest rate, the higher the exchange rate. Equation (20.5) also implies that when the domestic interest rate is equal to the foreign interest rate ($i = i^*$), the

Figure 20-1

The Relation between the Interest Rate and the Exchange Rate Implied by Interest Parity

A higher domestic interest rate leads to a higher exchange rate—an appreciation.

What happens to the line if
(1) i^* increases? (2) $\bar{E}^e$
increases?

exchange rate is equal to the expected future exchange rate $(E = \bar{E}^e)$. This implies that the line corresponding to the interest parity condition goes through point A in ▶ the figure.

20-3 Putting Goods and Financial Markets Together

We now have the elements we need to understand the movements of output, the interest rate, and the exchange rate.

Goods-market equilibrium implies that output depends, among other factors, on the interest rate and the exchange rate:

$$Y = C(Y - T) + I(Y, i) + G + NX(Y, Y^*, E)$$

The interest rate in turn is determined by the equality of money supply and money demand:

$$\frac{M}{P} = Y L(i)$$

And the interest parity condition implies a negative relation between the domestic interest rate and the exchange rate:

$$E = \frac{1 + i}{1 + i^*} \bar{E}^e$$

Together, these three relations determine output, the interest rate, and the exchange rate. Working with three relations is not very easy. But we can easily reduce them to two by using the interest parity condition to eliminate the exchange rate in the goods-market equilibrium relation. Doing this gives us the following two equations, the open economy versions of our familiar *IS* and *LM* relations:

$$IS: \quad Y = C(Y - T) + I(Y, i) + G + NX\left(Y, Y^*, \frac{1 + i}{1 + i^*} \bar{E}^e\right)$$

$$LM: \quad \frac{M}{P} = Y L(i)$$

Take the *IS* relation first and consider the effects of an increase in the interest rate on output. An increase in the interest rate now has two effects:

■ The first effect, which was already present in a closed economy, is the direct effect on investment: A higher interest rate leads to a decrease in investment, a decrease in the demand for domestic goods, and a decrease in output.
■ The second effect, which is only present in the open economy, is the effect through the exchange rate: An increase in the domestic interest rate leads to an increase in the exchange rate—an appreciation. The appreciation, which makes domestic goods more expensive relative to foreign goods, leads to a decrease in net exports, and therefore to a decrease in the demand for domestic goods and a decrease in output.

Both effects work in the same direction: An increase in the interest rate decreases demand directly, and indirectly—through the adverse effect of the appreciation on demand.

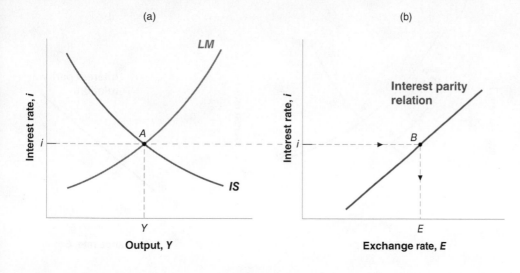

The *IS* relation between the interest rate and output is drawn in Figure 20-2(a), for given values of all the other variables in the relation—namely T, G, Y^*, i^*, and $\overline{E}^e$. The *IS* curve is downward sloping: An increase in the interest rate leads to lower output. The curve looks very much the same as in the closed economy, but it hides a more complex relation than before: The interest rate affects output not only directly, but also indirectly through the exchange rate.

◀ An increase in the interest rate leads, both directly and indirectly (through the exchange rate), to a decrease in output.

The *LM* relation is exactly the same as in the closed economy. The *LM* curve is upward sloping. For a given value of the real money stock, M/P, an increase in output leads to an increase in the demand for money, and to an increase in the equilibrium interest rate.

Equilibrium in the goods and financial markets is attained at point *A* in Figure 20-2(a), with output level Y and interest rate i. The equilibrium value of the exchange rate cannot be read directly from the graph. But it is easily obtained from Figure 20-2(b), which replicates Figure 20-1 and gives the exchange rate associated with a given interest rate found at point B. The exchange rate associated with the equilibrium interest rate i is equal to E.

Let's summarize: We have derived the *IS* and the *LM* relations for an open economy:

The *IS* curve is downward sloping: An increase in the interest rate leads directly, and indirectly (through the exchange rate), to a decrease in demand and a decrease in output.

The *LM* curve is upward sloping: An increase in income increases the demand for money, leading to an increase in the equilibrium interest rate.

Equilibrium output and the equilibrium interest rate are given by the intersection of the *IS* and the *LM* curves. Given the foreign interest rate and the expected future exchange rate, the equilibrium interest rate determines the equilibrium exchange rate.

20-4 The Effects of Policy in an Open Economy

Having derived the *IS–LM* model for the open economy, we now put it to use and look at the effects of policy.

The Effects of Fiscal Policy in an Open Economy

Let's look, again, at a change in government spending. Suppose that, starting from a balanced budget, the government decides to increase defense spending without

Figure 20-3

The Effects of an Increase in Government Spending

An increase in govern-ment spending leads to an increase in output, an in-crease in the interest rate, and an appreciation.

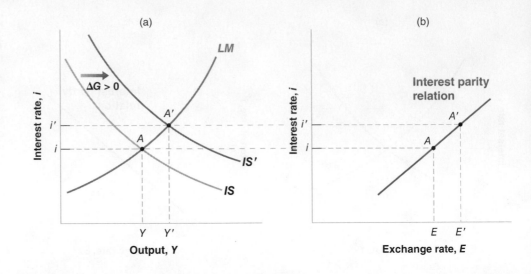

An increase in government spending shifts the *IS* curve to the right. It shifts neither the ▶ *LM* curve nor the interest parity line.

raising taxes, and so runs a budget deficit. What happens to the level of output? To the composition of output? To the interest rate? To the exchange rate?

The answers are given in Figure 20-3. The economy is initially at point A. The in-crease in government spending by, say, $\Delta G > 0$, increases output at a given interest rate, shifting the IS curve to the right, from IS to IS' in Figure 20-3(a). Because govern-ment spending does not enter the LM relation, the LM curve does not shift. The new equilibrium is at point A', with a higher level of output, Y', and a higher interest rate, i'. In panel (b), the higher interest rate leads to an increase in the exchange rate—an appreciation. So an increase in government spending leads to an increase in output, an increase in the interest rate, and an appreciation.

In words: An increase in government spending leads to an increase in demand, leading to an increase in output. As output increases, so does the demand for money, leading to upward pressure on the interest rate. The increase in the interest rate, which makes domestic bonds more attractive, leads to an appreciation. The higher interest rate and the appreciation both decrease the domestic demand for goods, offsetting some of the effect of government spending on demand and output.

Can we tell what happens to the various components of demand?

- Clearly, consumption and government spending both increase—consumption goes up because of the increase in income; government spending goes up by assumption.
- What happens to investment is ambiguous. Recall that investment depends on both output and the interest rate: $I = I(Y, i)$. On the one hand, output goes up, leading to an increase in investment. But on the other, the interest rate also goes up, leading to a decrease in investment. Depending on which of these two effects dominates, investment can go up or down. In short: The effect of government spending on investment was ambiguous in the closed economy; it remains am-biguous in the open economy.
- Recall that net exports depend on domestic output, foreign output, and the ex-change rate: $NX = NX(Y, Y^*, E)$. Thus, both the increase in output and the ap-preciation combine to decrease net exports: The increase in output increases imports, and the appreciation decreases exports and increases imports. As a result, the budget deficit leads to a deterioration of the trade balance. If trade is balanced to start, then the budget deficit leads to a trade deficit. Note that, while an increase

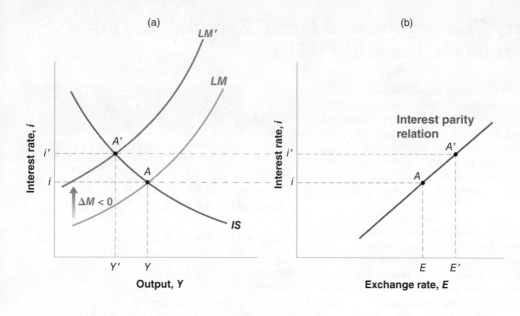

Figure 20-4

The Effects of a Monetary Contraction

A monetary contraction leads to a decrease in output, an increase in the interest rate, and an appreciation.

(a)

(b)

in the budget deficit increases the trade deficit, the effect is far from mechanical. It works through the effect of the budget deficit on output and on the exchange rate, and, in turn, on the trade deficit.

The Effects of Monetary Policy in an Open Economy

Now that we have looked at fiscal policy, we look at our other favorite policy experiment, a monetary contraction. Look at Figure 20-4(a). At a given level of output, a decrease in the money stock by, say, $\Delta M < 0$ leads to an increase in the interest rate: The *LM* curve shifts up, from *LM* to *LM'*. Because money does not directly enter the *IS* relation, the *IS* curve does not shift. The equilibrium moves from point *A* to point *A'*. ◄ In Figure 20-4(b), the increase in the interest rate leads to an appreciation.

A monetary contraction shifts the *LM* curve up. It shifts neither the *IS* curve nor the interest parity curve.

So *a monetary contraction leads to a decrease in output, an increase in the interest rate, and an appreciation.* The story is easy to tell. A monetary contraction leads to an increase in the interest rate, making domestic bonds more attractive and triggering an appreciation. The higher interest rate and the appreciation both decrease demand and output. As output falls, money demand falls, leading to a lower interest rate and offsetting some of the initial increase in the interest rate and some of the initial appreciation.

Can you tell what happens to consumption, to investment, ◄ and to net exports?

This version of the *IS–LM* model for the open economy was first put together in the 1960s by the two economists we mentioned at the outset of the chapter, Robert Mundell, at Columbia University, and Marcus Fleming, at the International Monetary Fund. How well does the Mundell-Fleming model fit the facts? The answer is: typically ◄ quite well, and this is why the model is still very much in use today. Like all simple models, it often needs to be extended; for example to take into account the liquidity trap or the role of risk in affecting portfolio decisions, two important aspects of the crisis. But it is always a good starting point to organize thoughts. (To test the predictions of the model, one could hardly design a better experiment than the sharp monetary and fiscal policy changes the U.S. economy went through in the late 1970s and early 1980s. This is the topic of the Focus box "Monetary Contraction and Fiscal Expansion: The United States in the Early 1980s." The Mundell-Fleming model and its predictions pass with flying colors.)

Robert Mundell was awarded ◄ the Nobel Prize in Economics in 1999.

Monetary Contraction and Fiscal Expansion: The United States in the Early 1980s

The early 1980s in the United States were dominated by sharp changes both in monetary policy and in fiscal policy.

We have already discussed the origins of the change in monetary policy in Chapter 8. By the late 1970s, the Chairman of the Fed, Paul Volcker, concluded that U.S. inflation was too high and had to be reduced. Starting in late 1979, Volcker embarked on a path of sharp monetary contraction, realizing this might lead to a recession in the short run but lower inflation in the medium run.

The change in fiscal policy was triggered by the election of Ronald Reagan in 1980. Reagan was elected on the promise of more conservative policies, namely a scaling down of taxation and the government's role in economic activity. This commitment was the inspiration for the Economic Recovery Act of August 1981. Personal income taxes were cut by a total of 23%, in three installments from 1981 to 1983. Corporate taxes were also reduced. These tax cuts were not, however, accompanied by corresponding decreases in government spending, and the result was a steady increase in budget deficits, which reached a peak in 1983 at 5.6% of GDP. Table 1 gives spending and revenue numbers for 1980–1984.

What were the Reagan administration's motivations for cutting taxes without implementing corresponding cuts in spending? These are still being debated today, but there is agreement that there were two main motivations:

One motivation came from the beliefs of a fringe, but influential, group of economists called the **supply siders**, who argued that a cut in tax rates would cause people and firms to work much harder and more productively, and that the resulting increase in activity would actually lead

Table 1	The Emergence of Large U.S. Budget Deficits, 1980–1984, (Percent of GDP)				
	1980	1981	1982	1983	1984
Spending	22.0	22.8	24.0	25.0	23.7
Revenues	20.2	20.8	20.5	19.4	19.2
Personal taxes	9.4	9.6	9.9	8.8	8.2
Corporate taxes	2.6	2.3	1.6	1.6	2.0
Budget surplus	−1.8	−2.0	−3.5	−5.6	−4.5

Numbers are for fiscal years, which start in October of the previous calendar year. All numbers are expressed as a percentage of GDP. A budget deficit is a negative budget surplus.

Source: Historical Tables, Office of Management and Budget

to an increase, not a decrease, in tax revenues. Whatever the merits of the argument appeared to be then, it proved wrong: Even if some people did work harder and more productively after the tax cuts, tax revenues decreased and the fiscal deficit increased.

The other motivation was more cynical. It was a bet that the cut in taxes, and the resulting increase in deficits, would scare Congress into cutting spending or, at the very least, into not increasing spending further. This motivation turned out to be partly right; Congress found itself under enormous pressure not to increase spending, and the

Table 2	Major U.S. Macroeconomic Variables, 1980–1984				
	1980	1981	1982	1983	1984
GDP growth (%)	−0.5	1.8	−2.2	3.9	6.2
Unemployment rate (%)	7.1	7.6	9.7	9.6	7.5
Inflation (CPI) (%)	12.5	8.9	3.8	3.8	3.9
Interest rate (real) (%)	11.5	14.0	10.6	8.6	9.6
	2.5	4.9	6.0	5.1	5.9
Real exchange rate	85	101	111	117	129
Trade surplus (% of GDP)	−0.5	−0.4	−0.6	−1.5	−2.7

Inflation: rate of change of the CPI. The nominal interest rate is the three-month T-bill rate. The real interest rate is equal to the nominal rate minus the forecast of inflation by DRI, a private forecasting firm. The real exchange rate is the trade-weighted real exchange rate, normalized so that 1973 = 100. A negative trade surplus is a trade deficit.

growth of spending in the 1980s was surely lower than it would have been otherwise. Nonetheless, the adjustment of spending was not enough to offset the shortfall in tax revenues and avoid the rapid increase in deficits.

Whatever the reason for the deficits, the effects of the monetary contraction and fiscal expansion were in line with what the Mundell-Fleming model predicts. Table 2 gives the evolution of the main macroeconomic variables from 1980 to 1984.

From 1980 to 1982, the evolution of the economy was dominated by the effects of the monetary contraction. Interest rates, both nominal and real, increased sharply, leading both to a large dollar appreciation and to a recession. The goal of lowering inflation was achieved; by 1982, inflation was down to about 4%, down from 12.5% in 1980. Lower output and the dollar appreciation had opposing effects on the trade balance (lower output leading to lower imports and an improvement in the trade balance; the appreciation of the dollar leading to a deterioration in the trade balance), resulting in little change in the trade deficit before 1982.

From 1982 on, the evolution of the economy was dominated by the effects of the fiscal expansion. As our model predicts, these effects were strong output growth, high interest rates, and further dollar appreciation. The effects of high output growth and the dollar appreciation were an increase in the trade deficit to 2.7% of GDP by 1984. By the mid-1980s, the main macroeconomic policy issue had become that of the **twin deficits**: the budget deficit and the trade deficit. The twin deficits were to remain one of the central macroeconomic issues throughout the 1980s and early 1990s.

20-5 Fixed Exchange Rates

We have assumed so far that the central bank chose the money supply and let the exchange rate freely adjust in whatever manner was implied by equilibrium in the foreign exchange market. In many countries, this assumption does not reflect reality: Central banks act under implicit or explicit exchange rate targets and use monetary policy to achieve those targets. The targets are sometimes implicit, sometimes explicit; they are sometimes specific values, sometimes bands or ranges. These exchange rate arrangements (or *regimes*, as they are called) come under many names. Let's first see what the names mean.

Pegs, Crawling Pegs, Bands, the EMS, and the Euro

At one end of the spectrum are countries with flexible exchange rates such as the United States, the United Kingdom, Japan, and Canada. These countries have no explicit exchange rate targets. Although their central banks probably do not ignore movements in the exchange rate, they have shown themselves quite willing to let their exchange rates fluctuate considerably.

At the other end are countries that operate under *fixed exchange rates*. These countries maintain a fixed exchange rate in terms of some foreign currency. Some **peg** their currency to the dollar. For example, from 1991 to 2001, Argentina pegged its currency, the peso, at the highly symbolic exchange rate of one dollar for one peso (more on this in Chapter 21). Other countries used to peg their currency to the French franc (most of these are former French colonies in Africa); as the French franc has been replaced by the euro, they are now pegged to the euro. Still other countries peg their currency to a basket of foreign currencies, with the weights reflecting the composition of their trade.

The label "fixed" is a bit misleading: It is not the case that the exchange rate in countries with fixed exchange rates never actually changes. But changes are rare. An extreme case is that of the African countries pegged to the French franc. When their exchange rates were readjusted in January 1994, this was the first adjustment in 45 years! Because these changes are rare, economists use specific words to distinguish them from the daily changes that occur under flexible exchange rates. A decrease in the exchange rate under a regime of fixed exchange rates is called a *devaluation* rather than a depreciation, and an increase in the exchange rate under a regime of fixed exchange rates is called a *revaluation* rather than an appreciation.

These terms were first introduced in Chapter 18.

Recall the definition of the real exchange rate $\epsilon = EP/P^*$.

If domestic inflation is higher than foreign inflation:
  P increases faster than P^*.
  If E is fixed, EP/P^* steadily increases.
Equivalently: There is a steady real appreciation. Domestic goods become steadily more expensive relative to foreign goods.

We will look at the 1992 crisis in Chapter 21.

You can think of countries adopting a common currency as adopting an extreme form of fixed exchange rates: Their "exchange rate" is fixed at one-to-one between any pair of countries.

Between these extremes are countries with various degrees of commitment to an exchange rate target. For example, some countries operate under a **crawling peg**. The name describes it well: These countries typically have inflation rates that exceed the U.S. inflation rate. If they were to peg their nominal exchange rate against the dollar, the more rapid increase in their domestic price level above the U.S. price level would lead to a steady real appreciation and rapidly make their goods uncompetitive. To avoid this effect, these countries choose a predetermined rate of depreciation against the dollar. They choose to "crawl" (move slowly) vis-à-vis the dollar.

Yet another arrangement is for a group of countries to maintain their bilateral exchange rates (the exchange rate between each pair of countries) within some bands. Perhaps the most prominent example was the **European Monetary System (EMS)**, which determined the movements of exchange rates within the European Union from 1978 to 1998. Under the EMS rules, member countries agreed to maintain their exchange rate relative to the other currencies in the system within narrow limits or **bands** around a **central parity**—a given value for the exchange rate. Changes in the central parity and devaluations or revaluations of specific currencies could occur, but only by common agreement among member countries. After a major crisis in 1992, which led a number of countries to drop out of the EMS altogether, exchange rate adjustments became more and more infrequent, leading a number of countries to move one step further and adopt a common currency, the **euro**. The conversion from domestic currencies to the euro began on January 1, 1999, and was completed in early 2002. We shall return to the implications of the move to the euro in Chapter 21.

We shall discuss the pros and cons of different exchange regimes in the next chapter. But first, we must understand how pegging (also called fixing) the exchange rate affects monetary policy and fiscal policy. This is what we do in the rest of this section.

Pegging the Exchange Rate, and Monetary Control

Suppose a country decides to peg its exchange rate at some chosen value, call it $\overline{E}$. How does it actually achieve this? The government cannot just announce the value of the exchange rate and remain idle. Rather, it must take measures so that its chosen exchange rate will prevail in the foreign exchange market. Let's look at the implications and mechanics of pegging.

Pegging or no pegging, the exchange rate and the nominal interest rate must satisfy the interest parity condition

$$(1 + i_t) = (1 + i_t^*)\left(\frac{E_t}{E_{t+1}^e}\right)$$

Now suppose the country pegs the exchange rate at $\overline{E}$, so the current exchange rate $E_t = \overline{E}$. If financial and foreign exchange markets believe that the exchange rate will remain pegged at this value, then their expectation of the future exchange rate, E_{t+1}^e, is also equal to $\overline{E}$, and the interest parity relation becomes

$$(1 + i_t) = (1 + i_t^*) \implies i_t = i_t^*$$

In words: If financial investors expect the exchange rate to remain unchanged, they will require the same nominal interest rate in both countries. *Under a fixed exchange rate and perfect capital mobility, the domestic interest rate must be equal to the foreign interest rate.*

This condition has one further important implication. Return to the equilibrium condition that the supply of money and demand for money be equal. Now that $i = i^*$, this condition becomes:

$$\frac{M}{P} = YL(i^*) \qquad (20.6)$$

Suppose an increase in domestic output increases the demand for money. In a closed economy, the central bank could leave the money stock unchanged, leading to an increase in the equilibrium interest rate. In an open economy, and under flexible exchange rates, the central bank can still do the same: The result will be both an increase in the interest rate and an appreciation. But under fixed exchange rates, the central bank cannot keep the money stock unchanged. If it did, the domestic interest rate would increase above the foreign interest rate, leading to an appreciation. To maintain the exchange rate, the central bank must increase the supply of money in line with the increase in the demand for money so the equilibrium interest rate does not change. Given the price level, P, nominal money, M, must adjust so that equation (20.6) holds.

Let's summarize: *Under fixed exchange rates, the central bank gives up monetary policy as a policy instrument.* With a fixed exchange rate, the domestic interest rate must be equal to the foreign interest rate. And the money supply must adjust so as to maintain the interest rate.

These results depend very much on the interest rate parity condition, which in turn depends on the assumption of perfect capital mobility— that financial investors go for the highest expected rate of return. The case of fixed exchange rates with imperfect capital mobility, which is more relevant for middle-income countries, such as in Latin America or Asia, is treated in the appendix to this chapter.

Fiscal Policy under Fixed Exchange Rates

If monetary policy can no longer be used under fixed exchange rates, what about fiscal policy? To answer this question, we use Figure 20-5.

Figure 20-5 starts by replicating Figure 20-3(a), which we used earlier to analyze the effects of fiscal policy under flexible exchange rates. In that case, we saw that a fiscal expansion ($\Delta G > 0$) shifted the IS curve to the right. Under flexible exchange rates, the money stock remained unchanged, leading to a movement in the equilibrium from point A to point B, with an increase in output from Y_A to Y_B, an increase in the interest rate, and an appreciation.

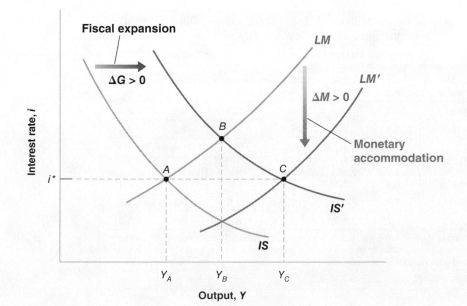

Figure 20-5

The Effects of a Fiscal Expansion under Fixed Exchange Rates

Under flexible exchange rates, a fiscal expansion increases output from Y_A to Y_B. Under fixed exchange rates, output increases from Y_A to Y_C.

German Reunification, Interest Rates, and the EMS

Under a fixed exchange rate regime such as the European Monetary System (EMS) (let's ignore here the degree of flexibility that was afforded by the bands), no individual country can change its interest rate if the other countries do not change theirs as well. So, how do interest rates actually change? Two arrangements are possible. One is for all the member countries to coordinate changes in their interest rates. Another is for one of the countries to take the lead and for the other countries to follow—this is in effect what happened in the EMS, with Germany as the leader.

During the 1980s, most European central banks shared similar goals and were happy to let the Bundesbank (the German central bank) take the lead. But in 1990, German unification led to a sharp divergence in goals between the Bundesbank and the central banks of the other EMS countries. Large budget deficits, triggered by transfers to people and firms in Eastern Germany, together with an investment boom, led to a large increase in demand in Germany. The Bundesbank's fear that this shift would generate too strong an increase in activity led it to adopt a restrictive monetary policy. The result was strong growth in Germany together with a large increase in interest rates.

This may have been the right policy mix for Germany. But for the other European countries, this policy mix was much less appealing. They were not experiencing the same increase in demand, but to stay in the EMS, they had to match German interest rates. The net result was a sharp decrease in demand and output in the other countries. These results are presented in Table 1, which gives nominal interest rates, real interest rates, inflation rates, and GDP growth from 1990 to 1992 for Germany and for two of its EMS partners, France and Belgium.

Note first how the high German nominal interest rates were matched by both France and Belgium. In fact,

nominal interest rates were actually higher in France than in Germany in all three years! This is because France needed higher interest rates than Germany to maintain the Deutsche Mark/franc parity. The reason is that financial markets were not sure that France would actually keep the parity of the franc relative to the DM. Worried about a possible devaluation of the franc, financial investors asked for a higher interest rate on French bonds than on German bonds.

Although France and Belgium had to match—or, as we have just seen, more than match—German nominal rates, both countries had less inflation than Germany. The result was very high real interest rates, much higher than the rate in Germany: In both France and Belgium, average real interest rates from 1990 to 1992 were close to 7%. And in both countries, the period 1990–1992 was characterized by slow growth and rising unemployment. Unemployment in France in 1992 was 10.4%, up from 8.9% in 1990. The corresponding numbers for Belgium were 12.1% and 8.7%.

A similar story was unfolding in the other EMS countries. By 1992, average unemployment in the European Union, which had been 8.7% in 1990, had increased to 10.3%. The effects of high real interest rates on spending were not the only source of this slowdown, but they were the main one.

By 1992, an increasing number of countries were wondering whether to keep defending their EMS parity or to give it up and lower their interest rates. Worried about the risk of devaluations, financial markets started to ask for higher interest rates in those countries where they thought devaluations were more likely. The result was two major exchange rate crises, one in the fall of 1992, and the other in the summer of 1993. By the end of these two crises, two countries, Italy and the United Kingdom, had left the EMS. We shall look at these crises, their origins, and their implications, in Chapter 21.

Table 1 German Reunification, Interest Rates, and Output Growth: Germany, France, and Belgium, 1990–1992					
	Nominal Interest Rates (%)			**Inflation** (%)		
	1990	1991	1992	1990	1991	1992
Germany	8.5	9.2	9.5	2.7	3.7	4.7
France	10.3	9.6	10.3	2.9	3.0	2.4
Belgium	9.6	9.4	9.4	2.9	2.7	2.4
	Real Interest Rates (%)			**GDP Growth** (%)		
	1990	1991	1992	1990	1991	1992
Germany	5.8	5.5	4.8	5.7	4.5	2.1
France	7.4	6.6	7.9	2.5	0.7	1.4
Belgium	6.7	6.7	7.0	3.3	2.1	0.8

The nominal interest rate is the short-term nominal interest rate. The real interest rate is the realized real interest rate over the year—that is, the nominal interest rate minus actual inflation over the year. All rates are annual.

Source: OECD Economic Outlook

However, under fixed exchange rates the central bank cannot let the currency appreciate. Because the increase in output leads to an increase in the demand for money, the central bank must accommodate this increased demand for money by increasing the money supply. In terms of Figure 20-5, the central bank must shift the *LM* curve down as the *IS* curve shifts to the right, so as to maintain the same interest rate and thus the same exchange rate. The equilibrium therefore moves from *A* to *C*, with higher output Y_C and unchanged interest and exchange rates. So, *under fixed exchange rates, fiscal policy is more powerful than it is under flexible exchange rates. This is because fiscal policy triggers monetary accommodation.*

As this chapter comes to an end, a question should have started to form in your mind: Why would a country choose to fix its exchange rate? You have seen a number of reasons why this appears to be a bad idea:

Is the effect of fiscal policy stronger in a closed economy or in an open economy with fixed exchange rates? (*Hint:* ◄ The answer is ambiguous.)

- By fixing the exchange rate, a country gives up a powerful tool for correcting trade imbalances or changing the level of economic activity.
- By committing to a particular exchange rate, a country also gives up control of its interest rate. Not only that, but the country must match movements in the foreign interest rate, at the risk of unwanted effects on its own activity. This is what happened in the early 1990s in Europe. Because of the increase in demand due to the reunification of West and East Germany, Germany felt it had to increase its interest rate. To maintain their parity with the Deutsche Mark, other countries in the European Monetary System were forced to also increase their interest rates, something that they would rather have avoided. (This is the topic of the Focus box "German Reunification, Interest Rates, and the EMS.")
- Although the country retains control of fiscal policy, one policy instrument may not be enough. As you saw in Chapter 19, for example, a fiscal expansion can help the economy get out of a recession, but only at the cost of a larger trade deficit. And a country that wants, for example, to decrease its budget deficit cannot, under fixed exchange rates, use monetary policy to offset the contractionary effect of its fiscal policy on output.

So why do some countries fix their exchange rate? Why have 17 European countries—with more to come—adopted a common currency? To answer these questions, we must do some more work. We must look at what happens not only in the short run—which is what we did in this chapter—but also in the medium run, when the price level can adjust. We must look at the nature of exchange rate crises. Once we have done this, we shall then be able to assess the pros and cons of different exchange rate regimes. These are the topics we take up in Chapter 21.

Summary

- In an open economy, the demand for domestic goods depends both on the interest rate and on the exchange rate. An increase in the interest rate decreases the demand for domestic goods. An increase in the exchange rate—an appreciation—also decreases the demand for domestic goods.
- The interest rate is determined by the equality of money demand and money supply. The exchange rate is determined by the interest parity condition, which states that domestic and foreign bonds must have the same expected rate of return in terms of domestic currency.

- Given the expected future exchange rate and the foreign interest rate, increases in the domestic interest rate lead to an increase in the exchange rate—an appreciation. Decreases in the domestic interest rate lead to a decrease in the exchange rate—a depreciation.
- Under flexible exchange rates, an expansionary fiscal policy leads to an increase in output, an increase in the interest rate, and an appreciation.

- Under flexible exchange rates, a contractionary monetary policy leads to a decrease in output, an increase in the interest rate, and an appreciation.
- There are many types of exchange rate arrangements. They range from fully flexible exchange rates to crawling pegs, to fixed exchange rates (or pegs), to the adoption of a common currency. Under fixed exchange rates, a country maintains a fixed exchange rate in terms of a foreign currency or a basket of currencies.

- Under fixed exchange rates and the interest parity condition, a country must maintain an interest rate equal to the foreign interest rate. The central bank loses the use of monetary policy as a policy instrument. Fiscal policy becomes more powerful than under flexible exchange rates, however, because fiscal policy triggers monetary accommodation, and so does not lead to offsetting changes in the domestic interest rate and exchange rate.

Key Terms

Mundell-Fleming model, 423
sudden stops, 428
safe haven, 428
supply siders, 434
twin deficits, 435
peg, 435

crawling peg, 436
European Monetary System (EMS), 436
bands, 436
central parity, 436
euro, 436

Questions and Problems

QUICK CHECK
All Quick Check questions and problems are available on MyEconLab.

1. Using the information in this chapter, label each of the following statements true, false, or uncertain. Explain briefly.
- a. A fiscal expansion tends to increase net exports.
- b. Fiscal policy has a greater effect on output in an economy with fixed exchange rates than in an economy with flexible exchange rates.
- c. Other things being equal, the interest parity condition implies that the domestic currency will appreciate in response to an increase in the expected exchange rate.
- d. If financial investors expect the dollar to depreciate against the yen over the coming year, one-year interest rates will be higher in the United States than in Japan.
- e. If the Japanese interest rate is equal to zero, foreigners will not want to hold Japanese bonds.
- f. Under fixed exchange rates, the money stock must be constant.

2. Consider an open economy with flexible exchange rates. Suppose output is at the natural level, but there is a trade deficit.
What is the appropriate fiscal and monetary policy mix?

3. In this chapter, we showed that a monetary expansion in an economy operating under flexible exchange rates leads to an increase in output and a depreciation of the domestic currency.
- a. How does a monetary expansion (in an economy with flexible exchange rates) affect consumption and investment?
- b. How does a monetary expansion (in an economy with flexible exchange rates) affect net exports?

4. Flexible exchange rates and foreign macroeconomic policy.
Consider an open economy with flexible exchange rates.
Let UIP stand for the uncovered interest parity condition.
- a. In an *IS–LM–UIP* diagram, show the effect of an increase in foreign output, Y^*, on domestic output, Y. Explain in words.
- b. In an *IS–LM–UIP* diagram, show the effect of an increase in the foreign interest rate, i^*, on domestic output, Y. Explain in words.
- c. Given the discussion of the effects of fiscal policy in this chapter, what effect is a foreign fiscal expansion likely to have on foreign output, Y^*, and on the foreign interest rate, i^*? Given the discussion of the effects of monetary policy in this chapter, what effect is a foreign monetary expansion likely to have on Y^* and i^*?
- d. Given your answers to parts (a), (b), and (c), how does a foreign fiscal expansion affect domestic output? How does a foreign monetary expansion affect domestic output? (*Hint*: One of these policies has an ambiguous effect on output.)

DIG DEEPER
All Dig Deeper questions and problems are available on MyEconLab.

5. Fixed exchange rates and foreign macroeconomic policy
Consider a fixed exchange rate system, in which a group of countries (called follower countries) peg their currencies to the currency of one country (called the leader country). Since the currency of the leader country is not fixed against the currencies of countries outside the fixed exchange rate system, the leader country can conduct monetary policy as it wishes. For this problem, consider the domestic country to be a follower country and the foreign country to be the leader country.
- a. Redo the analysis of Problem 4(a).
- b. Redo the analysis of Problem 4(b).

c. Using your answers to parts (a) and (b) and Problem 4(c), how does a foreign monetary expansion (by the leader country) affect domestic output? How does a foreign fiscal expansion (by the leader country) affect domestic output? (You may assume that the effect of Y^* on domestic output is small.) How do your answers differ from those in 4(d)?

6. The exchange rate as an automatic stabilizer

Consider an economy that suffers a fall in business confidence (which tends to reduce investment). Let UIP stand for the uncovered interest parity condition.

a. Suppose the economy has a flexible exchange rate. In an IS–LM–UIP diagram, show the short-run effect of the fall in business confidence on output, the interest rate, and the exchange rate. How does the change in the exchange rate, by itself, tend to affect output? Does the change in the exchange rate dampen (make smaller) or amplify (make larger) the effect of the fall in business confidence on output?

b. Suppose instead the economy has a fixed exchange rate. In an IS–LM–UIP diagram, show how the economy responds to the fall in business confidence. What must happen to the money supply in order to maintain the fixed exchange rate? How does the effect on output in this economy, with fixed exchange rates, compare to the effect you found for the economy in part (a), with flexible exchange rates?

c. Explain how the exchange rate acts as an automatic stabilizer in an economy with flexible exchange rates.

EXPLORE FURTHER

7. Demand for U.S. assets, the dollar, and the trade deficit

This question explores how an increase in demand for U.S. assets may have slowed the depreciation of the dollar that many economists believe is warranted by the large U.S. trade deficit and the need to stimulate the demand for domestic goods after the crisis. Here, we modify the IS–LM–UIP framework (where UIP stands for uncovered interest parity) to analyze the effects of an increase in demand for U.S. assets. Write the uncovered interest parity condition as

$$(1 + i_t) = (1 + i_t^*)(E_t/E_{t+1}^e) - x$$

where the parameter x represents factors affecting the relative demand for domestic assets. An increase in x means that investors are willing to hold domestic assets at a lower interest rate (given the foreign interest rate, and the current and expected exchange rates).

a. Solve the UIP condition for the current exchange rate, E_t.

b. Substitute the result from part (a) in the IS curve and construct the UIP diagram. As in the text, you may assume that P and P^* are constant and equal to one.

c. Suppose that as a result of a large trade deficit in the domestic economy, financial market participants believe that the domestic currency must depreciate in the future.

Therefore, the expected exchange rate, E_{t+1}^e, decreases. Show the effect of the decrease in the expected exchange rate in the IS–LM–UIP diagram. What are the effects on the exchange rate and the trade balance? (Hint: In analyzing the effect on the trade balance, remember why the IS curve shifted in the first place.)

d. Now suppose that the relative demand for domestic assets, x, increases. As a benchmark, suppose that the increase in x is exactly enough to return the IS curve to its original position, before the decrease in the expected exchange rate. Show the combined effects of the decrease in E_{t+1}^e and the increase in x in your IS–LM–UIP diagram. What are the ultimate effects on the exchange rate and the trade balance?

e. Based on your analysis, is it possible that an increase in demand for U.S. assets could prevent the dollar from depreciating? Is it possible that an increase in demand for U.S. assets could worsen the U.S. trade balance? Explain your answers.

By the time you read this book, it is possible that relative demand for U.S. assets could be weaker than it was at the time of this writing and that the dollar could be depreciating. Think about how you would use the framework of this problem to assess the current situation.

8. Expected depreciation of the dollar

Martin Feldstein, as mentioned at the end of Chapter 19, is one prominent economist who argues that the dollar may need to depreciate by as much as 20% to 40% in real terms to achieve a reasonable improvement in the trade balance.

a. Go the web site of The Economist (www.economist.com) and find data on 10-year interest rates. Look in the section "Markets & Data" and then the subsection "Economic and Financial Indicators." Look at the interest rates for the United States, Japan, China, Britain, Canada, and the Euro area. For each country (treating the Euro area as a country), calculate the spreads as that country's interest rate minus the U.S. interest rate.

b. From the uncovered interest parity condition, the spreads from part (a) are the annualized expected appreciation rates of the dollar against other currencies. To calculate the 10-year expected appreciation, you must compound. (So, if x is the spread, the 10-year expected appreciation is $[(1 + x)^{10} - 1]$. Be careful about decimal points.) Is the dollar expected to depreciate by much in nominal terms against any currency other than the yen?

c. Given your answer to part (b), if we accept that significant real depreciation of the dollar is likely in the next decade, how must it be accomplished? Does your answer seem plausible?

d. What do your answers to parts (b) and (c) suggest about the relative strength of demand for dollar assets, independent of the exchange rate? You may want to review Problem 7 before answering this question.

APPENDIX: Fixed Exchange Rates, Interest Rates, and Capital Mobility

The assumption of perfect capital mobility is a good approximation of what happens in countries with highly developed financial markets and few capital controls, such as the United States, the United Kingdom, Japan, and the Euro area. But this assumption is more questionable in countries that have less developed financial markets or have capital controls in place. In these countries, domestic financial investors may have neither the savvy nor the legal right to buy foreign bonds when domestic interest rates are low. The central bank may thus be able to decrease the interest rate while maintaining a given exchange rate.

To look at these issues, we need to have another look at the balance sheet of the central bank. In Chapter 4, we assumed the only asset held by the central bank was domestic bonds. In an open economy, the central bank actually holds two types of assets: (1) domestic bonds and (2) **foreign exchange reserves**, which we shall think of as foreign currency—although they also take the form of foreign bonds or foreign interest–paying assets. Think of the balance sheet of the central bank as represented in Figure 1:

On the asset side are bonds and foreign exchange reserves, and on the liability side is the monetary base. There are now two ways in which the central bank can change the monetary base: either by purchases or sales of bonds in the bond market, or by purchases or sales of foreign currency in the foreign exchange market. (If you did not read Section 4-4 in Chapter 4, replace "monetary base" with "money supply" and you will still get the basic argument.)

Perfect Capital Mobility and Fixed Exchange Rates

Consider first the effects of an open market operation under the joint assumptions of perfect capital mobility and fixed exchange rates (the assumptions we made in the last section of this chapter).

- Assume the domestic interest rate and the foreign interest rate are initially equal, so $i = i^*$. Now suppose the central bank embarks on an expansionary open market operation, buying bonds in the bond market in amount ΔB, and creating money—increasing the monetary base—in exchange. This purchase of bonds leads to a decrease in the domestic interest rate, i. This is, however, only the beginning of the story.

- Now that the domestic interest rate is lower than the foreign interest rate, financial investors prefer to hold foreign bonds. To buy foreign bonds, they must first buy foreign currency. They then go to the foreign exchange market and sell domestic currency for foreign currency.

- If the central bank did nothing, the price of domestic currency would fall, and the result would be a depreciation. Under its commitment to a fixed exchange rate, the central bank cannot allow the currency to depreciate. So it must intervene in the foreign exchange market and sell foreign currency for domestic currency. As it sells foreign currency and buys domestic money, the monetary base decreases.

- How much foreign currency must the central bank sell? It must keep selling until the monetary base is back to its pre-open market operation level, so the domestic interest rate is again equal to the foreign interest rate. Only then are financial investors willing to hold domestic bonds.

How long do all these steps take? Under perfect capital mobility, all this may happen within minutes or so of the original open market operation. After these steps, the balance sheet of the central bank looks as represented in Figure 2. Bond holdings are up by ΔB, reserves of foreign currency are down by ΔB, and the monetary base is unchanged, having gone up by ΔB in the open market operation and down by ΔB as a result of the sale of foreign currency in the foreign exchange market.

Let's summarize: Under fixed exchange rates and perfect capital mobility, the only effect of the open market operation is to change the *composition* of the central bank's balance sheet but not the monetary base (nor the interest rate.)

Imperfect Capital Mobility and Fixed Exchange Rates

Let's now move away from the assumption of perfect capital mobility. Suppose it takes some time for financial investors to shift between domestic bonds and foreign bonds.

Now an expansionary open market operation can initially bring the domestic interest rate below the foreign interest rate. But over time, investors shift to foreign bonds, leading to an increase in the demand for foreign currency in the foreign exchange market. To avoid a depreciation of the domestic currency, the central bank must again stand ready to sell foreign currency and buy domestic currency. Eventually, the central bank buys enough domestic currency to offset the effects of the initial open market operation. The monetary base is back to its pre-open market operation level, and so is the interest

Assets	Liabilities
Bonds Foreign exchange reserves	Monetary base

Figure 1

Balance Sheet of the Central Bank

Assets		Liabilities	
Bonds:	ΔB	Monetary base $\Delta B - \Delta B$	
Reserves:	$-\Delta B$		$= 0$

Figure 2

Balance Sheet of the Central Bank after an Open Market Operation, and the Induced Intervention in the Foreign Exchange Market

rate. The central bank holds more domestic bonds and smaller reserves of foreign currency.

The difference between this case and the case of perfect capital mobility is that, by accepting a loss in foreign exchange reserves, the central bank is now able to decrease interest rates *for some time*. If it takes just a few days for financial investors to adjust, the trade-off can be very unattractive—as many countries that have suffered large losses in reserves without much effect on the interest rate have discovered at their expense. But, if the central bank can affect the domestic interest rate for a few weeks or months, it may, in some circumstances, be willing to do so.

Now let's deviate further from perfect capital mobility. Suppose, in response to a decrease in the domestic interest rate, financial investors are either unwilling or unable to move much of their portfolio into foreign bonds. For example, there are administrative and legal controls on financial transactions, making it illegal or very expensive for domestic residents to invest outside the country. This is the relevant case for a number of emerging economies, from Latin America to China.

After an expansionary open market operation, the domestic interest rate decreases, making domestic bonds less attractive. Some domestic investors move into foreign bonds, selling domestic currency for foreign currency. To maintain the exchange rate, the central bank must buy domestic currency and supply foreign currency. However, the foreign exchange intervention by the central bank may now be small compared to the initial open market operation. And, if capital controls truly prevent investors from moving into foreign bonds at all, there may be no need for such a foreign exchange intervention.

Even leaving this extreme case aside, the net effects of the initial open market operation and the following foreign exchange interventions are likely to be *an increase in the monetary base; a decrease in the domestic interest rate; an increase in the central bank's bond holdings; and some—but limited—loss in reserves of foreign currency*. With imperfect capital mobility, a country has some freedom to move the domestic interest rate while maintaining its exchange rate. This freedom depends primarily on three factors:

- The degree of development of its financial markets, and the willingness of domestic and foreign investors to shift between domestic assets and foreign assets.
- The degree of capital controls it is able to impose on both domestic and foreign investors.
- The amount of foreign exchange reserves it holds: The higher the reserves it has, the more it can afford the loss in reserves it is likely to sustain if it decreases the interest rate at a given exchange rate.

With the large movements in capital flows we documented earlier in the chapter, all of these issues are hot topics. Many countries are considering a more active use of capital controls than in the past. Many countries are also accumulating large reserves as a precaution against large capital outflows.

Key Term

foreign-exchange reserves, 442

Exchange Rate Regimes

In July 1944, representatives of 44 countries met in Bretton Woods, New Hampshire, to design a new international monetary and exchange rate system. The system they adopted was based on fixed exchange rates, with all member countries other than the United States fixing the price of their currency in terms of dollars. In 1973, a series of exchange rate crises brought an abrupt

"Then it's agreed. Until the dollar firms up, we let the clamshell float."

end to the system—and an end to what is now called "the Bretton Woods period." Since then, the world has been characterized by many exchange rate arrangements. Some countries operate under flexible exchange rates; some operate under fixed exchange rates; some go back and forth between regimes. Which exchange rate regime to choose is one of the most debated issues in macroeconomics and, as the cartoon suggests, a decision facing every country in the world. This chapter discusses this issue.

Section 21-1 looks at the medium run. It shows that, in sharp contrast to the results we derived for the short run in Chapter 20, an economy ends up with the same real exchange rate and output level in the medium run, regardless of whether it operates under fixed exchange rates or flexible exchange rates. This obviously does not make the exchange rate regime irrelevant—the short run matters very much—but it is an important extension and qualification to our previous analysis.

Section 21-2 takes another look at fixed exchange rates and focuses on exchange rate crises. During a typical exchange rate crisis, a country operating under a fixed exchange rate is forced, often under dramatic conditions, to abandon its parity and to devalue. Such crises were behind the breakdown of the Bretton Woods system. They rocked the European Monetary System in the early 1990s, and were a major element of the Asian Crisis of the late 1990s. It is important to understand why they happen, and what they imply.

Section 21-3 takes another look at flexible exchange rates and focuses on the behavior of exchange rates under a flexible exchange rate regime. It shows that the behavior of exchange rates and the relation of the exchange rate to monetary policy are, in fact more complex than we assumed in Chapter 20. Large fluctuations in the exchange rate, and the difficulty of using monetary policy to affect the exchange rate, make a flexible exchange rate regime less attractive than it appeared to be in Chapter 20.

Section 21-4 puts all these conclusions together and reviews the case for flexible or fixed rates. It discusses two recent and important developments: the use of a common currency in much of Europe and the move toward strong forms of fixed exchange rate regimes, from currency boards to dollarization. ●

21-1 The Medium Run

When we focused on the short run in Chapter 20, we drew a sharp contrast between the behavior of an economy with flexible exchange rates and an economy with fixed exchange rates.

- Under flexible exchange rates, a country that needed to achieve a real depreciation (for example, to reduce its trade deficit or to get out of a recession) could do so by relying on an expansionary monetary policy to achieve both a lower interest rate and a decrease in the exchange rate—a depreciation.
- Under fixed exchange rates, a country lost both of these instruments: By definition, its nominal exchange rate was fixed and thus could not be adjusted. Moreover, the fixed exchange rate and the interest parity condition implied that the country could not adjust its interest rate; the domestic interest rate had to remain equal to the foreign interest rate.

This appeared to make a flexible exchange rate regime much more attractive than a fixed exchange rate regime: Why should a country give up two macroeconomic instruments—the exchange rate and the interest rate? As we now shift focus from the short run to the medium run, you shall see that this earlier conclusion needs to be qualified. Although our conclusions about the short run were valid, we shall see that, in the medium run, the difference between the two regimes fades away. More specifically, in the medium run, the economy reaches the same real exchange rate and the same level of output whether it operates under fixed or under flexible exchange rates.

The intuition for this result is actually easy to give. Recall the definition of the real exchange rate:

$$\epsilon = \frac{EP}{P^*}$$

The real exchange rate, ϵ, is equal to the nominal exchange rate, E (the price of domestic currency in terms of foreign currency) times the domestic price level, P, divided by the domestic price level, P^*. There are, therefore, two ways in which the real exchange rate can adjust:

- Through a change in the nominal exchange rate E: This can only be done under flexible exchange rates. And if we assume the domestic price level, P, and the foreign price level, P^*, do not change in the short run, it is the only way to adjust the real exchange rate in the short run.
- Through a change in the domestic price level, P, relative to the foreign price level, P^*. In the medium run, this option is open even to a country operating under a fixed (nominal) exchange rate. And this is indeed what happens under fixed exchange rates: The adjustment takes place through the price level rather than through the nominal exchange rate.

There are three ways in which a U.S. car can become cheaper relative to a Japanese car: First, through a decrease in the dollar price of the U.S car. Second, through an increase in the yen price of the Japanese car. Third, through a decrease in the nominal exchange rate—a decrease in the value of the dollar in terms of the yen.

Let us go through this argument step by step. To begin, let's derive the aggregate demand and aggregate supply relations for an open economy under a fixed exchange rate.

Aggregate Demand under Fixed Exchange Rates

In an open economy with fixed exchange rates, we can write the aggregate demand relation as

$$Y = Y\left(\frac{\overline{E}P}{P^*}, G, T\right) \tag{21.1}$$
$$(-, \ +, -)$$

Recall that the aggregate demand relation captures the effects of the price level on output. It is derived from equilibrium in goods and financial markets.

Output, Y, depends on the real exchange rate, $\overline{E}P/P^*$ ($\overline{E}$ denotes the fixed nominal exchange rate; P and P^* denote the domestic and foreign price levels, respectively), government spending, G, and taxes, T. An increase in the real exchange rate—a real appreciation—leads to a decrease in output. An increase in government spending leads to an increase in output; an increase in taxes to a decrease in output.

The derivation of equation (21.1) is better left to Appendix 1 at the end of this chapter, which is titled "Deriving Aggregate Demand under Fixed Exchange Rates." The intuition behind the equation is straightforward, however:

Recall that, in the closed economy, the aggregate demand relation took the same form as equation (21.1), except for the presence of the real money stock, M/P, instead of the real exchange rate, EP/P^*.

See equation (7.3).

- The reason for the presence of M/P in the closed economy was the following: By controlling the money supply, the central bank could change the interest rate and affect output. In an open economy, and under fixed exchange rates and perfect capital mobility, the central bank can no longer change the interest rate—which is pinned down by the foreign interest rate. Put another way, under fixed exchange rates, the central bank gives up monetary policy as a policy instrument. This is why the money stock no longer appears in the aggregate demand relation.

- At the same time, the fact that the economy is open implies that we must include a variable which we did not include when we looked at the closed economy earlier, namely the real exchange rate, $\overline{E}P/P^*$. As we saw in Chapter 19, an increase in the real exchange rate leads to a decrease in the demand for domestic goods and thus a decrease in output. Conversely, a decrease in the real exchange rate leads to an increase in output.

Note that, just as in the closed economy, the aggregate demand relation (21.1) implies a negative relation between the price level and output. But, while the sign of the effect of the price level on output remains the same, the channel is very different:

- In the closed economy, the price level affects output through its effect on the real money stock and, in turn, its effect on the interest rate.
- In the open economy under fixed exchange rates, the price level affects output through its effect on the real exchange rate. Given the fixed nominal exchange rate, $\overline{E}$, and the foreign price level, P^*, an increase in the domestic price level, P, leads to an increase in the real exchange rate $\overline{E}P/P^*$—a real appreciation. This real appreciation leads to a decrease in the demand for domestic goods, and, in turn, to a decrease in output. Put simply: An increase in the price level makes domestic goods more expensive, thus decreasing the demand for domestic goods, in turn decreasing output.

> Aggregate demand relation in the open economy under fixed exchange rates: P increases $\Rightarrow \overline{E}P/P^*$ increases $\Rightarrow Y$ decreases.

Equilibrium in the Short Run and in the Medium Run

The aggregate demand curve associated with equation (21.1) is drawn as the *AD* curve in Figure 21-1. It is downward sloping: An increase in the price level decreases output. As always, the relation is drawn for given values of the other variables; in this case for given values of $\overline{E}$, P^*, G, and T.

> Recall that the aggregate supply relation captures the effects of output on the price level. It is derived from equilibrium in labor markets.

For the aggregate supply curve, we rely on the relation we derived in the core. Going back to the *aggregate supply relation* we derived in Chapter 7, equation (7.2):

$$P = P^e \,(1 + m)\, F\!\left(1 - \frac{Y}{L}, z\right) \tag{21.2}$$

Figure 21-1

Aggregate Demand and Aggregate Supply in an Open Economy under Fixed Exchange Rates

An increase in the price level leads to a real appreciation and a decrease in output: The aggregate demand curve is downward sloping. An increase in output leads to an increase in the price level: The aggregate supply curve is upward sloping.

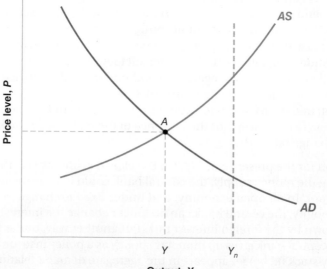

The price level, P, depends on the expected price level, P^e, and on the level of output, Y. Recall the two mechanisms at work:

■ The expected price level matters because it affects nominal wages, which in turn affect the price level.

■ Higher output matters because it leads to higher employment, which leads to lower unemployment, which leads to higher wages, which lead to a higher price level.

Aggregate supply relation: ◄ Y increases $\Rightarrow$ P increases.

The aggregate supply curve is drawn as the AS curve in Figure 21-1 for a given value of the expected price level. It is upward sloping: Higher output leads to a higher price level.

The short-run equilibrium is given by the intersection of the aggregate demand curve and the aggregate supply curve, point A in Figure 21-1. As was the case in the closed economy, there is no reason why the short-run equilibrium level of output, Y, should be equal to the natural level of output, Y_n. As the figure is drawn, Y is less than Y_n, so output is below the natural level of output.

What happens over time? The basic answer is familiar from our earlier look at adjustment in a closed economy, and is shown in Figure 21-2. As long as output remains below the natural level of output, the aggregate supply shifts down to AS'. The reason: When output is below the natural level of output, the price level turns out to be lower than was expected. This leads wage setters to revise their expectation of the price level downward, leading to a lower price level at a given level of output—hence, the downward shift of the aggregate supply curve. So, starting from point A, the economy moves over time along the aggregate demand curve, until it reaches point B. At point B, output is equal to the natural level of output. The price level is lower than it was at point A; by implication the real exchange rate is lower than it was at point A.

In words: As long as output is below the natural level of output, the price level decreases. The decrease in the price level over time leads to a steady real depreciation. This real depreciation then leads to an increase in output until output has returned to its natural level.

Make sure you understand this step. If you need a re-fresher, return to Section 7-1. ►

The result that the price level decreases along the path of adjustment comes from our assumption that the foreign price level is constant. If we had assumed instead that the foreign price level were increasing over time, what would be needed would be for the domestic price level to increase less than the foreign price level, or, put another way, for domestic inflation to be lower than foreign ◄ inflation for some time.

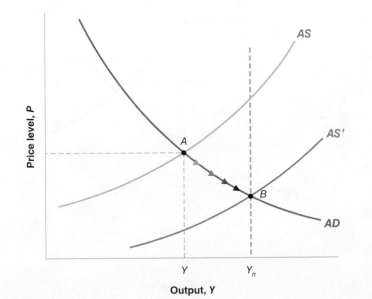

Figure 21-2

Adjustment under Fixed Exchange Rates

The aggregate supply curve shifts down over time, leading to a decrease in the price level, to a real depreciation, and to an increase in output. The process ends when output has returned to its natural level.

In the medium run, despite the fact that the nominal exchange rate is fixed, the economy still achieves the real depreciation needed to return output to its natural level. This is an important qualification to the conclusions we reached in the previous chapter—where we were focusing only on the short run:

- In the short run, a fixed nominal exchange rate implies a fixed real exchange rate.
- In the medium run, the real exchange rate can adjust even if the nominal exchange rate is fixed. This adjustment is achieved through movements in the price level.

The Case For and Against a Devaluation

The result that, even under fixed exchange rates, the economy returns to the natural level of output in the medium run is important. But it does not eliminate the fact that the process of adjustment may be long and painful. Output may remain too low and unemployment may remain too high for a long time.

Are there faster and better ways to return output to normal? The answer, within the model we have just developed, is a clear yes.

Suppose that the government decides, while keeping the fixed exchange rate regime, to allow for a one-time devaluation. For a given price level, a devaluation (a decrease in the nominal exchange rate) leads to a real depreciation (a decrease in the real exchange rate), and therefore to an increase in output. In other words, a devaluation shifts the aggregate demand curve to the right: Output is higher at a given price level.

This has a straightforward implication: A devaluation of the right size can take the economy directly from Y to Y_n. This is shown in Figure 21-3. Suppose the economy is initially at point A, the same point A as in Figure 21-2. The right size depreciation shifts the aggregate demand curve up from AD to AD', taking the equilibrium from points A to C. At point C, output is equal to the natural level of output, Y_n, and the real exchange rate is the same as at point B. (We know this because output is the same at points B and C. From equation (21.1), and without changes in G or T, this implies that the real exchange rate must also be the same.)

Figure 21-3

Adjustment with a Devaluation

The right size devaluation can shift aggregate demand to the right, leading the economy to go to point C. At point C, output is back to the natural level of output.

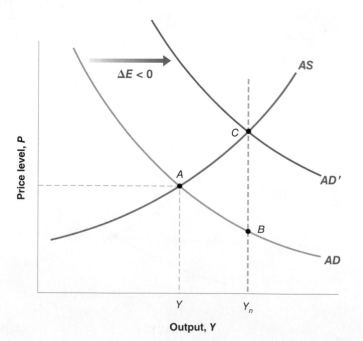

That the devaluation of the "right size" can return output to the natural level of output right away sounds too good to be true—and, in reality, it is. Achieving the "right size" devaluation—the devaluation that takes output to Y_n right away—is easier to achieve in a graph than in reality:

■ In contrast to our simple aggregate demand relation (21.1), the effects of the depreciation on output do not happen right away: As you saw in Chapter 19, the initial effects of a depreciation on output can be contractionary, as people pay more for imports, and the quantities of imports and exports have not yet adjusted. ◄ See Section 19-5 on the J-curve.

■ Also, in contrast to our simple aggregate supply relation (21.2), there is likely to be a direct effect of the devaluation on the price level. As the price of imported goods increases, the price of a consumption basket increases. This increase is likely to lead workers to ask for higher nominal wages, forcing firms to increase their prices as well.

But these complications do not affect the basic conclusion: A devaluation can hasten the return of output to its natural level. And so, whenever a country under fixed exchange rates faces either a large trade deficit or a severe recession, there is a lot of political pressure either to give up the fixed exchange rate regime altogether, or, at least, to have a one-time devaluation. Perhaps the most forceful presentation of this view was made 85 years ago by Keynes, who argued against Winston Churchill's decision to return the British pound in 1925 to its pre–World War I parity with gold. His arguments are presented in the Focus box "The Return of Britain to the Gold Standard: Keynes versus Churchill." Most economic historians believe that history proved Keynes right, and that overvaluation of the pound was one of the main reasons for Britain's poor economic performance after World War I.

Those who oppose a shift to flexible exchange rates or who oppose a devaluation argue that there are good reasons to choose fixed exchange rates, and that too much willingness to devalue defeats the purpose of adopting a fixed exchange rate regime in the first place. They argue that too much willingness on the part of governments to consider devaluations actually leads to an increased likelihood of exchange rate crises. To understand their arguments, we now turn to these crises: what triggers them, and what their implications might be.

21-2 Exchange Rate Crises under Fixed Exchange Rates

Suppose a country has chosen to operate under a fixed exchange rate. Suppose also that financial investors start believing there may soon be an exchange rate adjustment—either a devaluation or a shift to a flexible exchange rate regime accompanied by a depreciation.

We just saw why this might be the case:

■ The real exchange rate may be too high. Or, put another way, the domestic currency may be overvalued. In this case, a real depreciation is called for. Although this could be achieved in the medium run without a devaluation, financial investors might conclude that the government will take the quickest way out—and devalue.

Such an overvaluation often happens in countries that peg their nominal exchange rate to the currency of a country with lower inflation. Higher relative inflation implies a steadily increasing price of domestic goods relative to foreign goods, a steady real appreciation, and so a steady worsening of the trade position. As time passes, the need for an adjustment of the real exchange rate increases, and

The Return of Britain to the Gold Standard: Keynes versus Churchill

FOCUS

In 1925, Britain decided to return to the gold standard. The gold standard was a system in which each country fixed the price of its currency in terms of gold and stood ready to exchange gold for currency at the stated parity. This system implied fixed exchange rates between countries.

The gold standard had been in place from 1870 until World War I. Because of the need to finance the war, and to do so in part by money creation, Britain suspended the gold standard in 1914. In 1925, Winston Churchill, then Britain's Chancellor of the Exchequer (the British equivalent of Secretary of the Treasury in the United States), decided to return to the gold standard, and to return to it at the pre-war parity—that is, at the pre-war value of the pound in terms of gold. But, because prices had increased faster in Britain than in many of its trading partners, returning to the pre-war parity implied a large real appreciation: At the same nominal exchange rate as before the war, British goods were now relatively more expensive relative to foreign goods. (Go back to the definition of the real exchange rate, $\epsilon = EP/P^*$: The price level in Britain, P, had increased more than the foreign price level, P^*. At a given nominal exchange rate, E, this implied that ϵ was higher, that Britain suffered from a real appreciation.)

Keynes severely criticized the decision to return to the pre-war parity. In *The Economic Consequences of Mr. Churchill*, a book he published in 1925, Keynes argued as follows: If Britain were going to return to the gold standard, it should have done so at a lower price of currency in terms of gold; that is, at a lower nominal exchange rate than the pre-war nominal exchange rate. In a newspaper article, he articulated his views as follows:

"There remains, however, the objection to which I have never ceased to attach importance, against the return to gold in actual present conditions, in view of the possible consequences on the state of trade and employment. I believe that our price level is too high, if it is converted to gold at the par of exchange, in relation to gold prices elsewhere; and if we consider the prices of those articles only which are not the subject of international trade, and of services, i.e. wages, we shall find that these are materially too high—not less than 5 per cent, and probably 10 per cent. Thus, unless the situation is saved by a rise of prices elsewhere, the Chancellor is committing us to a policy of forcing down money wages by perhaps 2 shillings in the Pound.

I do not believe that this can be achieved without the gravest danger to industrial profits and industrial peace. I would much rather leave the gold value of our currency where it was some months ago than embark on a struggle with every trade union in the country to reduce money wages. It seems wiser and simpler and saner to leave the currency to find its own level for some time longer rather than force a situation where employers are faced with the alternative of closing down or of lowering wages, cost what the struggle may.

For this reason, I remain of the opinion that the Chancellor of the Exchequer has done an ill-judged thing—ill judged because we are running the risk for no adequate reward if all goes well."

Keynes's prediction turned out to be right. While other countries were growing, Britain remained in recession for the rest of the decade. Most economic historians attribute a good part of the blame to the initial overvaluation.

Source: "The Nation and Athenaeum," May 2, 1925

financial investors become more and more nervous. They start thinking that a devaluation might be coming.

- Internal conditions may call for a decrease in the domestic interest rate. As we have seen, a decrease in the domestic interest rate cannot be achieved under fixed exchange rates. But it can be achieved if the country is willing to shift to a flexible exchange rate regime. If a country lets the exchange rate **float** and then decreases its domestic interest rate, we know from Chapter 20 that this will trigger a decrease in the nominal exchange rate—a nominal depreciation.

As soon as financial markets believe a devaluation may be coming, then maintain the exchange rate requires an increase—often a large one—in the domestic interest rate.

To see this, return to the interest parity condition we derived in Chapter 18:

$$i_t = i_t^* - \frac{(E_{t+1}^e - E_t)}{E_t} \tag{21.3}$$

The expression to let a currency "float" is to allow a move from a fixed to a flexible exchange rate regime. A floating exchange rate regime is the same as a flexible exchange rate regime.

Because it is more convenient, we use the approximation, equation (18.4), rather than the original interest parity condition, equation (18.2).

In Chapter 18, we interpreted this equation as a relation among the *one-year* domestic and foreign nominal interest rates, the current exchange rate, and the expected exchange rate a year hence. But the choice of one year as the period was arbitrary. The relation holds over a day, a week, a month. If financial markets expect the exchange rate to be 2% lower a month from now, they will hold domestic bonds only if the one-month domestic interest rate exceeds the one-month foreign interest rate by 2% (or, if we express interest rates at an annual rate, if the annual domestic interest rate exceeds the annual foreign interest rate by 2% $\times$ 12 = 24%).

Under fixed exchange rates, the current exchange rate, E_t, is set at some level, say $E_t = \bar{E}$. If markets expect the parity will be maintained over the period, then $E^e_{t+1} = \bar{E}$, and the interest parity condition simply states that the domestic and the foreign interest rates must be equal.

Suppose, however, participants in financial markets start anticipating a devaluation—a decrease in the exchange rate. Suppose they believe that, over the coming month, there is a 75% chance the parity will be maintained and a 25% chance there will be a 20% devaluation. The term $(E^e_{t+1} - E_t)/E_t$ in the interest parity equation (21.3), which we assumed equal to zero earlier, now equals $0.75 \times 0\% + 0.25 \times (-20\%) = -5\%$ (a 75% chance of no change plus a 25% chance of a devaluation of 20%).

This implies that, if the central bank wants to maintain the existing parity, it must now set a monthly interest rate 5% higher than before—60% higher at an annual rate (12 months $\times$ 5% per month); 60% is the interest differential needed to convince investors to hold domestic bonds rather than foreign bonds! Any smaller interest differential, and investors will not want to hold domestic bonds.

What, then, are the choices confronting the government and the central bank?

◄ In most countries, the government is formally in charge of choosing the parity, the central bank is formally in charge of maintaining it. In practice, choosing and maintaining the parity are joint responsibilities of the government and the central bank.

- First, the government and the central bank can try to convince markets they have no intention of devaluing. This is always the first line of defense: Communiqués are issued, and prime ministers go on TV to reiterate their absolute commitment to the existing parity. But words are cheap, and they rarely convince financial investors.

◄ In the summer of 1998, Boris Yeltsin announced that the Russian government had no intention of devaluing the ruble. Two weeks later, the ruble collapsed.

- Second, the central bank can increase the interest rate, but by less than would be needed to satisfy equation (21.3)—in our example, by less than 60%. Although domestic interest rates are high, they are not high enough to fully compensate for the perceived risk of devaluation. This action typically leads to a large capital outflow, because financial investors still prefer to get out of domestic bonds and into foreign bonds. They sell domestic bonds, getting the proceeds in domestic currency. They then go to the foreign exchange market to sell domestic currency for foreign currency, in order to buy foreign bonds. If the central bank did not intervene in the foreign exchange market, the large sales of domestic currency for foreign currency would lead to a depreciation. If it wants to maintain the exchange rate, the central bank must therefore stand ready to buy domestic currency and sell foreign currency at the current exchange rate. In doing so, it often loses most of its reserves of foreign currency. (The mechanics of central bank intervention were described in the appendix to Chapter 20.)

- Eventually—after a few hours or a few weeks—the choice for the central bank becomes either to increase the interest rate enough to satisfy equation (21.3) or to validate the market's expectations and devalue. Setting a very high short-term domestic interest rate can have a devastating effect on demand and on output—no firm wants to invest; no consumer wants to borrow when interest rates are very high. This course of action makes sense only if (1) the perceived probability of a devaluation is small, so the interest rate does not have to be too high; and (2) the government believes markets will soon become convinced that no devaluation is coming, allowing domestic interest rates to decrease. Otherwise, the only option is to devalue. (All

The 1992 EMS Crisis

FOCUS

An example of the problems we discussed in this section is the exchange rate crisis that shook the European Monetary System in the early 1990s.

At the start of the 1990s, the European Monetary System (EMS) appeared to work well. The EMS had started in 1979. It was an exchange rate system based on fixed parities with bands: Each member country (among them, France, Germany, Italy, and, beginning in 1990, the United Kingdom) had to maintain its exchange rate vis-à-vis all other member countries within narrow bands. The first few years had been rocky, with many realignments—adjustment of parities—among member countries. From 1987 to 1992, however, there were only two realignments, and there was increasing talk about narrowing the bands further and even moving to the next stage—to the adoption of a common currency.

In 1992, however, financial markets became increasingly convinced that more realignments were soon to come. The reason was one we have already seen in Chapter 20, namely the macroeconomic implications of Germany's reunification. Because of the pressure on demand coming from reunification, the Bundesbank (the German central bank) was maintaining high interest rates to avoid too large an increase in output and an increase in inflation in Germany. While Germany's EMS partners needed lower interest rates to reduce a growing unemployment problem, they had to match the German interest rates to maintain their EMS parities. To financial markets, the position of Germany's EMS partners looked increasingly untenable. Lower interest rates outside Germany, and thus devaluations of many currencies relative to the Deutsche Mark (DM), appeared increasingly likely.

Throughout 1992, the perceived probability of a devaluation forced a number of EMS countries to maintain higher nominal interest rates than even those in Germany. Still, the first major crisis did not come until September 1992.

In early September 1992, the belief that a number of countries were soon going to devalue led to speculative attacks on a number of currencies, with financial investors selling in anticipation of an oncoming devaluation. All the lines of defense described earlier were used by the monetary authorities and the governments of the countries under attack. First, solemn communiqués were issued, but with no discernible effect. Then, interest rates were increased. For example, Sweden's overnight interest rate (the rate for lending and borrowing overnight) increased to 500% (expressed at an annual rate)! But interest rates were not increased by enough to prevent capital outflows and large losses of foreign exchange reserves by the central banks under pressure.

At that point, different countries took different courses of action: Spain devalued its exchange rate. Italy and the

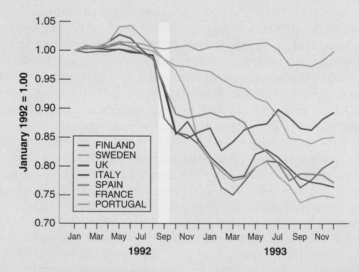

Figure 1 *Exchange Rates of Selected European Countries Relative to the Deutsche Mark, January 1992 to December 1993*

Source: IMF database

United Kingdom suspended their participation in the EMS. France decided to tough it out through higher interest rates until the storm was over. Figure 1 shows the evolution of the exchange rates relative to the DM for a number of European countries from January 1992 to December 1993: You can clearly see the effects of the September 1992 crisis , highlighted in the figure, and the ensuing depreciations/devaluations.

By the end of September, investors, by and large, believed that no further devaluations were imminent. Some countries were no longer in the EMS. Others had devalued but remained in the EMS, and those that had maintained their parity had shown their determination to stay in the EMS, even if this meant very high interest rates. But the underlying problem—the high German interest rates—was still present, and it was only a matter of time before the next crisis started. In November 1992, further speculation forced a devaluation of the Spanish peseta, the Portuguese escudo, and the Swedish krona. The peseta and the escudo were further devalued in May 1993. In July 1993, after yet another large speculative attack,

EMS countries decided to adopt large fluctuation bands (plus or minus 15%) around central parities, in effect moving to a system that allowed for very large exchange rate fluctuations.

This system with wider bands was kept until the adoption of a common currency, the Euro, in January 1999.

To summarize:

The 1992 EMS crisis came from the perception by financial markets that the high interest rates forced by Germany upon its partners under the rules of the EMS were becoming very costly.

The belief that some countries might want to devalue or get out of the EMS led investors to ask for even higher interest rates, making it even more costly for those countries to maintain their parity.

In the end, some countries could not bear the cost; some devalued, some dropped out. Others remained in the system, but at a substantial cost in terms of output. (For example, average growth in France from 1990 to 1996 was 1.2%, compared to 2.3% for Germany over the same period.)

these steps were very much in evidence during the exchange rate crisis which affected much of Western Europe in 1992. See the Focus box "The 1992 EMS Crisis.")

To summarize: Expectations that a devaluation may be coming can trigger an exchange rate crisis. Faced with such expectations, the government has two options:

■ Give in and devalue, or
■ Fight and maintain the parity, at the cost of very high interest rates and a potential recession. Fighting may not work anyway: The recession may force the government to change policy later on, or force the government out of office.

An interesting twist here is that a devaluation can occur even if the belief that a devaluation was coming was initially groundless. In other words, even if the government initially has no intention of devaluing, it might be forced to do so if financial markets believe that it will devalue: The cost of maintaining the parity would be a long period of high interest rates and a recession; the government might prefer to devalue instead.

This may remind you of our discussion of bank runs in ◄ Chapter 4. The rumor that a bank is in trouble may trigger a run on the bank and force it to close, whether or not there was truth to the rumor.

21-3 Exchange Rate Movements under Flexible Exchange Rates

In the model we developed in Chapter 20, there was a simple relation between the interest rate and the exchange rate: The lower the interest rate, the lower the exchange rate. This implied that a country that wanted to maintain a stable exchange rate just had to maintain its interest rate close to the foreign interest rate. A country that wanted to achieve a given depreciation just had to decrease its interest rate by the right amount.

In reality, the relation between the interest rate and the exchange rate is not so simple. Exchange rates often move even in the absence of movements in interest rates. Furthermore, the size of the effect of a given change in the interest rate on the exchange rate is hard to predict. This makes it much harder for monetary policy to achieve its desired outcome.

To see why things are more complicated, we must return once again to the interest parity condition we derived in Chapter 18 (equation (18.2)):

$$(1 + i_t) = (1 + i_t^*)\left(\frac{E_t}{E_{t+1}^e}\right)$$

As we did in Chapter 20 (equation (20.5)), multiply both sides by E_{t+1}^e, and reorganize to get

$$E_t = \frac{1 + i_t}{1 + i_t^*} E_{t+1}^e \tag{21.4}$$

Think of the time period (from t to $t + 1$) as one year. The exchange rate this year depends on the one-year domestic interest rate, the one-year foreign interest rate, and the exchange rate expected for next year.

We assumed in Chapter 20 that the expected exchange rate next year, E_{t+1}^e, was constant. But this was a simplification. The exchange rate expected one year hence is not constant. Using equation (21.4), but now for next year, it is clear that the exchange rate next year will depend on next year's one-year domestic interest rate, the one-year foreign interest rate, the exchange rate expected for the year after, and so on. So, any change in expectations of *current and future* domestic and foreign interest rates, as well as changes in the expected exchange rate in the far future, will affect the exchange rate today.

Let's explore this more closely. Write equation (21.4) for year $t + 1$ rather than for year t:

$$E_{t+1} = \frac{1 + i_{t+1}}{1 + i_{t+1}^*} E_{t+2}^e$$

The exchange rate in year $t + 1$ depends on the domestic interest rate and the foreign interest rate for year $t + 1$, as well as on the expected future exchange rate in year $t + 2$. So, the expectation of the exchange rate in year $t + 1$, held as of year t, is given by:

$$E_{t+1}^e = \frac{1 + i_{t+1}^e}{1 + i_{t+1}^{*e}} E_{t+2}^e$$

Replacing E_{t+1}^e in equation (21.4) with the expression above gives:

$$E_t = \frac{(1 + i_t)(1 + i_{t+1}^e)}{(1 + i_t^*)(1 + i_{t+1}^{*e})} E_{t+2}^e$$

The current exchange rate depends on this year's domestic and foreign interest rates, on next year's expected domestic and foreign interest rates, and on the expected exchange rate two years from now. Continuing to solve forward in time in the same way (by replacing E_{t+2}^e, E_{t+3}^e, and so on until, say, year $t + n$), we get:

$$E_t = \frac{(1 + i_t)(1 + i_{t+1}^e) \cdots (1 + i_{t+n}^e)}{(1 + i_t^*)(1 + i_{t+1}^{*e}) \cdots (1 + i_{t+n}^{*e})} E_{t+n+1}^e \tag{21.5}$$

Suppose we take n to be large, say 10 years (equation (21.5) holds for any value of n). This relation tells us that the current exchange rate depends on two sets of factors:

■ Current and expected domestic and foreign interest rates for each year over the next 10 years.
■ The expected exchange rate 10 years from now.

For some purposes, it is useful to go further and derive a relation among current and expected future domestic and foreign *real* interest rates, the current *real* exchange rate, and the expected future *real* exchange rate. This is done in Appendix 2 at the end of this chapter. (The derivation is not much fun, but it is a useful way of brushing up on the relation between real interest rates and nominal interest rates, and real exchange rates and nominal exchange rates.) Equation (21.5) is sufficient to make three important points, each outlined in more detail below:

■ The level of today's exchange rate will move one for one with the future expected exchange rate.

■ Today's exchange rate will move when future expected interest rates move in either country.

■ Because today's exchange rate moves with any change in expectations, the exchange rate will be volatile, that is, move frequently and perhaps by large amounts.

The basic lesson from Appendix 2: For all the statements below, you can put "real" in front of exchange rates and interest rates, and the statements will also hold.

Exchange Rates and the Current Account

Any factor that moves the expected future exchange rate, E^e_{t+n}, moves the current exchange rate, E_t. Indeed, if the domestic interest rate and the foreign interest rate are expected to be the same in both countries from t to $t + n$, the fraction on the right in equation (21.5) is equal to 1, so the relation reduces to $E_t = E^e_{t+n}$. In words: The effect of any change in the expected future exchange rate on the current exchange rate is one-for-one.

If we think of n as large (say 20 years or more), we can think of E^e_{t+n} as the exchange rate required to achieve current account balance in the medium or long run: Countries cannot borrow—run a current account deficit—forever, and will not want to lend—run a current account surplus—forever either. Thus, any news that affects forecasts of the current account balance in the future is likely to have an effect on the expected future exchange rate, and in turn on the exchange rate today. For example, the announcement of a larger-than-expected current account deficit may lead investors to conclude that a depreciation will eventually be needed to repay the increased debt. Thus, E^e_{t+n} will decrease, leading in turn to a decrease in E_t today.

News about the current account is likely to affect the exchange rate.

Exchange Rates and Current and Future Interest Rates

Any factor that moves current or expected future domestic or foreign interest rates between years t and $t + n$ moves the current exchange rate, too. For example, given foreign interest rates, an increase in current or expected future domestic interest rates leads to an increase in E_t—an appreciation.

This implies that any variable that causes investors to change their expectations of future interest rates will lead to a change in the exchange rate today. For example, the "dance of the dollar" in the 1980s that we discussed in earlier chapters—the sharp appreciation of the dollar in the first half of the decade, followed by an equally sharp depreciation later—can be largely explained by the movement in current and expected future U.S. interest rates relative to interest rates in the rest of the world during that period. During the first half of the 1980s, tight monetary policy and expansionary fiscal policy combined to increase both U.S. short-term interest rates and long-term interest rates; with the increase in long-term rates reflecting anticipations of high short-term interest rates in the future. This increase in both current and expected future interest rates was, in turn, the main cause of the dollar appreciation. Both fiscal and monetary policy were reversed in the second half of the decade, leading to lower U.S. interest rates and a depreciation of the dollar.

News about current and future domestic and foreign interest rates is likely to affect the exchange rate.

For more on the relation between long-term interest rates and current and expected future short-term interest rates, go back to Chapter 15.

Exchange Rate Volatility

The third implication follows from the first two. In reality, and in contrast to our analysis in Chapter 20, the relation between the interest rate, i_t, and the exchange rate, E_t, is anything but mechanical. When the central bank cuts the interest rate, financial markets have to assess whether this action signals a major shift in monetary policy and

We leave aside here other factors that move the exchange rate, such as perceptions of risk, which we discussed in a Focus box entitled "Sudden Stops, Safe Havens, and the Limits to the Interest Parity Condition" in Chapter 20.

the cut in the interest rate is just the first of many such cuts, or whether this cut is just a temporary movement in interest rates. Announcements by the central bank may not be very useful: The central bank itself may not even know what it will do in the future. Typically, it will be reacting to early signals, which may be reversed later. Investors also have to assess how foreign central banks will react: whether they will stay put or follow suit and cut their own interest rates. All this makes it much harder to predict what the effect of the change in the interest rate will be on the exchange rate.

Let's be more concrete. Go back to equation (21.5). Assume that $E^e_{t+n} = 1$. Assume that current and expected future domestic interest rates, and current and expected future foreign interest rates, are all equal to 5%. The current exchange rate is then given by:

If this reminds you of our discussion in Chapter 15 of how monetary policy affects stock prices, you are right. This is more than a coincidence: Like stock prices, the exchange rate depends very much on ▶ expectations of variables far into the future. How expectations change in response to a change in a current variable (here, the interest rate) determines the outcome.

$$E_t = \frac{(1.05)^n}{(1.05)^n} 1 = 1$$

Now consider a monetary expansion, which decreases the current domestic interest rate, i_t, from 5% to 3%. Will this lead to a decrease in E_t—to a depreciation—and if so by how much? The answer: It all depends:

Suppose the interest rate is expected to be lower for just one year, so the $n - 1$ expected future interest rates remain unchanged. The current exchange rate then decreases to:

$$E_t = \frac{(1.03)(1.05)^{n-1}}{(1.05)^n} = \frac{1.03}{1.05} = 0.98$$

The expansionary monetary policy leads to a decrease in the exchange rate—a depreciation—of only 2%.

Suppose instead that, when the current interest rate declines from 5% to 3%, investors expect the decline to last for five years (so $i_{t+4} = \cdots = i_{t+1} = i_t = 3\%$). The exchange rate then decreases to:

$$E_t = \frac{(1.03)^5(1.05)^{n-5}}{(1.05)^n} = \frac{(1.03)^5}{(1.05)^5} = 0.90$$

The expansionary monetary policy now leads to a decrease in the exchange rate—a depreciation—of 10%, a much larger effect.

You can surely think of still more outcomes. Suppose investors had anticipated that the central bank was going to decrease interest rates, and the actual decrease turns out to be smaller than they anticipated. In this case, the investors will revise their expectations of future nominal interest rates *upward*, leading to an appreciation rather than a depreciation of the currency.

When, at the end of the Bretton Woods period, countries moved from fixed exchange rates to flexible exchange rates, most economists had expected that exchange rates would be stable. The large fluctuations in exchange rates that followed—and have continued to this day—came as a surprise. For some time, these fluctuations were thought to be the result of irrational speculation in foreign exchange markets. It was not until the mid-1970s that economists realized that these large movements could be explained, as we have explained here, by the rational reaction of financial markets to news about future interest rates and the future exchange rate. This has an important implication:

A country that decides to operate under flexible exchange rates must accept the fact that it will be exposed to substantial exchange rate fluctuations over time.

21-4 Choosing between Exchange Rate Regimes

Let us now return to the question that motivates this chapter: Should countries choose flexible exchange rates or fixed exchange rates? Are there circumstances under which flexible rates dominate, and others under which fixed rates dominate?

Much of what we have seen in this and the previous chapter would seem to favor flexible exchange rates:

- Section 21-1 argued that the exchange rate regime may not matter in the medium run. But it is still the case that it matters in the short run. In the short run, countries that operate under fixed exchange rates and perfect capital mobility give up two macroeconomic instruments: the interest rate and the exchange rate. This not only reduces their ability to respond to shocks but can also lead to exchange rate crises.

- Section 21-2 argued that, in a country with fixed exchange rates, the anticipation of a devaluation leads investors to ask for very high interest rates. This in turn makes the economic situation worse and puts more pressure on the country to devalue. This is another argument against fixed exchange rates.

- Section 21-3 introduced one argument against flexible exchange rates, namely that, under flexible exchange rates, the exchange rate is likely to fluctuate a lot and be difficult to control through monetary policy.

On balance, it therefore appears that, from a macroeconomic viewpoint, flexible exchange rates dominate fixed exchange rates. This indeed appears to be the consensus that has emerged among economists and policy makers. The consensus goes like this:

In general, flexible exchange rates are preferable. There are, however, two exceptions: First, when a group of countries is already tightly integrated, a common currency may be the right solution. Second, when the central bank cannot be trusted to follow a responsible monetary policy under flexible exchange rates, a strong form of fixed exchange rates, such as a currency board or dollarization, may be the right solution.

Let us discuss in turn each of these two exceptions.

Common Currency Areas

Countries that operate under a fixed exchange rate regime are constrained to have the same interest rate. But how costly is that constraint? If the countries face roughly the same macroeconomic problems and the same shocks, they would have chosen similar policies in the first place. Forcing them to have the same monetary policy may not be much of a constraint.

This argument was first explored by Robert Mundell, who looked at the conditions under which a set of countries might want to operate under fixed exchange rates, or even adopt a common currency. For countries to constitute an **optimal currency area**, ◄ Mundell argued, they need to satisfy one of two conditions:

This is the same Mundell who put together the "Mundell–Fleming" model you saw in Chapter 20.

- The countries have to experience similar shocks. We just saw the rationale for this: If they experience similar shocks, then they would have chosen roughly the same monetary policy anyway.

- Or, if the countries experience different shocks, they must have high factor mobility. For example, if workers are willing to move from countries that are doing poorly to countries that are doing well, factor mobility rather than macroeconomic policy can allow countries to adjust to shocks. When the unemployment rate is high in a country, workers leave that country to take jobs elsewhere, and the unemployment rate in that country decreases back to normal. If the unemployment rate is low, workers come to the country, and the unemployment rate in the country increases back to normal. The exchange rate is not needed.

Each U.S. state could have its own currency that freely floated against other state currencies. But this is not the ▶ way things are: The United States is a common currency area, with one currency, the U.S. dollar.

Following Mundell's analysis, most economists believe, for example, that the common currency area composed of the 50 states of the United States is close to an optimal currency area. True, the first condition is not satisfied: Individual states suffer from different shocks. California is more affected by shifts in demand from Asia than the rest of the United States. Texas is more affected by what happens to the price of oil, and so on. But the second condition is largely satisfied. There is considerable labor mobility across states in the United States. When a state does poorly, workers leave that state. When it does well, workers come to that state. State unemployment rates quickly return to normal, not because of state-level macroeconomic policy, but because of labor mobility.

Clearly, there are also many advantages of using a common currency. For firms and consumers within the United States, the benefits of having a common currency are obvious; imagine how complicated life would be if you had to change currency every time you crossed a state line. The benefits go beyond these lower transaction costs. When prices are quoted in the same currency, it becomes much easier for buyers to compare prices, and competition between firms increases, benefiting consumers. Given these benefits and the limited macroeconomic costs, it makes good sense for the United States to have a single currency.

In adopting the euro, Europe made the same choice as the United States. When the process of conversion from national currencies to the euro ended in early 2002, the euro became the common currency for 11 European countries. (See the Focus box "The Euro: A Short History.") The count of countries using the euro at time of writing is now 17. Is the economic argument for this new common currency area as compelling as it is for the United States?

There is little question that a common currency yields for Europe many of the same benefits that it has for the United States. A report by the European Commission estimates that the elimination of foreign exchange transactions within the Euro area leads to a reduction in costs of 0.5% of the combined GDP of these countries. There are also clear signs that the use of a common currency is already increasing competition. When shopping for cars, for example, European consumers now search for the lowest euro price anywhere in the area using the euro. This has already led to a decline in the price of cars in a number of countries.

There is, however, less agreement on whether Europe constitutes an optimal common currency area. This is because neither of the two Mundell conditions appears to be satisfied. Although the future may be different, European countries have experienced very different shocks in the past. Recall our discussion of Germany's reunification and how differently it affected Germany and the other European countries. Furthermore, labor mobility is very low in Europe and likely to remain low. Workers move much less *within* European countries than they do within the United States. Because of language and cultural differences among European countries, mobility *between* countries is even lower.

The risk is, therefore, that one or more Euro area members suffers from a large decline in demand and output but is unable to use either the interest rate or the exchange rate to increase its level of economic activity. As we saw in Section 21-1, the adjustment can still take place in the medium run. But, as we also saw there, this adjustment is likely to be long and painful. This is no longer a hypothetical worry:

Some euro countries, in particular Greece and Portugal, are suffering from low output and a large trade deficit. Without the option of a devaluation, achieving a real

The Euro: A Short History

- As the European Union celebrated its 30th birthday in 1988, a number of governments decided the time had come to plan a move to a common currency. They asked Jacques Delors, the President of the European Union, to prepare a report, which he presented in June 1989.

  The Delors report suggested moving to a European Monetary Union (EMU) in three stages: Stage I was the abolition of capital controls. Stage II was the choice of fixed parities, to be maintained except for "exceptional circumstances." Stage III was the adoption of a single currency.

- Stage I was implemented in July 1990.

- Stage II began in 1994, after the exchange rate crises of 1992–1993 had subsided. A minor but symbolic decision involved choosing the name of the new common currency. The French liked "Ecu" (European currency unit), which is also the name of an old French currency. But its partners preferred euro, and the name was adopted in 1995.

- In parallel, EU countries held referendums on whether they should adopt the Maastricht treaty. The treaty,

negotiated in 1991, set three main conditions for joining the EMU: low inflation, a budget deficit below 3%, and a public debt below 60%. The Maastricht treaty was not very popular and, in many countries, the outcome of the popular vote was close. In France, the treaty passed with only 51% of the votes. In Denmark, the treaty was rejected.

- In 1996–1997, it looked as if few European countries would satisfy the Maastricht conditions. But a number of countries took drastic measures to reduce their budget deficit. When the time came to decide, in May 1998, which countries would be members of the Euro area, 11 countries made the cut: Austria, Belgium, Finland, France, Germany, Italy, Ireland, Luxembourg, The Netherlands, Portugal, and Spain. The United Kingdom, Denmark, and Sweden decided to stay out, at least at the beginning. Greece did not qualify initially, and didn't join until 2001. (In 2004, it was revealed that Greece had partly "cooked the books" and understated the size of its budget deficit in order to qualify.) Since then, five more small countries, Cyprus, Malta, Slovakia, Slovenia, and Estonia, have joined.

depreciation will require many years of high unemployment and downward pressure on wages and prices in Greece and Portugal relative to the rest of the Euro area. And, at the time of writing, worries are extending beyond these two countries. While in better economic shape than Greece and Portugal, other countries, notably Spain and Italy, are also in a slump, suffering from low output and high unemployment. As members of the Euro area, they also do not have the option of a devaluation. This, in turn, is leading to worries about the ability of these countries to limit their budget deficits and to repay their debt. This fiscal crisis, which we shall study at more length in Chapter 23, is the strongest challenge faced by Euro area countries since the creation of the euro.

Hard Pegs, Currency Boards, and Dollarization

The second case for fixed exchange rates is very different from the first. It is based on the argument that there may be times when a country may want to limit its ability to use monetary policy.

More on this in Chapter 22. ▶

Look at a country that has had very high inflation in the recent past—perhaps because it was unable to finance its budget deficit by any other means than through money creation, resulting in high money growth and high inflation. Suppose the country decides to reduce money growth and inflation. One way of convincing financial markets that it is serious about doing this is to fix its exchange rate: The need to use the money supply to maintain the parity then ties the hands of the monetary authority.

To the extent that financial markets expect the parity to be maintained, they will stop worrying about money growth being used to finance the budget deficit.

Note the qualifier "To the extent that financial markets expect the parity to be maintained." Fixing the exchange rate is not a magic solution. The country also needs to convince financial investors that, not only is the exchange rate fixed today, but it will remain fixed in the future. There are two ways in which it can do so:

■ Making the fixed exchange rate be part of a more general macroeconomic package. Fixing the exchange rate while continuing to run a large budget deficit will only convince financial markets that money growth will start again and that a devaluation is soon to come.

When Israel was suffering from high inflation in the 1980s, an Israeli finance minister proposed such a measure as part of a stabilization program. His proposal was perceived as an attack on the sovereignty of Israel, and he ▶ was quickly fired.

■ Making it symbolically or technically harder to change the parity, an approach known as a **hard peg**.

An extreme form of a hard peg is simply to replace the domestic currency with a foreign currency. Because the foreign currency chosen is typically the dollar, this is known as **dollarization**. Few countries are willing, however, to give up their currency and adopt the currency of another country. A less extreme way is the use of a **currency board**. Under a currency board, a central bank stands ready to exchange

Lessons from Argentina's Currency Board

When Carlos Menem became President of Argentina in 1989, he inherited an economic mess. Inflation was running at more than 30% per month. Output growth was negative.

Menem and his economy minister, Domingo Cavallo, quickly came to the conclusion that, under these circumstances, the only way to bring money growth—and, by implication, inflation—under control was to peg the peso (Argentina's currency) to the dollar, and to do this through a very hard peg. So, in 1991, Cavallo announced that Argentina would adopt a currency board. The central bank would stand ready to exchange pesos for dollars, on demand. Furthermore, it would do so at the highly symbolic rate of one dollar for one peso.

Both the creation of a currency board and the choice of a symbolic exchange rate had the same objective: to convince investors that the government was serious about the peg and to make it more difficult for future governments to give up the parity and devalue; and so, by making the fixed exchange rate more credible in this way, decrease the risk of a foreign exchange crisis.

For a while, the currency board appeared to work extremely well. Inflation, which had exceeded 2,300% in 1990, was down to 4% by 1994! This was clearly the result of the tight constraints the currency board put on money growth. Even more impressive, this large drop in inflation was accompanied by strong output growth. Output growth averaged 5% per year from 1991 to 1999.

Beginning in 1999, however, growth turned negative, and Argentina went into a long and deep recession. Was the recession due to the currency board? Yes and no:

■ Throughout the second half of the 1990s, the dollar steadily appreciated relative to the other major world currencies. Because the peso was pegged to the dollar, the peso also appreciated. By the late 1990s, it was clear that the peso was overvalued, leading to a decrease in demand for goods from Argentina, a decline in output, and an increase in the trade deficit.

■ Was the currency board fully responsible for the recession? No; there were other causes. But the currency board made it much harder to fight it. Lower interest rates and a depreciation of the peso would have helped the economy recover; but, under the currency board, this was not an option.

In 2001, the economic crisis turned into a financial and an exchange rate crisis, along the lines we described in Section 21-2:

■ Because of the recession, Argentina's fiscal deficit had increased, leading to an increase in government debt. Worried that the government might default on its debt, financial investors started asking for very high interest rates on government bonds, making the fiscal deficit

even larger, and, by doing so, further increasing the risk of default.

■ Worried that Argentina would abandon the currency board and devalue in order to fight the recession, investors started asking for very high interest rates in pesos, making it more costly for the government to sustain the parity with the dollar, and so making it more likely that the currency board would indeed be abandoned.

In December 2001, the government defaulted on part of its debt. In early 2002, it gave up the currency board and let the peso float. The peso sharply depreciated, reaching 3.75 pesos for 1 dollar by June 2002! People and firms that, given their earlier confidence in the peg, had borrowed in dollars found themselves with a large increase in the value of their dollar debts in terms of pesos. Many firms went bankrupt. The banking system collapsed. Despite the sharp real depreciation, which should have helped exports, GDP in Argentina fell by 11% in 2002, and unemployment increased to nearly 20%. In 2003, output growth turned positive and has been consistently high since—exceeding 8% a year—and unemployment has decreased. But it took until 2005 for GDP to reach its 1998 level again.

Does this mean that the currency board was a bad idea? Economists still disagree:

■ Some economists argue that it was a good idea but that it did not go far enough. They argue that Argentina should have simply dollarized (i.e., adopted the dollar outright as its currency and eliminated the peso altogether). Eliminating the domestic currency would have eliminated the risk of a devaluation. The lesson, they argue, is that even a currency board does not provide a sufficiently hard peg for the exchange rate. Only dollarization will do.

■ Other (indeed, most) economists argue that the currency board might have been a good idea at the start, but that it should not have been kept in place for so long. Once inflation was under control, Argentina should have moved from a currency board to a floating exchange rate regime. The problem is that Argentina kept the fixed parity with the dollar for too long, to the point where the peso was overvalued and an exchange rate crisis was inevitable.

The debate about "fix versus flex," about soft pegs, hard pegs, currency boards, and common currencies is likely to go on and has taken on new importance given the fiscal problems of the euro area.

For a fascinating, fun, and strongly opinionated book about Argentina's crisis, read Paul Blustein's *And the Money Kept Rolling In (and Out): Wall Street, the IMF, and the Bankrupting of Argentina* (Public Affairs, 2005).

foreign currency for domestic currency at the official exchange rate set by the government; furthermore, the bank cannot engage in open market operations (that is, buy or sell government bonds).

Perhaps the best known example of a currency board is that adopted by Argentina in 1991 but abandoned in a crisis at the end of 2001. The story is told in the Focus box "Lessons from Argentina's Currency Board." Economists differ on what conclusions one should draw from what happened in Argentina. Some conclude that currency boards are not *hard* enough: They do not prevent exchange rate crises. So, if a country decides to adopt a fixed exchange rate, it should go all the way and dollarize. Others conclude that adopting a fixed exchange rate is a bad idea. If currency boards are used at all, they should be used only for a short period of time, until the central bank has reestablished its credibility and the country returns to a floating exchange rate regime.

Summary

- Even under a fixed exchange rate regime, countries can adjust their *real* exchange rate in the medium run. They can do so by relying on adjustments in the price level. Nevertheless, the adjustment can be long and painful. Exchange rate adjustments can allow the economy to adjust faster and thus reduce the pain that comes from a long adjustment.

- Exchange rate crises typically start when participants in financial markets believe a currency may soon be devalued. Defending the parity then requires very high interest rates, with potentially large adverse macroeconomic effects. These adverse effects may force the country to devalue, even if there were no initial plans for such a devaluation.

- The exchange rate today depends on both (1) the difference between current and expected future domestic interest rates, and current and expected future foreign interest rates; and (2) the expected future exchange rate.

  Any factor that increases current or expected future domestic interest rates leads to an increase in the exchange rate today.

Any factor that increases current or expected future foreign interest rates leads to a decrease in the exchange rate today.

Any factor that increases the expected future exchange rate leads to an increase in the exchange rate today.

- There is wide agreement among economists that flexible exchange regimes generally dominate fixed exchange rate regimes, except in two cases:

1. When a group of countries is highly integrated and forms an optimal currency area. (You can think of a common currency for a group of countries as an extreme form of fixed exchange rates among this group of countries.) For countries to form an optimal currency area, they must either face largely similar shocks, or there must be high labor mobility across these countries.

2. When a central bank cannot be trusted to follow a responsible monetary policy under flexible exchange rates. In this case, a strong form of fixed exchange rates, such as dollarization or a currency board, provides a way of tying the hands of the central bank.

Key Terms

gold standard, 452
float, 452
optimal currency area, 459
Maastricht treaty, 461

European Central Bank (ECB), 462
hard peg, 462
dollarization, 462
currency board, 462

Questions and Problems

• •

QUICK CHECK

All Quick Check questions and problems are available on MyEconLab.

1. Using the information in this chapter, label each of the following statements true, false, or uncertain. Explain briefly.

a. Britain's return to the gold standard caused years of high unemployment.

b. A sudden fear that a country is going to devalue may force an exchange rate crisis, even if the fear initially had no basis.

c. Because economies tend to return to their natural level of output in the medium run, there is a never a reason to devalue.

d. High labor mobility within Europe makes the euro area a good candidate for a common currency.

e. Changes in the expected level of the exchange rate far in the future have little effect on the current level of the exchange rate.

2. Consider a country operating under fixed exchange rates, with aggregate demand and aggregate supply given by equations (21.1) and (21.2).

$$AD : Y = Y\left(\frac{\bar{E}P}{P^*}, G, T\right)$$

$$AS : P = P^e (1 + m) F\left(1 - \frac{Y}{L}, z\right)$$

Assume that the economy is initially in medium-run equilibrium, with a constant price level and output equal to the natural level of output. Foreign output, the foreign price level, and the foreign interest rate are fixed throughout the problem. Assume that expected (domestic) inflation remains constant throughout the problem.

a. Draw an *AD–AS* diagram for this economy.

b. Now suppose there is an increase in government spending. Show the effects on the *AD–AS* diagram in the short run and the medium run. How do output and the price level change in the medium run?

c. What happens to consumption in the medium run?

d. What happens to the real exchange rate in the medium run? [*Hint*: Consider the effect on the price level you identified in part (b).] What happens to net exports in the medium run?

e. Given that the exchange rate is fixed, what is the domestic nominal interest rate? Does the increase in government spending affect the domestic nominal interest rate? What happens to the real interest rate in the medium run? (*Hint*: Remember that expected inflation remains constant by assumption.) What happens to investment in the medium run?

f. In a closed economy, how does an increase in government spending affect investment in the medium run? (Refer to Chapter 7 if you need a refresher.)

g. Comment on the following statement. "In a closed economy, government spending crowds out investment. In an open economy with fixed exchange rates, government spending crowds out net exports."

3. Nominal and real interest parity

In equation (18.4), we wrote the nominal interest parity condition as

$$i_t \approx i_t^* - \frac{E_{t+1}^e - E_t}{E_t}$$

In Appendix 2 to this chapter, we derive a real interest parity condition. We can rewrite the real interest parity condition in a manner analogous to equation (18.4):

$$r_t \approx r_t^* - \frac{(\epsilon_{t+1}^e - \epsilon_t)}{\epsilon_t}$$

a. Interpret this equation. Under what circumstances will the domestic real interest rate exceed the foreign real interest rate?

Assume that the one-year nominal interest rate is 10% in the domestic economy and 6% in the foreign economy. Also assume that inflation over the coming year is expected to be 6% in the domestic economy and 3% in the foreign economy. Suppose that interest parity holds.

b. What is the expected nominal depreciation of the domestic currency over the coming year?

c. What is the expected real depreciation over the coming year?

d. If you expected a nominal appreciation of the currency over the coming year, should you hold domestic or foreign bonds?

4. Devaluation and interest rates

Consider an open economy with a fixed exchange rate, $\bar{E}$. Throughout the problem, assume that the foreign interest rate, i*, remains constant.

a. Suppose that financial market participants believe that the government is committed to a fixed exchange rate. What is the expected exchange rate? According to the interest parity condition, what is the domestic interest rate?

b. Suppose that financial market participants do not believe that the government is committed to a fixed exchange rate. Instead, they suspect that the government will either devalue or abandon the fixed exchange rate altogether and adopt a flexible exchange rate. If the government adopts a flexible exchange rate, financial market participants expect the exchange rate to depreciate from its current fixed value, $\bar{E}$. Under these circumstances, how does the expected exchange rate compare to $\bar{E}$? How does the domestic interest rate compare to i*?

c. Suppose that financial market participants feared a devaluation, as in part (b), and a devaluation actually occurs. The government announces that it will maintain a fixed exchange rate regime but changes the level of the fixed exchange rate to $\bar{E}'$, where $\bar{E}' < \bar{E}$. Suppose that financial market participants believe that the government will remain committed to the new exchange rate, $\bar{E}'$, and that there will be no further devaluations. What happens to the domestic interest rate after the devaluation?

d. Does a devaluation necessarily lead to higher domestic interest rates? Does fear of a devaluation necessarily lead to higher domestic interest rates?

DIG DEEPER

All Dig Deeper questions and problems are available on MyEconLab.

5. *Exchange rate overshooting*

a. Suppose there is a permanent 10% increase in M in a closed economy. What is the effect on the price level in the medium run? (*Hint*: If you need a refresher, review the analysis in Chapter 7.)

In a closed economy, we said that money was neutral because in the medium run, a change in the money stock affected only the price level. A change in the money stock did not affect any real variables. A change in the money stock is also neutral in an open economy with flexible exchange rates. In the medium run, a change in the money stock will not affect the real exchange rate, although it will affect the price level and the nominal exchange rate.

b. Consider an open economy with a flexible exchange rate. Write the expression for the real exchange rate. Suppose there is a 10% increase in the money stock and assume that it has the same effect on the price level in the medium run that you found in part (a). If the real exchange rate and the foreign price level are unchanged in the medium run, what must happen to the nominal exchange rate in the medium run?

c. Suppose it takes n years to reach the medium run (and everyone knows this). Given your answer to part (b), what happens to E_{t+n}^e (the expected exchange rate for n periods from now) after a 10% increase in the money stock?

d. Consider equation (21.5). Assume that the foreign interest rate is unchanged for the next n periods. Also assume, for the moment, that the domestic interest rate is unchanged for the next n periods. Given your answer to part (c), what happens to the exchange rate today (at time t) when there is a 10% increase in the money stock?

e. Now assume that after the increase in the money stock, the domestic interest rate decreases between time t and time $t + n$. Again assume that the foreign interest rate is unchanged. As compared to your answer to part (d), what happens to the exchange rate today (at time t)? Does the exchange rate move more in the short run than in the medium run?

The answer to part (e) is yes. In this case, the short-run depreciation is greater than the medium-run depreciation. This phenomenon is called overshooting and may help to explain why the exchange rate is so variable.

6. *Self-fulfilling exchange rate crises*

Consider an open economy with a fixed exchange rate, $\overline{E}$. Suppose that, initially, financial market participants believe that the government is committed to the fixed exchange rate. Suddenly, however, financial market participants become fearful that the government will devalue or allow the exchange rate

to float *(a decision that everyone believes will cause the currency to depreciate).*

a. What will happen to the expected exchange rate, E_{t+1}^e? (See your answer to Problem 4(b)).

Suppose that, despite the change in the expected exchange rate, the government keeps the exchange rate fixed today. Let UIP *stand for the uncovered interest parity condition.*

b. Draw an *IS–LM–UIP* diagram. How does the change in the expected exchange rate affect the *UIP* curve? As a result, how must the domestic interest rate change to maintain an exchange rate of $\overline{E}$?

c. Given your answer to part (b), what happens to the domestic money supply if the central bank defends the fixed exchange rate? How does the *LM* curve shift?

d. What happens to domestic output and the domestic interest rate? Is it possible that a government that was previously committed to a fixed exchange rate might abandon it when faced with a fear of depreciation (either through devaluation or abandonment of the fixed exchange rate regime)? Is it possible that unfounded fears about a depreciation can create a crisis? Explain your answers.

7. *Devaluation and credibility*

Consider an open economy with a fixed exchange rate, $\overline{E}$. Suppose that, initially, financial market participants believe that the government is committed to maintaining the fixed exchange rate. Let UIP *stand for the uncovered interest parity condition.*

Now suppose the central bank announces a devaluation. The exchange rate will remain fixed, but at a new level, $\overline{E}'$, such that $\overline{E}', < \overline{E}$. Suppose that financial market participants believe that there will be no further devaluations and that the government will remain committed to maintaining the exchange rate at $\overline{E}'$.

a. What is the domestic interest rate before the devaluation? If the devaluation is credible, what is the domestic interest rate after the devaluation? (See your answers to Problem 4.)

b. Draw an *IS–LM–UIP* diagram for this economy. If the devaluation is credible, how does the expected exchange rate change? How does the change in the expected exchange rate affect the *UIP* curve?

c. How does the devaluation affect the *IS* curve? Given your answer to part (b) and the shift of the *IS* curve, what would happen to the domestic interest rate if there is no change in the domestic money supply?

d. Given your answer to part (c), what must happen to the domestic money supply so that the domestic interest rate achieves the value you identified in part (a)? How does the *LM* curve shift?

e. How is domestic output affected by the devaluation?

f. Suppose that devaluation is not credible in the sense that the devaluation leads financial market participants to expect another devaluation in the future. How does the fear of further devaluation affect the expected exchange rate? How will the expected exchange rate in this case, where devaluation is not credible, compare to your answer to part (b)? Explain in words. Given this effect on the expected exchange rate, what must happen to the domestic interest rate, as compared to your answer to part (a), to maintain the new fixed exchange rate?

EXPLORE FURTHER

8. Exchange rates and expectations

In this chapter, we emphasized that expectations have an important effect on the exchange rate. In this problem, we use data to get a sense of how large a role expectations play. Using the results in Appendix 2 at the end of the book, you can show that the uncovered interest parity condition, equation (21.4), can be rewritten as

$$\frac{(E_t - E_{t-1})}{E_{t-1}} \approx (i_t - i_t^*) - (i_{t-1} - i_{t-1}^*) + \frac{(E_t^e - E_{t-1}^e)}{E_{t-1}^e}$$

In words, the percentage change in the exchange rate (the appreciation of the domestic currency) is approximately equal to the change in the interest rate differential (between domestic and foreign interest rates) plus the percentage change in exchange rate expectations (the appreciation of the expected domestic currency value). We shall call the interest rate differential the spread.

a. Go to the web site of the Bank of Canada (www.bank-banque-canada.ca) and obtain data on the monthly one-year Treasury bill rate in Canada for the past 10 years. Download the data into a spreadsheet. Now go to the web site of the Federal Reserve Bank of St. Louis (research.stlouisfed.org/fred2) and download data on the monthly U.S. one-year Treasury bill rate for the same time period. (You may need to look under "Constant Maturity" Treasury securities rather than "Treasury Bills.") For each

month, subtract the Canadian interest rate from the U.S. interest rate to calculate the spread. Then, for each month, calculate the change in the spread from the preceding month. (Make sure to convert the interest rate data into the proper decimal form.)

b. At the web site of the St. Louis Fed, obtain data on the monthly exchange rate between the U.S. dollar and the Canadian dollar for the same period as your data from part (a). Again, download the data into a spreadsheet. Calculate the percentage appreciation of the U.S. dollar for each month. Using the standard deviation function in your software, calculate the standard deviation of the monthly appreciation of the U.S. dollar. The standard deviation is a measure of the variability of a data series.

c. For each month, subtract the change in the spread [part (a)] from the percentage appreciation of the dollar [part (b)]. Call this difference the change in expectations. Calculate the standard deviation of the change in expectations. How does it compare to the standard deviation of the monthly appreciation of the dollar?

There are some complications we do not take into account here. Our interest parity condition does not include a variable that measures relative asset demand. We have explored the implications of changes in relative asset demands in Problem 7 at the end of Chapter 20. In addition, changes in interest rates and expectations may be related. Still, the gist of this analysis survives in more sophisticated work. In the short run, observable economic fundamentals do not account for much of the change in the exchange rate. Much of the difference must be attributed to changing expectations.

Further Readings

■ To get a sense of the problems of adjustment under a common currency, read Olivier Blanchard, "Adjustment within the Euro. The Difficult Case of Portugal," http://economics.mit.edu/files/740

■ For a skeptical view of the euro, read Martin Feldstein, "The European Central Bank and the Euro: The First Year," 2000, http://www.nber.org/papers/w7517, and "The Euro and the Stability Pact," 2005, http://www.nber.org/papers/w11249

APPENDIX 1: Deriving Aggregate Demand under Fixed Exchange Rates

To derive the aggregate demand for goods, start from the condition for goods market equilibrium we derived in Chapter 20, equation (20.1):

$$Y = C(Y - T) + I(Y, r) + G + NX(Y, Y^*, \epsilon)$$

This condition states that, for the goods market to be in equilibrium, output must be equal to the demand for domestic goods—that is, the sum of consumption, investment, government spending, and net exports.

Next, recall the following relations:

■ The real interest rate, r, is equal to the nominal interest rate, i, minus expected inflation, π^e (see Chapter 14):

$$r \equiv i - \pi^e$$

■ The real exchange rate, ϵ, is defined as (see Chapter 18):

$$\epsilon = \frac{EP}{P^*}$$

- Under fixed exchange rates, the nominal exchange rate, E, is, by definition, fixed. Denote by $\overline{E}$ the value at which the nominal exchange rate is fixed, so:

$$E = \overline{E}$$

- Under fixed exchange rates and perfect capital mobility, the domestic interest rate, i, must be equal to the foreign interest rate, i^* (see Chapter 18):

$$i = i^*$$

Using these four relations, rewrite equation (21.1) as:

$$Y = C(Y - T) + I(Y, i^* - \pi^e) + G + NX\left(Y, Y^*, \frac{\overline{E}P}{P^*}\right)$$

This is a rich—and complicated—equilibrium condition. It tells us that, in an open economy with fixed exchange rates, equilibrium output (or, more precisely, the level of output implied by equilibrium in the goods, financial, and foreign exchange markets) depends on:

- Government spending, G, and taxes, T. An increase in government spending increases output. So does a decrease in taxes.
- The foreign nominal interest rate, i^*, minus expected inflation, π^e. An increase in the foreign nominal interest rate requires a parallel increase in the domestic nominal interest rate. Given expected inflation, this increase in the domestic nominal interest rate leads to an increase in the domestic real interest rate, and so to lower demand and lower output.

- Foreign output, Y^*. An increase in foreign output increases exports, so increases net exports. The increase in net exports increases domestic output.
- The real exchange rate, ϵ, is equal to the fixed nominal exchange rate, $\overline{E}$, times the domestic price level, P, divided by the foreign price level, P^*. A decrease in the real exchange rate—equivalently, a real depreciation—leads to an increase in net exports, and so an increase in output.

We focused in this chapter on the effects of only three of these variables: the real exchange rate, government spending, and taxes. We shall therefore write:

$$Y = Y\left(\frac{\overline{E}P}{P^*}, G, T\right)$$
$$(\,-\,,\,+\,,\,-\,)$$

All the other variables that affect demand are taken as given and, to simplify notation, are simply omitted from the relation. This gives us equation (21.1) in the text.

Equation (21.1) gives us the *aggregate demand relation*, the relation between output and the price level implied by equilibrium in the goods market and in financial markets.

Note that, in the closed economy, we had to use both the *IS* and the *LM* relations to derive the aggregate demand relation. Under fixed exchange rates, we do not need the *LM* relation. The reason is that the nominal interest rate, rather than being determined jointly by the *IS* and *LM* relations, is determined by the foreign interest rate. (The *LM* relation still holds, but, as we saw in Chapter 20, it simply determines the money stock.)

APPENDIX 2: The Real Exchange Rate and Domestic and Foreign Real Interest Rates

We derived in Section 21-3 a relation among the current nominal exchange rate, current and expected future domestic and foreign nominal interest rates, and the expected future nominal exchange rate (equation (21.5)). This appendix derives a similar relation, but in terms of real interest rates and the real exchange rate. It then briefly discusses how this alternative relation can be used to think about movements in the real exchange rate.

Deriving the Real Interest Parity Condition

Start from the nominal interest parity condition, equation (19.2):

$$(1 + i_t) = (1 + i_t^*)\frac{E_t}{E_{t+1}^e}$$

Recall the definition of the real interest rate from Chapter 14, equation (14.3):

$$(1 + r_t) = \frac{(1 + i_t)}{(1 + \pi_{t+1}^e)}$$

where $\pi_{t+1}^e \equiv (P_{t+1}^e - P_t)/P_t$ is the expected rate of inflation. Similarly, the foreign real interest rate is given by:

$$(1 + r_t^*) = \frac{(1 + i_t^*)}{(1 + \pi_{t+1}^{*e})}$$

where $\pi_{t+1}^{*e} \equiv (P_{t+1}^{*e} - P_t^*)/P_t^*$ is the expected foreign rate of inflation.

Use these two relations to eliminate nominal interest rates in the interest parity condition, so:

$$(1 + r_t) = (1 + r_t^*)\left[\frac{E_t}{E_{t+1}^e}\frac{(1 + \pi_{t+1}^{*e})}{(1 + \pi_{t+1}^e)}\right] \quad (21.A1)$$

Note from the definition of inflation that $(1 + \pi_{t+1}^e) = P_{t+1}^e/P_t$ and, similarly, $(1 + \pi_{t+1}^{*e}) = P_{t+1}^{*e}/P_t^*$.

Using these two relations in the term in brackets gives:

$$\frac{E_t}{E_{t+1}^e}\frac{(1 + \pi_{t+1}^{*e})}{(1 + \pi_{t+1}^e)} = \frac{E_t}{E_{t+1}^e}\frac{P_{t+1}^{*e}}{P_t^*}\frac{P_t}{P_{t+1}^e}$$

Reorganizing terms:

$$\frac{E_t\, P^{*e}_{t+1}\, P_t}{E^e_{t+1}\, P^*_t P^e_{t+1}} = \frac{E_t\, P_t/P^*_t}{E^e_{t+1}P^e_{t+1}/P^{*e}_{t+1}}$$

Using the definition of the real exchange rate:

$$\frac{E_t\, P_t/P^*_t}{E^e_{t+1}P^e_{t+1}/P^{*e}_{t+1}} = \frac{\epsilon_t}{\epsilon^e_{t+1}}$$

Replacing in equation (21.A1) gives:

$$(1 + r_t) = (1 + r^*_t)\frac{\epsilon_t}{\epsilon^e_{t+1}}$$

or, equivalently,

$$\epsilon_t = \frac{1 + r_t}{1 + r^*_t}\, \epsilon^e_{t+1} \qquad (21.A2)$$

The real exchange rate today depends on the domestic and foreign real interest rates this year and the expected future real exchange rate next year. This equation corresponds to equation (21.4) in the text, but now in terms of the real rather than nominal exchange and interest rates.

Solving the Real Interest Parity Condition Forward

The next step is to solve equation (21.A2) forward, in the same way as we did it for equation (21.4). The equation above implies that the real exchange rate in year $t + 1$ is given by:

$$\epsilon_{t+1} = \frac{1 + r^e_{t+1}}{1 + r^{*e}_{t+1}}\, \epsilon^e_{t+2}$$

Taking expectations, as of year t:

$$\epsilon^e_{t+1} = \frac{1 + r^e_{t+1}}{1 + r^{*e}_{t+1}}\, \epsilon^e_{t+2}$$

Replacing in the previous relation:

$$\epsilon_t = \frac{(1 + r_t)(1 + r^e_{t+1})}{(1 + r^*_t)(1 + r^{*e}_{t+1})}\, \epsilon^e_{t+2}$$

Solving for ϵ^e_{t+2} and so on gives:

$$\epsilon_t = \frac{(1 + r_t)(1 + r^e_{t+1})\cdots(1 + r^e_{t+n})}{(1 + r^*_t)(1 + r^{*e}_{t+1})\cdots(1 + r^{*e}_{t+n})}\, \epsilon^e_{t+n+1}$$

This relation gives the current real exchange rate as a function of current and expected future domestic real interest rates, of current and expected future foreign real interest rates, and of the expected real exchange rate in year $t + n$.

The advantage of this relation over the relation we derived in the text between the nominal exchange rate and nominal interest rates, equation (21.5), is that it is typically easier to predict the future real exchange rate than to predict the future nominal exchange rate. If, for example, the economy suffers from a large trade deficit, we can be fairly confident that there will have to be a real depreciation—that ϵ^e_{t+n} will have to be lower. Whether there will be a nominal depreciation—what happens to E^e_{t+n}—is harder to tell: It depends on what happens to inflation, both at home and abroad over the next n years.

Back to Policy

Nearly every chapter of this book has looked at the role of policy. The next three chapters put it all together.

Chapter **22**

Chapter 22 asks two questions: Given the uncertainty about the effects of macroeconomic policies, wouldn't it be better not to use policy at all? And, even if policy can in principle be useful, can we trust policy makers to carry out the right policy? The bottom lines: Uncertainty limits the role of policy. Policy makers do not always do the right thing. But, with the right institutions, policy can help and should be used.

Chapter **23**

Chapter 23 looks at fiscal policy. It reviews what we have learned, chapter by chapter, and then looks more closely at the implications of the government budget constraint for the relation between debt, spending, and taxes. It then focuses on the implications and the dangers of high levels of public debt, a central issue in advanced countries today.

Chapter **24**

Chapter 24 looks at monetary policy. It reviews what we have learned, chapter by chapter, and then focuses on three issues. First, the optimal rate of inflation: High inflation is bad, but how low a rate of inflation should the central bank aim for? Second, the best design policy: Should the central bank target money growth, or should it target inflation? What rule should the central bank use to adjust the interest rate? Third, the two particular challenges to monetary policy raised by the crisis: How to deal with the liquidity trap and how to best use macroprudential tools.

Should Policy Makers Be Restrained?

A t many points in this book, we saw how the right mix of fiscal policy and monetary policies could potentially help a country out of a recession, improve its trade position without increasing activity and igniting inflation, slow down an overheating economy, stimulate investment and capital accumulation, and so on.

This conclusion, however, appears to be at odds with frequent demands that policy makers be tightly restrained:

In the United States, there are regular calls for the introduction of a balanced-budget amendment to the Constitution. Such a call was the first item in the "Contract with America," the program drawn by Republicans for the mid–term U.S. elections in 1994, and reproduced in Figure 22-1. It has regularly resurfaced, most recently in July 2011, when it was proposed by a group of Republicans with close ties to the Tea Party. In Europe, the countries that adopted the euro signed a "Stability and Growth Pact," which required them to keep their budget deficit under 3% of GDP or else face large fines. As we shall see, that pact eventually failed, but the Europeans are now exploring ways of making it stronger.

Monetary policy is also under fire. For example, the charter of the central bank of New Zealand, written in 1989, defines monetary policy's role as the maintenance of price stability, to the exclusion of any other macroeconomic goal. In the summer of 2011, Governor Rick Perry of Texas, running for the Republican presidential nomination, declared, "If this guy [Fed Chair Ben Bernanke] prints more money between now and the election, I dunno what y'all would do to him in Iowa but we would treat him pretty ugly down in Texas. Printing more money to play politics at this particular time in American history is almost treacherous—or treasonous in my opinion." Rick Perry, and a number of other Republicans, want the Fed Chair to be bound by rules, to have much less discretion.

This chapter looks at the case for such restraints on macroeconomic policy.

Sections 22-1 and 22-2 look at one line of argument, namely that policy makers may have good intentions, but they end up doing more harm than good.

Section 22-3 looks at another—more cynical—line, that policy makers do what is best for themselves, which is not necessarily what is best for the country. ●

House Republican
Contract with America

A Program for Accountability

Weʼve listened to your concerns and we hear you loud and clear. If you give us the majority, on the first day of Congress, a Republican House will:

Force Congress to live under the same laws as every other American
Cut one out of three Congressional committee staffers
Cut the Congressional budget

Then, in the first 100 days there will be votes on the following 10 bills:

1. Balanced budget amendment and the line item veto: Itʼs time to force the government to live within its means and restore accountability to the budget in Washington.

2. Stop violent criminals: Letʼs get tough with an effective, able, and timely death penalty for violent offenders. Letʼs also reduce crime by building more prisons, making sentences longer and putting more police on the streets.

3. Welfare reform: The government should encourage people to work, not have children out of wedlock.

4. Protect our kids: We must strengthen families by giving parents greater control over education, enforcing child support payments, and getting tough on child pornography.

5. Tax cuts for families: Letʼs make it easier to achieve the American Dream: save money, buy a home, and send their kids to college.

6. Strong national defense: We need to ensure a strong national defense by restoring the essentials of our national security funding.

7. Raise the senior citizensʼ earning limit: We can put an end to government age discrimination that discourages seniors from working if they want.

8. Roll back government regulations: Letʼs slash regulations that strangle small business and letʼs make it easier for people to invest in order to create jobs and increase wages.

9. Common-sense legal reform: We can finally stop excessive legal claims, frivolous lawsuits, and overzealous lawyers.

10. Congressional term limits: Letʼs replace career politicians with citizen legislators. After all, politics shouldnʼt be a lifetime job.
(Please see reverse side to know if the candidate from your district has signed the Contract as of October 5, 1994.)

IF WE BREAK THIS CONTRACT, THROW US OUT, WE MEAN IT.

Figure 22-1

The Contract with America

22-1 Uncertainty and Policy

A blunt way of stating the first argument in favor of policy restraints is that those who know little should do little. The argument has two parts: Macroeconomists, and by implication the policy makers who rely on their advice, know little; and they should therefore do little. Letʼs look at each part separately.

How Much Do Macroeconomists Actually Know?

Macroeconomists are like doctors treating cancer. They know a lot, but there is a lot they donʼt know.

Take an economy with high unemployment, where the central bank is considering the use of monetary policy to increase economic activity. Assume that it has room to decrease the interest rate; in other words, leave aside the even more difficult issue of what to do if the economy is in the liquidity trap. Think of the sequence of links between a reduction in the interest rate that the central bank controls and an increase in output—all the questions the central bank faces when deciding whether, and by how much, to reduce the interest rate:

- Is the current high rate of unemployment above the natural rate of unemployment, or has the natural rate of unemployment itself increased (Chapter 6)?
- If the unemployment rate is close to the natural rate of unemployment, is there a significant risk that an interest rate reduction through monetary expansion will

474   Back to Policy   **Back to Policy**

lead to a decrease in unemployment below the natural rate of unemployment and cause an increase in inflation (Chapter 8)?

■ What will be the effect of the decrease in the short-term interest rate on the long-term interest rate (Chapter 15)? By how much will stock prices increase (Chapter 15)? By how much will the currency depreciate (Chapters 21 and 22)?

■ How long will it take for lower long-term interest rates and higher stock prices to affect investment and consumption spending (Chapter 16)? How long will it take for the J-curve effects to work themselves out and for the trade balance to improve (Chapter 19)? What is the danger that the effects come too late, when the economy has already recovered?

When assessing these questions, central banks—or macroeconomic policy makers in general—do not operate in a vacuum. They rely, in particular, on macroeconometric models. The equations in these models show how these individual links have looked in the past. But different models yield different answers. This is because they have different structures, different lists of equations, and different lists of variables.

Figure 22-2 shows an example of this diversity. This example comes from a study commissioned by the Brookings Institution—a research institute in Washington, D.C.—asking the builders of the 12 main macroeconometric models to answer a similar set of questions. (The models are described in the Focus box "Twelve Macroeconometric Models.") The goal of the study was to see how the answers would differ across models. One question was:

"Consider a case where the U.S. economy is growing at its normal growth rate, and where unemployment is at its natural rate; call this the *baseline* case. Suppose now that over the period of a year, the Fed increases money faster than in the baseline, so that after a year, nominal money is 4% higher than it would have been in the baseline case. From then on, nominal money grows at the same rate as in the baseline case, so the level of nominal money remains 4% higher than it would have been without the change in monetary policy. Suppose further that interest rates in the rest of the world remain unchanged. What will happen to U.S. output?"

Try to think of the answer you would give based on what you have learned so far. Then look at Figure 22-2. Are you surprised?

Figure 22-2

The Response of Output to a Monetary Expansion. Predictions from 12 Models

Although all 12 models predict that output will increase for some time in response to a monetary expansion, the range of answers regarding the size and the length of the output response is large.

Twelve Macroeconometric Models

The Brookings study described in the text was carried out in the late 1980s (to my knowledge, this is the last time such a systematic comparison of a large class of models was made for the United States), so some of the models used in the study are no longer in use; others have changed names. The typology presented in the box remains relevant, however, and reflects the different approaches to modeling that are followed today.

■ Two models, DRI (Data Resources Incorporated) and WHARTON, were commercial models. Commercial models are used to generate and sell economic forecasts to firms and financial institutions.

■ Five were used to forecast and help design policy. MCM (for MultiCountry Model) was used by the Federal Reserve Board in Washington for the conduct of monetary policy; INTERLINK was used by the OECD in Paris; COMPACT was used by the Commission of the European Union in Brussels; EPA was used by the Japanese Planning Agency. Each of these four models was constructed by one team of researchers doing all the work, that is, building submodels for countries or groups of countries and linking them through trade and financial flows. In contrast, the fifth model, LINK, was composed of individual country models—models constructed in each country by researchers from that country and then linked together by trade and financial relations. The advantage of this approach is that researchers from a particular country are likely to understand that country very well; the disadvantage is that different country models may have quite different structures and may be hard to link to each other.

■ Four models incorporated rational expectations explicitly: the LIVERPOOL model, based in England; MINIMOD, used at the International Monetary Fund; MSG, developed by Warwick McKibbin and Jeffrey Sachs at Harvard University; and the TAYLOR model—which we saw in Section 7-4—developed by John Taylor of Stanford University. Because it is technically difficult to solve for large models under rational expectations, these models are typically smaller models, with less detail than those listed above. But they are better at capturing the expectation effects of various policies. Thanks to more and more powerful computers, researchers are building larger and larger models with rational expectations. The modern versions of these models are called **dynamic stochastic general equilibrium**—or **DSGE** models—and are the subject of active research (more on them in Chapter 25).

■ The last model, VAR (for Vector AutoRegression, the technique of estimation used to build the model), developed by Christopher Sims and Robert Litterman at the University of Minnesota, was very different from the others (Sims was awarded the Nobel Prize for his work on VARs in 2011). VAR models are not structural models but rather statistical summaries of the relations between the different variables, without an explicit economic interpretation. Their strength is in their fit of the data, with a minimum of theoretical restrictions. Their weakness is that they are, essentially, a (very big) black box.

A description of the models and of the study is given in Ralph Bryant et al., *Empirical Macroeconomics for Interdependent Economies* (Brookings Institution, 1988). The study shows the effects not only of monetary policy but also of fiscal policy.

A more recent study, but one that looks only at DSGE models, is given by Gunter Coenen et al., Effects of Fiscal Stimulus in Structural Models, in the *American Economic Journal Macroeconomics*, 2012 4(1): pp. 22–68.

Another study, which looks at simulations from a set of models for Canada, is found in Denise Coté et al., A Comparison of Twelve Macroeconomic Models of the Canadian Economy, *Journal of Policy Modeling*, 2006 28(5): pp. 523–562.

Figure 22-2 shows the deviation of output from the baseline predicted by each of the 12 models. All 12 models predict that output increases for some time after the increase in money. After one year, the average deviation of output from the baseline is positive. But the range of answers is large, from nearly no change to close to an increase of 3%; even leaving out the most extreme prediction, the range is still more than 1%. Two years out, the average deviation is 1.2%; again leaving out the most extreme prediction, the range is still 2%. And six years out, the average deviation is 0.6%, and the answers range from −0.3% to 2.5%. In short, if we measure uncertainty by the range of answers from this set of models, there is indeed substantial uncertainty about the effects of policy.

Should Uncertainty Lead Policy Makers to Do Less?

Should uncertainty about the effects of policy lead policy makers to do less? In general, the answer is: yes. Consider the following example, which builds on the simulations we have just looked at.

Suppose the U.S. economy is in recession. The unemployment rate is 7% and the Fed is considering using monetary policy to expand output. To concentrate on uncertainty about the effects of policy, let's assume the Fed knows, with certainty, everything else. Based on its forecasts, it *knows* that, absent changes in monetary policy, unemployment will still be 7% next year. It knows that the natural rate of unemployment is 5%, and therefore it knows that the unemployment rate is 2% above the natural rate. And it knows, from Okun's law, that 1% more output growth for a year leads to a 0.4% reduction in the unemployment rate.

Under these assumptions, the Fed knows that if it could use monetary policy to achieve 5% more output growth over the coming year, the unemployment rate a year from now would be lower by 0.4 times 5% = 2%, so would be down to the natural rate of unemployment, 5%. By how much should the Fed increase the money supply?

Taking the average of the responses from the different models in Figure 22-2, an increase in the money supply of 4% leads to a 0.85% increase in output in the first year. Equivalently, a 1% increase in the money supply leads to a $0.85/4 = 0.21\%$ increase in output.

Suppose the Fed takes this average relation as holding with *certainty*. What it should then do is straightforward. To return the unemployment rate to the natural rate in one year requires 5% more output growth. And 5% output growth requires the Fed to increase the supply of money by $5\%/0.21 = 23.8\%$. The Fed should therefore increase the money supply by 23.8%. If the economy's response is equal to the *average* response from the 12 models, this increase in money will return the economy to the natural rate of unemployment at the end of the year.

Suppose the Fed actually increases money by 23.8%. But let's now take into account uncertainty, as measured by the *range* of responses of the different models in Figure 22-2. Recall that the range of responses of output to a 4% increase in money after one year varies from 0 to 3%; equivalently, a 1% increase in money leads to a range of increases in output from 0 to 0.75%. These ranges imply that an increase in money of 23.8% leads, across models, to an output response anywhere between 0% and 17.9% (23.8% × 0.75). These output numbers imply, in turn, a decrease in unemployment anywhere between 0% and 7%. Put another way, the unemployment rate a year hence could be anywhere between 7% and 0%!

The conclusion is clear: Given the range of uncertainty about the effects of monetary policy on output, increasing the money supply by 23.8% would be irresponsible. If the effects of money on output are as strong as suggested by one of the 12 models, unemployment by the end of the year could be 5% below the natural rate of unemployment, leading to enormous inflationary pressures. Given this uncertainty, the Fed should increase money by much less than 23.8%. For example, increasing money by 10% leads to a range for unemployment a year hence of 7% to 4%, clearly a safer range of outcomes.

Uncertainty and Restraints on Policy Makers

Let's summarize: There is substantial uncertainty about the effects of macroeconomic policies. This uncertainty should lead policy makers to be more cautious and to use less active policies. Policies should be broadly aimed at avoiding large prolonged recessions, slowing down booms, and avoiding inflationary pressure. The higher

In the real world, of course, the Fed does not know any of these things with certainty. It can only make forecasts. It does not know the exact ◀ value of the natural rate of unemployment, or the exact coefficient in Okun's law. Introducing these sources of uncertainty would reinforce our basic conclusion.

This example relies on the notion of *multiplicative uncertainty*—that because the effects of policy are uncertain, more active policies lead to ◀ more uncertainty. See William Brainard, "Uncertainty and the Effectiveness of Policy," *American Economic Review* 1867 57(2): pp. 411–425 unemployment or the higher inflation, the more active the policies should be. But they should stop well short of **fine tuning**, of trying to achieve constant unemployment or constant output growth.

These conclusions would have been controversial 20 years ago. Back then, there was a heated debate between two groups of economists. One group, headed by Milton Friedman from Chicago, argued that because of long and variable lags, activist policy is likely to do more harm than good. The other group, headed by Franco Modigliani from MIT, had just built the first generation of large macroeconometric models and believed that economists' knowledge was becoming good enough to allow for and increasingly fine tuning of the economy. Today, most economists recognize there is substantial uncertainty about the effects of policy. They also accept the implication that this uncertainty should lead to less active policies.

Note, however, that what we have developed so far is an argument for *self-restraint by* policy makers, not for *restraints on* policy makers. If policy makers understand the implications of uncertainty—and there is no particular reason to think they don't—they will, on their own, follow less active policies. There is no reason to impose further restraints, such as the requirement that money growth be constant or that the budget be balanced. Let's now turn to arguments for restraints *on* policy makers.

▶ Friedman and Modigliani are the same two economists who independently developed the modern theory of consumption we saw in Chapter 16.

22-2 Expectations and Policy

One of the reasons why the effects of macroeconomic policy are uncertain is the interaction of policy and expectations. How a policy works, and sometimes whether it works at all, depends not only on how it affects current variables but also on how it affects expectations about the future (this was the main theme of Chapter 17). The importance of expectations for policy goes, however, beyond uncertainty about the effects of policy. This brings us to a discussion of *games*:

Until 30 years ago, macroeconomic policy was seen in the same way as the control of a complicated machine. Methods of **optimal control**, developed initially to control and guide rockets, were being increasingly used to design macroeconomic policy. Economists no longer think this way. It has become clear that the economy is fundamentally different from a machine, even from a very complicated one. Unlike a machine, the economy is composed of people and firms who try to anticipate what policy makers will do, and who react not only to current policy but also to expectations of future policy. Hence, macroeconomic policy must be thought of as a **game** between the policy makers and "the economy"—more concretely, the people and the firms in the economy. So, when thinking about policy, what we need is not **optimal control theory** but rather **game theory.**

▶ Even machines are becoming smarter: HAL, the robot in the 1968 movie 2001: A *Space Odyssey*, starts anticipating what humans in the space ship will do. The result is not a happy one. (See the movie.)

Warning: When economists say "game," they do not mean "entertainment"; they mean **strategic interactions** between **players**. In the context of macroeconomic policy, the players are the policy maker on one side and people and firms on the other. The strategic interactions are clear: What people and firms do depends on what they expect policy makers to do. In turn, what policy makers do depends on what is happening in the economy.

Game theory has given economists many insights, often explaining how some apparently strange behavior makes sense when one understands the nature of the game being played. One of these insights is particularly important for our discussion of restraints here: Sometimes you can do better in a game by giving up some of your options. To see why, let's start with an example from outside economics—governments' policies toward hostage takers.

▶ Game theory has become an important tool in all branches of economics. Both the 1994 and the 2005 Nobel Prizes in Economics were awarded to game theorists: in 1994 to John Nash from Princeton, John Harsanyi from Berkeley, and Reinhard Selten from Germany (John Nash's life is portrayed in the movie A *Beautiful Mind*); in 2005 to Robert Aumann, from Israel, and Tom Schelling, from Harvard.

Hostage Takings and Negotiations

Most governments have a stated policy that they will not negotiate with hostage takers. The reason for this stated policy is clear: to deter hostage taking by making it unattractive to take hostages.

Suppose, despite the stated policy, someone is taken hostage. Now that the hostage taking has taken place anyway, why not negotiate? Whatever compensation the hostage takers demand is likely to be less costly than the alternative—the likelihood that the hostage will be killed. So the best policy would appear to be: Announce that you will not negotiate, but if somebody is taken hostage, negotiate.

Upon reflection, it is clear this would in fact be a very bad policy. Hostage takers' decisions do not depend on the stated policy, but on what they expect will actually happen if they take a hostage. If they know that negotiations will actually take place, they will rightly consider the stated policy as irrelevant. And hostage takings will take place.

So what is the best policy? Despite the fact that once hostage takings have taken place negotiations typically lead to a better outcome, the best policy is for governments to commit *not* to negotiate. By giving up the option to negotiate, they are likely to prevent hostage takings in the first place.

Let's now turn to a macroeconomic example based on the relation between inflation and unemployment. As you will see, exactly the same logic is involved.

This example was developed by Finn Kydland, from Carnegie Mellon and now at UC Santa Barbara, and Edward Prescott, then from Minnesota and now at Arizona State University, in "Rules Rather than Discretion: The Inconsistency of Optimal Plans," *Journal of Political Economy*, 1977 85(3): pp. 473–492. Kydland and Prescott were awarded the Nobel Prize in Economics in 2004.

Inflation and Unemployment Revisited

Recall the relation between inflation and unemployment we derived in Chapter 8 (equation (8.9), with the time indexes omitted for simplicity):

$$\pi = \pi^e - \alpha(u - u_n) \tag{22.1}$$

Inflation π depends on expected inflation π^e, and on the difference between the actual unemployment rate u and the natural unemployment rate u_n. The coefficient α captures the effect of unemployment on inflation, given expected inflation: When unemployment is above the natural rate, inflation is lower than expected; when unemployment is below the natural rate, inflation is higher than expected.

Suppose the Fed announces it will follow a monetary policy consistent with zero inflation. On the assumption that people believe the announcement, expected inflation (π^e) as embodied in wage contracts is equal to zero, and the Fed faces the following relation between unemployment and inflation:

$$\pi = -\alpha(u - u_n) \tag{22.2}$$

If the Fed follows through with its announced policy, it will choose an unemployment rate equal to the natural rate; from equation (22.2), inflation will be equal to zero, just as the Fed announced and people expected.

Achieving zero inflation and an unemployment rate equal to the natural rate is not a bad outcome. But it would seem the Fed can actually do even better:

A refresher: Given labor market conditions, and given their expectations of what prices will be, firms and workers set nominal wages. Given the nominal wages firms have to pay, firms then set prices. So, prices depend on expected prices and labor market conditions. Equivalently, price inflation depends on expected price inflation and labor market conditions. This is what is captured in equation (22.1).

For simplicity, we assume the Fed can choose the unemployment rate—and, by implication, the inflation rate—exactly. In doing so, we ignore the uncertainty about the effects of policy. This was the topic of Section 22-1, but it is not central here.

■ Recall from Chapter 8 that in the United States, α is roughly equal to 0.5. So equation (22.2) implies that, by accepting just 1% inflation, the Fed can achieve an unemployment rate of 2% below the natural rate of unemployment. Suppose the Fed—and everyone else in the economy—finds the trade-off attractive and decides to decrease unemployment by 2% in exchange for an inflation rate of 1%. This incentive to deviate from the announced policy once the other player has made his move—in this case, once wage setters have set the wage—is known in game theory as the **time inconsistency** of optimal policy. In our example, the Fed

If $\alpha = 0.5$, equation (22.2) implies $\pi = -0.5(u - u_n)$. If $\pi = 1\%$, then $(u - u_n) = -2\%$.

Chapter 22   Should Policy Makers Be Restrained?   **479**

Remember that the natural rate of unemployment is neither natural nor best in any sense (see Chapter 6). It may be reasonable for the Fed and everyone else in the economy to prefer an unemployment rate lower than the natural rate of unemployment.

can improve the outcome this period by deviating from its announced policy of zero inflation: By accepting some inflation, it can achieve a substantial reduction in unemployment.

■ Unfortunately, this is not the end of the story. Seeing that the Fed has increased money growth by more than it announced it would, wage setters are likely to smarten up and begin to expect positive inflation of 1%. If the Fed still wants to achieve an unemployment rate 2% below the natural rate, it will now have to accept 2% inflation. However, if it does achieve 2% inflation, wage setters are likely to increase their expectations of inflation further, and so on.

■ The eventual outcome is likely to be high inflation. Because wage setters understand the Fed's motives, expected inflation catches up with actual inflation, and the Fed will eventually be unsuccessful in its attempt to achieve an unemployment rate below the natural rate. In short, attempts by the Fed to make things better lead in the end to things being worse. The economy ends up with the *same unemployment rate* that would have prevailed if the Fed had followed its announced policy, but with *much higher inflation*.

How relevant is this example? Very relevant. Go back to Chapter 8: We can read the history of the Phillips curve and the increase in inflation in the 1970s as coming precisely from the Fed's attempts to keep unemployment below the natural rate of unemployment, leading to higher and higher expected inflation, and higher and higher actual inflation. In that light, the shift of the original Phillips curve can be seen as the adjustment of wage setters' expectations to the central bank's behavior.

So what is the best policy for the Fed to follow in this case? It is to make a credible commitment that it will not try to decrease unemployment below the natural rate. By giving up the option of deviating from its announced policy, the Fed can achieve unemployment equal to the natural rate of unemployment and zero inflation. The analogy with the hostage-taking example is clear: By credibly committing not to do something that would appear desirable at the time, policy makers can achieve a better outcome: no hostage takings in our earlier example, no inflation here.

Establishing Credibility

How can a central bank credibly commit not to deviate from its announced policy?

One way to establish its credibility is for the central bank to give up—or to be stripped by law of—its policy-making power. For example, the mandate of the central bank can be defined by law in terms of a simple rule, such as setting money growth at 0% forever. (An alternative, which we discussed in Chapter 21, is to adopt a hard peg, such as a currency board or even dollarization: In this case, instead of giving up its ability to use money growth, the central bank gives up its ability to use the exchange rate and the interest rate.)

Such a law surely takes care of the problem of time inconsistency. But the tight restraint it creates comes close to throwing the baby out with the bath water. We want to prevent the central bank from pursuing too high a rate of money growth in an attempt to lower unemployment below the natural unemployment rate. But—subject to the restrictions discussed in Section 22-1—we still want the central bank to be able to expand the money supply when unemployment is far above the natural rate, and contract the money supply when unemployment is far below the natural rate. Such actions become impossible under a constant-money-growth rule. There are indeed better ways to deal with time inconsistency. In the case of monetary policy, our discussion suggests various ways of dealing with the problem.

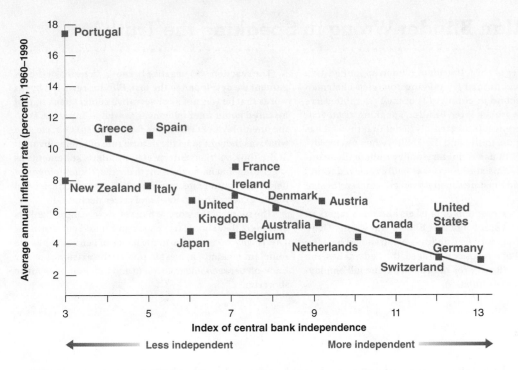

Figure 22-3

Inflation and Central Bank Independence

Across OECD countries, the higher the degree of central bank independence, the lower the rate of inflation.

Source: Vittorio Grilli, Donato Masciandaro, and Guido Tabellini, "Political and Monetary Institutions and Public Financial Policies in the Industrial Countries", *Economic Policy*, 1991 6(13): pp. 341–392.

A first step is to make the central bank independent. By an **independent central bank**, we mean a central bank where interest rate and money supply decisions are made independent of the influence of the currently elected politicians. Politicians, who face frequent reelections, are likely to want lower unemployment now, even if it leads to inflation later. Making the central bank independent, and making it difficult for politicians to fire the central banker, makes it easier for the central bank to resist the political pressure to decrease unemployment below the natural rate of unemployment.

This may not be enough, however. Even if it is not subject to political pressure, the central bank will still be tempted to decrease unemployment below the natural rate: Doing so leads to a better outcome in the short run. So, a second step is to give incentives to the central bankers to take the long view—that is, to take into account the long-run costs from higher inflation. One way of doing so is to give them long terms in office, so they have a long horizon and have the incentives to build credibility.

A third step may be to appoint a "conservative" central banker, someone who dislikes inflation very much and is therefore less willing to accept more inflation in exchange for less unemployment when unemployment is at the natural rate. When the economy is at the natural rate, such a central banker will be less tempted to embark on a monetary expansion. Thus, the problem of time inconsistency will be reduced.

These are the steps many countries have taken over the last two decades. Central banks have been given more independence. Central bankers have been given long terms in office. And governments typically have appointed central bankers who are more "conservative" than the governments themselves—central bankers who appear to care more about inflation and less about unemployment than the government. (See the Focus box "Was Alan Blinder Wrong in Speaking the Truth?")

Figure 22-3 suggests that giving central banks more independence has been successful, at least in terms of achieving lower inflation. The vertical axis gives the average inflation rate in 18 OECD countries over the period 1960–1990. The horizontal axis gives the value of an index of "central bank independence," constructed by looking at a number of legal provisions in the central bank's charter—for example, whether and

The figure is taken from a 1991 study and thus uses data only up to 1990. More recent evidence yields very similar conclusions.

Was Alan Blinder Wrong in Speaking the Truth?

In the summer of 1994, President Clinton appointed Alan Blinder, an economist from Princeton, vice-chairman (in effect, second in command) of the Federal Reserve Board. A few weeks later Blinder, speaking at an economic conference, indicated his belief that the Fed has both the responsibility and the ability, when unemployment is high, to use monetary policy to help the economy recover. This statement was badly received. Bond prices fell, and most newspapers ran editorials critical of Blinder.

Why was the reaction of markets and newspapers so negative? It was surely not that Blinder was wrong. There is no doubt that monetary policy can and should help the economy out of a recession. Indeed, the Federal Reserve Bank Act of 1978 requires the Fed to pursue full employment as well as low inflation.

The reaction was negative because, in terms of the argument we developed in the text, Blinder revealed by his words that he was not a conservative central banker, that he cared about unemployment as well as inflation. With the unemployment rate at the time equal to 6.1%, close to what was thought to be the natural rate of unemployment at the time, markets interpreted Blinder's statements as suggesting that he might want to decrease unemployment below the natural rate. Interest rates increased because of higher expected inflation—bond prices decreased.

The moral of the story: Whatever views central bankers may hold, they should try to look and sound conservative. This is why, for example, many heads of central banks are reluctant to admit, at least in public, the existence of any trade-off between unemployment and inflation, even in the short run.

A warning: Figure 22-3 shows correlation, not necessarily causality. It may be that countries that dislike inflation tend both to give more independence to their central bankers and have lower inflation. (This is another example of the difference between correlation and causality—discussed in Appendix 3 at the end of the book.)

how the government can remove the head of the bank. There is a striking inverse relation between the two variables, as summarized by the regression line: More central bank independence appears to be systematically associated with lower inflation.

Time Consistency and Restraints on Policy Makers

Let's summarize what we have learned in this section:

We have examined arguments for putting restraints on policy makers, based on the issue of time inconsistency.

When issues of time inconsistency are relevant, tight restraints on policy makers—like a fixed-money-growth rule in the case of monetary policy, or a balanced-budget rule in the case of fiscal policy—can provide a rough solution. But the solution has large costs because it prevents the use of macroeconomic policy altogether. Better solutions typically involve designing better institutions (like an independent central bank, or a better budget process) that can reduce the problem of time inconsistency while, at the same time, allowing the use of policy for the stabilization of output. This is not, however, easy to do.

22-3 Politics and Policy

We have assumed so far that policy makers were benevolent—that they tried to do what was best for the economy. However, much public discussion challenges that assumption: Politicians or policy makers, the argument goes, do what is best for themselves, and this is not always what is best for the country.

You have heard the arguments: Politicians avoid the hard decisions and they pander to the electorate, partisan politics leads to gridlock, and nothing ever gets done. Discussing the flaws of democracy goes far beyond the scope of this book. What we can do here is to briefly review how these arguments apply to macroeconomic policy, then look at the empirical evidence and see what light it sheds on the issue of policy restraints.

Games between Policy Makers and Voters

Many macroeconomic policy decisions involve trading off short-run losses against long-run gains—or, conversely, short-run gains against long-run losses.

Take, for example, tax cuts. By definition, tax cuts lead to lower taxes today. They are also likely to lead to an increase in demand, and therefore to an increase in output for some time. But unless they are matched by equal decreases in government spending, they lead to a larger budget deficit and to the need for an increase in taxes in the future. If voters are shortsighted, the temptation for politicians to cut taxes may prove irresistible. Politics may lead to systematic deficits, at least until the level of government debt has become so high that politicians are scared into action.

Now move on from taxes to macroeconomic policy in general. Again suppose that voters are shortsighted. If the politicians' main goal is to please voters and get reelected, what better policy than to expand aggregate demand before an election, leading to higher growth and lower unemployment? True, growth in excess of the normal growth rate cannot be sustained, and eventually the economy must return to the natural level of output: Higher growth now must be followed by lower growth later. But with the right timing and shortsighted voters, higher growth can win the elections. Thus, we might expect a clear **political business cycle**, with higher growth on average before elections than after elections.

We saw in Chapter 8 that, even if monetary policy is used to increase output in the short run, in the medium run, output returns to its natural level and unemployment to its natural rate.

You probably have heard these arguments before, in one form or another. And their logic appears convincing. The question is: How well do they fit the facts?

First, consider deficits and debt. The argument above would lead you to expect that budget deficits and high government debt have always been and will always be there. Figure 22-4 takes the long view. It gives the evolution of the ratio of government debt to GDP in the United States beginning in 1900 and shows that the reality is more complex.

Look first at the evolution of the ratio of debt to GDP from 1900 to 1980. Note that each of the three buildups in debt (represented by the shaded areas in the figure) was associated with special circumstances: World War I for the first buildup, the Great Depression for the second, and World War II for the third. These were times of unusually high military spending or unusual declines in output. Adverse circumstances—not pandering

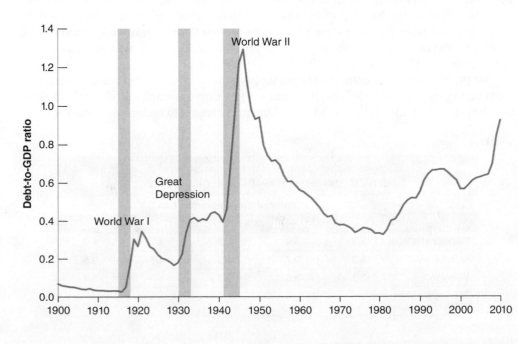

Figure 22-4

The Evolution of the U.S. Debt to GDP Ratio since 1900

The three major buildups of debt since 1900 have been associated with World War I, the Great Depression, and World War II. The buildup since 1980 appears different in nature.

Source: Historical Statistics of the United States, Department of Commerce, and Economic Report of the President, Tables B-1 and B-87

The precise relation between
the evolution of deficits, debt,
and the ratio of debt to GDP
is explored in detail in Chapter
23. For the moment, all you
need to know is that deficits
lead to increases in debt.

See the Focus box "The U.S.
Recession of 2001" in Chapter 5.

to voters—were clearly behind the large deficits and the resulting increase in debt during each of these three episodes. Note also how, in each of these three cases, the buildup was followed by a steady decrease in debt. In particular, note how the ratio of debt to GDP, which was as high as 130% in 1946, was steadily reduced to a postwar low of 33% in 1979.

The more recent evidence, however, fits the argument of shortsighted voters and pandering politicians much better. Clearly, the large increase since 2007 is due to the crisis. But, leaving it aside, note how the debt-to-GDP ratio increased from 33% in 1980 to 63% in 2007. This increase in debt can be largely traced back to two rounds of tax cuts, the first under the Reagan administration in the early 1980s, the second under the Bush administration in the early 2000s. Were these tax cuts, and the resulting deficits and increase in debt, best explained by pandering of politicians to shortsighted voters? We shall argue below that the answer is probably no, and that the main explanation lies in a game between political parties rather than in a game between policy makers and voters.

Before we do so, let us return to the political-business-cycle argument, that policy makers try to get high output growth before the elections so they will be reelected. If the political business cycle were important, we would expect to see faster growth before elections than after. Table 22-1 gives average output growth rates for each of the four years of each U.S. administration from 1948 to 2008, distinguishing between Republican and Democratic presidential administrations. Look at the last line of the table: Growth has indeed been highest on average in the last year of an administration. The average difference across years is small, however: 4.0% in the last year of an administration versus 3.3% in the first year. (We shall return below to another interesting feature in the table, namely the difference between Republican and Democratic administrations.) There is little evidence of manipulation—or at least of successful manipulation—of the economy to win elections.

Games between Policy Makers

Another line of argument shifts the focus from games between politicians and voters to games between policy makers.

Suppose, for example, that the party in power wants to reduce spending but faces opposition to spending cuts in Congress. One way of putting pressure both on Congress as well as on the future parties in power is to cut taxes and create deficits. As debt increases over time, the increasing pressure to reduce deficits may well, in turn, force Congress and the future parties in power to reduce spending—something they would not have been willing to do otherwise.

This strategy goes by the ugly
name of "Starve the Beast."

Or suppose that, either for the reason we just saw or for any other reason, the country is facing large budget deficits. Both parties in Congress want to reduce the deficit, but they disagree about the way to do it: One party wants to reduce deficits primarily

Table 22-1	Growth during Democratic and Republican Presidential Administrations since 1948 (percent per year)				
	Year of the Administration				
	First	**Second**	**Third**	**Fourth**	**Average**
Democratic	3.3	5.9	4.2	3.7	4.2
Republican	3.3	0.7	3.3	4.1	2.8
Average	3.3	2.8	3.6	4.0	3.4

Source: Calculated using Series GDPCA, from 1948 to 2008: Federal Reserve Economic Data (FRED) http://research.stlouisfed.org/fred2/

through an increase in taxes; the other wants to reduce deficits primarily through a decrease in spending. Both parties may hold out on the hope that the other side will give in first. Only when debt has increased sufficiently, and it becomes urgent to reduce deficits, will one party give up.

Game theorists refer to these situations as **wars of attrition**. The hope that the other side will give in leads to long and often costly delays. Such wars of attrition happen often in the context of fiscal policy, and deficit reduction occurs long after it should.

Wars of attrition arise in other macroeconomic contexts; for example, during episodes of hyperinflation. As we shall see in Chapter 23, hyperinflations come from the use of money creation to finance large budget deficits. Although the need to reduce those deficits is usually recognized early on, support for stabilization programs—which include the elimination of those deficits—typically comes only after inflation has reached such high levels that economic activity is severely affected.

These games go a long way in explaining the rise in the ratio of debt to GDP in the United States since the early 1980s. There is little doubt that one of the goals of the Reagan administration, when it decreased taxes from 1981 to 1983, was to slow down the growth of government spending. There is also little question that, by the mid-1980s, there was general agreement among policy makers that the deficits should be reduced. But, because of disagreements between Democrats and Republicans about whether this should happen primarily through tax increases or spending cuts, it was not until the late 1990s that deficit reduction was achieved. The motivation behind the Bush administration tax cuts of the early 2000s appears to be very similar to those of the Reagan administration. And the current fights between Congress and the Obama administration on how to reduce the large deficits triggered by the crisis are mostly driven by disagreements on whether deficit reduction should be achieved mainly through spending cuts or mainly through tax increases. At the time of this writing, we are clearly in the middle of a war of attrition.

Another example of games between political parties is the movements in economic activity brought about by the alternation of parties in power. Traditionally, Republicans have worried more than Democrats about inflation and worried less than Democrats about unemployment. So we would expect Democratic administrations to show stronger growth—and thus less unemployment and more inflation—than Republican administrations. This prediction appears to fit the facts quite well. Look at Table 22-1 again. Average growth has been 4.2% during Democratic administrations, compared to 2.8% during Republican administrations. The most striking contrast is in the second year: 5.9% during Democratic administrations compared to 0.7% during Republican administrations.

This raises an intriguing question: Why is the effect so much stronger in the administration's second year? It could just be a fluke. But the theory of unemployment and inflation we developed in Chapter 8 suggests a possible hypothesis: There are lags in the effects of policy, so it takes about a year for a new administration to affect the economy. And sustaining higher growth than normal for too long would lead to increasing inflation, so even a Democratic administration would not want to sustain higher growth throughout its term. Thus, growth rates tend to be much closer to each other during the second halves of Democratic and Republican administrations—more so than during first halves.

Politics and Fiscal Restraints

If politics sometimes lead to long and lasting budget deficits, can rules be put in place to limit these adverse effects?

Another example outside of economics: Think of the 2004–2005 National Hockey League lockout, where the complete season was canceled because owners and players could not reach an agreement. The National Basketball Association faced a similar lockout through the summer of 2011.

See the discussion in the Focus box "Monetary Contraction and Fiscal Expansion: The United States in the Early 1980s" in Chapter 20.

More on the current U.S. fiscal situation in Chapter 23.

The Stability and Growth Pact: A Short History.

The Maastricht treaty, negotiated by the countries of the European Union in 1991, set a number of convergence criteria that countries had to meet in order to qualify to join the Euro area (for more on the history of the euro, see the Focus box "The Euro: A Short History" in Chapter 21). Among them were two restrictions on fiscal policy: First, the ratio of the budget deficit to GDP had to be below 3%. Second, the ratio of its debt to GDP had to be below 60%, or at least "approaching this value at a satisfactory pace."

In 1997, would-be members of the Euro area agreed to make some of these restrictions permanent. The Stability and Growth Pact (SGP), signed in 1997, required members of the Euro area to adhere to the following fiscal rules:

- That countries commit to balance their budget in the medium run. That they present programs to the European authorities, specifying their objectives for the current and following three years in order to show how they are making progress toward their medium-run goal.
- That countries avoid excessive deficits, except under exceptional circumstances. Following the Maastricht treaty criteria, excessive deficits were defined as deficits in excess of 3% of GDP. Exceptional circumstances were defined as declines of GDP larger than 2%.
- That sanctions be imposed on countries that ran excessive deficits. These sanctions could range from 0.2 to 0.5% of GDP—so, for a country like France, up to roughly 10 billion dollars!

Figure 1 plots the evolution of budget deficits since 1990 for the Euro area as a whole. Note how from 1993 to 2000, budget balances went from a deficit of 5.8% of Euro area GDP to a surplus of 0.1%. The performance of some of the member countries was particularly impressive: Greece reduced its deficit from 13.4% of GDP to a reported 1.4% of GDP (it was discovered in 2004 that the Greek government had cheated in reporting its deficit numbers and that the actual improvement, although impressive, was less than reported; the deficit for 2000 is now estimated to have been 4.1%); Italy's deficit went from 10.1% of GDP in 1993 to only 0.9% of GDP in 2000.

Was the improvement entirely due to the Maastricht criteria and the SGP rules? Just as in the case of deficit reduction in the United States over the same period, the answer is no: The decrease in nominal interest rates, which decreased the interest payments on the debt, and the strong expansion of the late 1990s both played important roles. But, again as in the United States, the fiscal rules also played a significant role: The carrot—the right to become a member of the Euro area—was attractive enough to lead a number of countries to take tough measures to reduce their deficits.

Things turned around, however, after 2000. From 2000 on, deficits started increasing. The first country to break the limit was Portugal in 2001, with a deficit of 4.4%. The next two countries were France and Germany, both with deficits in excess of 3% of GDP in 2002. Italy soon followed. In each case, the government of the country decided it was more important to avoid a fiscal contraction that could lead to even slower output growth than to satisfy the rules of the SGP.

Faced with clear "excessive deficits" (and without the excuse of exceptional circumstances because output growth in each these countries was low but positive), European authorities found themselves in a quandary. Starting the excessive deficit procedure against Portugal, a small country, might have been politically feasible, although it is doubtful that Portugal would have ever been willing to pay the fine. Starting the same procedure against the two largest members of the Euro area, France and Germany, proved politically impossible. After an internal fight between the two main European authorities—the European Commission and the European Council—the European Commission wanted to proceed with the excessive deficit procedure, while the European Council, which represents the states, did not—the procedure was suspended.

The crisis made it clear that the initial rules were too inflexible. Romano Prodi, the head of the European Commission, admitted to that much: In an interview in October 2002, he stated, "I know very well that the Stability Pact is stupid, like all decisions that are rigid." And the attitudes of both France and Germany showed that the threat to impose large fines on countries with excessive deficits was simply not credible.

For two years, the European Commission explored ways to improve the rules so as to make them more flexible and, by implication, more credible. In 2005, a new, revised SGP was adopted. It kept the 3% deficit and 60% debt numbers as thresholds but allowed for more flexibility in deviating from the rules. Growth no longer had to be less than -2% for the rules to be suspended. Exceptions were also made if the deficit came from structural reforms, or from public investment. Fines were gone, and the plan was to rely on early public warnings as well as on peer pressure from other Euro area countries.

For a while, the ratio of the deficit to GDP declined, largely due to strong growth and higher revenues. The ratio reached a low of 0.5% in 2007. But the crisis, and the associated sharp decrease in revenues, led again to a sharp increase in budget deficits. In 2010, the ratio stood at close

Back to Policy   **Back to Policy**

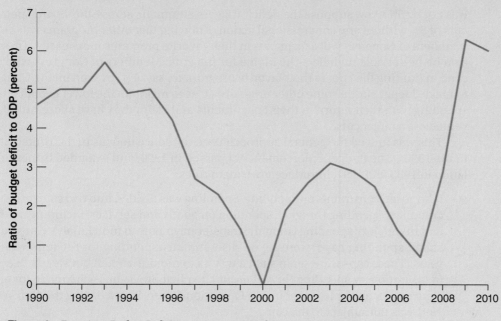

Figure 1 *Euro Area Budget Deficits as a Percentage of GDP, since 1990*

Source: Eurostat. General Government Deficit/Surplus, http://epp.eurostat.ec.europa.eu

to 6%, twice the SGP threshold; 23 out of 27 EU countries stood in violation of the 3% deficit limit, and it was clear that the rules had to be reconsidered. In March 2011 a new set of rules, known as the Euro Plus Pact, was adopted. It requires member countries to translate the SGP rules into national legislation, either through a constitutional amendment or a framework law. Whether or not these new rules work better than the initial pact remains to be seen.

A constitutional amendment to balance the budget each year, such as the amendment proposed by the Republicans in 1994, would surely eliminate the problem of deficits. But, just like a constant-money-growth rule in the case of monetary policy, it also would eliminate the use of fiscal policy as a macroeconomic instrument altogether. This is just too high a price to pay.

A better approach is to put in place rules that put limits either on deficits or on debt. This is, however, more difficult than it sounds. Rules such as limits on the ratio of the deficit to GDP or the ratio of debt to GDP are more flexible than a balanced-budget requirement; but they may still not be flexible enough if the economy is affected by particularly bad shocks. This has been made clear by the problems faced by the **Stability and Growth Pact** in Europe; these problems are discussed at more length in the Focus box "The Stability and Growth Pact: A Short History." More flexible or more complex rules, like rules that allow for special circumstances or rules that take into account the state of the economy, are harder to design and especially harder to enforce. For example, allowing the deficit to be higher if the unemployment rate is higher than the natural rate requires having a simple and unambiguous way of computing what the natural rate is, a nearly impossible task.

A complementary approach is to put in place mechanisms to reduce deficits, were such deficits to arise. Consider, for example, a mechanism that triggers automatic spending cuts when the deficit gets too large. Suppose the budget deficit is too large and it is desirable to cut spending across the board by 5%. Members of Congress will find it difficult to explain to their constituency why their favorite spending program was cut by 5%. Now suppose the deficit triggers automatic across-the-board spending cuts of 5% without any congressional action. Knowing that other programs will be cut, members of Congress will accept cuts in their favorite programs more easily. They will also be better able to deflect the blame for the cuts: Members of Congress who succeed in limiting the cuts to their favorite program to, say, 4% (by convincing Congress to make deeper cuts in some other programs so as to maintain the lower overall level of spending) can then return to their constituents and claim they have successfully prevented even larger cuts.

This was indeed the general approach used to reduce deficits in the United States in the 1990s. The Budget Enforcement Act passed in 1990, and extended by new legislation in 1993 and 1997, introduced two main rules:

- It imposed constraints on spending. Spending was divided into two categories: discretionary spending (roughly: spending on goods and services, including defense) and mandatory spending (roughly: transfer payments to individuals). Constraints, called **spending caps**, were set on discretionary spending for the following five years. These caps were set in such a way as to require a small but steady decrease in discretionary spending (in real terms). Explicit provisions were made for emergencies. For example, spending on Operation Desert Storm during the Gulf War in 1991 was not subject to the caps.
- It required that a new transfer program could only be adopted if it could be shown not to increase deficits in the future (either by raising new revenues or by decreasing spending on an existing program). This rule is known as the pay-as-you-go or the **PAYGO rule**.

The focus on spending rather than on the deficit itself had one important implication. If there was a recession, hence a decrease in revenues, the deficit could increase without triggering a decrease in spending. This happened in 1991 and 1992 when, because of the recession, the deficit increased—despite the fact that spending satisfied the constraints imposed by the caps. This focus on spending had two desirable effects: It allowed for a larger fiscal deficit during a recession—a good thing from the point of view of macroeconomic policy; and it decreased the pressure to break the rules during a recession—a good thing from a political point of view.

By 1998, deficits were gone, and, for the first time in 20 years, the federal budget was in surplus. Not all of the deficit reduction was due to the Budget Enforcement Act rules: A decrease in defense spending due to the end of the Cold War, and a large increase in tax revenues due to the strong expansion of the second half of the 1990s were important factors. But there is wide agreement that the rules played an important role in making sure that decreases in defense spending and increases in tax revenues were used for deficit reduction rather than for increases in other spending programs.

Once budget surpluses appeared, however, Congress became increasingly willing to break its own rules. Spending caps were systematically broken, and the PAYGO rule was allowed to expire in 2002. The lesson from this, as well as from the failure of the Stability and Growth Pact described in the Focus box "The Stability and Growth Pact: A Short History", is that, while rules can help, they cannot fully substitute for a lack of resolve from policy makers.

Summary

- The effects of macroeconomic policies are always uncertain. This uncertainty should lead policy makers to be more cautious and to use less active policies. Policies must be broadly aimed at avoiding prolonged recessions, slowing down booms, and avoiding inflationary pressure. The higher the level of unemployment or inflation, the stronger the policies should be. But they should stop short of fine tuning, of trying to maintain constant unemployment or constant output growth.

- Using macroeconomic policy to control the economy is fundamentally different from controlling a machine. Unlike a machine, the economy is composed of people and firms who try to anticipate what policy makers will do and who react not only to current policy but also to expectations of future policy. In this sense, macroeconomic policy can be thought of as a game between policy makers and people in the economy.

- When playing a game, it is sometimes better for a player to give up some of his options. For example: When a hostage taking occurs, it is better to negotiate with the hostage takers. But a government that credibly commits to not negotiating with hostage takers—a government that gives up the option of negotiation—is actually more likely to deter hostage takings.

- The same argument applies to various aspects of macroeconomic policy. By credibly committing not to use monetary policy to decrease unemployment below the natural rate of unemployment, a central bank can alleviate fears that money growth will be high, and in the process decrease both expected and actual inflation. When issues of time inconsistency are relevant, tight restraints on policy makers—such as a fixed-money-growth rule in the case of monetary policy—can provide a rough solution. But the solution can have large costs if it prevents the use of macroeconomic policy altogether. Better methods typically involve designing better institutions (such as an independent central bank) that can reduce the problem of time inconsistency without eliminating monetary policy as a macroeconomic policy tool.

- Another argument for putting restraints on policy makers is that policy makers may play games either with the public or among themselves, and these games may lead to undesirable outcomes. Politicians may try to fool a shortsighted electorate by choosing policies with short-run benefits but large long-term costs—for example, large budget deficits. Political parties may delay painful decisions, hoping that the other party will make the adjustment and take the blame. In cases like this, tight restraints on policy, such as a constitutional amendment to balance the budget, again provide a rough solution. Better ways typically involve better institutions and better ways of designing the process through which policy and decisions are made. However, the design and consistent implementation of such fiscal frameworks has proven very difficult in practice, as demonstrated both in the United States and the European Union.

Key Terms

dynamic stochastic general equilibrium (DSGE) models, 476

fine tuning, 478

optimal control, 478

game, 478

optimal control theory, 478

game theory, 478

strategic interactions, 478

players, 478

time inconsistency, 479

independent central bank, 481

political business cycle, 483

wars of attrition, 485

Euro Plus Pact, 487

Stability and Growth Pact, SGP, 487

spending caps, 488

PAYGO rule, 488

Questions and Problems

QUICK CHECK

All Quick Check questions and problems are available on MyEconLab.

1. Using the information in this chapter, label each of the following statements true, false, or uncertain. Explain briefly.

a. There is so much uncertainty about the effects of monetary policy that we would be better off not using it.

b. Elect a Democrat as president if you want low unemployment.

c. There is clear evidence of political business cycles in the United States: low unemployment during election campaigns and higher unemployment the rest of the time.

d. Rules are ineffective in reducing budget deficits.

e. Governments would be wise to announce a no-negotiation policy with hostage takers.

f. If hostages are taken, it is clearly wise for governments to negotiate with hostage takers, even if the government has announced a no-negotiation policy.

g. When a central bank announces a target inflation rate, it has no incentive to deviate from the target.

2. *Implementing a political business cycle*

You are the economic adviser to a newly elected president. In four years she will face another election. Voters want a low unemployment rate and a low inflation rate. However, you believe that voting decisions are influenced heavily by the values of unemployment and inflation in the last year before the election, and that the economy's performance in the first three years of a president's administration has little effect on voting behavior.

Assume that inflation last year was 10%, and that the unemployment rate was equal to the natural rate. The Phillips curve is given by

$$\pi_t = \pi_{t-1} - \alpha(u_t - u_n)$$

Assume that you can use fiscal and monetary policy to achieve any unemployment rate you want for each of the next four years. Your task is to help the president achieve low unemployment and low inflation in the last year of her administration.

a. Suppose you want to achieve a low unemployment rate (i.e., an unemployment rate below the natural rate) in the year before the next election (four years from today). What will happen to inflation in the fourth year?

b. Given the effect on inflation you identified in part (a), what would you advise the president to do in the early years of her administration to achieve low inflation in the fourth year?

c. Now suppose the Phillips curve is given by

$$\pi_t = \pi_t^e - \alpha(u_t - u_n)$$

In addition, assume that people form inflation expectations, π_t^e, based on consideration of the future (as opposed to looking only at inflation last year), and are aware that the president has an incentive to carry out the policies you identified in parts (a) and (b). Are the policies you described in parts (a) and (b) likely to be successful? Why or why not?

3. *Suppose the government amends the constitution to prevent government officials from negotiating with terrorists.*
What are the advantages of such a policy? What are the disadvantages?

4. *New Zealand rewrote the charter of its central bank in the early 1990s to make low inflation its only goal.*
Why would New Zealand want to do this?

DIG DEEPER
All Dig Deeper questions and problems are available on MyEconLab.

5. *Political expectations, inflation, and unemployment*

Consider a country with two political parties, Democrats and Republicans. Democrats care more about unemployment

than Republicans, and Republicans care more about inflation than Democrats. When Democrats are in power, they choose an inflation rate of π_D, and when Republicans are in power, they choose an inflation rate of π_R. We assume that

$$\pi_D > \pi_R$$

The Phillips curve is given by

$$\pi_t = \pi_t^e - \alpha(u_t - u_n)$$

An election is about to be held. Assume that expectations about inflation for the coming year (represented by π_t^e) are formed before the election. (Essentially, this assumption means that wages for the coming year are set before the election.) Moreover, Democrats and Republicans have an equal chance of winning the election.

a. Solve for expected inflation, in terms of π_D and π_R.

b. Suppose the Democrats win the election and implement their target inflation rate, π_D. Given your solution for expected inflation in part (a), how will the unemployment rate compare to the natural rate of unemployment?

c. Suppose the Republicans win the election and implement their target inflation rate, π_R. Given your solution for expected inflation in part (a), how will the unemployment rate compare to the natural rate of unemployment?

d. Do these results fit the evidence in Table 22-1? Why or why not?

e. Now suppose that everyone expects the Democrats to win the election, and the Democrats indeed win. If the Democrats implement their target inflation rate, how will the unemployment rate compare to the natural rate?

6. *Deficit reduction as a prisoner's dilemma game*

Suppose there is a budget deficit. It can be reduced by cutting military spending, by cutting welfare programs, or by cutting both. The Democrats have to decide whether to support cuts in welfare programs. The Republicans have to decide whether to support cuts in military spending.

The possible outcomes are represented in the following table:

		Welfare Cuts	
		Yes	No
Defense	Yes	$(R = 1, D = -2)$	$(R = -2, D = 3)$
Cuts	No	$(R = 3, D = -2)$	$(R = -1, D = -1)$

The table presents payoffs to each party under the various outcomes. Think of a payoff as a measure of happiness for a given party under a given outcome. If Democrats vote for welfare cuts, and Republicans vote against cuts in military spending, the Republicans receive a payoff of 3, and the Democrats receive a payoff of -2.

a. If the Republicans decide to cut military spending, what is the best response of the Democrats? Given this response, what is the payoff for the Republicans?

b. If the Republicans decide not to cut military spending, what is the best response of the Democrats? Given this response, what is the payoff for the Republicans?

c. What will the Republicans do? What will the Democrats do? Will the budget deficit be reduced? Why or why not? (A game with a payoff structure like the one in this problem, and that produces the outcome you have just described, is known as a *prisoner's dilemma*.) Is there a way to improve the outcome?

EXPLORE FURTHER

7. *Games, precommitment, and time inconsistency in the news*
    Current events offer abundant examples of disputes in which the parties are involved in a game, try to commit themselves to lines of action in advance, and face issues of time inconsistency. Examples arise in the domestic political process, international affairs, and labor–management relations.

   a. Choose a current dispute (or one resolved recently) to investigate. Do an internet search to learn the issues involved in the dispute, the actions taken by the parties to date, and the current state of play.

b. In what ways have the parties tried to pre-commit to certain actions in the future? Do they face issues of time inconsistency? Have the parties failed to carry out any of their threatened actions?

c. Does the dispute resemble a prisoner's dilemma game (a game with a payoff structure like the one described in Problem 6)? In other words, does it seem likely (or did it actually happen) that the individual incentives of the parties will lead them to an unfavorable outcome—one that could be improved for both parties through cooperation? Is there a deal to be made? What attempts have the parties made to negotiate?

d. How do you think the dispute will be resolved (or how has it been resolved)?

Further Readings

- If you want to learn more on these issues, a useful reference is Political Economy in Macroeconomics, by Alan Drazen (Princeton University Press, 2000).

- For an argument that inflation decreased as a result of the increased independence of central banks in the 1990s, read "Central Bank Independence and Inflation" in the 2009 Annual Report of the Federal Reserve Bank of St. Louis http://www.stlouisfed.org/publications/ar/2009/

- A leading proponent of the view that governments misbehave and should be tightly restrained is James Buchanan, from George Mason University. Buchanan received the Nobel Prize in 1986 for his work on public choice. Read, for example, his book with Richard Wagner, *Democracy in Deficit: The Political Legacy of Lord Keynes* (Academic Press, 1977).

- For an interpretation of the increase in inflation in the 1970s as the result of time inconsistency, see "Did Time Consistency Contribute to the Great Inflation?" by Henry Chappell and Rob McGregor, *Economics & Politics* 2004 16(3): pp. 233–251.

Fiscal Policy: A Summing Up

t the time of writing, fiscal policy is at the center of current policy discussions. In most advanced economies, the crisis has led to large budget deficits and a large increase in debt-to-GDP ratios. In Greece, the government has indicated that it will be unable to fully repay its debt and is negotiating with its creditors. The problem goes beyond Greece. In a number of countries, investors have started worrying about whether debt can indeed be repaid and are asking for higher interest rates to compensate for the risk of default. This calls for governments to strongly reduce deficits, stabilize the debt, and reassure investors. At the same time however, the recovery is weak and a fiscal contraction is likely to slow it down further, at least in the short run. Thus, governments face a difficult choice: Reduce deficits rapidly and reassure markets that they will pay their debt, at the risk of lower growth or even a recession; or reduce deficits more slowly in order to avoid further slowing the recovery, at the risk of not convincing investors that debt will be stabilized.

The purpose of this chapter is to review what we have learned about fiscal policy so far, to explore in more depth the dynamics of deficits and debt, and to shed light on the problems associated with high public debt.

Section 23-1 takes stock of what we have learned about fiscal policy in this book so far.

Section 23-2 looks more closely at the government budget constraint and examines its implications for the relation between budget deficits, the interest rate, the growth rate, and government debt.

Section 23-3 takes up three issues for which the government budget constraint plays a central role, from the proposition that deficits do not really matter, to how to run fiscal policy in the cycle, to whether to finance wars through taxes or through debt.

Section 23-4 discusses the dangers associated with high government debt, from higher taxes, to higher interest rates, to default, and to high inflation. ●

23-1 What We Have Learned

Let's review what we have learned about fiscal policy:

- In Chapter 3 we looked at how government spending and taxes affected demand and output in the short run.

  We saw how, in the short run, a fiscal expansion—increases in government spending, or decreases in taxes—increases output.

- In Chapter 5 we looked at the short-run effects of fiscal policy on output and on the interest rate.

  We saw how a fiscal expansion leads to an increase in output and an increase in the interest rate. We also saw how fiscal policy and monetary policy can be used together to affect both the level and the composition of output.

- In Chapter 7 we looked at the effects of fiscal policy in the short run and in the medium run.

  We saw that, in the medium run (that is, taking the capital stock as given), a fiscal expansion has no effect on output but is reflected in a different composition of spending. The interest rate is higher, and investment spending is lower.

- In Chapter 9 we looked at the case when the interest rate is equal to zero and the economy is in a liquidity trap.

  We saw that, in this case, conventional monetary policy cannot be used to increase output, and thus fiscal policy has an even more important role to play.

- In Chapter 11 we looked at how saving, both private and public, affects the level of capital accumulation and the level of output in the long run.

  We saw how, once capital accumulation is taken into account, a larger budget deficit, and, by implication, a lower national saving rate, decreases capital accumulation, leading to a lower level of output in the long run.

- In Chapter 17 we returned to the short-run effects of fiscal policy, taking into account not only fiscal policy's direct effects through taxes and government spending, but also its effects on expectations.

  We saw how the effects of fiscal policy depend on expectations of future fiscal and monetary policy. In particular, we saw how a deficit reduction may, in some circumstances, lead to an increase in output, even in the short run.

- In Chapter 19 we looked at the effects of fiscal policy when the economy is open in the goods market.

  We saw how fiscal policy affects both output and the trade balance, and we examined the relation between the budget deficit and the trade deficit. We saw how fiscal policy and exchange rate adjustments can be used together to affect both the level of output and its composition.

- In Chapter 20 we looked at the role of fiscal policy in an economy open in both goods markets and financial markets.

  We saw how, when capital is mobile, the effects of fiscal policy depend on the exchange rate regime. Fiscal policy has a stronger effect on output under fixed exchange rates than under flexible exchange rates.

- In Chapter 22 we looked at the problems facing policy makers in general, from uncertainty about the effects of policy to issues of time consistency and credibility. These issues arise in the analysis of fiscal policy as well as monetary policy. We looked at the pros and cons of putting restraints on the conduct of fiscal policy, from spending caps to a constitutional amendment to balance the budget.

In deriving these conclusions, we did not pay close attention to the government budget constraint—that is, the relation among debt, deficits, spending, and taxes. This relation is important, however, in understanding both how we got to where we are today and the choices faced by policy makers. It is the focus of the next section.

23-2 The Government Budget Constraint: Deficits, Debt, Spending, and Taxes

Suppose that, starting from a balanced budget, the government decreases taxes, creating a budget deficit. What will happen to the debt over time? Will the government need to increase taxes later? If so, by how much?

The Arithmetic of Deficits and Debt

To answer these questions, we must begin with a definition of the budget deficit. We can write the budget deficit in year t as

$$\text{deficit}_t = rB_{t-1} + G_t - T_t \tag{23.1}$$

All variables are in real terms:

- B_{t-1} is government debt at the end of year $t - 1$, or, equivalently, at the beginning of year t; r is the real interest rate, which we shall assume to be constant here. Thus rB_{t-1} equals the real interest payments on the government debt in year t.
- G_t is government spending on goods and services during year t.
- T_t is taxes minus transfers during year t.

In words: The budget deficit equals spending, including interest payments on the debt, minus taxes net of transfers.

Note two characteristics of equation (23.1):

- We measure interest payments as real interest payments—that is, the product of the *real* interest rate times existing debt—rather than as actual interest payments—that is, the product of the nominal interest rate and the existing debt. As the Focus box "Inflation Accounting and the Measurement of Deficits" shows, this is the correct way of measuring interest payments. Official measures of the deficit, however, use actual (nominal) interest payments and are therefore incorrect. When inflation is high, official measures can be seriously misleading. The correct measure of the deficit is sometimes called the **inflation-adjusted deficit**.
- For consistency with our earlier definition of G as spending on goods and services, G does not include transfer payments. Transfers are instead subtracted from T, so that T stands for *taxes minus transfers*. Official measures of government spending add transfers to spending on goods and services and define revenues as taxes, not taxes net of transfers.

These are only accounting conventions. Whether transfers are added to spending or subtracted from taxes makes a difference to the measurement of G and T, but clearly does not affect $G - T$, and therefore does not affect the measure of the deficit.

The **government budget constraint** then simply states that the *change in government debt during year t* is equal to the *deficit during year t*:

$$B_t - B_{t-1} = \text{deficit}_t$$

If the government runs a deficit, government debt increases. If the government runs a surplus, government debt decreases.

Do not confuse the words "deficit" and "debt." (Many journalists and politicians do.) Debt is a stock—what the government owes as a result of past deficits. The deficit is a flow—how much the government borrows during a given year.

Transfer payments are government transfers to individuals, such as unemployment benefits or Medicare.

Let G represent spending on goods and services; Tr, transfers; and Tax, total taxes. For simplicity, assume interest payments rB equal zero. Then

Deficit = G + Tr − Tax

This can be rewritten in two (equivalent) ways:

Deficit = G − (Tax − Tr)

The deficit equals spending on goods and services minus net taxes—that is, taxes minus transfers. This is the way we write it in the text.

Deficit = (G + Tr) − Tax

The deficit equals total spending—spending on goods and services plus transfers—minus total taxes. This is the way the government usually reports spending and revenues. Table A1-4 in Appendix 1 at the end of this book presents the U.S. federal budget in this way.

Inflation Accounting and the Measurement of Deficits

FOCUS

Official measures of the budget deficit are constructed (dropping the time indexes, which are not needed here) as nominal interest payments, iB, plus spending on goods and services, G, minus taxes net of transfers, T.

$$\text{official measure of the deficit} = iB + G - T$$

This is an accurate measure of the cash flow position of the government. If it is positive, the government is spending more than it receives and must therefore issue new debt. If it is negative, the government buys back previously issued debt.

But this is not an accurate measure of the *change in real debt*—that is, the change in how much the government owes, expressed in terms of goods rather than dollars.

To see why, consider the following example. Suppose the official measure of the deficit is equal to zero, so the government neither issues nor buys back debt. Suppose inflation is positive and equal to 10%. Then, at the end of the year, the real value of the debt has decreased by 10%. If we define—as we should—the deficit as the change in the real value of government debt, the government has decreased its real debt by 10% over the year. In other words, it has in fact run a budget surplus equal to 10% times the initial level of debt.

More generally: If B is debt and π is inflation, the official measure of the deficit overstates the correct measure by an amount equal to πB. Put another way, the correct measure of the deficit is obtained by subtracting πB from the official measure:

$$\begin{aligned}\text{correct measure of the deficit} &= iB + G - T - \pi B \\ &= (i - \pi)B + G - T \\ &= rB + G - T\end{aligned}$$

where $r = i - \pi$ is the (realized) real interest rate. The correct measure of the deficit is then equal to real interest payments plus government spending minus taxes net of transfers—this is the measure we have used in the text.

The difference between the official and the correct measures of the deficit equals πB. So, the higher the rate of inflation, π, or the higher the level of debt, B, the more inaccurate the official measure is. In countries in which both inflation and debt are high, the official measure may record a very large budget deficit, when in fact real government debt is decreasing. This is why we should always do the inflation adjustment before deriving conclusions about the position of fiscal policy.

Figure 1 plots the official measure and the inflation-adjusted measure of the (federal) budget deficit for the United States since 1969. The official measure shows a deficit in every year from 1970 to 1997. The inflation-adjusted measure shows instead alternating deficits and surpluses until the late 1970s. Both measures, however, show how much larger the deficit became after 1980, how things improved in the 1990s, and how they have deteriorated in the 2000s. Today, with inflation running at about 1–2% a year and the ratio of debt to GDP equal to roughly 90%, the difference between the two measures is roughly equal to 1–2% times 90%, or 0.9–1.8% of GDP.

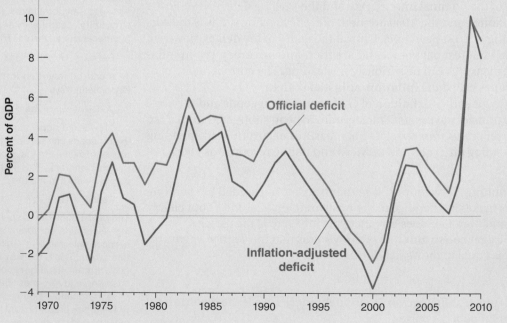

Figure 1 *Official and Inflation-Adjusted Federal Budget Deficits for the United States since 1969*

Source: Official Deficit and Debt as a Percent of GDP, Table B-79 Economic Report of the President; Inflation from Series CPIAUSL, Federal Reserve Economic Data (FRED) http://research.stlouisfed.org/fred2/

Using the definition of the deficit (equation (23.1)), we can rewrite the government budget constraint as

$$B_t - B_{t-1} = rB_{t-1} + G_t - T_t \qquad (23.2)$$

The government budget constraint links the change in government debt to the initial level of debt (which affects interest payments) and to current government spending and taxes. It is often convenient to decompose the deficit into the sum of two terms:

- Interest payments on the debt, rB_{t-1}.
- The difference between spending and taxes, $G_t - T_t$. This term is called the **primary deficit** (equivalently, $T_t - G_t$ is called the **primary surplus**).

Using this decomposition, we can rewrite equation (23.2) as

$$\underbrace{B_t - B_{t-1}}_{\text{Change in the debt}} = \underbrace{rB_{t-1}}_{\text{Interest Payments}} + \underbrace{(G_t - T_t)}_{\text{Primary Deficit}}$$

Or, moving B_{t-1} to the right side of the equation and reorganizing,

$$B_t = (1 + r)B_{t-1} + \underbrace{(G_t - T_t)}_{\text{Primary Deficit}} \qquad (23.3)$$

This relation states that the debt at the end of year t equals $(1 + r)$ times the debt at the end of year $t - 1$, plus the primary deficit during year t, $(G_t - T_t)$. Let's look at some of its implications.

Current versus Future Taxes

Consider first a one-year decrease in taxes for the path of debt and future taxes. Start from a situation where, until year 1, the government has balanced its budget, so that initial debt is equal to zero. During year 1, the government decreases taxes by 1 (think one billion dollars, for example) for one year. Thus, debt at the end of year 1, B_1, is equal to 1. The question we take up: What happens thereafter?

Full Repayment in Year 2

Suppose the government decides to fully repay the debt during year 2. From equation (23.3), the budget constraint for year 2 is given by

$$B_2 = (1 + r)B_1 + (G_2 - T_2)$$

If the debt is fully repaid during year 2, then the debt at the end of year 2 is equal to zero: $B_2 = 0$. Replacing B_1 by 1 and B_2 by 0 and transposing terms gives

$$T_2 - G_2 = (1 + r)1 = (1 + r)$$

To repay the debt fully during year 2, the government must run a primary surplus equal to $(1 + r)$. It can do so in one of two ways: a decrease in spending or an increase in taxes. We shall assume here and in the rest of this section that the adjustment comes through taxes, so that the path of spending is unaffected. It follows that the decrease in taxes by 1 during year 1 must be offset by an increase in taxes by $(1 + r)$ during year 2. ◀

Full repayment in year 2:
T_1 decreases by 1 $\Rightarrow$
T_2 increases by $(1 + r)$

The path of taxes and debt corresponding to this case is given in Figure 23-1(a): If the debt is fully repaid during year 2, the decrease in taxes of 1 in year 1 requires an increase in taxes equal to $(1 + r)$ in year 2.

Figure 23-1

Tax Cuts, Debt Repayment, and Debt Stabilization

(a): If the debt is fully repaid during year 2, the decrease in taxes of 1 in year 1 requires an increase in taxes equal to $(1 + r)$ in year 2. (b): If the debt is fully repaid during year 5, the decrease in taxes of 1 in year 1 requires an increase in taxes equal to $(1 + r)^4$ during year 5. (c): If the debt is stabilized from year 2 on, then taxes must be permanently higher by r from year 2 on.

Full Repayment in Year t

Now suppose the government decides to wait until year t to repay the debt. So, from year 2 to year $t - 1$, the primary deficit is equal to zero—taxes are equal to spending, not including interest payments on the debt.

During year 2, the primary deficit is zero. So, from equation (23.3), debt at the end of year 2 is:

$$B_2 = (1 + r)B_1 + 0 = (1 + r)1 = (1 + r)$$

where the second equality uses the fact that $B_1 = 1$.

With the primary deficit still equal to zero during year 3, debt at the end of year 3 is

$$B_3 = (1 + r)B_2 + 0 = (1 + r)(1 + r)1 = (1 + r)^2$$

Solving for debt at the end of year 4 and so on, it is clear that as long as the government keeps a primary deficit equal to zero, debt grows at a rate equal to the interest rate, and thus debt at the end of year $t - 1$ is given by

$$B_{t-1} = (1 + r)^{t-2} \tag{23.4}$$

Despite the fact that taxes are cut only in year 1, debt keeps increasing over time, at a rate equal to the interest rate. The reason is simple: Although the primary deficit is equal to zero, debt is now positive, and so are interest payments on the debt. Each year, the government must issue more debt to pay the interest on existing debt.

In year t, the year in which the government decides to repay the debt, the budget constraint is

$$B_t = (1 + r)B_{t-1} + (G_t - T_t)$$

If debt is fully repaid during year t, then B_t (debt at the end of year t) is zero. Replacing B_t by zero and B_{t-1} by its expression from equation (23.4) gives

$$0 = (1 + r)(1 + r)^{t-2} + (G_t - T_t)$$

Back to Policy   **Back to Policy**

Reorganizing and bringing $(G_t - T_t)$ to the left side of the equation implies

$$T_t - G_t = (1 + r)^{t-1}$$

◀ Add exponents: $(1 + r)$ $(1 + r)^{t-2} = (1 + r)^{t-1}$. See Appendix 2 at the end of this book.

To repay the debt, the government must run a primary surplus equal to $(1 + r)^{t-1}$ during year t. If the adjustment is done through taxes, the initial decrease in taxes of 1 during year 1 leads to an increase in taxes of $(1 + r)^{t-1}$ during year t. The path of taxes and debt corresponding to the case where debt is repaid in year 5 is given in Figure 23-1(b).

This example yields our first set of conclusions:

◀ Full repayment in year 5:

T_1 decreases by $1 \Rightarrow$ T_5 increases by $(1 + r)^4$

■ If government spending is unchanged, a decrease in taxes must eventually be offset by an increase in taxes in the future.
■ The longer the government waits to increase taxes, or the higher the real interest rate is, the higher the eventual increase in taxes must be.

Debt Stabilization in Year t

We have assumed so far that the government fully repays the debt. Let's now look at what happens to taxes if the government only stabilizes the debt. (Stabilizing the debt means changing taxes or spending so that debt remains constant from then on.)

Suppose the government decides to stabilize the debt from year 2 on. Stabilizing the debt from year 2 on means the debt at the end of year 2 and thereafter remains at the same level as it was at the end of year 1.

From equation (23.3), the budget constraint for year 2 is

$$B_2 = (1 + r)B_1 + (G_2 - T_2)$$

Under our assumption that debt is stabilized in year 2, $B_2 = B_1 = 1$. Setting $B_2 = B_1 = 1$ in the preceding equation yields

$$1 = (1 + r) + (G_2 - T_2)$$

Reorganizing, and bringing $(G_2 - T_2)$ to the left side of the equation,

$$T_2 - G_2 = (1 + r) - 1 = r$$

To avoid a further increase in debt during year 1, the government must run a primary surplus equal to real interest payments on the existing debt. It must do so in each of the following years as well: Each year, the primary surplus must be sufficient to cover interest payments, leaving the debt level unchanged. The path of taxes and debt is shown in Figure 23-1(c): Debt remains equal to 1 from year 1 on. Taxes are permanently higher from year 1 on, by an amount equal to r; equivalently, from year 1 on, the government runs a primary surplus equal to r.

The logic of this argument extends directly to the case where the government waits until year t to stabilize the debt. Whenever the government stabilizes, it must from then on run a primary surplus sufficient to pay the interest on the debt.

This example yields our second set of conclusions:

Stabilizing the debt from year 2 ◀ on:

T_1 decreases by $1 \Rightarrow$ $T_2, T_3, \ldots$ increase by r

■ The legacy of past deficits is higher government debt.
■ To stabilize the debt, the government must eliminate the deficit.
■ To eliminate the deficit, the government must run a primary surplus equal to the interest payments on the existing debt. This requires higher taxes forever.

The Evolution of the Debt-to-GDP Ratio

We have focused so far on the evolution of the *level* of debt. But in an economy in which output grows over time, it makes more sense to focus instead on the *ratio of debt to output*. To see how this change in focus modifies our conclusions, we need to go from equation (23.3) to an equation that gives the evolution of the **debt-to-GDP ratio**—the **debt ratio** for short.

Deriving the evolution of the debt ratio takes a few steps. Do not worry: The final equation is easy to understand.

First divide both sides of equation (23.3) by real output, Y_t, to get

$$\frac{B_t}{Y_t} = (1 + r) \frac{B_{t-1}}{Y_t} + \frac{G_t - T_t}{Y_t}$$

Next rewrite B_{t-1}/Y_t, as $(B_t/Y_{t-1})(Y_{t-1}/Y_t)$ (in other words, multiply the numerator and the denominator by Y_{t-1}):

$$\frac{B_t}{Y_t} = (1 + r) \left(\frac{Y_{t-1}}{Y_t} \right) \frac{B_{t-1}}{Y_{t-1}} + \frac{G_t - T_t}{Y_t}$$

Note that all the terms in the equation are now in terms of ratios to output, Y. To simplify this equation, assume that output growth is constant and denote the growth rate of output by g, so Y_{t-1}/Y_t can be written as $1/(1 + g)$. And use the approximation $(1 + r)/(1 + g) = 1 + r - g$.

Using these two assumptions, rewrite the preceding equation as

$$\frac{B_t}{Y_t} = (1 + r - g) \frac{B_{t-1}}{Y_{t-1}} + \frac{G_t - T_t}{Y_t}$$

Finally, reorganize to get

$$\frac{B_t}{Y_t} - \frac{B_{t-1}}{Y_{t-1}} = (r - g) \frac{B_{t-1}}{Y_{t-1}} + \frac{G_t - T_t}{Y_t} \qquad (23.5)$$

This took many steps, but the final relation has a simple interpretation.

The change in the debt ratio over time (the left side of the equation) is equal to the sum of two terms:

- The first term is the difference between the real interest rate and the growth rate times the initial debt ratio.
- The second term is the ratio of the primary deficit to GDP.

Compare equation (23.5), which gives the evolution of the ratio of debt to GDP, to equation (23.2), which gives the evolution of the level of debt itself. The difference is the presence of $r - g$ in equation (23.5) compared to r in equation (23.2). The reason for the difference is simple: Suppose the primary deficit is zero. Debt will then increase at a rate equal to the real interest rate, r. But if GDP is growing as well, the ratio of debt to GDP will grow more slowly; it will grow at a rate equal to the real interest rate minus the growth rate of output, $r - g$.

Equation (23.5) implies that the increase in the ratio of debt to GDP will be larger:

- the higher the real interest rate,
- the lower the growth rate of output,
- the higher the initial debt ratio,
- the higher the ratio of the primary deficit to GDP.

Start from $Y_t = (1 + g)Y_{t-1}$. Divide both sides by Y_t to get $1 = (1 + g)Y_{t-1}/Y_t$. Reorganize to get $Y_{t-1}/Y_t = 1/(1 + g)$.

This approximation is derived as proposition 6 in Appendix 2 at the end of this book.

If two variables (here debt and GDP) grow at rates r and g, respectively, then their ratio (here the ratio of debt to GDP) will grow at rate $(r - g)$. See proposition 8 in Appendix 2 at the end of this book.

How Countries Decreased Their Debt Ratios after World War II

FOCUS

After World War II, many countries had very high debt ratios, often in excess of 100% of GDP. Yet, two or three decades later, the debt ratios were much lower, often below 50%. How did they do it? The answer is given in Table 1.

Table 1 looks at four countries: Australia, Canada, New Zealand, and the United Kingdom. Column 1 gives the period during which debt ratios decreased. The first year is either 1945 or 1946. The last year is the year in which the debt ratio reached its lowest point; the period of adjustment varies from 13 years in Canada, to 30 years in the United Kingdom. Column 2 gives debt ratios at the start and at the end of the period. The most striking numbers here are those for the United Kingdom: an initial debt ratio of 270% of GDP in 1946 and an impressive decline, down to 47% in 1974.

To interpret the numbers in the table, go back to equation (23.5). It tells us that there are two, not mutually exclusive, ways in which a country can reduce its debt ratio. The first is through high primary surpluses. Suppose, for example, that $(r - g)$ was equal to 0. Then the decrease in the debt ratio over some period would just be the sum of the ratios of primary surpluses to GDP over the period. The second is through a low $(r - g)$, so either through low real interest rates or through high growth, or both.

With this in mind, columns 3 to 5 give first the average ratio of the primary balance to GDP, then the average growth rate of GDP and the average real interest rate, over the relevant period.

Look first at primary balances in column 3. Note how all four countries indeed ran primary surpluses on average over the period. But note also that these primary surpluses account only for a small part of the decline in the debt ratio. Look, for example, at the United Kingdom. The sum of the ratios of the primary surpluses to GDP over the period is equal to 2.1% times 30 = 63% of GDP, so accounting for less than a third of the decline in the debt ratio, 223% $(270 - 47)$ of GDP.

Now look at the growth rates and the real interest rates in columns 4 and 5. Note how high growth rates and how low real interest rates were during the period. Take Australia, for example. The average value of $(r - g)$ during the period was -6.9% $(-2.3\% - 4.6\%)$. This implies that, even if the primary balance had been equal to zero, the debt ratio would have declined each year by 6.9%. In other words, the decline in debt was not mainly the result of primary surpluses, but the result of sustained high growth and sustained negative real interest rates.

This leads to a final question: Why were real interest rates so low? The answer is given in column 6. During the period, average inflation was relatively high. This inflation, combined with consistently low nominal interest rates, is what accounts for the negative real interest rates. Put another way, a large part of the decrease in debt ratios was achieved by paying bond holders a negative real return on their bonds for many years.

Table 1 Changes in Debt Ratios Following World War II

Country	1 Start/End Year	2 Start/End Debt Ratio	3 Primary Balance	4 Growth Rate	5 Real Interest Rate	6 Inflation Rate
Australia	1946–1963	92–29	1.1	4.6	−2.3	5.7
Canada	1945–1957	115–59	3.6	4.3	−1.4	4.0
New Zealand	1946–1974	148–41	2.3	3.9	−2.9	4.9
United Kingdom	1946–1975	270–47	2.1	2.6	−1.5	5.5

Columns 2 and 3: Percent of GDP. Columns 4 to 6: Percent.

Source: S.M.A. Abbas et al., "Historical Patterns and Dynamics of Public Debt: Evidence from a New Database," IMF Economic Review 2011 59 (November): pp. 717–742

Building on this relation, the Focus box "How Countries Decreased Their Debt Ratios after World War II" shows how governments that inherited very high debt ratios at the end of the war steadily decreased them through a combination of low real interest rates, high growth rates, and primary surpluses. The next section shows how our analysis can also be used to shed light on a number of other fiscal policy issues.

23-3 Ricardian Equivalence, Cyclical Adjusted Deficits, and War Finance

Having looked at the mechanics of the government budget constraint, we can now take up three issues in which this constraint plays a central role.

Ricardian Equivalence

How does taking into account the government budget constraint affect the way we should think of the effects of deficits on output?

One extreme view is that once the government budget constraint is taken into account, neither deficits nor debt have an effect on economic activity! This argument is known as the **Ricardian equivalence** proposition. David Ricardo, a nineteenth-century English economist, was the first to articulate its logic. His argument was further developed and given prominence in the 1970s by Robert Barro, then at Chicago, now at Harvard University. For this reason, the argument is also known as the **Ricardo-Barro proposition**.

The best way to understand the logic of the proposition is to use the example of tax changes from Section 23-1:

- Suppose that the government decreases taxes by 1 (again, think one billion dollars) this year. And as it does so, it announces that, to repay the debt, it will increase taxes by $(1 + r)$ next year. What will be the effect of the initial tax cut on consumption?

- One possible answer is: No effect at all. Why? Because consumers realize that the tax cut is not much of a gift: Lower taxes this year are exactly offset, in present value, by higher taxes next year. Put another way, their human wealth—the present value of after-tax labor income—is unaffected. Current taxes go down by 1, but the present value of next year's taxes goes up by $(1 + r)/(1 + r) = 1$, and the net effect of the two changes is exactly equal to zero.

- Another way of coming to the same answer—this time looking at saving rather than looking at consumption—is as follows: To say that consumers do not change their consumption in response to the tax cut is the same as saying that *private saving increases one-for-one with the deficit.* So the Ricardian equivalence proposition says that if a government finances a given path of spending through deficits, private saving will increase one-for-one with the decrease in public saving, leaving total saving unchanged. The total amount left for investment will not be affected. Over time, the mechanics of the government budget constraint imply that government debt will increase. But this increase will not come at the expense of capital accumulation.

Under the Ricardian equivalence proposition, a long sequence of deficits and the associated increase in government debt are no cause for worry. As the government is dissaving, the argument goes, people are saving more in anticipation of the higher taxes to come. The decrease in public saving is offset by an equal increase in private saving. Total saving is therefore unaffected, and so is investment. The economy has the same capital stock today that it would have had if there had been no increase in debt. High debt is no cause for concern.

How seriously should we take the Ricardian equivalence proposition? Most economists would answer: "Seriously, but surely not seriously enough to think that deficits and debt are irrelevant." A major theme of this book has been that expectations matter, that consumption decisions depend not only on current income but also on future income. If it were widely believed that a tax cut this year is going to be followed by an

While Ricardo stated the logic of the argument, he also argued there were many reasons why it would not hold in practice. In contrast, Barro ▶ argued that not only the argument was logically correct, but it was also a good description of reality.

See Chapter 16 for a definition of human wealth and ▶ a discussion of its role in consumption.

offsetting increase in taxes *next year*, the effect on consumption would indeed probably be small. Many consumers would save most or all of the tax cut in anticipation of higher taxes next year. (Replace "year" by "month" or "week" and the argument becomes even more convincing.)

Of course, tax cuts rarely come with the announcement of corresponding tax increases a year later. Consumers have to guess when and how taxes will eventually be increased. This fact does not by itself invalidate the Ricardian equivalence argument: No matter when taxes will be increased, the government budget constraint still implies that the present value of future tax increases must always be equal to the decrease in taxes today. Take the second example we looked at in Section 23-1—drawn in Figure 23-1(b)—in which the government waits t years to increase taxes, and so increases taxes by $(1 + r)^{t-1}$. The present value in year 0 of this expected tax increase is $(1 + r)^{t-1}/(1 + r)^{t-1} = 1$—exactly equal to the original tax cut. The change in human wealth from the tax cut is still zero. ◀

The increase in taxes in t years is $(1 + r)^{t-1}$. The discount factor for a dollar t years from now is $1/(1 + r)^{t-1}$. So the value of the increase in taxes t years from now as of today is $(1 + r)^{t-1}/(1 + r)^{t-1} = 1$.

◀ Recall that this assumes that spending is unchanged. If people expect spending to be decreased in the future, what will they do?

But insofar as future tax increases appear more distant and their timing more uncertain, consumers are in fact more likely to ignore them. This may be the case because they expect to die before taxes go up, or, more likely, because they just do not think that far into the future. In either case, Ricardian equivalence is likely to fail.

So, it is safe to conclude that budget deficits have an important effect on activity—although perhaps a smaller effect than we thought before going through the Ricardian equivalence argument. In the short run, larger deficits are likely to lead to higher demand and to higher output. In the long run, higher government debt lowers capital accumulation and, as a result, lowers output.

Deficits, Output Stabilization, and the Cyclically Adjusted Deficit

The fact that budget deficits do, indeed, have long-run adverse effects on capital accumulation and, in turn, on output, does not imply that fiscal policy should not be used to reduce output fluctuations. Rather, it implies that deficits during recessions should ◀ be offset by surpluses during booms, so as not to lead to a steady increase in debt.

To help assess whether fiscal policy is on track, economists have constructed deficit measures that tell them what the deficit would be, under existing tax and spending rules, if output were at the natural level of output. Such measures come under many names, ranging from **the full-employment deficit**, to **the mid-cycle deficit**, to **the standardized employment deficit**, to **the structural deficit** (the term used by the OECD). We shall use **cyclically adjusted deficit**, the term we find the most intuitive.

Such a measure gives a simple benchmark against which to judge the direction of fiscal policy: If the actual deficit is large but the cyclically adjusted deficit is zero, then current fiscal policy is consistent with no systematic increase in debt over time. The debt will increase as long as output is below the natural level of output; but as output returns to its natural level, the deficit will disappear and the debt will stabilize.

It does not follow that the goal of fiscal policy should be to maintain a cyclically adjusted deficit equal to zero at all times. In a recession, the government may want to run a deficit large enough that even the cyclically adjusted deficit is positive. In this case, the fact that the cyclically adjusted deficit is positive provides a useful warning. The warning is that the return of output to its natural level will not be enough to stabilize the debt: The government will have to take specific measures, from tax increases to cuts in spending, to decrease the deficit at some point in the future.

The theory underlying the concept of cyclically adjusted deficit is simple. The practice of it has proven tricky. To see why, we need to look at how measures of the cyclically adjusted deficit are constructed. Construction requires two steps. First,

Note the analogy with monetary policy: The fact that higher money growth leads in the long run to more inflation does not imply that monetary policy should not be used for output stabilization.

◀ We ignore output growth in this section, and so ignore the distinction between stabilizing the debt and stabilizing the debt-to-GDP ratio. (Verify that the argument extends to the case where output is growing.)

establish how much lower the deficit would be if output were, say, 1% higher. Second, assess how far output is from its natural level.

- The first step is straightforward. A reliable rule of thumb is that a 1% decrease in output leads automatically to an increase in the deficit of about 0.5% of GDP. This increase occurs because most taxes are proportional to output, whereas most government spending does not depend on the level of output. That means a decrease in output, which leads to a decrease in revenues and not much change in spending, naturally leads to a larger deficit.

  If output is, say, 5% below its natural level, the deficit as a ratio to GDP will therefore be about 2.5% larger than it would be if output were at the natural level of output. (This effect of activity on the deficit has been called an **automatic stabilizer**: A recession naturally generates a deficit, and therefore a fiscal expansion, which partly counteracts the recession.)

- The second step is more difficult. Recall from Chapter 6 that the natural level of output is the output level that would be produced if the economy were operating at the natural rate of unemployment. Too low an estimate of the natural rate of unemployment will lead to too high an estimate of the natural level of output and therefore to too optimistic a measure of the cyclically adjusted deficit.

  This difficulty explains in part what happened in Europe in the 1980s. Based on the assumption of an unchanged natural unemployment rate, the cyclically adjusted deficits of the 1980s did not look that bad: If European unemployment had returned to its level of the 1970s, the associated increase in output would have been sufficient to reestablish budget balance in most countries. But, it turned out, much of the increase in unemployment reflected an increase in the natural unemployment rate, and unemployment remained very high during the 1980s. As a result, the decade was characterized by high deficits and large increases in debt ratios in most countries.

Wars and Deficits

Wars typically bring about large budget deficits. As we saw in Chapter 22, the two largest increases in U.S. government debt in the twentieth century took place during World War I and World War II. We examine the case of World War II further in the Focus box "Deficits, Consumption, and Investment in the United States during World War II."

Look at the two peaks associated with World War I and World War II in Figure 22-4.

Is it right for governments to rely so much on deficits to finance wars? After all, war economies are usually operating at low unemployment, so the output stabilization reasons for running deficits we just examined are irrelevant. The answer, nevertheless, is yes. In fact, there are two good reasons to run deficits during wars:

- The first is distributional: Deficit finance is a way to pass some of the burden of the war to those alive after the war, and it seems only fair for future generations to share in the sacrifices the war requires.
- The second is more narrowly economic: Deficit spending helps reduce tax distortions.

  Let's look at each reason in turn:

Passing on the Burden of the War

Wars lead to large increases in government spending. Consider the implications of financing this increased spending either through increased taxes or through debt. To distinguish this case from our earlier discussion of output stabilization, let's also assume that output is fixed at the natural level of output.

- Suppose that the government relies on deficit finance. With government spending sharply up, there will be a very large increase in the demand for goods. Given

Deficits, Consumption, and Investment in the United States during World War II

FOCUS

In 1939, the share of U.S. government spending on goods and services in GDP was 15%. By 1944, it had increased to 45%! The increase was due to increased spending on national defense, which went from 1% of GDP in 1939 to 36% in 1944.

Faced with such a massive increase in spending, the U.S. government reacted with large tax increases. For the first time in U.S. history, the individual income tax became a major source of revenues; individual income tax revenues, which were 1% of GDP in 1939, increased to 8.5% in 1944. But the tax increases were still far less than the increase in government expenditures. The increase in federal revenues, from 7.2% of GDP in 1939 to 22.7% in 1944, was only a little more than half the increase in expenditures.

The result was a sequence of large budget deficits. By 1944, the federal deficit reached 22% of GDP. The ratio of debt to GDP, already high at 53% in 1939 because of the deficits the government had run during the Great Depression, reached 110%!

Was the increase in government spending achieved at the expense of consumption or private investment? (As we saw in Chapter 19, it could in principle have come from higher imports and a current account deficit. But the United States had nobody to borrow from during the war. Rather, it was lending to some of its allies: Transfers from the U.S. government to foreign countries were equal to 6% of U.S. GDP in 1944.)

■ It was met in large part by a decrease in consumption: The share of consumption in GDP fell by 23 percentage points, from 74% to 51%. Part of the decrease in consumption may have been due to anticipations of higher taxes after the war; part of it was due to the unavailability of many consumer durables. Patriotism also probably motivated people to save more and buy the war bonds issued by the government Summing to finance the war.

■ It was also met by a 6% decrease in the share of (private) investment in GDP—from 10% to 4%. Part of the burden of the war was therefore passed on in the form of lower capital accumulation to those living after the war.

---

our assumption that output stays the same, the interest rate will have to increase enough so as to maintain equilibrium. Investment, which depends on the interest rate, will decrease sharply.

■ Suppose instead that the government finances the spending increase through an increase in taxes—say income taxes. Consumption will decline sharply. Exactly how much depends on consumers' expectations: The longer they expect the war to last, then the longer they will expect higher taxes to last, and the more they will decrease their consumption. In any case, the increase in government spending will be partly offset by a decrease in consumption. Interest rates will increase by less than they would have increased under deficit spending, and investment will therefore decrease by less.

In short, for a given output, the increase in government spending requires either a decrease in consumption and/or a decrease in investment. Whether the government relies on tax increases or deficits determines whether consumption or investment does more of the adjustment when government spending goes up.

How does this affect who bears the burden of the war? The more the government relies on deficits, the smaller the decrease in consumption during the war and the larger the decrease in investment. Lower investment means a lower capital stock after the war, and therefore lower output after the war. By reducing capital accumulation, deficits become a way of passing some of the burden of the war onto future generations.

◄ Assume that the economy is closed, so that $Y = C + I + G$. Suppose that G goes up, and Y remains the same. Then, $C + I$ must go down. If taxes are not increased, most of the decrease will come from a decrease in I. If taxes are increased, most of the decrease will come from a decrease in C.

Reducing Tax Distortions

There is another argument for running deficits, not only during wars but, more generally, in times when government spending is exceptionally high. Think, for example, of reconstruction after an earthquake or the costs involved in the reunification of Germany in the early 1990s.

The argument is as follows: If the government were to increase taxes in order to finance the temporary increase in spending, tax rates would have to be very high. Very high tax rates can lead to very high economic distortions: Faced with very high income tax rates, people work less or engage in illegal, untaxed activities. Rather than moving the tax rate up and down so as to always balance the budget, it is better (from the point of view of reducing distortions) to maintain a relatively constant tax rate—to *smooth taxes*. **Tax smoothing** implies running large deficits when government spending is exceptionally high, and small surpluses the rest of the time.

23-4 The Dangers of High Debt

Suppose that, for good or bad reasons, large deficits have led to a high debt ratio. What should the government do then? Simply trying to stabilize the debt at this high level is unwise: The lesson from history is that high debt can lead to vicious cycles and makes the conduct of fiscal policy extremely difficult. Let's look at this more closely.

High Debt, Default Risk, and Vicious Cycles

Return to equation (23.5):

$$\frac{B_t}{Y_t} - \frac{B_{t-1}}{Y_{t-1}} = (r - g)\frac{B_{t-1}}{Y_{t-1}} + \frac{(G_t - T_t)}{Y_t}$$

Take a country with a high debt ratio, say, 100%. Suppose the real interest rate is 3% and the growth rate is 2%. The first term on the right is $(3\% - 2\%)$ times $100\% = 1\%$ of GDP. Suppose further that the government is running a primary surplus of 1%, thus just enough to keep the debt ratio constant (the right side of the equation equals $(3\% - 2\%)$ times $100\% + (-1\%) = 0\%$).

Now suppose financial investors start to worry that the government may not be able to fully repay the debt. They ask for a higher interest rate, to compensate for what they perceive as a higher risk of default on the debt. But this in turn makes it more difficult for the government to stabilize the debt. Suppose, for example, that the interest rate increases from 3% to, say, 8%. Then, just to stabilize the debt, the government now needs to run a primary surplus of 6% (the right side of the equation is then equal to $(8\% - 2\%) \times 100 + (-6 = 0)$. Suppose that, in response to the increase in the interest rate, the government indeed takes measures to increase the primary surplus to 6%. The spending cuts or tax increases that are needed are likely to prove politically costly, potentially generating more political uncertainty, a higher risk of default, and thus a further increase in the interest rate. Also, the sharp fiscal contraction is likely to lead to a recession, decreasing the growth rate. Both the increase in the real interest rate and the decrease in growth further increase $(r - g)$, requiring an even larger surplus to stabilize the debt. At some point, the government may become unable to increase the primary surplus sufficiently, and the debt ratio starts increasing, leading financial markets to become even more worried and require an even higher interest rate. Increases in the interest rate and increases in the debt ratio feed on each other. The result is a debt explosion.

In short, the higher the ratio of debt to GDP, the larger the potential for catastrophic debt dynamics. Even if the fear that the government may not fully repay the debt was initially unfounded, it can easily become self-fulfilling. The increased interest the government must pay on its debt can lead the government to lose control of its budget and lead to an increase in debt to a level such that the government is unable to repay the debt, thus validating the initial fears.

The lesson is clear. When a government inherits a high debt ratio, it should aim at decreasing it over time. As equation (23.5) made clear, it can achieve this through a combination of primary surpluses, high growth rates, and low real interest rates.

We saw earlier how countries relied on such a combination to reduce their debt ratios after World War II. Another example of debt reduction is that of England in the nineteenth century. By the end of its wars against Napoleon in the early 1800s, England had run up a debt ratio in excess of 200% of GDP. It spent most of the nineteenth century reducing the ratio, so that by 1900 the ratio stood at only 30% of GDP.

The U.S. Budget Deficit Challenge

So far, investors do not so far appear worried about U.S. budget deficits. Even long-term interest rates on U.S. government bonds are very low. Nevertheless, it is clear that first stabilizing and then decreasing the U.S. debt ratio will require major adjustments in fiscal policy.

A useful starting point is to look at the evolution of federal deficits from 2011 to 2021 as projected by the Congressional Budget Office (or CBO for short). The CBO is a nonpartisan agency of Congress that helps Congress assess the costs and the effects of fiscal decisions; one of CBO's tasks is to prepare projections of revenues, spending, and deficits under current fiscal rules. Figure 1 presents these projections, by fiscal year, as of January 2011. (The fiscal year runs from October 1 of the previous calendar year to September 30 of the current calendar year.)

The orange line shows projected deficits under current rules (these are called **baseline projections**). According to this projection, the future looks better than the present: The deficit decreases from close to 10% in 2011 to close to 3% in 2014.

Unfortunately, this projection is misleading. It is based on three assumptions—three budget rules that Congress has said it would follow, but is in fact unlikely to follow:

The first assumption is that nominal discretionary spending will increase only at the rate of inflation—in other words, will remain constant in real terms. A more realistic assumption, based on past experience, is that discretionary spending will increase at the same rate as GDP—in other words, that the ratio of discretionary spending to GDP will remain constant. The red line shows what will happen under this alternative assumption. The deficit stabilizes not at 3% of GDP but at more than 4% of GDP.

The second assumption is the provision that most of the tax cuts introduced by the Bush administration in 2001 and extended by the Obama administration will expire in 2012. It seems very likely that most of these tax reductions will instead continue past 2012.

The third assumption is that the rules governing the **alternative minimum tax, or AMT, will not be changed.** This alternative tax was introduced to ensure that the richest taxpayers would pay at least some taxes. Because the income threshold at which it is triggered is not indexed to

◄ This is not CBO's fault. In making projections, it is not allowed to second guess Congress.

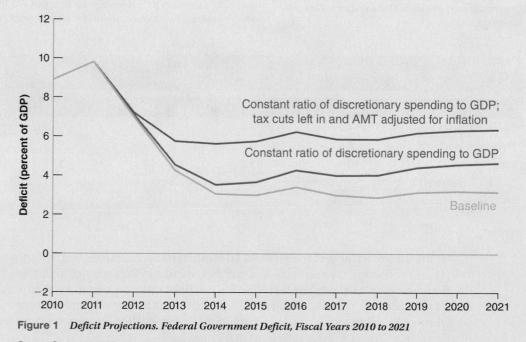

Figure 1 *Deficit Projections. Federal Government Deficit, Fiscal Years 2010 to 2021*

Source: Congressional Budget Office. Tables 1-6 and 1-7; The Budget and Economic Outlook: Fiscal Years 2011 to 2021, January 2011

inflation, the number of taxpayers subject to this alternative tax has steadily increased. It is widely believed that the tax will be redefined and the income threshold will be indexed.

The dark blue line shows the projected path of the deficit under the joint assumptions that discretionary spending will increase with nominal GDP, that tax cuts will be extended, and that the AMT will be indexed for inflation. Under these assumptions, the deficit stabilizes at 6% of GDP in 2012.

In short, looking at the medium run, the fiscal situation looks bad. And even more serious challenges arise in the longer run.

About half of U.S. federal spending is on **entitlement programs**. These are programs that require the payment of benefits to all who meet the eligibility requirements established by the law. The three largest programs are Social Security (which provides benefits to retirees), Medicare (which provides health care to retirees), and Medicaid (which provides health care to the poor). Table 1 shows actual and projected spending on each of these three programs, under current rules, as a percent of GDP, from 2011 to 2050.

The numbers are striking: Under current rules, Social Security benefits are projected to increase from 4.8% of GDP in 2011 to 5.9% in 2050. Medicare and Medicaid benefits are projected to increase from 5.6% to 11.8%. The ratio of entitlement spending to GDP (the sum of the two numbers) is projected therefore to increase by 7.3% of GDP over the next 40 years. These projected increases have two main sources:

■ The first is the aging of America, the rapid increase in the proportion of people over 65 that will take place as the Baby Boom generation begins to reach retirement age, from year 2011 on. The old age dependency ratio—the ratio of the population 65 years old or more to the population between 20 and 64 years—is projected to increase from about 20% in 2000 to above 40% in 2050. This evolution explains the projected growth in Social Security benefits and some of the increase in Medicare.

■ The second, which explains the rest of the growth of Medicare and all the growth in Medicaid, is the steadily and rapidly increasing cost of health care.

Can these increases in entitlement spending be offset by decreases in other government expenditures? The answer is a clear no. Even if all expenditures other than transfers were eliminated, there would still not be enough to cover the projected increase in entitlement spending: In 2010, total government expenditures, excluding interest payments and transfers, were equal to 7.9% of GDP, about the same as the 7.3% projected increase in entitlement spending.

It is therefore clear that major changes in entitlement programs will have to take place. Social Security benefits may have to be reduced (relative to projections), and the provision of medical care will have to be limited (again, relative to projections). There is also little doubt that taxes, such as the payroll taxes used to finance Social Security, will have to be increased. If such changes are not achieved, there will be good reasons to worry about U.S. debt dynamics.

Table 1 Projected Spending on Social Security, Medicare, and Medicaid (Percent of GDP), 2011–2050

	2011	2020	2030	2050
Social Security	4.8	5.2	6.0	5.9
Medicare/Medicaid	5.6	6.7	8.4	11.8
Total	10.4	11.9	14.4	17.7

Source: Congressional Budget Office. Figure 3-2 and Figure 4-1; CBO's 2011 Long-Term Budget Outlook

At the time of writing, this is far from an abstract issue. Investors' worries about default risk are affecting interest rates in a number of European countries in Europe. (For the time being, and despite the fact that the U.S. debt ratio is close to 100%, investors do not appear overly worried about the U.S. budget situation, and interest rates on U.S. government bonds have remained low. Whether investors should worry is discussed in the Focus box "The U.S. Budget Deficit Challenge.")

Figure 23-2 shows the evolution of interest rates on government bonds for Italy, Spain, and Belgium from January to October 2011. For each country, it plots the difference, also called the **spread**, between the two-year interest rate on the country's government bond and the two-year interest rate on German government bonds. The reason for comparing interest rates to German interest rates is that German bonds are considered nearly riskless. Thus, the spreads plotted in the figure reflect the risk

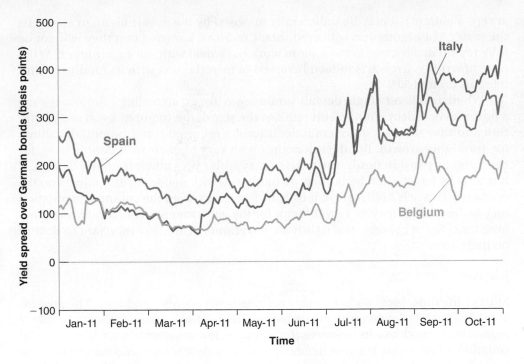

Figure 23-2

The Increase in European Bond Spreads

The spreads on Italian, Spanish, and Belgian two-year bonds over German two-year bonds have increased between January and October 2011, making it harder for those countries to stabilize their debt ratios.

Source: International Monetary Fund

premia that investors require in order to hold the bonds of each of the three countries. The spreads are measured, on the vertical axis, in **basis points** (a basis point is a hundredth of a percent).

◀ For more on risk premia, see Chapter 15.

Note how all three spreads have increased since the beginning of 2011. As of October 2011, the spread on Italian bonds exceeded 400 basis points (equivalently, 4%), the spread on Spanish bonds exceeded 300 basis points, and the spread of Belgian bonds exceeded 200 basis points. These spreads make it more difficult for the governments to decrease their debt ratios. The worry is that, were the spreads were to increase further, the primary surpluses that would be needed to stabilize debt might not be politically feasible. So, in all three countries, governments are taking strong measures to convince markets that they will not only stabilize their debt ratios, but decrease them over time. If they succeed, interest rates will indeed come down, making it easier for governments to achieve their goal. When we read this book, we are likely to know whether they have succeeded or not.

We can now turn to the next question: What if a government does not succeed in stabilizing the debt, and debt and interest rates explode? Then, historically, one of two things happens: Either the government explicitly defaults on its debt; or the government relies increasingly on money finance, which typically leads to very high inflation. Let's look at each outcome in turn.

Debt Default

At some point, when a government finds itself facing very high interest rates, it may decide to default. Default is often partial, and creditors take what is known as a **haircut**: A haircut of 30%, for example, means that creditors receive only 70% of what they were owed. Default also comes under many names, many of them euphemisms—probably to make the prospects more appealing (or less unappealing) to creditors. It is called **debt restructuring**, or **debt rescheduling** (when interest payments are deferred rather than cancelled), or, quite ironically, **private sector involvement** (the private sector, i.e., the creditors, are asked to *get involved*, i.e., to accept a haircut). It may be unilaterally imposed by the government, or it may be the result of a negotiation with creditors: Creditors, knowing that they will not be fully repaid in any case, may prefer to work out a deal with the government. At the time of writing, Greece is indeed involved in negotiations with its creditors, with haircuts around 50%.

When debt is very high, default would seem like an appealing solution: Having a lower level of debt after default reduces the size of the required fiscal consolidation and thus makes it more credible. It lowers required taxes, potentially allowing for higher growth. But default comes with very high costs. If debt is held, for example, by pension funds, the retirees may suffer very much from the default. If it is held by banks, then banks may go bankrupt, with major adverse effects on the economy. If debt is held instead mostly by foreigners, then the country's reputation may be lost, and it may be very difficult for the government to borrow abroad for a long time. So, in general, and rightly so, governments are very reluctant to default on their debt.

Money Finance

Most of the time, fiscal and monetary policies proceed independently. The government finances its deficit through borrowing. The central bank chooses the supply of money so as to achieve its objective (for example, low inflation). But, when the fiscal situation is bad, either because deficits are large or debt is high, and the interest rate faced by the government is high, it becomes increasingly tempting for the government to want to finance itself through money finance. Fiscal policy then determines the behavior of the money supply, a case known as **fiscal dominance.**

Governments do not literally finance themselves through money creation. As we saw in Chapter 4, it is the central bank that creates money. But when the central bank finds itself in the fiscal dominance case, the central bank must do what the government tells it to do. The government issues new bonds and tells the central bank to buy them. The central bank then pays the government with the money it creates, and the government uses that money to finance its deficit. This process is called **debt monetization**.

For a refresher on central bank money, see Section 4-3. ▶

How large a deficit can a government finance through such money creation? Let H be the amount of central bank money in the economy. (We shall refer to central bank money simply as money for short in what follows.) Let ΔH be money creation; that is, the change in the nominal money stock from one month to the next. (When we look at numbers below, you will understand why we use the month rather than, say, the year, as the unit of time.) The revenue, in real terms (that is, in terms of goods), that the government generates by creating an amount of money equal to ΔH is therefore $\Delta H / P$—money creation during the period divided by the price level. This revenue from money creation is called **seignorage.**

The word is revealing: The right to issue money was a precious source of revenue for the "seigneurs" of the past: ▶ They could buy the goods they wanted by issuing their own money and using it to pay for the goods.

We can summarize what we have just learned by writing

$$\text{seignorage} = \frac{\Delta H}{P}$$

Seignorage is equal to money creation divided by the price level. To see what rate of (central bank) nominal money growth is required to generate a given amount of seignorage, we can rewrite $\Delta H / P$ as

$$\frac{\Delta H}{P} = \frac{\Delta H}{H} \frac{H}{P}$$

In words: We can think of seignorage ($\Delta H/P$) as the product of the rate of nominal money growth ($\Delta H/H$) and the real money stock (H/P). Replacing this expression in the previous equation gives

$$\text{seignorage} = \frac{\Delta H}{H} \frac{H}{P}$$

This gives us a relation between seignorage, the rate of nominal money growth, and real money balances. To think about relevant magnitudes, it is convenient to take one more step and divide both sides of the equation by monthly GDP, Y, to get:

$$\frac{\text{seignorage}}{Y} = \frac{\Delta H}{H} \left(\frac{H/P}{Y} \right) \tag{23.6}$$

Suppose the government is running a budget deficit equal to 10% of GDP and decides to finance it through seignorage, so $(\text{deficit}/Y) = (\text{seignorage}/Y) = 10\%$. The average ratio of central bank money to monthly GDP in advanced countries is roughly equal to 1, so choose $(H/P)/Y = 1$. This implies that nominal money growth must satisfy

$$\frac{\Delta H}{H} \text{ times } 1 = 10\% \Rightarrow \frac{\Delta H}{H} = 10\%$$

To finance a deficit of 10% of GDP through seignorage, given a ratio of central bank money to monthly GDP of 1, the monthly growth rate of nominal money must be equal to 10%.

This is surely a very high rate of money growth, but one might conclude that this is an acceptable price to pay to finance the deficit. Unfortunately, this conclusion would be wrong. As money growth increases, inflation is likely to follow. And very high inflation is likely to lead people to want to reduce their demand for money, and in turn the demand for central bank money. In other words, as the government increases $\Delta H/H$, H/P is likely to decrease. As it does so, the government needs to increase the rate of money growth further to achieve the same level of revenues. But higher money growth leads to further inflation, a further decrease in H/P, and the need for further money growth. Soon, high inflation is likely to turn into **hyperinflation**, the term that economists use for very high inflation—typically inflation in excess of 30% per month.

This scenario has been replayed many times in the past. You probably have heard of the hyperinflation that existed in post World War I Germany: In 1913, the value of all currency circulating in Germany was 6 billion marks. Ten years later, in October 1923, 6 billion marks was barely enough to buy a one-kilo loaf of rye bread in Berlin. A month later, the price of the same loaf of bread had increased to 428 billion marks. But the German hyperinflation is not the only one. Table 23-1 summarizes the seven major hyperinflations that followed World War I and World War II. They share a number of features. They were all short (lasting a year or so) but intense, with money growth and inflation running at 50% *per month* or more. In all, the increases in the price levels were staggering. As we can see, the largest price increase actually occurred not in Germany, but in Hungary after World War II. What cost one Hungarian pengö in August 1945, cost 3,800 trillions of trillions of pengös less than a year later!

Inflation rates of that magnitude have not been seen since the 1940s. But many countries have experienced very high inflation as a result of money finance. Monthly inflation ran above 20% in many Latin American countries in the late 1980s. The most recent example of very high inflation is Zimbabwe, where, in 2008, monthly inflation reached 500% before a stabilization program was adopted in early 2009.

Hungary has the distinction of having not one, but two hyperinflations in this period, one after World War I and one after World War II.

Table 23-1 Seven Hyperinflations of the 1920s and 1940s					
Country	Start	End	P_T/P_0	Average Monthly Inflation Rate (%)	Average Monthly Money Growth (%)
Austria	Oct. 1921	Aug. 1922	70	47	31
Germany	Aug. 1922	Nov. 1923	1.0×10^{10}	322	314
Greece	Nov. 1943	Nov. 1944	4.7×10^{6}	365	220
Hungary 1	Mar. 1923	Feb. 1924	44	46	33
Hungary 2	Aug. 1945	Jul. 1946	3.8×10^{27}	19,800	12,200
Poland	Jan. 1923	Jan. 1924	699	82	72
Russia	Dec. 1921	Jan. 1924	1.2×10^{5}	57	49

P_T/P_0: Price level in the last month of hyperinflation divided by the price level in the first month.

Source: Philip Cagan, "The Monetary Dynamics of Hyperinflation," in Milton Friedman ed., *Studies in the Quantity Theory of Money* (University of Chicago Press, 1956), Table 1

It will come as no surprise that hyperinflations have enormous economic costs:

- The transaction system works less and less well. One famous example of inefficient exchange occurred in Germany at the end of its hyperinflation: People actually had to use wheelbarrows to cart around the huge amounts of currency they needed for their daily transactions.

- Price signals become less and less useful: Because prices change so often, it is difficult for consumers and producers to assess the relative prices of goods and to make informed decisions. The evidence shows that the higher the rate of inflation, the higher the variation in the relative prices of different goods. Thus the price system, which is crucial to the functioning of a market economy, also becomes less and less efficient.

- Swings in the inflation rate become larger. It becomes harder to predict what inflation will be in the near future, whether it will be, say, 500% or 1,000% over the next year. Borrowing at a given nominal interest rate becomes more and more of a gamble. If we borrow at, say, 1,000% for a year, we may end up paying a real interest rate of 500% or 0%: a large difference! The result is that borrowing and lending typically come to a stop in the final months of hyperinflation, leading to a large decline in investment.

So, as inflation becomes very high, there is typically an increasing consensus that it should be stopped. Eventually, the government reduces the deficit and no longer has recourse to money finance. Inflation stops, but not before the economy has suffered substantial costs.

How likely is such a scenario to play again in the future? Much depends on the relation between the government and the central bank. To the extent that central banks have become more independent, the danger is lower than in the past. But it cannot be excluded.

A joke heard in Israel during the high inflation of the 1980s: "Why is it cheaper to take the taxi rather than the bus? Because in the bus, you have to ▶ pay the fare at the beginning of the ride. In the taxi, you pay only at the end."

We are discussing here the costs of very high inflation. The discussion today in OECD countries is about the costs of, ▶ say, 4% inflation versus 0%. The issues are quite different in that case, and we return to this topic in Chapter 24.

Summary

- The government budget constraint gives the evolution of government debt as a function of spending and taxes. One way of expressing the constraint is that the change in debt (the deficit) is equal to the primary deficit plus interest payments on the debt. The primary deficit is the difference between government spending on goods and services, G, and taxes net of transfers, T.

- If government spending is unchanged, a decrease in taxes must eventually be offset by an increase in taxes in the future. The longer the government waits to increase taxes or the higher the real interest rate, the higher the eventual increase in taxes.

- The legacy of past deficits is higher debt. To stabilize the debt, the government must eliminate the deficit. To eliminate the deficit, it must run a primary surplus equal to the interest payments on the existing debt.

- The evolution of the ratio of debt to GDP depends on four factors: the interest rate, the growth rate, the initial debt ratio, and the primary surplus.

- Under the Ricardian equivalence proposition, a larger deficit is offset by an equal increase in private saving. Deficits have no effect on demand and on output. The accumulation of debt does not affect capital accumulation. In practice however, Ricardian equivalence fails and larger deficits lead to higher demand and higher output in the short run. The accumulation of debt leads to lower capital accumulation, and thus to lower output in the long run.

- To stabilize the economy, the government should run deficits during recessions and surpluses during booms. The cyclically adjusted deficit tells us what the deficit would be, under existing tax and spending rules, if output were at the natural level of output.

- Deficits are justified in times of high spending, such as wars. Relative to an increase in taxes, deficits lead to higher consumption and lower investment during wars. They therefore shift some of the burden of the war from people living during the war to those living after the war. Deficits also help smooth taxes and reduce tax distortions.

- High debt ratios increase the risk of vicious cycles. A higher perceived risk of default can lead to a higher interest rate and an increase in debt. The increase in debt in turn can lead to a higher perceived risk of default and a higher interest rate. Together, both can combine to lead to a debt explosion. Governments may have no choice than to default or to rely on money finance. Money finance may in turn lead to hyperinflation. In either case, the economic costs are likely to be high.

Key Terms

inflation-adjusted deficit, 495
government budget constraint, 495
primary deficit (primary surplus), 497
debt-to-GDP ratio, debt ratio, 500
Ricardian equivalence, Ricardo-Barro proposition, 502
full-employment deficit, 503
mid-cycle deficit, 503
standardized employment deficit, 503
structural deficit, 503
cyclically adjusted deficit, 503
automatic stabilizer, 504
tax smoothing, 506
Congressional Budget Office (CBO), 507

baseline projections, 507
alternative minimum tax (AMT), 507
entitlement programs, 508
spread, 508
basis points, 509
haircuts, 509
debt restructuring, 509
debt rescheduling, 509
private sector involvement, 509
fiscal dominance, 510
debt monetization, 510
seignorage, 510
hyperinflation, 510

Questions and Problems

QUICK CHECK
All Quick Check questions and problems are available on MyEconLab.

1. Using information in this chapter, label each of the following statements true, false, or uncertain. Explain briefly.

a. Tax smoothing and deficit finance help spread the burden of war across generations.

b. The government should always take immediate action to eliminate a cyclically adjusted budget deficit.

c. If Ricardian equivalence holds, then an increase in income taxes will affect neither consumption nor saving.

d. The ratio of debt to GDP cannot exceed 100%.

e. Because the United States is able to finance investment by borrowing from abroad, the low U.S. saving rate is not a cause for concern.

f. Social security benefits will have to be decreased in the future.

g. Inflation has not played a role in the reduction of the ratio of debt to GDP.

h. In 2009 the United States government was in surplus

i. A hyperinflation is an inflation rate greater than 30% per month.

j. Hyperinflations may distort prices, but they have no effect on real output.

2. Consider the following statement:

"A deficit during a war can be a good thing. First, the deficit is temporary, so after the war is over, the government can go right back to its old level of spending and taxes. Second, given that the evidence supports the Ricardian equivalence proposition, the deficit will stimulate the economy during wartime, helping to keep the unemployment rate low."

Identify the mistakes in this statement. Is anything in this statement correct?

3. Consider an economy characterized by the following facts:

i. The official budget deficit is 4% of GDP.

ii. The debt-to-GDP ratio is 100%.

iii. The nominal interest rate is 10%.

iv. The inflation rate is 7%.

a. What is the primary deficit/surplus ratio to GDP?

b. What is the inflation-adjusted deficit/surplus ratio to GDP?

c. Suppose that output is 2% below its natural level. What is the cyclically adjusted, inflation-adjusted deficit/surplus ratio to GDP?

d. Suppose instead that output begins at its natural level and that output growth remains constant at the normal rate of 2%. How will the debt-to-GDP ratio change over time?

4. Assume that money demand takes the form

$$\frac{M}{P} = Y[1 - (r + \pi^e)]$$

where $Y = 1,000$ and $r = 0.1$.

a. Assume that, in the short run, π^e is constant and equal to 25%. Calculate the amount of seignorage for each annual rate of money growth, $\Delta M/M$, listed below.

i. 25%

ii. 50%

iii. 75%

b. In the medium run, $\pi^e = \pi = \Delta M/M$. Compute the amount of seignorage associated with the three rates of annual money growth in part (a). Explain why the answers differ from those in part (a).

DIG DEEPER
All Dig Deeper questions and problems are available on MyEconLab.

5. Consider the economy described in Problem 3 and assume that there is a fixed exchange rate, $\overline{E}$. Suppose that financial investors worry that the level of debt is too high and that the government may devalue to stimulate output (and therefore tax revenues) to help pay down the debt. Financial investors begin to expect a devaluation of 10%. In other words, the expected exchange rate, E^e_{t+1}, decreases by 10% from its previous value of $\overline{E}$.

a. Recall the uncovered interest parity condition:

$$i_t = i^*_t - \frac{E^e_{t+1} - \overline{E}}{\overline{E}}$$

If the foreign interest rate remains constant at 5% a year, what must happen to the domestic interest rate when E^e_{t+1} decreases by 10%?

b. Suppose that domestic inflation remains the same. What happens to the domestic real interest rate? What is likely to happen to the growth rate?

c. What happens to the official budget deficit? What happens to the inflation-adjusted deficit?

d. Suppose the growth rate decreases from 2% to 0%. What happens to the change in the debt ratio? (Assume that the primary deficit/surplus ratio to GDP is unchanged, even though the fall in growth may reduce tax revenues.)

e. Were the investors' fears of investors justified?

6. Ricardian equivalence and fiscal policy

First consider an economy in which Ricardian equivalence does not hold.

a. Suppose the government starts with a balanced budget. Then, there is an increase in government spending, but there is no change in taxes. Show in an IS–LM diagram the effect of this policy on output in the short run. How will the government finance the increase in government spending?

b. Suppose, as in part (a), that the government starts with a balanced budget and then increases government spending. This time, however, assume that taxes increase by the same amount as government spending. Show in an IS–LM diagram the effect of this policy on output in the short run. (It may help to recall the discussion of the multiplier in Chapter 3. Does government spending or tax policy have a bigger multiplier?) How does the output effect compare with the effect in part (a)?

Now suppose Ricardian equivalence holds in this economy. [Parts (c) and (d) do not require use of diagrams.]

c. Consider again an increase in government spending with no change in taxes. How does the output effect compare to the output effects in parts (a) and (b)?

d. Consider again an increase in government spending combined with an increase in taxes of the same amount. How does this output effect compare to the output effects in parts (a) and (b)?

e. Comment on each of the following statements:

i. "Under Ricardian equivalence, government spending has no effect on output."

ii. "Under Ricardian equivalence, changes in taxes have no effect on output."

EXPLORE FURTHER
7. Consider an economy characterized by the following facts:

i. The debt-to-GDP ratio is 40%.

ii. The primary deficit is 4% of GDP.

iii. The normal growth rate is 3%.

iv. The real interest rate is 3%.

a. Using your favorite spreadsheet software, compute the debt-to-GDP ratio in 10 years, assuming that the primary deficit stays at 4% of GDP each year; the economy grows at the normal growth rate in each year; and the real interest rate is constant, at 3%.

b. Suppose the real interest rate increases to 5%, but everything else remains as in part (a). Compute the debt-to-GDP ratio in 10 years.

c. Suppose the normal growth rate falls to 1%, and the economy grows at the normal growth rate each year. Everything else remains as in part (a). Calculate the debt-to-GDP ratio in 10 years. Compare your answer to part (b).

d. Return to the assumptions of part (a). Suppose policy-makers decide that a debt-to-GDP ratio of more than 50% is dangerous. Verify that reducing the primary deficit to 1% immediately, and that maintaining this deficit for 10 years, will produce a debt-to-GDP ratio of 50% in 10 years.

Thereafter, what value of the primary deficit will be required to maintain the debt-to-GDP ratio of 50%?

e. Continuing with part (d), suppose policy makers wait five years before changing fiscal policy. For five years, the primary deficit remains at 4% of GDP. What is the debt-to-GDP ratio in five years? Suppose that after five years, policy makers decide to reduce the debt-to-GDP ratio to 50%. In years 6 through 10, what constant value of the primary deficit will produce a debt-to-GDP ratio of 50% at the end of year 10?

f. Suppose that policy makers carry out the policy in either parts (d) or (e). If these policies reduce the growth rate of output for a while, how will this affect the size of the reduction in the primary deficit required to achieve a debt-to-GDP ratio of 50% in 10 years?

g. Which policy—the one in part (d) or the one in part (e)—do you think is more dangerous to the stability of the economy?

Further Readings

- The modern statement of the Ricardian equivalence proposition is Robert Barro's "Are Government Bonds Net Wealth?", *Journal of Political Economy*, 1974 82 (6): pp. 1095–1117.

- Each year, the Congressional Budget Office publishes *The Economic and Budget Outlook* for the current and future fiscal years. The document provides a clear and unbiased presentation of the current budget, of current budget issues, and of budget trends available at: http://www.cbo.gov/.

- As indicated in Chapter 11, a good site to follow current discussions about Social Security reform is the site run by the nonpartisan Concord Coalition: www.concordcoalition.org/socialsecurity/.

- For more on the German hyperinflation, read Steven Webb, *Hyperinflation and Stabilization in the Weimar Republic* (Oxford University Press, 1989).

- A good review of what economists know and don't know about hyperinflation is given in Rudiger Dornbusch, Federico Sturzenegger, and Holger Wolf, "Extreme Inflation: Dynamics and Stabilization," *Brookings Papers on Economic Activity*, 1990 (2): pp. 1–84.

Monetary Policy:
A Summing Up

The crisis has led to a major reassessment of monetary policy. For the two decades before the crisis, central banks had largely converged toward a framework for monetary policy, called **inflation targeting**. It was based on two principles. The first was that the primary goal of monetary policy was to keep inflation stable and low. The second was that the best way to achieve this goal was to follow an **interest rate rule**, a rule allowing the interest rate directly controlled by the central bank to respond to movements in inflation and in activity.

The first central bank to adopt this framework was the Reserve Bank of New Zealand in 1990. The European Central Bank, when created in 2000, also adopted this framework. The latest central bank to do so is the Fed, which announced a formal 2% inflation target in early 2012, just as this book went to print.

Until the crisis, this framework appeared to work well. Inflation decreased and remained low and stable in most countries. Output fluctuations decreased in amplitude. The period became known as the **Great Moderation**. Many researchers looked for the causes of this moderation, and many concluded that better monetary policy was one of the main factors behind the improvement.

The crisis has forced macroeconomists and central bankers to reassess along at least two dimensions.

The first is the set of issues raised by the liquidity trap, which we already touched upon at various points in the book, in particular in Chapter 9. When an economy is in a liquidity trap, the interest rate can no longer be used to increase activity. This raises two questions. First, can monetary policy be conducted in such a way as to avoid getting in the liquidity trap in the first place? Second, once the economy is in a liquidity trap, are there other tools that the central bank can use to help increase activity?

The second, and a deeper set of issues, is about the mandate of the central bank and the tools of monetary policy. From the early 2000s to the start of the crisis, most advanced economies appeared to do well, with sustained output growth and stable inflation. Yet, as we saw in Chapter 9, not everything was fine behind the scenes. Important changes were taking place in the financial system, such as the large increase in leverage and the increased reliance on wholesale funding by banks. In many countries, also, there were sharp increases in housing prices. These factors turned out to be at the source of the crisis. Put another way—and the cartoon below makes the point—the economy that Alan Greenspan, the previous chairman of the Fed, left to his successor, Ben Bernanke, was no gift. This again raises at least two sets of issues. Looking forward, should the central bank worry not only about inflation and the overall level of economic activity, but also about asset prices, stock market booms, housing booms, and creating and implementing regulations to avoid excessive risk in the financial sector? And if so, what tools does it have at its disposal?

Daryl Cagle, MSNBC.com

The purpose of this chapter is to review what we have learned about monetary policy so far, then describe the logic of inflation targeting and the use of an interest rate rule, and finally we discuss where we stand on the issues raised by the crisis.

Section 24-1 takes stock of what we have learned.

Section 24-2 reviews the costs and benefits of inflation and draws implications for the choice of a target inflation rate by central banks.

Section 24-3 describes the inflation-targeting framework.

Section 24-4 describes the challenges raised by the crisis and how they may affect the design of monetary policy in the future. ●

24-1 What We Have Learned

■ In Chapter 4 we looked at money demand and money supply and the determination of the interest rate.

We saw how an increase in the money supply, achieved through an open market operation, leads to a decrease in the interest rate.

- In Chapter 5 we looked at the short-run effects of monetary policy on output.

  We saw how an increase in money leads, through a decrease in the interest rate, to an increase in spending and to an increase in output.

- In Chapter 7 we looked at the effects of changes in money on output and prices, not only in the short run but also in the medium run.

  We saw that in the medium run, money is neutral: Changes in the level of money are reflected one-for-one in changes in the price level.

- In Chapter 8 we looked at the relation between nominal money growth, inflation, and unemployment.

  We saw that in the medium run, an increase in nominal money growth is reflected one-for-one in an increase in inflation, leaving the unemployment rate unaffected.

- In Chapter 9 we looked at the implications of the liquidity trap, the fact that monetary policy cannot decrease the nominal interest rate below zero.

  We saw that, in this case, conventional monetary policy can no longer be used. Other tools, such as quantitative or credit easing, can be used but they are not as reliable.

- In Chapter 14 we introduced the concept of the natural real rate of interest, the real rate of interest associated with output being at its natural level.

  We saw that, when money growth increases, the nominal interest rate eventually increases one-for-one with money growth and inflation, leaving the real interest rate unaffected.

- In Chapter 17 we returned to the short-run effects of monetary policy on output, taking into account the effects of monetary policy on expectations.

  We saw that monetary policy affects the short-term nominal interest rate, but that spending depends on current and expected future short-term real interest rates. We saw how the effects of monetary policy on output depend on how expectations respond to monetary policy.

- In Chapter 20 we looked at the effects of monetary policy in an economy open in both goods markets and financial markets.

  We saw how, in an open economy, monetary policy affects spending and output not only through the interest rate, but also through the exchange rate. An increase in money leads both to a decrease in the interest rate and a depreciation, both of which increase spending and output.

- In Chapter 21 we discussed the pros and cons of different monetary policy regimes, namely flexible exchange rates versus fixed exchange rates.

  We discussed the pros and cons of adopting a common currency such as the euro, or even giving up monetary policy altogether through the adoption of a currency board or dollarization.

- In Chapter 22 we looked at the problems facing macroeconomic policy in general, and monetary policy in particular.

  We saw that uncertainty about the effects of policy should lead to more cautious policies. We saw that even well-intentioned policy makers may sometimes not do what is best, and that there is a case to be made for putting restraints on policy makers. We also looked at the benefits of having an independent central bank and appointing a conservative central banker.

In this chapter we extend the analysis to look, first, at the optimal inflation rate; second, at inflation targeting; and third, at the challenges raised by the crisis.

24-2 The Optimal Inflation Rate

Table 24-1 shows how inflation has steadily decreased in rich countries since the early 1980s. In 1981, average inflation in the OECD was 10.5%; in 2010, it was down to 1.2%.

Table 24-1	Inflation Rates in the OECD, 1981–2010						
Year	**1981**	**1985**	**1990**	**1995**	**2000**	**2005**	**2010**
OECD average*	10.5%	6.6%	6.2%	5.2%	2.8%	2.3%	1.2%
Number of countries with inflation below 5%**	2	10	15	21	24	28	27

*Average of GDP deflator inflation rates, using relative GDPs measured at PPP prices as weights.
**Out of 30 countries.

The three countries with inflation above 5% in 2010: Australia (5.1%), Luxembourg (5.3%), Turkey (6.4%).

In 1981, two countries (out of 30) had an inflation rate below 5%; in 2010, the number had increased to 27.

Should central banks aim for an even lower inflation rate, perhaps 0%? Or have they have overshot their goal? The answer depends on the costs and benefits of inflation.

The Costs of Inflation

We saw in Chapter 23 how very high inflation, say a rate of 30% per month or more, can disrupt economic activity. The debate in OECD countries today, however, is not about the costs of inflation rates of 30% or more per month. Rather, it centers on the advantages of, say, 0% versus, say, 4% inflation per year. Within that range, economists identify four main costs of inflation: (1) shoe-leather costs, (2) tax distortions, (3) money illusion, and (4) inflation variability.

Shoe-Leather Costs

Recall that in the medium run, a higher inflation rate leads to a higher nominal interest rate, and so to a higher opportunity cost of holding money. As a result, people decrease their money balances by making more trips to the bank—thus the expression **shoe-leather costs.** These trips would be avoided if inflation were lower and people could be doing other things instead, such as working more or enjoying leisure.

During hyperinflations, shoe-leather costs become indeed quite large. But their importance in times of moderate inflation is limited. If an inflation rate of 4% leads people to go the bank, say, one more time every month, or to do one more transaction between their money market fund and their checking account each month, this hardly qualifies as a major cost of inflation.

Tax Distortions

The second cost of inflation comes from the interaction between the tax system and inflation.

Consider, for example, the taxation of capital gains. Taxes on capital gains are typically based on the change in the price in dollars of the asset between the time it was purchased and the time it is sold. This implies that the higher the rate of inflation, the higher the tax. An example will make this clear:

- Suppose inflation has been running at π % a year for the last 10 years.
- Suppose also that you bought your house for $50,000 10 years ago, and you are selling it today for $50,000 times $(1 + \pi\%)^{10}$—so its real value is unchanged.

The numerator of the fraction equals the sale price minus the purchase price. The denominator is the sale price.

- If the capital-gains tax is 30%, the *effective tax rate* on the sale of your house—defined as the ratio of the tax you pay to the price for which you sell your house—is

$$(30\%) \frac{50,000 (1 + \pi\%)^{10} - 50,000}{50,000 (1 + \pi\%)^{10}}$$

- Because you are selling your house for the same real price at which you bought it, your real capital gain is zero, so you should not be paying any tax. Indeed, if $\pi = 0$ —if there has been no inflation—then the effective tax rate is 0. But if, for example, $\pi = 4\%$, then the effective tax rate is 9.7%: Despite the fact that your real capital gain is zero, you end up paying a high tax.

The problems created by the interactions between taxation and inflation extend beyond capital-gains taxes. Although we know that the real rate of return on an asset is the real interest rate, not the nominal interest rate, income for the purpose of income taxation includes nominal interest payments, not real interest payments. Or, to take yet another example, until the early 1980s in the United States, the income levels corresponding to different income-tax rates were not increased automatically with inflation. As a result, people were pushed into higher tax brackets as their nominal income—but not necessarily their real income—increased over time, an effect known as **bracket creep.**

You might argue this cost is not a cost of inflation per se, but rather the result of a badly designed tax system. In the house example we just discussed, the government could eliminate the problem if it *indexed* the purchase price to the price level—that is, it adjusted the purchase price for inflation since the time of purchase—and computed the tax on the difference between the sale price and the adjusted purchase price. Under this computation, there would be no capital gains and therefore no capital–gains tax to pay. But because tax codes rarely allow for such systematic adjustment, the inflation rate matters and leads to distortions.

Some economists argue that the costs of bracket creep were much larger. As tax revenues steadily increased, there was little pressure on the government to control spending. The result, they argue, was an increase in the overall size of the government in the 1960s and 1970s far beyond what would have been desirable.

Money Illusion

The third cost comes from **money illusion**—the notion that people appear to make systematic mistakes in assessing nominal versus real changes in incomes and interest rates. A number of computations that would be simple when prices are stable become more complicated when there is inflation. When they compare their income this year to their income in previous years, people have to keep track of the history of inflation. When choosing between different assets or deciding how much to consume or save, they have to keep track of the difference between the real interest rate and the nominal interest rate. Casual evidence suggests that many people find these computations difficult and often fail to make the relevant distinctions. Economists and psychologists have gathered more formal evidence, and it suggests that inflation often leads people and firms to make incorrect decisions (see the Focus box "Money Illusion"). If this is the case, then a seemingly simple solution is to have zero inflation.

Inflation Variability

Another cost comes from the fact that higher inflation is typically associated with *more variable inflation*. And more variable inflation means financial assets such as bonds, which promise fixed nominal payments in the future, become riskier.

Take a bond that pays $1,000 in 10 years. With constant inflation over the next 10 years, not only the nominal value, but also the real value of the bond in 10 years is known with certainty—we can compute exactly how much a dollar will be worth in 10 years. But with variable inflation, the real value of $1,000 in 10 years becomes uncertain. The more variability there is, the more uncertainty it creates. Saving for retirement becomes more difficult. For those who have invested in bonds, lower inflation than they expected means a better retirement; but higher inflation may mean poverty. This is one of the reasons retirees, for whom part of their income is fixed in dollar terms, typically worry more about inflation than other groups in the population.

A good and sad movie about surviving on a fixed pension in post–World War II Italy: *Umberto D*, by Vittorio de Sica, 1952.

You might argue, as in the case of taxes, that these costs are not due to inflation per se, but rather to the financial markets' inability to provide assets that protect their

Money Illusion

There is a lot of anecdotal evidence that many people fail to adjust properly for inflation in their financial computations. Recently, economists and psychologists have started looking at money illusion more closely. In a recent study, two psychologists, Eldar Shafir from Princeton and Amos Tversky from Stanford, and one economist, Peter Diamond from MIT, designed a survey aimed at finding how prevalent money illusion is and what causes it. Among the many questions they asked of people in various groups (people at Newark International Airport, people at two New Jersey shopping malls, and a group of Princeton undergraduates) is the following:

Suppose Adam, Ben, and Carl each received an inheritance of $200,000 and each used it immediately to purchase a house. Suppose each sold his house one year after buying it. Economic conditions were, however, different in each case:

- During the time Adam owned the house, there was a 25% deflation—the prices of all goods and services decreased by approximately 25%. A year after Adam bought the house, he sold it for $154,000 (23% less than what he had paid).

- During the time Ben owned the house, there was no inflation or deflation—the prices of all goods and services did not change significantly during the year. A year after Ben bought the house, he sold it for $198,000 (1% less than what he had paid).

- During the time Carl owned the house, there was a 25% inflation—the prices of all goods and services

increased by approximately 25%. A year after Carl bought the house, he sold it for $246,000 (23% more than what he had paid).

Please rank Adam, Ben, and Carl in terms of the success of their house transactions. Assign "1" to the person who made the best deal and "3" to the person who made the worst deal.

In nominal terms, Carl clearly made the best deal, followed by Ben, followed by Adam. But what is relevant is how they did in real terms—adjusting for inflation. In real terms, the ranking is reversed: Adam, with a 2% real gain, made the best deal, followed by Ben (with a 1% loss), followed by Carl (with a 2% loss).

The survey's answers were the following:

Rank	Adam	Ben	Carl
1st	37%	15%	48%
2nd	10%	74%	16%
3rd	53%	11%	36%

Carl was ranked first by 48% of the respondents, and Adam was ranked third by 53% of the respondents. These answers suggest that money illusion is very prevalent. In other words, people (even Princeton undergraduates) have a hard time adjusting for inflation.

Source: Eldar Shafir, Peter Diamond, Amos Tversky, "Money Illusion", *Quarterly Journal of Economics*, 1997 112(2): pp. 341–374.

holders against inflation. Rather than issuing only nominal bonds (bonds that promise a fixed nominal amount in the future), governments or firms could also issue *indexed bonds*—bonds that promise a nominal amount adjusted after inflation so people do not have to worry about the real value of the bond when they retire. Indeed, as we saw in Chapter 15, a number of countries, including the United States, have now introduced such bonds so people can better protect themselves against movements in inflation.

The Benefits of Inflation

This may surprise you, but inflation is actually not all bad. There are three benefits of inflation: (1) seignorage, (2) the option of negative real interest rates for macroeconomic policy, and (3) (somewhat paradoxically) the use of the interaction between money illusion and inflation in facilitating real wage adjustments.

Seignorage

Money creation—the ultimate source of inflation—is one of the ways in which the government can finance its spending. Put another way, money creation is an alternative to borrowing from the public or raising taxes.

As we saw in Chapter 23, the government typically does not "create" money to pay for its spending. Rather, the government issues and sells bonds, and spends the proceeds. But if the bonds are bought by the central bank, which then creates money to pay for them, the result is the same: Other things equal, the revenues from money creation—that is, *seignorage*—allow the government to borrow less from the public or to lower taxes.

How large is seignorage in practice? When looking at hyperinflations in Chapter 23, we saw that seignorage can be an important source of government finance in countries with very high inflation rates. But its importance in OECD economies today, and for the range of inflation rates we are considering, is much more limited. Take the case of the United States. The ratio of the monetary base—the money issued by the Fed (see Chapter 4)—to GDP is usually about 6%. An increase in the rate of nominal money growth of 4% per year (which eventually leads to a 4% increase in the inflation rate) would lead therefore to an increase in seignorage of $4\% \times 6\%$, or 0.24% of GDP. This is a small amount of revenue to get in exchange for 4% more inflation.

Therefore, while the seignorage argument is sometimes relevant (for example, in economies that do not yet have a good fiscal system in place), it hardly seems relevant in the discussion of whether OECD countries today should have, say, 0% versus 4% inflation.

The Option of Negative Real Interest Rates

This argument follows from our discussion of the liquidity trap in Chapter 9. A numerical example will help here.

- Consider two economies, both with a *natural real interest rate equal to 2%*.
- In the first economy, the central bank maintains an average inflation rate of 4%, so the nominal interest rate is on average equal to $2\% + 4\% = 6\%$.
- In the second economy, the central bank maintains an average inflation rate of 0%, so the nominal interest rate is on average equal to $2\% + 0\% = 2\%$.
- Suppose both economies are hit by a similar adverse shock, which leads, at a given interest rate, to a decrease in spending and a decrease in output in the short run.
- In the first economy, the central bank can decrease the nominal interest rate from 6% to 0% before it hits the liquidity trap, thus a decrease of 6%. Under the assumption that expected inflation does not change immediately and remains equal to 4%, the real interest rate decreases from 2% to -4%. This is likely to have a strong positive effect on spending and help the economy recover.
- In the second economy, the central bank can only decrease the nominal interest rate from 2% to 0%, a decrease of 2%. Under the assumption that expected inflation does not change right away and remains equal to 0%, the real interest rate decreases only by 2%, from 2% to 0%. This small decrease in the real interest rate may not increase spending by very much.

In short, an economy with a higher average inflation rate has more room to use monetary policy to fight a recession. An economy with a low average inflation rate may find itself unable to use monetary policy to return output to the natural level of output. As we saw in Chapter 9, this possibility is far from being just theoretical. Many countries today find themselves in the liquidity trap, unable to decrease interest rates further. The question is whether this should lead the country to choose slightly higher average inflation in the future. Some economists argue that the current crisis is an exceptional event, that it is unlikely that countries will face a liquidity trap again in the future, and so there is no need to adopt a higher average inflation rate. Others argue that the problems faced by a country in a liquidity trap are so serious that we should avoid taking the risk that it happens again, and that a higher rate of inflation is in fact justified. The debate is far from settled.

Because of quantitative easing, the ratio of the monetary base to GDP is higher than it was pre-crisis. But it is expected to return to its normal level when the U.S. economy emerges from the liquidity trap.

Recall equation (23.6): Let H denote the monetary base—the money issued by the central bank. Then

$$\frac{\text{Seignorage}}{Y} = \frac{\Delta H}{PY} = \frac{\Delta H}{H} \frac{H}{PY}$$

where $\Delta H/H$ is the rate of growth of the monetary base, and H/PY is the ratio of the monetary base to nominal GDP.

Money Illusion Revisited

See, for example, the results of a survey of managers by Alan Blinder and Don Choi, in "A Shred of Evidence on Theories of Wage Rigidity," *Quarterly Journal of Economics*, 1990 105 (4): pp. 1003–1015.

Paradoxically, the presence of money illusion provides at least one argument *for* having a positive inflation rate.

To see why, consider two situations. In the first, inflation is 4% and your wage goes up by 1% in nominal terms—in dollars. In the second, inflation is 0% and your wage goes down by 3% in nominal terms. Both lead to the same 3% decrease in your real wage, so you should be indifferent. The evidence, however, shows that many people will accept the real wage cut more easily in the first case than in the second case.

Why is this example relevant to our discussion? As we saw in Chapter 13, the constant process of change that characterizes modern economies means some workers must sometimes take a real pay cut. Thus, the argument goes, the presence of inflation allows for these downward real wage adjustments more easily than when there is no inflation. This argument is plausible. Economists have not established its importance; but, because so many economies now have very low inflation, we may soon be in a position to test it.

A conflict of metaphors: Because inflation makes these real wage adjustments easier to achieve, some economists say inflation "greases the wheels" of the economy. Others, emphasizing the adverse effects of inflation on relative prices, say that inflation "puts sand" in the economy.

The Optimal Inflation Rate: The Current Debate

At this stage, most central banks in richer countries have an inflation target of about 2%. They are, however, being challenged on two fronts. Some economists want to achieve price stability—that is, 0% inflation. Others want, instead, a higher target rate of inflation, say 4%.

Those who want to aim for 0% make the point that 0% is a very different target rate from all others: It corresponds to price stability. This is desirable in itself. Knowing the price level will be roughly the same in 10 or 20 years as it is today simplifies a number of complicated decisions and eliminates the scope for money illusion. Also, given the time consistency problem facing central banks (discussed in Chapter 22), credibility and simplicity of the target inflation rate are important. Some economists and some central bankers believe price stability—that is, a 0% target—can achieve these goals better than a target inflation rate of 2%. So far, however, no central bank has actually adopted a 0% inflation target.

Those who want to aim for a higher rate argue that it is essential not to fall in the liquidity trap in the future, and that, for these purposes, a higher target rate of inflation, say 4%, would be helpful. Their argument has gained little support among central bankers. They argue that if central banks increase their target from its current value of 2% to 4%, people may start anticipating that the target will soon become 5%, then 6%, and so on, and inflation expectations will no longer be anchored. Thus, they see it as important to keep current target levels.

This reasoning is sometimes known as the "slippery slope" argument.

The debate goes on. For the time being, most central banks appear to be aiming for low but positive inflation—that is, inflation rates of about 2%.

24-3 The Design of Monetary Policy

Until the early 1990s, the design of monetary policy typically centered around nominal money growth. Central banks chose a nominal money growth target for the medium run; and they thought about short-run monetary policy in terms of deviations of nominal money growth from that target. In the last two decades, however, this design has evolved. Most central banks have adopted an inflation rate target rather than a nominal money growth rate target. They think about short-run monetary policy in terms of movements in the nominal interest rate rather than in terms of movements in the rate of nominal money growth. The current crisis has shown however some of the limits of this approach and raises the question of whether and how monetary policy should be modified. In this section, we look at the evolution of monetary policy up to the crisis. We then take up the issues raised by the crisis in the next section.

Money Growth Targets and Target Ranges

Until the 1990s, monetary policy, in the United States and in other advanced countries, was typically conducted as follows:

■ The central bank chose a target rate for nominal money growth corresponding to the inflation rate it wanted to achieve in the medium run. If, for example, it wanted to achieve an inflation rate of 4% and the normal rate of growth of output (the rate of growth implied by the rate of technological progress and the rate of population growth) was 3%, the central bank chose a target rate of nominal money growth of 7%.

■ In the short run, the central bank allowed for deviations of nominal money growth from the target. If, for example, the economy was in a recession, the central bank increased nominal money growth above the target value, so as to allow for a decrease in the interest rate and a faster recovery of output. In an expansion, it might do the reverse, so as to slow output growth.

■ To communicate to the public both what it wanted to achieve in the medium run and what it intended to do in the short run, the central bank announced a range for the rate of nominal money growth it intended to achieve. Sometimes this range was presented as a commitment from the central bank; sometimes it was presented simply as a forecast rather than as a commitment.

Over time, central banks became disenchanted with this way of conducting monetary policy. Let's now see why.

Money Growth and Inflation Revisited

The design of monetary policy around nominal money growth is based on the assumption that there is a close relation between inflation and nominal money growth in the medium run. Theory tells us that there should be such a relation. The problem is that, in practice, this relation is not very tight. If nominal money growth is high, inflation will also be high; and if nominal money growth is low, inflation will be low. But the relation is not tight enough that, by choosing a rate of nominal money growth, the central bank can achieve precisely its desired rate of inflation, not even in the medium run.

◀ See Chapter 8.

The relation between inflation and nominal money growth is shown in Figure 24-1, which plots 10-year averages of the U.S. inflation rate against 10-year averages of the growth rate of money from 1970 up to the crisis (the way to read the figure: the numbers for inflation and for money growth for 2000 for example are the average inflation rate and the average growth rate of money from 1991 to 2000). The inflation rate is constructed using the CPI as the price index. The growth rate of nominal money is constructed using $M1$ as the measure for the money stock. The reason for using 10-year averages should be clear: In the short run, changes in nominal money growth affect mostly output, not inflation. It is only in the medium run that a relation between nominal money growth and inflation should emerge. Taking 10-year averages of both nominal money growth and inflation is a way of detecting such a medium-run relation.

From Chapter 4: $M1$ measures the amount of money in the economy and is constructed as the sum of currency and checkable deposits. The Fed ◀ does not directly control $M1$. What it controls is H, the monetary base; but it can choose H to achieve the value of $M1$ it wants. It is therefore reasonable to think of the Fed as controlling $M1$.

Figure 24-1 shows that, for the United States, the relation between $M1$ growth and inflation has not been very tight. True, both went up in the 1970s, and both have come down since. But note how inflation started declining in the early 1980s, while nominal money growth remained high for another decade and came down only in the 1990s. Average inflation from 1981 to 1990 was down to 4%, while average money growth over the same period was still running at 7.5%.

Figure 24-1

M1 Growth and Inflation: 10-Year Averages, 1970 to the crisis

There is no tight relation between *M*1 growth and inflation, not even in the medium run.

Source: Series CPIAUSL and M1SL Federal Reserve Economic Data (FRED) http://research.stlouisfed.org/fred2/

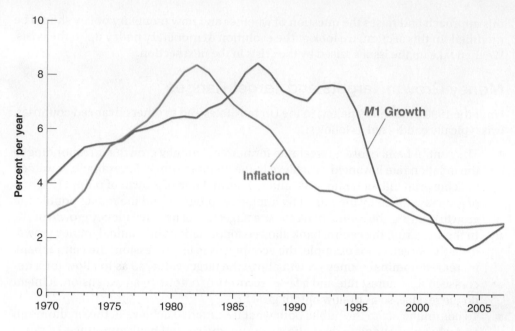

From equation (5.3) (the *LM* equation): The real money supply (the left side) must be equal to the real demand for money (the right side):

$$\frac{M}{P} = Y L(i)$$

If, as a result of the introduction of credit cards, the real demand for money halves, then

$$\frac{M}{P} = \frac{1}{2} Y L(i)$$

For a given level of output and a given interest rate, *M/P* must also halve. Given *M*. this implies *P* must double.

Why is the relation between *M*1 growth and inflation not tighter? Because of *shifts in the demand for money*. An example will help. Suppose, as the result of the introduction of credit cards, people decide to hold only half the amount of money they held before; in other words, the real demand for money decreases by half. In the medium run, the real money stock must also decrease by half. For a given nominal money stock, the price level must double. Even if the nominal money stock were to remain constant, there would still be a period of inflation as the price level doubles. During this period, there would be no tight relation between nominal money growth (which is zero) and inflation (which would be positive). The Focus box "The Unsuccessful Search for the Right Monetary Aggregate" explores this further.

Throughout the 1970s and the 1980s, these frequent and large shifts in money demand created serious problems for central banks. They found themselves torn between trying to keep a stable target for money growth and staying within announced bands (in order to maintain credibility), or adjusting to shifts in money demand (in order to stabilize output in the short run and inflation in the medium run). Starting in the early 1990s, a dramatic rethinking of monetary policy took place, based instead on inflation targeting rather than money growth targeting, and the use of interest rate rules. Let's look at the way monetary policy has evolved.

Inflation Targeting

In most countries, central banks have defined as their primary goal the achievement of a low inflation rate, both in the short run and in the medium run. This is known as *inflation targeting*.

■   Trying to achieve a given inflation target *in the medium run* would seem, and indeed is, a clear improvement over trying to achieve a nominal money growth target. After all, in the medium run, the primary goal of monetary policy is to achieve a given rate of inflation. Better to have an inflation rate as the target than a nominal money growth target, which, as we have seen, may not lead to the desired rate of inflation.

The Unsuccessful Search for the Right Monetary Aggregate

FOCUS

The reason why the demand for money shifts over time goes beyond the introduction of credit cards. To understand why, we must challenge an assumption we have maintained until now, namely that there is a sharp distinction between money and other assets. In fact, there are many financial assets that are close to money. They cannot be used for transactions—at least not without restrictions—but they can be exchanged for money at little cost. In other words, these assets are very liquid; this makes them attractive substitutes for money. Shifts between money and these assets are the main factor behind shifts in the demand for money.

Take, for example, money market fund shares. Money market funds are financial intermediaries that hold as assets short-maturity securities (typically, Treasury bills) and have deposits (or shares, as they are called) as liabilities. The funds pay depositors an interest rate close to the T-bill rate minus the administrative costs of running the fund. Deposits can be exchanged for money on notice and at little cost. Most money market funds allow depositors to write checks, but only above a certain amount, typically $500. Because of this restriction, money market funds are not included in $M1$. When these funds were introduced in the mid-1970s, people were able for the first time to hold a very liquid asset while receiving an interest rate close to that on T-bills. Money market funds quickly became very attractive, increasing from nothing in 1973 to $321 billion in 1989. (For comparison: Checkable deposits were $280 billion in 1989.) Many people reduced their bank account balances and moved to money market funds. In other words, there was a large negative shift in the demand for money.

The presence of such shifts between money and other liquid assets led central banks to construct and report measures that include not only money, but also other liquid assets. These measures are called **monetary aggregates** and come under the names of $M2$, $M3$, and so on. In the United States, $M2$—which is also sometimes called **broad money**—includes $M1$ (currency and checkable deposits), plus money market mutual fund shares, money market deposit accounts (the same as money market shares, but issued by banks rather than money market funds), and time deposits (deposits with an explicit maturity of a few months to a few years and with a penalty for early withdrawal). In 2010, $M2$ was $8.6 trillion, compared to $1.7 trillion for $M1$.

The construction of $M2$ and other monetary aggregates would appear to offer a solution to our earlier problem: If most of the shifts in the demand for money are between $M2$ and other assets within $M2$, the demand for $M2$ should be more stable than the demand for $M1$, and so there should be a tighter relation between $M2$ growth and inflation than between $M1$ growth and inflation. If so, the central bank could choose targets for $M2$ growth rather than for $M1$ growth. This is indeed the solution that

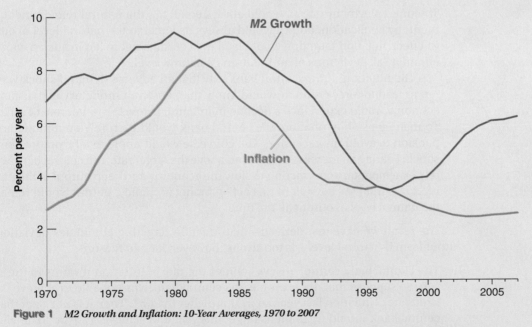

Figure 1 *M2 Growth and Inflation: 10-Year Averages, 1970 to 2007*

Source: Series CPIAUSL and M2NS Federal Reserve Economic Data (FRED) *http://research.stlouisfed.org/fred2/*

- The relation between $M2$ growth and inflation is no tighter than the relation between $M1$ growth and inflation. This is shown in Figure 1, which plots 10-year averages of the inflation rate and of the rate of growth of $M2$ from 1970 to 2007. $M2$ growth was nearly 5% above inflation in the early 1970s. This difference disappeared over time, only to reappear and grow in the 2000s.
- More importantly, while the central bank controls $M1$, it does not control $M2$. If people shift from T-bills to money market funds, this will increase $M2$—which includes money market funds but does not include T-bills. There is little the central bank can do about this increase in $M2$. Thus, $M2$ is a strange target: It is neither under the direct control of the central bank nor what the central bank ultimately cares about.

In short, the relation between inflation and the growth of monetary aggregates such as $M2$ is no tighter than the relation between inflation and the growth rate of $M1$. And the central bank has little control over the growth of these monetary aggregates anyway. This is why, in most countries, monetary policy has shifted its focus from monetary aggregates, be it $M1$ or $M2$, to inflation.

- Trying to achieve a given inflation target *in the short run* would appear to be much more controversial. Focusing exclusively on inflation would seem to eliminate any role monetary policy could play in reducing output fluctuations. But, in fact, this is not necessarily the case.

To see why, return to the Phillips curve relation among inflation, π_t, lagged inflation, π_{t-1}, and the deviation of the unemployment rate, u_t from the natural rate of unemployment, u_n (equation (8.10)):

$$\pi_t = \pi_{t-1} - \alpha(u_t - u_n)$$

Let the inflation rate target be π^*. Suppose the central bank could achieve its inflation target exactly in every period. Then the relation would become:

$$\pi^* = \pi^* - \alpha(u_t - u_n)$$

$0 = -\alpha(u_t - u_n) \Rightarrow u_t = u_n.$ ▶

The unemployment rate u_t would always equal u_n, the natural rate of unemployment; by implication, output would always be equal to the natural level of output. In effect, inflation targeting would lead the central bank to act in such a way as to eliminate all deviations of output from its natural level.

The intuition: If the central bank saw that an adverse demand shock was going to lead to a recession, it would know that, absent a monetary expansion, the economy would experience a decline in inflation below the target rate of inflation. To maintain stable inflation, the central bank would then rely on a monetary expansion to avoid the recession. The converse would apply to a favorable demand shock: Fearing an increase in inflation above the target rate, the central bank would rely on a monetary contraction to slow the economy and keep output at the natural level of output. As a result of this active monetary policy, output would remain at the natural level of output all the time.

The result we have just derived—that inflation targeting eliminates deviations of output from its natural level—is too strong, however, for two reasons:

1. The central bank cannot always achieve the rate of inflation it wants in the short run. So suppose that, for example, the central bank was not able to achieve its desired rate of inflation last year, so π_{t-1} is higher than π^*. Then it is not clear that the central bank should try to hit its target this year and achieve $\pi_t = \pi^*$: The Phillips curve relation implies that such a decrease in inflation would require a potentially large increase in unemployment.

2. Like all other macroeconomic relations, the Phillips curve relation above does not hold exactly. It will happen that, for example, inflation increases even when unemployment is at the natural rate of unemployment. In this case, the central bank will face a more difficult choice: whether to keep unemployment at the natural rate and allow inflation to increase, or to increase unemployment above the natural rate to keep inflation in check.

These qualifications are important, but the basic point remains: Inflation targeting makes good sense in the medium run and allows for monetary policy to stabilize output close to its natural level in the short run.

Interest Rate Rules

Given the discussion so far, the question now is how to achieve the inflation target. Inflation is clearly not under the direct control of the central bank. In answer to this question, John Taylor, from Stanford University, argued in the 1990s that, since the central bank affects spending through the interest rate, the central bank should think directly in terms of the choice of an interest rate rather than a rate of nominal money growth. He then suggested a rule that the central bank should follow to set the interest rate. This rule, which is now known as the **Taylor rule**, goes as follows:

■ Let π_t be the rate of inflation and π^* be the target rate of inflation.
■ Let i_t be the nominal interest rate controlled by the central bank and i^* be the target nominal interest rate—the nominal interest rate associated with the target rate of inflation, π^*, in the medium run.
■ Let u_t be the unemployment rate and u_n be the natural unemployment rate.

Think of the central bank as choosing the nominal interest rate, i. (Recall, from Chapter 4, that, through open market operations, and ignoring the liquidity trap, the central bank can achieve any short-term nominal interest rate that it wants.) Then, Taylor argued, the central bank should use the following rule:

$$i_t = i^* + a(\pi_t - \pi^*) - b(u_t - u_n)$$

where a and b are positive coefficients.

Let's look at what the rule says:

■ If inflation is equal to target inflation ($\pi_t = \pi^*$) and the unemployment rate is equal to the natural rate of unemployment ($u_t = u_n$), then the central bank should set the nominal interest rate, i_t, equal to its target value, i^*. This way, the economy can stay on the same path, with inflation equal to the target inflation rate and unemployment equal to the natural rate of unemployment.
■ If inflation is higher than the target ($\pi_t > \pi^*$), the central bank should increase the nominal interest rate, i_t, above i^*. This higher interest rate will increase unemployment, and this increase in unemployment will lead to a decrease in inflation. The coefficient a should therefore reflect how much the central bank cares about inflation. The higher a, the more the central bank will increase the interest rate in response to inflation, the more the economy will slow down, the more unemployment will increase, and the faster inflation will return to the target inflation rate. In any case, Taylor pointed out, a should be larger than one. Why? Because what matters for spending is the real interest rate, not the nominal interest rate. When inflation increases, the central bank, if it wants to decrease spending and output, must increase the *real* interest rate. In other words, it must increase the nominal interest rate more than one-for-one with inflation.

Recall from Chapter 14 that, in the medium run, the real interest rate is equal to the natural real interest rate, r_n, so the nominal interest rate moves one-for-one with the inflation rate: If $r_n = 2\%$ and the target inflation rate $\pi^* = 4\%$, then the target nominal interest rate $i^* = 2\% + 4\% = 6\%$. If the target inflation rate π^* is 0%, then $i^* = 2\% + 0\% = 2\%$.

Some economists argue that the increase in U.S. inflation in the 1970s was due to the fact that the Fed increased the nominal interest rate less than one-for-one with inflation. The result, they argue, was that an increase in inflation led to a decrease in the real interest rate, which led to higher demand, lower unemployment, more inflation, a further decrease in the real interest rate, and so on.

- If unemployment is higher than the natural rate of unemployment $(u_t > u_n)$, the central bank should decrease the nominal interest rate. The lower nominal interest rate will increase output, leading to a decrease in unemployment. The coefficient b should reflect how much the central bank cares about unemployment. The higher b, the more the central bank will be willing to deviate from target inflation to keep unemployment close to the natural rate of unemployment.

In stating this rule, Taylor did not argue that it should be followed blindly: Many other events, such as an exchange rate crisis or the need to change the composition of spending on goods, and thus the mix between monetary policy and fiscal policy, justify changing the nominal interest rate for other reasons than those included in the rule. But, he argued, the rule provided a useful way of thinking about monetary policy: Once the central bank has chosen a target rate of inflation, it should try to achieve it by adjusting the nominal interest rate. The rule it should follow should take into account not only current inflation, but also current unemployment.

Since it was first introduced, the Taylor rule has generated a lot of interest, both from researchers and from central banks:

- Interestingly, researchers looking at the behavior of both the Fed in the United States and the Bundesbank in Germany have found that, although neither of these two central banks thought of itself as following a Taylor rule, this rule actually described their behavior fairly well over the last 15–20 years before the crisis.
- Other researchers have explored whether it is possible to improve on this simple rule: for example, whether the nominal interest rate should be allowed to respond not only to current inflation, but also to expected future inflation.
- Yet other researchers have discussed whether central banks should adopt an explicit interest rate rule and follow it closely, or whether they should use the rule more informally, and feel free to deviate from the rule when appropriate.
- In general, most central banks have now shifted from thinking in terms of nominal money growth to thinking in terms of an interest rate rule. Whatever happens to nominal money growth as a result of following such a nominal interest rate rule is increasingly seen as unimportant, both by the central banks and by financial markets.

24-4 Challenges from the Crisis

Until 2007, most central banks believed that inflation targeting provided them with a solid framework for monetary policy. In most countries, inflation was stable, and output fluctuations were smaller than they had been in the past. The crisis has presented them with two challenges:

- The liquidity trap has prevented them from decreasing the interest rate as much as they wanted. At the time of this writing, given high unemployment and low inflation, the nominal interest rate implied by the Taylor rule for the United States should be around −3%. Yet the actual nominal interest rate cannot go below zero.
- It has become clear that stable inflation is not, by itself, a guarantee of macroeconomic stability: The crisis can clearly be traced to problems in the housing and the financial sectors, that built up long before 2007.

   Let's take each challenge from the crisis in turn.

The Liquidity Trap

When an economy falls into the liquidity trap, conventional monetary policy (namely, the use of the nominal interest rate) can no longer be used. This raises three issues: first, whether economies can avoid falling into the trap in the first place; second, whether and how they can get out of the trap; and third, if an economy is in the trap, are there unconventional monetary policy tools available. We have already discussed these issues at various points in the book. What follows puts things together.

See, in particular, Chapter 9 on the crisis, the box on quantitative easing in Chapter 17, and the discussion of optimal inflation earlier in this chapter.

Avoiding Falling into the Trap

A way of dealing with the liquidity trap is simply to avoid falling into it! One way to do so is to have higher average inflation. We discussed this argument in Section 24-2. The higher is average inflation, the higher is the average nominal interest rate, and the more room the central bank has to decrease the nominal interest rate in response to an adverse shock before falling in the liquidity trap.

Whether or not this should lead central banks to adopt a higher target inflation depends on the probability that, once this crisis has passed, the economy is hit again by an adverse shock so large that the central bank hits the zero interest bound again. Most central banks have concluded that the shocks that triggered this crisis were so exceptional, that shocks of this magnitude are very unlikely to happen again. Thus, they do not appear willing to increase their target inflation rate.

Getting Out of the Trap

In the strange world of the liquidity trap, higher expected inflation can help get out of the trap and help the economy recover. We went through the argument in the Focus box "The Liquidity Trap, Quantitative Easing, and the Role of Expectations" in Chapter 17: The liquidity trap puts a floor on the nominal interest rate, but not necessarily on the real interest rate. If people expect higher inflation, then the real rate of interest (which is equal to the nominal interest rate, namely zero in this case, minus expected inflation) decreases. A lower real interest rate is likely to increase investment and consumption, leading to an increase in demand and an increase in output and thus help the economy to recover.

This is one of the reasons why, before the crisis, most central banks did not worry much about the liquidity trap. Even if they could not decrease the nominal interest rate, they thought they could decrease the real interest rate by increasing inflation expectations. The issue, however, is how to actually get people to expect higher inflation. There is a bootstrap aspect to the reasoning: If people indeed increase their inflation expectations, the economy will indeed recover, unemployment will decrease, and, from the Phillips curve relation, lower unemployment and higher expected inflation are likely to lead to higher inflation, validating the initial increase in expected inflation. But if expectations of inflation do not increase in the first place, neither will the real rate, activity, nor inflation.

One of the ways that central banks have tried to affect inflation expectations during the crisis has been their use of *quantitative easing*, a large increase in the money stock. One of the arguments given by proponents of quantitative easing was that people, seeing large increases in the money supply, would expect more inflation. Has it worked? So far, the evidence is mixed at best. There is not much evidence that quantitative easing, which has now been used in a number of countries (in particular, the United States, the United Kingdom, and Japan) has had much effect on inflation expectations.

For more on quantitative easing, see the Focus box "The Liquidity Trap, Quantitative Easing and the Role of Expectations" in Chapter 17.

Dealing with the Trap

An economy is said to be in the liquidity trap when the *short-term nominal interest rate on government bonds* is down to zero. But when this interest rate is equal to zero, many other interest rates may still be positive. This raises the issue of whether the central bank can decrease some of those other interest rates by buying some of the corresponding assets directly. Such actions go by the name of *credit easing*, or *qualitative easing,* or *targeted easing.* These actions need not lead to an increase in the money supply: This depends on whether the purchases of specific assets are offset by sales of other assets. In most cases, however, credit easing has been associated with an increase in the money supply.

We looked at the effects of such actions by the Fed in the Focus box in Chapter 17. To summarize, the verdict is still out. When, for some reason, investors are forced or decide to leave a specific market, the central bank can, in effect, replace them and thus limit the increase in that market's interest rate. When, however, markets function well and investors arbitrage across markets, the effects of central bank purchases are likely to be limited.

To summarize: While unconventional monetary policy tools can help, they do not work as reliably as does conventional monetary policy, namely movements in the short-term nominal interest rate. Even taking unconventional monetary policy tools into account, being in the liquidity trap considerably reduces the scope of monetary policy.

Macro Prudential Regulation

For a discussion of bubbles versus fundamentals, see ▶ Chapter 15.

Before the crisis, central bankers did not ignore bubbles. Indeed, starting in the mid-2000s, the Fed became worried about the increase in housing prices. But the Fed and other central banks facing similar housing price increases were reluctant to intervene. This was for a number of reasons. First, they found it difficult to assess whether the price increases reflected increases in fundamentals (for example, low interest rates) or reflected a bubble (i.e., increases in prices above what were justified by fundamentals). Second, they worried that an increase in the interest rate, while it might indeed stop the increase in housing prices, would also slow down the whole economy and trigger a recession. Third, they thought that, even if the increase in housing prices was indeed a bubble, and the bubble were to burst and lead to a decrease in housing prices later, they could counter the adverse effects on demand through an appropriate decrease in the interest rate.

The crisis has forced them to reconsider. As we saw throughout this book, and especially in Chapter 9, housing price declines combined with the buildup of risk in the financial system, led to a major financial and macroeconomic crisis.

As a result, a broad consensus is emerging, along two lines:

- It is risky to wait. Even if in doubt about whether an increase in asset prices reflects fundamentals or a bubble, it may be better to do something than not: Better to stand for a while in the way of a fundamental increase and turn out to be wrong, than to let a bubble build up and burst, with major adverse macroeconomic effects. The same applies to buildups of financial risk; for example, excessive bank leverage. Better to prevent high leverage, at the risk of decreasing bank credit, than allow it to build up, increasing the risk of a financial crisis.
- To deal with bubbles, credit booms, or dangerous behavior in the financial system, the interest rate is not the right policy instrument. It is too blunt a tool, affecting the whole economy rather than resolving the problem at hand. The right instruments are **macro prudential tools**, rules that are aimed directly at borrowers, or lenders, or banks and other financial institutions, as the case may require.

What form might some of the macro prudential tools take? Some tools may be aimed at borrowers:

- Suppose the central bank is worried about what it perceives to be an excessive increase in housing prices. It can tighten conditions under which borrowers can obtain mortgages. A measure used in many countries is a ceiling on the size of the loan borrowers can take relative to the value of the house they buy, a measure known as the maximum **loan-to-value ratio**, or maximum **LTV** for short. Reducing the maximum loan-to-value ratio is likely to decrease demand and thus slow down the price increase. (The Focus box "LTV Ratios and Housing Price Increases from 2000 to 2007" examines the relation between maximum LTVs and housing price increases in the period leading up to the crisis.)

■ Suppose the central bank is worried that people are borrowing too much in foreign currency. An example will help to make the point. At the time of writing, more than two-thirds of mortgages in Hungary are denominated in Swiss francs! The reason is simple. Swiss interest rates have been very low, making it apparently very attractive for Hungarians to borrow at the Swiss rather than the Hungarian interest rate. The risk that borrowers did not take into account, however, was the risk that the Hungarian currency, the forint, would depreciate vis-à-vis the Swiss franc. Such a depreciation has, in fact, taken place, increasing, on average, the real value of the mortgages Hungarian have to pay by more than 50%. Many households can no longer make their mortgage payment, thus leading to a macroeconomic crisis. This suggests that it would have been wise to put restrictions on the amount of borrowing in foreign currency by households.

Some tools may aimed at lenders, such as banks or foreign investors:

■ Suppose the central bank is worried about an increase in bank leverage. We saw why this should be a concern in Chapter 9: High leverage was one of the main reasons why housing price declines led to the financial crisis. The central bank can impose minimum capital ratios, so as to limit leverage. These may take various forms (for example, a minimum value for the ratio of capital to all assets, or a minimum value for the ratio of capital to risk weighted assets, with more risky assets having a higher weight). In fact, in a series of agreements known as **Basel II** and **Basel III**, many countries have agreed to impose the same minima on their banks. A more difficult and unresolved issue is whether and how such capital ratios should be adjusted over time as a function of economic and financial conditions (whether, for example, they should be increased if there appears to be excessive credit growth).

Go back to Chapter 9 for a refresher on the relation between leverage and capital ratios.

■ Suppose the central bank is worried about high capital inflows. This matches the Hungarian case we discussed above. The central bank worries that, while investors are willing to lend at low interest rates to the country, they may change their mind, and this might lead to a sudden stop. The central bank may then want to limit the capital inflows by imposing **capital controls** on inflows. These may take the form of taxes on different types of inflows, with lower taxes on capital flows that are less prone to sudden stops, such as **foreign direct investment**, the purchase of physical assets by foreigner-sor a direct limit on the ability of domestic residents to take out foreign loans.

See the Focus box "Sudden Stops, Safe Havens, and the Limits to the Interest Parity Condition" in Chapter 20.

While there is large agreement that the use of such *macro prudential* tools is desirable, many questions remain:

■ In many cases, we do not know how well these tools work (for example, how much a decrease in the maximum LTV ratio affects the demand for housing, or whether foreign investors can find ways of avoiding capital controls).

■ There are likely to be complex interactions between the traditional monetary policy tools and these macro prudential tools. For example, there is some evidence that very low interest rates lead to excessive risk taking, be it by investors or by financial institutions. If this is the case, a central bank that decides, for macroeconomic reasons, to lower interest rates may have to use various macro prudential tools to offset the potential increase in risk taking. Again, we know very little about how to correctly go about this.

LTV Ratios and Housing Price Increases from 2000 to 2007

Is it the case that countries that had more stringent restrictions on borrowing had lower housing price increases from 2000 to 2007? The answer is given in Figure 1. The figure, taken from an IMF study, shows the evidence for 21 countries for which the data could be obtained.

The horizontal axis plots the maximum loan-to-value (LTV) ratio on new mortgages across countries. This maximum is not necessarily a legal maximum, but may be a guideline, or a limit over which additional requirements, such as mortgage insurance, may be asked of the borrower. A ratio of 100% means that a borrower may be able to get a loan equal to the value of the house. Actual values vary from 60% in Korea; to 100% in a large number of countries, including the United States; to 125% in The Netherlands. The vertical axis plots the increase in the nominal price of housing from 2000 to 2007 (measuring the real price increase would lead to a very similar picture). The figure also plots the regression line, the line that best fits the set of observations.

The figure suggests two conclusions:

The first is that there indeed appears to be a positive relation between the LTV ratio and the housing price increase. Korea and Hong Kong, which imposed low LTV ratios, had smaller housing price increases. Spain and the United Kingdom, with much higher ratios, had much larger price increases.

The second is that the relation is far from tight. This should not come as a surprise, as surely many other factors played a role in the increase in housing prices. But, even controlling for other factors, it is difficult to identify with much confidence the precise effect of the LTV ratio. Looking forward, we shall have to learn a lot more about how an LTV-based regulatory tool might work before it can be used as a reliable macro prudential tool.

Source: Christopher Crowe, Giovanni Dell'Ariccia, Deniz Igan, Pau Rabanal, "Policies for Macrofinancial Stability: Options to Deal with Real Estate Booms," Staff Discussion Note, International Monetary Fund, February 2011

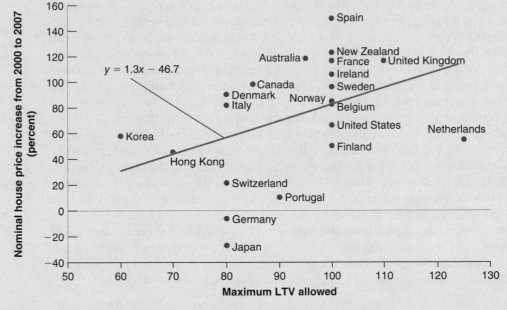

Figure 1 *Maximum LTV Ratios and Housing Price Increases, 2000–2007*

■ The question arises of whether macro prudential tools should be, together with traditional monetary policy tools, under the control of the central bank or under the control of a separate authority. The argument for having the central bank in charge of both monetary and macro prudential tools is that these tools interact, and thus only one centralized authority can use them in the right way. The argument against it is the worry that such a consolidation of tools may give too much power to an independent central bank.

At this stage, some countries have taken one route, while others took another. In the United Kingdom, the central bank has been given power over both monetary and macro prudential tools. In the United States, the responsibility has been given to a council under the formal authority of the U.S. Treasury, but with the Fed playing a major role within the council.

To summarize: The crisis has shown that macroeconomic stability requires the use not only of traditional monetary instruments, but also of macro prudential tools. How best to use them is one of the challenges facing macroeconomic policy makers today.

Summary

On the optimal rate of inflation

- Arguments in favor of low or even zero inflation are:
  1. Inflation, together with an imperfectly indexed tax system, leads to tax distortions.
  2. Because of money illusion, inflation leads people and firms to make incorrect decisions.
  3. Higher inflation typically comes with higher inflation variability, creating more uncertainty and making it more difficult for people and firms to make decisions.
  4. As a target, price stability has a simplicity and a credibility that a positive inflation target does not have.
- Arguments for maintaining positive inflation are:
  1. Positive revenues from nominal money growth—seignorage—allow for decreases in taxes elsewhere in the budget. However, this argument is quantitatively unimportant when comparing inflation rates of 0% versus, say, 4%.
  2. Positive actual and expected inflation allow the central bank to achieve negative real interest rates, an option that is useful when fighting a recession.
  3. Positive inflation allows for real wage cuts when they are needed, without requiring nominal wage cuts.
  4. Further decreasing inflation from its current rate to zero would require an increase in unemployment for some time, and this transition cost might exceed whatever benefits come from zero inflation.

On the design of monetary policy

- Traditionally, the design of monetary policy was focused on nominal money growth. But, because of the poor relation between inflation and nominal money growth, this approach was abandoned by most central banks.

- Central banks now typically focus on an inflation rate target rather than a nominal money growth rate target. And they think about monetary policy in terms of determining the nominal interest rate rather than determining the rate of nominal money growth.
- The Taylor rule gives a useful way of thinking about the choice of the nominal interest rate. The rule states that the central bank should move its interest rate in response to two main factors: the deviation of the inflation rate from the target rate of inflation, and the deviation of the unemployment rate from the natural rate of unemployment. A central bank that follows this rule will stabilize activity and achieve its target inflation rate in the medium run.

On the lessons from the crisis for monetary policy

- The fact that a number of countries have hit the liquidity trap has led them to explore unconventional monetary policy tools, such as quantitative easing or credit easing. These policies work through their effect on expectations, and through their effect on interest rates other than the short-term nominal interest rate.
- The crisis has shown that stable inflation is not a sufficient condition for macroeconomic stability. This is leading central banks to explore the use of macro prudential tools. These tools can, in principle, help limit bubbles, control credit growth, and decrease risk in the financial system. How best to use them, however, is still poorly understood and is one the challenges facing monetary policy today.

Key Terms

Questions and Problems

QUICK CHECK
All Quick Check questions and problems are available on MyEconLab.

1. *Using the information in this chapter, label each of the following statements true, false, or uncertain. Explain briefly.*

  a. The most important argument in favor of a positive rate of inflation in OECD countries is seignorage.

  b. The Fed should target $M2$ growth because it moves quite closely with inflation.

  c. Fighting inflation should be the Fed's only purpose.

  d. Because most people have little trouble distinguishing between nominal and real values, inflation does not distort decision making.

  e. The Fed announced an inflation target of 2% in early 2012.

  f. The higher the inflation rate, the higher the effective tax rate on capital gains.

  g. The Taylor rule describes how central banks adjust the growth rate of money across recessions and booms.

  h. The only policy tools available to central banks are interest rates and the money stock.

2. *Explain how each of the developments listed in (a) through (d) would affect the demand for M1 and M2.*

  a. Banks reduce penalties on early withdrawal from time deposits.

  b. The government forbids the use of money market funds for check-writing purposes.

  c. The government legislates a tax on all ATM transactions.

  d. Congress decides to impose a tax on all transactions involving government securities with maturities of more than one year.

3. *Taxes, inflation, and home ownership*

    In this chapter, we discussed the effect of inflation on the effective capital-gains tax rate on the sale of a home. In this question, we explore the effect of inflation on another feature of the tax code—the deductibility of mortgage interest.

    Suppose you have a mortgage of $50,000. Expected inflation is π^e, and the nominal interest rate on your mortgage is i. Consider two cases.

      i. $\pi^e = 0\%$; i = 4%

      ii. $\pi^e = 10\%$; i = 14%

  a. What is the real interest rate you are paying on your mortgage in each case?

  b. Suppose you can deduct nominal mortgage interest payments from your income before paying income tax (as is the case in the United States). Assume that the tax rate is 25%. So, for each dollar you pay in mortgage interest, you pay 25 cents less in taxes, in effect getting a subsidy from the government for your mortgage costs. Compute, in each case, the real interest rate you are paying on your mortgage, taking this subsidy into account.

  c. Considering only the deductibility of mortgage interest (and not capital-gains taxation), is inflation good for homeowners in the United States?

4. *Inflation targets*

Consider a central bank that has an inflation target, π^*. The Phillips curve is given by

$$\pi_t - \pi_{t-1} = -\alpha(u_t - u_n)$$

  a. If the central bank is able to keep the inflation rate equal to the target inflation rate every period, will there be dramatic fluctuations in unemployment?

  b. Is the central bank likely to be able to hit its inflation target every period?

  c. Suppose the natural rate of unemployment, u_n, changes frequently. How will these changes affect the central bank's ability to hit its inflation target? Explain.

DIG DEEPER
All Dig Deeper questions and problems are available on MyEconLab.

5. *Suppose you have been elected to Congress. One day, one of your colleagues makes the following statement:*

    The Fed chair is the most powerful economic policy maker in the United States. We should not turn over the keys to the economy to someone who was not elected and therefore has no accountability. Congress should impose an explicit Taylor rule on the Fed. Congress should choose not only the target inflation rate but the relative weight on the inflation and unemployment targets. Why should the preferences of an individual substitute for the will of the people, as expressed through the democratic and legislative processes?

    Do you agree with your colleague? Discuss the advantages and disadvantages of imposing an explicit Taylor rule on the Fed.

6. *Inflation targeting and the Taylor rule in the IS–LM model*

    Consider a closed economy in which the central bank follows an interest rate rule. The IS relation is given by

$$Y = C(Y - T) + I(Y,r) + G$$

where r is the real interest rate.

    The central bank sets the nominal interest rate according to the rule

$$i = i^* + a(\pi^e - \pi^*) + b(Y - Y_n)$$

where π^e is expected inflation, π^* is the target rate of inflation, and Y_n is the natural level of output. Assume that a > 1 and b > 0. The symbol i* is the target interest rate the central bank chooses when expected inflation equals the target rate and output equals the natural level. The central bank will increase the nominal interest rate when expected inflation rises above the target, or when output rises above the natural level.

    (Note that the Taylor rule described in this chapter uses actual inflation instead of expected inflation, and it uses unemployment instead of output. The interest rate rule we use in this problem simplifies the analysis and does not change the basic results.)

    Real and nominal interest rates are related by

$$r = i - \pi^e$$

a. Define the variable r^* as $r^* = i^* - \pi^*$. Use the definition of the real interest rate to express the interest rate rule as

$$r = r^* + (a - 1)(\pi^e - \pi^*) + b(Y - Y_n)$$

(*Hint:* Subtract π^* from each side of the nominal interest rate rule and rearrange the righthand side of the equation.)

b. Graph the *IS* relation in a diagram, with r on the vertical axis and Y on the horizontal axis. In the same diagram, graph the interest rate rule (in terms of the real interest rate) you derived in part (a) for given values of π^e, π^*, and Y_n. Call the interest rate rule the monetary policy (*MP*) relation.

c. Using the diagram you drew in part (b), show that an increase in government spending leads to an increase in output and the real interest rate in the short run.

d. Now consider a change in the monetary policy rule. Suppose the central bank reduces its target inflation rate, π^*. How does the fall in π^* affect the *MP* relation? (Remember that $a > 1$.) What happens to output and the real interest rate in the short run?

7. *Consider the economy described in Problem 6.*

a. Suppose the economy starts with $Y = Y_n$ and $\pi^e = \pi^*$.

Now suppose there is an increase in π^e. Assume that Y_n does not change. Using the diagram you drew in Problem 6(b), show how the increase in π^e affects the *MP* relation. (Again, remember that $a > 1$.) What happens to output and the real interest rate in the short run?

b. Without attempting to model the dynamics of inflation explicitly, assume that inflation and expected inflation will increase over time if $Y > Y_n$, and that they will decrease over time if $Y < Y_n$. Given the effect on output you found

in part (a), will π^e tend to return to the target rate of inflation, π^*, over time?

c. Redo part (a), but assuming this time that $a < 1$. How does the increase in π^e affect the *MP* relation when $a < 1$? What happens to output and the real interest·rate in the short run?

d. Again assume that inflation and expected inflation will increase over time if $Y > Y_n$, and that they will decrease over time if $Y < Y_n$. Given the effect on output you found in part (c), will π^e tend to return to the target rate of inflation, π^*, over time? Is it sensible for the parameter a (in the interest rate rule) to have values less than 1?

EXPLORE FURTHER

8. Current monetary policy

Problem 10 in Chapter 4 asked you to consider the current stance of monetary policy. Here, you are asked to do so again, but with the additional understanding of monetary policy you have gained in this and previous chapters.

Go to the Web site of the Federal Reserve Board of Governors (**www.federalreserve.gov**) and download either the press release you considered in Chapter 4 (if you did Problem 10) or the most recent press release of the Federal Open Market Committee (FOMC).

a. What is the stance of monetary policy, as described in the press release?

b. Is there evidence that the FOMC considers both inflation and unemployment when setting interest rate policy, as would be implied by the Taylor rule?

c. Does the language make specific reference to a target for inflation?

d. Does the language raise any issues related to macro prudential regulation of financial institutions?

Further Readings

■ For more on the optimal rate of inflation, see *The Economist*'s debate, at http://www.economist.com/debate/days/view/696

■ For an early statement of inflation targeting, read "Inflation Targeting: A New Framework for Monetary Policy?", by Ben Bernanke and Frederic Mishkin, *Journal of Economic Perspectives*, 1997 11(Spring): pp. 97–116. (This article was written by Ben Bernanke before he became Chairman of the Fed.)

■ For more institutional details on how the Fed actually functions, see *http://www.federalreserve.gov/aboutthefed/default.htm*

■ A time frame giving financial developments and the actions of the Fed during the crisis is given at *http://www.nytimes.com/interactive/2008/09/27/business/economy/20080927_WEEKS_TIMELINE.html*

■ On the relaxed attitude of the Fed vis-à-vis the housing bubble, see "Inside the Fed in 2006: A Coming Crisis, and Banter" New York Times, January 12, 2012, http://www.nytimes.com/2012/01/13/business/transcripts-show-an-unfazed-fed-in-2006.html?pagewanted=all

Epilogue: The Story of Macroeconomics

W e have spent 24 chapters presenting the framework that most economists use to think about macroeconomic issues, the major conclusions they draw, and the issues on which they disagree. How this framework has been built over time is a fascinating story. It is the story we want to tell in this chapter.

Section 25-1 starts at the beginning of modern macroeconomics—with Keynes and the Great Depression.

Section 25-2 turns to the *neoclassical synthesis*, a synthesis of Keynes's ideas with those of earlier economists—a synthesis that dominated macroeconomics until the early 1970s.

Section 25-3 describes the *rational expectations critique*, the strong attack on the neoclassical synthesis that led to a complete overhaul of macroeconomics starting in the 1970s.

Section 25-4 gives you a sense of the main lines of research in macroeconomics up to the crisis.

Section 25-5 takes a first pass at assessing the effects of the crisis on macroeconomics. ●

25-1 Keynes and the Great Depression

The history of modern macroeconomics starts in 1936, with the publication of Keynes's *General Theory of Employment, Interest, and Money.* As he was writing the *General Theory*, Keynes confided to a friend: "I believe myself to be writing a book on economic theory which will largely revolutionize—not, I suppose at once but in the course of the next ten years, the way the world thinks about economic problems."

John Maynard Keynes

Keynes was right. The book's timing was one of the reasons for its immediate success. The Great Depression was not only an economic catastrophe, but also an intellectual failure for the economists working on **business cycle theory**—as macroeconomics was then called. Few economists had a coherent explanation for the Depression, either for its depth or for its length. The economic measures taken by the Roosevelt administration as part of the New Deal had been based on instinct rather than on economic theory. The *General Theory* offered an interpretation of events, an intellectual framework, and a clear argument for government intervention.

The *General Theory* emphasized **effective demand**—what we now call *aggregate demand.* In the short run, Keynes argued, effective demand determines output. Even if output eventually returns to its natural level, the process is slow at best. One of Keynes's most famous quotes is: "In the long run, we are all dead."

In the process of deriving effective demand, Keynes introduced many of the building blocks of modern macroeconomics:

- The relation of consumption to income, and the multiplier, which explains how shocks to demand can be amplified and lead to larger shifts in output.
- **Liquidity preference** (the term Keynes gave to the demand for money), which explains how monetary policy can affect interest rates and aggregate demand.
- The importance of expectations in affecting consumption and investment; and the idea that *animal spirits* (shifts in expectations) are a major factor behind shifts in demand and output.

The *General Theory* was more than a treatise for economists. It offered clear policy implications, and they were in tune with the times: Waiting for the economy to recover by itself was irresponsible. In the midst of a depression, trying to balance the budget was not only stupid, it was dangerous. Active use of fiscal policy was essential to return the country to high employment.

25-2 The Neoclassical Synthesis

Within a few years, the *General Theory* had transformed macroeconomics. Not everyone was converted, and few agreed with it all. But most discussions became organized around it.

Paul Samuelson

By the early 1950s a large consensus had emerged, based on an integration of many of Keynes's ideas and the ideas of earlier economists. This consensus was called the **neoclassical synthesis**. To quote from Paul Samuelson, in the 1955 edition of his textbook *Economics*—the first modern economics textbook:

"In recent years, 90 per cent of American economists have stopped being 'Keynesian economists' or 'Anti-Keynesian economists.' Instead, they have worked toward a synthesis of whatever is valuable in older economics and in modern theories of income determination. The result might be called neoclassical economics and is accepted, in its broad outlines, by all but about five per cent of extreme left-wing and right-wing writers."

The neoclassical synthesis was to remain the dominant view for another 20 years. Progress was astonishing, leading many to call the period from the early 1940s to the early 1970s the golden age of macroeconomics.

Progress on All Fronts

The first order of business after the publication of the *General Theory* was to formalize mathematically what Keynes meant. While Keynes knew mathematics, he had avoided using it in the *General Theory*. One result was endless controversies about what Keynes meant and whether there were logical flaws in some of his arguments.

The *IS – LM* Model

A number of formalizations of Keynes's ideas were offered. The most influential one was the *IS–LM* model, developed by John Hicks and Alvin Hansen in the 1930s and early 1940s. The initial version of the *IS–LM* model—which was actually very close to the version presented in Chapter 5 of this book—was criticized for emasculating many of Keynes's insights: Expectations played no role, and the adjustment of prices and wages was altogether absent. Yet the *IS–LM* model provided a basis from which to start building, and as such it was immensely successful. Discussions became organized around the slopes of the *IS* and *LM* curves, what variables were missing from the two relations, what equations for prices and wages should be added to the model, and so on.

Theories of Consumption, Investment, and Money Demand

Keynes had emphasized the importance of consumption and investment behavior, and of the choice between money and other financial assets. Major progress was soon made along all three fronts.

In the 1950s, Franco Modigliani (then at Carnegie Mellon, later at MIT) and Milton Friedman (at the University of Chicago) independently developed the theory of consumption we saw in Chapter 16. Both insisted on the importance of expectations in determining current consumption decisions.

Franco Modigliani

James Tobin, from Yale, developed the theory of investment, based on the relation between the present value of profits and investment. The theory was further developed and tested by Dale Jorgenson, from Harvard. You saw this theory in Chapter 16.

Tobin also developed the theory of the demand for money and, more generally, the theory of the choice between different assets based on liquidity, return, and risk. His work has become the basis not only for an improved treatment of financial markets in macroeconomics, but also for finance theory in general.

James Tobin

Growth Theory

In parallel with the work on fluctuations, there was a renewed focus on growth. In contrast to the stagnation in the pre–World War II era, most countries were experiencing rapid growth in the 1950s and 1960s. Even if they experienced fluctuations, their standard of living was increasing rapidly. The growth model developed by MIT's Robert Solow in 1956, which we saw in Chapters 11 and 12, provided a framework to think about the determinants of growth. It was followed by an explosion of work on the roles saving and technological progress play in determining growth.

Macroeconometric Models

All these contributions were integrated in larger and larger macroeconometric models. The first U.S. macroeconometric model, developed by Lawrence Klein from the University of Pennsylvania in the early 1950s, was an extended *IS* relation, with 16 equations.

Robert Solow

Lawrence Klein

Milton Friedman

With the development of the National Income and Product Accounts (making available better data) and the development of econometrics and of computers, the models quickly grew in size. The most impressive effort was the construction of the MPS model (MPS stands for MIT-Penn-SSRC, for the two universities and the research institution—the Social Science Research Council—involved in its construction), developed during the 1960s by a group led by Modigliani. Its structure was an expanded version of the *IS–LM* model, plus a Phillips curve mechanism. But its components—consumption, investment, and money demand—all reflected the tremendous theoretical and empirical progress made since Keynes.

Keynesians versus Monetarists

With such rapid progress, many macroeconomists—those who defined themselves as **Keynesians**—came to believe that the future was bright. The nature of fluctuations was becoming increasingly well understood; the development of models allowed policy decisions to be made more effectively. The time when the economy could be fine-tuned, and recessions all but eliminated, seemed not far in the future.

This optimism was met with skepticism by a small but influential minority, the **monetarists**. The intellectual leader of the monetarists was Milton Friedman. Although Friedman saw much progress being made—and was himself the father of one of the major contributions to macroeconomics, the theory of consumption—he did not share in the general enthusiasm. He believed that the understanding of the economy remained very limited. He questioned the motives of governments as well as the notion that they actually knew enough to improve macroeconomic outcomes.

In the 1960s, debates between "Keynesians" and "monetarists" dominated the economic headlines. The debates centered around three issues: (1) the effectiveness of monetary policy versus fiscal policy, (2) the Phillips curve, and (3) the role of policy.

Monetary Policy versus Fiscal Policy

Keynes had emphasized *fiscal* rather than *monetary* policy as the key to fighting recessions. And this had remained the prevailing wisdom. The *IS* curve, many argued, was quite steep: Changes in the interest rate had little effect on demand and output. Thus, monetary policy did not work very well. Fiscal policy, which affects demand directly, could affect output faster and more reliably.

Friedman strongly challenged this conclusion. In their 1963 book *A Monetary History of the United States, 1867–1960*, Friedman and Anna Schwartz painstakingly reviewed the evidence on monetary policy and the relation between money and output in the United States over a century. Their conclusion was not only that monetary policy was very powerful, but that movements in money did explain most of the fluctuations in output. They interpreted the Great Depression as the result of a major mistake in monetary policy, a decrease in the money supply due to bank failures—a decrease that the Fed could have avoided by increasing the monetary base, but had not.

Friedman and Schwartz's challenge was followed by a vigorous debate and by intense research on the respective effects of fiscal policy and monetary policy. In the end, a consensus was reached. Both fiscal policy and monetary policy clearly affected the economy. And if policy makers cared about not only the level but also the composition of output, the best policy was typically a mix of the two.

The Phillips Curve

The second debate focused on the Phillips curve. The Phillips curve was not part of the initial Keynesian model. But because it provided such a convenient (and apparently reliable) way of explaining the movement of wages and prices over time, it had become part of the neoclassical synthesis. In the 1960s, based on the empirical evidence up until then, many Keynesian economists believed that there was a reliable trade-off between unemployment and inflation, even in the long run.

Milton Friedman and Edmund Phelps (from Columbia University) strongly disagreed. They argued that the existence of such a long-run trade-off flew in the face of basic economic theory. They argued that the apparent trade-off would quickly vanish if policy makers actually tried to exploit it—that is, if they tried to achieve low unemployment by accepting higher inflation. As we saw in Chapter 8 when we studied the evolution of the Phillips curve, Friedman and Phelps were definitely right. By the mid-1970s, the consensus was indeed that there was no long-run trade-off between inflation and unemployment.

Edmund Phelps

The Role of Policy

The third debate centered on the role of policy. Skeptical that economists knew enough to stabilize output and that policy makers could be trusted to do the right thing, Friedman argued for the use of simple rules, such as steady money growth (a rule we discussed in Chapter 24). Here is what he said in 1958:

> "A steady rate of growth in the money supply will not mean perfect stability even though it would prevent the kind of wide fluctuations that we have experienced from time to time in the past. It is tempting to try to go farther and to use monetary changes to offset other factors making for expansion and contraction . . . The available evidence casts grave doubts on the possibility of producing any fine adjustments in economic activity by fine adjustments in monetary policy—at least in the present state of knowledge. There are thus serious limitations to the possibility of a discretionary monetary policy and much danger that such a policy may make matters worse rather than better.
>
> Political pressures to 'do something' in the face of either relatively mild price rises or relatively mild price and employment declines are clearly very strong indeed in the existing state of public attitudes. The main moral to be drawn from the two preceding points is that yielding to these pressures may frequently do more harm than good."

Source: "The Supply of Money and Changes in Prices and Output," Testimony to Congress, 1958

As we saw in Chapter 22, this debate on the role of macroeconomic policy has not been settled. The nature of the arguments has changed a bit, but they are still with us today.

25-3 The Rational Expectations Critique

Despite the battles between Keynesians and monetarists, macroeconomics at around 1970 looked like a successful and mature field. It appeared to successfully explain events and guide policy choices. Most debates were framed within a common intellectual framework. But within a few years, the field was in crisis. The crisis had two sources.

One was events. By the mid-1970s, most countries were experiencing *stagflation*, a word created at the time to denote the simultaneous existence of high unemployment and high inflation. Macroeconomists had not predicted stagflation. After the fact and after a few years of research, a convincing explanation was provided, based on the effects of adverse supply shocks on both prices and output. (We discussed the effects of such shocks in Chapter 7.) But it was too late to undo the damage to the discipline's image.

Robert Lucas

The other was ideas. In the early 1970s, a small group of economists—Robert Lucas from Chicago; Thomas Sargent, then from Minnesota and now at New York University; and Robert Barro, then from Chicago and now at Harvard—led a strong attack against mainstream macroeconomics. They did not mince words. In a 1978 paper, Lucas and Sargent stated:

> "That the predictions [of Keynesian economics] were wildly incorrect, and that the doctrine on which they were based was fundamentally flawed, are now simple matters of fact, involving no subtleties in economic theory. The task which faces contemporary students of the business cycle is that of sorting through the wreckage, determining what features of that remarkable intellectual event called the Keynesian Revolution can be salvaged and put to good use, and which others must be discarded."

The Three Implications of Rational Expectations

Lucas and Sargent's main argument was that Keynesian economics had ignored the full implications of the effect of expectations on behavior. The way to proceed, they argued, was to assume that people formed expectations as rationally as they could, based on the information they had. Thinking of people as having *rational expectations* had three major implications, all highly damaging to Keynesian macroeconomics.

Thomas Sargent

The Lucas Critique

The first implication was that existing macroeconomic models could not be used to help design policy. Although these models recognized that expectations affect behavior, they did not incorporate expectations explicitly. All variables were assumed to depend on current and past values of other variables, including policy variables. Thus, what the models captured was the set of relations between economic variables as they had held in the past, under past policies. Were these policies to change, Lucas argued, the way people formed expectations would change as well, making estimated relations—and, by implication, simulations generated using existing macroeconometric models—poor guides to what would happen under these new policies. This critique of macroeconometric models became known as the Lucas critique. To take again the history of the Phillips curve as an example, the data up to the early 1970s had suggested a trade-off between unemployment and inflation. As policy makers tried to exploit that trade-off, it disappeared.

Robert Barro

Rational Expectations and the Phillips Curve

The second implication was that when rational expectations were introduced in Keynesian models, these models actually delivered very un-Keynesian conclusions. For example, the models implied that deviations of output from its natural level were short lived, much more so than Keynesian economists claimed.

This argument was based on a reexamination of the aggregate supply relation. In Keynesian models, the slow return of output to the natural level of output came from the slow adjustment of prices and wages through the Phillips curve mechanism. An increase in money, for example, led first to higher output and to lower unemployment. Lower unemployment then led to higher nominal wages and to higher prices. The adjustment continued until wages and prices had increased in the same proportion as nominal money, until unemployment and output were both back at their natural levels.

But this adjustment, Lucas pointed out, was highly dependent on wage setters' backward-looking expectations of inflation. In the MPS model, for example, wages responded only to current and past inflation and to current unemployment. But once the assumption was made that wage setters had rational expectations, the adjustment was likely to be much faster. Changes in money, to the extent that they were anticipated, might have no effect on output: For example, anticipating an increase in money of 5% over the coming year, wage setters would increase the nominal wages set in contracts for the coming year by 5%. Firms would in turn increase prices by 5%. The result would be no change in the real money stock, and no change in demand or output.

Within the logic of the Keynesian models, Lucas therefore argued, only *unanticipated changes in money* should affect output. Predictable movements in money should have no effect on activity. More generally, if wage setters had rational expectations, shifts in demand were likely to have effects on output for only as long as nominal wages were set—a year or so. Even on its own terms, the Keynesian model did not deliver a convincing theory of the long-lasting effects of demand on output.

Optimal Control versus Game Theory

The third implication was that if people and firms had rational expectations, it was wrong to think of policy as the control of a complicated but passive system. Rather, the right way was to think of policy as a game between policy makers and the economy. The right tool was not *optimal control*, but *game theory*. And game theory led to a different vision of policy. A striking example was the issue of *time inconsistency* discussed by Finn Kydland (then at Carnegie Mellon, now at UC Santa Barbara) and Edward Prescott (then at Carnegie Mellon, now at Arizona State University), an issue that we discussed in Chapter 22: Good intentions on the part of policy makers could actually lead to disaster.

To summarize: When rational expectations were introduced, Keynesian models could not be used to determine policy; Keynesian models could not explain long-lasting deviations of output from the natural level of output; the theory of policy had to be redesigned, using the tools of game theory.

The Integration of Rational Expectations

As you might have guessed from the tone of Lucas and Sargent's quote, the intellectual atmosphere in macroeconomics was tense in the early 1970s. But within a few years, a process of integration (of ideas, not people, because tempers remained high) had begun, and it was to dominate the 1970s and the 1980s.

Fairly quickly, the idea that rational expectations was the right working assumption gained wide acceptance. This was not because macroeconomists believed that people, firms, and participants in financial markets always form expectations rationally. But rational expectations appeared to be a natural benchmark, at least until economists have made more progress in understanding whether, when, and how actual expectations systematically differ from rational expectations.

Work then started on the challenges raised by Lucas and Sargent.

The Implications of Rational Expectations

First, there was a systematic exploration of the role and implications of rational expectations in goods markets, in financial markets, and in labor markets. Much of what was discovered has been presented in this book. For example:

■ Robert Hall, then from MIT and now at Stanford, showed that if consumers are very foresighted (in the sense defined in Chapter 16), then changes in consumption should be unpredictable: The best forecast of consumption next year would be consumption this year! Put another way, changes in consumption should be very hard to predict. This result came as a surprise to most macroeconomists at the time, but it is in fact based on a simple intuition: If consumers are very foresighted, they will change their consumption only when they learn something new about

Robert Hall

Rudiger Dornbusch

the future. But, by definition, such news cannot be predicted. This consumption behavior, known as the **random walk of consumption**, became the benchmark in consumption research thereafter.

■ Rudiger Dornbusch from MIT showed that the large swings in exchange rates under flexible exchange rates, which had previously been thought of as the result of speculation by irrational investors, were fully consistent with rationality. His argument—which we saw in Chapter 21—was that changes in monetary policy can lead to long-lasting changes in nominal interest rates; changes in current and expected nominal interest rates lead in turn to large changes in the exchange rate. Dornbusch's model, known as the *overshooting* model of exchange rates, became the benchmark in discussions of exchange rate movements.

Wage and Price Setting

Second, there was a systematic exploration of the determination of wages and prices, going far beyond the Phillips curve relation. Two important contributions were made by Stanley Fischer, then at MIT, now governor of the Central Bank of Israel, and John Taylor, then from Columbia University and now at Stanford. Both showed that the adjustment of prices and wages in response to changes in unemployment can be slow *even under rational expectations.*

Stanley Fischer

Fischer and Taylor pointed out an important characteristic of both wage and price setting, the **staggering** of wage and price decisions. In contrast to the simple story we told earlier, where all wages and prices increased simultaneously in anticipation of an increase in money, actual wage and price decisions are staggered over time. So there is not one sudden synchronized adjustment of all wages and prices to an increase in money. Rather, the adjustment is likely to be slow, with wages and prices adjusting to the new level of money through a process of leapfrogging over time. Fischer and Taylor thus showed that the second issue raised by the rational-expectations critique could be resolved, that a slow return of output to the natural level of output can be consistent with rational expectations in the labor market.

The Theory of Policy

Third, thinking about policy in terms of game theory led to an explosion of research on the nature of the games being played, not only between policy makers and the economy but also between policy makers—between political parties, or between the central bank and the government, or between governments of different countries. One of the major achievements of this research was the development of a more rigorous way of thinking about fuzzy notions such as "credibility," "reputation," and "commitment." At the same time, there was a distinct shift in focus from "what governments should do" to "what governments actually do," an increasing awareness of the political constraints that economists should take into account when advising policy makers.

John Taylor

In short: By the end of the 1980s, the challenges raised by the rational-expectations critique had led to a complete overhaul of macroeconomics. The basic structure had been extended to take into account the implications of rational expectations, or, more generally, of forward-looking behavior by people and firms. As we have seen, these themes have played a central role in this book.

25-4 Developments in Macroeconomics Up to the 2009 Crisis

From the late 1980s to the crisis, three groups dominated the research headlines: the new classicals, the new Keynesians, and the new growth theorists. (Note the generous use of the word "new." Unlike producers of laundry detergents, economists stop short of using "new and improved." But the subliminal message is the same.)

New Classical Economics and Real Business Cycle Theory

The rational-expectations critique was more than just a critique of Keynesian economics. It also offered its own interpretation of fluctuations. Lucas argued that instead of relying on imperfections in labor markets, on the slow adjustment of wages and prices, and so on to explain fluctuations, macroeconomists should see how far they could go in explaining fluctuations as the effects of shocks in competitive markets with fully flexible prices and wages.

This research agenda was taken up by the **new classicals**. The intellectual leader is Edward Prescott, and the models he and his followers developed are known as **real business cycle (RBC)** models. Their approach was based on two premises.

Edward Prescott

The first was methodological. Lucas had argued that, in order to avoid earlier pitfalls, macroeconomic models should be constructed from explicit microfoundations (i.e., utility maximization by workers, profit maximization by firms, and rational expectations). Before the development of computers, this was hard, if not impossible, to achieve: Models constructed in this way would have been too complex to solve analytically. Indeed, much of the art of macroeconomics was in finding simple shortcuts to capture the essence of a model while keeping the model simple enough to solve (it still remains the art of writing a good textbook). The development of computing power made it possible to solve such models numerically, and an important contribution of RBC theory was the development of more and more powerful numerical methods of solution, which allowed for the development of richer and richer models.

The second was conceptual. Until the 1970s, most fluctuations had been seen as the result of imperfections, of deviations of actual output from a slowly moving natural level of output. Following up on Lucas's suggestion, Prescott argued in a series of influential contributions, that fluctuations could indeed be interpreted as coming from the effects of technological shocks in competitive markets with fully flexible prices and wages. In other words, he argued that movements in actual output could be seen as movements in—rather than as deviations from—the natural level of output. As new discoveries are made, he argued, productivity increases, leading to an increase in output. The increase in productivity leads to an increase in the wage, which makes it more attractive to work, leading workers to work more. Productivity increases therefore lead to increases in both output and employment, just as we observe in the real world. Fluctuations are desirable features of the economy, not something policy makers should try to reduce.

Not surprisingly, this radical view of fluctuations was criticized on many fronts. As we discussed in Chapter 12, technological progress is the result of many innovations, each taking a long time to diffuse throughout the economy. It is hard to see how this process could generate anything like the large short-run fluctuations in output that we observe in practice. It is also hard to think of recessions as times of technological *regress*, times in which productivity and output both go down. Finally, as we have seen, there is strong evidence that changes in money, which have no effect on output in RBC models, in fact have strong effects on output in the real world. Still, the conceptual RBC approach proved influential and useful. It made an important point, that not all fluctuations in output are deviations of output from its natural level, but movements in the natural level itself.

New Keynesian Economics

The term **new Keynesians** denotes a loosely connected group of researchers who shared a common belief that the synthesis that emerged in response to the rational-expectations critique was basically correct. But they also shared the belief that much remained to be learned about the nature of imperfections in different markets and about the implications of those imperfections for macroeconomic fluctuations.

There was further work on the nature of **nominal rigidities**. As we saw earlier in this chapter, Fischer and Taylor had shown that with staggering of wage or price decisions, output can deviate from its natural level for a long time. This conclusion raised a number of questions: If staggering of decisions is responsible, at least in part, for fluctuations, why don't wage setters/price setters synchronize decisions? Why aren't prices and wages adjusted more often? Why aren't all prices and all wages changed, say, on the first day of each week? In tackling these issues, George Akerlof (from Berkeley) and N. Gregory Mankiw (from Harvard University) derived a surprising and important result, often referred to as the **menu cost** explanation of output fluctuations:

George Akerlof

Each wage setter or price setter is largely indifferent as to when and how often he changes his own wage or price (for a retailer, changing the prices on the shelf every day versus every week does not make much of a difference to the store's overall profits). Therefore, even small costs of changing prices—like the costs involved in printing a new menu, for example—can lead to infrequent and staggered price adjustment. This staggering leads to slow adjustment of the price level and to large aggregate output fluctuations in response to movements in aggregate demand. In short, decisions that do not matter much at the individual level (how often to change prices or wages) lead to large aggregate effects (slow adjustment of the price level, and shifts in aggregate demand that have a large effect on output).

Another line of research focused on the imperfections in the labor market. We discussed in Chapter 6 the notion of *efficiency wages*—the idea that wages, if perceived by workers as being too low, may lead to shirking by workers on the job, to problems of morale within the firm, to difficulties in recruiting or keeping good workers, and so on. One influential researcher in this area was Akerlof, who explored the role of "norms," the rules that develop in any organization—in this case, the firm—to assess what is fair or unfair. This research led him and others to explore issues previously left to research in sociology and psychology, and to examine their macroeconomic implications. In another direction, Peter Diamond (from MIT), Dale Mortensen (from Cornell), and Christopher Pissarides (from the London School of Economics) looked at the labor market as the market characterized by constant reallocation, large flows, and bargaining between workers and firms, a characterization that has proven extremely useful and that we relied upon in Chapter 6.

Ben Bernanke

Yet another line of research, which turned out to be precious when the crisis took place, explored the role of imperfections in credit markets. Most macro models assumed that monetary policy worked through interest rates, and that firms could borrow as much as they wanted at the market interest rate. In practice, many firms can borrow only from banks. And banks often turn down potential borrowers, despite the willingness of these borrowers to pay the interest rate charged by the bank. Why this happens, and how it affects our view of how monetary policy works, was the focus of research by, in particular, Ben Bernanke (then from Princeton, and now the Chairman of the Fed) and Mark Gertler (from New York University).

New Growth Theory

After being one of the most active topics of research in the 1960s, growth theory had gone into an intellectual slump. Since the late 1980s however, growth theory has made a strong comeback. The set of new contributions went under the name of **new growth theory**.

Two economists, Robert Lucas (the same Lucas who spearheaded the rational-expectations critique) and Paul Romer, then from Berkeley, now at New York University, played an important role in defining the issues. When growth theory faded in the late 1960s, two major issues were left largely unresolved. One issue was the role of increasing returns to scale—whether, say, doubling capital and labor can actually cause output to more than double. The other was the determinants of technological progress. These are the two major issues on which new growth theory concentrated.

Paul Romer

The discussions of the effects of R&D on technological progress in Chapter 12, and of the interaction between technological progress and unemployment in Chapter 13, both reflect some of the advances made on this front. An important contribution here was the work of Philippe Aghion (from Harvard University) and Peter Howitt (from Brown University), who developed a theme first explored by Joseph Schumpeter in the 1930s, the notion that growth is a process of *creative destruction* in which new products are constantly introduced, making old ones obsolete. Institutions that slow this process of reallocation (for example, by making it harder to create new firms or by making it more expensive for firms to lay off workers) may slow down the rate of technological progress and thus decrease growth.

Research also tried to identify the precise role of specific institutions in determining growth. Andrei Shleifer (from Harvard University) explored the role of different legal systems in affecting the organization of the economy, from financial markets to labor markets, and, through these channels, the effects of legal systems on growth. Daron Acemoglu (from MIT) explored how to go from correlations between institutions and growth—democratic countries are on average richer—to causality from institutions to growth: Does the correlation tell us that democracy leads to higher output per person, or does it tell us that higher output per person leads to democracy, or that some other factor leads to both more democracy and higher output per person? Examining the history of former colonies, Acemoglu argued that their growth performance has been shaped by the type of institutions put in place by their colonizers, thus showing a strong causal role of institutions in economic performance.

Philippe Aghion

Toward an Integration

In the 1980s and 1990s, discussions between these three groups, and in particular between "new classicals" and "new Keynesians," were often heated. New Keynesians would accuse new classicals of relying on an implausible explanation of fluctuations and ignoring obvious imperfections; new classicals would in turn point to the ad hocery of some of the new Keynesian models. From the outside—and indeed sometimes from the inside—macroeconomics looked like a battlefield rather than a research field.

Peter Howitt

By the 2000s however, a synthesis appeared to be emerging. Methodologically, it built on the RBC approach and its careful description of the optimization problems of people and firms. Conceptually, it recognized the potential importance, emphasized by the RBC and the new growth theory, of changes in the pace of technological progress. But it also allowed for many of the imperfections emphasized by the New Keynesians, from the role of bargaining in the determination of wages, to the role of imperfect information in credit and financial markets, to the role of nominal rigidities

Andrei Shleifer

Daron Acemoglu

Michael Woodford

Jordi Gali

in creating a role for aggregate demand to affect output. There was no convergence on a single model or on a single list of important imperfections, but there was broad agreement on the framework and on the way to proceed.

A good example of this convergence was the work of Michael Woodford (from Columbia) and Jordi Gali (from Pompeu Fabra in Catalonia). Woodford, Gali, and a number of coauthors developed a model, known as the *new Keynesian model*, that embodies utility and profit maximization, rational expectations, and nominal rigidities. You can think of it as a high-tech version of the model that was presented in Chapter 17. This model proved extremely useful and influential in the redesign of monetary policy—from the focus on inflation targeting to the reliance on interest rate rules—that we described in Chapter 24. It led to the development of a class of larger models that build on its simple structure but allow for a longer menu of imperfections and thus must be solved numerically. These models, which are now standard work horses in most central banks, are known as "*dynamic stochastic general equilibrium*," or *DSGE*, models.

25-5 First Lessons for Macroeconomics after the Crisis

Just at the time at which a new synthesis appeared to be in sight and macroeconomists felt that they had the tools to understand the economy and design policy, the crisis started, and, at the time of writing this chapter, is still continuing. We saw in Section 25-1 how the Great Depression had led to a dramatic reassessment of macroeconomics and started the Keynesian revolution. You may ask: Will this crisis have the same effect on macroeconomics, leading yet to another revolution? It is too early to say, but our guess is: probably not.

There is no question that the crisis reflects a major intellectual failure on the part of macroeconomics. The failure was in not realizing that such a large crisis *could happen*, that the characteristics of the economy were such that a relatively small shock, in this case the decrease in U.S. housing prices, could lead to a major financial and macroeconomic global crisis. The source of the failure, in turn, was a lack of focus on the role of the financial institutions in the economy. (To be fair, a few macroeconomists, who were looking more closely at the financial system, sounded the alarm; best known among them Nouriel Roubini, from New York University, and the economists at the Bank for International Settlements in Basel, whose job it is to follow financial developments closely.)

By and large, the financial system, and the complex role of banks and other financial institutions in the intermediation of funds between lenders and borrowers, was ignored in most macroeconomic models. There were exceptions. Work by Doug Diamond (from Chicago) and Philip Dybvig (from Washington University in Saint Louis) in the 1980s had clarified the nature of bank runs (which we examined in Chapter 4): Illiquid assets and liquid liabilities created a risk of runs even for solvent banks. The problem could only be avoided by the provision of liquidity by the central bank if and when needed. Work by Bengt Holmström and Jean Tirole (both from MIT) had shown that liquidity issues were endemic to a modern economy. Not only banks, but firms could well find themselves in a position where they were solvent, but illiquid, unable to raise the additional cash to finish a project or unable to repay investors when they wanted repayment. An important paper by Andrei Shleifer, called "The Limits of Arbitrage" had shown that, after a decline in an asset price below its fundamental value, investors might not be able to take advantage of the arbitrage opportunity; indeed they may themselves be forced to sell the asset, leading to a further decline in the price and a further deviation from fundamentals. Behavioral economists (for example, Richard Thaler, from Chicago) had pointed to the way in which individuals differ from the rational individual model typically used in economics, and had drawn implications for financial markets.

Thus, most of the elements needed to understand the crisis were available. Much of the work, however, was carried out outside macroeconomics, in the fields of finance or corporate finance. The elements were not integrated in a consistent macroeconomic model, and their interactions were poorly understood. Leverage, complexity, and liquidity, the factors which, as we saw in Chapter 9, combined to create the crisis, were nearly fully absent from the macroeconomic models used by central banks.

Bengt Holmström

Several years after the beginning of the crisis, things have changed dramatically. Not surprisingly, researchers have turned their attention to the financial system and the nature of macro financial linkages. Further work is taking place on the various pieces, and these pieces are starting to be integrated into the large macroeconomic models. The lessons for policy are also being drawn, be it on the use of *macro prudential* tools or the dangers of very high public debt. There is still a long way to go, but, in the end, our macroeconomic models will be richer, with a better understanding of the financial system. Yet, one has to be realistic: If history is any guide, the economy will be hit by yet another type of shock we have not thought about.

The lessons from the crisis probably go beyond adding the financial sector to macroeconomic models and analysis. The Great Depression had, rightly, led most economists to question the macroeconomic properties of a market economy and to suggest a larger role for government intervention. The crisis is raising similar questions. Both the new classical and new Keynesian models had in common the belief that, in the medium run at least, the economy naturally returned to its natural level. The new classicals took the extreme position that output was always at its natural level. The new Keynesians took the view that, in the short run, output would likely deviate from its natural level. But they maintained that, eventually, in the medium run, natural forces would return the economy to the natural level. The Great Depression and the long slump in Japan were well known; they were seen however as aberrations and thought to be caused by substantial policy mistakes that could have been avoided. Many economists today believe that this optimism was excessive. After three years in the liquidity trap, it is clear that the usual adjustment mechanism—namely, a decrease in interest rates in response to low output—is not operational. It is also clear that the room for policy, be it monetary policy, or fiscal policy, is also more limited than previously thought.

Jean Tirole

If there is a consensus, it might be that with respect to small shocks and normal fluctuations, the adjustment process works; but that, in response to large, exceptional shocks, the normal adjustment process may fail, the room for policy may be limited, and it may take a long time for the economy to repair itself. For the moment, the priority is for researchers is to better understand what has happened, and for policy makers to use as best they can, the monetary and fiscal policy tools they have, to steer the world economy back to health.

Summary

- The history of modern macroeconomics starts in 1936, with the publication of Keynes's *General Theory of Employment, Interest, and Money*. Keynes's contribution was formalized in the *IS–LM* model by John Hicks and Alvin Hansen in the 1930s and early 1940s.

- The period from the early 1940s to the early 1970s can be called the golden age of macroeconomics. Among the major developments were the development of the theories of consumption, investment, money demand, and portfolio choice; the development of growth theory; and the development of large macroeconometric models.

- The main debate during the 1960s was between Keynesians and monetarists. Keynesians believed developments in macroeconomic theory allowed for better control of the economy. Monetarists, led by Milton Friedman, were more skeptical of the ability of governments to help stabilize the economy.

- In the 1970s, macroeconomics experienced a crisis. There were two reasons. One was the appearance of stagflation, which came as a surprise to most economists. The other was a theoretical attack led by Robert Lucas. Lucas and his followers showed that when rational expectations were introduced, (1) Keynesian models could not be used to determine policy, (2) Keynesian models could not explain long-lasting deviations of output from its natural level, and (3) the theory of policy needed to be redesigned using the tools of game theory.

- Much of the 1970s and 1980s was spent integrating rational expectations into macroeconomics. As is reflected in this book, macroeconomists are now much more aware of the role of expectations in determining the effects of shocks and policy and of the complexity of policy than they were two decades ago.

- Recent research in macroeconomic theory, up to the crisis, proceeded along three lines. New classical economists explored the extent to which fluctuations can be explained as movements in the natural level of output, as opposed to movements away from the natural level of output. New Keynesian economists explored more formally the role of market imperfections in fluctuations. New growth theorists explored the determinants of technological progress. These lines were increasingly overlapping, and, on the eve of the crisis, a new synthesis appeared to be emerging.

- The crisis reflects a major intellectual failure on the part of macroeconomics: the failure to understand the macroeconomic importance of the financial system. While many of the elements needed to understand the crisis had been developed before the crisis, they were not central to macroeconomic thinking and were not integrated in large macroeconomic models. Much research is now focused on macro financial linkages.

- The crisis has also raised a larger issue, about the adjustment process through which output returns to its natural level. If there is a consensus, it might be that with respect to small shocks and normal fluctuations, the adjustment process works, and policy can accelerate this return; but that, in response to large, exceptional shocks, the normal adjustment process may fail, the room for policy may be limited, and it may take a long time for the economy to repair itself.

Key Terms

business cycle theory, 540

effective demand, 540

liquidity preference, 540

neoclassical synthesis, 540

Keynesians, 542

monetarists, 542

random walk of consumption, 546

staggering (of wage and price decisions), 546

new classicals, 547

real business cycles, RBC models, 547

new Keynesians, 548

nominal rigidities, 548

menu costs, 548

new growth theory, 549

Further Readings

- Two classics are J. M. Keynes, *The General Theory of Employment, Interest, and Money* (Macmillan Press, 1936), and Milton Friedman and Anna Schwartz, *A Monetary History of the United States, 1867–1960* (Princeton University Press, 1963). Warning: The first makes for hard reading, and the second is a heavy volume.

- For an account of macroeconomics in textbooks since the 1940s, read Paul Samuelson's, "Credo of a Lucky Textbook Author," *Journal of Economic Perspectives*, 1997 11 (Spring): pp. 153–160.

- In the introduction to *Studies in Business Cycle Theory* (MIT Press, 1981), Robert Lucas develops his approach to macroeconomics and gives a guide to his contributions.

- The paper that launched real business cycle theory is Edward Prescott, "Theory Ahead of Business Cycle

Measurement," *Federal Reserve Bank of Minneapolis Review*, 1996 (Fall): pp. 9–22. It is not easy reading.

- For more on new Keynesian economics, read David Romer, "The New Keynesian Synthesis," *Journal of Economic Perspectives*, 1993 7 (Winter): pp. 5–22.

- For more on new growth theory, read Paul Romer, "The Origins of Endogenous Growth," *Journal of Economic Perspectives*, 1994 8 (Winter): pp. 3–22.

- For a detailed look at the history of macroeconomic ideas, with in-depth interviews of most of the major researchers, read Brian Snowdon and Howard Vane, *Modern Macroeconomics: Its Origins, Development and Current State* (Edward Elgar, 2005).

- For two points of view on the state of macroeconomics pre crisis, read V. V. Chari and Patrick Kehoe, "Macroeconomics in Practice: How Theory Is Shaping Policy," *Journal of Economic Perspectives*, 2006 20 (4): pp. 3–28; and N. Greg Mankiw, "The Macroeconomist as Scientist and Engineer," *Journal of Economic Perspectives*, 2006 20 (4): pp. 29–46.

- For a skeptical view of financial markets and the contributions of Thaler and Shleifer among others, read *The Myth of the Rational Market. A History of Risk, Reward, and Delusion on Wall Street* by Justin Fox (HarperCollins, 2009).

- For an assessment of macroeconomic policy post-crisis, read *In the Wake of the Crisis: Leading Economists Reassess Economic Policy*, edited by Olivier Blanchard et al. (MIT Press, 2012).

If you want to learn more about macroeconomic issues and theory:

- Most economics journals are heavy on mathematics and are hard to read. But a few make an effort to be more friendly. The *Journal of Economic Perspectives,* in particular, has nontechnical articles on current economic research and issues. The *Brookings Papers on Economic Activity*, published twice a year, analyze current macroeconomic problems. So does *Economic Policy*, published in Europe, which focuses more on European issues.

- Most regional Federal Reserve Banks also publish reviews with easy-to-read articles; these reviews are available free of charge. Among these are the *Economic Review* published by the Cleveland Fed, the *Economic Review* published by the Kansas City Fed, the *New England Economic Review* published by the Boston Fed, and the *Quarterly Review* published by the Minneapolis Fed.

- More advanced treatments of current macroeconomic theory—roughly at the level of a first graduate course in macroeconomics—are given by David Romer, *Advanced Macroeconomics* (McGraw-Hill, fourth edition, 2011) and by Olivier Blanchard and Stanley Fischer, *Lectures on Macroeconomics* (MIT Press, 1989).

Appendices

APPENDIX 1 An Introduction to National Income and Product Accounts

This appendix introduces the basic structure and the terms used in the national income and product accounts. The basic measure of aggregate activity is gross domestic product, or GDP. The **national income and product accounts** (**NIPA**, or simply **national accounts**) are organized around two decompositions of GDP.

One decomposes GDP from the *income side*: Who receives what?

The other decomposes GDP from the *production side* (called the *product side* in the national accounts): What is produced, and who buys it?

The Income Side

Table A1-1 looks at the income side of GDP—who receives what.

The top part of the table (lines 1–8) goes from GDP to national income—the sum of the incomes received by the different factors of production:

- The starting point, in line 1, is **gross domestic product**, **GDP**. GDP is defined as *the market value of the goods and services produced by labor and property located in the United States.*

- The next three lines take us from GDP to **GNP**, the **gross national product** (line 4). GNP is an alternative measure of aggregate output. It is defined as *the market value of the goods and services produced by labor and property supplied by U.S. residents.*

Until the 1990s, most countries used GNP rather than GDP as the main measure of aggregate activity. The emphasis in the U.S. national accounts shifted from GNP to GDP in 1991. The difference between the two comes from the distinction between "located in the United States" (used for GDP) and "supplied by

Table A1-1 GDP: The Income Side, 2010 (billions of dollars)		
From gross domestic product to national income:		
1 **Gross domestic product** (GDP)	14,660	
2 Plus: receipts of factor income from the rest of the world		+706
3 Minus: payments of factor income to the rest of the world		−518
4 Equals: **Gross national product**	14,848	
5 Minus: consumption of fixed capital		−1,868
6 Equals: **Net national product**	12,980	
7 Minus: Statistical Discrepancy		152
8 Equals: **National income**	12,828	
The Decomposition of National Income:		
9 Indirect taxes	1,000	
10 Compensation of employees	7,991	
11 Wages and salaries		6,405
12 Supplements to wages and salaries		1,586
13 Corporate profits and business transfers	1,743	
14 Net interest	738	
15 Proprietors' income	1,055	
16 Rental income of persons	301	

Source: Survey of Current Business, May 2011, Tables 1-7-5 and 1-12

U.S. residents" (used for GNP). For example, profit from a U.S.-owned plant in Japan is not included in U.S. GDP, but is included in U.S. GNP.

So, to go from GDP to GNP, we must first add **receipts of factor income from the rest of the world**, which is income from U.S. capital or U.S. residents abroad (line 2); then subtract **payments of factor income to the rest of the world**, which is income received by foreign capital and foreign residents in the United States (line 3).

In 2010, payments from the rest of the world exceeded receipts to the rest of the world by $188 billion, so GNP was larger than GDP by $188 billion.

- The next step takes us from GNP to **net national product**, or **NNP** (line 6). The difference between GNP and NNP is the depreciation of capital, called **consumption of fixed capital** in the national accounts.

- Finally, lines 7 and 8 take us from NNP to **national income** (line 8). National income is defined as the *income that originates in the production of goods and services supplied by residents of the United States*. In theory, national income and net national product should be equal. In practice, they typically differ, because they are constructed in different ways:

Net national product is constructed from the top down, starting from GDP and going through the steps we have just gone through in Table A1-1. National income is constructed instead from the bottom up, by adding the different components of factor income (compensation of employees, corporate profits, and so on). If we could measure everything exactly, the two measures should be equal. In practice, the two measures differ, and the difference between the two is called the "statistical discrepancy." In 2010, national income computed from the bottom up (the number in line 8) was smaller than the net national product computed from the top down (the number in line 6) by $152 billion. The statistical discrepancy is a useful reminder of the statistical problems involved in constructing the national income accounts. Although $152 billion seems like a large error, as a percentage of GDP, the error is about 1 percentage point.

The bottom part of the table (lines 9–15) decomposes national income into different types of income.

- **Indirect taxes** (line 9). Some of the national income goes directly to the state in the form of sales taxes. (Indirect taxes are just another name for sales taxes.)

The rest of national income goes either to employees, or to firms:

- **Compensation of employees** (line 10), or labor income, is what goes to employees. It is by far the largest component of national income, accounting for 62% of national income. Labor income is the sum of wages and salaries (line 11) and of supplements to wages and salaries (line 12). These range from employer contributions for social insurance (by far the largest item) to such exotic items as employer contributions to marriage fees to justices of the peace.

- **Corporate profits and business transfers** (line 13). Profits are revenues minus costs (including interest payments) and minus depreciation. (Business transfers, which account for $132 billion out of $1,743 billion, are items such as liability payments for personal injury, and corporate contributions to nonprofit organizations.)

- **Net interest** (line 14) is the interest paid by firms minus the interest received by firms, plus interest received from the rest of the world minus interest paid to the rest of the world. In 2010, most of net interest represented net interest paid by firms: The United States received about as much in interest from the rest of the world as it paid to the rest to the world. So the sum of corporate profits plus net interest paid by firms was approximately $1,743 billion + $738 billion = $2,481 billion, or about 19% of national income.

- **Proprietors' income** (line 15) is the income received by persons who are self-employed. It is defined as *the income of sole proprietorships, partnerships, and tax-exempt cooperatives*.

- **Rental income of persons** (line 16) is the income from the rental of real property, minus depreciation on this real property. Houses produce housing services; rental income measures the income received for these services.

If the national accounts counted only actual rents, rental income would depend on the proportion of apartments and houses that were rented versus those that were owner occupied. For example, if everybody became the owner of the apartment or the house in which he or she lived, rental income would go to zero, and thus measured GDP would drop. To avoid this problem, national accounts treat houses and apartments as if they were all rented out. So, rental income is constructed as actual rents plus *imputed* rents on those houses and apartments that are owner occupied.

Before we move to the product side, Table A1-2 shows how we can go from national income to personal disposable income—the income available to persons after they have received transfers and paid taxes.

Table A1-2 From National Income to Personal Disposable Income, 2010 (billions of dollars)

1	National income	12,828
2	Minus: indirect taxes	−1,000
3	Minus: corporate profits and business transfers	−1,743
4	Minus: net interest	−738
5	Plus: income from assets	+1,908
6	Plus: personal transfers	+2,296
7	Minus: contributions for social insurance	−1,004
8	Equals: **Personal income**	12,547
9	Minus: personal tax payments	−1,167
10	Equals: **Personal disposable income**	11,380

Source: *Survey of Current Business*, May 2011, Tables 1-7-5, 1-12, and 2-1

■ Not all national income (line 1) is distributed to persons:

Some of the income goes to the state in the form of indirect taxes, so the first step is to subtract indirect taxes. (Line 2 in Table A1-2 is equal to line 9 in Table A1-1.)

Some of the corporate profits are retained by firms. Some of the interest payments by firms go to banks, or go abroad. So the second step is to subtract all corporate profits and business transfers (line 3—equal to line 13 in Table A1-1) and all net interest payments (line 4—equal to line 14 in Table A1-1), and add back all income from assets (dividends and interest payments) received by persons (line 5).

■ People receive income not only from production, but also from public transfers (line 6). Transfers accounted for $1,908 billion in 2010. From these transfers must be subtracted personal contributions for social insurance, $1,004 billion (line 7).

■ The net result of these adjustments is **personal income**, the income actually received by persons (line 8). **Personal disposable income** (line 10) is equal to personal income minus personal tax and nontax payments (line 9). In 2010, personal disposable income was $11,380 billion, or about 78% of GDP.

The Product Side

Table A1-3 looks at the product side of the national accounts—what is produced, and who buys it.

Start with the three components of domestic demand: consumption, investment, and government spending.

■ Consumption, called **personal consumption expenditures** (line 2), is by far the largest component of demand. It is defined as *the sum of goods and services purchased by persons resident in the United States.*

In the same way that national accounts include imputed rental income on the income side, they include imputed housing services as part of consumption. Owners of a house are assumed to consume housing services, for a price equal to the imputed rental income of that house.

Consumption is disaggregated into three components: purchases of **durable goods** (line 3), **nondurable goods** (line 4), and **services** (line 5). Durable goods are commodities that can be stored and have an average life of at least three years; automobile purchases are the largest item here. Nondurable goods are commodities that can be stored but have a life of less than three years. Services are commodities that cannot be stored and must be consumed at the place and time of purchase.

■ Investment, called **gross private domestic fixed investment** (line 6), is the sum of two very different components:

Nonresidential investment (line 7) is the purchase of new capital goods by firms. These may be either **structures** (line 8)—mostly new plants—or **equipment and software** (line 9)—such as machines, computers, or office equipment.

Residential investment (line 10) is the purchase of new houses or apartments by persons.

■ **Government purchases** (line 11) equal the purchases of goods by the government plus the compensation of government employees. (The government is thought of as buying the services of the government employees.)

Government purchases equal the sum of purchases by the federal government (line 12) (which

Table A1-3 GDP: The Product Side, 2010 (billions of dollars)

1	**Gross domestic product**	14,660	
2	Personal consumption expenditures	10,348	
3	Durable goods		1,089
4	Nondurable goods		2,336
5	Services		6,923
6	Gross private domestic fixed investment	1,756	
7	Nonresidential		1,415
8	Structures			383
9	Equipment and Software			1,032
10	Residential		341
11	Government purchases	3,001	
12	Federal		1,215
13	National Defense			818
14	Nondefense			397
15	State and local		1,786
16	Net exports	−516	
17	Exports		1,838
18	Imports		−2,354
19	Change in business inventories	71	

Source : Survey of Current Business, May 2010, Table 1-1-5

themselves can be disaggregated between spending on national defense (line 13) and nondefense spending (line 14) and purchases by state and local governments (line 15).

Note that government purchases do not include transfers from the government or interest payments on government debt. These do not correspond to purchases of either goods or services, and so are not included here. This means that the number for government purchases you see in Table A1-3 is substantially smaller than the number we typically hear for government spending—which includes transfers and interest payments.

■ The sum of consumption, investment, and government purchases gives the demand for goods by U.S. firms, U.S. persons, and the U.S. government. If the United States were a closed economy, this would be the same as the demand for U.S. goods. But because the U.S. economy is open, the two numbers are different. To get to the demand for U.S. goods, we must make two adjustments. First, we must add the foreign purchases of U.S. goods, **exports** (line 17). Second, we must subtract U.S. purchases of foreign goods, **imports** (line 18). In 2010, exports were smaller

than imports by $516 billion. Thus, **net exports** (or, equivalently, the **trade balance**), was equal to −$516 billion (line 16).

■ Adding consumption, investment, government purchases, and net exports gives the *total purchases of U.S. goods.* Production may, however, be less than purchases if firms satisfy the difference by decreasing inventories. Or production may be greater than purchases, in which case firms are accumulating inventories. The last line of Table A1-3 gives **changes in business inventories** (line 19), also sometimes called (rather misleadingly) "inventory investment." It is defined as the *change in the volume of inventories held by business.* The change in business inventories can be positive or negative. In 2010, it was small and positive: U.S. production was higher than total purchases of U.S. goods by $71 billion.

The Federal Government in the National Income Accounts

Table A1-4 presents the basic numbers describing federal government economic activity in fiscal year 2010, using NIPA numbers.

The reason for using the fiscal year rather than the calendar year is that budget projections—as presented in Chapter 23—are typically framed in terms of fiscal year rather than calendar year numbers. The fiscal year runs from October 1 of the previous calendar year to September 30 of the current calendar year, so in this case from October 2009 to September 2010.

The reason for using NIPA rather than the official budget numbers is that they are economically more meaningful; that is, the NIPA numbers are a better representation of what the government is doing in the economy than the numbers presented in the various budget documents. Budget numbers presented by the government need not follow the national income accounting conventions and sometimes involve creative accounting.

In 2010, federal revenues were $2,329 billion (line 1). Of those, personal taxes (also called "income taxes") accounted for $884 billion, or 38% of revenues; social insurance contributions (also called "payroll taxes") accounted for $965 billion, or 41% of revenues.

Expenditures excluding interest payments but including transfer payments to individuals were $3,385 billion (line 7). Consumption expenditures (mostly wages and salaries of public employees and depreciation of capital) accounted for $1,041 billion, or 30% of expenditures. Excluding defense, expenditures were only $349 billion. **Transfers to persons**. (also called "entitlement programs," mostly unemployment, retirement, and health benefits) were a much larger $1,703 billion. Table A1-3 shows how the expenditures on goods and services by state and local government are much larger than those of the federal government.

The federal government was therefore running a primary deficit of $1,056 billion (line 1 minus line 7, here recorded as a negative **primary surplus** in line 14). This is a very large primary deficit, equal to one-third of expenditures, nearly one-half of revenues, and nearly 9% of GDP.

Net interest payments on the debt held by the public totaled $249 billion (line 15). The **official deficit** was therefore equal to $1,305 billion (line 14 plus line 15). We know, however, that this measure is incorrect (see the Focus box "Inflation Accounting and the Measurement of Deficits" in Chapter 23.). It is appropriate to correct the official deficit measure for the role of inflation in reducing the real value of the public debt. The correct measure, the **inflation adjusted deficit**, namely the sum of the official deficit plus *real* interest payments, was still a very large $1,208 billion (line 19).

Warning

National accounts give an internally consistent description of aggregate activity. But underlying these accounts are many choices of what to include and what not to include, where to put some types of income or spending, and so on. Here are five examples:

- Work within the home is not counted in GDP. If, for example, two women decide to babysit each other's child rather than take care of their own child and pay each other for the babysitting services, measured GDP will go up, while true GDP clearly does not change. The solution would be to count work within the home in GDP, the same way that we impute rents for owner-occupied housing. But, so far, this has not been done.

- The purchase of a house is treated as an investment, and housing services are then treated as part of consumption. Contrast this with the treatment of automobiles. Despite the fact that they provide services for a long time—although not as long a time as houses do—purchases of automobiles are not treated as investment. They are treated as consumption and appear in the national accounts only in the year in which they are bought.

- Firms' purchases of machines are treated as investment. The purchase of education is treated as consumption of education services. But education is clearly in part an investment: People acquire education in part to increase their future income.

- Many government purchases have to be valued in the national accounts in the absence of a market transaction. How do we value the work of teachers in teaching children to read when that transaction is mandated by the state as part of compulsory education? The rule used is to value it at cost, so using the salaries of teachers.

- The correct calculation of the government's deficit (and debt) is a very challenging task. Here is one aspect of the problem: Suppose the teachers in the example above are paid partly with cash and partly with the promise of a future retirement pension. There is an important sense that the pension is just like government debt (i.e., a future liability of taxpayers). However, these liabilities are not counted in the deficit measure in Table A1-4 or in our standard measures of public debt. Another problem lies in the treatment of private sector debt guarantees by federal or state government. Should such contingent liabilities be counted as part of public debt?

The list could go on. However, the point of these examples is not to make you conclude that national accounts are wrong. Most of the accounting decisions you just saw were made for good reasons, often because of data availability or for simplicity. The point is that to use national accounts best, you should understand their logic, but also understand the choices that have been made and thus their limitations.

Table A1-4 U.S. Federal Budget Revenues and Expenditures, fiscal year 2010 (billions of dollars)

1 Revenues	2,329		
2 Personal taxes		884	
3 Corporate profit taxes		281	
4 Indirect taxes		99	
5 Social insurance contributions		965	
6 Other		100	
7 Expenditures, excluding net interest payments	3,385		
8 Consumption expenditures		1,041	
9 Defense			692
10 Nondefense			349
11 Transfers to persons		1,703	
12 Grants to state/local governments		523	
13 Other		118	
14 Primary surplus (+ sign: surplus)	−1,056		
15 Net interest payments	249		
16 Real interest payments		152	
17 Inflation component		97	
18 Official surplus: (1) minus (7) minus (15)	−1,305		
19 Inflation adjusted surplus: (18) plus (17)	−1,208		

Source: Survey of Current Business March 2011, Table 10. Inflation adjustment calculated by using the debt-to-GDP ratio from Table B-79, Economic Report of the President and inflation from CPI series CPIAUSL, Federal Reserve Economic Data (FRED) http://research.stlouisfed.org/fred2/

Key Terms

- national income and product accounts (NIPA), national accounts, A-1
- gross domestic product (GDP), A-1
- gross national product (GNP), A-1
- receipts of factor income from the rest of the world, payments of factor income to the rest of the world, A-2
- net national product (NNP), A-2
- consumption of fixed capital, A-2
- national income, A-2
- indirect taxes, A-2
- compensation of employees, A-2
- corporate profits, A-2
- net interest, A-2
- proprietors' income, A-2
- rental income of persons, A-2
- personal income, A-3
- personal disposable income, A-3
- personal consumption expenditures, A-3
- durable goods, nondurable goods, and services, A-3
- gross private domestic fixed investment, A-3
- nonresidential investment, structures, equipment, and software, A-3
- residential investment, A-3
- government purchases, A-3
- exports, imports, A-4
- net exports, trade balance, A-4
- changes in business inventories, A-4
- transfers to persons, A-5
- primary surplus (deficit), A-5
- official surplus (deficit), A-5
- inflation-adjusted surplus (deficit), A-5

Further Readings

For more details, read "A Guide to the National Income and Product Accounts of the United States," September 2006 (www.bea.gov/national/pdf/nipaguid.pdf).

APPENDIX 2 A Math Refresher

This appendix presents the mathematical tools and the mathematical results that are used in this book.

Geometric Series

Definition. A geometric series is a sum of numbers of the form:

$$1 + x + x^2 + \cdots + x^n$$

where x is a number that may be greater or smaller than one, and x^n denotes x to the power n; that is, x times itself n times.

Examples of such series are:

■ The sum of spending in each round of the multiplier (Chapter 3). If c is the marginal propensity to consume, then the sum of increases in spending after $n + 1$ rounds is given by:

$$1 + c + c^2 + \cdots + c^n$$

■ The present discounted value of a sequence of payments of one dollar each year for n years (Chapter 14), when the interest rate is equal to i:

$$1 + \frac{1}{1 + i} + \frac{1}{(1 + i)^2} + \cdots + \frac{1}{(1 + i)^{n-1}}$$

We usually have two questions we want to answer when encountering such a series:

1. What is the sum?
2. Does the sum explode as we let n increase, or does it reach a finite limit (and, if so, what is that limit)?

The following propositions tell you what you need to know to answer these questions.

Proposition 1 tells you how to compute the sum:

Proposition 1:

$$1 + x + x^2 + \cdots + x^n = \frac{1 - x^{n+1}}{1 - x} \quad \text{(A2.1)}$$

Here is the proof: Multiply the sum by $(1 - x)$, and use the fact that $x^a x^b = x^{a+b}$ (that is, you must add exponents when multiplying):

$$(1 + x + x^2 + \ldots + x^n)(1 - x) = 1 + x + x^2 + \ldots + x^n$$
$$- x - x^2 - \ldots - x^n - x^{n+1}$$
$$= 1 \qquad\qquad\qquad - x^{n+1}$$

All the terms on the right except for the first and the last cancel. Dividing both sides by $(1 - x)$ gives equation (A2.1).

This formula can be used for any x and any n. If, for example, x is 0.9 and n is 10, then the sum is equal to 6.86. If x is 1.2 and n is 10, then the sum is 32.15.

Proposition 2 tells you what happens as n gets large:

Proposition 2:   If x is less than one, the sum goes to $1/(1 - x)$ as n gets large. If x is equal to or greater than one, the sum explodes as n gets large.

Here is the proof: If x is less than one, then x^n goes to zero as n gets large. Thus, from equation (A2.1), the sum goes to $1/(1 - x)$. If x is greater than one, then x^n becomes larger and larger as n increases, $1 - x^n$ becomes a larger and larger negative number, and the ratio $(1 - x^n)/(1 - x)$ becomes a larger and larger positive number. Thus, the sum explodes as n gets large.

Application from Chapter 14: Consider the present value of a payment of $1 forever, starting next year, when the interest rate is i. The present value is given by:

$$\frac{1}{(1 + i)} + \frac{1}{(1 + i)^2} + \cdots \quad \text{(A2.2)}$$

Factoring out $1/(1 + i)$, rewrite this present value as:

$$\frac{1}{(1 + i)}\left[1 + \frac{1}{(1 + i)} + \cdots\right]$$

The term in brackets is a geometric series, with $x = 1/(1 + i)$. As the interest rate i is positive, x is less than 1. Applying Proposition 2, when n gets large, the term in brackets equals

$$\frac{1}{1 - \frac{1}{(1 + i)}} = \frac{(1 + i)}{(1 + i - 1)} = \frac{(1 + i)}{i}$$

Replacing the term in brackets in the previous equation by $(1 + i)/i$ gives:

$$\frac{1}{(1 + i)}\left[\frac{(1 + i)}{i}\right] = \frac{1}{i}$$

The present value of a sequence of payments of one dollar a year forever, starting next year, is equal to $1 divided by the interest rate. If i is equal to 5% per year, the present value equals $1/0.05 = $20.

Useful Approximations

Throughout this book, we use a number of approximations that make computations easier. These approximations are most reliable when the variables x, y, z below are small, say between 0 and 10%. The numerical examples in Propositions 3–10 below are based on the values $x = .05$ and $y = .03$.

Proposition 3:

$$(1 + x)(1 + y) \approx (1 + x + y) \qquad \text{(A2.3)}$$

Here is the proof. Expanding $(1 + x)(1 + y)$ gives $(1 + x)(1 + y) = 1 + x + y + xy$. If x and y are small, then the product xy is very small and can be ignored as an approximation (for example, if $x = .05$ and $y = .03$, then $xy = .0015$). So $(1 + x)(1 + y)$ is approximately equal to $(1 + x + y)$.

For the values x and y above, for example, the approximation gives 1.08 compared to an exact value of 1.0815.

Proposition 4:

$$(1 + x)^2 \approx 1 + 2x \qquad \text{(A2.4)}$$

The proof follows directly from Proposition 3, with $y = x$. For the value of $x = .05$, the approximation gives 1.10, compared to an exact value of 1.1025.

Application from Chapter 15: From arbitrage, the relation between the two-year interest rate and the current and the expected one-year interest rates is given by:

$$(1 + i_{2t})^2 = (1 + i_{1t})(1 + i_{1t+1}^e)$$

Using Proposition 4 for the left side of the equation gives:

$$(1 + i_{2t})^2 \approx 1 + 2i_{2t}$$

Using Proposition 3 for the right side of the equation gives:

$$(1 + i_{1t})(1 + i_{1t+1}^e) \approx 1 + i_{1t} + i_{1t+1}^e$$

Using this expression to replace $(1 + i_{1t})(1 + i_{1t+1}^e)$ in the original arbitrage relation gives:

$$1 + 2i_{2t} = 1 + i_{1t} + i_{1t+1}^e$$

Or, reorganizing:

$$i_{2t} = \frac{(i_{1t} + i_{1t+1}^e)}{2}$$

The two-year interest rate is approximately equal to the average of the current and the expected one-year interest rates.

Proposition 5:

$$(1 + x)^n \approx 1 + nx \qquad \text{(A2.5)}$$

The proof follows by repeated application of Propositions 3 and 4. For example, $(1 + x)^3 = (1 + x)^2(1 + x) \approx (1 + 2x)(1 + x)$ by Proposition 4, $\approx (1 + 2x + x) = 1 + 3x$ by Proposition 3.

The approximation becomes worse as n increases, however. For example, for $x = .05$ and $n = 5$, the approximation gives 1.25, compared to an exact value of 1.2763. For $n = 10$, the approximation gives 1.50, compared to an exact value of 1.63.

Proposition 6:

$$\frac{(1 + x)}{(1 + y)} \approx (1 + x - y) \qquad \text{(A2.6)}$$

Here is the proof: Consider the product of $(1 + x - y)(1 + y)$. Expanding this product gives $(1 + x - y)(1 + y) = 1 + x + xy - y^2$. If both x and y are small, then xy and y^2 are very small, so $(1 + x - y)(1 + y) \approx (1 + x)$. Dividing both sides of this approximation by $(1 + y)$ gives the proposition above.

For the values of $x = .05$ and $y = .03$, the approximation gives 1.02, while the correct value is 1.019.

Application from Chapter 14: The real interest rate is defined by:

$$(1 + r_t) = \frac{(1 + i_t)}{(1 + \pi_{t+1}^e)}$$

Using Proposition 6 gives

$$(1 + r_t) \approx (1 + i_t - \pi_{t+1}^e)$$

Simplifying:

$$r_t \approx i_t - \pi_{t+1}^e$$

This gives us the approximation we use at many points in this book: The real interest rate is approximately equal to the nominal interest rate minus expected inflation.

These approximations are also very convenient when dealing with growth rates. Define the rate of growth of x by $g_x \equiv \Delta x / x$, and similarly for z, g_z, and y, g_y. The numerical examples below are based on the values $g_x = .05$ and $g_y = .03$.

Proposition 7: If $z = xy$, then:

$$g_z \approx g_x + g_y \qquad \text{(A2.7)}$$

Here is the proof: Let Δz be the increase in z when x increases by Δx and y increases by Δy. Then, by definition:

$$z + \Delta z = (x + \Delta x)(y + \Delta y)$$

Divide both sides by z.
The left side becomes:

$$\frac{(z + \Delta z)}{z} = \left(1 + \frac{\Delta z}{z}\right)$$

The right-hand side becomes

$$\frac{(x + \Delta x)(y + \Delta y)}{z} = \frac{(x + \Delta x)}{x}\frac{(y + \Delta y)}{y}$$

$$= \left(1 + \frac{\Delta x}{x}\right)\left(1 + \frac{\Delta y}{y}\right)$$

where the first equality follows from the fact that $z = xy$, the second equality from simplifying each of the two fractions.

Using the expressions for the left and right sides gives:

$$\left(1 + \frac{\Delta z}{z}\right) = \left(1 + \frac{\Delta x}{x}\right)\left(1 + \frac{\Delta y}{y}\right)$$

Or, equivalently,

$$(1 + g_z) = (1 + g_x)(1 + g_y)$$

From Proposition 3, $(1 + g_z) \approx (1 + g_x + g_y)$, or, equivalently,

$$g_z \approx g_x + g_y$$

For $g_x = 0.05$ and $g_y = 0.03$, the approximation gives $g_z = 8\%$, while the correct value is 8.15%.

Application from Chapter 13: Let the production function be of the form $Y = NA$, where Y is production, N is employment, and A is productivity. Denoting the growth rates of Y, N, and A by g_Y, g_N, and g_A; respectively, Proposition 7 implies

$$g_Y \approx g_N + g_A$$

The rate of output growth is approximately equal to the rate of employment growth plus the rate of productivity growth.

Proposition 8: If $z = x/y$, then

$$g_z \approx g_x - g_y \qquad \text{(A2.8)}$$

Here is the proof: Let Δz be the increase in z, when x increases by Δx and y increases by Δy. Then, by definition:

$$z + \Delta z = \frac{x + \Delta x}{y + \Delta y}$$

Divide both sides by z.
The left side becomes:

$$\frac{(z + \Delta z)}{z} = \left(1 + \frac{\Delta z}{z}\right)$$

The right side becomes:

$$\frac{(x + \Delta x)}{(y + \Delta y)}\frac{1}{z} = \frac{(x + \Delta x)}{(y + \Delta y)}\frac{y}{x} = \frac{(x + \Delta x)/x}{(y + \Delta y)/y} = \frac{1 + (\Delta x/x)}{1 + (\Delta y/y)}$$

where the first equality comes from the fact that $z = x/y$, the second equality comes from rearranging terms, and the third equality comes from simplifying.

Using the expressions for the left and right sides gives:

$$1 + \Delta z/z = \frac{1 + (\Delta x/x)}{1 + (\Delta y/y)}$$

Or, substituting:

$$1 + g_z = \frac{1 + g_x}{1 + g_y}$$

From Proposition 6, $(1 + g_z) \approx (1 + g_x - g_y)$, or, equivalently,

$$g_z \approx g_x - g_y$$

For $g_x = .05$ and $g_y = .03$, the approximation gives $g_z = 2\%$, while the correct value is 1.9%.

Application from Chapter 8: Let M be nominal money, P be the price level. It follows that the rate of growth of the real money stock M/P is given by:

$$g_{M/P} \approx g_M - \pi$$

where π is the rate of growth of prices or, equivalently, the rate of inflation.

Functions

We use functions informally in this book, as a way of denoting how a variable depends on one or more other variables.

In some cases, we look at how a variable Y moves with a variable X. We write this relation as

$$Y = f(X)$$
$$+$$

A plus sign below X indicates a positive relation: An increase in X leads to an increase in Y. A minus sign below X indicates a negative relation: An increase in X leads to a decrease in Y.

In some cases, we allow the variable Y to depend on more than one variable. For example, we allow Y to depend on X and Z:

$$Y = f(X, Z)$$
$$(+, -)$$

The signs indicate that an increase in X leads to an increase in Y, and that an increase in Z leads to a decrease in Y.

An example of such a function is the investment function (5.1) in Chapter 5:

$$I = I(Y, i\ )$$
$$(+, -)$$

This equation says that investment, I, increases with production, Y, and decreases with the interest rate, i.

In some cases, it is reasonable to assume that the relation between two or more variables is a **linear relation**. A given increase in X always leads to the same increase in Y. In that case, the function is given by:

$$Y = a + bX$$

This relation can be represented by a line giving Y for any value of X.

The parameter a gives the value of Y when X is equal to zero. It is called the **intercept** because it gives the value of Y when the line representing the relation "intercepts" (crosses) the vertical axis.

The parameter b tells us by how much Y increases when X increases by one unit. It is called the **slope** because it is equal to the slope of the line representing the relation.

A simple linear relation is the relation $Y = X$, which is represented by the 45-degree line and has a slope of 1. Another example of a linear relation is the consumption function (3.2) in Chapter 3:

$$C = c_0 + c_1 Y_D$$

where C is consumption and Y_D is disposable income. c_0 tells us what consumption would be if disposable income were equal to zero. c_1 tells us by how much consumption increases when income increases by 1 unit; c_1 is called the marginal propensity to consume.

Logarithmic Scales

A variable that grows at a constant growth rate increases by larger and larger increments over time. Take a variable X that grows over time at a constant growth rate, say at 3% per year.

- Start in year 0 and assume $X = 2$. So a 3% increase in X represents an increase of 0.06 (0.03 times 2).
- Go to year 20. X is now equal to $2(1.03)^{20} = 3.61$. A 3% increase now represents an increase of 0.11 (0.03 times 3.61).
- Go to year 100. X is equal to $2(1.03)^{100} = 38.4$. A 3% increase represents an increase of 1.15 (0.03 times 38.4), so an increase about 20 times larger than in year 0.

If we plot X against time using a standard (linear) vertical scale, the plot looks like Figure A2-1(a). The increases in X become larger and larger over time (0.06 in year 0, 0.11 in year 20, 1.15 in year 100). The curve representing X against time becomes steeper and steeper.

Another way of representing the evolution of X is to use a *logarithmic scale* to measure X on the vertical axis. The property of a logarithmic scale is that the same *proportional* increase in this variable is represented by the same vertical distance on the scale. So the behavior of a variable such as X that increases by the same proportional increase (3%) each year is now represented by a line. Figure A2-1(b) represents the behavior of X, this time using a logarithmic scale on the vertical axis. The fact that the relation is represented by a line indicates that X is growing at a constant rate over time. The higher the rate of growth, the steeper the line.

In contrast to X, economic variables such as GDP do not grow at a constant growth rate every year. Their

Figure A2-1

(a) The Evolution of X (using a linear scale) (b) The evolution of X (using a logarithmic scale) growth rate may be higher in some decades, lower in others; A recession may lead to a few years of negative growth. Yet, when looking at their evolution over time, it is often more informative to use a logarithmic scale rather than a linear scale. Let's see why.

Figure A2-2(a) plots real U.S. GDP from 1890 to 2011 using a standard (linear) scale. Because real U.S. GDP is about 51 times bigger in 2011 than in 1890, the same proportional increase in GDP is 51 times bigger in 2011 than in 1890. So the curve representing the evolution of GDP over time becomes steeper and steeper over time. It is very difficult to see from the figure whether the U.S. economy is growing faster or slower than it was 50 years or 100 years ago.

Figure A2-2(b) plots U.S. GDP from 1890 to 2011, now using a logarithmic scale. If the growth rate of GDP was the same every year—so the proportional increase in GDP was the same every year—the evolution of GDP would be represented by a line—the same way as the evolution of X was represented by a line in Figure A2-1(b). Because the growth rate of GDP is not constant from year to year—so the proportional increase in GDP is not the same every year—the evolution of GDP is no longer represented by a line. Unlike in Figure A2-2(a), GDP does not explode over time, and the graph is more informative. Here are two examples:

■ If, in Figure A2-2(b), we were to draw a line to fit the curve from 1890 to 1929, and another line to fit the curve from 1950 to 2011 (the two periods are separated by the shaded area in Figure A2-2(b)), the two lines would have roughly the same slope. What this tells us is that the average growth rate was roughly the same during the two periods.

■ The decline in output from 1929 to 1933 is very visible in Figure A2-2(b). (By contrast, the current crisis looks so far very small relative to the Great Depression.) So is the strong recovery of output that follows. By the 1950s, output appears to be back to its old trend line. This suggests that the Great Depression was not associated with a permanently lower level of output.

Note, in both cases, how you could not have derived these conclusions by looking at Figure A2-2(a), but you can derive them by looking at Figure A2-2(b). This shows the usefulness of using a logarithmic scale.

Key Terms

■ linear relation, A-9
■ intercept, A-10
■ slope, A-10

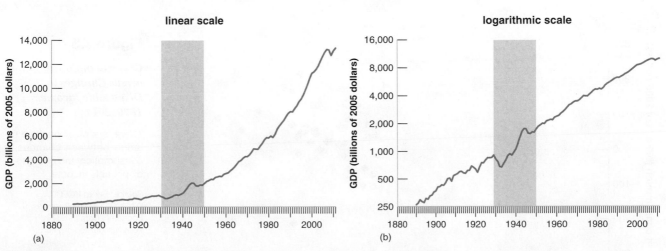

Figure A2-2

(a) U.S. GDP since 1890 (using a linear scale) (b) U.S. GDP since 1890 (using a logarithmic scale)

Source: 1890–1928: Historical Statistics of the United States, Table F1-5, adjusted for level to be consistent with the post 1929 series. 1929–2011: BEA, billions of chained 2005 dollars. http://www.bea.gov/national/index.htm#gdp

APPENDIX 3 An Introduction to Econometrics

How do we know that consumption depends on disposable income?

How do we know the value of the propensity to consume?

To answer these questions and, more generally, to estimate behavioral relations and find out the values of the relevant parameters, economists use *econometrics*—the set of statistical techniques designed for use in economics. Econometrics can get very technical, but we outline in this appendix the basic principles behind it. We shall do so using as an example the consumption function introduced in Chapter 3, and we shall concentrate on estimating c_1, the propensity to consume out of disposable income.

Changes in Consumption and Changes in Disposable Income

The propensity to consume tells us by how much consumption changes for a given change in disposable income. A natural first step is simply to plot changes in consumption versus changes in disposable income and see how the relation between the two looks. You can see this in Figure A3-1.

The vertical axis in Figure A3-1 measures the annual change in consumption minus the average annual change in consumption, for each year from 1970 to 2011. More precisely:

Let C_t denote consumption in year t. Let ΔC_t denote $C_t - C_{t-1}$, the change in consumption from year $t - 1$ to year t. Let $\overline{\Delta C}$ denote the average annual change in consumption since 1970. The variable measured on the vertical axis is constructed as $\Delta C_t - \overline{\Delta C}$. A positive value of the variable represents an increase in consumption larger than average, while a negative value represents an increase in consumption smaller than average.

Similarly, the horizontal axis measures the annual change in disposable income, minus the average annual change in disposable income since 1970, $\Delta Y_{Dt} - \overline{\Delta Y_D}$.

A particular square in the figure gives the deviations of the change in consumption and disposable income from their respective means for a particular year between 1970 and 2011. In 2011, for example, the change in consumption was higher than average by $39 billion, and the change in disposable income was lower than average by $78 billion. (For our purposes, it is not important to know which year each square refers to, just what the set of points in the diagram looks like. So, except for 2011, the years are not indicated in Figure A3-1.)

Figure A3-1 suggests two main conclusions:

■ One, there is a clear positive relation between changes in consumption and changes in disposable income. Most of the points lie in the upper-right and lower-left quadrants of the figure: When disposable income increases by more than average, consumption also typically increases by more than average; when disposable income increases by less than average, so typically does consumption.

■ Two, the relation between the two variables is good but not perfect. In particular, some points lie in the upper-left quadrant: These points correspond to

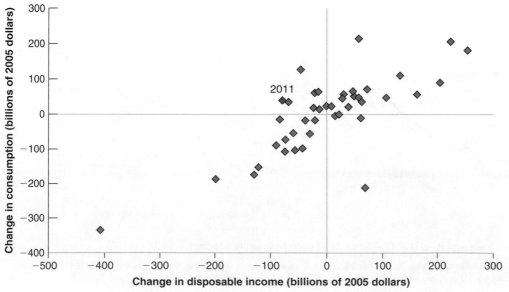

Figure A3-1

Changes in Consumption versus Changes in Disposable Income, 1970–2011

There is a clear positive relation between changes in consumption and changes in disposable income.

Source: Series PCECCA, DSPIC96 Federal Reserve Economic Data (FRED) http://research.stlouisfed.org/fred2/)

Figure A3-2

Changes in Consumption and Changes in Disposable Income: The Regression Line

The regression line is the line that fits the scatter of points best.

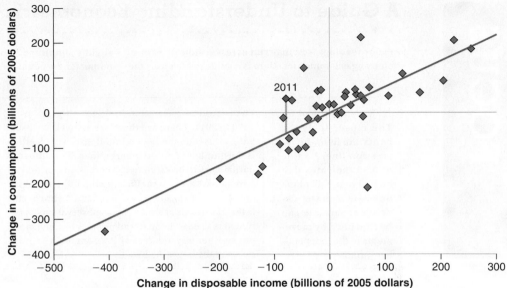

years when smaller-than-average changes in disposable income were associated with higher-than-average changes in consumption. (This is indeed what happened in 2011.)

Econometrics allows us to state these two conclusions more precisely and to get an estimate of the propensity to consume. Using an econometrics software package, we can find the line that fits the cloud of points in Figure A3-1 best. This line-fitting process is called **ordinary least squares** (OLS).[1] The estimated equation corresponding to the line is called a **regression**, and the line itself is called the **regression line**.

In our case, the estimated equation is given by

$$(\Delta C_t - \overline{\Delta C}) = 0.74(\Delta Y_{Dt} - \overline{\Delta Y_D}) + \text{residual}$$

$$\overline{R}^2 = 0.59 \qquad (A3.1)$$

The regression line corresponding to this estimated equation is drawn in Figure A3-2. Equation (A3.1) reports two important numbers (econometrics packages give more information than those reported above; a typical printout, together with further explanations, is given in the Focus box "A Guide to Understanding Econometric Results"):

■ The first important number is the estimated propensity to consume. The equation tells us that an increase

in disposable income of $1 billion above normal is typically associated with an increase in consumption of $0.74 billion above normal. In other words, the estimated propensity to consume is 0.74. It is positive but smaller than 1.

■ The second important number is $\overline{R}^2$, which is a measure of how well the regression line fits:

Having estimated the effect of disposable income on consumption, we can decompose the change in consumption for each year into that part that is due to the change in disposable income—the first term on the right in equation (A3.1)— and the rest, which is called the **residual**. For example, the residual for 2011 is indicated in Figure A3-2 by the vertical distance from the point representing 2011 to the regression line.

If all the points in Figure A3-2 were exactly on the estimated line, all residuals would be zero; all changes in consumption would be explained by changes in disposable income. As you can see, however, this is not the case. $\overline{R}^2$ is a statistic that tells us how well the line fits. $\overline{R}^2$ is always between 0 and 1. A value of 1 would imply that the relation between the two variables is perfect, that all points are exactly on the regression line. A value of zero would imply that the computer can see no relation between the two variables. The value of $\overline{R}^2$ of 0.59 in equation (A3.1) is high, but not very high. It confirms the message from Figure A3-2: Movements in disposable income clearly affect consumption, but there is still quite a bit of movement in consumption that cannot be explained by movements in disposable income.

---

[1] The term "least squares" comes from the fact that the line has the property that it minimizes the sum of the squared distances of the points to the line—thus gives the "least" "squares." The word "ordinary" comes from the fact that this is the simplest method used in econometrics.

A Guide to Understanding Econometric Results

In your readings, you may run across results of estimation using econometrics. Here is a guide, which uses the slightly simplified, but otherwise untouched computer output for the equation (A3.1):

$\bar{R}^2$ is a measure of fit. The closer to 1, the better the fit of the regression line. A value of 0.59 indicates that much but not all of the movement in the dependent variable can be explained by movements in the independent variables.

The period of estimation includes all years from 1970 to 2011. There are therefore 42 **usable observations** used in the regression. **Degrees of freedom** is the number of observations minus the number of parameters to be estimated. There is one estimated parameter here: the coefficient on *DYD*. Thus, there are 42 − 1 = 41 degrees of freedom. A simple rule is that one needs at least as many observations as parameters to be estimated, and preferably much more; put another way, degrees of freedom must be positive, and the larger the better.

The variable we are trying to explain is called the **dependent variable**. Here the dependent variable is *DC*—the annual change in consumption minus its mean.

Dependent Variable DC—Estimation by Least Squares
Annual Data from 1970 to 2011
Usable Observations: 42
Degrees of Freedom: 41
$\bar{R}^2$: 0.59

Variable	Coefficient	*t*-Statistic
DYD	0.74	7.6

The variables that we use to explain the dependent variable are called the **independent variables**. Here there is only one independent variable, *DYD*—the annual change in disposable income minus its mean.

For each independent variable, the computer then gives the estimated coefficient, as well as a *t*-**statistic**. The *t*-statistic associated with each estimated coefficient tells us how confident we can be that the true coefficient is different from zero. A *t*-statistic above 2 indicates that we can be at least 95% sure that the true coefficient is different from zero. A *t*-statistic of 7.6, as on the coefficient associated with disposable income, is so high that we can be nearly completely sure (more than 99.99% sure) that the true coefficient is different from zero.

Correlation versus Causality

What we have established so far is that consumption and disposable income typically move together. More formally, we have seen that there is a positive **correlation**—the technical term for "co-relation"—between annual changes in consumption and annual changes in disposable income. And we have interpreted this relation as showing **causality**—that an increase in disposable income causes an increase in consumption.

We need to think again about this interpretation. A positive relation between consumption and disposable income may reflect the effect of disposable income on consumption. But it may also reflect the effect of consumption on disposable income. Indeed, the model we developed in Chapter 3 tells us that if, for any reason, consumers decide to spend more, then output, and therefore income and, in turn, disposable income will increase. If part of the relation between consumption and disposable income comes from the effect of consumption on disposable income, interpreting equation (A3.1) as telling us about the effect of disposable income on consumption is not right.

An example will help here: Suppose consumption does not depend on disposable income, so that the true value of c_1 is zero. (This is not very realistic, but it will make the point most clearly.) So draw the consumption function as a horizontal line (a line with a zero slope) in Figure A3-3. Next, suppose disposable income equals Y_D, so that the initial combination of consumption and disposable income is given by point A.

Now suppose that, because of improved confidence, consumers increase their consumption, so the consumption line shifts up. If demand affects output, then income and, in turn, disposable income, increase, so that the new combination of consumption and disposable income will be given by, say, point B. If, instead, consumers become more pessimistic, the consumption line shifts down, and so does output, leading to a combination of consumption and disposable income given by point D.

If we look at the economy described in the previous two paragraphs, we observe points A, B, and D. If, as we did above, we draw the best-fitting line through these points, we estimate an upward-sloping line, such as CC', and so estimate a positive value for propensity to consume, c_1. Remember, however, that the true value of c_1 is zero. Why do we get the wrong answer—a positive value for c_1 when the true value is zero? Because we interpret the positive relation between disposable income and consumption as showing the effect of disposable income on consumption, where, in fact, the relation reflects the effect of consumption on disposable income: Higher consumption leads to higher demand, higher output, and so higher disposable income.

There is an important lesson here: *the difference between correlation and causality*. The fact that two variables move together does not imply that movements in the first variable cause movements in the second variable. Perhaps the causality runs the other way: Movements in the second variable cause movements in the first variable. Or perhaps, as is likely to be the case here, the causality runs both ways: Disposable income affects consumption, *and* consumption affects disposable income.

Is there a way out of the correlation-versus-causality problem? If we are interested—and we are—in the effect of disposable income on consumption, can we still learn that from the data? The answer: yes, but only by using more information.

Suppose we *knew* that a specific change in disposable income was not caused by a change in consumption. Then, by looking at the reaction of consumption to *this*

Figure A3-3

A Misleading Regression

The relation between disposable income and consumption comes from the effect of consumption on income rather than from the effect of income on consumption.

change in disposable income, we could learn how consumption responds to disposable income; we could estimate the propensity to consume.

This answer would seem to simply assume away the problem: How can we tell that a change in disposable income is not due to a change in consumption? In fact, sometimes, we can tell. Suppose, for example, that the government embarks on a major increase in defense spending, leading to an increase in demand and, in turn, an increase in output. In that case, if we see both disposable income and consumption increase, we can safely assume that the movement in consumption reflects the effect of disposable income on consumption, and thus estimate the propensity to consume.

This example suggests a general strategy:

■ Find exogenous variables—that is, variables that affect disposable income but are not in turn affected by it.

■ Look at the change in consumption in response not to all changes in disposable income—as we did in our earlier regression—but in response to those changes in disposable income that can be explained by changes in these exogenous variables.

By following this strategy, we can be confident that what we are estimating is the effect of disposable income on consumption, and not the other way around.

The problem of finding such exogenous variables is known as the **identification problem** in econometrics. These exogenous variables, when they can be found, are called **instruments**. Methods of estimation that rely on the use of such instruments are called **instrumental variable methods**.

When equation (A3.1) is estimated using an instrumental variable method—using current and past changes in government defense spending as the instruments—rather than ordinary least squares as we did earlier, the estimated equation becomes

$$(\Delta C_t - \overline{\Delta C}) = 0.58(\Delta Y_{Dt} - \overline{\Delta Y_D})$$

Note that the coefficient on disposable income, 0.58, is smaller than 0.74 in equation (A3.1). This decrease in the estimated propensity to consume is exactly what we would expect: Our earlier estimate in equation (A3.1) reflected not only the effect of disposable income on consumption, but also the effect of consumption back on disposable income. The use of instruments eliminates this second effect, which is why we find a smaller estimated effect of disposable income on consumption.

This short introduction to econometrics is no substitute for a course in econometrics. But it gives you a sense of how economists use data to estimate relations and parameters and to identify causal relations between economic variables.

Key Terms

■ ordinary least squares (OLS), A-13
■ regression, regression line, A-13
■ residual, $\overline{R}^2$, A-13
■ dependent, independent variables, A-14
■ usable observations, degrees of freedom, A-14
■ t-statistic, A-14
■ correlation, causality, A-14
■ identification problem, A-16
■ instruments, instrumental variable methods, A-16

Glossary

AAA, BBB Different credit ratings, AAA being the higher quality rating, BBB being lower.

above the line, below the line In the balance of payments, the items in the *current account* are above the line drawn to divide them from the items in the *financial account*, which appear below the line.

accelerationist Phillips curve See *modified Phillips curve*.

adaptive expectations A backward-looking method of forming expectations by adjusting for past mistakes.

aggregate demand relation The demand for output at a given price level. It is derived from equilibrium in goods and financial markets.

aggregate output The total amount of output produced in the economy.

aggregate private spending The sum of all nongovernment spending. Also called *private spending*.

aggregate production function The relation between the quantity of aggregate output produced and the quantities of inputs used in production.

aggregate supply relation The price level at which firms are willing to supply a given level of output. It is derived from equilibrium in the labor market.

American International Group (AIG) Insurance company, which in the 2000s, issued large amounts of insurance contracts, called credit default swaps, against the risk of default of various securities.

American Recovery and Reinvestment Act (ARRA) The fiscal stimulus program introduced in February 2009 by the U.S. administration.

animal spirits A term introduced by Keynes to refer to movements in investment that could not be explained by movements in current variables.

appreciation (nominal) An increase in the value of domestic currency in terms of foreign currency. Corresponds to an increase in the exchange rate E, as defined in this text.

appropriability (of research results) The extent to which firms benefit from the results of their research and development efforts.

arbitrage The proposition that the expected rates of return on two financial assets must be equal. Also called *risky arbitrage* to distinguish it from *riskless arbitrage*, the proposition that the actual rates of return on two financial assets must be the same.

automatic stabilizer The fact that a decrease in output leads, under given tax and spending rules, to an increase in the budget deficit. This increase in the budget deficit in turn increases demand and thus stabilizes output.

autonomous spending The component of the demand for goods that does not depend on the level of output.

balance of payments A set of accounts that summarize a country's transactions with the rest of the world.

balanced budget A budget in which taxes are equal to government spending.

balanced growth The situation in which output, capital, and effective labor all grow at the same rate.

band (for exchange rates) The limits within which the exchange rate is allowed to move under a fixed exchange rate system.

bank reserves Holdings of central bank money by banks. The difference between what banks receive from depositors and what they lend to firms or hold as bonds.

bank run Simultaneous attempts by depositors to withdraw their funds from a bank.

bargaining power The relative strength of each side in a negotiation or a dispute.

base year When constructing real GDP by evaluating quantities in different years using a given set of prices, the year to which this given set of prices corresponds.

behavioral equation An equation that captures some aspect of behavior.

bilateral exchange rate The real exchange rate between two countries.

bond A financial asset that promises a stream of known payments over some period of time.

bond rating The assessment of a bond based on its default risk.

broad money See *M2*.

budget deficit The excess of government expenditures over government revenues.

business cycle theory The study of macroeconomic fluctuations.

business cycles See *output fluctuations*.

capital accumulation Increase in the capital stock.

capital controls Restrictions on the foreign assets domestic residents can hold, and on the domestic assets foreigners can hold.

capital ratio Ratio of the capital of a bank to its assets.

cash flow The net flow of cash a firm is receiving.

causality A relation between cause and effect.

central bank money Money issued by the central bank. Also known as the *monetary base* and *high-powered money*.

central parity The reference value of the exchange rate around which the exchange rate is allowed to move under a fixed exchange rate system. The center of the *band*.

change in business inventories In the national income and product accounts, the change in the volume of inventories held by businesses.

checkable deposits Deposits at banks and other financial institutions against which checks can be written.

churning The concept that new goods make old goods obsolete, that new production techniques make older techniques and worker skills obsolete, and so on.

collateral The asset pledged in order to get a loan. In case of default, the asset goes to the lender.

collateralized debt obligation (CDO) Security based on an underlying portfolio of assets.

collective bargaining Wage bargaining between unions and firms.

compensation of employees In the national income and product accounts, the sum of wages and salaries and of supplements to wages and salaries.

confidence band When estimating the dynamic effect of one variable on another, the range of values where we can be confident the true dynamic effect lies.

Congressional Budget Office (CBO) An office of Congress in charge of constructing and publishing budget projections.

constant returns to scale The proposition that a proportional increase (or decrease) of all inputs leads to the same proportional increase (or decrease) in output.

consumer confidence index An index computed monthly that estimates consumer confidence regarding current and future economic conditions.

consumer price index (CPI) The cost of a given list of goods and services consumed by a typical urban dweller.

consumption (C) Goods and services purchased by consumers.

consumption function A function that relates consumption to its determinants.

consumption of fixed capital Depreciation of capital.

contractionary open-market operation An open-market operation in which the central bank sells bonds to decrease the money supply.

convergence The tendency for countries with lower output per capita to grow faster, leading to convergence of output per capita across countries.

corporate bond A bond issued by a corporation.

corporate profits In the national income and product accounts, firms' revenues minus costs (including interest payments) and minus depreciation.

correlation A measure of the way two variables move together. A positive correlation indicates that the two variables tend to move in the same direction. A negative correlation indicates that the two variables tend to move in opposite directions. A correlation of zero indicates that there is no apparent relation between the two variables.

cost of living The average price of a consumption bundle.

coupon bond A bond that promises multiple payments before maturity and one payment at maturity.

coupon payments The payments before maturity on a coupon bond.

coupon rate The ratio of the coupon payment to the face value of a coupon bond.

crawling peg An exchange rate mechanism in which the exchange rate is allowed to move over time according to a pre-specified formula.

creative destruction The proposition that growth simultaneously creates and destroys jobs.

credibility The degree to which people and markets believe that a policy announcement will actually be implemented and followed through.

credit channel The channel through which monetary policy works by affecting the amount of loans made by banks to firms.

credit default swap (CDS) A contract in which insures the buyer against the risk of default on a particular financial instrument.

currency Coins and bills.

currency board An exchange rate system in which: (i) the central bank stands ready to buy or sell foreign currency at the official exchange rate; (ii) the central bank cannot engage in open-market operations, that is buy or sell government bonds.

current account In the balance of payments, the summary of a country's payments to and from the rest of the world.

Current Population Survey (CPS) A large monthly survey of U.S. households used, in particular, to compute the unemployment rate.

current yield The ratio of the coupon payment to the price of a coupon bond.

cyclically adjusted deficit A measure of what the government deficit would be under existing tax and spending rules, if output were at its natural level. Also called a *full-employment deficit, midcycle deficit,* *standardized employment deficit,* or *structural deficit.*

debt finance Financing based on loans or the issuance of bonds.

debt monetization The printing of money to finance a deficit.

debt ratio See *debt-to-GDP ratio.*

debt-to-GDP ratio The ratio of debt to gross domestic product. Also called simply the *debt ratio.*

decreasing returns to capital The property that increases in capital lead to smaller and smaller increases in output as the level of capital increases.

decreasing returns to labor The property that increases in labor leads to smaller and smaller increases in output as the level of labor increases.

default risk The risk that the issuer of a bond will not pay back the full amount promised by the bond.

deflation Negative inflation.

degrees of freedom The number of usable observations in a *regression* minus the number of parameters to be estimated.

demand or checkable deposit A bank account that allows depositors to write checks or get cash on demand, up to an amount equal to the account balance.

demand for domestic goods The demand for domestic goods by people, firms, and governments, both domestic and foreign. Equal to the domestic demand for goods plus net exports.

dependent variable A variable whose value is determined by one or more other variables.

depreciation (nominal) A decrease in the value of domestic currency in terms of a foreign currency. Corresponds to a decrease in the exchange rate E, as defined in this text.

depreciation rate A measure of how much usefulness a piece of capital loses from one period to the next.

depression A deep and long-lasting recession.

devaluation A decrease in the exchange rate (E) in a fixed exchange rate system.

discount bond A bond that promises a single payment at maturity.

discount factor The value today of a dollar (or other national currency unit) at some time in the future.

discount rate (i) The interest rate used to discount a sequence of future payments. Equal to the nominal interest rate when discounting future nominal payments and to the real interest rate when discounting future real payments. (ii) The interest rate at which the Fed lends to banks.

discouraged worker A person who has given up looking for employment.

disinflation A decrease in inflation.

disposable income The income that remains once consumers have received transfers from the government and paid their taxes.

dividends The portion of a corporation's profits that the firm pays out each period to its shareholders.

dollar GDP See *nominal GDP*.

dollarization The use of dollars in domestic transactions in a country other than the United States.

domestic demand for goods The sum of consumption, investment, and government spending.

durable goods Commodities that can be stored and have an average life of at least three years.

duration of unemployment The period of time during which a worker is unemployed.

dynamic stochastic general equilibrium models (DSGE) Macro models derived from optimization by firms, consumers, and workers.

dynamics Movements of one or more economic variables over time.

econometrics Statistical methods applied to economics.

effective demand Synonym for *aggregate demand*.

effective labor The number of workers in an economy times the state of technology.

effective real exchange rate See *multilateral exchange rate*.

efficiency wage The wage at which a worker is performing a job most efficiently or productively.

endogenous variable A variable that depends on other variables in a model and is thus explained within the model.

entitlement programs Programs that require the payment of benefits to all who meet the eligibility requirements established by law.

equilibrium The equality between demand and supply.

equilibrium condition The condition that supply be equal to demand.

equilibrium equation An equation that represents an equilibrium condition.

equilibrium in the goods market The condition that the supply of goods be equal to the demand for goods.

equity finance Financing based on the issuance of shares.

equity premium Risk premium required by investors to hold stocks rather than short-term bonds.

euro A European currency that replaced national currencies in 11 countries in 2002 and is now used in 15 countries.

European Central Bank (ECB) The central bank, located in Frankfurt, in charge of determining monetary policy in the euro area.

European Monetary System (EMS) A series of rules that implemented bands for bilateral exchange rates between member countries in Europe that operated from 1979 to roughly 1982.

European Union A political and economic organization of 25 European nations. Formerly called the European Community.

exogenous variable A variable that is not explained within a model, but rather, is taken as given.

expansion A period of positive GDP growth.

expansionary open-market operation An open-market operation in which the central bank buys bonds to increase the money supply.

expectations hypothesis The hypothesis that financial investors are risk neutral, which implies that expected returns on all financial assets have to be equal.

expectations-augmented Phillips curve See *modified Phillips curve*.

experiment A set of test conditions in which one variable is altered while the others are kept constant.

expected present discounted value The value today of an expected sequence of future payments. Also called *present discounted value* or *present value*.

exports (*X*) The purchases of domestic goods and services by foreigners.

face value (on a bond) The single payment at maturity promised by a discount bond.

fad A period of time during which, for reasons of fashion or over-optimism, financial investors are willing to pay more for a stock than its fundamental value.

Fed accommodation A change in the money supply by the Fed to maintain a constant interest rate in the face of changes in money demand or in spending.

federal deposit insurance Insurance provided by the U.S. government that protects each bank depositor up to $100,000 per account.

federal funds market The market where banks that have excess reserves at the end of the day lend them to banks that have insufficient reserves.

federal funds rate The interest rate determined by equilibrium in the federal funds market. The interest rate affected most directly by changes in monetary policy.

Federal Reserve Bank (Fed) The U.S. central bank.

fertility of research The degree to which spending on research and development translates into new ideas and new products.

financial intermediary A financial institution that receives funds from people, firms, or other financial institutions, and uses these funds to make loans or buy financial assets.

financial investment The purchase of financial assets.

financial markets The markets in which financial assets are bought and sold.

financial wealth The value of all of one's financial assets minus all financial liabilities. Sometimes called *wealth*, for short.

fine-tuning A macroeconomic policy aimed at precisely hitting a given target, such as constant unemployment or constant output growth.

fire sale prices Very low asset prices, reflecting the need for sellers to sell, and the absence of sufficient buyers, because of liquidity constraints.

fiscal consolidation See *fiscal contraction*.

fiscal contraction A policy aimed at reducing the budget deficit through a decrease in government spending or an increase in taxation. Also called *fiscal consolidation*.

fiscal expansion An increase in government spending or a decrease in taxation, which leads to an increase in the budget deficit.

fiscal policy A government's choice of taxes and spending.

fiscal year An accounting period of 12 months. In the United States, the period from October 1 of the previous calendar year through September 30 of the current calendar year.

Fisher effect or Fisher hypothesis The proposition that, in the long run, an increase in nominal money growth is reflected in an identical increase in both the nominal interest rate and the inflation rate, leaving the real interest rate unchanged.

Fisher hypothesis See *Fisher effect*.

fixed exchange rate An exchange rate between the currencies of two or more countries that is fixed at some level and adjusted only infrequently.

fixed investment See *investment* (*I*).

flexible exchange rate An exchange rate determined in the foreign exchange market without central bank intervention.

float The exchange rate is said to float when it is determined in the foreign exchange market, without central bank intervention.

flow A variable that can be expressed as a quantity per unit of time (such as income).

foreign direct investment The purchase of existing firms or the development of new firms by foreign investors.

foreign exchange Foreign currency; all currencies other than the domestic currency of a given country.

foreign exchange reserves Foreign assets held by the central bank.

four tigers The four Asian economies of Singapore, Taiwan, Hong Kong, and South Korea.

full-employment deficit See *cyclically adjusted deficit*.

fully funded social security system A retirement system in which the contributions of current workers are invested in financial assets, with the proceeds (principal and interest) given back to the workers when they retire.

fundamental value (of a stock) The present value of expected dividends.

G20 The group of 20 countries, representing about 85% of world production, which has met regularly during the crisis, and has served as a forum for coordination of economic policies.

game *Strategic interactions* between *players*.

game theory The prediction of outcomes from *games*.

GDP adjusted for inflation See *real GDP*.

GDP deflator The ratio of nominal GDP to real GDP; a measure of the overall price level. Gives the average price of the final goods produced in the economy.

GDP growth The growth rate of real GDP in year *t*; equal to $(Y_t - Y_{t-1})/Y_{t-1}$.

GDP in chained (2000) dollars See *real GDP*.

GDP in constant dollars See *real GDP*.

GDP in current dollars See *nominal GDP*.

GDP in terms of goods See *real GDP*.

GNP See *Gross National Product*

geometric series A mathematical sequence in which the ratio of one term to the preceding term remains the same. A sequence of the form $1 + c + c^2 + \cdots + c^n$.

gold standard A system in which a country fixed the price of its currency in terms of gold and stood ready to exchange gold for currency at the stated parity.

golden-rule level of capital The level of capital at which steady-state consumption is maximized.

government bond A bond issued by a government or a government agency.

government budget constraint The budget constraint faced by the government. The constraint implies that an excess of spending over revenues must be financed by borrowing, and thus leads to an increase in debt.

government purchases In the national income and product accounts, the sum of the purchases of goods by the government plus compensation of government employees.

government spending (G) The goods and services purchased by federal, state, and local governments.

government transfers Payments made by the government to individuals that are not in exchange for goods or services. Example: Social Security payments.

Great Depression The severe worldwide depression of the 1930s.

gross domestic product (GDP) A measure of aggregate output in the national income accounts. (The market value of the goods and services produced by labor and property located in the United States.)

gross national product (GNP) A measure of aggregate output in the national income accounts. (The market value of the goods and services produced by labor and property supplied by U.S. residents.)

gross private domestic fixed investment In the national income and product accounts, the sum of nonresidential investment and residential investment.

growth The steady increase in aggregate output over time.

hedonic pricing An approach to calculating real GDP that treats goods as providing a collection of characteristics, each with an implicit price.

high-powered money See *central bank money*.

hires Workers newly employed by firms.

housing wealth The value of the housing stock.

human capital The set of skills possessed by the workers in an economy.

human wealth The labor-income component of wealth.

hyperinflation Very high inflation.

hysteresis In general, the proposition that the equilibrium value of a variable depends on its history. With respect to unemployment, the proposition that a long period of sustained actual unemployment leads to an increase in the equilibrium rate of unemployment.

identification problem In econometrics, the problem of finding whether correlation between variables *X* and *Y* indicates a causal relation from *X* to *Y*, or from *Y* to *X*, or both. This problem is solved by finding exogenous variables, called *instruments*, that affect *X* and do not affect *Y* directly, or affect *Y* and do not affect *X* directly.

identity An equation that holds by definition, denoted by the sign $\equiv$.

imports (Q) The purchases of foreign goods and services by domestic consumers, firms, and the government.

income The flow of revenue from work, rental income, interest, and dividends.

independent variable A variable that is taken as given in a relation or in a model.

index number A number, such as the GDP deflator, that has no natural level and is thus set to equal some value (typically 1 or 100) in a given period.

indexed bond A bond that promises payments adjusted for inflation.

indirect taxes Taxes on goods and services. In the United States, primarily sales taxes.

inflation A sustained rise in the general level of prices.

inflation rate The rate at which the price level increases over time.

inflation targeting The conduct of monetary policy to achieve a given inflation rate over time.

inflation-adjusted deficit The correct economic measure of the budget deficit: The sum of the *primary deficit* and real interest payments.

instrumental variable methods In econometrics, methods of estimation that use *instruments* to estimate causal relations between different variables.

instruments In econometrics, the exogenous variables that allow the identification problem to be solved.

intercept In a linear relation between two variables, the value of the first variable when the second variable is equal to zero.

interest parity condition See *uncovered interest parity*.

intermediate good A good used in the production of a final good.

International Monetary Fund (IMF) The principal international economic organization. Publishes the *World Economic Outlook* annually and the *International Financial Statistics (IFS)* monthly.

inventory investment The difference between production and sales.

investment (I) Purchases of new houses and apartments by people, and purchases of new capital goods (machines and plants) by firms.

IS curve A downward-sloping curve relating output to the interest rate. The curve corresponding to the *IS relation*, the equilibrium condition for the goods market.

IS relation An equilibrium condition stating that the demand for goods must be equal to the supply of goods, or equivalently that investment must be equal to saving. The equilibrium condition for the goods market.

J-curve A curve depicting the initial deterioration in the trade balance caused by a real depreciation, followed by an improvement in the trade balance.

junk bond A bond with a high risk of default.

labor force The sum of those employed and those unemployed.

labor in efficiency units See *effective labor*.

labor market rigidities Restrictions on firms' ability to adjust their level of employment.

labor productivity The ratio of output to the number of workers.

layoffs Workers who lose their jobs either temporarily or permanently.

leverage ratio Ratio of the assets of the bank to its capital (the inverse of the capital ratio).

libor rate Rate at which banks lend to each other.

life cycle theory of consumption The theory of consumption, developed initially by Franco Modigliani, which emphasizes that the planning horizon of consumers is their lifetime.

linear relation A relation between two variables such that a one-unit increase in one variable always leads to an increase of *n* units in the other variable.

liquid asset An asset that can be sold easily and at little cost.

liquidity preference The term introduced by Keynes to denote the demand for money.

liquidity trap The case where nominal interest rates are equal to zero, and monetary policy cannot, therefore, decrease them further.

LM curve An upward-sloping curve relating the interest rate to output. The curve corresponding to the *LM relation*, the equilibrium condition for financial markets.

LM relation An equilibrium condition stating that the demand for money must be equal to the supply of money. The equilibrium condition for financial markets.

logarithmic scale A scale in which the same proportional increase is represented by the same distance on the scale, so that a variable that grows at a constant rate is represented by a straight line.

long run A period of time extending over decades.

Lucas critique The proposition, put forth by Robert Lucas, that existing relations between economic variables may change when policy changes. An example is the apparent trade-off between inflation and unemployment, which may disappear if policymakers try to exploit it.

M1 The sum of currency, traveler's checks, and checkable deposits—assets that can be used directly in transactions. Also called *narrow money*.

M2 $M1$ plus money market mutual fund shares, money market and savings deposits, and time deposits. Also called *broad money*.

M3 A *monetary aggregate* constructed by the Fed that is broader than $M2$.

Maastricht treaty A treaty signed in 1991 that defined the steps involved in the transition to a common currency for the European Union.

macroeconomics The study of aggregate economic variables, such as production for the economy as a whole, or the average price of goods.

marginal propensity to consume (mpc or c_1) The effect on consumption of an additional dollar of disposable income.

marginal propensity to import The effect on imports from an additional dollar in income.

marginal propensity to save The effect on saving of an additional dollar of disposable income. (Equal to one minus the marginal propensity to consume.)

Marshall–Lerner condition The condition under which a real depreciation leads to an increase in net exports.

maturity The length of time over which a financial asset (typically a bond) promises to make payments to the holder.

medium run A period of time between the *short run* and the *long run*.

menu cost The cost of changing a price.

microeconomics The study of production and prices in specific markets.

midcycle deficit See *cyclically adjusted deficit*.

model A conceptual structure used to think about and interpret an economic phenomenon.

models of endogenous growth Models in which accumulation of physical and human capital can sustain growth even in the absence of technological progress.

modified Phillips curve The curve that plots the change in the inflation rate against the unemployment rate. Also called an *expectations-augmented Phillips curve* or an *accelerationist Phillips curve*.

monetarism, monetarists A group of economists in the 1960s, led by Milton Friedman, who argued that monetary policy had powerful effects on activity.

monetary aggregate The market value of a sum of liquid assets. *M*1 is a monetary aggregate that includes only the most liquid assets.

monetary base See *central bank money*.

monetary contraction A change in monetary policy, which leads to an increase in the interest rate. Also called *monetary tightening*.

monetary expansion A change in monetary policy, which leads to a decrease in the interest rate.

monetary policy The use of the money stock by the central bank to affect interest rates, and by implication, economic activity and inflation.

monetary-fiscal policy mix The combination of monetary and fiscal policies in effect at a given time.

monetary tightening See *monetary contraction*.

money Those financial assets that can be used directly to buy goods.

money illusion The proposition that people make systematic mistakes in assessing nominal versus real changes.

money market funds Financial institutions that receive funds from people and use them to buy short-term bonds.

money multiplier The increase in the money supply resulting from a one-dollar increase in central bank money.

mortgage based security (MBS) A security based on an underlying portfolio of mortgages.

mortgage lenders The institutions that make housing loans to households.

multilateral exchange rate (multilateral real exchange rate) The real exchange rate between a country and its trading partners, computed as a weighted average of bilateral real exchange rates. Also called the *trade-weighted real exchange rate* or *effective real exchange rate*.

multiplier The ratio of the change in an *endogenous variable* to the change in an *exogenous variable* (for example, the ratio of the change in output to a change in autonomous spending).

Mundell–Fleming model A model of simultaneous equilibrium in both goods and financial markets for an open economy.

narrow banking Restrictions on banks that would require them to hold only short-term government bonds.

narrow money See *M1*.

national accounts See *national income and product accounts*.

national income In the United States, the income that originates in the production of goods and services supplied by residents of the United States.

national income and product accounts (NIPA) The system of accounts used to describe the evolution of the sum, the composition, and the distribution of aggregate output.

natural level of employment The level of employment that prevails when unemployment is equal to its natural rate.

natural level of output The level of production that prevails when employment is equal to its natural level.

natural rate of unemployment The unemployment rate at which price and wage decisions are consistent.

neoclassical synthesis A consensus in macroeconomics, developed in the early 1950s, based on an integration of Keynes' ideas and the ideas of earlier economists.

net capital flows Capital flows from the rest of the world to the domestic economy, minus capital flows to the rest of the world from the domestic economy.

net exports The difference between exports and imports. Also called the *trade balance*.

net income payments (NI) the excess of foreign income earned by domestic residents over domestic income earned by foreigners

net interest In the national income and product accounts, the interest paid by firms minus the interest received by firms, plus interest received from the rest of the world minus interest paid to the rest of the world.

net national product (NNP) Gross national product minus capital depreciation.

net transfers received In the current account, the net value of foreign aid received minus foreign aid given.

neutrality of money The proposition that an increase in nominal money has no effect on output or the interest rate, but is reflected entirely in a proportional increase in the price level.

new classicals A group of economists who interpret fluctuations as the effects of shocks in competitive markets with fully flexible prices and wages.

new growth theory Recent developments in growth theory that explore the determinants of technological progress and the role of increasing returns to scale in growth.

New-Keynesian model Model based on utility maximization, profit maximization, and nominal rigidities.

New Keynesians A group of economists who believe in the importance of nominal rigidities in fluctuations, and who are exploring the role of market imperfections in explaining fluctuations.

nominal exchange rate The price of domestic currency in terms of foreign currency. The number of units of foreign currency you can get for one unit of domestic currency.

nominal GDP The sum of the quantities of final goods produced in an economy times their current price. Also known as *dollar GDP* and *GDP in current dollars*.

nominal interest rate The interest rate in terms of the national currency (in terms of dollars in the United States). It tells us how many dollars one has to repay in the future in exchange for borrowing one dollar today.

nominal rigidities The slow adjustment of nominal wages and prices to changes in economic activity.

nonaccelerating inflation rate of unemployment (NAIRU) The unemployment rate at which inflation neither decreases nor increases. See *natural rate of unemployment*.

nondurable goods Commodities that can be stored but have an average life of less than three years.

nonhuman wealth The financial and housing component of wealth.

noninstitutional civilian population The number of people potentially available for civilian employment.

nonresidential investment The purchase of new capital goods by firms: *structures* and *producer durable equipment*.

North American Free Trade Agreement (NAFTA) An agreement signed by the United States, Canada, and Mexico in which the three countries agreed to establish all of North America as a free-trade zone.

not in the labor force The number of people who are neither employed nor looking for employment.

***n*-year interest rate** See *yield to maturity*.

Okun's law The relation between GDP growth and the change in the unemployment rate.

open-market operation The purchase or sale of government bonds by the central bank for the purpose of increasing or decreasing the money supply.

openness in factor markets The opportunity for firms to choose where to locate production, and for workers to choose where to work and whether or not to migrate.

openness in financial markets The opportunity for financial investors to choose between domestic and foreign financial assets.

openness in goods markets The opportunity for consumers and firms to choose between domestic and foreign goods.

optimal control The control of a system (a machine, a rocket, an economy) by means of mathematical methods.

optimal control theory The set of mathematical methods used for *optimal control*.

ordinary least squares A statistical method to find the best-fitting relation between two or more variables.

Organisation for Economic Co-operation and Development (OECD) An international organization that collects and studies economic data for many countries. Most of the world's rich countries belong to the OECD.

output fluctuations Movements in output around its trend. Also called *business cycles*.

output per person A country's gross domestic product divided by its population.

overshooting The large movement in the exchange rate triggered by a monetary expansion or contraction.

panel data set A data set that gives the values of one or more variables for many individuals or many firms over some period of time.

paradox of saving The result that an attempt by people to save more may lead both to a decline in output and to unchanged saving.

parameter A coefficient in a behavioral equation.

participation rate The ratio of the labor force to the noninstitutional civilian population.

patent The legal right granted to a person or firm to exclude anyone else from the production or use of a new product or technique for a certain period of time.

pay-as-you-go Social Security system A retirement system in which the contributions of current workers are used to pay benefits to current retirees.

payments of factor income to the rest of the world In the United States, income received by foreign capital and foreign residents.

peg The exchange rate to which a country commits under a fixed exchange rate system.

permanent income theory of consumption The theory of consumption, developed by Milton Friedman, that emphasizes that people make consumption decisions based not on current income, but on their notion of permanent income.

personal consumption expenditures In the national income and product accounts, the sum of goods and services purchased by persons resident in the United States.

personal disposable income *Personal income* minus personal tax and non-tax payments. The income available to consumers after they have received transfers and paid taxes.

personal income The income actually received by persons.

Phillips curve The curve that plots the relation between movements in inflation and unemployment. The original Phillips curve captured the relation between the

inflation rate and the unemployment rate. The *modified Phillips curve* captures the relation between (i) the change in the inflation rate and (ii) the unemployment rate.

players The participants in a *game*. Depending on the context, players may be people, firms, governments, and so on.

policy coordination (of macroeconomic policies between two countries) The joint design of macroeconomic policies to improve the economic situation in the two countries.

policy mix See *monetary-fiscal policy mix*.

political business cycle Fluctuations in economic activity caused by the manipulation of the economy for electoral gain.

present value See *expected present discounted value*.

price level The general level of prices in an economy.

price-setting relation The relation between the price chosen by firms, the nominal wage, and the markup.

primary deficit Government spending, excluding interest payments on the debt, minus government revenues. (The negative of the *primary surplus*.)

primary surplus Government revenues minus government spending, excluding interest payments on the debt.

private saving (S) Saving by the private sector. The value of consumers' disposable income minus their consumption.

producer price index (PPI) A price index of domestically produced goods in manufacturing, mining, agricultural, fishing, forestry, and electric utility industries.

production function The relation between the quantity of output and the quantities of inputs used in production.

profitability The expected present discounted value of profits.

propagation mechanism The dynamic effects of a *shock* on output and its components.

proprietors' income In the national income and product accounts, the income of sole proprietorships, partnerships, and tax-exempt cooperatives.

propensity to consume (c_1) The effect of an additional dollar of disposable income on consumption.

propensity to save The effect of an additional dollar of disposable income on saving (equal to one minus the propensity to consume).

public saving Saving by the government; equal to government revenues minus government spending. Also called the *budget surplus*. (A *budget deficit* represents public dissaving.)

purchasing power Income in terms of goods.

purchasing power parity (PPP) A method of adjustment used to allow for international comparisons of GDP.

quits Workers who leave their jobs for better alternatives.

quotas Restrictions on the quantities of goods that can be imported.

$\bar{R}^2$ A measure of fit, between zero and one, from a *regression*. An R^2 of zero implies that there is no apparent relation between the variables under consideration. An R^2 of 1 implies a perfect fit: all the *residuals* are equal to zero.

random walk The path of a variable whose changes over time are unpredictable.

random walk of consumption The proposition that, if consumers are foresighted, changes in their consumption should be unpredictable.

rate of growth of multifactor productivity See *Solow residual*.

rational expectations The formation of expectations based on rational forecasts, rather than on simple extrapolations of the past.

rational speculative bubble An increase in stock prices based on the rational expectation of further increases in prices in the future.

real appreciation An increase in the relative price of domestic goods in terms of foreign goods. An increase in the real exchange rate.

real business cycle (RBC) models Economic models that assume that output is always at its natural level. Thus, all output fluctuations are movements of the natural level of output, as opposed to movements away form the natural level of output.

real depreciation A decrease in the relative price of domestic goods in terms of foreign goods. An increase in the real exchange rate.

real exchange rate The relative price of domestic goods in terms of foreign goods.

real GDP A measure of aggregate output. The sum of quantities produced in an economy times their price in a base year. Also known as *GDP in terms of goods*, *GDP in constant dollars*, or *GDP adjusted for inflation*. The current measure of real GDP in the United States is called *GDP in (chained) 2000 dollars*.

real GDP in chained (2000) dollars See *real GDP*.

real interest rate The interest rate in terms of goods. It tells us how many goods one has to repay in the future in exchange for borrowing the equivalent one good today.

receipts of factor income from the rest of the world In the United States, income received from abroad by U.S. capital or U.S. residents.

recession A period of negative GDP growth. Usually refers to at least two consecutive quarters of negative GDP growth.

regression The output of *ordinary least squares*. Gives the equation corresponding to the estimated relation between variables, together with information about the degree of fit and the relative importance of the different variables.

regression line The best-fitting line corresponding to the equation obtained by using *ordinary least squares*.

rental cost of capital See *user cost*.

rental income of persons In the national income and product accounts, the income from the rental of real property, minus depreciation on this property.

research and development (R&D) Spending aimed at discovering and developing new ideas and products.

reservation wage The wage that would make a worker indifferent between working and being unemployed.

reserve ratio The ratio of bank reserves to checkable deposits.

residential investment The purchase of new homes and apartments by people.

residual The difference between the actual value of a variable and the value implied by the *regression line*. Small residuals indicate a good fit.

revaluation An increase in the exchange rate (E) in a fixed exchange rate system.

Ricardian equivalence The proposition that neither government deficits nor government debt have an effect on economic activity. Also called the *Ricardo-Barro proposition*.

Ricardo-Barro proposition See *Ricardian equivalence*.

risk averse A person is risk averse if he/she prefers to receive a given amount for sure to an uncertain amount with the same expected value.

risk neutral A person is risk neutral if he/she is indifferent between receiving a given amount for sure or an uncertain amount with the same expected value.

risk premium The difference between the interest rate paid on a given bond and the interest rate paid on a bond with the highest rating.

riskless arbitrage See *arbitrage*.

risky arbitrage See *arbitrage*.

saving The sum of private and public saving, denoted by S.

saving rate The proportion of income that is saved.

savings The accumulated value of past saving. Also called *wealth*.

scatter diagram A graphic presentation that plots the value of one variable against the value of another variable.

secondary labor market A labor market where jobs are poor, wages are low, and turnover is high. Contrast to the *primary labor market*.

securitization The issuance of securities, based on an underlying portfolio of assets, such as mortgages, or commercial paper.

seignorage The revenues from the creation of money.

separations Workers who are leaving or losing their jobs.

services Commodities that cannot be stored and thus must be consumed at the place and time of purchase.

shadow banking system The set of non-bank financial institutions, from SIVs to hedge funds.

share A financial asset issued by a firm that promises to pay a sequence of payments, called dividends, in the future. Also called *stock*.

shocks Movements in the factors that affect aggregate demand and/or aggregate supply.

shoe-leather costs The costs of going to the bank to take money out of a checking account.

short run A period of time extending over a few years at most.

simulation The use of a model to look at the effects of a change in an exogenous variable on the variables in the model.

skill-biased technological progress The proposition that new machines and new methods of production require skilled workers to a greater degree than in the past.

Social Security Trust Fund The funds accumulated by the U.S. Social Security system as a result of surpluses in the past.

slope In a linear relation between two variables, the amount by which the first variable increases when the second increases by one unit.

Solow residual The excess of actual output growth over what can be accounted for by the growth in capital and labor.

stabilization program A government program aimed at stabilizing the economy. Often used in the context of stopping a high inflation or even a hyperinflation. Sometimes used to describe a plan to reduce a large deficit. Often the two may be combined.

stagflation The combination of stagnation and inflation.

staggering of wage decisions The fact that different wages are adjusted at different times, making it impossible to achieve a synchronized decrease in nominal wage inflation.

standardized employment deficit See *cyclically adjusted deficit*.

state of technology The degree of technological development in a country or industry.

statistical discrepancy A difference between two numbers that should be equal, coming from differences in sources or methods of construction for the two numbers.

steady state In an economy without technological progress, the state of the economy where output and capital per worker are no longer changing. In an economy with technological progress, the state of the economy where output and capital per effective worker are no longer changing.

stock A variable that can be expressed as a quantity at a point in time (such as wealth). Also a synonym for *share*.

stocks An alternative term for inventories. Also, an alternative term for shares.

strategic interactions An environment in which the actions of one player depend on and affect the actions of another player.

structural deficit See *cyclically adjusted deficit*.

structural rate of unemployment See *natural rate of unemployment*.

structured investment vehicle (SIV) Financial intermediaries set up by banks. SIVs borrow from investors, typically in the form of short term debt, and invest in securities.

structures In the national income and product accounts: plants, factories, office buildings, and hotels.

subprime mortgages Mortgages with a higher risk of default by the borrower.

supply-siders A group of economists in the 1980s who believed that tax cuts would increase activity by enough to increase tax revenues.

tariffs Taxes on imported goods.

tax smoothing The principle of keeping tax rates roughly constant, so that the government runs large deficits when government spending is exceptionally high and small surpluses the rest of the time.

Taylor rule A rule, suggested by John Taylor, telling a central bank how to adjust the nominal interest rate in response to deviations of inflation from its target, and of the unemployment rate from the natural rate.

technological progress An improvement in the state of technology.

technological unemployment Unemployment brought about by technological progress.

term structure of interest rates See *yield curve*.

time inconsistency In game theory, the incentive for one player to deviate from his previously announced course of action once the other player has moved.

Tobin's *q* The ratio of the value of the capital stock, computed by adding the stock market value of firms and the debt of firms, to the replacement cost of capital.

total wealth The sum of human wealth and nonhuman wealth.

toxic assets Nonperforming assets, from subprime mortgages to non performing loans.

tradable goods Goods that compete with foreign goods in domestic or foreign markets.

trade balance The difference between exports and imports. Also called *net exports*.

trade deficit A negative trade balance, that is, imports exceed exports.

trade surplus A positive trade balance, that is, exports exceed imports.

transfers See *government transfers*.

Treasury bill (T-bill) A U.S. government bond with a maturity of up to one year.

Treasury bond A U.S. government bond with a maturity of 10 years or more.

Treasury note A U.S. government bond with a maturity of one to 10 years.

Troubled Asset Relief Program (TARP) The program introduced in October 2008 by the U.S. administration, aimed at buying toxic assets, and, later, providing capital to banks and other financial institutions in trouble.

t-statistic A statistic associated with an estimated coefficient in a regression that indicates how confident one can be that the true coefficient differs from zero.

twin deficits The budget and trade deficits that characterized the United States in the 1980s.

uncovered interest parity An arbitrage relation stating that domestic and foreign bonds must have the same expected rate of return, expressed in terms of a common currency.

underground economy That part of a nation's economic activity that is not measured in official statistics, either because the activity is illegal or because people and firms are seeking to avoid paying taxes.

unemployment rate The ratio of the number of unemployed to the labor force.

usable observation An observation for which the values of all the variables under consideration are available for *regression* purposes.

user cost of capital The cost of using capital over a year, or a given period of time. The sum of the real interest rate and the depreciation rate. Also called the *rental cost of capital*.

value added The value a firm adds in the production process, equal to the value of its production minus the value of the intermediate inputs it uses in production.

wage indexation   A rule that automatically increases wages in response to an increase in prices.

wage-price spiral   The mechanism by which increases in wages lead to increases in prices, which lead in turn to further increases in wages, and so on.

wage-setting relation   The relation between the wage chosen by wage setters, the price level, and the unemployment rate.

war of attrition   When both parties to an argument hold their grounds, hoping that the other party will give in.

wealth   See *financial wealth*.

wholesale funding   Financing through the issuance of short term debt than through deposits.

yield curve   The relation between yield and maturity for bonds of different maturities. Also called the *term structure of interest rates*.

yield to maturity   The constant interest rate that makes the price of an *n*-year bond today equal to the present value of future payments. Also called the *n-year interest rate*.

Index

G

G20, 409
Gali, Jordi, 550
Game theory, 478, 545
Garber, Peter, 331
GDP. *See* gross domestic product
GDP deflator, 29
GDP growth, 24
The General Theory of Employment, Interest, and Money (Keynes), 56, 85, 540
Geometric series, 53, 308, A7
Germany
    EMS currency crisis, 454–455
    hyperinflation, 511, 512 (table)
    spread, 508–509
    unemployment rate (figure), 174
    unification, 438
Gertler, Mark, 548
Getty, J. Paul, 65
Global Financial Stability Report (GFSR), 18
GNP. *See* gross national product
Goffe, Bill, 18
Golden-rule level of capital, 235, 237–238, 241–242
Gold standard, Britain's return to, 452
Goods
    demand for, 45–49
    domestic and foreign, 382
    domestic demand for, 400
    final, 21
    intermediate, 20–21
    tradable, 381
Goods market
    domestic vs. foreign goods, 382
    equilibrium in, 49–57, 57–58, 403–404, 424–425
    exports and imports, 380–382
    IS relation and, 86–90, 400–403
    openness in, 379, 380–388
    together with financial markets, 430–431
Government, role in choosing output, 59
Government bonds, 315
Government budget constraints, 495–501
Government purchases, A3–A4
Government spending, 44, 48–49
    choosing output level and, 58–59
    decrease in, 370–371
    determinants of, 400–401
    effects of increase, 432
    in national income accounts, A4–A5
    plus taxes: fiscal policy described by, 48–49
    ratios to GDP, 100 (figure)
Government transfers, 44–45
Graph, equilibrium, 51–53. *See also* Equilibrium
Great Britain, return to gold standard, 452
Great Depression, 8
    adverse effects of deflation, 296
    fears of, 55–56
    Keynes and, 540
    monetarists' view, 542
    natural employment rate and, 178
Great Moderation, 517
Greece
    debt-to-GDP ratio, 493
    hyperinflation, 512 (table)
    unemployment rate (figure), 174
Greenspan, Alan, 99, 102, 518
Griliches, Zvi, 258

Gross domestic product (GDP), A1
    composition of, 44–45
    debt-to-GDP ratio, 500–501
    deflator, 29
    exports exceeding, 382
    to GNP, A2
    GNP vs.: Kuwait, 392
    hedonic pricing and, 25
    level versus growth rate, 24–25
    national income and product accounts (NIPA), A1–A6
    nominal and real, 22–24
    production and income, 20–22
    in United States, 23, 23 (figure), 24 (figure), 208 (figure), A11 (figure)
    vs. GNP: Kuwait, 392
Gross national product (GNP), 20, A1–A2
Gross private domestic fixed investment, A3
Growth, 207, 217–221
    across millenia, 215
    aggregate production function, 217–218
    among rich countries, 211–215, 260–262
    balanced, 254–255
    capital accumulation vs. technological progress, 260–262
    endogenous, models, 244
    happiness and, 212–213
    importance of institutions, 281–283
    money, 298–304, 525–526
    M1 and M2, 527–528
    OECD countries, 215–217
    output per worker and capital per worker, 219–220
    post–WWII France, 232
    returns to scale and returns to factors, 218–219
    in rich countries since 1950, 211, 215–216
    sources of, 220–221
    theory, 541
Growth rate, technological progress and, 249–262

H

Haircut, 509–510
Hall, Robert, 545–546
Hansen, Alvin, 85, 541
Hard peg, 462
Harsanyi, John, 478
Hedonic pricing, 25
Hicks, John, 85, 541
High-powered money, 80
Hires, 113
Historical Statistics of the United States, Colonial Times to 1970, 18
Holland, tulip bubble, 331
Holmstrom, Bengt, 550
Hong Kong, 534
Hostage takings, 479
Housing prices, 184–185
    maximum loan-to-value (LTV) ratios, 534
Housing wealth, 338
Howitt, Peter, 549
Human capital, 242
    endogenous growth, 244
    extending production function, 242–243
    output and, 243–244
Human wealth, 338
Hungary, hyperinflation in, 511, 512 (table)

Hybrid corn, 258
Hyperinflation, 511
    Germany, 512 (table)

I

Identification problem, A17
Identity, 46
Illiquidity, 186
Imports, 45, 380–382
    determinants of, 401
Imports, A4
Income, 43, 65
    consumption and current, 343–344
    determinants of, 400–401
    disposable, 46
    GDP as sum of, 21
    real, 90–91
Income
    national income and product accounts, A1–A3
Income balance, 390
Independent central bank, 481
Index
    chain type, 39–40
    Nikkei, 330
Indexed bonds, 315
Index number, 29
India, 15
Indirect taxes, A2
Inflation, 31. *See also* disinflation; hyperinflation
    accounting, 496
    benefits of, 522–524
    bracket creep, 31
    China, 13–14, 14 (table)
    costs of, 520–522
    economists' view of, 30–31
    European Union, 10, 10 (table)
    expected, 162–164, 294
    high, Phillips curve relation and, 177–178
    money growth and, 525–526
    nominal interest rates, 303
    Okun's law, 31–32
    optimal, 519–524
    Phillips curve, 32–33
    relation to expected inflation and unemployment, 182
    targeting, 517, 526, 528–529
    unemployment and, 165, 479–480
    in United States, 152 (figure), 162 (figure), 166–168, 175–176
    variability, 521–522
Inflation-adjusted deficit, 495
Inflation rate, 7, 8, 29–31
    optimal, 519–524
Institutions, technological progress and growth, 281–283
Instrumental variable methods, A17
Instruments, A17
Insurance, deposit, 75
Insurance, unemployment, 173
Interest parity condition, 393, 427–428
Interest rate
    on bonds, 64
    constant, 307–308
    deficit reduction and, 147–148
    demand for money and, 77
    determination of, 67–79

Credits

Chapter 2

Chapter 3

Chapter 5

Chapter 6

Chapter 7

Chapter 8

Chapter 9

Chapter 10

International Comparisons of Production, Income and Prices at the University of Pennsylvania, May 2011.

p. 214: SOURCE: Alan Heston, Robert Summers and Bettina Aten, Penn World Table Version 7.0, Center for International Comparisons of Production, Income and Prices at the University of Pennsylvania, May 2011.

p. 216: SOURCE: Alan Heston, Robert Summers and Bettina Aten, Penn World Table Version 7.0, Center for International Comparisons of Production, Income and Prices at the University of Pennsylvania, May 2011.

Chapter 11

p. 232: POSTWAR ECONOMIC RECONSTRUCTION AND LESSONS FOR THE EAST TODAY by Rudiger Dornbusch, Wilhelm Nolling, and Richard Layard, eds. Copyright © 1993 MIT Press. Reprinted by permission.

Chapter 12

p. 258: "Hybrid Corn: An Exploration in the Economics of Technological Change," by Zvi Griliches from ECONOMETRICA, October 1957. Copyright © 1957 The Econometric Society. Reprinted by permission.

p. 259: © Chappatte in "L'Hebdo", Lausanne—www.globecartoon.com

Chapter 13

p. 271: Graphs and Charts from FRED, Federal Reserve Bank of St. Louis. Copyright © 2012 Federal Reserve Bank of St. Louis. Reprinted by permission.

p. 277: © Chappatte in "Die Weltwoche", Zurich—www.globecartoon.com

p. 278: "Earnings of Displaced Male Workers before and after Displacement" by Steven J. Davis and Till M. von-Wachter, from BROOKINGS PAPERS ON ECONOMIC ACTIVITY, Fall 2011. Copyright © 2011 Steven J. Davis and Till M. vonWachter. Reprinted by permission.

p. 281: "Understanding Institutions" by Daron Acemoglu from the Lionel Robbins lectures. Copyright © 2004 Daron Acemoglu. Reprinted by permission.

p. 282: "Understanding Institutions" by Daron Acemoglu from the Lionel Robbins lectures. Copyright © 2004 Daron Acemoglu. Reprinted by permission.

Chapter 14

p. 295: Graphs and Charts from FRED, Federal Reserve Bank of St. Louis. Copyright © 2012 Federal Reserve Bank of St. Louis. Reprinted by permission.

p. 296: "Nominal Interest Rates and Inflation: Latin America, 1992-1993" in IMF INTERNATIONAL FINANCIAL STATISTICS. Copyright © 2012 International Monetary Fund. Reprinted by permission.

p. 304: Graphs and Charts from FRED, Federal Reserve Bank of St. Louis. Copyright © 2012 Federal Reserve Bank of St. Louis. Reprinted by permission.

Chapter 15

p. 314: Graphs and Charts from FRED, Federal Reserve Bank of St. Louis. Copyright © 2012 Federal Reserve Bank of St. Louis. Reprinted by permission.

p. 322: Graphs and Charts from FRED, Federal Reserve Bank of St. Louis. Copyright © 2012 Federal Reserve Bank of St. Louis. Reprinted by permission.

p. 323: Graphs and Charts from FRED, Federal Reserve Bank of St. Louis. Copyright © 2012 Federal Reserve Bank of St. Louis. Reprinted by permission.

p. 329: © Tribune Media Services, Inc. All Rights Reserved. Reprinted with permission.

Chapter 16

p. 340: Cartoon Excerpted by permission from Cartoon Bank. Copyright © 1997 by Roz Chast/The New Yorker Collection/The Cartoon Bank.

p. 344: Surveys of Consumers by Thomson Reuters/University of Michigan. Copyright © 2012 Thomson Reuters/University of Michigan. Reprinted by permission.

p. 353: Graphs and Charts from FRED, Federal Reserve Bank of St. Louis. Copyright © 2012 Federal Reserve Bank of St. Louis. Reprinted by permission.

Chapter 18

p. 380: "Growth in Advanced and Emerging Economies Since 2005" in WORLD ECONOMIC OUTLOOK, July 8, 2009. Copyright © 2009 International Monetary Fund. Reprinted by permission.

Chapter 21

p. 445: Copyright © 1971 by Ed Fisher/The New Yorker Collection/The Cartoon Bank.

Chapter 23

p. 512: "The Monetary Dynamics of Hyperinflation" by Milton Friedman from STUDIES IN THE QUANTITY THEORY OF MONEY. Copyright © 1956

University of Chicago Press. Reprinted by permission of the publisher.

Chapter 24

p. 518: Daryl Cagle/MSNBC.com/Cagle Cartoons

p. 522: "Money Illusion" by Eldar Shafir, Peter Diamond, and Amos Tversky from the QUARTERLY JOURNAL OF ECONOMICS, 1997 (No. 2): 341–374. Copyright © 1997 Oxford University Press. Reprinted by permission of the publisher.

Chapter 25

p. 540 (top): Bettmann/Corbis

p. 541 (top): Plinio Lepri/AP Images

p. 541 (middle): AFP/Newscom

p. 542 (bottom): Chuck Nacke/Alamy

p. 546 (middle): Achmad Ibrahim/AP Images

p. 546 (bottom): Michael Probst/AP Images

p. 547: Giuseppe Aresu/AP Images

p. 548 (bottom): Jay L. Clendenin/Aurora Photos/Aurora Photos

p. 551 (bottom): Antoine Devouard/REA/Redux

The Pearson Series in Economics

Abel/Bernanke/Croushore
Macroeconomics*

Bade/Parkin
Foundations of Economics*

Berck/Helfand
The Economics of the Environment

Bierman/Fernandez
Game Theory with Economic Applications

Blanchard
Macroeconomics*

Blau/Ferber/Winkler
The Economics of Women, Men and Work

Boardman/Greenberg/Vining/ Weimer
Cost-Benefit Analysis

Boyer
Principles of Transportation Economics

Branson
Macroeconomic Theory and Policy

Brock/Adams
The Structure of American Industry

Bruce
Public Finance and the American Economy

Carlton/Perloff
Modern Industrial Organization

Case/Fair/Oster
Principles of Economics*

Caves/Frankel/Jones
World Trade and Payments: An Introduction

Chapman
Environmental Economics: Theory, Application, and Policy

Cooter/Ulen
Law & Economics

Downs
An Economic Theory of Democracy

Ehrenberg/Smith
Modern Labor Economics

Farnham
Economics for Managers

Folland/Goodman/Stano
The Economics of Health and Health Care

Fort
Sports Economics

Froyen
Macroeconomics

Fusfeld
The Age of the Economist

Gerber
International Economics*

González-Rivera
Forecasting for Economics and Business

Gordon
Macroeconomics*

Greene
Econometric Analysis

Gregory
Essentials of Economics

Gregory/Stuart
Russian and Soviet Economic Performance and Structure

Hartwick/Olewiler
The Economics of Natural Resource Use

Heilbroner/Milberg
The Making of the Economic Society

Heyne/Boettke/Prychitko
The Economic Way of Thinking

Hoffman/Averett
Women and the Economy: Family, Work, and Pay

Holt
Markets, Games and Strategic Behavior

Hubbard/O'Brien
Economics*
Money, Banking, and the Financial System*

Hubbard/O'Brien/Rafferty
Macroeconomics*

Hughes/Cain
American Economic History

Husted/Melvin
International Economics

Jehle/Reny
Advanced Microeconomic Theory

Johnson-Lans
A Health Economics Primer

Keat/Young
Managerial Economics

Klein
Mathematical Methods for Economics

Krugman/Obstfeld/Melitz
International Economics: Theory & Policy*

Laidler
The Demand for Money

Leeds/von Allmen
The Economics of Sports

Leeds/von Allmen/Schiming
Economics*

Lipsey/Ragan/Storer
Economics*

Lynn
*Economic Development:
Theory and Practice for a
Divided World*

Miller
Economics Today*
Understanding Modern Economics

Miller/Benjamin
The Economics of Macro Issues

Miller/Benjamin/North
The Economics of Public Issues

Mills/Hamilton
Urban Economics

Mishkin
*The Economics of Money, Banking,
and Financial Markets**
*The Economics of Money, Banking,
and Financial Markets,
Business School Edition**
*Macroeconomics: Policy and
Practice**

Murray
*Econometrics: A Modern
Introduction*

Nafziger
*The Economics of Developing
Countries*

O'Sullivan/Sheffrin/Perez
*Economics: Principles, Applications
and Tools**

Parkin
Economics*

Perloff
Microeconomics*
*Microeconomics: Theory and
Applications with Calculus**

Perman/Common/McGilvray/Ma
*Natural Resources and
Environmental Economics*

Phelps
Health Economics

Pindyck/Rubinfeld
Microeconomics*

**Riddell/Shackelford/Stamos/
Schneider**
*Economics: A Tool for Critically
Understanding Society*

Ritter/Silber/Udell
*Principles of Money, Banking &
Financial Markets**

Roberts
*The Choice: A Fable of Free Trade
and Protection*

Rohlf
*Introduction to Economic
Reasoning*

Ruffin/Gregory
Principles of Economics

Sargent
Rational Expectations and Inflation

Sawyer/Sprinkle
International Economics

Scherer
*Industry Structure, Strategy, and
Public Policy*

Schiller
*The Economics of Poverty and
Discrimination*

Sherman
Market Regulation

Silberberg
Principles of Microeconomics

Stock/Watson
Introduction to Econometrics

Studenmund
*Using Econometrics: A Practical
Guide*

Tietenberg/Lewis
*Environmental and Natural
Resource Economics*
*Environmental Economics and
Policy*

Todaro/Smith
Economic Development

Waldman
Microeconomics

Waldman/Jensen
*Industrial Organization: Theory
and Practice*

**Walters/Walters/Appel/Callahan/
Centanni/Maex/O'Neill**
*Econversations: Today's Students
Discuss Today's Issues*

Weil
Economic Growth

Williamson
Macroeconomics

---

* denotes MyEconLab titles Visit www.myeconlab.com to learn more